JONATHAN HOLSLAG

A Political History of the World
Three Thousand Years of War and Peace

A PELICAN BOOK

PELICAN
an imprint of
PENGUIN BOOKS

PELICAN BOOKS

UK | USA | Canada | Ireland | Australia
India | New Zealand | South Africa

Penguin Books is part of the Penguin Random House
group of companies whose addresses can be found at
global.penguinrandomhouse.com.

Penguin
Random House
UK

First published 2018
002

Text copyright © Jonathan Holslag, 2018

The moral right of the author has been asserted

Book design by Matthew Young
Set in 10/14.664 pt FreightText Pro
Typeset by Jouve (UK), Milton Keynes
Printed and bound in Great Britain by Clays Ltd, Elcograf S.p.A.

A CIP catalogue record for this book is available from the British Library

ISBN: 978-0-241-35204-5

Penguin Random House is committed to a
sustainable future for our business, our readers
and our planet. This book is made from Forest
Stewardship Council® certified paper.

www.greenpenguin.co.uk

Contents

INTRODUCTION

Why History Matters   1

CHAPTER 1

Heavens Obscured   15

CHAPTER 2

Solomon's Peacock   53

CHAPTER 3

The Persian Takeover   89

CHAPTER 4

Gold and Iron   127

CHAPTER 5

The World Like a Chariot Run Wild   165

CHAPTER 6

Barbarians at the Gates   205

CHAPTER 7

The Great Imperial Crisis   239

CHAPTER 8

In the Name of the Prophet   279

CHAPTER 9
The Earth between Hope and Calamity   315

CHAPTER 10
The Mongol Shockwave   357

CHAPTER 11
Huddling in the Darkness   393

CHAPTER 12
A New Age of Islamic Conquest   433

CHAPTER 13
The Primacy of the West   475

CONCLUSION
Horror as a Friend   535

NOTES AND REFERENCES   557

FURTHER READING   601

ACKNOWLEDGEMENTS   615

INDEX   617

| | EUROPE | | AFRICA |
AMERICAS		MEDITERRANEAN		NEAR EAST

CHAPTER 2

Olmec city states · **Libyan Dynasty**

CHAPTER 3

Greek city states · Biblical Kingdoms

CHAPTER 4

Gauls · Corinth · Athens · Sparta

CHAPTER 5

Carthage · Rome · Antigonids · Ptolemaics

CHAPTER 6

Germanic tribes

CHAPTER 7

Roman Empire

CHAPTER 8

Teotihuacán and Maya city states

Carolingian Kingdom

CHAPTER 9

Cordoba · **East Roman Empire**

CHAPTER 10

Venice

CHAPTER 11

Kingdoms in East, Central and West Africa

Inca Empire · **Spanish Empire**

CHAPTER 12

Habsburg Empire · **Russian Empire**

CHAPTER 13

French Empire · **Ottoman Empire**
British Empire · German Empire
· **Soviet Union**
Brazil · **United States** · EU · Russia

Overview of the chapters, time, geography and main polities

CENTRAL ASIA

NORTH & SOUTHEAST ASIA

MESOPOTAMIA　　　　INDIA　　　　CHINA

1000 BCE

Assyrian Empire　　　Vedic city states　　　Zhou Empire

Hong Bang

Achaemenid Empire　　　Mahajanapadas　　　Spring and Autumn　　　500 BCE

Gojoseon

Macedonian Empire　　　Warring States

Maurya Empire　　　Qin Empire

Seleucids　　　　　　　　　　0

Parthian Empire　　　Bactria　　　West Han Empire

Ziongnu

Kushan Empire　　　East Han Empire

Qiang

500

Gupta Empire

Sasanian Empire　　　Goguryeo

Funan

Himyar　　　Yamato

Umayyad Empire　　　Tang Empire　　　1000

Abbasid Empire

Srivijaya

Seljuk Empire　　　Song　　　Liao　　　1500

Goryeo

Mongol Empire　　　Yuan Empire

Timurid Empire

Ming Empire　　　2000

Safavid Empire

Mughal Empire　　　Qing Empire

Japanese Empire

India　　　Indonesia　　　China　　　2000

A R C T I C

W E S T E R N
H E M I S P H E R E

ROCKY MOUNTAINS

MISSISSIPPI
DELTA

SIERRA MADRE

Gulf of
Mexico

Caribbean Sea

ATLANTIC
OCEAN

Amazon

PACIFIC
OCEAN

ANDES

WESTERN
EUROPEAN
COASTAL PLA

ALP

PYRENEES

Mediterra

St. Gibraltar

SAHA
DESE

S O U T H E R

A Concise Map of the World

OCEAN

EASTERN
HEMISPHERE

PONTIC-CASPIAN
STEPPE

Black
Sea

KAN   CAUCASUS

ANATOLIA

MESOPOTAMIA

Caspian
Sea

TIAN SHAN

HINDU KUSH

ZAGROS

Hormuz

HIMALAYA

INDO
GANGETIC
PLAIN

MANCHURIAN
STEPPE

NORTII CIIINA
PLAIN

East China
Sea

South
China
Sea

PACIFIC
OCEAN

Nile

Red Sea

Arabian Sea

Gulf of
Bengal

MEKONG
DELTA

St. Malacca

INDIAN
OCEAN

ic
a

OCEAN

Why History Matters

A few kilometres outside the Hungarian capital, Budapest, archaeologists made a remarkable discovery. In a grave from the sixth century BCE they found the remains of a Scythian woman and young boy. They were not rich. Still, their relatives had dressed them in fine clothes and laid them to rest in a tender embrace. Mother and son were victims of war, one of the many conflicts that the Scythian tribes fought with each other. Staring at them, I started wondering. How was it possible that these people could show so much love and care for their kin, yet repeatedly stumble from one bout of carnage to another? How is it possible today for countries to continue to arm themselves to the teeth, for wars still to tear apart so many loving families, and for diplomacy to fail so miserably to prevent military rivalry? Why has a planet that has always yearned for peace never managed to preserve it?

Peace and war, the famous American statesman Henry Kissinger noted, are the core business of world politics. Even if the international agenda has been broadened by environmental issues and matters as trivial as the curve of bananas, it is still diplomacy that bears an enormous responsibility when situations of great peril arise. This explains why diplomacy has remained such a weighty business, mystical almost, dignified by protocol and shrouded in secrecy. It also explains why young people remain attracted to it. Each year, numerous graduates compete in demanding entrance exams all over the world to join the *corps diplomatique*. Many more seek to be involved in international politics from the sidelines. I have written this book mostly for them, for the men and women that aspire to study, report or shape world politics, whether as politicians, diplomats, military officers, professors, or journalists.

World politics is again poised precariously at a tipping point. At one end of the balance sits a large crowd of cosmopolitans, the airborne elite that hops from one city to another and considers the success of diplomacy to be measured by the number of dialogues established or the flocks of cameramen present at international conferences. It insists that the bloody history of great power politics has ended and that major wars have become much less likely. Competition, such reasoning continues, is much less likely to spark major wars because of economic interdependence. This opinion was particularly dominant in politics after the collapse of the Soviet Union in 1991: in Europe, which has aspired to lead by example rather than by force; in China, which has designed the doctrine of peaceful rise; and in the United States of America, where conservatives and progressives alike have championed a foreign policy premised on liberal values.

At the other end sit the many who believe that the free and open world has not benefited them, that globalization is responsible for economic turbulence, and that both migrants and multinationals are a threat. They are angry and rally around strong nationalistic leaders. They want to be protected against a world of injustice and insecurity. As the cosmopolitans went on to revel in their flat, borderless world, this group has grown bigger and now severely limits the scope for international compromise and moderation.

This shift comes at a moment when the global levels of military spending are once again higher than during the darkest hours of the Cold War.[1] The number of armed conflicts is also growing and other international disputes have become tenser. It is in this confusing world that a new generation has to chart its way and develop the wisdom to make the important decisions that face it. These leaders of tomorrow should be guided by good understanding of the people's wellbeing, of economics, of ethics – and of history. As the ancient Roman statesman Marcus Tullius Cicero put it: 'To be ignorant of what occurred before you were born is to remain always a child.'[2]

If theory and ideology give you a vantage point on the world much like that gained from a helicopter ride, history brings you to the same point only after a long and arduous mountain expedition. A journey through history strengthens the mind in the same way that an expedition in nature hardens body and soul. It requires perseverance and concentration to interpret the many events along the way. It develops the perceptiveness and awareness that are needed to detect and overcome hurdles. And it ultimately leads to great heights, from where one can look back, draw conclusions, and search for the best possible route towards the horizon ahead.

There is no shortcut for this voyage. However much we trust in the rigour of theory and the clarity of ideology, if we do not accept the challenge of coming to grips with history, it is like claiming to be religious without having read any sacred texts. Compared to ideology, history can be a moderating force. It reveals not only how much progress the world has made in improving living conditions, but also how hard-fought such progress – and its preservation – has been. From this perspective, world history can be viewed as an upward curve; but it has experienced dramatic setbacks along the way, which need to be understood in order to help prevent – or at least ameliorate – new crises in the future.

However, the study of history has increasingly become marginalized in the programmes of schools and universities. What remains often summarizes history in support of theories or preconceived ideas. In courses of international politics, for example, history is at best limited to the same handful of case studies, like the Peloponnesian War, the rise of ancient Rome, or the workings of the nineteenth-century Congress System.[3] It instantly becomes clear that the subjects that are always focused on relate to only a small area of the globe: Europe. This has led scholars outside Europe to claim that the strategic culture of their own countries is fundamentally different and stands apart from vicious European power politics. I have heard this argument many times: from Chinese colleagues and diplomats who refer to an alleged tradition of harmoniousness innate to the Middle Kingdom; or from Indian officials who consider their nation to have been founded on Gandhi's principles of peace. Such geographical limitations in the study of history inevitably cause misunderstanding and disagreement.

Writing History

So, what should readers expect from this book? In order to answer that question, I should first explain what this book is not. It is not a specialized work that reveals new discoveries from archaeological sites or archives. It does sometimes draw upon primary sources, but it also gratefully relies on numerous excellent secondary sources. Nor is this book another history promoting a single great idea: that there is a 'clash of civilizations' brewing, for instance; or that we are nearing 'the end of history'; or that humans have always been rational optimists who advanced their prosperity through trade. Neither is this a work of historical revisionism that tries to provoke controversy by attacking earlier studies. To be sure, like any other student of international affairs I do have predispositions, but I have not set out merely to confirm them. In fact, I did not know what to expect when I embarked on the research for this book, as much of what I had to explore was new to me.

In writing this book, I have been guided by a single question. What do I want the shapers of this world to know about the history of world politics, given that they have so many other issues to engage with, so many other courses to take? The result is a bird's-eye view of 3,000 years of history: an introduction that acquaints the reader with essential events, allows him or her to draw some conclusions about the functioning of international relations, and hopefully awakens enough interest in some aspects that they go on to explore them in greater detail themselves. It can be used by students at university, but equally by any reader with a desire to make sense of our restless world, to understand where we come from, and to gain some idea of what the future might bring.

To that end, this book integrates different aspects of history that are usually treated separately. There are magnificent works about the causes of war, but they do not dwell on periods of peace.[4] There are masterful studies of the historic shifts in the balance of power, but they overlook much of the way international politics has been conducted:[5] how international organizations have been founded, how treaties have been negotiated both in cramped back rooms and in marble ballrooms, how the personal beliefs of participants have played significant roles, and how diplomats have shaped the rules of world politics. My challenge has been to unpack these different but interrelated layers into one consistent enquiry.

The first of these layers concerns the history of the distribution of power across the globe from the earliest times onwards. Power, as the political scientist Robert Dahl put it, is the ability to make people do what they otherwise would not have done.[6] For a polity or state this has both an internal dimension – that is, its influence over its citizens – and also an external one – that is, its influence over other polities. Power, in these terms, has two aspects: its inputs, or capabilities, and its outputs, or effective influence. This effective influence can be both hard and soft. It can involve everything between forceful subjugation and subtle inducement – with diplomacy merely the art of mediating between one's own country's domestic interests and those of others.

When we focus on inputs, a polity's capabilities can be

measured in terms of its land and natural resources, its treasure, its military power, its political system, its legitimacy as a state, and so forth. These are never static, but their relative distribution among polities shapes the balance of power at any one point in time. Many scholars study the processes by which polities accumulate and lose capabilities. One of the most critical areas of discussion in this regard concerns the ways social, economic, and political organization – as well as individual leadership – affect the accumulation and conservation of capabilities. Is Western capitalism really a superior form of economic organization? Is democracy necessary for prosperity, or do we need authoritarian leadership? Another important area of debate concerns the impact of ideas on the value of material assets. For example, why do polities appear to value military power differently at certain times? Do the wealthiest economic powers shape the way in which other states define their own needs?

This leads us to the second layer: the history of political organization. Polities have taken numerous different forms: cities, city states, nation states, multinational unions, and empires ranging from indirect trading ones to the directly territorial. They have been organized as monarchies or republics, dictatorships or democracies, and so on. And they have coexisted with other influential agents such as religious groupings, international corporations, and even pirates.

Until a few years ago, the predominant assumption was that we would live in an egalitarian, borderless world, and that states were about to become powerless. We observe a completely different reality today. Nationalism is back, people call for well-protected borders, military expenditure is on the rise, and governments interfere incessantly in economic affairs. The current debate about the importance of geographically delimited political power versus cosmopolitan trade, capital, ideas, and culture is by no means new. This book pays attention to the factors that historically have caused shifts between cosmopolitanism, fixated with openness, and protectionism, obsessed with borders and defence.

The third layer concerns the history of interaction between political units. Time and again, people have stood up to proclaim that the very nature of international relations was about to change for the better: competition would continue, but it would become less violent. Just as, in the fifth century BCE, the Athenian statesman Pericles promised other Greek cities peace and security if they joined his Delian League, so, twenty-five centuries later, the American president Harry Truman vowed to protect the free world, and, in the last few years, the Chinese president Xi Jinping has held up the vision of a harmonious new world order. But according to the great political scientist Hans Morgenthau, underneath the chaos of international politics there are perennial forces that shape all societies, such as humans' limitless lust for power and the consequent rivalry between states.[7] So, can we deduce any pattern in the occurrence of war and peace throughout history? What has made war more prevalent than peace? And what, on the contrary, has driven powerful agents to champion the cause of peace and tie themselves to conventions, to international organizations, and to rules restricting sovereignty? To what extent have international relations been driven by a desire for defensive security, or territorial aggrandizement, or economic profit, or by ideas of religion, nationalism, or justice, or simply by ignorance and folly? Do states become more restrained in the use of force and more keen to cooperate as a result of economic interdependence, increased communication, and shared values?

The fourth layer to consider is the history of the relationship between people and the planet; in other words, the importance of nature and environmental change. Some of the first writers about politics – such as the Indian court advisor Kautilya and the Chinese strategist Sun Tzu – were already advising leaders to husband their natural resources carefully. For much of history one of the principal tasks of monarchs has been to intercede with the gods for favourable weather. Climatic changes, food scarcity, and the migrations instigated by them have caused social upheaval and war at least since Egypt was first ruled by the pharaohs. So, in the twenty-first century, what is new in this regard? Should we consider global warming a new component of the international agenda? Or is it just as Kautilya and Sun Tzu wrote over two thousand years ago, that any leader who wants to be successful must strike a balance between the desires of his people and the resources of nature?

The fifth, and final, layer concerns thinking how the nature of world politics has evolved throughout history. After the fall of the Soviet Union, the debate was dominated by optimistic scholars, so-called liberals, who advocated that trade made polities more dependent on each other and that this interdependence made conflict more expensive, and so-called constructivists, who assumed that international norms dissuaded polities from using force against each other and that even their very DNA could be changed, away from a predisposition to selfish national interests and towards a greater focus on the common good. Within the last few years, however, politically realist intellectuals have become more audible. They believe that polities will always strive for autonomy, security, and power; as a result, cooperation and peace are unlikely to be sustainable. The world remains gripped by anarchy, which for students of international politics means the perpetual competition between polities and the absence of a durable force that can arbitrate or solve their disputes. This shift from optimist idealism to pessimist realism is nothing new, as this book will show. It will keep track of the two schools of thought as they alternate through history, and pay particular attention to the reasons why each viewpoint gained its momentary prominence and then declined in turn.

In total, this book surveys 3,000 years of history, from the beginning of the first millennium BCE to the beginning of the twenty-first century CE. Each chapter covers two to three centuries and concentrates on the geographical region that the historical evidence suggests at that time was most important: because of the size of its population, because of its strength, or because of its leadership in international affairs. This way, the focus will move from east to west, north to south, as it follows the ever-shifting centres of power. Inevitably, some regions will figure less prominently than others, like sub-Saharan Africa and the Americas. For most of their history they were less densely populated than other areas – until the nineteenth century they probably accounted between them for less than 10 per cent of the world's population – and sources for their pre-colonial political organizations are also much scarcer. Nevertheless, this work does at least touch on polities like the ancient Olmec cities of Central America and the medieval kingdoms of Central Africa, as well as addressing the fate of other less prominent actors in world affairs: the wary countries on the fringes of big empires, the peoples enslaved during wars, and the shrewd trading cities that cautiously sought to hedge their bets between the political giants.

Throughout, the book takes a keen interest in the impact of world politics on the lives of ordinary people. Besides the effects of economic change, it was often the outbreak of war that had the greatest ramifications, and so we will attempt to trace the causes and consequences of conflicts, investigate how they were won and lost, analyse how they were perceived, as well as follow the diplomats in their desperate attempts to stop them. Even if our aim is to try and abstract timeless underlying themes from the history of war and peace, it must remain above all a story of human beings, of their hopes and fears, their capacity for violence and their suffering. That is the only way we will ever understand the hard choices that define the nature of true leadership.

CHAPTER 1

Heavens Obscured

THE PRELUDE: BEFORE 1000 BCE

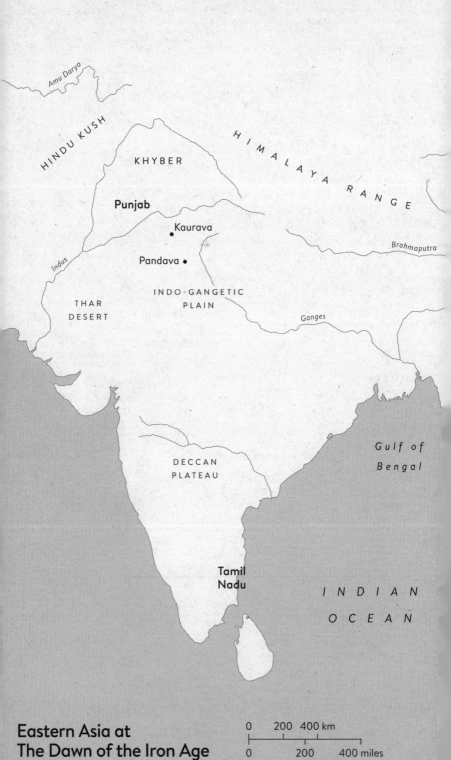

Eastern Asia at
The Dawn of the Iron Age

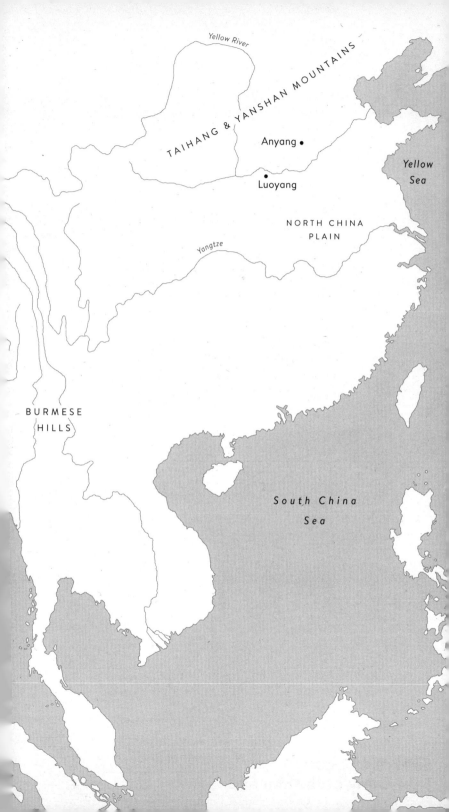

The Middle East at
The Dawn of the Iron Age

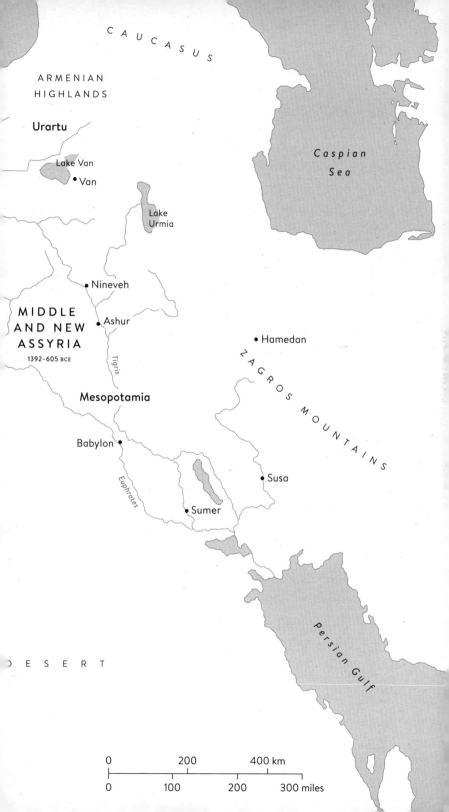

CAUCASUS

ARMENIAN
HIGHLANDS

Urartu

Lake Van
• Van

Lake
Urmia

*Caspian
Sea*

• Nineveh

**MIDDLE
AND NEW
ASSYRIA**
1392–605 BCE

• Ashur

Tigris

• Hamedan

Z A G R O S

M O U N T A I N S

Mesopotamia

Babylon •

Euphrates

• Susa

• Sumer

Persian Gulf

D E S E R T

0		200		400 km

0	100	200	300 miles

'O, tell me of the wilderness of this world!' the blind Kaurava king Dhritarashtra cries when he learns his hundred sons have all been butchered in battle. It had been an apocalyptic struggle: the field was 'strewn with bones and hair, overflowing with torrents of blood, covered on every side with thousands upon thousands of corpses, littered with the blood-smeared remains of elephants, horses, chariots and warriors, and with headless bodies and bodiless heads . . . swarming with jackals, jungle crows, ravens, storks and crows'.[1] Dhritarashtra had been warned against this carnage. The gods had counselled him to negotiate a truce and share his territory with his rivals. The queen had told him to defend his kingdom's prosperity by mild means, not by force. It was to no avail. The monarch underestimated the threat of war, the resentment between the Kauravas and the enemy Pandava tribe, and the boundless ambitions of his own belligerent son.

Thus concludes the tragic episode at the heart of the *Mahabharata*: the power brokers have overruled the voices of peace and evil has prevailed over good. One of the oldest known works of literature to address the struggle between the ideal of peace and the reality of war, this anonymous epic poem can be traced back to origins in North India in around 1000 BCE. Although the actual conflicts from that era were fought between tiny kingdoms, and with relatively rudimentary weapons, it is no surprise that war in the *Mahabharata* appears as a form of universal deluge, as mass destruction. Even spears and arrows, clubs and axes, can wipe out entire communities, raze farms and settlements – to all intents and purposes destroying the victims' entire world.

The *Mahabharata*, though, is not unique, as the rest of this chapter will reveal. There are other representations of foreign relations to be found in the art and literature, the archives and inscriptions, prior to the first millennium BCE. This period, commonly referred to as the transition from the Bronze Age to the Iron Age, is the earliest to leave us sufficiently widespread written evidence from around the world to understand how foreign relations were organized and how people thought about them.

This chapter begins, though, with the geographical context. It explains where on the globe the first polities were established. It clarifies the importance of both natural barriers, such as mountains, and natural junctures, such as plains and valleys. Having set the scene, it goes on to discuss foreign relations in their most primitive incarnation, among tribes and wandering peoples – the so-called 'natural state'. Subsequently, its focus shifts towards the first cities and kingdoms. We end in the four chief centres of political power in that time: Egypt; the 'fertile crescent' of Mesopotamia; the North China Plain; and the Indo-Gangetic Plain.

Worlds Apart

Before we can make sense of the politics of the ancient world, it is crucial to appreciate its geography. As many features will recur throughout this book, let us sketch a mental map. The world can be divided into two main geopolitical complexes: the Eastern Hemisphere, comprising Africa, Asia, and Europe; and the Western Hemisphere, consisting of the Americas. These two hemispheres can be regarded as discrete entities until the establishment of permanent long-distance maritime trade routes between them at the beginning of the sixteenth century CE.

In the Eastern Hemisphere – which was the 'cradle of civilization' – human settlement is conditioned by the vast band of mountain ranges running from west to east, sometimes referred to as the Alpide Belt. It includes the Pyrenees, Alps, Balkans, Caucasus, Zagros, Hindu Kush, Tian Shan, and the Himalaya. Along this chain, one finds temperate and subtropical climate zones in the presence of rivers, ideal for permanent human settlement, unlike the regions of snow, desert, or tropical forest found further to the north or south. The most attractive areas are the North China Plain and the Western European Coastal Plain, followed by vast stretches of flat land both in much warmer areas, like the Mekong Delta, the Indo-Gangetic Plain, Mesopotamia, and the valley of the River Nile, and also in colder ones, like the grasslands of the Pontic-Caspian Steppe, Siberia, Mongolia, and Manchuria. Smaller, but similarly promising for human development, are the coastal plains in today's Japan, Korea, Oman, Kenya,

Georgia, Azerbaijan, Greece, Italy, and Senegal, as well as the fertile plateaus of Afghanistan, Armenia, and Macedonia. In addition to the connections provided by overland routes and rivers, seas (the Baltic, Mediterranean, Black and Red Seas, and so on) formed crucial strategic interfaces, with narrows such as the Kattegat, Gibraltar, the Bab-el-Mandeb, and the Strait of Malacca proving of particular significance.

In the Western Hemisphere – which was occupied by humans far later – it is hard to find any substantial region that matched those of the Eastern Hemisphere as an incubator of power. The east coast of North America does enjoy a temperate climate, but these littoral flatlands are less than half the size of the North China Plain or the Western European Coastal Plain. The Mississippi and Amazon rivers have wide deltas, like the Nile, but their discharge is so unpredictable that it discourages farming. What comes nearest to the Nile Valley and Mesopotamia are the middle reaches of the Mississippi, where there are large plateaus right in between the subtropical and moderate continental climate zones. The narrow coastal plains south of the Gulf of Mexico and along the Pacific Coast of South America also benefited from fertile soil and abundant water. These areas are mostly tropical and again lacked the scale necessary to generate great agricultural centres like those in the Eastern Hemisphere. Natural potential was not turned effectively into prosperity everywhere. One of the chief reasons for this was the astounding emptiness of the world. Only about 60 million people – the equivalent of the population of Italy today – inhabited the planet at the dawn of the first millennium BCE, and their distribution was very uneven. In most regions of the globe,

communities existed from day to day entirely independent-
ly of each other. 'Abroad' was the next village. Family clans
were the main social unit. Sometimes they coalesced into
tribes – in defence of land and other natural resources for
instance – but even the very largest cities had fewer than
100,000 inhabitants. [2]

Nevertheless, the world's political map was fundamentally determined by how generously geography had distributed
a holy trinity of natural resources: water, fertile soil, and a
temperate climate. In places where all three were bountiful,
ploughs, shovels, and bare hands slowly pushed the frontier
of civilization forward: villages evolved into cities, cities into
kingdoms, and kingdoms into empires.

The earliest imperial powers were the civilizations of
Egypt and Mesopotamia. By the beginning of the first millennium BCE, they had known well over a thousand years of
uninterrupted development in agriculture, of high population density, complex social and administrative structures,
and political unity of some sort. Numerous smaller kingdoms existed in the North China and Indo-Gangetic Plains,
in the oases and fertile valleys of Central Asia, in Anatolia
and the Eastern Mediterranean, as well as in Central America. Powerful federations of nomadic peoples had emerged
on the steppes of Mongolia and Central Asia. Small tribes inhabited most of the rest of the globe.

The Natural State

How did the majority of the world's population that lived
in simple tribal cultures at the dawn of the first millennium

conduct political relations and exchanges with other groups? Was there ever an 'age of innocence' or 'natural state' in international relations before the evolution of kingdoms and empires? This question goes right to the heart of the age-old debate over whether humans' natural state is one of peace or war. The Enlightenment philosopher Jean-Jacques Rousseau (1712–78 CE) famously asserted that primitive people needed to cooperate. Consider, he said, a group of hungry men hoping to bring home the large amount of meat provided by a stag. If they are to succeed, the first condition is that they do not prey on each other. The second condition is that they track the stag together, and resist the temptation to go after smaller quarry by themselves.[3]

To some extent, Rousseau's theory has been borne out by modern anthropologists, who affirm that tribal peoples are generally less inclined to fight than those from more developed societies, precisely because the strength of the entire group together is required to survive in the natural environment. Human life is also more precious. The loss of an able-bodied man means fewer hands to help hunt, till the land, or keep predators away. The loss of a father renders a family at the mercy of other men. The loss of a son means no protection for his parents when they grow old. The more tribes are separated from each other, therefore, the less contact there is and so less risk of conflict. This is certainly the case in environments where there is no real scarcity, but where it just takes a long time to forage and to track game, and where it is difficult to hoard foodstuffs.

We know that traditional societies today – such as tribes in the Amazon forest – have a clear understanding of borders and employ rituals involving drugs and gifts to avoid conflict and reinforce good relations. Friendship between tribes is cultivated through marriage. Messengers enjoy special rights to enter alien territory. Agreements exist about the responsibility to maintain trails. But this is only one side of the picture: even the remotest tribes today indulge in bloody conflicts.

Archaeological evidence for tribal diplomacy before the Iron Age is scarce. We know from excavations that goods were exchanged; and markers hint at an effort to delineate territory.[4] But the fact that the archaeological layers before the Iron Age are strewn with flints, axes, daggers, and crushed skulls suggests that these peoples did not escape the anguish of war. The rock carvings of Tanumshede in Sweden, for example, include a depiction of a man peacefully tilling his land. But, adjacent to him, men brandish spears, and crush heads, and attack ships with battering rams; while nearby, a woman grieves over a dead body.[5] In 2006, archaeologists discovered an even older mass grave near Frankfurt in Germany. It contained the remains of at least twenty-six people: victims of torture.[6] The absence of the remains of young women and teenagers suggests that they were carried away as slaves. Comparable mass graves have been found in Austria and Hungary, confirming that warfare before the Iron Age often led to the extermination of entire communities. It is also telling that primitive people first used the demanding process of metal casting for weapons. Swords, halberds, and axes – not to mention the rare examples of helmets with huge horns that have been found from the period – were symbols of masculinity and of the readiness to fight. We can, however, only guess at the causes of early wars. Archaeologists and historians generally assume they were caused by issues such as the theft of livestock or crops, attempts to abduct women, competition over water wells and other natural resources, feuds, and rivalry for leadership and status.

Despite, or perhaps because of, this backdrop of violence, early peoples clearly understood the value of life and cherished it. There is plentiful archaeological evidence proving they liked to dress up in finery, play music, and make toys for their children. They also cared for the weaker members of society. In the Bronze Age cemetery at Man Bac in Vietnam, for example, archaeologists discovered the body of a man whose bones were so fragile that he must have been cared for throughout his life before his relatives buried him with great care and affection.

Bringer of Spoils

The picture we gain of the minor kingdoms and trading cities of the late second millennium in many ways is similar to that of its tribal peoples, although the nature of the evidence is often far more plentiful and sophisticated. The remains of one such community were discovered by farmers in the north of present-day Afghanistan, near the Amu Darya (Oxus River), when they unearthed a series of silver cups. The images decorating these cups display almost exactly the same dichotomy between war and peace as the Tanumshede rock carvings in Sweden. On one cup we see men leisurely sipping from goblets, a basket of fruit between them, while dancing or ploughing takes place beneath them.[7] On another, a muscleman – who could have escaped from a Hollywood action movie – shoots an arrow into the spine of his rival.[8] The people who crafted these cups lived in a city surrounded by lush, well-irrigated fields. They were part of a trade network that reached as far as the Persian Gulf and brought great wealth to the city by exporting lapis lazuli from its only known source in the ancient world. But despite these trading ties, their city was well fortified. When archaeologists excavated, they found a vast rectangular clay wall, within which broad concentric rings of buildings surrounded the circular citadel where the inhabitants placed their gods and hoarded their grain.[9]

Similar walled trading cities from that era are scattered across the mountain ranges and valleys of Eurasia. Perhaps the best-known example remains Mycenae, the citadel that looms over a wide valley in the Greek Peloponnese. It was almost entirely built from colossal stones, and visitors entered it via the famous Lion Gate. Mycenae was part of the world described by the great poet Homer and characterized by anarchy. In his *Iliad*, an epic that takes place against the backdrop of the Trojan War, he presents numerous kingdoms, all ruled from walled cities, and in almost perpetual competition for wealth, power, and honour. Their kings were called *wanakes*, which it is thought originally meant 'bringers of spoils'. The story of Helen, the most beautiful woman in Greece, introduces an important element in early interstate relations; the use of marriages to establish and strengthen diplomatic partnerships. The *Iliad* gives a glimpse of the role of messengers, who race back and forth between cities, and of treaties and alliances based on oaths. We do not know a lot about the life of Homer, whether he might have witnessed the Trojan War himself, or even whether he existed at all. Still, his work expresses his longing for peace and good kings who understand the limits of force, and so does this hymn to the god of war, Ares:

> Shed down a kindly ray from above upon my life . . . that I may be able to drive away bitter cowardice from my head and crush down the deceitful impulses of my soul. Restrain also the keen fury of my heart which provokes me to tread the ways of blood-curdling strife. Rather, O blessed one, give you me boldness to abide within the harmless laws of peace, avoiding strife and hatred and the violent fiends of death.[10]

We can also scrutinize the international relations of the Eastern Mediterranean world at this time more directly, through the archives of the small but wealthy kingdom of Ugarit. From the ruins of this walled city, located in present-day Syria, archaeologists have recovered hundred of clay tablets. These record not only how its inhabitants made their fortunes from agriculture, crafts, and trade, but also how its rulers conducted diplomatic relations. Squeezed between the powerful states of Egypt and Mesopotamia, Ugarit tried to gain influence by controlling trade in the Levant: a first wave of merchants would be followed by soldiers and conquest. Ugarit also formed alliances with similar neighbouring states, in order to counterbalance the great powers: solemn oaths were sworn, sumptuous gifts exchanged, and envoys called *akero* (angels) by the Greeks shuttled back and forth with letters and dispatches. One tablet from around 1200 describes how Ugarit worked with its allies to strangle the economy of Assyria, the leading power in Mesopotamia at that time. 'Since the king of Assyria is my majesty's enemy, he shall be your enemy,' it read. 'Your merchant shall not go to Assyria and you shall not allow his merchants into your land.'[11] This was economic warfare *avant la lettre*.

But even shrewd diplomacy could not save Ugarit from disaster in the end. During the early years of the twelfth century mysterious invaders – referred to by later historians as 'the Sea Peoples' – wrought havoc across the Eastern Mediterranean. When they reached the Levant, they sacked one city after another. The despairing king of Ugarit found himself overstretched: 'The enemy's ships came here, my cities were burned, and they did evil things in my country. Does not my father know that all my troops and chariots are in the Land of Hatti, and all my ships are in the land of Lukka? . . . Thus, the country is abandoned to itself.'[12] The ruined city was left forsaken by its inhabitants; the kingdom of Ugarit was never revived. These were the Dark Ages of the Eastern Mediterranean, the beginning of the Bronze Age Collapse.

The Dark Ages (roughly 1200–1000 BCE) resulted from a combination of environmental crisis, growing drought as a result of deforestation, mass migration-turned-invasion, the advance of iron working techniques at the expense of bronze making, and the collapse of trade networks. Ugarit was not the only city to succumb. Hattusha, the capital of the kingdom of the Hittites, was far greater than Ugarit. Its ruins, which lie in the heart of Anatolia, share similarities with those of Mycenae. Its citadel overlooked a large fertile plateau, pasturelands, woods, and important trade routes connecting the Aegean, the Black Sea, and Mesopotamia. Its walls were built with similar gigantic masonry blocks; a pair of lions even flanked one of its main gates. In the thirteenth century, the Hittites controlled Anatolia. In 1274, they even defeated the Egyptian armies at the Battle of Kadesh.

The surviving diplomatic correspondence from the time shows that the Hittite kings demanded to be treated as the equals of the rulers of Assyria and Egypt: if the Hittite king addressed the pharaoh respectfully as 'the king of the sun', he expected to be called the 'king of the storm' in return. From less powerful peoples, the Hittite kings demanded tribute. Advanced iron weapons and fast chariots enabled them to enforce their will. But civil war weakened the kingdom at a moment when the Assyrians were on the rise in Mesopotamia.

The new Hittite ruler, Hattushili III, went all out to gain diplomatic recognition from Egypt and to secure an anti-Assyrian alliance. After lengthy negotiations, delegations from the two sides finally signed the Treaty of Kadesh in 1259. It remains as the world's oldest completely preserved peace treaty.[13] Diplomatic tensions were renewed, however, when Hattushili deferred the marriage of his daughter to the pharaoh. The Hittites also complained that Egyptian propaganda belittled the Hittite victory of 1274. In the end, they never obtained the promised Egyptian support to repel the Assyrian advance and the invasion of the so-called Sea Peoples. It was probably this coalition of Northern and Western Mediterranean peoples – emboldened to attack the Eastern and Southern Mediterranean by climatic change, migration pressures, and the richness of Egypt, Anatolia, and the Levant – that finally burned Hattusha to the ground in around 1180.[14]

Egypt

The cities of Ugarit and Hattusha existed on the fringes of the mighty agricultural centres of Egypt and Mesopotamia. These great societies had mastered the art of taming rivers through countless dikes, basins, and irrigation canals. Rivers carried fertile silt from the mountains to the plains. Here, once the irrigation canals were in place, farmers could have two harvests per year; and high agricultural productivity allowed populations to flourish. Flash floods still frequently erased the maze of locks and mud ditches and embankments, but surpluses of grain could be stocked in abundant years. Whoever held the granaries held political power: the power to arm soldiers, to erect monuments, and to buy luxury goods, for surpluses allowed for specialization in different crafts, and grain was traded up and down the River Nile. Cities like Memphis, Thebes, and Amarna in Egypt counted 50,000 inhabitants or more. About 3 to 4 million people lived around the River Nile and its delta.[15]

Despite their prosperity, even these rich agricultural centres remained unsentimental places. People usually did not live beyond the age of thirty. They shared their short stay on earth in damp settlements with flies, lice, fleas, mosquitos, and dangerous predators; disease often meant death. Toil was unrelenting. A story from the Mesopotamian state of Akkad conveys the anguish of a citizen of Nippur. Despite hard work, he complains, his storage bin is empty, his insides 'burn' from hunger; worst of all, he cannot even afford some mediocre beer. But the art and literature of Egypt and

Mesopotamia also reveal another side of daily life. They attest to the remarkable phlegmatism of peoples reconciled to their fate of hard work and the premature loss of loved ones. 'Seize the day! hold holiday,' an Egyptian poem from about 1160 advised:

> Be unwearied, unceasing, alive,
> you and your own true love;
> let not your heart be troubled during your
> sojourn on Earth,
> But seize the day as it passes.[16]

The ideal world of the early Iron Age was a verdant garden, a paradise of abundance. Wall paintings and relief carvings depict gracefully flowing rivers, bountiful grain fields, palms with sweet dates, reed beds full of fat ducks, ponds abundant with fish, and perfumed lotus blossoms. In this world of sodden or dusty mud shacks, the lotus was a universal symbol of purity.

Egypt enjoyed a unique geopolitical position. From the Great Lakes in Central Africa, the River Nile flows thousands of kilometres to the Mediterranean Sea. But only over the last thousand kilometres or so has the presence of soft sandstone allowed it to wear out the well-known wide valley and delta: the ancient world's largest oasis. Already, by around 3150, the lands adjacent to these stretches of the Nile – Upper and Lower Egypt – were unified by a pharaoh named Menes. Over the 2,000 years that followed, twenty different dynasties ruled the territory. This characterized the frequent periods of instability, division, and subjugation by foreign invaders. Egypt, however, was never a political monolith, and the major cities, like Memphis and Thebes, frequently competed to be the centre of power.

Upstream, towards what is now Sudan, geological formations of hard granite prevented the valley from widening, and created cataracts that were often impassable by boat. This was the land of the Nubians. Their settlements grew up in places where the Nile valley became wider, but these oases were never large enough to support significant populations. As a result, Nubia was often too weak to repel the Egyptian troops that sought to take control of its abundant gold mines and the trade routes that gave access to the ivory, ebony, and spices of the Horn of Africa.

In the north of Egypt, around the Nile Delta, the Mediterranean coast was still partially forested in the early Iron Age and suitable for dry farming. From the coastal oases around present-day Benghazi, Libyan warlords repeatedly tried to take advantage of weak Egyptian rulers. The pharaohs also had to guard against incursions across the Sinai Desert – which formed the land bridge to Mesopotamia and the Levant – and sporadic raids from the sea.

In a quiet corner of the Egyptological section of the Musée du Louvre sits a simple wooden burial sculpture: a farmer, with his ankles in the mud, guides a primitive plough pulled by two fat oxen and gazes towards a granary.[17] Tilling, sowing, harvesting, and waiting for the next flood season in order to begin again – these determined the rhythm of life for most ancient Egyptians. Above all, they desired peace – both political stability and secure borders. But for outsiders, Egypt was the ultimate trophy. Just as commoners were required to protect their homes against thieves, kings had to defend their realms from foreign predators. Like jackals in their lairs, they lay continuously on the watch for even the slightest opportunity as Egypt sat like a fat goose on its nest.

The most important role for Egyptian rulers, therefore, was to provide security, stability, and, ideally, harmony. The Egyptians called this *Maat*. The divine force that prevailed in times of prosperity, it regulated the stars, the floods, and the seasons, and represented obedience, order, justice, and morality in people and nations. *Isfet*, or chaos, was the alternative. If ideas of just war, proportionality, and arbitration in the *Mahabharata* and other Indian epics reflected the anarchical context of multiple competing kingdoms, Egyptian writings exemplify the imperial tradition. Harmony meant hierarchy. This was made clear in every possible way. In the relief carvings on temples, the pharaoh towered high above long lines of obedient Egyptian subjects and subservient foreign envoys.

The Amarna Tablets offer a fascinating window on this thinking. These diplomatic letters from the fourteenth century depict the Egyptian pharaoh as the supreme leader among the kings of Babylon, Assyria, the Hittites, and many others.[18] His official in charge of relations with these realms was called the 'overseer of all northern lands'.[19] Court protocol helped affirm the idea of Egyptian supremacy. 'At the feet of the king my lord,' a delegate testified, 'seven times and again seven times I prostrate myself upon my back and upon my breast.'[20] Envoys were made to linger for hours in the scorching sun before presenting their sumptuous gifts of horses, chariots, gems, slave girls, and exotic woods. One unfortunate ambassador was kept waiting four years for an audience. The pharaoh expected inferior kings to send their daughters to his palace, but dispatching an Egyptian princess abroad was considered a humiliation. Such marriage alliances were sealed when Egypt was weak and needed support. But the great rulers of the New Kingdom era (1550–1069), such as Tuthmosis III (1479–1425) and Ramesses II (1279–1213), expanded the realm far into Nubia and into the Levant, deploying tens of thousands of soldiers in their campaigns. Their preferred tools of propaganda included ostentatious displays of gold – jewellery, weapons, and regalia – and the construction of vast temple complexes, like that of Ramesses II at Abu Simbel, where imposing victory scenes adorned almost every wall.

Fortunes turned, and the splendour of the New Kingdom gradually dissolved into anarchy. Already, early in the reign of Ramesses II, there were signs of war fatigue. 'Peace is better than fighting. Give us breath!' we read in the *Poem of Pentaur*.[21] The real descent from the golden age began at the end of the thirteenth century.[22] The death of Ramesses II in 1213 sparked a succession struggle, harem conspiracies, and civil war. Politically weakened, Egypt struggled with a violent influx of immigrants and raiders from the Mediterranean. The impact of these Sea Peoples seems to have been traumatic. On one of the walls of Ramesses III's temple at Medinet Habu, near Luxor, an epic sea battle dominates the representations of his military campaigns. The drama and dynamism of the relief – the hundreds of wrestling bodies, the bristling forests of oars and spears – encapsulate the sense of shock and awe felt by the Egyptians. The Sea Peoples could be defeated, but only at the cost of thousands of lives, famine, inflation, and social upheaval. Meanwhile, Libyan raiders continued to lurk on the borders. Eventually, in 1107, the high priests of Thebes seized control of Upper Egypt, dividing the kingdom, and prompting the Nubians to cast off the Egyptian yoke. But the fatal blow came only in the tenth century, when the Great Chief of the Libyan Meshwesh, Shoshenq I (943–922), became pharaoh. A foreign dynasty ruled over Egypt.

Once again, poetry gives us a vivid impression of how such turmoil was experienced by the common people:

> A strange bird will breed in the Delta marsh,
> Having made its nest beside the people,
> The people having let it approach by default . . .
> All happiness has vanished,
> The land is bowed down in distress,
> Owing to those feeders,
> Asiatics who roam the land.
> Foes have risen in the East,
> Asiatics have come down to Egypt . . .
> Men will seize weapons of warfare,
> The land will live in uproar.
> Men will make arrows of copper,
> Will crave blood for bread,
> Will laugh aloud at distress.
> None will weep over death,
> None will wake fasting for death,
> Each man's heart is for himself.
> Mourning is not done today,
> Hearts have quite abandoned it.

A man sits with his back turned,
While one slays another.
I show you the son as enemy, the brother as foe,
A man slaying his father.[23]

Egypt owed its power to the large fertile valley of the Nile, which enabled it to become one of the first regions in the world to develop an imperial tradition. Within this, the political manifestation of *Maat* took the form of hierarchy: the gods supported the pharaoh's efforts to preserve harmony, and the pharaoh demanded obeisance not only from his subjects but also from lesser kings in the Egyptian sphere of influence. In the then ideal incarnation of international politics, those lesser kings brought tribute, sent their daughters to the palace, and dispatched delegates to prostrate themselves at the feet of the pharaoh. The reality, however, was far more turbulent. Even within Egypt, the Nile Valley could form an arena of competition between cities. And the country's prosperity always made it an attractive target for predators. Any moment of weakness could therefore trigger invasion by one of the powers lurking on its fringes. But most conquerors, like the Libyan warlord Shoshenq, preferred to adopt the Egyptian imperial tradition and its symbols wholesale instead of destroying them. Despite changing overlords, the imperial interpretation of *Maat* always lived on.

Mesopotamia

Compared to Egypt, the geography and environment of Mesopotamia are rather more complex. The rivers Tigris and

Euphrates – from which Mesopotamia (Greek for the land 'between the rivers') takes its name – run roughly parallel for almost 2,000 kilometres, cutting the area into a patchwork of valleys and oases that are difficult for a single power to control. The first to impose an empire on this area was the central city state of Akkad in around 2300. Over the centuries the Akkadians were succeeded by other indigenous states: the Sumerians, who ruled from the city of Ur in the south; the Babylonians, in the centre; and the Assyrians, whose ancestral capital was Assur, in the north.

And those were not the only contenders for power in the region. The tributaries of the Tigris and Euphrates led into the Taurus Mountains, the Armenian Highlands, and the Zagros Mountains. Advantageously located high above the plains of Mesopotamia, these ranges formed strategic bridgeheads – locations that were close to water, rich in farmland, gateways to trade, and well defended by rock formations – and gave rise to ambitious kingdoms, such as Mitanni, Uratu, Elam, and Media. The hills of the Levant too offered sanctuary to kingdoms, but these were too small to threaten the Mesopotamian plains.

Archaeological traces of thinking about governance lead us deep into the history of Mesopotamia. Clay tablets from the kingdom of Ur promulgate laws to curb violence, tax abuse, income inequality, and mistreatment of women. Displayed in the Musée du Louvre is the oldest complete code of law, issued by the Babylonian king Hammurabi in around 1750. The Code of Hammurabi contains detailed stipulations concerning property, the treatment of prisoners, and the rights of women in divorce. There are representations of Shamash, the popular Babylonian god of justice, who bestowed authority and wisdom on the kings. There is the *Epic of Gilgamesh*, which describes a ruler who oppresses his people and sleeps with their brides on the nights of their weddings, but then finds friendship and becomes a good king who digs wells, tames floods, builds walls that gleam like copper – a king, so the story goes, who is righteous, beautiful, and perfect. 'There is no rival who can raise his weapon against him.'[24]

All these elements add up to what can be thought of as a Mesopotamian imperial culture. Shamash, the Babylonian god of justice, was also embraced by the Assyrian kings, as were the Code of Hammurabi and the *Epic of Gilgamesh*. Even the Assyrian kings' robes, magnificent beards, and regalia were inherited in part from Babylon. And, just like the Babylonians, the Assyrians also depicted their king as a gardener, surrounded by paradisiacal landscapes, as a metaphor for peace and prosperity. 'I dug out a canal from the Upper Zab, cutting through a mountain peak, and called it Abundance Canal,' boasted one Assyrian king.

> I watered the meadows of the Tigris and planted orchards with all kinds of fruit trees in the vicinity. I planted seeds and plants that I had found in the countries through which I had marched and in the highlands which I had crossed: pines of different kinds, cypresses and junipers of different kinds, almonds, dates, ebony, rosewood, olive, oak, tamarisk, walnut, terebinth and ash, fir, pomegranate, pear, quince, fig, grapevine . . .[25]

But, as the texts and artworks also attest, for paradise to reign at home, the king had to be strong abroad – subduing other kings, and receiving their tribute and homage.

As in Egypt, the Iron Age in Mesopotamia originated in turmoil. The climate became drier, so that plants no longer grew.[26] This drove the Cimmerians from the plains around the Black Sea to the Caucasus; the semi-nomadic Arameans from Anatolia into Mesopotamia; several other peoples, such as the Dorians, towards the Mediterranean; and the Sea Peoples towards the Levant and Egypt. This period of mass migration was an age of darkness, unrest, and destruction, in which the walled cities of the periphery – such as Ugarit and Mycenae – succumbed first.

In Mesopotamia, Babylon was a shadow of its former great imperial self. It had never really recovered from the turmoil that followed the death of the great King Hammurabi in 1699. Now it was invaded by the Hittites, the Kassites, the Elamites, and the Assyrians. In 1082, the region was afflicted by famine and Aramean attacks. In 1025, the native Babylonian king was deposed. Chronicles state that important religious processions were suspended, there was famine once again, and lions, wolves, and panthers roamed the streets. Assyria too trembled before the onslaught of the Aramean hordes from the north. Destruction, murder, and slavery, later kings recorded, fell upon the people of Assyria.[27] Just before the dawn of the first millennium, the whole of the Middle East was in flames.

China

Another region with the potential to form an imperial heart-land was located in the North China Plain.[28] This vast flat and fertile land of over 400,000 square kilometres is the work of the Yellow River. It stretches from present-day Beijing in the north to Shanghai in the south and extends over 1,000 kilometres inland to the mountain ranges of Yanshan and Taihang. It comprises about 5 per cent of the territory of modern China.

By the beginning of the Iron Age, most of the forest that once covered this plain had disappeared and made way for farmland. The centre was inhabited by several societies, like the Wei and the Qi. They were surrounded by societies that had their power bases in the valleys that gave on to the plains, like the Qin and the Zhou. Further out lived barbarian peoples like the Xirong, the Beidi, and the Nanman. We often praise China for its long imperial history, but for long periods it has been fragmented and ravaged by war. Indeed, the territory that we know as China today would not finally be united until the eighteenth century CE.

A large part of the North China Plain was unified for the first time in its history by the Shang kingdom in around 1600 BCE. Primary sources about the Shang are scarce. From the tomb of Fu Hao we know that the dynasty's rulers were buried with only a handful of slaves, unadorned bronze vessels, and rather primitive jade sculptures.[29] Texts engraved on tortoise shells testify to a world of permanent war against the 'devil's lands'. The absence of any further shells after around 1200 could indicate that these precious tributary gifts from coastal states no longer reached the Shang capital. If so, this was perhaps an early sign of the decline of the Shang Dynasty, which was noticeable for more than a century before the Zhou state and its allies eventually overthrew it at the Battle of Muye in 1046. This was an event of cataclysmic proportions: records speak of a million fighters taking part.[30] To the people of the North China Plain, the arrival of the Zhou from their stronghold deep in the Yellow River Valley must have been as perplexing as the Libyan putsch in Egypt or the entry of the Kassites into Babylon.

The Zhou's rulers justified the overthrow of the Shang Dynasty as being mandated by heaven, because the latter had let the country slip into corruption, drunkenness, and insecurity. Duke Dan of Zhou, a powerful advisor to the first king of the Zhou Dynasty, refined this theory of legitimization down to its essence: the king was the son of heaven, and he ruled with the mandate of heaven (*tian ming*) the centre of the world under heaven.[31] And thus the notion of China as 'the Middle Kingdom' was born.

An inscription on the Shi Qiang *pan*, a bronze basin, describes how the first kings of Zhou united 10,000 states and restored order. 'Steadfast and at peace is the Son of Heaven,' it goes. 'Heavenly radiant and incorruptible, the Lord on High and the witch protectors give the Son of Heaven an extensive mandate, thick blessings, and abundant harvests. Among the borderland peoples and the *man*-savages, there are none who do not hasten to appear at court.'[32] 'Great peace', that was the ultimate goal. 'When the ruler, above, insists on wanting to conduct his affairs imperially, then he is submitting to upholding the way of heaven,' the later Confucian scholar Shao Bowen asserted. 'When, at the middling level, he conducts kingly affairs, then he is submitted to upholding the way of man. When, at the lowest level, he conducts affairs tyrannically, then he is submitting to upholding the way of earth. Among these three ways, only this first one ought to be raised.'[33]

China's political landscape at the outset of the Iron Age, therefore, was in many ways comparable to the situation in Mesopotamia and Egypt. A large fertile plain allowed the population to expand – in the case of China probably to around 10 million – but it was divided between separate cities and kings that competed incessantly for influence.[34] The small city of Fenghao was located on the periphery of the North China Plain; but, as the capital of the Zhou kings, it became one of the first states to bring some degree of unity to the region and to establish an imperial ideology based on the mandate of heaven.

South Asia

The North China Plain was separated by almost 3,000 kilometres of forests, mountains, and glaciers from another important potential cradle of empire, the Indo-Gangetic Plain. For millions of years, the waters discharged by the monsoon against the southern slopes of the Himalaya ran south in hundreds of small rivers that fed the Indus, the Ganges, and the Brahmaputra as they carved their way to the Arabian Sea and the Bay of Bengal. The plain they formed measures over 2.5 million square kilometres and is the most important food basket in the world. Like a horseshoe it bends around the hard rock formation of the Deccan Plateau to the south. To the north, it is bordered by the Hindu Kush, the Himalaya, and the Shan Hills of Myanmar. Until the arrival of European colonists in the sixteenth century CE, external threats were mostly limited to the nomadic people that dwelt along the Amu Darya in Central Asia, but they had to cross the long and dangerous mountain trails of the Hindu Kush before the Khyber Pass gave them entry to the plains of South Asia.

During the Bronze Age, the western half of the Indo-Gangetic Plain was dominated by the Indus Valley or Harappa Civilization (3000–1300 BCE). After its great mud-brick cities of Mohenjodaro and Harappa were abandoned around 1900, there is no evidence of any new major polity filling the void in the centuries afterwards. Instead, when the so-called 'Indo-Aryan Migration' began to advance south, probably via the Hindu Kush in around 1500, it encountered a patchwork of tribes and little kingdoms. At first, these incomers developed a stronghold in the grasslands of the Swat Valley in the north of what is now Pakistan; but over the course of centuries they multiplied, gained influence over the existing inhabitants, and advanced on to the fertile plains of the Indus and the Ganges.[35]

Although this long process is probably more appropriately described as a 'migration' than an 'invasion', it caused a profound social transformation. This new culture is usually referred to as the Vedic Civilization, after the Vedas, or sacred texts written in Sanskrit, on which Hinduism is founded. The primitive painted greyware ceramics of the Vedic Civilization did not come close to the artistic splendours of Egypt and Mesopotamia, but it did leave a literature unparalleled for richness in that epoch. During this period, iron working was introduced, society was divided into castes, and new kingdoms were established. If we are to believe epics such as the *Mahabharata*, relations between these states seem to have been characterized by anarchy, as they formed alliances against one another, quarrelled, and fought almost endlessly. It was not until the fifth century that one state – the kingdom of Panchala – was able to create a kind of hegemony over its neighbours. And it was not until the fourth century that a large part of the Indian subcontinent fell under the control of a single empire, the Maurya.

In the Hindu tradition, harmony is represented by the goddess of fortune, Lakshmi, and her husband, Vishnu, the god of justice and peace. The ancient Sanskrit epics, like the *Mahabharata* and the *Ramayana*, highlight the desire for peace and harmony – for parents to see their children grow up, farmers to bring in their harvest, and kings to rule justly. But they also stress how difficult it is to uphold. The concept of proportionality (*desha dharma*) is promulgated in order to avoid the excessive use of violence, only to be abandoned to the folly of hatred. Arbitration (*panchayat*) is introduced, but that too rarely prevents conflict. Emissaries are treated with contempt, and preparations for war continue regardless.

Even if the gods in the *Mahabharata* warned against war, cunning ministers knew how to play on the king's pride and insecurity. 'Kings should ever be ready with uplifted maces to strike when necessary and they should ever increase their prowess,' the evil counsellor Kanika advises. 'Carefully avoiding all faults themselves they should ceaselessly watch over the faults of their foes and take advantage of them.'[36] Kanika goes on to explain that a king should behave like a wily jackal, and destroy his foes preferably without resorting to open warfare, through diplomacy, financial power, or provoking internal disunity. It is perhaps unsurprising that the ideal polity on earth, according to the Vedas, was a city of iron, well protected against the forces of nature and men.

Security and Power

Vice, virtue, and violence in international relations: at the dawn of the first millennium, these had already become important themes about which people reflected, wrote, painted, and sculpted. In modern terms, power distribution – the first historical layer to be studied in this book – depended on the holy trinity of natural resources. Even if the world was still sparsely populated and natural barriers slowed communication immensely, the Eastern Mediterranean, the North China Plain, and the Indo-Gangetic Plain had clearly transformed into restless arenas of power politics. Elsewhere, throughout the thick forest, the mountain ranges, and the grass plains that still covered much of the rest of the globe, power politics took place on a smaller scale. Its impact on human lives, however, was no less important.

The second historical layer we identified for consideration was the evolution in political organization. The late Bronze Age world was dotted with small cities and towns, seldom with more than a few thousand inhabitants. Many of these cities were ruled by kings and controlled a tract of surrounding territory, and were thus city states. Especially in the four regions of the globe where agriculture was most advanced – Egypt, Mesopotamia, the Indo-Gangetic and North China Plains – the density of these city states was relatively high, enabling them to interact more intensively culturally, commercially – and militarily. They generally shared cultural, religious, and political customs, which in turn contributed to the birth of imperial traditions in the form of common symbols to legitimize hierarchy. Thus political reality in these regions was shaped by small city states vying for power and, ultimately, possession of the insignia of empire.

If there was a 'natural state' – that is, a primitive stage – of international relations, it was already characterized by the tension between the desire for peace and the failure to preserve it. Burial sites, the visual arts, and poetry all testify to the value attached to human life, the desire to live life to the fullest, even in very tough conditions, the anguish of losing loved ones, and the horror of war. Even for people living in the most primitive conditions, in temporary huts or tiny villages, war meant massacre, torture, abduction, and enslavement. It was little different for the farmers and craftsmen of the more developed states. Threats might be met on distant borders, but such wars still often resulted in higher taxes, the neglect of the irrigation infrastructure essential for agricultural surpluses, and conscription.

As a result, people everywhere dreamt of an ideal world of harmony. In Egypt, this was embodied in *Maat*; in China, in the 'mandate of heaven'; in Mesopotamia, in the Code of Hammurabi; and in India, in the deities Vishnu and Lakshmi. The main tasks of the state and its ruler were to preserve peace internally and to provide security on the border. The

ideal images of the polity, therefore, were those of a sanctuary against an evil world, a garden in the desert, a walled
refuge, a city of iron. So, when we consider the fifth historical
layer identified at the outset of this book – the evolution of
thinking about the nature of world politics – the late Bronze
Age already reveals a striking dichotomy. The ideal king was
a fair-minded father to his own people, but a fearless fighter
against foreign threats.

This brings us to an important aspect of the third historical layer identified earlier: namely, why was war more prevalent
than peace? Paradoxically, it was the pursuit of security that
caused so much misery. Borders were fluid, so that the scope
of the pursuit of security was hard to define: any firm distinction between defensive and offensive wars could seldom be
made. What one side saw as a just defensive war was, from
the opposing viewpoint, brutal aggression. In the same vein,
if a king from Egypt, Assyria, or China considered the establishment of an empire as the way to transform anarchy into
stability, the subjugated parties saw it very differently. Any dif-
ferentiation between a state's search for security and its desire
for power maximization could rarely be made.

Already, at the threshold of the first millennium, war
could be immensely profitable, if not for the common people
then certainly for the king and his court. Cities and temples
were treasuries of gold and other luxuries; farmlands could
generate large tax incomes, and so could the control of trade
routes. The search for security and profit were thus inextricably entwined. The same was also true for the strength and
weakness of states. The rise of a polity, its economic success,
its political unity, or its technological progress could all spell

war with jealous or frightened rivals. But a polity's weakness could encourage predators to intervene, as happened to the New Kingdom in Egypt and the Shang Dynasty in China.

One final aspect merits mention: nature, which is the fourth historical layer considered in this book. Just before the first millennium, the world experienced a change of climate. It destabilized entire societies – especially those in the most precarious environments, like the steppes – and caused large-scale migration and strife. Fear, greed, power, and natural scarcity – these were the factors shaping early international relations.

CHAPTER 2

Solomon's Peacock

1000–750 BCE

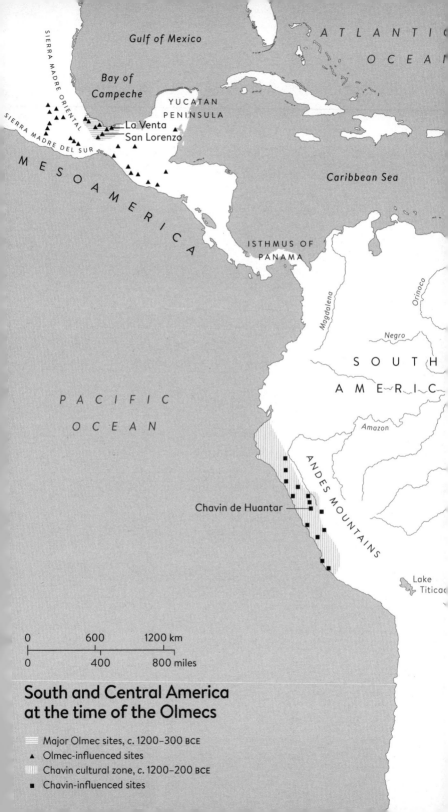

South and Central America at the time of the Olmecs

≡ Major Olmec sites, c. 1200–300 BCE
▲ Olmec-influenced sites
▥ Chavín cultural zone, c. 1200–200 BCE
■ Chavín-influenced sites

At the dawn of the Iron Age, around 1000 BCE, the world remained an empty place. Most of the planet was inhabited by isolated tribes and wandering peoples. Those tribal societies which we encountered in the previous chapter valued life, and sought to coexist with others by demarcating borders, exchanging goods, and engaging in diplomacy. Still, the natural state of foreign relations was as much about war as about peace. The same state of affairs, as we have also seen, was true for the first kingdoms. The ideal was again a life of harmony. Kings communicated with each other, wrote letters, and dispatched envoys. But kings were also expected to win spoils: to benefit their subjects and advance their own personal prestige. The Nile Valley, Mesopotamia, the Indo-Gangetic Plain, and the North China Plain were the main demographic and political centres. They too desired harmony, prayed to *Maat* or Lakshmi, or hoped the emperor would uphold the mandate of heaven.

This chapter describes how, at the turn of the new millennium, Egypt, Mesopotamia, and the eastern part of the Mediterranean became a single vast political arena. The ambitions of Egypt and Assyria – whose rise seemed unstoppable – collided in the Levant, where numerous lesser states failed to unite to resist them. Both wanted to control trade; both believed their rulers chosen by the gods. This chapter also reconstructs how the designs of the Zhou emperors of China clashed with those of their powerful neighbours and, as a result, the dynasty foundered and the North China Plain fragmented into anarchy. Finally, it explores one of the first empires in the Western Hemisphere, that of the enigmatic Olmec, and the role of the humble maize pancake, the tortilla, in creating it.

The Rise of Assyria

By the beginning of the first millennium, the Dark Ages had spread over the shores of the Mediterranean like the smoke from a bushfire. Invaders from the Northern Mediterranean, known as the Sea Peoples, engulfed the southern and eastern shores of the Mediterranean. Egypt descended into turmoil. Beyond, Babylon was on the verge of collapse. The invaders that swarmed across the Mesopotamian plains now started to fight each other. Assyria was the only tree left standing with its roots intact. This was Assyria's chance and it seized it. The turning point was 910, the year that King Adad-nirari II (911–891) confronted the Arameans, a people in the north of present-day Syria, and dealt them a major blow. From then on, the Assyrian kings rapidly spread their influence across the Middle East.

The victories of Adad-nirari II would not have been possible, however, without the twenty years of domestic reform carried out by his father. King Ashur-dan II (934–912) had organized the realm into formal provinces and regulated their administration, fortified the capital, restored the fortresses along important trade routes, and increased agricultural production. 'I brought back the weary people of Assyria, who in the face of famine, hunger, and shortage had abandoned their cities,' Ashur-dan had bragged. 'I hitched up plows in the districts of my land; I heaped up more grain than ever before.'[1]

As soon as he had dealt with the Arameans, Adad-nirari turned his attention to Babylon. Although his troops prevailed again, the victory was not decisive and so a marriage alliance was arranged between the two courts. Subsequent campaigns concentrated on the small kingdoms of the mountains to the north, including the enfeebled Hittites. Adad-nirari's grandson Ashurnasirpal II (883–859) advanced all the way to the Mediterranean and the Red Sea. In 879, Ashurnasirpal showed his self-confidence by throwing a grandiose party to inaugurate a new palace in a renewed capital: Nimrud.[2] For over two decades, thousands of men had laboured to complete it. Now the king 'treated for ten days with food and drink 47,074 persons, men and women, who were bid to come from across my entire country; also 5,000 important persons, delegates from other countries,' he recorded on a stone stele. 'I did them due honors and sent them back, healthy and happy.'[3] His successor pushed the Assyrian conquests even further. By the late ninth century, the Assyrian Empire controlled almost the entirety of Mesopotamia as well as large parts of the Levant and Anatolia.[4]

The spectacular rise of Assyria was possible because several capable kings occupied the throne without any dispute over the succession. Their strength lay in a combination of economic reforms, needed to keep the population satisfied, and innovation on the battlefield.[5] The Assyrians perfected their siege tactics, using battering rams and mobile towers. They experimented with camels and cavalry as an alternative to chariot warfare. They improved technologies for hardening iron into steel. Propaganda designed to terrorize enemies posed a clear choice: pay tribute or perish. 'Their men, young and old, I took prisoners. Of some I cut off the feet and hands; of others I cut off the noses, ears and lips,' we read in inscriptions on the walls of Ashurnasirpal II's palace in Nimrud. 'Of the young men's ears I made a heap; of the old men's heads I made a minaret . . . The male children and the female children I burnt in the flames.'[6]

The result was predatory imperialism. Conquest allowed for tribute and tribute allowed for new conquests. Administrative records give us an impression of the spoils: gold, silver, tin, copper, linen garments with coloured trimmings, monkeys, ebony, boxwood, and sea-creatures' tusks. Some of the conquered lands were turned into imperial provinces, ruled by governors who upheld Assyrian law, spread Assyrian culture, and levied Assyrian taxes. Others became client states, ruled indirectly through puppet kings who had to forego independent foreign relations, pay tribute, and send their children as hostages to the Assyrian court.

From the annals of the Assyrian kings – punched into tablets of clay and carved into steles of stone – a clear imperial order emerges. At the centre resided Ashur. He was the chief god, who instructed the king. The king lived in a palace, surrounded by paradisiacal gardens, which in turn was surrounded by a city with immense walls and gates and inhabited by craftsmen, around which lay farmland, idealized in sculpture as a lush habitat of bountiful date trees, fecund grain fields, and rivers full of fish. This was 'the middle kingdom', the land chosen by the gods. The lands beyond – the periphery – were thought to have been abandoned by the gods and left as a 'failed cosmos'.

This failed cosmos proved a restless place. The Assyrians were fortunate that their neighbours recovered more slowly from the collapse of the Bronze Age and were busy quarrelling among themselves. In Egypt, for instance, the new Libyan Dynasty – which famously identified itself with the holy cat – was able to deliver only two strong kings. King Shoshenq I (943–922), the founder of the dynasty, was an unrelenting campaigner. One of the temples at Karnak still shows him towering above bound and defeated enemies, neatly lined up and labelled, a bit like a collection of insects. Shoshenq held sway over much of present-day Israel and Lebanon. He signed a trade agreement with the king of Tyre. The latter expressed his diffidence by placing a small granite statue of the pharaoh in the main temple of Byblos.[7]

But King Shoshenq's death was followed by succession conflicts and it was only with a stroke of luck that Osorkon II (872–837) was able to establish and consolidate power. Osorkon briefly campaigned in the north, but his foreign policy was one of restraint. Already he was haunted by the prospect of further succession conflicts after his death. 'Establish my children to the offices which I shall give to them,' he prayed to the god Amon, 'so that no brother is jealous of the other brother.'[8] Yet Egypt did plunge into dynastic struggle. A few years after Osorkon's death, it split in two. The south regained autonomy and even the Nile Delta gradually disintegrated into various statelets. The Assyrians came dangerously close to the Sinai Desert.[9] Only around 710 would a new king reunify Egypt: a black pharaoh, from Nubia.

The Bible and the Battlefield

Much like today, the Levant in the early Iron Age was a warren of political intrigue and ambition. For Shoshenq I and Osorkon II this patchwork of small cities and kingdoms was an attractive target: politically weak, but wealthy from trade. From the city of Memphis in the Nile Delta one trade route, the 'Way of the Sea', led via numerous Mediterranean coastal cities all the way to Damascus. Another, the 'King's Highway', led via the northern reaches of the Red Sea, the Dead Sea, and the River Jordan also to Damascus, and then on to the Euphrates and Anatolia.

The Jordan Rift Valley divides the Levant into western and eastern parts. Moving from west to east, first there is the coastal strip, which receives plenty of rain; then the valley of the River Jordan; and finally the arid Jordanian plateau. In the north of the region was the great city of Tyre. Tyre was to the Iron Age Levant what Venice became to Italy from the twelfth century CE. Much as medieval Venice in its protected lagoon drew upon its overseas possessions – the vast *Stato da Màr* – the Phoenicians of Tyre wove the entire Mediterranean into a web of commerce centred on their island city, protected by its location just off the coast of modern Lebanon. They possessed colonies as far as the Strait of Gibraltar. The Phoenicians were indispensable for the supply of cedar wood and iron. East of Tyre was the kingdom of Aram, home of the Arameans. South of it, stretching along the Sea of Galilee and the River Jordan, were the kingdoms of Israel, Ammon, Judah, Edom, and Moab.

The perpetual struggle between these kingdoms forms the historical background of the Old Testament. Under King Saul (1043–1012 BCE), Israel emerged as the hegemon of the Levant. After leading a heterogeneous alliance of tribes to victory against the Ammonites, Saul had been crowned as their king and united them as the kingdom of Israel. His successors, David (1010–1002) and Solomon (970–931), enlarged the kingdom. The Old Testament describes Solomon as a competent ruler. He wanted the state to control all trade, built furnaces for smelting iron, commissioned a navy, and founded a standing army. Solomon gained control over the Way of the Sea, oversaw most of the traffic on the King's Highway, and established a trade agreement with the king of Tyre.

There is evidence of trade between the Middle East, the Mediterranean, the Red Sea, and even the Indian Ocean. 'Once every three years came the fleet bringing gold, silver, ivory, apes, and peacocks,' the Old Testament reports.[10] It also refers to a visit by the queen of Sheba to Solomon's court. This could be explained by the fact that Sheba, located in today's Yemen, was already a crucial trade hub between the worlds of the Indian Ocean and the Mediterranean. Solomon also cemented alliances by adding to his harem princesses from Egypt, Moab, Ammon, Edom, and other kingdoms. But after Solomon's death, Israel split in two, with the southern half becoming the independent kingdom of Judah.

Immediately after its secession, Judah was besieged by Shoshenq I, who had been brought into the region by Israel,

Egypt's new ally. Around 890, King Asa of Judah took all the gold from the main temple to bribe the king of Aram to terminate his treaty with Israel and open a second front in the north. Around 860, Judah was invaded by the kingdoms of Moab and Ammon. When Aramean troops also arrived, Judah was forced to sue for peace.

In 853, the whole region found itself threatened by imminent Assyrian invasion. Mutual conflicts were brought to an end to form a formidable alliance. It gathered at Qarqar, in modern Syria, to waylay the Assyrian army. The coalition consisted of troops from Babylon, Egypt, Persia, Israel, Aram, and ten other nations. According to one stele, over 60,000 warriors clashed during the battle. For the peoples of the Middle East, this was akin to a world war. Assyria prevailed, possibly thanks to its larger and better cavalry. It forced most of its defeated foes into vassalage.

Less than three years later, the Arameans and Israelites were back at war with each other. On the Tel Dan Stele, the Aramean king describes how he took revenge for the defeat of his father, 'subduing seventy kings with thousands of chariots and horses'.[11] In 849, Israel and Judah fought side by side against the Arameans, sealing the alliance with the superior northern kingdom by marrying a princess. In 815, the Arameans could have defeated Israel entirely if the Assyrians had not descended once again on Damascus, so that the threat from the north temporarily subsided. In 814, the Arameans gathered with the Babylonians and the Elamites to ward off a further Assyrian strike.[12] Judah, meanwhile, was plagued by rivalry with Edom and raids by the Philistines. But then the wars between Aram and Israel rekindled.

Although the Assyrians continued to campaign against Babylon and the Aramean kingdom into the eighth century, their war machine slowly lost traction. This was because of succession conflicts, governors gaining power at the expense of the king, and the growing influence of the chief of staff, the *turtanu*. By 763, the power of the Assyrian king was severely weakened. An eclipse that year was seen as the harbinger of misfortune. Plague struck, and the Assyrian kingdom plunged into a decade of revolt and anarchy. The records report violations of border agreements by the Babylonians, rebellions against Assyrian influence in the Levant, and even the breaking of a treaty by Mati'-ilu, king of the small state of Arpad. 'If Mati'ilu sins against this treaty,' we read in the Assyrian records, 'may Mati'ilu become a prostitute.'[13] But curses like these could not prevent the empire from descending into forty years of stagnation. Luckily for Assyria, however, nobody was able to take advantage. After several decades of uncertainty, another sequence of great kings would embark on the campaign that doubled the Assyrian Empire's size, extending its borders all the way to Nubia, Cyprus, and the Persian Gulf.

Treaties and Curses

If the aggression of the Sea Peoples was the most remarkable event of the late second millennium, the rise of Assyria shaped the outlook of a large part of the Eastern Hemisphere in the centuries that followed. Compared to Egypt and Babylon, Assyria is often portrayed as a merciless empire. The reliefs on Assyrian palace walls leave nothing to the imagination.

They show the amputation of the ears, noses, and limbs of prisoners of war. This was propaganda based on terror. But the differences with other ancient empires were not that great. The Egyptian pharaohs, too, covered their temples with representations of enemies being dismembered or enslaved. Ramesses III, for instance, made his bid for immortality with the true temple of terror he built at Medinet Habu. In every corner of the compound he can be seen smiting rivals and towering over the field of battle. On one wall, he is even depicted taking receipt of piles of chopped hands and penises as evidence of the success of the campaigns of his generals. The ideology underlying Assyrian and Egyptian imperial rule was also similar. Both cultures' kings were tasked by the gods to preserve the stability and the prosperity of the people that prayed to them. The Assyrian king was the representative of the god Ashur. Wherever he reigned, there was peace, tranquillity, and justice. Wherever he did not rule, was chaos.[14]

The ancient sources show that the conquests made by Egypt and Assyria were driven by the need for security. Above all, it was crucial to secure the agricultural production centred in the river valleys, both to prevent social unrest arising from hunger, and also to preserve a steady flow of taxes from farmers. The sheer size and fragmentation of Mesopotamia made this much more difficult for the Assyrians than for the Egyptians. There were many ambitious cities, each with its own strong cultural identity, that had to be brought under control. Neither Egypt nor Assyria had the luxury of clearly defined natural frontiers; and so security also implied that the whole periphery had to be brought under control too.

For Egypt, the focus was mostly on the populous Eastern Mediterranean. For Assyria, efforts were required in every direction: west to the Levant, north to Anatolia, east to the Zagros Mountains, and south to the Persian Gulf and Arabian Peninsula.

It was in this pursuit of a sphere of influence that the difference between security seeking and power maximization blurred. Security was no longer just a matter of defending the capital city or the kingdom's borders, but required the borders to be extended in order to keep enemies as far from the capital as possible. Kings prided themselves on the spoils they seized in war, the slaves they captured, and the immense wealth they gained by forcing other states into tributary obedience. The Black Obelisk of Shalmaneser III gives an impression of the curious gifts brought to the court by foreign missions. 'I received tribute from Musri: two-humped camels, a water buffalo, a rhinoceros, an antelope, female elephants, female monkeys and apes,' it reports. 'I received tribute from Iaua, son of Omri: silver, gold, a golden bowl, a golden tureen, golden pails, tin, the staffs of the king's hand and a spear.'[15] From the eighth century onwards, Assyria also strove to control the trade routes to the Levant and to secure the supply of timber.

Egypt and Assyria, like other polities, used terror as propaganda. Still, life was valuable, even that of people outside the realm. The Musée du Louvre has a relief that shows the deportation of men and women, probably to work in or around the Assyrian capital.[16] Much like recent photographs from war zones, one sees unfortunate people carrying belongings, a cart pulled by a bony ox, its ribs clearly visible, with four children on top of the load. In the left-hand corner one discerns what looks like a refugee camp: Assyrian men hand out fish, figs, and water, and tend to children and a weak old man. Strength is vital, the relief seems to state, but so is magnanimity for fellow human beings.

Besides brute force, Assyria's kings used a raft of diplomatic tools to affirm their power. They demanded tributary states send princes to their courts as hostage and princesses to become one of many royal wives. If princesses were sent in both directions, it signalled that Assyria was not yet in a position to enforce its superiority. This was the case, for example, with the treaty between Adad-nirari II and the king of Babylon. It fixed the two states' border and it was sealed after the monarchs exchanged daughters as wives.

Peace treaties were often concluded in the presence of a priest and endorsed with a curse. In a treaty between Assyria and Arpad, the latter's king is warned: 'This head is not the head of a spring lamb, it is the head of Mati'-ilu, it is the head of his sons, his magnates and the people of his land. If Mati'-ilu should sin against this treaty, so may, just as the head of this spring lamb is cut off, and its knuckle placed in its mouth, the head of Mati'-ilu be cut off.'[17] Lesser states copied these oaths in treaties between themselves. The Sefire Stele records a treaty between two minor Levantine rulers, King Barga'yah and King Matti'el. The consequences of any violations are clear: 'As this wax is consumed by fire, thus Matti'el shall be consumed by fire . . . As this calf is cut up, thus Matti'el and his nobles shall be cut up.'[18]

No work offers a better picture of the power politics in the region than the Old Testament. As a historical account, it is an astounding story of wars, shifting alliances, and the permanent threat of great powers like Assyria. It venerates the Israelites as a nation chosen by God and inhabiting cities 'walled up to heaven', as the Book of Deuteronomy has it, destined to keep their promised land and to make it prosperous through farming and trade.[19] The ideal was that of a society of disparate tribes united in a common front against external enemies.

The Book of Judges recounts how Israel emerged from a period of chaos and civil war, when 'there was no king in Israel; all the people did whatever seemed right in their own eyes'.[20] Unity was brought by powerful monarchs. The Book of Kings describes Saul, David, and Solomon above all as fighters, as ruthless unifiers and defenders of their kingdom. But their power led to abuse and arbitrary decisions. This is why the Book of Deuteronomy listed very clear criteria that a good king had to fulfil. He needed to be an Israelite in the first place. The number of his horses had to be limited. He had to refrain from accumulating large amounts of silver and gold. He had to abide by the law.[21] He was not allowed to marry many wives. Thus the Old Testament defines good governance not as an authoritarian monarchy, but more as a federation bound by the divine rules of the Torah and served by a ruler who had only limited power.

When it came to defending the state, however, there were almost no limitations on the use of force. Deuteronomy prescribed that the enemy had to be given the opportunity to surrender before the fighting started: 'When you approach a city to fight against it, you shall offer it terms of peace. If it agrees to make peace with you and opens to you, then all the people who are found in it shall become your forced labor and shall serve you.' If the city did not surrender, the Israelites were called to 'strike all the men in it with the edge of the sword' and to take 'the women and the children and the animals and all that is in the city . . . as booty for yourself'.[22] The Old Testament calls for nothing less than a holy war and mass destruction. 'The Lord your God will deliver them over to you, throwing them into great confusion until they are destroyed. He will give their kings into your hand, and you will wipe out their names from under heaven. No one will be able to stand up against you; you will destroy them.'[23]

Such aggression was by no means exceptional in the early Iron Age. It bears resemblances not least to Hindu sacred epics like the *Mahabharata*, and it is also similar to inscriptions about international affairs from the ancient Levant. From the kingdom of Sam'al, north of Israel, we have a ninth-century stele that says:

> I am Kilamuwa, the son of King Haya. My own father did nothing with his reign. Predatory kings beset our kingdom. I raged amongst them like a fire . . . Under previous kings, the people howled like dogs. I was a father, a mother and a brother to them. I gave gold, silver and cattle to men who had never so much as seen the face of a sheep before. Those who had never even seen linen I dressed in byssus-cloth from head to foot.[24]

The early eighth-century stele of King Zakkur, who ruled the city of Hamath (in present-day Syria), first describes a border agreement with Assyria and curses possible violators. It goes on to report how the king was aided by the gods in a holy war against a mighty alliance of rivals who challenged his annexation of the neighbouring state of Hadrach.

> Bar-Hadad, the King of Aram, formed a great alliance with seventeen kings . . . All these kings set up a siege against Hadrach. They raised a wall higher than the wall of Hadrach. They dug a moat deeper than its moat. But I lift my hands to Baalshamin and He said: fear not, for I made you king and I will deliver you from all these kings who forced a siege against you.[25]

Both sources confirm the image from the Old Testament of warfare in the Levant, in particular the fact that the divinely ordained use of force – meaning holy war – was crucial for warding off threats and preserving a state's prosperity.

The Mediterranean World

Whereas the world of the Assyrians, the Egyptians, and the minor kingdoms of the Eastern Mediterranean is often well documented, the struggle for mastery in the Middle East also involved a number of more enigmatic actors. In the north, the Caucasus and the steppes between the Black Sea and Mongolia were the hunting ground of nomadic peoples. One important group was the Cimmerians, who were first mentioned in Assyrian documents in the eighth century. They combined cattle raising and farming. They traded with Mesopotamia along the mountain passes of the Caucasus, and also with Central Europe via the Danube.

The Cimmerians passed important knowledge on to the peoples of Anatolia – and, through them, indirectly to the

Levant and Mesopotamia – which helped improve horse riding and cavalry tactics: the use of cheek pieces and bits, for example.[26]As the Cimmerians pushed south to the Armenian Highlands, they were followed by a much more warlike people: the Scythians. From the ninth century, they poured through Central Asia and on to the Pontic-Caspian Steppe, terrifying the Cimmerians, conquering numerous mountain kingdoms, and ultimately advancing into Mesopotamia. It is not clear how numerous these steppe peoples were, but the nomadic migrations of the early Iron Age are usually conceived of in terms of hundreds of thousands of individuals – far fewer than the populaces of the great agricultural centres of Egypt and Mesopotamia, which numbered in the millions.[27]

Two of the first societies to encounter the Cimmerian thrust to the south were the Mannean kingdom and the kingdom of Urartu. The latter had evolved out of a number of tribes that had confederated in response to the growing might of Assyria. By the ninth century, it had expanded to occupy the region between the Black Sea and Lake Urmia and the upper Euphrates. Urartu became known for its monumental walled cities, its fortresses guarding strategic mountain passes, its irrigation engineering, and its underground canals. Its main legacy is the ruin of a mighty citadel of basalt and mud bricks that looks over Lake Van. It maintained an army tens of thousands strong. Neighbouring Phrygia was the main victim of Urartu's expansion. Its capital was destroyed in 800.[28]

Meanwhile, on the other side of the Aegean Sea, the Greek world slowly recovered from its Dark Ages. Between the tenth and the eighth centuries, the population around the

Aegean Sea grew rapidly. This was the beginning of a major revival. Dorian settlers transformed Corinth and Sparta into thriving towns with populations of up to 10,000.[29] All over the Greek Peninsula new land was brought into cultivation. If the plains were used mostly for wheat production, the hills were turned into olive groves, in turn boosting the trade in olive oil. By the eighth century, Greek trading settlements were established in modern-day Syria and on Cyprus. It brought Greek traders into contact with the Phoenicians and their mighty emporium of Tyre. The Greeks derived their alphabet from the Phoenicians. They were inspired by Phoenician art to replace the austere geometric decoration on their pottery with oriental themes like lions, bulls, and elegantly dressed people. As the economy boomed and the climate became milder, the Dorian settlements became too large for their farmers to support. Greek colonies were established in Asia Minor, Sicily, and the Italian Peninsula to cope with the excess population. Nevertheless, the competition for land between the Greek cities escalated.[30]

One of the chief victors of this struggle was the city state of Sparta, which by the end of the eighth century had annexed most of the southern Peloponnese. The Spartan conception of the world was straightforward. Conquered people were sold into slavery or forced to work the land as helots and yield half their harvest to Spartan citizens. Other neighbouring states became *perioikoi*: they enjoyed more freedom than the helots, but never acquired full Spartan citizenship. At the centre of it all were the citizens of Sparta itself. They believed that they were descendants of Heracles, the paragon of masculinity and son of Zeus, the supreme deity of the Greek pantheon. Given the perpetual struggle for land in the Peloponnese, manliness was key. The Spartans cultivated it through a series of commandments promulgated by the legendary lawgiver Lycurgus in the eighth century. He prescribed that all Spartan men had to be able to fight, to eat together, and to share the land equally.

The Spartan constitution – which was presumably conceived by Lycurgus – established a popular assembly of all adult male citizens. The assembly in turn elected a council of elders and five ephors. These ephors were in charge of the most important matters of state. The two Spartan kings had a largely symbolical function and maintained contact with the gods via the sanctuary of Delphi. Delphi was the centre of the Greek world. Representatives from all cities came to the sanctuary to consult its famous oracle. It was an important symbol of the growing awareness of a common Greek culture, of the idea that – the many conflicts notwithstanding – the people of Greece were set apart by divine blessing, common language, and a shared history as recorded by epic poets such as Homer. In 776, the Greek cities for the first time sent their best sportsmen to a tournament at the sanctuary of Zeus in Olympia. This was the start of the Olympic Games. They were a celebration of the strength and collective identity of all the people of Greece; during them, a truce was declared throughout the Greek world.

Just a couple of decades after the first Olympic Games, on the other side of the Ionian Sea, a city was founded that would upset the entire balance of power of the Mediterranean. The first inhabitants of this kingdom, which comprised barely a few hundred people in huts of twigs, named it Rome, after its founding father, Romulus. According to the myth, a wolf discovered abandoned twins on the banks of the River Tiber. They were the sons of the god of war and started killing from the moment they became adult. Rome's mythical founding itself was the outcome of fratricide. Romulus killed his brother Remus in an outburst of anger.

In its first years, Rome was a settlement of thugs and adventurers, more a tribe than a real city. The myth describes how Romulus and his followers tricked the neighbouring Sabine people in order to abduct their virgin daughters. They waged war with the surrounding towns and murdered their envoys when they came to sue for peace. However, the underlying conditions for Rome to become a thriving city were good. The town was protected by the Tiber, benefited from fertile land, and looked out over important trade routes. Rivers, hills, and marshes formed a natural buffer against the main centres of power at that time: the Etruscans, who lived in the north of the peninsula, and the growing Greek colonies in the south.

By the eighth century, the Mediterranean world and the Middle East had thus both fully recovered from the Bronze Age Collapse. Trade had picked up and new cities been built. The region lived in the shadow of the Assyrian Empire, which had set its eye on the other main power, Egypt. Thanks to the use of standing armies and chariots, Egypt and Assyria could project massive military power to control the large plains of Mesopotamia and the Nile and advance along the trade roads of the Levant. It was here that the two giants clashed. It was here also that they developed relations with lesser powers, like the Phoenicians and the kingdoms of Israel and

Judah. Sometimes these minor powers responded to the incursions of the Assyrians and Egyptians by joining them. At others they temporarily formed large coalitions, like the one that fought at the Battle of Qarqar.

There were also efforts made to preserve the peace between states. Sacred oaths were sworn during peace treaties. Greek statelets gathered together at shared religious sanctuaries and competed in athletic contests. Rules were established to limit the destructiveness of war. Nevertheless, anarchy between states prevailed and turned the region into a world of walls: walls of stone, and walls of myths that supported the idea of being chosen and blessed by the gods. There was also extensive trade. The Phoenician city of Tyre was in many ways the Venice or the New York of the Levant: prosperous, outward-looking, and free. Solomon traded with the Red Sea. Yet, the objective of rulers was not to let trade be free, but to control it, by means of monopolies, by sending troops to seize trade routes and natural resources, and through tributary policies.

Chinese Rites

If the rise of Assyria was the most important event to shape the western side of Eurasia in the early first millennium, in the east it was the decline of the Zhou Dynasty, which would have an enormous impact on the lives of millions of people in the North China Plain.[31] After their great victory over the Shang Dynasty at the Battle of Muye in 1046, the Zhou were instantly confronted with internal unrest. As soon as the dynasty's first king died, envious uncles rebelled against his son, Prince Cheng of Zhou. Thanks to the support of one loyal uncle, the Duke of Zhou, Cheng survived and became king in 1042.

The Duke of Zhou – who is still regarded as one of the great strategic thinkers in Chinese history – taught the new king to be moderate and to shun opulence and self-indulgence. 'Oh! the superior man rests in this, – that he will indulge in no luxurious ease,' the duke is recorded as saying. 'He first understands how the painful toil of sowing and reaping conducts to ease, and thus he understands how the lower people depend on this toil for their support,' he continued. 'I have observed among the lower people, that where the parents have diligently laboured in sowing and reaping, their sons often do not understand this painful toil, but abandon themselves to ease, and to village slang, and become quite disorderly.'[32] Cheng of Zhou consolidated his power over the North China Plain and also campaigned in the central flatlands of China. He and his immediate successors were forceful leaders. They ruled from a large new capital, Chengzhou. Chengzhou was a perfect quadrangle, defended by high walls, and accessible through three fortified gates on each side.

The *Book of Rites* offers a fascinating view of the institutions that kept the Zhou kingdom together. Regional leaders were divided in five ranks from duke to baron. At his court, the king was assisted by ministers, but the regions too had their own administrations. The king was the supreme arbiter. He held a long inspection tour once every five years and summoned regional leaders to visit his court regularly. 'This is the way to cherish the princes of the states: to make time for their visits, to welcome their coming with small contributions, and to send them away after liberal treat-ment.'[33] To handle those relations, there was a 'grand min-ister of war', but also a 'grand peace maintainer'. There were three inspectors and a 'grand minister of instruction' to supervise the ceremonies.

External trade was promoted. There were markets at the border and the *Book of Rites* advised limiting charges at the frontier gates. 'When merchants and others collect from all quarters, and come from the most distant parts, then the re-sources of the government do not fail.'[34] To support trade with foreigners, the kingdom dispatched envoys and inter-preters. In his testament, King Cheng of Zhou advised con-tinuing to invest in diplomacy. 'Make pliable those distant and make capable those near,' he urged. 'Pacify and encour-age the many countries, small and large.'[35] Such a peaceable monarch was known as a 'tranquillizing king'. The *Book of Documents* also explains that there were rules for war: do not steal cattle, jump over enclosures, or decoy away female attendants.[36]

One of the military innovations of the Zhou was to man chariots with archers.[37] The main rivals of the Zhou were the Dongyi, who continued to resist Zhou power from their stronghold around the Shandong Peninsula, the Xianyun in the Ordos region, the Guifang in what is now Shanxi Province, and the Chu, whose state was centred on the middle reaches of the Yangtze River.[38] The Zhou wrote mockingly of their enemies. 'The tribes on the east were called [the Dongyi]. They had their hair unbound, and tattooed their bodies. Some of them ate their food without it being cooked.'[39]

From texts on bronze vessels, the image emerges of an era

of savage fighting. Around 1000, King Kang of Zhou launched two campaigns against the Guifang and dispatched eight armies against the Dongyi. One bronze cauldron describes how Kang's general entered the capital in triumph in 979 with two shackled chiefs, 482 trophies, 13,081 men, thirty chariots, 355 oxen and thirty-eight sheep.[40] Soon after this victory parade, the Zhou suffered a series of setbacks. Around 970, King Zhao of Zhou attacked the Chu. The powerful Chu confederation controlled a realm that was almost as large as that of the Zhou. The Zhou used to recruit Chu ministers for their court, but the Zhou seemed to have become antagonized by their growing arrogance. That the Chu possessed important reserves of minerals for the bronze industry could have been another reason. Open hostilities finally broke out after one of the smaller tribes that was supposed to form a buffer against the Chu called for Zhou support against alleged aggression. It was a disastrous defeat for King Zhao. 'There was a comet . . . The heavens were greatly obscured and the pheasants and hares were all shaken. They lost the six armies in the Han River; the king died.'[41]

Zhao's successor in 956, King Mu of Zhou, initially concentrated on administrative reforms, establishing a promotion system based on merit. But, for unknown reasons, he started an offensive against the Xianyun and the Dongyi. The records explain that the campaign provoked opposition at the Zhou court because both states already paid tribute. Although Mu won his war, the Xianyun and Dongyi never paid tribute again. During the next sixty years, only two more major campaigns were launched by the Zhou. Inscriptions on ritual bronze vessels describe how six armies were raised and how they seized thousands of horses. The Zhou sacrificed some of the prisoners of war to the dynasty's ancestors. But their courtiers and the people grew tired of these wars and of ever-increasing taxes. On one bronze the following poem was found:

> Let us gather the thorn-ferns, let us gather the
>   thorn-ferns;
> The thorn-ferns are now springing up.
> When shall we return? When shall we return?
> It will be late in the next year.
> Wife and husband will be separated,
> Because of the Xianyun.
> We shall have no leisure to rest,
> Because of the Xianyun.[42]

During the ninth century, things continued to change for the worse as the Zhou's enemies forged alliances against them; the Chu even formed a coalition of thirty-six eastern states to attack them.[43] From then on, the annals are a litany of military defeats, barbarian incursions, and peasant revolts against excessive taxation. 'The superiors and inferiors flattered each other and the common people became perverse and indecisive,' the annals report. 'The royal house thereupon declined and poets wrote satires.'[44] It was not until the accession of King Xuang of Zhou in 828 that royal authority and the social order were restored. Then he turned his attention to external threats. According to the inscription recorded on one bronze vessel: 'It was the fifth year, third month, after the dying brightness [waning half-moon]; the king first approached to attack the Xianyun at Tuyu. Xi Jia followed the king, cutting off heads and manacling prisoners . . . The king awarded Xi Jia four horses and a colt chariot.'[45] Xuang also intervened in the succession crises of lesser states, like the Qi and the Lu, and invaded the Hua Yi for failing to pay tribute. 'The Hua Yi were our tribute money men. They must deliver their tribute, their taxes, their men and their goods. If they dare not to obey the command, then strike and attack them.'[46]

In 780, Xuan was succeeded by King You of Zhou. The omens were not good: a major earthquake hit the capital just before his coronation. Prophets preached the end of the dynasty. The annals describe how the king deposed his queen after she had given birth, prompting his father-in-law, the Marquess of Shen, to join forces with the Xianyun. Not much later, the king was killed and barbarian hordes sacked the capital. It was the year 771. The Zhou's heavenly mandate was challenged.

In the decades that followed, the Zhou capital was relocated to Luoyang. More and more vassals turned their backs on the king. While the Zhou retained nominal power, the dream of unity gave way to naked anarchy. For more than five centuries, the North China Plain was the arena of relentless competition and fighting between states, an era known as the Spring and Autumn (771–476) and Warring States (476–221) periods.

The rise and the demise of the Zhou Dynasty in China coincided with the spread of important new technology in East Asia. Along with bronze casting, the wet-rice cultivation that had flourished in China for centuries – where farmers planted rice on dry land and transferred the seedlings to flooded fields – was now gradually adopted in Japan, Korea, and Southeast Asia.

Until the seventh century, however, Korea remained sparsely populated. There were no large cities and most people lived as semi-nomads in pit dwellings, or as fisherfolk along the coast.[47] Korean myths refer to the kingdom of Gojoseon. Primitive clay statues and utensils of stone are the only objects that have been unearthed from this kingdom. Northern Vietnam was also one of the first neighbours to be exposed to Chinese influence. The Hong Bang kingdom was an important trade partner and introduced bronze casting from the eighth century. Most of the rest of East Asia remained in the Stone Age for several centuries; the first real cities emerged there only from the fifth century onwards. India, meanwhile, continued to be afflicted by perpetual fighting between tribes and small kingdoms. Gradually, however, the Indo-Gangetic Plain became more densely populated. Trade grew and villages coalesced into cities. Only in the sixth century, however, would they start to form real states, known as the Mahajanapadas.

In the same way that Assyria and Egypt had projected their power across the plains of the Middle East, the Zhou state used chariots and large armies to gain control of the North China Plain. Once that was done, it benefited from the output of millions of farmers, which in turn financed wars of expansion. In China, as in the Middle East, smaller states responded either by forming alliances against the more powerful – a strategy often referred to in international relations as 'balancing' – or by cooperating with the strongest state, a process sometimes referred to as 'bandwagoning'. Even if the Zhou kings claimed to be preserving harmony with their mandate of heaven, their bragging about severed heads was no less crude than that of the Assyrians. However, the North China Plain was still separated from the rest of Asia. Its natural borders may not have entirely stopped the spread of trade and technology, but they were formidable enough to prevent the Zhou from attempting to invade the neighbouring regions of Southeast Asia, South Asia, Central Asia, or the Korean Peninsula.

The Olmec

This chapter would not be complete without a few words about another tropical region that was home to an important civilization, Central America. The coast of the Gulf of Mexico was inhabited by the earliest significant American culture, the Olmec. There were other societies in the Western Hemisphere, such as the Chavín in what is now Peru, but their polity remained very small, and almost all of the rest of the Americas was still predominantly inhabited by hunters and hunter-gatherers.

Central America was a challenging environment, known for its dense jungle, sweltering climate, heavy rains, and dangerous predators like the jaguar. The Olmec flourished, not only because they learned to master nature – by means of extensive irrigation infrastructure – but because they learned to live with its vagaries, adapting their agriculture to the specific environmental conditions. Some farmers grew food on small grasslands on riverbanks. Others worked on plots that had been cleared by burning trees, and left as soon as the thin layer of fertile soil had been exhausted. Farming was combined with food gathering: fruit and meat from the forest, fish and shellfish from the rivers and the sea. Domesticated dogs were an additional source of protein. By the first millennium, farmers had perfected production methods for beans, potatoes, and maize, so that the population grew steadily. People began to specialize in crafts and trade began to flourish.

The agricultural surpluses must have been significant in order for so much labour to be diverted to the extraordinary objects of prestige that allow us to glimpse the Olmec civilization. The wooden huts and shelters of the Olmec may have been consumed by the forest centuries ago, but archaeologists have unearthed a series of colossal stone sculpted heads of kings or gods, some weighing over twenty tons. The remains of a pyramid have been found at La Venta, alongside large columns and a mosaic pavement. Around 900, this site had become the Olmec capital after the decline of their previous main city, at San Lorenzo. Both of these cities had fewer than 20,000 inhabitants. They were primarily religious centres, and probably the seats of rulers.[48] They dominated a large number of smaller agricultural settlements. San Lorenzo enjoyed a monopoly in the obsidian trade, while La Venta became an important trading centre for jade and other luxury goods. The best way to imagine the role of La Venta and San Lorenzo is that of the economic, political, and religious centres of federations of small villages.

Although the control of trade was certainly important for the rise of the Olmec city states, we do not know how they handled international affairs. The projection of military power must have been tremendously difficult. Campaigns were inevitably restricted by the dense forest and the long rainy season. The Olmec also lacked horses, so soldiers had to move on foot. As a result of such factors, scholars believe that the use of military force was not so common in Olmec society compared to the cultures of the Eastern Hemisphere. This might explain the absence of fortifications around cities. Contrary to the walled cities of Eurasia, La Venta was essentially an open settlement: a centre of stone buildings, probably surrounded by wooden structures, which in turn gradually blended into the forest. Several of the sculptures found at these sites appear to show foreigners, but they are not represented expressing inferiority, performing humiliating prostrations, or as prisoners.[49] One relief of an ambassador or envoy depicts him standing proudly upright bearing a flag. Another group of carvings gives the most important figure prominence without degrading the foreigners around him.[50]

Although some sculptures depict babies, or men and women holding children, most of the arts of the Olmec expressed masculine strength. The angry-looking giant heads were clearly meant to deter. Statues portray rulers as imposing figures holding staffs as weapons. Although war is certainly not as common in Olmec art as in Egyptian or Assyrian, carvings have been found of warriors and slain enemies. The late period of Olmec expansion, after the ninth century, marked by the spread of monuments like the colossal stone heads, also left archaeological finds of fire-hardened wooden spears, obsidian projectile points, and sling stones.[51] Interestingly, this moment of expansion coincided with the introduction of a food that is still very common in the region today: the tortilla. Experts argue that the tortilla was the first form of food that could be carried easily over long distances in such a humid environment. War thus might not have been so prominent in the external relations of the Olmec, but it was certainly an inseparable part of them.

Battle-Hardened Societies

At the beginning of the Iron Age, the Nile, Mesopotamia, and the North China Plain remained the leading economic centres and consequently also the centres of political power. As regards the distribution of power, the first layer studied in this book, not much had changed. The main form of political organization remained the city state. After the Dark Ages, many new city states had been founded. From some of these urban centres, many others had been conquered, dominated, and absorbed into empires, like those of Assyria and Zhou China. Their periphery was still dotted by smaller city states in Libya, the Levant, around the rest of the Mediterranean Sea, in Nubia, Anatolia, the Zagros, and in the valleys that gave way on to the agricultural heartland of China.

The ideal world remained one of abundantly irrigated fields: a paradise of golden grain, lush fruit, and herds of healthy cattle. Beyond its borders lay a lawless, godless realm: the 'failed cosmos' of the Assyrians; the *Isfet*, or chaos, of the Egyptians; the domain of tattooed barbarians who devoured raw meat, according to the Zhou. It was the king's or emperor's task to defend his people against invasion by this periphery. The same held true for smaller kingdoms. The Greek poet Homer's ideal king was a warrior. Lycurgus wanted all Spartan men to be able to fight. The Old Testament praised Saul, David, and Solomon as ruthless defenders of their kingdoms.

But the difference between defence and offence was not all that clear, and this remained an important cause of war. For the Assyrian King Adad-nirari II, the campaign against the Arameans was defensive, as they had raided his territory; but this defensive war opened the way to other kingdoms in the Levant. Similarly, the control of the Sinai Desert east of the Nile Delta was key for the defence of Egypt; but once this had been secured, the Levant was up for grabs. Security also still implied that, in order to preserve the imperial capital, other cities had to be subjugated. This was the reason why Assyria went to war with Babylon, and why the Zhou attacked the capital of the Chu. Zhou rulers relentlessly tried to absorb smaller kingdoms, calling this 'pacification'. If one did not conquer, one ran the risk of being conquered. And the ability to make conquests was now aided by increasing mobility, such as the large-scale use of chariots for military purposes and mounted archery, and by other more mundane innovations, such as the tortilla, which helped the Olmec feed their troops on campaign.

Trade also remained a cause for conflict. There is ample evidence in both hemispheres of growing trade and of greater cultural exchange along trade routes. Yet still the main objective was not to set trade free, but to control it. Even though some Zhou sources advised limiting the taxes levied at frontier gates, the Zhou kings were determined to govern the supply of strategic resources. King Solomon sought to monopolize trade with the Red Sea region. Assyria, Egypt, and the Greek city states all attempted to take over the commercial networks of the Phoenicians. The Olmec fought for territory that was rich in obsidian, jade, and other resources.

Strength encouraged new conquests, but weakness encouraged conquest by others. The Xianyun saw the chance to attack the Zhou kingdom when it struggled with heavy taxation and corruption. Succession conflicts in Egypt triggered an invasion from Nubia. When Assyria was struck with plague and the eruption of anarchy, subject states seized the opportunity to rebel, although none of them was able to take the Assyrian capital. Lesser powers also elicited war against each other, often inviting the great powers to intervene on their behalf. This was the case, for instance, with the biblical kingdoms of the Levant.

To be sure, there was diplomacy. But diplomacy's purpose was the preservation of security, status, and power, not maintaining peace. The major powers used diplomacy to force tribute from lesser states. Yet border agreements guaranteed territorial sovereignty of some sort. Alliances were cemented by exchanging princesses, and by calling the gods to bear witness to the terms of treaties and curse any party that broke them. Nevertheless, a good king was expected constantly to be ready for war. The ideal of peace was always counterbalanced by the ideal of a battle-hardened society.

CHAPTER 3

The Persian Takeover

750–500 BCE

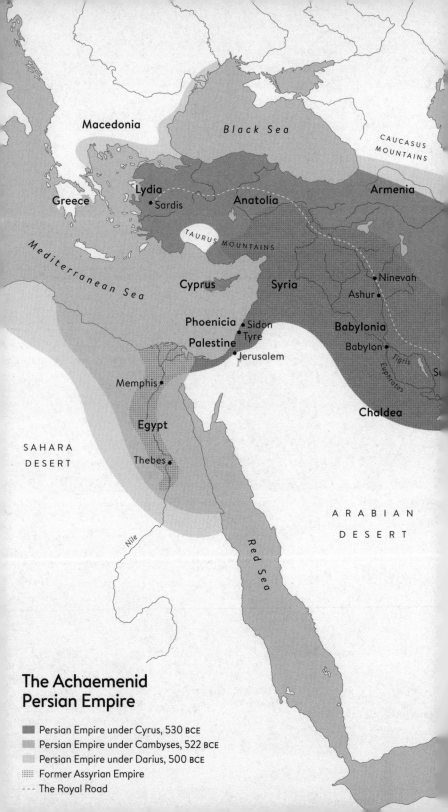

Macedonia

Black Sea

CAUCASUS
MOUNTAINS

Lydia

Greece

• Sardis

Anatolia

Armenia

Mediterranean Sea

TAURUS MOUNTAINS

Cyprus

Syria

• Ninevah

Ashur •

Babylonia

Phoenicia   • Sidon

Palestine   • Tyre

• Jerusalem

Babylon •

Tigris

Si

Memphis •

Euphrates

Egypt

Chaldea

SAHARA
DESERT

Thebes •

ARABIAN

DESERT

Nile

Red Sea

The Achaemenid
Persian Empire

▉ Persian Empire under Cyrus, 530 BCE

▉ Persian Empire under Cambyses, 522 BCE

▉ Persian Empire under Darius, 500 BCE

▦ Former Assyrian Empire

- - - The Royal Road

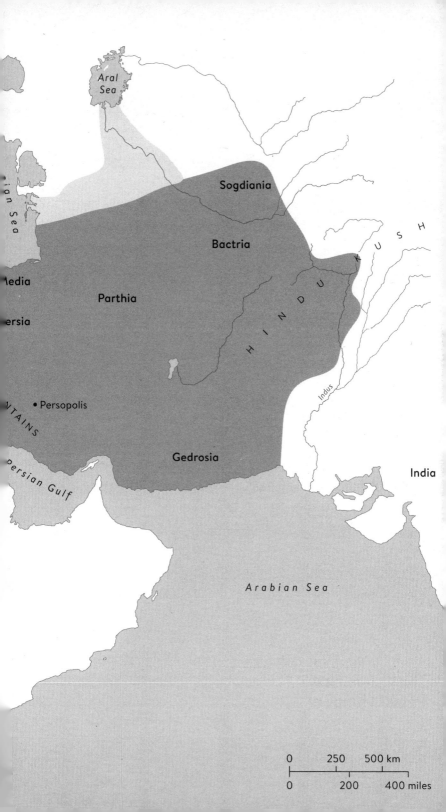

Aral
Sea

Sogdiania

Bactria

Media

Parthia

ersia

H I N D U   K U S H

Indus

Persopolis

Gedrosia

India

Persian Gulf

Arabian Sea

| 0 | 250 | 500 km |
| 0 | 200 | 400 miles |

In 650 BCE, a young prince arrived in Nineveh, the new capital of the Assyrian Empire. His name was Arukku. He was the son of a king who ruled over a small plateau deep in the Zagros Mountains. It was located on the periphery of the more powerful kingdom of Elam, which the Assyrians had ravaged a few years earlier. 'When Kurash, king of Parsumash, heard of the mighty victory, which I had inflicted on Elam with the help of Ashur, Bel, Nabu and the great gods, my lords, and that I had overwhelmed the whole of Elam like a flood,' King Ashurbanipal later recorded, 'he sent Arukku, his eldest son, together with his tribute, as hostage to Nineveh, my lordly city, and implored my lordship.'[1] Nobody at the Assyrian court would have guessed that, barely a hundred years later, this small state with just a few thousand inhabitants would conquer a realm far larger than the Assyrians ever ruled. This chapter starts with an account of this remarkable takeover: of how the Assyrian Empire reached its zenith, of how its neighbours exploited its decline, and of how one of them – the Persians under the Achaemenid Dynasty – laid the foundations of their own empire.

Between 750 and 500, the world's population grew steadily. Innovations such as the iron plough-tip and the waterwheel spread across the Eastern Hemisphere. Urbanization picked up and the Eastern Hemisphere became dotted with cities. These cities were seldom inhabited by more than 20,000 people, but even this small scale allowed for specialization in crafts, as had already been the case in Egypt, Mesopotamia and the Levant for many centuries. Surpluses of wheat, olives, and rice were bartered for luxury goods, timber, and metals. With growing surpluses and trade came new writing systems, the introduction of coins, and more shipping.

In the absence of an imperial power like the one in Mesopotamia, anarchy took hold of the rest of the world. In the Mediterranean, South Asia, and the North China Plain, the transformation of towns into cities sparked relentless competition. This was the time of infighting between Greek city states, of wars between Rome and its neighbours, and of continued struggle in the Levant. In India, it was a period of rivalry between the ambitious states known as the Mahajanapadas. In China, this epoch of anarchy was lyrically named the Spring and Autumn period. The most important event in this era, however, was the downfall of the Assyrian Empire and the rise of the Persian Achaemenid Dynasty.

Assyria at Its Zenith

Assyria entered the eighth century in turmoil. Cities in the empire revolted. Lesser kingdoms refused to pay tribute. In 745, a general staged a coup, determined to end this time of trouble. He named himself Tiglath-Pileser III (745–727 BCE). The new king instantly addressed the core of Assyria's problems. Previous conquests had become too heavy a burden.

Tiglath-Pileser's solution was once more to make conquest pay. He established a system of direct rule over the conquered peoples and made them deliver tribute and troops. Soldiers from different parts of the empire were combined in the same units and dressed uniformly. An Assyrian elite force was kept in reserve at the centre. To prevent insurrection, provinces were kept small. For his governors, the king chose eunuchs, officials whose loyalty was ensured through castration, which prevented them from founding their own dynasties. Even so, governors were rotated in their posts frequently and instructed to report on neighbouring provinces. Inspectors, spies, and courtiers formed a parallel network of control.

The result was a predatory economy such as the world had never seen. Territorial expansion was not only meant to defend the Assyrian Empire, but also to enrich it, strengthen it, and enlarge its armed forces. Under Tiglath-Pileser, the number of soldiers grew from 44,000 to 72,000. King Sennacherib (705–681) raised it to 208,000 men. Ashurbanipal (668–627) fielded over 300,000. This was a stunning achievement if one considers that the Assyrian heartland counted no more than a few million inhabitants. It also points to another explanation for Assyria's revival: the fact that it was ruled by five forceful kings in a row. Once again, the Assyrians marched across the Middle East as if there was no resistance. In barely two decades, Tiglath-Pileser overpowered Cyprus and the whole of the Levant; Phrygia, Urartu, and the Cimmerians in the north; Persia, Media, and Elam in the east; and the most desired prize for any Mesopotamian ruler: Babylon.

The speed of conquest not only showed how decisively the balance of power had swung in Assyria's favour, but also reflected the fact that most of the neighbouring countries were small and often divided. Around 723, the king of Judah, for instance, called upon Assyria to intervene, as he felt threatened by an alliance between Israel and Aram. The dust had not even settled before other parties tried to benefit from the situation. Pharaoh Osorkon IV of Egypt sought to exploit the confusion in the Levant by backing a revolt in Judah, yet was shrewd enough to send twelve horses as a token of friendship to Assyria. Beginning in 720, Assyrian spies reported that the Cimmerians had left their power base on the Black Sea and started to encroach upon Urartu and Phrygia. This led the kings of the city states in Asia Minor to form an alliance and to call on Assyria for assistance. The Assyrians, however, cynically allied with the Cimmerians in order to attack Urartu, with whom both Assyria and the Cimmerians competed for control of the Caucasian trade routes.

When Sennacherib took the throne in 705, he ordered a new campaign in the Levant. 'The Lord is bringing the mighty flood waters of the River, the king of Assyria and all his glory; it will rise above all its channels and overflow all its banks,' the Old Testament prophesied. 'Band together, you peoples!'[2] In 700, Sennacherib defeated the Elamites, Chaldeans, and Babylonians and placed his son on the throne of Babylon. Eight years later, these subject peoples revolted. The Chaldean king now formed an even larger alliance with the Elamites, the Persians, and other kingdoms from the Zagros Mountains. Sennacherib engaged with them at the

Battle of Halule in 691, bragging that he had killed 150,000 enemy soldiers.[3] Babylon was set ablaze.

Less than ten years later, Sennacherib was on his way to Egypt to fight the Pharaoh Taharqa. Taharqa belonged to a dynasty of pharaohs that originated in Nubia. He was seen by Assyria as a troublemaker in the Levant. The great Egyptian city of Memphis was sacked, but the Assyrian armies failed to capture the pharaoh, and a few months after the bulk of Assyrian troops had left Egypt, riots broke out. In the Levant, Sennacherib replaced the city of Tyre with an Assyrian trade hub after an official reported that its king was 'turning all of the boat trade for himself'.[4] By now, however, a much more formidable threat was looming. In 678, the Medes, the Cimmerians, and the Manneans, together with a new entrant on the scene – the Scythians – formed a coalition against the Assyrians. When their attack failed in 676, the Scythian king opportunistically changed sides and married his daughter to the Assyrian king.

For the time being, the Assyrian records reported no internal unrest. 'The Palace Gate was normal; the Peace was there.'[5] The economy flourished. Sennacherib moved the capital from Nimrud to Nineveh, which grew to 150,000 inhabitants. Nineveh must have been an astounding place with huge walls, towers, wide squares, botanical gardens, a zoo, aqueducts, workshops, a boatyard, and, above all, two newly built palaces.[6] 'There is no end to Nineveh's treasures – its vast uncounted wealth,' the Old Testament proclaimed.[7] In 694, Sennacherib completed his 'palace without a rival'.[8] Winged bulls guarded the gates and the walls were finely carved with scenes of victories. His grandson Ashurbanipal's palace was intended to be even bigger. Its library held ancient works from the whole empire – such as the *Epic of Gilgamesh* – as well as texts on astronomy, medicine, and diplomacy. This Mesopotamian renaissance later inspired Alexander the Great to build his own library in Alexandria. Archaeological finds reveal scientific activity using crystal lenses and complex hydraulic systems. In the British Museum, we can still experience the sensitive yet realistic relief carvings of lion hunts that adorned Ashurbanipal's palace walls.[9] By any standard, they comprise a landmark in the history of art. Less dramatic, perhaps, but profoundly symbolic is the relief of the king and his queen reposing in a garden of vines, palm trees, and birds, with the head of one of his rivals dangling from a branch.[10]

Ashurbanipal had succeeded to the throne in 668. Determined to complete his father's work in Egypt, he swiftly reduced it to a puppet state. Two years later, he defeated the Medes, the Persians, and the Parthians. He kept the Scythians and Cimmerians at bay by playing one off against the other. By 650, however, a sequence of events had set off Assyria's decline. Around that time, a severe drought struck the Middle East, where population growth already strained agricultural resources. In one prayer that has been preserved, Ashurbanipal begged for the alleviation of the resulting inflation in food prices. Meanwhile, unrest in Egypt and Babylon grew. About this time, the Arameans, Elamites, Medes, Egyptians, and Arab tribes formed a grand alliance. Even Ashurbanipal's own brother, the king of Babylon, joined it secretly. 'Outwardly with his lips he spoke friendly things, while inwardly his heart plotted murder'.[11]

Ashurbanipal was able to contain this threat, but the whole region plunged into disorder with his death in 627. In the following year, the Babylonians rebelled, backed by the Scythians and the Medes. The Medes at that time were led by Cyaxares, a capable king, who exploited the power vacuum to conquer most of the kingdoms in the Zagros Mountains, and who forged a marriage alliance with Babylon. In 612, the coalition destroyed Nineveh. In 605, it overpowered a combined force of Assyrians and Egyptians at the Battle of Carchemish. And in 585, it defeated the wealthy Anatolian kingdom of Lydia at the Battle of Halys. The main beneficiary of these triumphs were the Medes, who now controlled an empire of their own in eastern Mesopotamia.

This Median Empire served as the launch pad for the far more successful push for mastery by the Persians. We do not know exactly how the Persians gained control over the Median Empire. But their power base in the Zagros Mountains towered above the eastern fringes of Median territory like a natural citadel.[12] This plateau had numerous advantages: the presence of a large tract of flat farmland that could feed tens of thousands of inhabitants, natural walls of limestone cliffs, rivers, a moderate climate, and the proximity of trade routes. Besides this strategic location, the Persians had no particular asset that made them bound to predominate. Their first three kings were simple vassal rulers, first under the Assyrians and then the Medes.

It was only with the third of these kings, Cambyses I (580–559), that Persia's growing influence became noticeable. The Greek historian Herodotus reported prestigious marriages with a princess of Lydia and a princess of Media. It was the son of this latter marriage, Cyrus II (559–530), who would challenge his Median grandfather. By that time, the Medes were already struggling to keep their empire together, and Herodotus informs us about court intrigues and border skirmishes.[13] In 553, the Persians openly revolted against the Medes. A punitive expedition was dispatched, but its soldiers mutinied and were crushed by the Persians. This defeat sent a tremor through the Middle East. Babylonian records show how the subsequent campaigns of Cyrus II were observed with trepidation. The great god 'Bel did not come out,' we read in the *Nabonidus Chronicle*.[14] It describes how Cyrus' troops swept into Mesopotamia, encircling Babylon before they sacked it in 539. 'All of the people bared their heads.'[15]

The Persian Takeover

A new imperial dynasty was born: the Achaemenids.[16] What allowed the Achaemenid King Cyrus II to push so far was, once again, the weakness of his neighbours. In the east, the Persian heartland did not have much to fear from a slew of smaller mountain kingdoms. In the west, the Median Empire was overstretched, crumbling, and challenged from all sides. Once the Median dynasty was decapitated, Cyrus II could expropriate its resources and take on the cities of Mesopotamia one by one. The Persians were confronted by various alliances. But, according to the Greek historian Xenophon's biography of Cyrus, they gained the support of the Cadusians, the Sacians, the Bactrians, the Hyrcanians, and many others.[17]

The Persians were thus picking up the shards of an old imperial order that had splintered into warring kingdoms.

From the many accounts of Cyrus' campaigns, it is clear that he displayed his leadership at the most decisive moments. When, in 539, his troops initially failed to storm the walls of Babylon, he diverted the course of the Euphrates so that they could enter the city along the river bed. To counter the threat of the Lydian cavalry at the Battle of Thymbra in 546, Cyrus reportedly deployed camels against them so that their smell frightened the horses, rendering the cavalry ineffective. Cyrus' armies also launched bombs filled with petroleum from siege towers, employed engineers to undermine fortifications, and experimented with surprise strikes by fast cavalry.

Another explanation for the Persians' advance was their magnanimity. Cyrus was often generous to those people who surrendered. He spared the king of Media after he had been defeated. According to the inscription on a clay cylinder found in Babylonia, Cyrus allowed the locals to continue worshipping their own gods. But he could also be ruthless. When the king of Lydia rejected Cyrus' offer to keep his throne as a vassal ruler and instead asked the Greek city states for mercenaries, the Persian ruler seems to have ordered him burned alive, although he might have been spared at the last minute. By the death of Cyrus in 530, the Persian Empire stretched from the Aegean Sea to the River Indus and from the Caucasus to the Nubian Desert. Leadership, luck, and magnanimity had all helped create it.

The key to maintaining so vast a realm was efficiency: maximizing the gains and limiting the sacrifices. Like the Assyrians, the Persians developed a system of incorporation. As Cyrus himself put it: 'If I make my friends rich I shall have treasures in them and at the same time more trusty watchers.'[18] The provinces were ruled by satraps, or governors. Under Darius I (522–486), there were thirty-six of them, and they were responsible for collecting a fixed amount of tribute. Some of these governors were local rulers. They were often aided by native power brokers; plots of land in the provinces were allocated to them in exchange for services, and their daughters married Persian noblemen. For example, the rulers of the Phoenician cities became vassals of the Persian Empire after their conquest in 539. They could continue to mint their own coins, as long as they paid tribute, obeyed the satrap, and put their ships at his disposal in time of war. After the defeat of Egypt in 525, the Persians allied with the clan chiefs of Egyptian provinces to administer the kingdom on their behalf.

The conqueror of Egypt, King Cambyses II (530–522), also recruited a senior official called Udjahorresnet from the former regime to advise him. The Egyptian counselled the Persians on how to win the hearts and minds of the locals. When the holy bull of Egypt died, Cambyses oversaw his burial. On a wall of a temple, he had himself named the restorer of order. The Persian kings were eager to be seen as benevolent leaders by their new citizens elsewhere in the empire, and here too religious propaganda was vital. During his campaigns in Asia Minor, Cyrus had bribed the oracle of Apollo near Miletus to appeal to its followers to surrender. In Babylon, he distributed inscribed cylinders claiming that the native gods had abandoned their king and chosen Cyrus to liberate the city from previous rulers. He released the Jewish exiles from their captivity in Babylon, and ordered the return of their holy golden vessels, which the Babylonians had stolen, and the rebuilding of the great temple in Jerusalem.

The unequalled mastermind of such propaganda was Darius I. When he campaigned on the Aegean Sea, he did not let his troops land on Delos – which was sacred to the Greeks – but ordered a golden statue of the island's patron deity, Apollo, to be erected instead. In Judah, he ordered the codification of local laws, which scholars assume contributed to the compilation of the Jewish Torah.[19] In Egypt, too, he had the local laws compiled into a codex intended to guide non-Egyptian administrators. When Darius entered Memphis in 521 to suppress a revolt, he did so at the very moment the locals were mourning the death of the Apis bull. He quickly turned it to his advantage by promising a vast sum of silver to whoever provided a new bull. He even had himself carved on a stele kneeling before the falcon god Horus. Keeping the temples and priests happy was important. Not only could they legitimize Persian rule, but in the agricultural economies of the Middle East, they were indispensable in collecting taxes and administering reserves.

Archaeological evidence points to expanding settlements throughout the Persian Empire – a clear sign of economic prosperity.[20] Roads and ingenious messenger networks were established, reaching as far as present-day Pakistan. 'There is nothing in the world which travels faster than these Persian couriers.'[21] Records show how the Persians regularly presented gifts to rulers in the Zagros Mountains in exchange for commodities like wool, and to Arab tribes in exchange for keeping desert caravan routes safe. In 510, Darius convened a conference of architects in Persepolis, his new capital, to plan a canal between the Nile and the Red Sea. The project was a success. Along the entire canal, vast steles were erected with the king's image. 'Ships went from Egypt through this canal to Persia, as was my desire.'[22] Darius organized maritime expeditions between the Nile and the Indian Ocean, introduced weight standards, extended the Royal Road, and promoted coins as a means of trade instead of a means of propaganda. Trade meant taxes, and taxes were used to gain control over even more trade. All this was administered by an immense bureaucracy. It corresponded in all the different languages spoken in the empire. 'An edict . . . was written to the king's satraps and to the governors over all the provinces and to the officials of all the peoples,' we read in the Old Testament, 'to every province in its own script and every people in its own language.'[23] All those achievements were only possible because the Achaemenid Dynasty provided a near-unbroken chain of strong leaders for almost two centuries.

Once it was established, the Persian Empire faced no genuine rivals for over a century. This concentration of power in a single state was unprecedented. With the annexation of Egypt, the empire may well have controlled a third of the world's farmland and a quarter of its population. It had an abundance of iron mines, needed for weapons and tools, and forests, for construction and ship building. Economic statecraft helped to exploit the potential of such resources: the organization into provinces, the role of the satraps, the advanced transportation networks, and the exchanges with peoples on the periphery that we have already mentioned.

The Persians outshone the Assyrians not only by establishing more solid rule over Egypt, but also by more firmly integrating the trading kingdoms of the Levant and those on the threshold of South Asia into their empire. There is no denying that Assyria had tried to control these important trade hubs as well, hence the many expeditions against the Phoenician kingdom of Tyre, into timber-rich Anatolia, and along the eastern trade routes, as well as the persistent focus on Egypt.[24] 'I opened the sealed-off harbour of Egypt, mixed Assyrians with Egyptians and let them trade with each other,' Sargon II had boasted in 716.[25] The Assyrians had done the groundwork. The Persians built on it.

Mediterranean Mayhem

The most enigmatic challengers on Persia's fringes were the Scythians. In the seventh century, they had penetrated from the Pontic-Caspian Steppe into the heart of the Middle East, helped sack Nineveh, and even infested the borders of Egypt. Riding stocky horses, and extravagantly tattooed, they were feared fighters, lightly armed, but extremely versatile.[26] Those Scythian warriors who entered Mesopotamia formed a relatively small group of mercenaries which gradually assimilated. Around the sixth century, the climate in the Pontic-Caspian Steppe became more favourable, so that the pressure to migrate abated.[27] From then onwards, the Scythians withdrew into their heartlands, from where they made occasional forays into the Balkans and the Armenian Highlands in pursuit of loot. The strategic position occupied by the Scythians allowed their elite to accumulate vast wealth from a mixture of pastoralism, agriculture, gold mining, slave

trading, and other forms of commerce which reached as far
afield as Western Europe and China.[28]

Yet, however impressive some of the Scythians' treasures
are, and however large some of their wooden fortresses,
such as the remains excavated near Bilsk in Ukraine, their
steppe homeland did not allow for wealth accumulation on
the scale of that by the Persians. One hectare of irrigated
land in Mesopotamia could feed more than five persons, but
one hectare of cropland in the steppes north of the Black Sea
could support only one or two people, and the pastoralists
further north required several hectares to feed each mouth.[29]
There was thus enough to survive, but not to flourish. A
Greek traveller in the sixth century described the Scythians
as plagued with arthritis and other diseases.[30] Altogether,
their population could not have exceeded 1 or 2 million. As
long as the Persians stayed strong, the Scythian challenge
could be handled.

In the shadow of the Scythians and Persians, the Greek
city states continued to grow and their populations expanded
steadily. Forests rapidly gave way to olive farms and vineyards. This was the ideal world, as one of Homer's heroes
described it in the *Iliad*: 'a great estate on the banks of a
river, lovely in its vineyards and grain-bearing fields'.[31] The
eighth-century poet Hesiod's *Works and Days* also idealized
the peaceful life of the farmer:

> Neither famine nor disaster ever haunt men who do true
> justice; but light-heartedly they tend the fields which are all
> their care. The earth bears them victual in plenty, and on
> the mountains, the oak bears acorns upon the top and bees

in the midst. Their woolly sheep are laden with fleeces; their women bear children like their parents. They flourish continually with good things, and do not travel on ships, for the grain-giving earth bears them fruit.[32]

He contrasted it with a gloomy world in which men foolishly sought to maximize their possessions, leading to war, hunger, disease, and starvation:

for a man grows eager to work when he considers his neighbour, a rich man who hastens to plough and plant and put his house in good order; and neighbour vies with his neighbour as he hurries after wealth. This Strife is wholesome for men. And potter is angry with potter, and craftsman with craftsman, and beggar is jealous of beggar, and minstrel of minstrel.[33]

One of the main causes of strife in Greece was *stenochoria*, which means 'confined space': there was just not enough suitable land available to feed the growing population. It was also one of the reasons why Greek philosophers from the sixth century – more than 2,300 years before the Enlightenment scholar Robert Malthus – posited that a society could no longer be governed if its population became too large. The consequences were relentless migration around the coastal plains of the Mediterranean and the Black Sea as well as immense pressure to trade. Trade brought about new elites and changed the political organization of the city states. Wealthy trade hubs were the first to experience coups against their traditional rulers. In around 657, Cypselus, a powerful military leader in Corinth, overthrew the king. He claimed that he was obeying the oracle of Delphi and gained support by promising justice. About the same time, a general in the army of Sicyon called Orthagoras toppled that city's king. Shortly after, Theagenes seized power in Megara, slaughtering the cattle of the rich to win the support of the poor. And in 632, Cylon, an Olympic wrestling champion, staged a putsch in Athens.[34] The Greeks called these autocrats *tyrannoi*, or tyrants.

Shared gods, oracles, epics, and language helped the Greek city states develop a sense of common identity. On occasion it led to treaties formalizing cooperation between neighbouring states. One of the earliest examples was the Amphictyonic League protecting the sanctuary at Delphi, which established a council to arbitrate in cases of conflict between members. But, more often, the common language was used by poets to praise heroic exploits in the wars the Greeks fought against each other. 'By doing mighty deeds let him learn how to fight,' proclaimed Tyrtaeus in his so-called 'Spartan Creed'.[35] Archilochus celebrated the courageous soldiers of Pharos, 'desiring to plunge in the phalanxes of Naxos'.[36] 'When will you show some courage, young comrades?' another poet admonished. 'Lazing in shabby peace on our land bled by war, have you no shame?'[37] Alcaeus warned: 'Not homes with beautiful roofs, nor walls of permanent stone, nor canals and piers for ships make the city – but men of strength.'[38]

Those 'men of strength' fought many wars: the Messenian Wars (743–724, 685–668), for instance, in which Sparta won the fertile coastal plains of the Messinian Gulf; the Lelantine War (around 710–650), which involved many cities in the fight to control the central fertile plain of Euboea; the Meliac War (around 690–670) between the Ionian cities in Asia Minor; or the First Sacred War (595–585), in which the Amphictyonic League destroyed the city of Cirrha for its impiety. Greek historians like Herodotus distinguished three forms of territorial aggrandizement: conquest, colonization, and *synoecism*. The latter – a kind of imperialism for pygmies – involved the incorporation by a city of smaller neighbouring towns; in this way, for example, Athens assimilated the settlements of the Attica.

Throughout the seventh and sixth centuries, Corinth and Sparta were the two dominant powers in Greece. During their seventy years in power (657–587), the tyrants Cypselus and Periander made Corinth the centre of commerce and industry. They promoted the manufacture of pottery, boosted exports by setting up trading posts in the Adriatic and Ionian Seas, and paved a trackway so that ships could be pulled overland across the narrow isthmus between the Aegean and Ionian. Showcasing its might, Corinth invited smaller cities to its own sporting contest, the Isthmian Games, set up in the early sixth century to rival the Olympics. In 525, Corinth brokered an alliance with its main rival, Sparta. If Corinth dominated the seas and was one of the first Greek states to build the large warships known as triremes, Sparta was the land power *par excellence*, reliant on its military training and hoplite phalanx, a formation of heavy infantry armed with spears. But by the end of the sixth century, Corinth's star had started to fade, as another city shrewdly diverted trade away and established itself as an industrial centre: Athens.

The boom in Corinth's trade had initially benefited

CHAPTER 3

Athens, which was favourably located to exploit the sea routes of the Aegean. Athens had roughly 10,000 inhabitants in 700, and this increased to around 20,000 over the next two centuries.[39] Meanwhile, it quietly built up an impressive network of colonies in Corinth's shadow. Its currency was pegged to Corinth's and the two rivals traded intensively. In the early sixth century, a new popular leader called Solon was responsible for steering Athens on its path to greatness. A cunning mercantilist, Solon created a local maritime sphere of influence for Athens in the Saronic Gulf by conquering the neighbouring island of Salamis. He improved the investment climate so that the pottery industry gradually moved away from Corinth. The first Athenian producers had copied the Corinthian style of vase painting, but they gradually made its black figures more refined, before setting new standards of artistry with their innovative 'red figure' style.

As Corinth's export economy waned, Athens assumed the mantle of the leading sea power in Greece. After the populist politician Themistocles gained power in the early fifth century, he urged the Athenians to spend the profits from a newly discovered large silver mine on strengthening the fleet and fortifying the port of Piraeus with long walls that would connect it with Athens; he also introduced tax breaks that attracted foreign artisans and traders to the city. The Athenian statesman Pericles later extolled this period of expansion, stating: 'Our adventurous spirit has forced an entry into every sea and into every land.' His credo, that 'Sea-power is of enormous importance', remains the motto of the Hellenic navy today.[40]

By the sixth century, the Greeks had long been embroiled

in a fierce struggle with the Phoenicians for trade in the Mediterranean. The Phoenicians historically had controlled trade routes across much of the region, and were important suppliers of metals and timber to both Mesopotamia and Egypt. According to Homer, the Phoenicians, unlike the Greeks, were not especially organized and they generally tried to open markets peacefully rather than by force. Hesiod wrote that their primary objective was not colonization but trade.

Phoenicia's trade dominance was under pressure from two sides: the interior of Asia to the east, as well as the maritime west.[41] However, the Persian Empire was resolutely a land power: controlling the Levant and Asia Minor as the gateways for trade was profitable enough. The Greek city states were far more aggressive. Competition with the Phoenicians became so fierce that piracy was lauded by the Greeks as an act of bravery. In the seventh century, Greek merchants had already taken over much of the trade with Sicily and supported whoever was willing to fight the Phoenicians. When the Assyrians cracked down on an uprising against taxes by the traders of Tarsus in 697, the Greeks fought on the Assyrian side.[42] When the Persians conquered the main Phoenician cities in the Levant in 539, the Greeks rapidly filled the void and became the dominant traders in the Eastern Mediterranean. Phoenician influence survived and continued to flourish in the Western Mediterranean under the hegemony of a power that would become a protagonist in one of the best-known conflicts in ancient history: the city of Carthage.

By the sixth century, then, the Greek world had more than recovered from its Dark Ages. This was the time when the first famous Greek philosophers and mathematicians were born, like Anaximander and Pythagoras. It was also the time now known as the Archaic period of Greek art (700–480), when sober geometric patterns on pottery gave way to elegantly painted figurative designs. Sculptors carved the famously enigmatic *korai* and *kouroi*, robed female and nude male youths. The first monumental stone temples in the austere Doric style were erected, for example the Temple of Apollo at Corinth.

Through trade and the influence of the Greek colonies in Italy, the Archaic style was eagerly embraced by the peoples on the other side of the Ionian Sea. None more so than the Etruscans, whose characteristic terracotta sarcophagi with their lifesize figures are clearly indebted to Greek sculpture. The Etruscans were a confederation of twelve towns located in the hills of Central Italy. Their assembly gathered once a year at the Shrine of Voltumna and elected a leader to represent the confederation. They expanded into the Po Valley and established colonies as far afield as Spain.

Although Greece and Etruria traded intensively – the latter was an important market for Athenian pottery – they soon became locked in a fierce contest for colonies and commercial opportunities, much like Corinth and Athens in earlier times. Before long, the Etruscans came to use Greek weapons against Greek citizens. In 540, an allied Carthaginian and Etruscan force engaged a Greek fleet near Alalia, in Corsica, repelling Greek attempts to colonize the island. In the north, the Etruscans also interacted with the Gauls. A spectacular archaeological find of Etruscan and Greek objects in a Celtic settlement in France in 2015 shows how extensive these relations were.[43] But in this case too, trade led to friction. Enticed by the wealth of Etruria, tribes like the Insubres crossed the Alps and settled in Northern Italy.

In the context of these struggles, the early history of Rome was a relatively unimportant affair. In the two centuries after the death of its legendary first king, Rome grew into a city of about 30,000 inhabitants. Throughout that period, the Romans maintained much the same political system: male citizens elected a senate and the senate appointed the king, who was the chief priest, justice, and military leader.

Rome's earliest wars were petty affairs, often sparked by cattle rustling. The army of the second Roman king consisted of only 1,800 soldiers. Besides Rome's advantageous geographical position, it is difficult to explain its early military success. But once the first neighbouring towns were conquered, their citizens were forced to migrate to Rome and their soldiers were incorporated into the Roman army. The balance of power thus shifted with each conquest, sparking yet further wars, both of aggression and defence. The neighbouring city of Fidenae, Livy wrote, did not wait till Rome's potential strength was realized, but began a preventive war itself. There are also examples of Rome sowing division among its rivals. King Lucius Tarquinius Superbus (534–510) convened a peace conference of neighbouring leaders in a sacred grove. During the meeting, he had weapons put into the tent of one of the attendees so that the latter attracted the ire of the others.

However, the stronger Rome got, the more it could show its magnanimous side. King Servius Tullius (575–535) coaxed the nobles of neighbouring cities into a 'community of harmony and worship'. After a series of successful wars against the Latins, Lucius Tarquinius Priscus erected a shrine of Diana where those same former enemies were welcome to pray. Following the conquest of the Latin towns on the eastern bank of the Tiber, the Etruscans loomed as the next challenge. 'Great is their strength on land,' the historian Livy had a Latin leader warn, 'exceedingly great on the sea.'[44] But, for now, the Romans avoided confrontation. Tarquinius Superbus even concluded a treaty with the Etruscans and tried to attract their artisans to Rome with the offer of a major project: the construction of a vast new temple to Jupiter on the Capitoline Hill. The artisans came in such numbers that the Romans became disgruntled with the heavy spending on infrastructure and the influx of immigrants, and deposed their king. In 509, the year that Tarquinius Superbus' temple was consecrated, Rome became a republic.

By the end of the sixth century, Rome had grown into one of the largest cities on the coastal plain around the River Tiber. Its population had increased to such an extent that its sacred boundary – the so-called *pomerium* – had to be extended for the first and only time until the first century. It had gained the sea port of Ostia, bridged the Tiber, erected the first apartment blocks, or *insulae*, and, significantly, built one of the world's first permanent underground sewerage systems, the Cloaca Maxima.

But although the city was flourishing, Rome continued to play only a modest, regional role. Looking back over the preceding two and a half centuries of power politics, it was great Middle Eastern empires like the Assyrians and the Persians that still predominated. Even if Hesiod was far from alone in yearning for tranquillity, the Eastern Mediterranean remained one large arena of rivalry. *Stenochoria*, commercial imperatives, ambitious tyrants – all inflamed the competition for land, trade, prestige, and power.

Beyond the Indus

In 538, the army of King Cyrus II of Persia reached the Indus. It found the political landscape on the other side of the river fragmented and marred by anarchy, as city states contended for territory, commercial advantage, and influence. Referred to in ancient Buddhist sources as the sixteen Mahajanapadas, these city states experimented with monarchical and republican forms of government, the latter known in Sanskrit as *gana-sangha*, which literally means 'equal assembly'. By the sixth century, four main competitors emerged out of the Mahajanapadas' struggle: Koshala, Magadha, Vatsa, and Avanti. Finally, there was a showdown between Avanti and Magadha. The Buddhist sources explained that, in the past, Avanti had conquered Magadha, but then the latter's people rebelled against their foreign overlords and established a new, native dynasty. Throughout the sixth century, a precarious balance of power existed between the two states. Relations were sufficiently cordial at one point for King Bimbisara of Magadha famously to send his doctor to the Avanti ruler, Chanda Pradyota, when he fell ill. Around 490, Bimbisara was murdered by an ambitious son who embarked on a policy of attacking Avanti's allies.

It is not clear exactly how it happened, but probably by the mid-fifth century, Magadha had emerged as the supreme power of the Indo-Gangetic Plain. Advantageously situated on the middle reaches of the Ganges, Magadha was a large city, according to the sources, protected by five surrounding hills and with the intervening valleys barred by walls. Most of the writings of that time propagated the idea of a universal kingdom that brought stability. Considering the behaviour of the sixteen Mahajanapadas, the *Numerical Discourses of the Buddha* concluded: 'human kingship is poor compared to celestial happiness'.[45] Great emphasis was placed on the idea of the righteous king. The same text described a good king as cultivated, the shield and protector of his people, caring for the lives of his soldiers, guarding his vassals, and even minding the fate of animals and birds. 'He is rich, with great wealth and property, with full treasuries and storerooms. He is powerful, possessing an army of four divisions that is obedient and compliant to his commands. His counselor is wise, competent, and intelligent, able to consider benefits pertaining to the past, future, and present.'[46]

Further north and east, China too had dissolved into a remorseless struggle between states after the weakening of the Zhou Dynasty. 'The world was fallen into decay,' wrote the famous fourth-century philosopher Mencius, 'and right principles had dwindled away. Perverse discourses and oppressive deeds were again waxen rife. Cases were occurring of ministers who murdered their rulers, and of sons who murdered their fathers.'[47] One man who experienced this at first hand was the pre-eminent sage Confucius (551–479), who served as advisor to the kings of Lu. The state of Lu had once been very powerful, controlling the core of the fertile North China Plain. But it was surrounded by rivals, and a moment of unrest at the court in around 700 proved fatal.

One neighbouring state seized the opportunity: the Qi, who had grown rich on the salt trade, and had been mandated by the Zhou king to lead the fight against the barbarians. In 642, this role of *ba*, or hegemon, under the symbolic fiat of the Zhou, was seized by another of the Lu's neighbours, the Song. Ten years later, the Jin in turn became hegemon, and spearheaded a campaign against the Chu, before the title was bestowed first upon the Qin and then on the Chu, each promising to restore peace between the Chinese kingdoms and to fight the common threat of the barbarians. The kingdom of Zhou by now had atrophied to the point that it conferred little more than a veneer of legitimacy to the ambitions of these warring states.

As a young man, Confucius had seen his world gird itself for major conflict as the short-haired, tattooed, barbarian Wu prepared to challenge the Chu. The Wu had grown powerful thanks to their proficiency in metal working, and they had as their chief strategic advisor a man who would later be regarded as one of China's most famous thinkers: Sun Tzu (544–496). Focusing on military strategy and tactics, especially spying and deception, he was the intellectual antipode of Confucius. Sun Tzu served his Wu masters well, bringing them five important military victories. For a short period, the Wu became hegemon, before the advent of another challenger, the Yue, which was witnessed by Confucius as his life drew to a close.

The annals of this Spring and Autumn period (771–476) confirm that there was no sustained peace for any of the Chinese states. If one part of their border was secure, it was almost inevitable that challenges were building up in another part. But however much it was an era of conflict, it was also an era of consolidation.[48] If there were still 148 separate states mentioned in the chronicles of the seventh century, the number had been brought down to eighteen by the sixth century. As in India, this period in China witnessed the rise of larger city states, which absorbed surrounding towns and enabled the specialization of crafts. As manufactures like bronze vessels, iron utensils, and silk developed, trade became ever more important, facilitated by the introduction first of shell tokens and then true coins. Fan Li, one of the earliest Chinese economists, counselled kings to promote commerce as well as agriculture. Cities evolved on a grandiose scale, with vast temple complexes, palaces, iron workings, huge walls, and wide roads that allowed the passage of nine carriages side by side.[49] Competition to serve the most powerful kings was ruthless: advisors, craftsmen, soldiers, and even ministers, would go to great lengths to place their knowledge and skills at the disposal of rulers. States could field armies numbering hundreds of thousands. Innovative military technologies – such as the crossbow, initially imported from Southeast Asia – spread rapidly.

Although the Spring and Autumn period was plagued by numerous wars, with kingdoms seemingly always ready to sacrifice their young men, it was also an era of intense diplomacy, as lesser states swung pragmatically between allies. The annals list hundreds of treaties, bilateral visits, and international conferences, where more powerful states forced weaker ones to acknowledge their will. Duke Ding of Jin, for instance, convened a summit that concluded: 'No family is to amass military equipment. No town may have a wall of one hundred zhi.'[50] The Jin themselves, though, were not bound by this agreement. Conferences could also legitimize a state's hegemonic status as guardian of the heavenly mandate of the Zhou kings. In 667, the Qi assembled an important convention for the purpose of 'supporting the prince and expelling the barbarians'.[51] In 656, the Qi called another conference, this time to check the rise of the Chu and to sanction humiliating the king of Zhou. Equally, meetings were held to challenge the hegemon. In 598, for example, the Jin gathered the Qi, Song, Cai, Zheng, Wei, and Ju at Jiantu in order to broker an alliance against the Chu, who had just toppled the Jin hegemony.

The scope of those international meetings and treaties, however, was often much broader than security. In 651, an agreement signed between seven states at Kuiqiu stipulated that: 'The contracting parties shall not build dykes on a river; shall not store grain for speculation; shall not change successors; shall not make concubines as wives; shall not let women be involved in state affairs.'[52] A conference in 554 vowed to protect the king, give mutual aid in case of insurrection or at times of famine, extradite fugitives, eliminate barriers to the trade in corn, and refrain from distorting trade by means of monopolies. Rules were written down to protect envoys and treaties were submitted to the oversight of the gods. 'May the gods of the hills and rivers, the spirits of former emperors and dukes, and the ancestors of our seven tribes and twelve states, watch over its implementation,' the conclusion of the treaty proclaimed. 'If any one proves unfaithful, may the all-seeing gods smite him, so that his people shall forsake him, his life be lost, and his posterity cut off.'[53]

Such dire penalties recall the oaths sworn as part of Meso-potamian treaties. Among the Chinese states, treaties were ratified by the participants slitting their palm, mingling wine with their blood, and laying their hand on the head of a sacri-ficial ox, goat, or white horse. Each state possessed a special archive known as the *mengfu*, or 'palace of treaties', where copies of agreements were usually carefully stored.

Scepticism about such diplomatic endeavours was already prevalent in the *Spring and Autumn Annals* themselves. Its an-onymous authors clearly portrayed treaties as instruments of the strong, nothing more than a reflection of military power on paper. 'And thus the states are kept quiet and do service to the great powers, securing their own preservation and escaping ruin,' we read. 'The lawless are kept in awe and accomplished virtue is displayed.'[54] The withering of the authority of the heavenly mandate and the consequent anarchy in China in-spired a series of intellectuals who are still widely read today. One of them was Guan Zhong, prime minister to Duke Huan of Qi in the seventh century. Guan Zhong counselled the duke to be on his guard and to spend enough on defence. 'When talk of universal love prevails, the troops will not fight . . . knights who are skilled in archery and charioteering and who possess courage and strength will go abroad. How will we be able to avoid attacks from others?' But military power could not exist without good governance. 'Heaven and Earth alternate hard times with the good,' he insisted, but a prince who was 'overly aggressive, he would fall as a withered leaf'. The key to power was prosperity: 'The pres-ervation of territory depends on walls; the preservation of walls depends on arms. The preservation of arms depends on men, and the preservation of men depends on grain.' He warned against decadence, called for dignity at the court, and emphasized the importance of just legislation: 'Laws are created to make use of the people's strength.'[55]

Confucius also emphasized the need for wise government. 'In carrying on your government, why should you use killing at all?' he asked rhetorically in his *Analects*. He recognized the need for military strength, but seemed to stress that the effective use of hard power required an educated people. 'To lead an uninstructed people to war,' he said, 'is to throw them away.' The ideal was harmony, but harmony meant hierarchy, both between and within states: 'There is government, when the prince is prince, and the minister is minister; when the father is father, and the son is son.'[56] Lao Tzu, the legendary founder of Taoism, loathed violence. 'Where armies are, thorns and brambles grow.'[57] Yet he, too, implicitly admitted the need for defensive wars. His plea was that force should be used prudently and proportionately: violence should be employed for limited ends, it should not be rejoiced in, and it should cease as soon as victory was achieved. Peace and tranquillity were what a prince should prize above all; the ideal was always to advance one's interests without creating resistance: 'Nothing under heaven is softer or more yielding than water, but when it attacks things hard and resistant there is not one of them that can prevail. For they can find no way of altering it. That the yielding conquers the resistant and the soft becomes the hard is a fact known by all men, yet utilised by none.'[58]

Even Sun Tzu, who is known today mostly for his shrewd prescriptions for waging war, subscribed to the same fundamental viewpoint as his contemporaries Confucius and Lao Tzu. While the bulk of *The Art of War* is about how to fight, the introduction makes it clear that what is most important in the struggle between states is their internal strength. Out of the seven conditions for winning a war identified by Sun Tzu, only the last three related to the waging of war itself. Most important was the quality of the leader and his understanding of how 'the moral law causes the people to be in complete accord with their ruler'.[59] Next was the balance of power with the primacy of economic resources: lengthy wars should be avoided, and conquests must pay off. 'The proximity of an army causes prices to go up; and high prices cause the people's substance to be drained away.'[60]

In the eastern part of Eurasia, South Asia and the North China Plain remained separate arenas. Both, however, were beset by disorder: India by fighting between the Mahajanapadas and China by a sequence of wars contesting the hegemony under the Zhou. As in the Mediterranean and the Middle East, war coincided with economic rivalry and technological competition; but, as in the Mediterranean and the Middle East, states also combined to preserve peace. The writings of Buddhist intellectuals from India and Chinese thinkers such as Guan Zhong, Sun Tzu, Confucius, and Lao Tzu reveal to us both a search for order and also a fixation with hard power. Without peace and stability, they argued, the farmer could not farm. If agricultural production fell, the king's position would weaken too. Good governance was important for preserving peace, but so was the readiness to fight – even if everyone understood the consequences when two neighbours fought.

Harmony and Anarchy

Between 750 and 500, the Achaemenid Dynasty of Persia founded the largest empire that the world had ever seen. Never before had Egypt, Mesopotamia, and the Levant been so firmly under the control of a single monarch. The world's centre of political prowess and prestige was clearly in the Middle East.

What permitted a small kingdom on the fringes of Mesopotamia to embark on so ambitious a political project was the fact that it encountered an Assyrian Empire whose body was severely weakened, but whose skeleton of laws and conventions, institutions, economic structures, trade networks, and infrastructure still operated. It was a hostile takeover of a decaying empire by a fresh, ambitious contender. But although the first Achaemenid rulers may have been fierce military commanders, they also recognized the wisdom of sponsoring trade, soft power, and an imperial doctrine of harmony. They accentuated their Persian origins while absorbing the imperial tradition of Mesopotamia. They also highlighted the importance of magnanimity and justice throughout their realm.

If the Achaemenid Empire brought unprecedented political unity to the heart of the Eastern hemisphere, everywhere else – especially the Mediterranean and the Indo-Gangetic and North China Plains – comprised arenas of conflict. Beyond the bounds of empire, the situation of anarchy gave birth to fresh debates about politics and diplomacy. Some intellectuals were pragmatic, if not cynical. It is the nature of man, asserted the Greek poet Hesiod, that he envies his neighbour.

The Chinese statesman Guan Zhong insisted that societies had to be alert and that neglecting the army would lead to decline. Sun Tzu was of the same opinion. The king had to be just towards his citizens, he said, in order to prioritize economic prosperity, but also to be constantly ready for combat. Others, like Confucius, Lao Tzu, and the Indian writers in the Buddhist tradition, were more idealistic and placed greater emphasis on the pursuit of harmony.

Yet whatever their belief in the feasibility of harmony in international politics, all of these thinkers acknowledged the importance of peace for the countryside – a reflection of the fact that agricultural production remained a crucial attribute of power. Farmland meant food, food meant population growth, and population growth meant more soldiers. City states that lacked the ability to feed themselves had to go to great lengths to secure their food supply through trade or colonization. The lack of enough fertile land prompted the Greek city states both to fight each other and to establish colonies across the Mediterranean. Drought had made the Assyrian Empire vulnerable to the Persians. Nature thus remained a decisive factor.

But there were other causes of conflict too. Trade, in particular, was a principal source of discord. Commerce might bring polities closer together, but it could also cause them to clash. Military and political weakness continued to elicit aggression from predators. But strength, equally, could draw states into wars: each conquest led to a further campaign in order to protect the previous gains, as the Persians discovered. Offence often remained the best defence.

The ability of culture and religion to foster accord also had its limitations. States in China, India, and around the Aegean Sea often shared the same language, customs, rituals, and even gods, to whom they made solemn pledges when they signed treaties and attended international conventions. Yet despite the ceremony with which the Chinese cities stored diplomatic documents in their 'palaces of treaties', many thinkers remained sceptical about the enforceability of these agreements; military might, they argued, was a far more reliable guarantee of security. Many so-called peace conferences were little more than a means of enforcing the recognition of one state's superiority over others. Despite the lip service paid to high ideals, shared values, and common heritage, all over the Eastern Hemisphere, diplomacy was a seething cauldron of opportunism and expediency as alliances were opportunistically built and broken in an endless struggle for advantage. Between 750 and 500, the ideal throughout the Eastern Hemisphere may have been harmony, but the overwhelming reality remained anarchy.

CHAPTER 4

Gold and Iron

500–250 BCE

Among the objects on display in the National Archaeological Museum of Athens is a modest vase from the second half of the fifth century BCE, its white sides painted with fine dark lines and delicate coloured tints.[1] The scene which forms the main part of the decoration depicts a seated woman and an armed man, most probably a husband and wife. The man glances lovingly at the beautiful woman; she smiles, her foot resting against the instep of her husband, who holds out his helmet towards her. She wants him to stay. But this is a departure, a definite departure. The vase was a funerary offering, most likely left at the grave of a fallen soldier. Ancient Greece was a martial society. Still, the painter of this vase, who lived just before the outbreak of the Peloponnesian War (431–404), makes a statement: however much a society gets used to war, one never gets accustomed to personal loss, the death of relatives, families being ripped apart – even if it is for the sacred duty of defending one's country.

History books often present this Peloponnesian War as the bedrock of Western strategic culture, a culture defined by anarchy and by a fixation with the balance of power. The rise of one state, it presupposes, must be a threat to the other. Yet, as this chapter shows, this obsession was not present only in ancient Greece. Asian civilizations, like China and India, became possessed by it too, as they saw the ideal of imperial harmony collapse into chaos.

The world in around 500 contained one large empire. Ruled by the Persian Achaemenid Dynasty, and building on the traditions of Babylon, Assyria, and the Medes, it subjugated a realm of unprecedented scale, encompassing the rich irrigation economies of Egypt and Mesopotamia, the east–west trade routes between Central Asia and the Mediterranean and the north–south ones between the Pontic-Caspian Steppe and the Indian Ocean. After the empire's downfall, and its short occupation by Alexander the Great (336–323), the Middle East would not be so unified again until the early Islamic conquests of the seventh century CE, more than 900 years later.

The century after the death of Alexander the Great in 323 BCE was characterized by fighting between city states in the Mediterranean, South Asia, and the North China Plain. Diplomatic relations between these city states twisted and turned, with federations being built and destroyed, peace treaties signed and abandoned. This turmoil slowly gave way to a Eurasian order dominated by two of the dynasties that fought over the remains of Alexander's empire – the Ptolemies and the Seleucids – as well as by the Romans in the Western Mediterranean, the Maurya Dynasty in India, and the Han Dynasty in China. The appearance of the world was also markedly different: expanding populations in Europe, China, Southeast Asia, and Central America had by now transformed a large part of the primeval forest into farmland.

The Fall of Persia

In 522, after a series of successful campaigns in Egypt, King Cambyses II of Persia died in circumstances that remain unclear. Even less clear is the turmoil that followed. We do know that a usurper ruled the Persian Empire for almost seven months, rallying support mostly by promising tax relief to the poor. Seeing the threat posed to their privileges, and the empire at severe risk, a small group of leading Persian families backed the rival claim of a young soldier called Darius.

It was a decisive moment in the history of the Persian Empire. When Darius I (522–486) succeeded to the throne, he was confronted by insurrections in Babylon, Elam, Assyria, Egypt, Parthia, and Bactria. Remarkably, Darius overcame them all. After a long siege, Babylon fell back into submission. Other rebels were crushed as Persian troops marched against the kingdom of Bactria, and even crossed the Hindu Kush to reach the River Indus in 515. Barely two years later, Darius spurred his troops west, crossed the Bosporus over a pontoon bridge, and pushed the Scythians back deep into the Pontic-Caspian Steppe. Having fortified the border, he promptly swung back south to batter the Greek city states of Ionia into obedience.

The Persian victory on the eastern shores of the Aegean Sea, however, was short-lived. The cities of the Greek islands and mainland supported their brothers' resistance, partly because they wanted to keep Persia at bay, partly because of trade interests, and partly because the Persian king had by now become the most hated figure in the Greek world. With the exception of a few aristocrats and intellectuals, most Greeks imagined the Persian monarch to be decadent, deceitful, and tyrannical. In 499, the Ionian Revolt broke out when several of the Greek cities in Asia Minor rebelled, supported by forces from Greece. The Persians acted vigorously. The Ionians and their allies were defeated at the Battle of Ephesus in 498, recovered, and were finally destroyed four years later at the Battle of Lade. The revolt was over, but Darius realized that he had to go after its sponsors.

What followed was not Persia's only border war, but it was certainly its best-documented border war, appearing in most history books as *the* Persian Wars (499–449). In 491, Darius dispatched envoys to Greece to demand water and earth, the symbols of submission. Although many cities gave in, there were two notable exceptions: Sparta and Athens. The Spartans threw the envoys into a well and told them to find earth and water there. Six months later, a punitive expedition was under sail. After the Persian troops had disembarked in the Bay of Marathon, near Athens, they were heavily defeated by predominantly Athenian forces, who held the slightly higher ground above the beachhead.

Darius' attempt to mount a second invasion was thwarted by his death in 486. Rebellions against Persian rule broke out in Egypt and Babylon. The new king, Xerxes (486–465), Darius' son, soon crushed them, and shortly after began preparations to punish those Greeks who had so brazenly humiliated his father. When the vast Persian army finally marched in 480, it invaded Greece by land, from the north. The Greeks attempted to halt their advance at Thermopylae, a narrow plain with mountains on one side and sea on the other. Despite the favourable geographical conditions, the Greek army led by King Leonidas and a small unit of Spartan spearmen could delay the Persian troops for only three days. The turning point came a few weeks later, when the Greek fleet, led by Athens, defeated the Persians in the narrow Bay of Salamis. The following year, the Persian army in Greece was decisively defeated at Plataea and its fleet destroyed at Mycale.

Although the invasion of Greece was over, the conflict with Persia was not. Rebellion reignited all over Asia Minor. The Delian League – the large anti-Persian alliance of Greek states led by Athens – went on to support uprisings in Cyprus and Egypt in the 470s and 460s. Only in 449 did hostilities formally end when Persia and Athens signed the Peace of Callias. It provided autonomy for the Greek cities in Asia Minor. The Aegean Sea became a buffer zone. The Persians promised to stay out as long as Athens and the Delian League did not interfere with Egypt and Cyprus.

Decadence: that was how ancient Greek writers explained the troubles that dogged the Persian Empire in the fifth century. Hence, they thought, the numerous court intrigues. This theory was not entirely accurate. The Persian court was no more unstable than in the past. There may have been widespread unrest, but it was not necessarily worse than in previous times. There is evidence of inflation, higher interest rates and tax revolts in the late fifth century, but administrative archives also show that commercial life continued to flourish.[2] And the Persians were still able to field vast armies. At the Battle of Papremis in 460, hundreds of thousands of soldiers crushed an Egyptian revolt.

Persian rulers were also strategically astute. They took advantage of the Peloponnesian War – fought between Athenian-led and Spartan-led alliances – to play the Greek cities off against each other. In 413, Persia sent a delegation to Sparta with the aim to seal an alliance against Athens. In 409, Persian troops put down a rebellion in Asia Minor, as well as ones in Egypt, and the eastern part of the empire. Finally, in 387, Persia forced a revision of the Peace of Callias upon the exhausted Greeks so that it regained full control over Asia Minor.

In the first half of the fourth century, the Persian kings Artaxerxes II (404–359) and Artaxerxes III (359–338) were able to devote enormous resources to the seemingly endless struggle to keep Egypt as part of the empire. In 343, resistance was finally crushed when Artaxerxes III deployed 330,000 troops in Egypt, ousted the last native pharaoh, and tore down the city walls of Memphis.

Contrary to being effete and ineffective leaders, therefore, these Persian kings displayed a great deal of vigour. In the mid-fourth century, their empire remained by far the greatest power in the region. It controlled an enormous agricultural economy. It dominated many of the gateways for trade, and facilitated commerce wherever it benefited the imperial coffers, modernizing the Royal Road and maintaining a canal between the Nile Delta and the Red Sea. The size of its armies was still unmatched. Nothing indicated that the Persian Empire was about to face a greater danger than ever before.

Alexander the Great

This apparent strength is probably what made King Darius III (336–332) underestimate the threat posed by the accession of a new, immensely ambitious king in the northern Greek state of Macedon: Alexander the Great. It would be a fatal error.

Conflict with Macedon had slowly been brewing for a long time. Alexander's father, King Philip II (350–336), conquered a large part of the Greek Peninsula and advanced the Macedonian border towards the Hellespont, the modern Dardanelles. In 341 the father of Darius III, Artaxerxes III, responded positively to an Athenian request for support against Macedon. When Philip closed in on the Hellespont in 340, Artaxerxes ordered his satrapies to supply mercenaries and weapons. At that moment, nobody would have bet money on a Macedonian victory. Artaxerxes had proved himself to be a capable commander and his forces dwarfed those of Philip.

But, in 338, Artaxerxes was murdered. The same year, Philip defeated the Athenians and their allies, leaving his hands free to exploit the turmoil at the Persian court. Acting swiftly, in the spring of 337, he formed the League of Corinth to unite the Greeks in a sacred war against the Persians and liberate their compatriots in Asia Minor. That autumn, he dispatched two generals across the Hellespont to establish a bridgehead. In the spring of 336, they advanced with 10,000 troops south along the coast of Ionia as far as Magnesia. It was one of these moments when a whole region braced for the coming collision.

In the summer, Macedonian troops clashed for a first time with mercenaries in the service of Persia. While the swords were being unsheathed, a new wave of astonishment rippled across the Aegean: King Philip had been murdered. Alexander, then only twenty-one years old, faced rebellion and unrest. He dealt with them briskly and continued preparations for the sacred war against Persia. His dynamism revealed his training as a prince, his education by the finest teachers, including Aristotle, and the fact that he had commanded his first battles at the age of sixteen.

In 334, Alexander crossed the Hellespont. Darius, however, still left the defence of Asia Minor to Greek mercenaries, who suffered defeat on the muddy banks of the River Granicus, near the site of Troy. The region's cities swung over to Alexander one after the other, leaving Darius' satraps powerless. Once Asia Minor had been secured, Alexander forged on to the Levant, Egypt, and Mesopotamia, where he decisively defeated Persian troops under the command of Darius himself at the Battle of Gaugamela in the autumn of 331. The heartlands of the Persian Empire now lay open before the advancing Macedonians. By 328, the last organized Persian resistance was defeated. Once again, Mesopotamia had fallen to a lesser power on its fringes.

Historians still debate what made the Macedonian victory possible. That Alexander would come to rule an empire even bigger than Darius III's was as improbable as Cyrus II establishing the Persian Empire in the sixth century in the first place. The discovery by the conquering Macedonians of vast amounts of gold in the Persian royal treasuries showed that the empire still had plenty of reserves to draw upon.

Even during the last battles, Darius commanded hundreds of thousands of troops; although he bemused his opponents by entering the field with hundreds of personal cooks and dozens of servants to perfume him. Darius' biggest mistakes, however, were undoubtedly allowing the Macedonians to gain a foothold across the Hellespont and leaving the defence of Asia Minor to mercenaries. He was certainly too slow in shifting the bulk of the Persian armed forces to try to deter and defeat Alexander.

Once the Persians were on the defensive, Alexander proved a superior commander. He inspired his troops by leading from the front, surrounded himself with capable generals, carefully cultivated his image as a demigod, and used propaganda to present each victory as a personal achievement. He benefited from the magnificent army he inherited from his father: above all, the formidable Macedonian phalanx, but also elite cavalry and highly skilled military engineers. But his political leadership did not match his military astuteness. When Alexander died in Babylon in 323, aged thirty-two, cracks were appearing in both his reputation and his empire. He had neglected to consolidate his conquests, failing to replace the Persian imperial administration with his own or to make efforts to win the loyalty of subjugated peoples. His biographer, the Greek author Plutarch, described how Alexander succumbed to Persian luxury, estranged his Macedonian troops, and grew arrogant and tyrannical. Above all, he neglected to designate a successor. As Alexander lay dying, he merely whispered that his empire should be inherited by 'the strongest'.

The Persian Imperial Tradition

So strong was the Persian imperial tradition that it entirely captivated Alexander. Persepolis, the ceremonial capital, left an enormous impression. It was a dazzling architectural representation of how the Persians dreamt of ruling their empire for eternity. Its giant walls gave way first to an inner court and the Gate of All Nations, guarded by two intimidating pairs of human-headed winged bulls. This led to a second court, where visitors would look up to the Apadana, a vast columned hall. Its base, three metres high, was decorated with endless rows of carved Persian spearmen and tribute bearers from all parts of the empire, including Scythians, Parthians, Ionians, and many more. Having climbed the broad processional stairs, visitors arrived at a pair of bronze doors and finally entered the great audience hall itself, with its heavily decorated coffered ceiling supported by thirty-six columns over twenty metres high. Hidden behind the Apadana were the private palaces, the harem, and, most importantly, the royal treasury. Alexander had to employ a thousand camels to carry all its gold away.

Persepolis was a temple as much as a palace. The Persian kings ruled over the world with divine blessing. Nothing illustrates this better than the carved frontage of the rock tomb of Artaxerxes II. At the top is the god Ahuramazda and below him stands the king on a platform that is carried by two rows of subjects. On Mount Behistun, a rock relief shows Darius I, enthroned beneath the wings of Ahuramazda, inspecting a line of nine bound and captive rulers. Below this scene, Darius explains how, by the grace and with the aid of Ahuramazda, he restored the universal order that was lost through the misconduct of previous kings and maintained the wellbeing of his subjects.

The Persian kings preserved much of the imperial traditions of Babylon and Assyria. The ancient *Epic of Gilgamesh* and Code of Hammurabi continued to circulate widely. The iconography of the Assyrian god Ashur was even adopted to represent Ahuramazda. Mesopotamia remained the empire's demographic and economic centre. We see its influence throughout the art of the Persians, their architecture, infrastructure, agriculture, bureaucracy, and the organization of their empire. Royal depots and garrisons were scattered over the empire, connected by the same roads and routes that linked together the major cities in previous times.

In the same way that the Assyrians divided the realm into provinces administered by governors, the Persians divided it into satrapies. The satraps who ruled these provinces were responsible for taxation, maintaining stability, upholding law, monitoring events beyond the empire's border, and reporting anything of importance to the court. They received delegations from subject peoples. An early fourth-century frieze from Xanthos in south-western Asia Minor depicts a satrap – or a local ruler who acted like one – seated under a royal parasol, admonishing a Greek embassy.[3] But the Persians also expected such delegations regularly to attend on the 'king of kings' himself in order to pay homage – and tribute. The works of Greek historians like Herodotus, Thucydides, and Xenophon bear witness to a maze of diplomatic activity, with embassies being sent hither and thither between the Persian court and places as far afield as India. The strategy was to treat leniently those who accepted Persian rule and harshly those who resisted it. 'The man who cooperates,' Darius I proclaimed in his epitaph, 'him according to his cooperative action, him thus do I reward.'[4] In his idealized biography of Cyrus II, Xenophon explained the Persian rationale: 'There are two things that it were well for us to look out for: that we make ourselves masters of those who own this property, and that they stay where they are. For a land destitute of people becomes likewise destitute of produce.'[5]

When the Persians encountered unrest, their first response was for the local satrap to restore order. The crackdown against the Ionian Revolt, for example, was depicted as just such a restoration of justice. The satrap Mardonius imposed agreements on the Ionian cities that replaced their hated tyrants with democratically elected leaders, made them swear an oath of perpetual peace with each other, facilitated trade between them, and obliged them to settle their border disputes through Persian arbitration, abide by a common law, and tear down their walls. Local self-government under Persian supervision: that was the objective. It was probably what the Persians had had in mind when they dispatched their envoys to demand water and earth from the city states on the other side of the Aegean. When Sparta and Athens refused, the Persians responded by trying to divide the league that had been established to defend Greece. Before long, they succeeded: Thessaly, the gateway to central and southern Greece, sent a messenger to Darius to propose an alliance. Argos and Thebes soon followed.

One of the Persians' chief diplomatic weapons was money. Near the end of the Persian Wars, when Athens, as leader of the Delian League, seemed to be emerging as the main beneficiary of the conflict, Artaxerxes I tried to win over the Spartans, who were not members of the league. In 456, he ordered an official called Megabazus to bribe them to attack Athens so as to stop the latter's campaigns in Cyprus and Egypt. In 449, when the Athenian general Callias returned with the terms of the treaty he had agreed with Persia to bring the fifty-year hostilities to a formal close, he was accused of bribery by his fellow citizens who deemed the concessions he had negotiated insufficient.[6] Persia's policy of divide-and-rule saw it first subsidize Sparta's fleet, then aid Athens when Sparta supported a revolt against Artaxerxes II. In 395, the Persians sent an agent called Timocrates – who was a Greek from Rhodes – to Greece with gold to distribute among politicians in Athens, Thebes, Corinth, and Argos to try to persuade them to form an alliance against Sparta.

The Persians liked to cajole the Greek cities with 'special relationships', sometimes based on the emotional appeal of common ancestors, at others on pragmatic arguments of common interests. Yet occasionally Greek diplomacy could leave the Persians bewildered. After the Spartans sent a mission to Persia in 425, the Persian king wrote a letter in reply urging them in future to speak with one voice: 'The King did not understand what they wanted, since the many ambassadors who had come to him all said different things.'[7]

CHAPTER 4

The Greek March into Disaster

Scandalous! That was the Greek verdict on diplomats who succumbed to the allure of Persian gold. In Athens, a comic dramatist called Plato mocked the prominent populist politician Epicrates for being more obsessed with Persian luxury than with the city's interests, while an envoy called Timagoras was put to death after he returned not only with gold but also with a Persian bed – an insult to the frugal Greek lifestyle. Nothing disturbed Greek intellectuals more than the lack of Hellenic unity. Herodotus championed the cause of a common front against the barbarian Persians, emphasizing the kinship of all Greeks. But Hellenic unity never really existed. Even Athens, a flourishing commercial city connected to all corners of the Greek world, was often profoundly nativist. Immigrants from other cities were frequently expelled, had their property expropriated, or were even murdered.

Inter-Greek tensions reached their apogee with the Peloponnesian War. The Athenian historian Thucydides (460–400) portrayed the conflict as an unprecedented tragedy, a march into disaster. 'The state of affairs everywhere in Hellas was such that nothing very remarkable could be done by any combination of powers,' he wrote. 'For a short time the wartime alliance held together, but it was not long before quarrels took place and Athens and Sparta, each with her own allies, were at war with each other.'[8] In Aristophanes' comic play *Lysistrata* (411), the women of Greece stage a sex-strike to stop the fighting. In his *Peace* (421), an Athenian farmer is so desperate to end the conflict that he flies to heaven

142

on a giant dung beetle in order to free Irene, the goddess of peace, who is being held in a cage by Polemos, the god of war. Spears are turned into vine props, breastplates into pots, and war trumpets into scales for weighing figs. In 415, Euripides staged his tragedy *The Women of Troy* to protest against the massacres and the destitution that the Greeks were inflicting on themselves. Even after the Peloponnesian War had nearly destroyed Athens, the politician Demosthenes thundered at the Greek cities for neglecting to act against the threat now posed by Macedon. The lack of orchestrated response – the desire to avoid war even if territory was chipped away and trade interfered with – was 'an act of stupidity'.[9]

Although many Greeks longed for unity and peace, most thinkers remained sceptical they could ever be achieved. The Athenian philosopher Plato (424–348) insisted that all people depended on each other, yet greed and envy prevented them from seeing the merits of a harmonious city where inhabitants coexisted in peace and good health before dying at a ripe old age; instead they lived in 'fevered' cities ravaged by infighting. The only way to attain the harmonious city was to educate all citizens properly, train them to be soldiers, and cherish peace as the bedrock of political legitimacy. 'Being Greeks they should not ravage Greece,' he asserted.[10]

Plato's former pupil, the philosopher Aristotle (384–322), endorsed this view; but, far more than his old master, he counselled the statesman to watch the balance of power. 'He should know whether the military power of another country is like or unlike that of his own; for this is a matter that may affect their relative strength.'[11] War, Aristotle continued, was often necessary to defend freedom. But, he added cynically, the pursuit of peace was a powerful cause of war. We do business in order that we may have leisure, he summarized, and we fight wars in order to have peace. A preoccupation with the balance of power was also present in Herodotus' history. 'The power of Persia was steadily increasing,' he wrote. 'This gave Croesus food for thought, and he wondered if he might be able to check Persian expansion before it had gone too far.'[12]

In very similar terms, Thucydides explained the outbreak of the Peloponnesian War between Athens and Sparta. Thucydides posited that human nature was dominated by fear, honour, and self-interest, but that what most fundamentally shaped international politics was the balance of power. 'What made war inevitable,' he famously declared, 'was the growth of Athenian power and the fear which this caused in Sparta.'[13] Thucydides went on to explain the contribution of the lesser powers to the outbreak of war. Open hostilities were triggered by unrest in the small town of Epidamnos. One party gained the support of Corcyra, which in turn appealed for support from Athens. The opposing party in Epidamnos meanwhile called on Corinth, which called on its ally, Sparta. And Sparta called for Persian support.

Thucydides also exposed the limits of law, arbitration, and justice in relations between states. Even though arbitration was a common practice, Corcyra and Corinth disagreed about its terms. The lengthy speeches of the Corcyrans and Corinthians before the assemblies of Sparta and Athens showed how the validity and justness of treaties could be subject to the way opposing sides interpreted them in the light of past and present events. 'The Spartans voted that the treaty had been broken and that war should be declared not so much because they were influenced by the speeches of their allies as because they were afraid of the further growth of Athenian power, seeing, as they did, that already the greater part of Hellas was under the control of Athens.'[14] Although Thucydides concluded sceptically that it had always been the natural order of things for the weak to be subject to the strong, he insisted: 'This is what a leader should do – to look after his own interests as everyone else does, but also, in return for all the honour he receives from others, to give a special consideration to the general interest.'[15]

The permanent state of threat that existed between states turned Greece into a laboratory of diplomacy. As monarchs and tyrants were replaced by assemblies based on greater or lesser degrees of popular representation, cities during diplomatic missions turned to the most gifted communicators to plead their case before these citizen bodies. Thucydides repeatedly showed how such orators passionately defended the interests of their cities before the assemblies of Athens and Sparta, observing in turn how the leading politicians of Athens and Sparta had to try and steer the assemblies' responses to such rhetoric. There were also more familiar types of diplomat: message bearers with very limited mandates to negotiate; true envoys with the authority to agree terms within parameters established by their assembly; and *proxenoi*, who were a kind of honorary consul. From the state whose interests they represented, *proxenoi* could receive official protection or tax-exemptions in exchange for assisting negotiations, providing grain, or contributing ships. They could be ordinary citizens, eminent generals, or even kings or poets.[16] The Acropolis Museum in Athens contains several relief panels commemorating the contributions of these 'official friends', including one depicting the *proxenos* standing as symbolic intermediary between the patron goddesses of two cities, whose hands rest meaningfully on him.[17] Treaties were sworn with binding oaths before the gods and chiselled into stone, so that citizens could read them. But, as Thucydides put it, they had often been violated before the parties had even left the shrine.

Far more ambitious in scope were the leagues formed around a hegemonic power, such as the famous Delian League around Athens, the rival Peloponnesian League around Sparta, or the League of Corinth around Macedon. The smaller members usually had to pay taxes, and contribute troops, to the leading state, which provided security in return. Both Athens and Sparta also tried to install sympathetic regimes with similar political constitutions in fellow league members. Interestingly, one of the first attempts to form a union after the Amphictyonic League was the attempt by the Persian satrap Mardonius to make the Greek cities of Asia Minor cooperate in the aftermath of the Ionian Revolt. But there were also leagues formed *against* possible hegemons: the league formed to defend Greece against the Persian invasions in the early fifth century was perhaps the most notable one.

Some smaller leagues achieved a remarkable degree of integration. The Arcadian League (370–230), for example, required cities to surrender a significant degree of their autonomy if they wanted to join, to subscribe to a democratic constitution, to designate representatives to a council in the newly founded capital of Megalopolis, and to conduct a common foreign and security policy. The Achaean League (281–146) took matters even further and developed a quasi-federal government. The Epirote League (around 300–170) also had a federal constitution, a council with regular meetings, joint rules on taxation, a common currency, freedom of personal movement, and was one of the first polities to give citizenship to women.

We know of numerous peace treaties from the period of the Persian Wars and the Peloponnesian War, as well as an almost equal number of breaches. The Peace of Callias held for only two years. In 446, Sparta and Athens agreed a thirty years peace that confirmed the division of most of the Greek world into Athenian and Spartan spheres of influence. It was violated four years later. In 421, the agreement of seventeen cities to the Peace of Nicias brought a partial end to the Peloponnesian War. Intended to last for fifty years, it was completely abandoned six years later. In 387, the Treaty of Antalcidas introduced the idea of the 'common peace', based on the principle of autonomy for all city states but with Sparta guaranteeing it as a sort of hegemon. But at a peace conference in 371, Sparta was famously criticized by Autocles, an Athenian envoy: 'Now you always say, "The cities must be independent," but you are yourselves the greatest obstacle in the way of their independence. For the first stipulation you make with your allied cities is this, that they follow wherever you may lead. And yet how is this consistent with independence?'[18] The Theban ambassador Epaminondas added that there could be peace only if the Spartans recognized their own provincial towns as free communities. The conference ended in war. Nevertheless fresh attempts were made in 363 and 338 to establish a 'common peace', the latter occasion in response to the rise of Macedon.

The idea of peace was closely related to the idea of free trade. One of the first Greeks to promote its importance was Xenophon:

> Whereas in other trading cities merchants are forced to barter one commodity for another, in regard their coin is not current abroad, we abound not only in manufactures, and products of our own growth, sufficient to answer the demands of foreign traders, but in case they refused to export our goods, in return for their own, they may trade with us to advantage, by receiving silver in exchange for them, which transported to any other market, would pass for more than they took it for at Athens.[19]

The Persian Peace of the Ionian states, the Peace of Antalcidas, championed free trade as well. The Peace of Callias aimed to guarantee that 'all might sail without fear'.[20] Alexander the Great is reported to have issued an edict to his Persian subjects: 'I intend to bring prosperity to your lands and to see that the roads of Persia are used for trade and business in total peace, so that people from Greece may trade with you and you with them.'[21] But mutual commercial interests seldom prevented Greek states from going to war again and again.

Rome's First Steps to Primacy

With the death of Alexander the Great in 323, the prospect of unity in the Eastern Mediterranean and the Middle East disappeared. In the wars fought between his former generals to succeed him, the empire became divided into four main parts. Eventually, after much blood had been spilled, the Antigonid Dynasty ruled over the Macedonian heartland, the Attalids over Asia Minor, the Ptolemies over Egypt, and the Seleucids over Mesopotamia. The unipolar era was over, making way for an age of multipolar regional orders. In 306, Antigonus was the first openly to proclaim himself king and heir of Alexander. Together with his son, Demetrius, he gained control over the Levant, Asia Minor, Cyprus, and a part of the Peloponnese. It was not enough: Babylon remained the ultimate prize. As much as it had captivated Alexander, and all the other great Mesopotamian rulers of the past, Antigonus too was determined to conquer it.

He came close, but at the Battle of Ipsus in 301, he was defeated by a coalition of his rival dynasts, and killed. They pushed the Antigonid realm, now under Demetrius, out of the Levant and Asia Minor. In 281, one of these dynasts, King Seleucus, took sole control of Asia Minor. As he prepared to cross the Hellespont in order to add Macedon to his domains, he was assassinated. His son, Antiochus I, had the greatest difficulty standing his ground against the hugely ambitious King Ptolemy II, who ruled Egypt. In an echo of events from centuries ago, once again a king of Egypt was fighting a king of Mesopotamia for control of the Levant. These wars between the successor dynasties of Alexander would continue for another century, until the growing power of Rome eclipsed them all.

In the third century, Rome gradually emerged as the leading state in the Western Mediterranean. The small city on the banks of the River Tiber had come to maturity through centuries of warfare. After having dealt a series of defeats to the

Etruscans, Rome was faced by the fearsome threat posed by the Gallic migrations. Numbering in their hundreds of thousands, the Gauls crossed the Alps into present-day France, Spain, Italy, and the Balkans. In 387, Rome only escaped total destruction when the Gallic leader Brennus, who had captured the city, was bribed to withdraw from it. The Gauls had been repelled, but Rome still faced other dangers. The Volsci and the Etruscans still resisted Roman hegemony in the north. In the south, Rome competed with mercantile powers like the Greek cities of Syracuse and Tarentum, and the former Phoenician colony of Carthage, each of which contained more than 100,000 inhabitants. In 348, Carthage was able to impose a humiliating treaty that locked Rome out of Sardinia and North Africa. In 303, Rome had to accept an agreement with Tarentum that limited its access to the Ionian Sea.

Still, the balance of power was slowly altering. By the beginning of the third century, Rome had emerged as the victor of a series of wars with a coalition of Samnites, Gauls, and the Etruscans, giving it effective control over most of the Italian Peninsula. The last meaningful resistance came from King Pyrrhus of Epirus, who sailed across the Ionian Sea to the aid of Tarentum in 280. Despite his twenty war elephants – the first encountered by the Romans in battle – not even this experienced general was able to turn the tide against Rome's seemingly endless supply of manpower. '[Even] if we are victorious in one more battle with the Romans,' he stated, 'we shall be utterly ruined.'[22]

In 264, the Sicilian city of Messina appealed to Rome for support in a conflict with Syracuse. Carthage considered this appeal a violation of earlier treaties and occupied Messina itself, provoking Rome to respond. This chain of events marked the start of the Punic Wars (264–146), a struggle for control of the Western Mediterranean that lasted more than a century and transformed Rome into Europe's foremost power. The Greek historian Polybius, who provided a first-hand account of the latter stages of the conflict, explained the underlying causes:

> [The Romans] saw that Carthaginian aggrandisement was not confined to Libya, but had embraced many districts in Iberia as well; and that Carthage was, besides, mistress of all the islands in the Sardinian and Tyrrhenian seas: they were beginning, therefore, to be exceedingly anxious lest, if the Carthaginians became masters of Sicily also, they should find them very dangerous and formidable neighbours, surrounding them as they would on every side, and occupying a position which commanded all the coasts of Italy.[23]

Initially, the power struggles in the Western Mediterranean involving Rome and the power struggles in the Eastern Mediterranean and Middle East between the successor dynasties of Alexander the Great were not connected. This changed, first when Pyrrhus crossed the Ionian Sea, and then in 273, when Ptolemy II sought an alliance with Rome to check his powerful North African neighbour, Carthage. As the First Punic War (264–241) advanced, though, Ptolemy changed sides and lent Carthage money.

Between 500 and 250, the Mediterranean, Middle East, and North Africa continued their slow transformation into a single vast arena of power politics. This metamorphosis had been instigated by the Persian Achaemenid Dynasty's wars west of the Aegean Sea and in Egypt. The Achaemenids combined hard power with the mollifying effects of gold, both of which were funded by a tributary order that reconnected with the imperial traditions of Assyria and Babylon and followed in the footsteps of their earlier efforts to control trade. For a moment, in the mid-fourth century, it looked as if Alexander the Great would permanently establish an even larger empire. After his death, however, the region fractured politically, while remaining connected through rivalry, trade, and travel. Rome, meanwhile, took a growing interest in securing trade through the Adriatic Sea, which would be followed in the next centuries by the conquest of Greece and the whole Eastern Mediterranean.

Writers from this era have left us with a stream of information about this intriguing theatre of diplomacy. From their works, it becomes clear that republics and monarchies, democracies and oligarchies, were not that different in their zeal for power. Even if some thinkers stressed the importance of welfare, free trade, and cooperation, they also placed a great deal of emphasis on maintaining the balance of power. Thucydides, in his history of the Peloponnesian War, explored the tragic dilemmas that arise when two powers try to defend overlapping interests; and Polybius, in discussing the tensions between Rome and Carthage over Sicily, highlighted the tendency of lesser powers to play larger states off against each other and the destabilizing effects of commercial ambitions. 'Thus,' concluded Xenophon, 'strife and anger beget war, avarice stifles benevolence, envy produces hate.'[24]

The Maurya Empire

Beyond the borders of Persia, east of the River Indus, a new empire was slowly being shaped. Already, in 326, its might was such that Alexander the Great's soldiers refused to march beyond the Beas River lest they encountered the army of the Nanda kingdom, which they believed numbered more than 200,000 warriors and 3,000 war elephants.[25]

The Nanda kingdom had been established in the preceding decades by Mahapadma Nanda (345–321). Mahapadma – the name means 'ruler of great wealth' – had seized the throne of the Magadha kingdom, which had been founded by King Bimbisara. By the time that Mahapadma came to power, the realm already encompassed a large part of the plain along the middle reaches of the Ganges. He expanded it all the way to the southern slopes of the Hindu Kush and the Deccan Plateau. The Nanda triumph was short-lived: Mahapadma's heirs were overthrown by Chandragupta Maurya (324–298). He would turn India into a true empire, one of the largest that the world had seen.

Little is known about how Chandragupta became powerful enough to seize the Nanda kingdom; he probably made use of widespread resentment against the dynasty to start a guerrilla campaign, and bribed the regime's generals. But once the Nanda had been dethroned, Chandragupta marched west in order to prevent King Seleucus from carrying out Alexander's dream of conquering India. After two years of war, a peace treaty was signed in 303 and sealed with a marriage alliance. In return for 500 war elephants – which were instrumental in the defeat of Antigonus at Ipsus in 301 – Seleucus ceded to Chandragupta control of the mountain passes of the Hindu Kush, the crossroads between Southern, Central, and Western Asia. The Maurya king instantly set to work developing a new highway – the Grand Trunk Road – and deploying soldiers to guard it. From then on, trade between Southern Asia and the Middle East flourished. Chandragupta's son, Bindusara Maurya, expanded the realm to the south and sealed alliances with the Tamils and the Cholas. When Chandragupta's grandson, Ashoka (268–232), came to the throne, the Maurya Empire stretched from the Zagros Mountains to the Brahmaputra River.

For most of Ashoka's lengthy reign, the subjects of the Maurya Empire enjoyed peace. This remarkable achievement was at least partly attributable to the royal advisor Kautilya, whose treatise on statecraft, the *Arthashastra*, is still read today. Kautilya was most respected for his 'mandala' system, a scheme of concentric geopolitical circles which showed kings that the way to keep a neighbour in check was to form alliances with the states situated on its other borders. But his principal advice was to keep society at home satisfied. 'A wise king can make even the poor and miserable elements of his sovereignty happy and prosperous,' he explained; for 'strength is power and happiness is the end.'[26] Land had to be cultivated, wild beasts kept at a distance, conspirators eliminated, and treasure built up. Powerful kings could embark on conquest, whereas weak kings needed to sue for peace. The *Arthashastra* lists the many ways to enforce a peace treaty: swearing by fire or on the shoulder of an elephant, by giving children or adult members of the royal family as hostages – although Kautilya judged a hostage princess more trouble to the recipient than a hostage prince. But whatever form guarantees took, Kautilya warned, rising powers could not be prevented from breaking a peace agreement.

King Ashoka replaced this realist strategic culture, which emphasized the state of anarchy existing between many small polities, with a true doctrine of empire, which presupposed hierarchy under a major power. After the defeat of the stubborn kingdom of Kalinga, Ashoka adopted the tenets of Buddhism. Renouncing violence, he propagated a benign form of rule over his subjects. He became the *chakravartin* – 'he who lets the wheel roll throughout the whole world' – the Buddhist symbol for the precepts that lead to enlightenment. Since its origins in northern India in the fifth century, Buddhism had spread widely across Southern Asia. Now, its doctrine of universal truth and harmony proved convenient for legitimizing the emperor. All over the Maurya Empire, pillars were erected with Ashoka's Buddhist edicts. 'In the past, kings used to go out on pleasure tours,' we read. 'I consider the welfare of all to be my duty.'[27] The thirteenth of these 'rock edicts' speaks of 'moral conquest'; to put that into practice, envoys (*dutas*) were dispatched not only across the empire, but as far afield as Sri Lanka, Greece, and Egypt, in order to preach Buddhism, set up hospitals, and cultivate gardens. But Ashoka's doctrine of harmony still rested on hard power. He maintained a well-structured military establishment of 600,000 soldiers. He continued to use a large network of spies and royal emissaries, the so-called *pulisanis*, to keep him informed about the situation in the empire's four provinces. Each province was administered by a governor-prince, the *kumara*, who was responsible for maintaining order and levying taxes.

At the heart of the empire, which contained between 50 and 60 million inhabitants, was the capital, Pataliputra, near modern Patna. According to Megasthenes, a Greek diplomat residing at the Maurya court, Pataliputra and its wooden palaces were rivalled in splendour only by the great cities of Persia. It was a centre of politics, culture, and science, attracting intellectuals like Aryabhata, the mathematician and astronomer who calculated *pi* to four decimal places. Bindusara Maurya asked the Seleucid king Antiochus I for sweet wine, dried figs – and a philosopher. The sudden flourishing of the arts under the Maurya still puzzles historians. In less than a century, primitive works of clay had been replaced by elaborate stone carvings, such as the capitals of the Pillars of Ashoka – which clearly show Persian influences – or the voluptuous Yakshi goddesses. The Maurya cities had become the world's new crucibles of culture and science. In the wake of its Buddhist monks, its influence spread from Greece to Southeast Asia. The centre of the world had shifted from the Middle East to India.

Warring States

The contrast between India during the Ashokan era of harmony and China at the same time could not have been more stark. Here, relentless struggle defined the age. Ever since the Zhou Dynasty lost its heavenly mandate in the eighth century, the North China Plain had been convulsed by city states and slightly larger kingdoms competing for primacy.

Formally, there was still a Zhou king, but his status was ceremonial and he depended entirely on the support of other rulers. Numerous diplomatic conferences were held, to talk about disarmament, for example, or about the rules of war, or even to try and agree peace. But, more often than not, they were in vain. 'While the conference was still in session, and before the ceremonies recognizing the new status of Wu were completed,' we read in the annals about the congress held at Huangchi in 482, 'word came that King Goujian had invaded Wu, captured its capital, and ravaged the country. King Fuchai killed the messenger who brought the news in hopes of keeping it a secret until the conference ended, but the information leaked out and he was forced to beat a hasty retreat.'[28]

Between the fifth and the third centuries, the pack of warring states after whom this era is named, was thinned down from fourteen to seven, and then down to one. The Warring States period (476–221) started with the split of the Jin state into three parts: Wei, Zhao, and Han. The rest of the North China Plain was divided between the Chu, the Qin, the Qi, and the Yan, and, at the centre, the shrivelled rump state of the Zhou, whose king was now held in almost negligible esteem. This was the cultured world; beyond it lurked barbarians: the Gojoseon, who controlled the Korean Peninsula; the nomadic Xiongnu in the north; in the west, the Wuzhong mountain tribes and the Qiang; in the south, the Shu, the Yelang, the Dian, and the diverse conglomeration of Yue tribes that reached beyond the Red River.

After the state of Jin split, the Wei were the first to benefit. Records explain how Marquess Wen of Wei shrewdly played off the Zhao against the Han, and sacked one of the

Xiongnu states in 406. It was the state of Zhao, however, that outsmarted the others by integrating the mounted archery of the Xiongnu into its army. It was a masterstroke that gave it a decisive advantage against chariots, which often proved sluggish on mountainous battlefields. In 354, the Zhao pulverized the Wei in the Battle of Guiling; but, by that time, a new pretender had already thrown down the gauntlet: Duke Xiao of Qin. The Qin had several advantages over other states. Their motherland along the Wei River was protected from the plains by mountain passes. Behind this barrier, the Qin developed a flourishing agricultural economy by recognizing land ownership in exchange for tax and services, resettling farmers from overpopulated areas, and providing advanced irrigation. 'Thereupon the land within the passes became a fertile plain, and there were no more bad years,' the records report. 'Qin thus became rich and powerful.'[29] On the battlefield, the Qin benefited from lightly armoured cavalry, again inspired by the Xiongnu. Their soldiers fought in small units, often drawn from one family or village. In 260, about half a million Qin troops and a similar number of Zhao men took up positions near Changping. The ensuing confrontation was fiercely fought and decisive. Hundreds of thousands of Zhao soldiers were killed; the advance of the Qin was now unstoppable. In 221, the Qin Empire was established.

When the Qin Empire was founded, bringing to an end the Warring States period, the population of China had reached approximately 40 million. The many conflicts had slowed population growth and inflicted enormous damage. Technological innovations, however, were plentiful. As in other parts of the world, iron became more commonly used.

In farming, crop rotation and fertilizers were introduced, alongside feudal land holding, which gave families some security of tenure. Cities grew. The largest of them was the Qi capital of Linzi, with over 350,000 inhabitants. 'If the people only lifted their sleeves, they would cover the sky,' a visitor wrote. 'If they shook the sweat from them, it would appear to rain.'[30] Protected by lofty walls and towers, Linzi was laid out around a grid of avenues, some more than twenty metres wide. Central to such cities was the market place; here, besides the traditional staple crops, an increasingly diverse array of products was found – furniture, iron utensils, silk, and, of course, jade. Powerful tycoons emerged, like the infamous Lu Buwei, who bought himself the position of prime minister of Qin.

As trade grew, court advisors wondered how to manage it. The famous Qin counsellor Shang Yang insisted that statecraft remained a matter of 'promoting farming and confining trade'.[31] But Confucian thinkers believed that a new sort of political harmony would evolve, under the king, if states specialized in what they produced. 'The north sea has running horses and barking dogs,' summarized the Confucian philosopher some 2,000 years before the English economist David Ricardo formulated his theory of economic specialization: 'The south sea has feathers, plumes, elephant tusks, rhinoceros hides, copper, and cinnabar . . . The eastern sea has purple-dye plants, white silks, fish, and salt . . . The western sea has skins, hides, and patterned yak tails.'[32] Mencius thought that a kingdom would attract traders and travellers if no taxes were charged at frontier gates; while the *Book of Rites* advised that tariffs at border crossings should be reduced, so that merchants come from the most distant parts and 'the resources of the government do not fail'.[33]

Commerce with other continents, however, was negligible: if trade in luxury goods connected India, the Middle East, and the Mediterranean, China was not yet a part of this network, or at best only very marginally. But the Chinese states did start to extend their might to areas where it had previously been unknown. In 316, the Qin defeated the state of Shu and, two years later, the last hostile Rong tribe. In 300, the Yan invaded the Gojoseon kingdom in Korea. In 257, Shu refugees, headed by Prince Thuc Phan, founded the Au Lac state in the north of modern Vietnam.

Because there was still no single unified state, a dynamic intellectual diversity – the so-called Hundred Schools of Thought – could flourish. Wandering thinkers travelled from court to court, attracted more often than not by how much kings would pay. There was intense and sophisticated debate about governance, diplomacy, war, and peace. The violent context led some thinkers to urge for law and order. These 'legalists', such as Shang Yang and Han Fei, asserted that, in the absence of a strong ruler, humans' innate selfish nature led to chaos, and that there could be no peace without power. 'Generally, war is a thing that people hate,' argued Shang Yang. 'He who succeeds in making people delight in war, attains supremacy.'[34] 'Men of remote antiquity strove to be known as moral and virtuous; those of the middle age struggled to be known as wise and resourceful; and now men fight for the reputation of being vigorous and powerful,' asserted Han Fei. 'Peoples everywhere that could be reached by transportation came to pay homage. They were not won over by

Qin's goodness, but were intimidated by its military power. Whoever has great strength sees others visit his court; whoever has little strength visits the courts of others.'[35]

As the Zhou kings lost all authority, and other lords did not even bother to be proclaimed hegemon any more, scholars contemplated how to manage relations between states. Realists advocated so-called 'horizontal alliances', which implied that the weak should side with the strong. Others promoted 'vertical alliances', in which the weak would join forces against the strong. Even many Confucian scholars shifted towards realism. Xunzi wrote that struggle was inevitable. Men are evil, he stated, because of their innate greed, sensuality, and quarrelsomeness. But these realist Confucians still maintained that kings should be morally superior. 'You speak of the values of plots and of moving by sudden attack,' Xunzi observed, 'but these are matters appropriate only to lesser lords. What is really essential is to be good at winning the support of the people.'[36]

No matter how wise the advice of philosophers and sages, it made little difference. The annals of this period are a catalogue of wars and broken treaties, even more so than the *Spring and Autumn Annals*. This passage summarizes it all perfectly:

> Envoys rush along the roads in such haste that the hubs of their carriage wheels bumped against each other. Bound by each other by means of conversations, they form alliances, specious ministers in collusion cleverly gloss their artful schemes. The code of laws is in order, but the many people act falsely. The official documents are numerous

but obscure. The hundred families are in want. There are arguments by scholars in their strange dress, but wars do not cease.[37]

Strength and Happiness

For most of the period between 500 and 250, the Eastern Hemisphere was afflicted by political fragmentation. The North China Plain suffered from the warring states and their violent attempts at unification. The empire of the Achaemenids and Alexander the Great imploded. This left the densely populated Indo-Gangetic Plain under its Maurya kings as the centre of power and a vital conduit between the East Asian and Middle Eastern worlds.

During this era, there was also a slow change in political organization. In between tiny polities and vast empires, a growing number of middling large states emerged. The Eastern Mediterranean after the death of Alexander the Great, for example, was dominated by the successor kingdoms of the Seleucids and Attalids in Asia Minor, the Ptolemies in Egypt, and the Antigonids in Macedon; while the Western Mediterranean was shared between Carthage and the growing power of Rome. In East Asia, the number of Chinese warring states was first whittled down to seven, and then to one, the Qin, and the Korean Peninsula became dominated by the kingdom of Gojoseon.

As regards thinking about politics, the Mesopotamian imperial tradition was continued by the Achaemenid Dynasty right to the end, before Alexander the Great also invested heavily in it during his brief reign. Much as with the Zhou kings' heavenly mandate in China, Persian monarchs based the legitimacy of their rule on divine approval of the way they fostered the welfare of their citizens. Preserving harmony inside the realm was key, but so was preserving security along the border. Both the suppression of the Ionian Revolt and the consequent interventions in Greece were seen as efforts to restore the just order. The Maurya Dynasty in India, meanwhile, founded its own imperial tradition on Buddhism. Ashoka saw himself as the *chakravartin*, duty-bound to nurture the welfare of the whole world. The Maurya kings also drew on the teachings of the *Arthashastra*, a text that today is mostly known for its realist divide-and-rule strategy towards neighbouring states, but which is fundamentally concerned with wise and righteous government and the pursuit of public wellbeing.

Beyond the peaceful empires, in regions scarred by war, people also pondered the nature of politics. In both Greece and China, pacifism grew in popularity. Intellectuals like Xenophon and Xun Kuang highlighted the importance of trade for facilitating cooperation between states. Others, such as Thucydides and Han Fei, were more jaundiced, arguing that the selfishness and opportunism of human nature wrought havoc. In reality, wars were fought for many reasons: some shift in the balance of power, tensions between overlapping spheres of influence, competition over trade, not to mention the long legacy of nationalism, distrust, and hatred.

Nevertheless, diplomatic efforts were often intense; although even here cynicism and idealism both found free rein. International conferences intended to settle disagreements were often regarded with distrust. States formalized relationships between each other by establishing leagues: some were voluntary, with common institutions; others were hegemonies in all but name, subservient to the interests of the most powerful member. The Persians employed gold and offers of special partnership both to mollify the Greek city states and to undermine Hellenic unity. Around the Mediterranean, citizen assemblies increasingly had a say in decisions relating to war and peace – and often demonstrated a ruthlessness and aggressiveness to match even the most warmongering of monarchs.

CHAPTER 5

The World Like a Chariot Run Wild

250–1 BCE

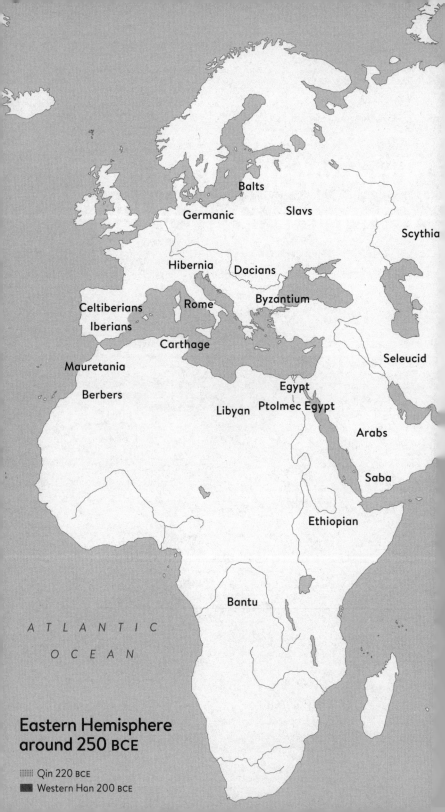

Balts

Slavs

Scythia

Germanic

Hibernia

Dacians

Byzantium

Celtiberians

Rome

Iberians

Seleucid

Carthage

Mauretania

Egypt

Berbers

Libyan Ptolmec Egypt

Arabs

Saba

Ethiopian

Bantu

A T L A N T I C

O C E A N

Eastern Hemisphere
around 250 BCE

Qin 220 BCE

Western Han 200 BCE

Xiongnu

Qiang

Wei Yan

Zhao

Qi

Tibetans

Qin

Chu (State)

Maurya

PACIFIC

OCEAN

Chola

N D I A N

O C E A N

500 1000 1500 km

500 1000 miles

Just as the kingdoms of the Warring States period struggled for mastery of the North China Plain, so Rome, Carthage, and some of the remnants of the empire of Alexander the Great vied for dominance over the Mediterranean, its trade, and the rich agricultural regions on its shores. From these twin contests, two empires emerged: the Han Empire and the Roman Empire. By the end of the first century BCE, they both ruled over roughly 50 million people. Although the Italian Peninsula itself did not have the same agricultural potential as the North China Plain, Rome was able to draw much of its food from overseas provinces, like Sicily and Spain, that were no more difficult to reach by ship than some parts of China were by inland transportation. In terms of connectivity and prosperity, the Mediterranean became to Rome what the plains around the Yellow River and the Yangtze were to Han China.

Many theories have been put forward to explain the ascents of Rome and the Han. The truth is that both were relatively small fringe powers who had the knack of emerging victorious from close-fought battles which, in turn, opened the way to further conquests. By the beginning of the second century, Rome had become a formidable military power on land and sea, while Han China was unmatched in terms of its infantry, chariots, and fortresses. The strategies of both powers now shifted from defence to offence. Rome's epic battle with Carthage in the Second Punic War (218–201) was a horrific struggle for survival. Its subsequent campaigns in Spain and north of the Alps were not. While the Han state still faced challenges to its rule from rival Chinese kingdoms, it sought to conciliate the northern nomads. Yet, once Han domestic power was unrivalled, Emperor Wu chose to attack them: the control of external trade routes had become a much more pressing concern.

By contrast with Roman and Han dominance of the western and eastern edges of the hemisphere, elsewhere the political situation was far less stable. Egypt under the Ptolemaic kings was in decline, its population falling below 10 million. Seleucid weakness in the mid-third century allowed the inception of the Parthian Empire in what had once been the eastern provinces of Achaemenid Persia. But Parthia's military strength belied a demographic frailty arising from agricultural stagnation. In the Indo-Gangetic Plain, anarchy prevailed as the Maurya Empire crumbled after the death of Ashoka. The heart of Eurasia, meanwhile, witnessed an astounding tournament of power as the nomadic Xiongnu, driven west by Han China, collided with the Yuezhi. This was a conflict not only for survival, but also for the riches of the Silk Road trade between China, the Mediterranean, and the Indian Ocean. It destroyed the once-flourishing kingdom of Bactria and, in the process, gave rise to the Kushan Empire, which would come to play a prominent role in Central and South Asia.

The Struggle between Chinese Dynasties

The Qin victory at the Battle of Changping in 260 was the decisive moment in a grinding war of attrition. The annals tell that the Qin mobilized every man over fifteen years old. Tens of thousands of captives were buried alive. Alarmed by this ruthlessness, the Zhao, the Wei, and the Han combined their forces. It was to no avail: the Qin deposed the last Zhou king in 256, and unleashed a campaign to eradicate the Zhao. The death of the powerful king Zhaoxiang of Qin in 251 and the subsequent struggle at court gave the rest of China a short period of relief. In 230, Zhaoxiang's grandson instigated a fresh decade of campaigns, which came to be known as the Wars of Unification. The weakened kingdom of Han was the first to succumb; Zhao, Wei, Chu, and Qi all followed. In 221, King Ying Zheng of Qin proclaimed himself emperor. The first dynasty of imperial China was born: the Qin.

The success of the Qin came at a tremendous cost. If the annals are to be trusted, the history of the Qin's rise to supremacy reads like an endless massacre.[1] Battles were fought between hundreds of thousands of soldiers, farmland was ravaged, cities burned, and countless civilians lost their lives. That the Qin prevailed was due to their superior power base. It was easy to defend and endowed with both farmland and iron mines. Some scholars have argued that the Qin's weapons gave them a significant advantage, but this is not clear. More importantly, the Qin diplomatic strategy created a beneficial domino effect. The historian Sima Qian (145–86) explained the Qin approach in terms of befriending the far and attacking the near – somewhat like the 'mandala' system of Kautilya. Their first step was to appease the Qi so that they could concentrate on more proximate rivals, the weakened Han and Zhao states. Once these had been easily conquered, their territories and resources helped defeat the Wei. As a result of these annexations, the balance of power swung decisively against the Qin's strongest rival, the Chu.

In the aftermath of his victories, Ying Zheng – who ruled under the title of Qin Shi Huang, or 'first emperor of Qin' (221–210) – initiated reform after reform to promote unity. Former kingdoms were divided up into commanderies with directly appointed leaders. Major infrastructure works were undertaken, such as the construction of a vast wall to defend against incursions by the nomadic Xiongnu, the Linqu canal to improve communications between north and south, as well as hundreds of kilometres of roads. A single official written script was introduced across the entire empire. Measures, coins, and even the axles of carts were standardized in order to facilitate trade. But the quest for control also led the first Qin emperor to impose the doctrine of legalism, which, in contrast to Confucianism, held power, law, and order more important than morality. Hundreds of scholars of other philosophies were burned alive. This at least partly explains why the Qin Empire came to be so widely portrayed as malicious and brutish. 'It failed to rule with humanity and righteousness, and did not realize that the power to attack, and the power to retain what one has thereby won, are not the same,' wrote the later Confucian thinker Jia Yi in his *Faults of the Qin*. 'Its downfall was merely a matter of time.'[2]

Three years after Qin Shi Huang was consigned to the afterlife under the protection of the famous Terracotta Army, the empire died too. When Shi Huang died, his courtiers had been so afraid of the resulting power vacuum that for several months they pretended he was still alive, scrupulously dressing him every morning, and – at least as Sima Qian records – placing carts of rotten fish on either side of the corpse to mask the smell. Only when the courtiers had managed to manoeuvre their preferred successor into power did this macabre theatre end. The new emperor, Qin Er Shi, was soon shown to be not up to the tasks of consolidating Shi Huang's work of unification and administering a realm that extended 2,500 kilometres from north to south. The military was in permanent overstretch: rebellions broke out and soldiers mutinied. Yet, fearful of the new emperor's ire, nobody dared to inform him of the true scope of the problems. Eventually, in 207, the army in desperation forced him to commit suicide. It was too late: the Qin Dynasty collapsed.

Immediately two pretenders, the Chu and the Han, began to fight over the spoils. With its vast power base in the south, the Chu kingdom seemed bound to win. But then the foremost Chu warlord had the largely ceremonial king executed. That, combined with the cruelty with which the Chu enforced their regime, sparked further unrest and encouraged five other kingdoms to side with the Han. From then on, the Han ruler, Liu Bang, claimed to be waging a just war against Chu tyranny. Although Liu Bang was able to muster 560,000 troops at the Battle of Pengcheng in 205, he was defeated. Barely a year later, the Han and Chu armies faced each other across the Wei River. In a masterly stratagem, the Han secretly dammed the river with sandbags, lowering its level. The Chu were encouraged by the apparent shallows to cross, at which point the Han released the pent-up waters. Close to 50,000 Chu soldiers drowned. 'Although Liu Bang lost 100 battles in 100 battles,' it was said, 'he became the king as he won one decisive victory in the end.'[3] In the autumn of 204, the Han sacked the Chu capital. Two years later, the last Chu troops, ill-equipped, exhausted, and starving, were finally defeated.

The Han

Imperial China's second dynasty – the Han – would rule for four centuries. Most Chinese historians regarded this as a moment of fundamental change, from tyrannical repression to imperial harmony. However, many of those historians were adherents of Confucianism, recruited by the Han emperors after their victory. In fact, as recent research has confirmed, what Liu Bang – now Emperor Gaozu of Han (202–195) – did was strike a balance between the centralism of the Qin and the looser political structures of the Zhou. One third of the empire was organized in commanderies under direct control, the rest assigned to vassal kings. Taxes were reduced, soldiers sent home, and laws enforced less harshly.

Following a brief period of instability, when Dowager Empress Lu served as regent on behalf of a trio of weak emperors, the empire enjoyed a century of relative stability under three capable rulers. The first, Wen of Han (180–157), concentrated on reforming the political system – he was responsible for the meritocratic civil service exams that were such a characteristic feature of the imperial Chinese administration – while the second, Jing of Han, devoted himself to subduing rebellious princes. But it was under the third, Wu of Han (141–87) that the dynasty's power reached its apex. Nothing expressed that more clearly than the teachings of Dong Zhongshu (179–104). Dong was the architect of a new but by no means innovative Confucian imperial doctrine. 'If the son of heaven takes orders from heaven, the nobles take orders from the son of heaven, the son takes orders from the father, the wife takes orders from the husband,' he prescribed. 'Then there will be unity of heaven and men.'[4] Rigid hierarchy – with the emperor at the top – that was Dong's formula for preventing men's innate wickedness and greed from shoving China back into anarchy.

According to Dong, the legitimacy of the emperor depended on his ability to guarantee stability and prosperity. Self-criticism was due in case of missteps. Thus far, Emperor Wu enthusiastically embraced the Confucian's teachings. But when Dong went on to say that the cosmological cycle meant no dynasty would last forever, he was thrown in jail and almost beheaded. Not that there was much reason for Emperor Wu to fear any downfall during his lifetime. China's population recovered from the impact of so many wars and increased rapidly to about 50 million. Demographic growth led to the reclamation of new land for farming, unprecedented irrigation works, the development of towns with markets, and a boom in silk-weaving and other crafts. The capital, Chang'an, surged to 400,000 inhabitants. There was relentless territorial expansion, with expeditions as far as the Korean Peninsula, Vietnam, and the Tien Shan. Han China had become the world's most powerful empire.

The emperors flaunted their wealth. The annals testify to a sumptuousness at court unseen in previous dynasties: it became a mysterious microcosm of embroidered silk and intricate protocol. Spectacular temples were constructed; artworks of bronze, jade, glazed ceramic, and gold became ever more elaborate. The modest clay sculptures found in the tombs of the common people, their poems and songs, all reveal their desire to be part of this world of seemingly exquisite refinement and sensitivity – and also their resignation that they would never attain it. In that regard, there is little difference between the poems of the Han and those from Egypt almost two thousand years earlier. Chinese farmers still lamented the brevity of life and an existence blighted by lice and sodden hovels.[5]

But life for rural communities would become even harder. Although the early Han emperors had supported smallholders, they were gradually replaced by large landowners who acquired monopolies to supply cities. The imperial counsellor Chao Cuo wrote about the shocking inequality that resulted. 'Great merchants get profits of two hundred per cent by hoarding stocks of commodities while the lesser ones sit in rows in the market stalls to buy and sell. They deal in superfluous luxuries and lead an easy life in cities,' he wrote. 'Though they never engage in farming and their women neither tend silkworms nor weave, they always wear embroidered and multicoloured clothes and always eat fine millet and meat. Without experiencing the farmers' sufferings, they make vast gains.' Life in the countryside, by contrast, was marked by toil: 'Farmers plough in spring, weed in summer, reap in autumn and store in winter; they cut undergrowth and wood for fuel and render labour services to the government.'[6]

That labour still included military service. If internal wars had ceased, emperors continued to embark on campaigns against foreign foes. The situation was movingly captured by a Han poet:

> When I was fifteen I went on a military campaign,
>   and didn't get to return until I was eighty.
> On the road back I ran into some folks from home:
>   'Who is still in my family?' I asked.
> 'Behold! Far over there is your home:
>   under pine and cypress, the cluster of graves.'
> Rabbits entered through holes in the wall for dogs,
>   pheasants flew up from the beams.[7]

The Han imperial order was envisaged as five concentric circles. The first consisted of the royal domain. Second was the rest of the Han power base, centrally located in the North China Plain. Third were directly ruled provinces and commanderies. Fourth were the vassal kingdoms, which retained some autonomy but were overseen from Chang'an by the 'director of dependent states'. These served as a protective buffer against the outer, fifth circle of barbarians – that is, everyone else.

At times, the barbarians were approached by ambassadors with gifts and economic concessions; at others – such as when they refused peaceful submission – by large armies. Whenever possible, the Han followed the old strategy of setting barbarian against barbarian. Those who submitted to the Han paid tribute and were supervised by the 'prefect grand usher'. The Han were well aware of their power. Explorers like Zhang Qian, in the later second century, reached as far afield as Mesopotamia and the Indus Basin. Travel seems not to have broadened Zhang's mind: he repeatedly sneered at the many 'petty chieftains' outside China.

Inside China, the domestic might of the Han emperor became overwhelming. Scholars worried that such concentration of power would end up inescapable. If thinkers like Dong Zhongshu called for absolute political centralization and cultural uniformity, others warned about the dangers of using Confucianism as a pretext for the abuse of power, and of cunning courtiers using the administration of the empire as a vehicle for advancing their own personal interests. Checks and balances were key, they insisted in the collection of their deliberations known as the *Huainanzi*, and the mind needed to be free. Thousands of things needed to return to their own roots, they concluded, and diversity was better than uniformity. Debate, however, soon shifted to another urgent question: how to maintain order beyond the frontier.

The Han Empire had been plagued by incursions from the start. The first emperors had sought to defuse foreign threats peacefully so that they could focus on domestic affairs. The chief danger came from the Xiongnu nomads that frequently raided across the northern borders. They were bought off with economic concessions and marital alliances: Emperor Wen married at least four princesses off to Xiongnu commanders. The rationale of this appeasement policy was spelled out by Wen in an imperial edict from around 163. 'Since we are not perspicacious,' it stated:

We have been unable to extend the influence of Our virtue
to distant regions. This has caused states outside the
borders sometimes to be disquiet and discontented. Hence
We have sent envoys in rapid succession, so that their wheel
tracks were uninterrupted on the road, in order to enlighten
the Xiongnu concerning our intentions. Now the Xiongnu
has returned to the path of the ancients; he has sought for
the peace of Our gods of the soils and grains . . . Recently,
together with Us, we have both bound ourselves together
in the relationship of brotherhood in order to conserve the
good people of the world.[8]

This was the Confucian ideal of imperial harmony expressed
as practical diplomacy.

The strategy of appeasement towards the Xiongnu did
have critics. Jia Yi, who served as a Han official, complained
that it was utterly unacceptable that the mighty empire
bowed to their demands. The Xiongnu 'are arrogant and insolent on the one hand, and invade and plunder us on the
other, which must be considered as an expression of extreme
disrespect towards us', he fulminated. 'The population of the
Xiongnu does not exceed that of a large Chinese district.'[9] Although Jia's arguments fell on deaf ears, the debate continued.
Thirty years later, one of Emperor Wu's advisors, Wang Hui,
was more successful. In a famous dialogue with the general
Han Anguo, Wang proposed deploying elite troops deep into
Xiongnu territory. He inveighed against the disrespect of the
barbarians for agreements, and the hardship of the people
on the border caused by the many incursions. Security could

only be achieved if the enemy was forced to submit totally. Han Anguo maintained that this sort of offensive strategy could never work. The Xiongnu were difficult to subjugate because they never stayed in the same place. A war would also end five generations of profitable economic relations and devastate the region's agriculture.

Wang won the debate. Emperor Wu decided that enough was enough and embarked on a series of punitive campaigns. The Confucian policy of peaceful accommodation had given way before a much more hard-headed understanding of the Han's burgeoning power. Wu's army had grown from 400,000 to 600,000 soldiers. Greater emphasis had been placed on cavalry, so that long-range offensive campaigns were now feasible. Even so, the expeditions against the Xiongnu were not a success. But Wu's ambitions were not confined to the northern border. He also pursued control over the trade routes to Central Asia, particularly the strategic Hexi Corridor, which was vitally important for the supply of horses and to separate the Xiongnu from possible allies. He annexed the Korean Peninsula and the kingdom of Nanyue in the southeast, which was an important supplier of rice and luxury goods like pearls. His fleet conquered Hainan and explored Taiwan. The rise of realism at the expense of Confucianism was also visible in a debate about the empire's economy. In the famous *Discourses on Salt and Iron*, the imperial secretary Sang Hongyang defended state monopolies on the grounds that they paid for the wars against the barbarians. See those Confucians, in their coarse gowns and worn shoes, he mocked. 'See them now present us with nothingness and consider it substance, with emptiness and call it plenty!'[10]

Between the reigns of Emperor Wen and Emperor Wu, those who lived in the inner two circles of the Han Empire enjoyed a century of relative peace, unity, and prosperity. 'Relative', because vast numbers of young men continued to be drafted for military service on the frontier. But in the century following the death of Wu, although the Han Dynasty preserved power, clan rivalries erupted. In the mid-first century, Emperor Yuan of Han expanded the empire's influence into Central Asia, but against a backdrop of worsening inequality, social unrest, and court intrigues by conniving courtiers that undermined the emperor's power. The death of Emperor Ai of Han in 1 BCE caused a bloody succession struggle. After thirty years of conflict, the empire would live on, but under a new branch of the Han. This reborn Han Empire remained the largest realm in Eurasia.

A Chain Reaction of Migrations

None of the societies visited by Han travellers instilled more fear than the Xiongnu. Their power base in the Orkhon Valley lay deep in Mongolia. Hemmed in by protective mountains, it provided water, some woodland, and, most of all, a vast tract of grassland. Whoever controlled the Orkhon Valley had a major advantage over its smaller neighbours in the Mongolian hills. Once those had been absorbed, the way was open to the endless plains in the south and to the Chinese Empire.

Not much is known of the origins of the nomadic Xiongnu. From the third century, they assimilated most of the tribes between the Orkhon Valley and the Chinese border into a confederation. By the second century, its powerful kings ruled between 1 and 2 million souls and were able to field hundreds of thousands of warriors on tough Mongolian horses.[11] Impressive works of gold and fine jade carvings found in their royal tombs are evidence of enormous wealth. This affluence depended on the control of the cattle herds of the Mongolian plains and the taxing of peasants to the south.

In all respects, the balance of power lay with China. But the Xiongnu excelled in surprise attack. Chinese horses could not match the Xiongnu's 'for going up and down mountains and hills or in and out of streams', the Han counsellor Chao Cuo complained. 'For going through narrow and twisting paths or shooting and riding at the same time, the horsemen of China cannot match [the Xiongnu]. For facing wind, rain, fatigue, hunger, and thirst and not succumbing, the men of China cannot match them.'[12] This, in essence, was why it took more than a century for the Chinese to turn the Xiongnu federation into a tributary.

China's pressure on the Xiongnu helped trigger a cataclysm that was felt even in the Indian subcontinent and the Mediterranean. Halted in the east, the Xiongnu turned west. Their campaigns terrorized the nomadic peoples in Central Asia, whose flight in turn accelerated the shattering of kingdoms in the Middle East and South Asia. Around 180, Xiongnu raids sparked an exodus of the neighbouring Yuezhi. The Yuezhi – the skull of whose king the Xiongnu reportedly turned into a drinking vessel – poured into the lands of the Wusun, who responded by brokering an alliance with the Xiongnu. The ensuing conflict forced the Yuezhi back on to the trail, this time along the Ili River into Central Asia. There, on the banks of the Amu Darya (Oxus), they were visited by the Han explorer Zhang

Qian, who had been sent as an envoy of the Emperor of China to negotiate an alliance against the Xiongnu. His reports leave a vivid impression of the Yuezhi's turmoil.[13]

In 145, the Yuezhi burned the capital of Bactria. One of the richest kingdoms in the region, Bactria had broken away from the Seleucid Empire, but had then forged an alliance with its former Seleucid overlords because they too feared the advance of the nomadic hordes.[14] The prosperity of Bactria was based on the fertile valleys of the Amu Darya and the Ferghana. The Greek historian Diodorus Siculus described how its fortresses stood high above the trade routes between East, South, and Central Asia.[15] The legacy of its Greek artistic culture had an enormous impact on Indian sculpture and Buddhist art in general. Bactria's role as a cultural crucible lived on after its conquest and into the Kushan Empire that evolved out of the Yuezhi a century later.

Once Bactria had succumbed, the mountain passes lay open to the Indo-Gangetic Plain and its tremendous wealth. The situation for invaders was ideal. After the death of Ashoka in 232, the Maurya Empire had fallen into disrepair. Kings in Kashmir were the first to reclaim their independence. As others followed their example, the map of India frayed into a mishmash of warring states. Around the ancient city of Magadha coalesced the Shunga kingdom, which controlled the lower reaches of the Ganges and the Brahmaputra. The Satavahanas dominated the Deccan Plateau. In the south were the kingdoms of Kalinga and Pandya.

One of the few contemporary sources testifying to the relations between these realms is the Hathigumpha Inscription, which one of the kings of Kalinga had chiselled opposite one of the 'rock edicts' of Ashoka in the second century. The inscription depicts a world much like that of the *Mahabharata*: a world of war elephants, chariots, and plunder, riven by internecine bloodshed. There is faint evidence of a religious element to this strife: Pushyamitra, founder of the Shunga dynasty, campaigned under the pretext of defending Jainism and had Buddhist monks murdered.

Few other sources survive from this period. There are the cries for compassion of Thiruvalluvar, one of the most celebrated Tamil poets, who warned that infighting would leave states exposed to attack:

> Internal dissension is a small seed
> That harbours huge growth.[16]

Thiruvalluvar also insisted that trade, industry, and agricultural productivity should be used to prevail over enemies, not war. Energy, moral courage, wisdom, and a liberal hand were therefore the most important qualities for a king. Another source from this era is the Hindu text known as the *Manusmriti*. It called for empathy and pacifism, but also provided a sobering description of the balance of power. 'When a king feels that his army is strong and kingdom prosperous, and notices that the case is [the] reverse with his opponents, he is at liberty to declare a war against them.'[17]

Even if these indigenous realms fought each other savagely, most Indian writers were more embittered about incursions of barbarian hordes. Much like Herodotus in his portrait of fifth-century Greece, they deplored that India failed to stand united and that rulers collaborated with the enemy. Nevertheless, resistance to the invaders was fierce: it took a century of warfare before the Yuezhi gained control over both large parts of Central Asia and the Indo-Gangetic Plain. In 30 CE, the Yuezhi proclaimed their territories the Kushan Empire.

The rise of the Han and the collapse of the Maurya were the most important events in the eastern part of Eurasia during the last two and a half centuries BCE. The Han emerged as victors from their wars with the Qin and the Chu. The new dynasty promised peace and harmony, but their growing power coincided with a shift from defensive to offensive strategies. The resulting wars of expansion – along with exploration, trade, and cultural soft power – spread Han influence into the Korean Peninsula, Southeast Asia, Mongolia, and Central Asia. They also helped spark the wave of migrations in Central Asia that, in turn, contributed to the destruction of the Maurya Empire.

Parthia's Cosmopolitan Empire

After Zhang Qian's failure to secure an alliance for the Han with the crumbling kingdom of Bactria, Emperor Wu tried to persuade another state to join forces against the Xiongnu. In 121, a mission led by Han Wudi arrived in Parthia. The most cosmopolitan empire of its time, Parthia encompassed cities inhabited by Greeks, Persians, and numerous other ethnicities, all enjoying more freedom than they had under the Achaemenids, the Medes, or the Assyrians. It tolerated Buddhists, Jews, and Zoroastrians. Its royal palaces blended Greek, Persian, and nomadic Central Asian influences. Princes were taught Greek philosophy, but also memorized the Code of Hammurabi. Such tolerance was a necessity if the empire was to survive. That the Parthian kings had the legend *philhellenos*, or 'friend of the Greeks', emblazoned on their coins showed how much they feared a revolt of the powerful merchant class of the Greek community that had inhabited so many eastern cities since the era of Alexander the Great.

Like so many other great dynasties in the Middle East, the Parthian kings arose from a semi-nomadic tribe on the periphery of a great power. In 238, a tribe known as the Parni crossed the Kopet Dag mountain range, located to the south-east of the Caspian Sea, and seized a satrapy that had broken away from the Seleucid Empire. At first, they joined forces with the Bactrians to repel the Seleucids, before turning against their erstwhile allies. Fortune favoured them: both the Seleucids and the Bactrians were under pressure from other enemies. Meanwhile, the Parni – or Parthians, as they were now known – secured a strong agricultural power base from where its feared armies of mounted archers could issue forth. The Parthian shot, fired back at a pursuing enemy while at full gallop, surprised enemies more than once.

King Mithridates I (165–132) consolidated Parthia's previous gains and conquered Mesopotamia. The Seleucids fought back, but the Parthians saw a new opportunity in the arrival of the Scythians. Instead of trying to halt the Scythians as they fled from the Yuezhi, they routed them to the southeast of the Taurus Mountains and directed their fighting power to the west. It was a clever move, which allowed the Parthians to hold their ground. Around 100, King Mithridates II decided that it was time to add the Parthians to that great gallery of fame on Mount Behistun. A rock carving still shows him towering on horseback over four vassals, close to the depiction of the Achaemenid king Darius I. Like the Persians and Assyrians before them, Parthian rulers now called themselves the 'king of kings'.

If Darius I had reigned like a lion over the Middle East, then the rule of the Parthian kings was rather more like that of a sheepdog around a flock. Parthia's vassals retained a great deal of autonomy; the presence of two royal councils and powerful warlords also checked the king's power. This, perhaps, is why history does not treat the Parthians generously. Even though the empire lasted more than four centuries, and even though it withstood formidable challenges, its cosmopolitanism meant that it left little impression on the imagination of posterity: no images of appalling terror like the Assyrians, no powerful cultural symbols like the Egyptians, no myths even. Its legacy, as it were, was to preserve that of others. It was a syncretic empire *par excellence*.

The image of Parthia was also negatively influenced by Roman authors, in much the same way that historiography about Persia had been negatively influenced by Greek opinions. The politician Lucius Cornelius Lentulus Crus, for example, claimed that the Parthians were predisposed by the warmth of the climate to softness and decadence. The philosopher Seneca wrote that their kings ruled by fear. Such disparagement was little surprise, as the Romans sought to get rid of Parthia's role as commercial gatekeeper between the Mediterranean and Asia. Official relations with Rome were established in 96, but they started on a bad note. When the Roman general Lucius Cornelius Sulla received the ambassador of Parthia, he took the seat of honour for himself, leaving the envoy a place appropriate for the representative of a minor kingdom. The unfortunate envoy was executed when the Parthian king came to hear of the humiliation. After such an inauspicious beginning, ties with Rome only worsened.

The Struggle for Italy

Long before Rome's legions reached the east, it faced an epic battle closer to home. By the early third century, Rome controlled almost all of peninsular Italy, from the southern tip of the Italian boot to the River Arno in the north. Only the fertile plain of the River Po, between the Alps and the Apennines, was still held by Gallic tribes. Carthage, meanwhile, which already controlled Corsica and Sardinia, had been strengthening its influence in Sicily. Rome risked getting caught in a pincer and decided to act. When Rome took up arms in 264, on the pretext of Carthaginian interference in a local conflict in Sicily, it was an enormous gamble. Rome had proved its fighting skills on land, but had no experience at sea whatsoever with which to fight the powerful Carthaginian navy. In just a few years, though, Rome had built up its sea power sufficiently to be able to compete. The historian Polybius – the best ancient source for the Punic Wars – described how inexperienced Roman shipwrights built a hundred warships and how equally inexperienced rowers trained on benches on dry land.[18] Rome initially surprised its rival by installing swing bridges on the bows of its ships, so that legionaries could more easily storm the Carthaginian vessels, thereby turning naval engagements into floating land battles.

Eventually, both sides lost so many ships, causing such a drain on resources, that a truce was signed in 241. Carthage evacuated Sicily and paid a large indemnity. Rome subsequently took advantage of Carthaginian weakness to seize Corsica and Sardinia. The three islands formed the first provinces in Rome's nascent overseas empire. Meanwhile, on the other side of Italy, in the Adriatic Sea, the Illyrians threatened Roman trading interests. In 229, after an envoy was killed, the Roman senate ordered a surprise attack. But it required Greek assistance before Rome could secure a treaty with the Illyrians that gave it control over most of the Adriatic Sea. In 225, disgruntled Italian peoples joined forces with the Cisalpine Gauls of the Po Valley. According to Polybius, a new generation of Gallic leaders, who had forgotten the cost of earlier defeats by Rome, was filled with an unthinking desire to fight and recklessly broke the peace by marching south. The Gauls were only halted after three years of relentless fighting. But it was as if the city of Rome had been cursed. Almost immediately, reports began to arrive from Spain that a young Carthaginian general was amassing an army capable of striking Rome at its heart.

The general's name was Hannibal, and he was sworn to revenge Carthage's humiliating losses from the First Punic War. In 218, he marched out of Spain with a large army and brought it across the Alps – a feat that had been thought impossible. Benefiting initially from the support of the Cisalpine Gauls, Hannibal inflicted a string of costly defeats on the Romans, culminating in the Battle of Cannae in 215. Tactically supreme, and seemingly unstoppable in set-piece battles, Hannibal roamed almost at will across the length and breadth of Italy for fifteen years. But he never succeeded in landing the knockout blow. Perhaps the closest he came was in 211, when he briefly marched within sight of the walls of Rome before turning back.

Rome's vast resources of manpower and wealth were tested to breaking point. Erstwhile allies either turned actively against it or cautiously adopted positions of neutrality. The Roman currency was debased several times. Yet somehow the senate still managed to raise legion after legion. The tide began to turn with the adoption of a new strategy after Cannae: rather than seeking decisive battle with Hannibal, the Romans would slowly wear him down with attritional irregular warfare, denying him supplies and reinforcements. To that end, armies were dispatched to retake Sicily, and to Spain in order to cut off the main source of support for Hannibal. While Italy remained stuck in a debilitating stalemate, and the Carthaginian senate grew increasingly critical of the expense and conduct of the war, the Romans under a young general of their own, called Scipio, terminated Carthage's control of Spain at the Battle of Ilipa in 206.

The following year, the senate gave its blessing to an operation that would finally bring an end to the conflict. In the spring of 204, Scipio sailed with an army from Sicily to North Africa, and established a beachhead from where he set about laying waste to the environs of Carthage. In desperation, the Carthaginian senate recalled Hannibal from Italy. In 202, after attempts to negotiate a peace had broken down in mutual recrimination, the two armies met in open battle at Zama. But this time, despite the presence of their talismanic general, and eighty war elephants, it was the Carthaginians who were decisively defeated. The war had been won, leaving Rome as undisputed master of the Western Mediterranean and all its resources.

The price Rome paid for its victory, however, was colossal. During the Second Punic War, one third of the Roman male population served in the army. Close to 100,000 of them lost their lives. Many women widowed by the wars faced destitution, reduced to earning a pittance sewing clothes for the army or working as prostitutes in the capital. The economic drain was immense. Countless farms – still the backbone of the Roman economy – were lost to the policy of not challenging Hannibal in battle. In 214, in the aftermath of the disaster of Cannae, the senate decreed that even orphans, widows, and unmarried women had to contribute their possessions to the treasury. Rome at this time was not a city of triumphal arches, marble squares, and citizens decadently wallowing in the spoils of distant wars. It was a beleaguered city of lice-infested apartment blocks, claustrophobic back-streets, and filthy slums; a city afflicted by famine and torn by the loss of loved ones.

In such a context, it is hard to imagine why, barely five years after the ending of the Second Punic War, Rome embarked on a fresh series of campaigns, in Spain, the Balkans, and the Levant. How did the Romans find the will to endure in such circumstances? It appears from the writings of Polybius that the Romans simply believed they had no choice. Their view of the world was bleak: either they conquered their neighbours, or their neighbours would conquer them.[19] Even though Rome had tried to preserve the status quo through treaties and the delimitation of spheres

of influence, its growing strength and the reaction that provoked in neighbours simply made war inevitable, in much
the same way that, in Thucydides' account, the rise of Athens
led to the Peloponnesian War. Tensions were exacerbated
not just by the balance of power, but by hatred too: Hannibal
and a new generation of Cisalpine Gauls thirsted to avenge
the humiliation of defeats suffered by previous generations
and to reverse the deleterious terms under which they had
been granted peace. Rome, it was generally thought, thus had
to keep on expanding or die.

This sense of insecurity created a warrior cult. The archetypal Roman citizen was a soldier-farmer, like the legendary
Cincinnatus summoned from his plough to save the city, or
Cato the Elder – one of the leading public figures in second-
century Rome – who returned from campaigns to tend his
olive trees and to salt hams. The archetypal Roman woman
was equally austere, devoted to hearth and home, and the
rearing of fine sons, proud to wear homespun and eschew-
ing costly finery. Roman sculpture from this period was not
inspired by the youthful male nudes or sensual Aphrodites
of contemporary Greek art. What the Romans sculpted were
unflatteringly grim-faced statesmen – the very personifica-
tions of the city's power. Writers like Polybius saw Rome as
the successor of that other fearless city, Sparta. Like the Spartan, the Roman warrior was supposed to fight solely in the
causes of patriotism and justice. In the eyes of the Romans, it
was always the other side's egregious behaviour that left them
with no alternative but to go to war to defend their interests.

In that pursuit of justice, the Romans made every effort to
ensure the gods were on their side. Animals were sacrificed so

that their entrails could be studied for omens. One of Rome's worst defeats in the First Punic War was attributed to the general's sacrilegious dismissal of unfavourable portents. The responsibility for ensuring that a war was just lay in the hands of the priests of Jupiter. These *fetiales* were dispatched as ambassadors to convey the grievances of Rome and – if those complaints remained unsatisfied – to declare war formally by hurling a javelin dipped in blood across the border. As with most other ancient societies, Roman war almost by definition was a sacred war.

Such was the idealized picture. But as the second century wore on, the Romans increasingly found themselves confronted by a very different reality. There is evidence that the sacred rituals were manipulated to ensure the 'right' decision was endorsed – often one that served more worldly ends than the principle of justice. The First Punic War, for instance, was eagerly promoted by the so-called 'Campanian connection', a group of wealthy businessmen from Southern Italy that had greedily eyed the rich soils of Sicily.[20] In the ultra-competitive environment of republican Rome, would-be generals were well aware of how the honour and riches of a successful war could be parlayed into political advantage.

War changed Roman society profoundly. The traditional farmer-soldier and his values became increasingly redundant. Ever longer campaigns, and ever more years of poorly paid military service, meant he was seldom free to tend his crops. In any case, he could no longer compete against the imports of cheap grain from overseas provinces or against the armies of slaves who worked the vast estates of the rich – even though it was his sword and his blood that had won them for Rome. As the wealthy snapped up the debt-laden farms of poor citizens for a trifle, a restless mass of dangerously destitute and disillusioned young men was driven to the city.

Crossing the Rubicon

One of the defining moments in Rome's rise to power came in 146. In that one year, Roman armies laid waste the cities of Corinth and Carthage – finally fulfilling the oft-repeated call of Cato the Elder that 'Carthage must be destroyed'.[21] The conquests sent shockwaves around the Mediterranean and heralded Rome's status as the pre-eminent power in the region. The richness of the spoils that flooded back into the city was unprecedented. Gone forever were the counsels for austerity by the likes of Cato. 'Where can such a body be of service to the state, when everything between its gullet and its groin is devoted to belly?' he lamented at the sight of a wealthy businessman, but few if any were listening.[22] The culture of war, self-sacrifice, and blood had became a culture of wine, women, and profit. When the rewards for victory were so vast, and so unequally distributed, the sacred duty to fight for Rome was no longer credible.

'This was the beginning of civil bloodshed and of the free reign of swords in the city of Rome,' wrote the historian Velleius Paterculus, referring to the events of 133 when the attempt by the populist politician Tiberius Gracchus to reverse the tide of history and redistribute public land to the poor led to the murder of him and hundreds of supporters.[23] In 107, the consul Gaius Marius tried another remedy.

Previously, the poorest citizens had not been eligible for military service. Now he sought to rid the city of the growing threat that they posed to the social order by enrolling them in the army and rewarding their service not only with pay but with the promise of land won in far-flung provinces.

War was increasingly becoming a safety valve to release the steam from the overheating furnace of Rome's social order. But it was still not enough. Rome's spiralling wealth elicited envy from the Italian cities whose manpower helped swell the ranks of the legions. Now they demanded Roman citizenship, and all the benefits that came with it. The result was civil war – the so-called Social War (91–88) – in which thousands of people died before the allied cities were granted their rights. Rome's primacy was being threatened from within.

In a bid to relieve the pressures that exploded into civil war, Roman generals started new conflicts overseas. But this only briefly postponed the inevitable. In 82, the general Lucius Cornelius Sulla returned from a successful campaign abroad, marched his troops to the capital, and demanded the senate reward his veterans with land. The senate baulked. In the days following the senate's refusal, Sulla's battle-hardened troops killed tens of thousands of their compatriots just outside the barricaded Colline Gate. Sulla in the end prevailed. The Roman Republic was dead. Appointed dictator, Sulla started a reign of terror. The poet Virgil lamented:

> So many wars, so many shapes of crime!
> The plough dishonored, fields left lying waste . . .
> Unholy Mars bends all to his mad will:
> The world is like a chariot run wild.[24]

After Sulla's death in 78, new warlords entered the lists. Rome continued to slide deeper into mayhem. Conventional politics was overshadowed by the ferocious rivalry between Julius Caesar and Pompey the Great. Both men had amassed immense wealth through foreign conquest – in Gaul and Asia respectively – which they employed to finance networks of patronage and further their personal ambitions. Open warfare finally broke out when Caesar led his army across the River Rubicon and into Italy. The ensuing civil war (49–45) engulfed the entire Mediterranean region. After the Pompeians had been decisively defeated, and their leader killed, the senate declared Caesar dictator for life.

Caesar's rule brought some brief stability and much-needed reform. The poet Tibullus echoed the desire of Romans to return to a simple country life: 'the hero is he whom, when his children are begotten, old age's torpor overtakes in his humble cottage. He follows his sheep, his son the lambs, while the good wife heats the water for his weary limbs. So let me live till the white hairs glisten on my head . . .'[25] But in 44, Caesar was murdered by his former senatorial peers. Their claim that they had acted to restore Roman liberty gained little traction. Instead, one of Caesar's former lieutenants, Mark Antony, and his teenaged adoptive son and heir, Octavian, shouldered the responsibility of wreaking vengeance on the dictator's killers. Once again, the Mediterranean region erupted into civil war (44–31), first as Caesar's assassins were brought to book, and then as Mark Antony and Octavian turned against each other. Despite his youth and lack of military experience, Octavian was a skilled political operator and utterly ruthless. There was only ever going to be one winner.

It is perhaps unsurprising that, after a century of political turmoil and civil war, many Romans began to long for strong leadership that would bring them peace. Although there were a few diehards who resisted the idea of autocracy until the bitter end, most citizens were more pragmatic: in reality, the traditional republican rights and freedoms had long been in abeyance. Thus, when Octavian finally stood triumphant, the majority of ordinary Romans breathed a cautious sigh of relief. 'While [Augustus] Caesar guards the state, not civil rage, nor violence, nor wrath that forges swords, embroiling hapless towns, shall banish peace,' asserted the poet Horace.[26] In 27, the senate formally recognized the reality of the situation when they acknowledged Octavian was 'the first', or *princeps*, and declared him 'the illustrious' or *Augustus*. The same decree in effect charged him with relieving the hardship of the people of Rome and inaugurating a deep and lasting Pax Romana.

That Rome not only survived but expanded during this century of infighting is remarkable. But it was not unique. Other powers, such as Han China or the earlier empires of Mesopotamia, went through similarly contradictory processes of expanding borders and eroding political structures. As with Rome, the two evolutions even enforced each other. Rome is the first polity, though, where so much written about such turmoil has survived. We have the letters and speeches of Cicero – one of the leading spokesmen for the virtues of traditional republicanism – as well as Caesar's first-hand reports of his campaigns in Gaul and during the civil war.

It comes across very clearly in these and the other sources that, even during the darkest hours of the civil wars, Rome's existence was never imperilled by external enemies. There were no imminent threats against the Italian Peninsula, the nerve centre of Roman power. Rome controlled Gaul and the gateways of the Alps, as well as almost the entire Mediterranean littoral. When the Helvetii and other tribes started to move down from the Alps, they posed nowhere near the same threat as the Gauls who sacked Rome in 387 or who were recruited by Hannibal during the Second Punic War. Whereas the warfare of the tribes had hardly changed, Rome's legions had progressed immensely in their weaponry, their tactics, their engineering, and their supply chains. After Caesar defeated the Helvetii, his conquest of Gaul was an unequal fight between a superbly commanded fighting machine and brave but divided guerrilla warriors.

Rome was also protected by the naval power it had maintained since the mid-third century. Its hundreds of warships protected grain supplies, combated piracy, besieged port cities, and carried troops to fight remote enemies – none of whom, after the defeat of Carthage in the Second Punic War, possessed the ability to emulate Rome's expeditionary power. The whole Mediterranean had now effectively become a Roman lake, a true *mare nostrum*.

Equally important was the fact that the main powers of the Eastern Mediterranean were locked in mutual conflicts. Ptolemaic Egypt continued to quarrel with the Seleucids, the Seleucids with the Parthians, the Parthians with the kingdom of Pontus in Asia Minor, and the kingdom of Pontus with the Seleucids. Even so, when Rome's legions crossed the Aegean Sea, they found these states very stubborn opponents. In the end, however, they were defeated, and the eastern border of Rome's empire was planted on the River Euphrates. But this achievement came with stern warnings from men like Cicero: 'It is difficult to put into words,' the statesman admonished, 'just how hated we Romans are among foreign peoples, because of the greed and the damage our governors, men sent by us, have done in recent years.'[27]

The Roman Republic was a war machine. It not only resembled Sparta's militarism, but also turned to Sparta and the other Greek states for cultural inspiration, symbols of power, and military technology. As with the Han in China, success in initial defensive wars made it confident enough to embark on foreign conquests. Rome's expansionist wars were said to be decreed – or at least supported – by the gods, but in reality they were driven by much more earthly interests: prestige, the ambitions of consuls and generals, the desire to control trade and grain supplies. 'With the blessing of the gods and the senate, any war could be justified,' concluded the soldier and historian Sempronius Asellio.[28]

The World of Zhang Qian and Herodotus

By the turn of the new millennium, the political world map was dominated by Han China at one end of Eurasia and the Roman Empire at the other. In between were the smaller Parthian and Kushan Empires, as well as nomadic federations like the Xiongnu. Most of the rest of the Eastern Hemisphere continued to be inhabited by small tribes and city states. In North Africa, Carthage and Egypt, and lesser kingdoms like Numidia and Mauretania, fell under the sway of Rome. Further south, the African continent remained the domain of tribes like the Bantu, whose migration led to friction and wars with other ethnic groups. The north of Eurasia remained the realm of wandering peoples: migrating farmers in search of better farmland and nomads in search of pasture and plunder. The human remains unearthed by archaeologists testify to the hard lives of these people, blighted by malnourishment and violence. But even if vast swathes of these nomadic northern regions were unsuitable for agriculture and militated against the accumulation of wealth, they were important channels of connection. Much as city states used maritime power to colonize the resource-rich regions of the Mediterranean, nomadic peoples like the Xiongnu exploited the mobility of horses on wide plains to benefit from the resource-rich fringes of the great plains.

Traders gradually wove the Eastern Hemisphere into a flimsy network of economic and cultural exchange. There was no true transcontinental trade, however: goods were relayed from one city to another, and volumes were small. Yet such trade as there was did contribute to the dissemination of ideas. Zhang Qian, and Herodotus before him, were the first important international correspondents, albeit their books constitute a very slow form of journalism. The maps of the ancient Greek geographers, such as Anaximander, Hecataeus, and Hipparchus, show how knowledge of the Eastern Hemisphere became more fine-grained over the centuries.

The reports of Zhang and Herodotus are particularly interesting because they give international politics a human face. They certainly evaluated the respective power of different nations, their economic prosperity and their military strengths and weaknesses, and described the scheming of kings and diplomats. But their obvious fascination with the peoples, cultures, and places they encountered bring them to life. Zhang recorded the intrinsic violence of a society of pig-headed plunderers, the dimensions of city walls, and the skill of archers, but also the taste of peaches and the use of a drinking bowl made from a human skull. Similarly, Herodotus carefully delineated the workings of the balance of power during the Persian Wars; yet he also noted the crushed bones left lying on the battlefield, the diseases and hardships endured by the peoples he visited, the constant fear of being enslaved in war, and the cruel treatment of those who had been enslaved, for instance, the Scythian habit of blinding their slaves and making them blow into the vulvas of mares in order to produce more milk. Life was harsh in the world of Zhang and Herodotus and it was only made worse by the endless armed conflicts. The only places that seemed to come close to the ideals of peace, harmony, and prosperity, were the heartlands of empire in times of political stability, far removed as they were from border wars and bands of pillagers, pirates, and slave raiders.

For most people, the ideal life was a peaceful existence of bucolic simplicity. Such a rural idyll was celebrated not only by Confucian scholars like Dong Zhongshu, but also by Roman statesmen like Cicero and Cato the Elder. Like all previous imperial dynasties, the Han considered their realm the centre of the universe. Foreign policy was primarily a question of taming the barbarians beyond the border. But opinion was divided between the Confucians, who espoused peaceful diplomacy, and a growing band of realists who advocated the use of force. The same debate took place in India, where Thiruvalluvar hymned the benefits of trade, while the *Manusmriti* insisted that strong kings had the right to attack weaker ones.

In China, the realists got their way. As the power of the Han grew, so did their ambition. Military might, the need for resources, the desire to control trade routes, and the fear of being humiliated by primitive barbarians inspired conquests that reached into Southeast Asia and Central Asia. Similarly, Republican Rome believed that its wars were just and even commanded by the gods to teach others a lesson. Yet once Rome's rivals, first in the Italian Peninsula, and then for supremacy over the Mediterranean Sea, had been defeated, what mattered was that the way lay open for further conquests, that the growing population of the capital required wheat from overseas, and that groups of businessmen were willing to support military action that advanced their interests abroad.

Far beyond the world of Zhang and Herodotus, in the Western Hemisphere, the forces of nature kept civilizations in a state of flux. Earthquakes, changing courses of rivers, and flooding probably all contributed to the downfall of the Olmec culture in Central America. We do not know much about the period that followed: whatever still lies buried under the thick tropical forest can only be left to the imagination – for now, at least.

Nevertheless, those sites that have been unearthed bear witness to a rapidly changing political landscape. New city states emerged. Like those in Eurasia, they evolved through *synoecism*, the amalgamation of several villages. They were generally small, like Monte Albán, the centre of the Zapotec culture, which possessed around 10,000 inhabitants in the first century. Its hilltop ruins still tower over the wide valley of the River Atoyac in southern Mexico. Remains of earthen dams for irrigation have been discovered on the slopes of its site. Finds of ceramic, jade, and gems indicate the existence of continental trade routes. Much bigger than Monte Albán was Teotihuacán, near present-day Mexico City, which benefited from the surrounding large fertile plateaus and its control of important trade routes. In Yucatán, city states were founded that would later become the source of the Maya civilization. In South America, a belt of cities stretched along the Andes. They gave birth to enigmatic cultures like the Chavín (900–200) and the Moche (1–800). The rest of the Americas were thinly populated by nomadic peoples.

It feels like an injustice to devote only a couple of paragraphs to these peoples. But up to this point in time, the societies of the Western Hemisphere remained relatively small, and there is very little evidence that sheds clear light on their political history.

CHAPTER 6

Barbarians at the Gates

1–250 CE

At the beginning of the first millennium CE, China and Rome remained the world's largest and most powerful empires. Each held sway over approximately 60 million people. Rome's might was centred on the control of trade and agriculture around the Mediterranean. Expansion was its defence, in the south as far as the Sahara, in the east as far as Mesopotamia, and in the north along the shores of the Black Sea, the Danube, and the Rhine and the fringes of the Scottish Highlands. The empire was kept together by the superior organization and mobility of its armed forces, on land and at sea, as well as by the immense lure of trade. Italy, the heart of the empire, enjoyed an unprecedented period of stability known as the Pax Romana.

During the two centuries following the start of Augustus' reign as emperor (27 BCE–14 CE), the city of Rome experienced major incidents of violence in only eight years. It was an era in which foreigners from all corners of the empire came to pay tribute as Rome ruthlessly tapped its provinces for food, gold, and luxury. The Roman world was tripartite: there was the capital city, the empire, and *barbaricum* – the uncivilized region beyond the frontier. The only possible way for Rome seemed to be up, much like the victorious scenes that spiral ever higher around Trajan's Column in the heart of Rome. This very success, according to ancient Roman writers, caused the empire's decadence and moral decline. By the third century, as the defence of the empire's borders was increasingly outsourced to barbarian *foederati* and unrest plagued the society inside the borders, Rome's peace and prosperity were drawing to an end.

The situation in China was similar. After a period of civil war, the Han emperor Guangwu (25–57) ushered in a century of peace across the North China Plain. He and his immediate successors demilitarized the empire, abolished slavery, and implemented a series of other popular reforms. This era coincided with a weakening of the nomadic threat: when these barbarians regained strength, the golden age was over. The Han emperors opted for retrenchment, withdrawing from forward bases along the Silk Road and using proxies, similar to the Roman *foederati*, to defend the border. Meanwhile, members of the court had gained so much power that they came to control much of China's farmland. It caused major rebellions. By 220, the last emperor of the Han Dynasty was deposed, fracturing the empire.

In the shadow of Rome and Han China, lesser powers sought to organize themselves in various different ways. Sometimes they attempted to accommodate themselves with their imperial neighbours, at other times they were stubbornly defiant. In the great swathes of Eurasia that lay between Rome and China, a contest unfolded for control of the trade corridor between East and West: the Silk Road. It was a struggle in which polities like the Kushan Empire, the Parthian Empire, and the Xiongnu competed for fertile valleys and trade emporiums, and occasionally solicited China and Rome to support their endeavours.

The Donkey's Master

In 13 BCE, the Emperor Augustus returned to Rome from a military campaign in Spain and Gaul. The senate decided to celebrate his arrival by erecting the Altar of Augustan Peace, the *Ara Pacis Augustae*. The relief panel on one wall of the shrine depicts the goddess Peace, or Pax, reposing with two infants on her lap and surrounded by flowers, grain, and livestock. This was the earthly paradise that Augustus promised to his people. The relief on the opposite wall depicts a female warrior – possibly the personification of Rome – seated on a pile of captured weapons to remind citizens of one of Augustus' most famous maxims: peace is only born out of military victory. Rome was thus entering a period of prosperity thanks to its military success. A new imperial tradition was born.

Augustus made sure that the Romans continued to regard themselves as a chosen people. Under the emperor's patronage, Livy embarked on his celebrated history. From the poet Virgil, Augustus commissioned the *Aeneid*, a jubilant work of patriotism celebrating the mythic origins of Rome. Virgil had Rome's future supreme deity proclaim:

> young Romulus
> Will take the leadership, build walls of Mars,
> And call it by his own name his people Romans.
> For these I set no limits, world or time,
> But make the gift of an empire without end.[1]

Under the rule of Augustus, Rome gradually became a metropolis of travertine and marble. He built a new forum, a temple in memory of Julius Caesar, and a temple dedicated to Mars, the god of war, filled with the spoils of battle. As the capital was embellished, the emperor sought to rid it of many of its poor. The free distribution of wheat – the grain dole – was reduced. Veterans and destitute young men were encouraged to try their luck elsewhere in the empire. Augustus established a record number of colonies. They were an opportunity for Rome to externalize the problems of over-population and poverty.

Even though Virgil wrote of an empire without end, Augustus' foreign strategy was one of moderation. He reduced the army from 500,000 to 300,000 men, and fixed the empire's frontiers behind protective natural features: the Rhine, the Danube, the Euphrates, and the Sahara. The empire, Augustus insisted, had to stay within its existing borders.[2] He described his foreign policy as combining hardness and softness, conciliation and repression. 'I brought peace to the Alps from the region which is near the Adriatic Sea to the Tuscan, with no unjust war waged against any nation,' he boasted:

> I sailed my ships on the ocean from the mouth of the Rhine
> to the east region up to the borders of the Cimbri, where
> no Roman had gone before that time by land or sea, and
> the Cimbri and the Charydes and the Semnones and the
> other Germans of the same territory sought by envoys the
> friendship of me and of the Roman people.[3]

Yet at the same time, he described fierce punitive campaigns against those who opposed the establishment of the Pax

Romana: 'By my order and auspices two armies were led . . . into Ethiopia and into that part of Arabia which is called Happy and the troops of each nation of enemies were slaughtered.'[4]

Augustus was portrayed by contemporaries as a demigod, combining wisdom with military valour. The appointment of senators, consuls, praetors, and other officials who had previously been freely elected now required his approval. The senate continued to select governors for the so-called 'senatorial' provinces. For 'imperial' provinces, the largest part of the empire, Augustus picked his own legates. There were only a few client states. The objective of Augustus was to exert his power as directly as possible in all corners of the empire. The majority of the army was deployed in garrisons on the periphery of Roman territory, where they were protected by fortresses and connected by an ever-expanding network of roads. Leaders of defeated tribes were forced to prostrate themselves in submission. In return for clemency, they paid an indemnity and regular tax, accepted Roman law, and often surrendered their children as hostages.

Beyond the empire, Augustus sought to stabilize relations with foreign powers. He negotiated a peace with the Parthians and made a spectacle of the reception of foreign ambassadors: 'Emissaries from the Indian kings were often sent to me,' he reported. 'The Bastarnae, the Scythians, and the Sarmatians . . . and the kings of the Albanians, of the Iberians, and of the Medes, sought our friendship through emissaries . . . King Phrates of the Parthians, son of Orodes, sent all his sons and grandsons into Italy to me, though defeated in no war, but seeking our friendship through the pledges of his children.'[5] To keep himself informed, Augustus overhauled the courier system; although there were state archives, there was no particular ministry or bureaucracy in charge of foreign affairs. The emperor took the important decisions himself; the senate handled what was left.

Nevertheless, the Roman peace was shaky. The historian Tacitus (54–120) famously described how the prospect of Roman rule was perceived by many when he recorded the purported words of Calgacus – the leader of the Caledonian tribes in what is now northern Scotland – on the eve of battle against an invading Roman army:

> Nature has willed that every man's children and kindred should be his dearest objects. Yet these are torn from us by conscriptions to be slaves elsewhere. Our wives and our sisters, even though they may escape violation from the enemy, are dishonoured under the names of friendship and hospitality. Our goods and fortunes they collect for their tribute, our harvests for their granaries. Our very hands and bodies, under the lash and in the midst of insult, are worn down by the toil of clearing forests and morasses.[6]

There were many more such resistance leaders, so that the Roman legions seldom had any rest. 'Heaven knows,' complained one soldier, 'lashes and wounds are always with us! So are hard winters and hardworking summers, grim war and unprofitable peace.'[7] When Augustus died, the legions along the German border promptly mutinied.

Augustus' legacy fell heavily on the shoulders of his successors. The Emperor Tiberius (14–37) grappled with a flash flood that destroyed parts of Rome, insurrections along the Rhine, a power grab by the Praetorian Guard – who protected the emperor in Rome and formed the only significant body of troops in Italy – rising food prices, and tax revolts in Macedonia and Syria. Gradually, stability in Rome gave way to violence. 'Frenzied with bloodshed, the emperor now ordered the execution of all those arrested for complicity with Sejanus,' wrote Tacitus following the uncovering of an alleged plot centred on the commander of the Praetorian Guard in 31. 'It was a massacre. Without discrimination of sex or age, eminence or obscurity, there they lay, strewn about – or in heaps . . . Terror had paralysed human sympathy.'[8] Generosity and justice were recurring themes in the pages of Tacitus, as well as those of that other celebrated writer of the age, Suetonius; but most emperors, they bitterly reported, abused their power.

Senators complained about the growing number of immigrants acquiring citizenship and gaining political influence. 'Do we have to import foreigners in hordes, like gangs of prisoners, and leave no careers for our own surviving aristocracy?'[9] The situation continued to deteriorate. In an episode that established a damaging precedent for the imperial succession, the Emperor Caligula (37–41) was murdered by the Praetorians, who then supported the succession of his uncle, Claudius (41–53), and received a handsome reward from him for their 'loyalty'. Under Nero (54–68), Rome burst into flames: both literally, when a great fire devastated much of the city, and figuratively, as the emperor's increasingly outlandish and authoritarian behaviour provoked open rebellion. 'Traditional morals,' complained critics of the regime, 'have been utterly ruined by this imported laxity! It makes everything potentially corrupting and corruptible flow into the capital – foreign influences demoralize our young men into shirkers, gymnasts, and perverts.'[10]

Between the death of Nero in 68 and the death of Philip the Arab in 249, emperors ruled on average for only six years. There were strong rulers, to be sure, like Trajan (98–117) and Hadrian (117–38). Yet Trajan, in particular, overstretched the empire's resources. He embarked on campaigns in Dacia (part of modern Romania), Parthia, and Arabia, the cost of which forced him to debase the currency. His successor, Hadrian, had to withdraw from Mesopotamia, lower taxes, and rely more on local soldiers. Hadrian prided himself on his efforts to restore Rome's prosperity. A marble statue in the Musée du Louvre, for example, portrays him as Mars, the god of war, embraced by Venus, the goddess of love.[11] But even Hadrian's endeavours were not enough. Subsequent emperors, like Marcus Aurelius (161–80), tried to manage Rome's overstretched capabilities and to quell growing unrest along the borders. Others were more irresponsible and reckless: the megalomaniacal Caracalla (198–217) aimed at world domination.

A prime witness to the turmoil and violent repression experienced by most Romans in the late second and early third centuries was the Greek-born historian and senator Cassius Dio. His writings comprise a forceful condemnation of the abuse of power, the corruption, and the endless wars that were waged to try to keep gold flowing into the imperial coffers. Gone were any illusions about the nature of Roman rule. In response to a rebellion in Britain, the Emperor Septimius Severus (193–211) ordered: 'Let no one escape sheer destruction, no one our hands, not even the babe in the womb of the mother.'[12] But Severus realized that never-ending campaigns could make emperors unpopular. 'On the occasion of the tenth anniversary of his coming to power,' Dio recorded, 'Severus presented to the entire populace that received the grain dole and to the soldiers of the pretorian guard gold pieces equal in number to the years of his reign.'[13]

Other emperors were less astute: Caracalla spent so heavily on the army and on gladiatorial games to entertain the masses that he was forced to debase the currency and to declare all male non-slaves in the empire Roman citizens in a desperate attempt to expand the tax base. 'He would appoint some freedman or other wealthy person to be director of the games in order that the man might spend money in this way also; and he would salute the spectators with his whip from the arena below and beg for gold pieces like a performer of the lowest class.'[14] Dio decried the disintegration of the social order: the ruling through terror, the armed gangs roaming the Italian countryside, the orgies in the imperial palace. 'He carried his lewdness to such a point,' he wrote about one emperor, 'that he asked the physicians to contrive a woman's vagina in his body.'[15] The omens for Rome were not good and the gods issued stern warnings: 'Thy house shall perish utterly in blood.'[16]

But the empire survived this descent into anarchy. Part of the reason is that, externally, nobody could challenge its military power. Rome had a single peer: Parthia. Parthia could at worst threaten Roman possessions in Armenia and the Levant. Most of the imperial frontier was inhabited by tribes. Guerrilla tactics in the forests of Germany or the Highlands of Scotland tormented the Roman legions, but were curbed as soon as reinforcements arrived. 'The Germans wear no breastplates or helmets,' Tacitus has a general reassure his troops. 'Even their shields are not reinforced . . . Spears, of a sort, are limited to their front rank. The rest only have clubs burnt at the end, or with short metal points. Physically, they look formidable and are good for a short rush. But they cannot stand being hurt.'[17] Crucially, the Romans had an unmatched capacity for long-range power projection, thanks to their roads, the navy that dominated the Mediterranean Sea, and small galleys that could patrol rivers like the Rhine and Danube. At its peak, Rome had more than 80,000 kilometres of paved roads, built a fleet of over a thousand ships, and constructed dozens of ports in the Mediterranean and the Black Seas and, to a much lesser extent, the North Sea. The Romans were also adept at playing tribes off against each other: allowing one to trade freely while excluding another, proclaiming one community a friend of the Roman people while declaring another their enemy.

The other part of the reason for the empire's survival is that, internally, the elite mollified the masses. Inequality among the 1 million inhabitants of Rome was staggering. While the rich erected extravagant villas on the hills of the capital, the poor lived in an impenetrable maze of apartment blocks and dark alleyways occupied by beggars, criminals, and prostitutes. As much as one third of the population in the capital might have been slaves.[18] A worker earned about four sestertii per day, but more than 400,000 sestertii were required for a citizen to qualify for the leading social class, the equestrians. Landowners could be tremendously rich. One of them, Marcus Antonius Pallas, was even reputed to have been worth over 300 million sestertii.[19] The masses were conditioned to accept their poverty. Virgil, Seneca, and many other writers praised hard work.

Popular poems and plays took poverty as a given, sometimes humorously so. 'I was in agony from the cold,' says the donkey in the second-century Greek writer Lucius Apuleius' novel the *Golden Ass*; 'but my master was no better off. Indeed, because of his extreme poverty, he is unable to buy straw or even the smallest blankets for his bed.'[20] To ameliorate the living conditions of poor citizens, spectacular gladiatorial games and chariot races were regularly staged: this was the time of grandiose projects like the building of the Colosseum, the renovation of the Circus Maximus, and the construction of giant public bath houses. Emperors did everything in their might to guarantee a steady supply of grain from the provinces. In extreme cases, there was the army to restore order. 'Many uprisings were begun by many persons, some of which caused great alarm,' wrote Cassius Dio, 'but they were all put down.'[21] Imperial Roman society was inequality permanently pushed to the limits of acceptability.

Controlling *Barbaricum*

Outside the borders of the Roman Empire lay *barbaricum*. The attitudes of those people that lived on the fringes of the empire were ambivalent. Even the fiercest opponents of military domination sought to benefit economically. The Caledonian tribes, for instance, obstinately resisted the legions from their redoubts in the Scottish Highlands, but the graves of their leaders were full of Roman artefacts. Germanic tribes fought countless wars with the Romans. The Frisii, who lived north of the lower Rhine, hanged Roman tax collectors and rebelled against an oppressive Roman governor. Yet some Frisian clans were among the many Germanic peoples who supplied auxiliary troops to fight in the Roman army.

One of the larger societies on Rome's northern frontier were the Dacians. Initially, the Romans bribed them not to cross the Danube. But as turmoil within the empire grew, enterprising Dacian kings began to raid across the border. The Roman counterstroke, when it came, was ferocious: the Dacians were defeated, their king hunted down and killed, and the kingdom incorporated into the empire in 105. Still the Dacians continued to resist the influx of Romans keen to exploit the region's many gold mines. That resistance ultimately forced the Emperor Commodus (180–92) to grant the tribes greater autonomy.

Many factors influenced the behaviour of these tribal peoples. Their political organization shifted between fragmentation into clans and cohesion under strong kings. Most of them were small-scale farmers with a clear interest in stability. But they were also known for their warrior ethos and the ability to mobilize young and old, women as well as men, to fight. The security of their domains remained permanently in flux. Migrating peoples from the east, attracted by the more temperate climate and the region's growing wealth, exerted growing pressure on the tribes already settled next to the Roman border.

The empire was not always able to defend its frontiers with the same degree of vigour. The defensive system – the so-called *limes* – frequently suffered from undermanning. Instead, more diplomatic policies were often adopted. The desire to become part of the empire was fostered by promoting trade or granting elites certain privileges. Tribes just beyond the border were invited to become *tributarii*: a trade-off between access to Roman markets and a degree of Roman protection on the one hand, and the payment of taxes and the performance of military service on the other. Some tribes became *leati*, granted land inside the empire in exchange for providing men for the army. The most favoured tribes became *foederati*, able to settle inside the empire, retain their leaders, and even receive subsidies in return for serving as auxiliary troops.

The tribes in Britain and along the Rhine and Danube have not left us any written sources concerning their relations with the Romans. The main texts available are those of historians like Tacitus and Cassius Dio. Matters are different when it comes to Greece, the Levant, and Egypt, where native written sources do exist. In Greece, intellectuals during this period were divided. Some tried to reconcile their countrymen to Roman rule: the historian Dionysius of Halicarnassus and the geographer Strabo both argued that Rome provided protection from rival states in Asia Minor, the scourge of piracy, and the restless hordes around the coast of the Black Sea; while the philosopher Aristides praised the freedom of movement in the empire. Others were less reconciled: the geographer Pausanias, for example, argued that the Roman conquest had ushered in 'the period when Greece sank to the lowest depth of weakness'.[22] He deplored the way that the Greek cities had lost their freedom and their leaders rushed to become part of the imperial elite. 'The foulest of all crimes,' he insisted, was 'the betrayal of native land

and fellow-countrymen for personal gain.'[23] He testified to Roman looting, the forced depopulation of great cities like Corinth, and the arbitrary behaviour of governors.

The last of these was also one of the chief complaints of Philo of Alexandria, a Jewish-Greek philosopher who lived in Egypt in the first century, and who described – in his tract *Against Flaccus* – how a Roman governor incited popular unrest against Jews in the country. But perhaps the most vivid account of life in the Middle East under the Roman regime is provided by the story of Jesus Christ – his peaceful resistance, his passion, and his crucifixion – as it is recorded in the New Testament. For many in the centuries since, this narrative has come to symbolize imperial oppression. The apostle John deplored how the Romans came and took away both the land and soul of the Jews. Yet he was even more critical of the many locals who collaborated with their conquerors, not least those who let themselves be manipulated and bribed when Jesus was put on trial alongside the criminal Barabbas by the Roman governor, Pontius Pilate. The gospel account is contextualized by Philo of Alexandria and the late first-century Jewish-Greek historian Flavius Josephus, both of whom record how the arbitrary rule of Pilate, and his disdain for Jewish customs, caused unrest in Palestine. Both writers, however, had become Romanized in their outlook, suggesting that Roman rule over the Jews was the will of God.

At its height, during the reign of Trajan in the early second century, the Roman Empire was one of the largest the world had seen. But if the land area controlled by the Han and the Achaemenids was probably more extensive, Rome also controlled a vast maritime zone stretching from the North Sea, via the Mediterranean, all the way to the Black Sea and the northern part of the Red Sea. The degree of Roman imperialism was arguably greater too. Rome had the power not only to conquer, but also to integrate its conquests – through stringent administrative practices, harmonized standards, common languages for the elite, shipping, and unrivalled engineering prowess, which is visible in the harbours, roads, bridges, and aqueducts that still survive from antiquity. Sea and land combined, the Roman Empire was one of the largest ever.

Along the Silk Road

Parthia, the cosmopolitan empire that stretched between the Euphrates and the Hindu Kush, remained Rome's most significant rival according to the ancient historians. Tacitus, for example, referred to Rome and Parthia as the two greatest empires (*maxima imperia*), while Pompeius Trogus visualized the world as divided between Romans and Parthians. Nevertheless, the Parthian Empire was under pressure. From a Roman viewpoint, the desired relationship with the Parthians was clear: Parthia had to be treated like a major power, yet still inferior to Rome. The famous white marble Prima Porta statue of Augustus, now in the Vatican Museums, shows on its breastplate a Parthian soldier diffidently returning one of the military standards captured from the Roman legions in earlier wars. The Parthian king even gave his sons as hostages to Augustus to ensure that the next ruler would be of Roman blood.

The peace did not last. The two powers became locked

into a geopolitical zero-sum game, where the gains of one side were regarded as a loss by the other, over the kingdom of Armenia, which acted as a buffer state between the empires. There were also persistent tensions over the Euphrates border. Initially, Rome's ambitions stopped on the western banks of the river. But in 115, the Emperor Trajan crossed it. According to Tacitus, Roman campaigns in the east historically were regarded as a way of consolidating the domestic prestige of emperors. And Trajan did indeed allude to the Persian conquests of Alexander the Great in relation to his own war. However, Parthia had initially provoked Rome by replacing the king of Armenia. Another contributory factor was Roman 'mission creep'. After his Dacian campaign, Trajan had led his troops to the Black Sea. Beyond the gold of Dacia, the trade of the Caucasus and the Middle East beckoned. The Parthians, however, opposed the Roman invasion fiercely. Trajan's successor, Hadrian, withdrew from Mesopotamia. In 198, the Emperor Septimius Severus returned. He sacked the Parthian capital, Ctesiphon, and annexed northern Mesopotamia. In 217, Parthia and Rome readied for another major confrontation: the Emperor Caracalla was poised to descend with his troops from the Anatolian mountains into Mesopotamia. The expedition was aborted when Caracalla was assassinated during a toilet break, and the Romans were forced to sue for peace.

But the Parthian Empire was now so exhausted that it fell prey to a tiny vassal kingdom situated a mere two kilometres from the ruins of Persepolis, in the historic heartland of the Achaemenids. Its ruler, Ardashir I, crowned himself 'king of kings' – in the tradition of the Assyrians and the Persians – in

Ctesiphon in 224. A new empire was founded. This Sasanian Empire would rule over large parts of the Middle East and Central Asia until the birth of Islam in the seventh century.

Even as the Parthian Empire was clearly weakening, it remained an important trading hub connecting the Mediterranean and Asia. The Greek-born Roman official and historian Herodian described the flourishing trade at the beginning of the third century and argued that specialization could smooth political relations: 'Since the Parthians produced spices and excellent textiles and the Romans metals and manufactured articles, these products would no longer be scarce and smuggled by merchants; rather, when there was one world under one supreme authority, both peoples would enjoy these goods and share them in common.'[24] But the reality was not so straightforward. Chinese and Roman sources hint that the Parthians tried to preserve their position as the gatekeeper of Asian commerce. In 97, a Chinese envoy requested permission from the Parthian court to travel on to Rome via the Persian Gulf. The Parthians seemingly convinced him that the journey would be too arduous. 'The ocean is huge,' they said. '[It] urges men to think of their country, and get homesick, and some of them die.'[25] The Chinese were probably well aware that they were being tricked. The Roman emperor 'always wanted to send envoys to the Han', we read in the Chinese records, 'but Anxi [Parthia], wishing to control the trade in multi-colored Chinese silks, blocked the route'.[26]

Parthia's designs on monopolizing the trade of the Silk Road were not the only economic concern in Rome, where writers also worried about the trade deficit with the East. Pliny the Elder believed that Roman women's thirst for Eastern luxuries cost the empire a fortune: 'In no year does India drain our empire of less than five hundred and fifty millions of sesterces.'[27] Tacitus warned that too much wealth was being transferred to foreign hostile countries for the sake of female extravagance. Instead of trying to regulate the consumption of rich Romans, the objective became to control the trade. First, Rome sought to dominate entrepôts in the Levant, such as Palmyra and Petra, in order to avoid additional tariffs. At the same time, it promoted maritime trade via the Red Sea with the ports of the Arabian Peninsula, with India, and even with China. Most trade with China was indirect, even though Rome probably sent an embassy as early as 166. Yet the Chinese, for the time being, remained unimpressed. 'The tribute they brought,' we read in the records, 'was neither precious nor rare.'[28]

The Kushan Empire

While direct overland trade between Rome and China was blocked by Parthia, maritime trade with India grew. Under Augustus, ships sailed to India each year, mooring in the many ports on the subcontinent's western coast. A traveller from the first century recounted this long, tiring journey from the port of Alexandria, via the Red Sea, where Roman warships patrolled against pirates, along the dangerous coasts of the Indian Ocean.[29] His *periplus* (literally 'voyage around') described how the ports on the coast of South Asia were primarily independent city states or part of small kingdoms, which took a keen interest in controlling trade through designated harbours, official pilots, customs officers, patrols against pirates, and ancient claims to authority of the region. In the case of a valuable spice such as frankincense, 'neither openly nor by stealth can it be loaded on board ship without the King's permission; if a single grain were loaded without this, the ship could not clear from the harbour'.[30] These ports were connected with their hinterland by rivers along which gold, gems, textiles, and spices were transported. They also held regular markets with more primitive tribes. 'They come with their wives and children, carrying great packs and plaited baskets of what looks like green grape-leaves . . . There they hold a feast for several days, spreading out the baskets under themselves as mats, and then return to their own places in the interior.'[31] The traveller also testified to what he thought were 'signs of the expedition of Alexander the Great, such as ancient shrines, walls of forts and great wells'.[32]

The hinterlands of India and Central Asia remained a perilous arena of war. The south of the subcontinent was divided between kingdoms such as those of the Satavahanas, the Kshaharatas, the Pandyans, and the Cholas. In the north, the Kushan Empire of the Yuezhi took advantage of the Parthian decline to continue to expand. As the *Book of the Later Han* put it: 'It was when the Yuezhi triumphed over the Parthians that they took Kabul.'[33] The Yuezhi were able to field hundreds of thousands of horsemen, a capability that no other power in the region could match.

The Yuezhi conquered the kingdoms of the Indo-Gangetic Plain one after another. The impact of the Yuezhi is reflected in biographies of the early second-century Buddhist monk Ashvaghosha. The ideal state was a world 'made peaceable, with a long-lived king, plentiful harvests, and joy throughout the land, with none of the myriad calamaties'.[34] But then came the Yuezhi, demanding tribute: one kingdom was expected to pay a sum three times greater than its entire wealth. Its compassionate Buddhist king gave in: 'We will provide for you whatever you require. Why must the people suffer and be distressed by your extended presence?'[35] The kingdom was overrun nonetheless.

The Romans may have believed that there were only two great emperors – their own and Parthia's – but the Kushan ruler regarded himself as their equal. On their coins, Kushan monarchs described themselves as 'august', in imitation of Roman emperors, but also 'king of kings', in the Mesopotamian tradition, and 'son of heaven', like Chinese rulers. According to legend, the powerful emperor Kanishka (127–63) had supernatural powers and defeated an evil serpent king. The Rabatak Inscription honoured Kanishka as 'the great salvation, Kanishka the Kushan, the righteous, the just, the autocrat, the god worthy of worship, who has obtained the kingship from Nana and from all the gods'.[36] The Mathura Inscription described him as 'steadfast in the true law'.[37] The Kushan emperors prided themselves on their irrigation schemes. Projects like the Dargom dam, which controlled much of the water supply for the city of Samarkand in the Ferghana Valley, were unmatched.

Although the Kushan Empire was divided into satrapies, they were probably not as tightly controlled as those of the Achaemenid Empire. Nevertheless, Chinese travellers admired the strength and brilliance of the Kushan realm. It is striking that, even though there were no significant gold mines in the area, the Kushans minted an immense volume of gold coinage. The only possible explanation is a large economic surplus with Parthia, Rome, and other trading partners. The combination of the South Asian plains and the Central Asian oases had immense agricultural potential. At their peak, the Kushans controlled the main caravan routes connecting South Asia, Mesopotamia, the Tarim Basin in present-day China, and even Siberia, as well as major ports in the Gulf of Aden. Like Ashoka Maurya four centuries earlier, Kanishka adopted Buddhism as the official religion of his realm and as justification for his righteous rule over hundreds of different tribes and languages.

The Kushan Empire emerged as a pivotal player in an ancient version of the 'Great Game', and contested with Rome, Parthia, the Xiongnu, and China for control over the fertile plateaus and trade corridors of Central Asia. Around 50, the Kushan Empire was at war with the Parthians over the control of the green valleys of the eastern Zagros Mountains. Cassius Dio reported a Kushan alliance with Rome: 'The people of India, who had already made overtures, now made a treaty of friendship, sending among other gifts tigers, which were then for the first time seen by the Romans.'[38] At the same time, the Kushans agreed a pact with China. It was short-lived. Insulted by the Chinese refusal of a royal marriage and alarmed by the scale of their advances into Central Asia, the Kushan Empire declared war. When it lost, China demanded humiliating terms. The Kushan Empire took revenge by forming a coalition with the Xiongnu. But when the Sasanians overthrew the sclerotic Parthian Empire, the Kushan emperor Vasudeva I sought a new alliance with

China. To flatter the Chinese, he even issued coins with his name stamped in Chinese. It was a sign of weakness. After Vasudeva's death in around 235, the Kushan realm first divided in two and later splintered into smaller kingdoms.

Even without the Kushan Empire, South Asia, Central Asia, the Middle East, the Mediterranean, and China remained more connected than before. After having absorbed Greek influences, South Asia now also took an interest in Roman culture. In the other direction, Roman citizens became very keen on Asian luxuries. Trade, culture, and travel helped cement ties across Eurasia. So did power politics. Diplomatic relations were established between China, Rome, Parthia, Kushan, and India. But more wars were fought between them too. Because the more that trade travelled the Silk Road and penetrated the mountains of the Hindu Kush and the Tian Shan, the fiercer the competition to control it.

Closing the Jade Gate

Along with Parthia and Kushan, the other major contender for mastery of Central Asia was thus Han China. The Han adhered to the traditional notion that China was 'the Middle Kingdom'. As we have seen, they conceived the world order as concentric rings surrounding the imperial domain; the emperor's task was to preserve this peaceful Chinese realm and keep out the world of the barbarians. At the end of the first century BCE, however, that peace was threatened from within.

After the death of Emperor Ai of Han in 1 BCE, the empire collapsed into turmoil over the succession that fed into the bitter resentments of poor farmers. A military command-er called Wang Mang made a particular bid to win over the masses. 'The rich had dogs and horses fed on more grain and vegetables than they could eat,' he observed. 'The poor could not get their fill of dregs, and were driven by poverty to crime.'[39] The reforms he proposed were sweeping. As soon as he prised the regency from his aunt, the dowager empress, he outlawed slavery, nationalized farmland, and embarked on in-frastructure works. He also tried to curb food prices, appoint-ing a superintendent of the market to buy goods when they were cheap and sell them when they were expensive.[40] His radical undertakings were halted, however, by massive floods, famine, and opposition to his apparent usurpation of the im-perial throne. Rebels and robbers organized themselves into armed bands such as the Red Eyebrows Army.

Meanwhile, another scion of the imperial family, Liu Xiu, turned the chaos to his advantage. Seizing the decisive moment in the struggle against Wang Mang, Liu displayed re-markable military leadership to achieve the victory that won him most of the North China Plain. In 25 CE, he proclaimed himself emperor of a restored Han Dynasty, the so-called 'Eastern Han', and adopted the name Guangwu. As the new imperial colour, he chose red, the colour of fire and vigour. Emperor Guangwu did everything to boost his legitimacy as rightful inheritor of the heavenly mandate. Like Augustus, he cultivated important writers. One of them was the court his-torian Ban Gu, who narrated how the new Han Dynasty 'mag-nified imperial discipline'.[41] He made a forceful case for the centralization of authority and revived the Confucian imper-ial theory of Dong Zhongshu. Guangwu understood, though, that he also had to placate the masses to stay in power and therefore upheld some of Wang Mang's populist policies. He confirmed the abolition of slavery, reduced the number of noblemen at court, redistributed land to the poor, and relieved farmers from the burden of compulsory military service.

One objective of this last, remarkable reform was to disarm Chinese society and so make civil war more difficult. But it had severe consequences for the empire's foreign policy. With only a palace guard of 2,400 soldiers, and a further five commanders each with 3,500 troops, the Chinese army was now far smaller than that of many neighbours. The solution was to conscript criminals and recruit non-Han warriors.[42] More than ever, security depended on a strategy of setting barbarian against barbarian. In such circumstances, Ban Gu advised against campaigning beyond the border. The barbarians 'are separated from us by mountains and valleys and cut off by the desert. By these means did Heaven and Earth divide inner from outer,' he asserted. 'To conclude agreements with them is to waste gifts and suffer deception. To attack them is to exhaust our armies and provoke raids.'[43]

The ensuing strategy of restraint conveniently coincided with a period of weakness among the barbarians. In 24, the Xiongnu had baulked at the demand for tribute, arguing that Liu Xiu should pay them in return for the support he had received against Wang Mang. But in 50, after the Xiongnu federation had been riven by succession conflicts, the Southern Xiongnu accepted their obligation to pay tribute, sent a prince as hostage to the Han court, and aligned themselves as a buffer state. The Northern Xiongnu lacked the power to threaten the Chinese Empire and were also harassed by

Han-sponsored rivals like the Wuhuan and the Xianbei. In such circumstances, Chinese commanders grew contemptuous. 'Why does it take five Xiongnu to match one Han soldier? It is because their sword blades are dull and their crossbows worthless.'[44] The counsellor Chao Cuo, meanwhile, likened the Xiongnu to 'flying birds or running beasts in the vast, open fields'.[45] This dismissiveness did not last long.

Guangwu's successor, Emperor Ming (57–75), was greeted on his accession by growing assertiveness from the Northern Xiongnu. They raided trading posts on the border and attacked their poorly equipped garrisons. Their conflicts with the Southern Xiongnu generated large inflows of immigrants, who were promptly bribed to return home. The military challenge was met with punitive expeditions. Emperor Zhang (75–88) ordered his troops to push deeply into Central Asia and end the Xiongnu problem once and for all. The general Ban Chao succeeded in pacifying most of these 'Western Regions', assisted by the Kushan and lesser local rulers. When famine also struck the Xiongnu, several of their leaders came to the border to submit. 'Overawed by our military strength and attracted by our wealth, all the rulers presented exotic local products as tribute and their beloved sons as hostages. They bared their heads and kneeled down towards the east to pay homage to the Son of Heaven,' the records boasted.[46] China reinstated the office of protector-general of the Western Regions to oversee the payment of tribute.[47] If a ruler was unable to meet his dues, he was stripped of his authority and the official imperial ribbon was bestowed on a new puppet.

Under Emperors Ming and Zhang, China lived through a golden age. Internal stability returned, taxes remained low, and the majority of farmers were spared conscription. Zhang successfully managed a disastrous cattle epidemic and experimented with social security policies, including tax relief for young fathers, grants of grain to any wife that gave birth, and subsidies to parents that could not feed their children. In 79, in an apparent effort to shore up his credentials as a just ruler, Zhang summoned renowned scholars from across the realm to participate in the so-called 'Virtuous Discussions of White Tiger Hall'. The result was a new manifesto for governance based on Confucian principles. It dealt with court rituals, social justice, law, and public administration within the empire. Beyond the borders, meanwhile, the Confucian principle of harmony was propagated through increasingly ritualized relationships and ceremonies designed to overawe envoys with their magnificence, as well as ever more extravagant gifts.

This age of prosperity, however, was short-lived. The policy of demilitarization proved untenable. Distrustful of barbarian intentions, officials recommended that more troops were needed to guard the border. The cost of subsidies to foreign leaders grew alarmingly high. The weakening of the Northern Xiongnu also diminished the need for the Southern Xiongnu, the Xianbei, and the Wuhuan to collaborate. As their subsidies were cut, they started to pillage Chinese farmers. In 94, the Southern Xiongnu formally joined forces with the Northern Xiongnu against the Han Empire.

Meanwhile, another neighbour tried to profit from the mayhem: the nomadic Qiang people, who lived west of the North China Plain. In 104, tensions escalated into a full-blown war. The Han regime panicked and withdrew several frontier garrisons in order to preserve security 'east of the passes'. A leading intellectual warned of the geopolitical domino effect: 'If you lose Liang province, then the Three Adjuncts will be the border. If the people of the Three Adjuncts move inward, then Hongnong will be the border. If the people of Hongnong move inward, then Luoyang will be the border. If you carry on like this, you will reach the edge of the Eastern Sea.'[48]

This was the beginning of the Han Dynasty's collapse. Beset by growing unrest not only beyond but within the border, Emperor An (106–25) opted for isolationism. He closed the Jade Gate – the main Silk Road pass connecting China with Central Asia – and terminated tributary relations with the peoples to its west, which were no longer sustainable. An was a notoriously miserly and incompetent ruler: records speak of a 'gradual diminishment of benevolence' in his reign. One of his first decrees abolished the redistribution of land and grain to the poor, while landowning families grew more powerful again. In the *Monthly Instructions for the Four Classes of People*, Ts'ui Shih deplored how land was systematically transferred to courtiers and how the emperor's desire to increase taxes incited local officials to sequestrate peasants' farms. The landless peasantry were then left at the mercy of rich landowners, who exploited them as labourers. According to Ts'ui, the countryside grew increasingly restless, causing landowners to fortify their homes and hire private guards.[49] Under An's successors, major revolts erupted, like the Five Pecks of Grain Uprising in 142 and the Yellow Turban Rebellion in 182. Popular poems from the time depict a world of impermanence and sorrow.

Seasons of growth and decay march on and on,

The years allotted to man are like morning dew.

Man's life is as transient as a sojourn,

His frame is not as firm as metal or stone . . .

Some take drugs and hope to become immortals,

Many of them only end their life with poison.

Far better to drink fine wine

And wear clothes of choice white silk.[50]

War with the Qiang made the situation worse. 'The Qiang invade our frontiers so frequently,' it was reported, 'that hardly a year goes by in peace and it is only when the trading season arrives that they come forward in submission.'[51] The records speak of hundreds of thousands of casualties, the loss of large stretches of farmland, and an immense drain on the empire's coffers. Officials now proposed relinquishing all claims on the areas inhabited by the Qiang, tacitly admitting that the Han had become unable to stop the loss of influence on the periphery. The elite had become largely uninterested in the restless western part of the empire and aligned its interests more than ever with the rich agricultural areas in the east. Here the economic centre of gravity had shifted from the North China Plain to the banks of the River Yangtze, and thus even further from the western frontier.[52]

The Han court was dominated by scholar-officials from rich agricultural families. 'Since the times of the Qin and Han, Shandong produces civil ministers and Shanxi produces military generals,' it was said.[53] Those officials were loath to surrender their influence to military men at the head of powerful armies and so they continued to prefer the old policies involving soft power or the fighting of wars by proxy. 'The men of Bing and Liang, as well as the Xiongnu, the Tuge, the voluntary followers from the Huangzhong area, and the eight stocks of the Western Qiang are the most vigorous fighters [of] all under Heaven and are feared by the people,' asserted one courtier in a conversation with the emperor. 'They are all under the command of Your Excellency and serve as teeth and claws.'[54] Another official ordered books on filial piety to be distributed in the Qiang's territories.

The mellow eastern heartland of the empire failed to come to grips with the rough power politics of the west. But if the imperial court was reluctant to defend the border, growing internal unrest and more frequent coup attempts made it invest in large militias. When the court fractured into its constituent clans, the militias followed suit. China had become ungovernable. By 190, the whole empire was beset with fighting, very much like the Spring and Autumn or the Warring States periods centuries earlier. Battles often involved hundreds of thousands of warriors. Powerful warlords first sidelined the scholar-officials, and then the emperor. In 220, the last Han emperor was relieved from more than a decade's existence as a puppet ruler and deposed. He was lucky and allowed to retire peacefully. The empire was less fortunate. It split into three kingdoms: the Shu, the Wu, and the Wei. The subsequent century of infighting cost millions of lives.

The foundering of the Han Empire affected the whole of East Asia. In the Korean Peninsula, the kingdom of Goguryeo, which had replaced the Gojoseon kingdom, seized the opportunity to escape from Chinese tutelage. Goguryeo had been established in the late first century BCE as a federation of hunting tribes and had only recently been consolidated into a centrally governed realm under King Gogukcheon (179–97 CE). The *Samguk Sagi*, a compilation from ancient Korean records, credited Gogukcheon with being a capable commander and a just ruler. Encountering an impoverished town, the legend went, he shared his clothes with its inhabitants and later instituted a grain-subsidy system. The Goguryeo kingdom had probably been a client state of the Han Empire, although skirmishes between them were frequent. This was primarily because Goguryeo straddled the Yalu River, so that there was no natural border with the Han Empire, and persistent competition for the grasslands of Manchuria. When the Han Dynasty collapsed, Goguryeo briefly expanded, but was pushed back by the newly established Wei kingdom.

In Japan, meanwhile, state building also advanced slowly. Chinese sources inform us that the archipelago of Wa, the ancient name for Japan, was still atomized in hundreds of statelets throughout the first century, but that by 230 it had been united under the Yamatai kingdom. With the Han emperor gone, the Japanese monarch decided to make overtures to the Wei, which instantly adopted traditional tributary practice, bestowing the title 'Kingdom of Wa Friendly to Wei' along with a special purple ribbon. These ribbons had also been used by the Han to legitimize rulers in Southeast Asia. In present-day Vietnam, for example, China subsidized and protected kings. When the Trung Sisters rebelled against Chinese hegemony in around 41, the Han dispatched a 'wave-calming general' to Vietnam, together with 20,000 soldiers.

'Wherever he passed, the general promptly established pre-fectures and districts to govern walled towns.'[55] But guerrilla attacks from the dense forests continued to be mounted on Chinese-supported fortresses, and the Han returned to their previous policy of indirect control through trade and diplo-matic flattery.[56] After the Han's demise, the same practices were continued by the Wu kingdom.

Even though the Han Empire crumbled, China's cultural and economic influence remained vast. Looking at the Han's down-fall, some parallels with the contemporary Roman Empire are striking. In both cases, imperialism initially brought security to the heartland, but subsequently caused destabilizing in-equality and decadence in the elite. This weakened the core of the empire at the same time as its borders continued to be pushed outwards. The result was overstretch. It is perhaps no coincidence that the Han closed the Jade Gate at almost exactly the same time as Hadrian ordered the legions to pull back from Mesopotamia.

World of Extremes

The world of the Emperors Augustus and Guangwu was thus one of extremes. It was an era of unprecedented transcontin-ental trade and exploration. Merchants and envoys travelled vast distances. We have already encountered the Chinese delegate stuck in Parthia on his way to Rome in 97; but in 166, a Roman emissary made the journey east, arriving in what is now Vietnam in the hope of presenting gifts to the Chinese emperor.

The empires of Rome, Parthia, Kushan, and the Han all

promised peace and harmony of some sort. Indeed, Rome and the Han achieved it for several decades. But, even there, peace was always relative. Violence never ceased along the borders. In any case, such peace as there was mostly bene-fited a small elite in the centre, who controlled the food supply, the luxury trade, and the state monopolies. In the Roman Empire, around 15 per cent of the population might have consisted of slaves.[57] In Han China, only 1–2 per cent of the population consisted of slaves, although the propor-tion was higher in the cities, and peasants often did not fare much better. Tribal peoples also kept slaves and were feared among the inhabitants of sedentary societies for their slave-taking raids.

Unless they lived in the imperial capitals at times of pol-itical stability, therefore, most men, women, and children were never entirely safe, and rarely free from hardship. People often survived on only a fistful of cereals and beans per day, occasionally enriched with some oil, fruit, or vege-tables.[58] Undernourishment was rampant and so was disease, particularly in the crowded cities. Infant mortality in the first two years of life was 50 per cent.[59] At its heart, empire was about advancing the privileges of a small capital area over those of a large surrounding hinterland, and about promot-ing the interests of a small rich elite over those of the large numbers of poor and needy.

CHAPTER 7

The Great Imperial Crisis

250–500 CE

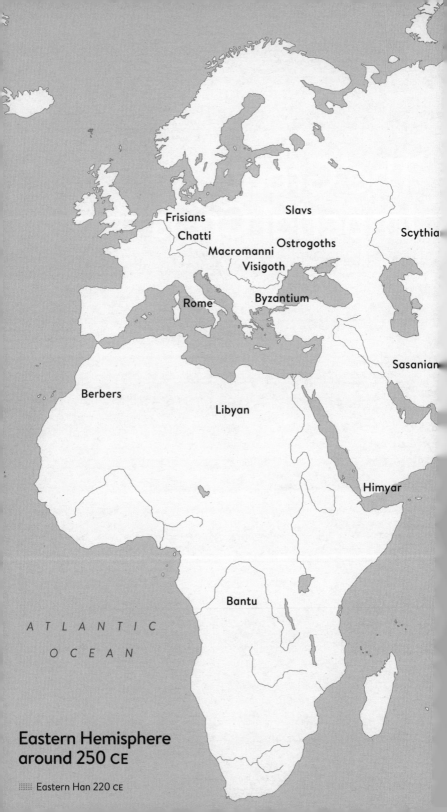

Frisians

Chatti

Macromanni

Slavs

Ostrogoths

Visigoth

Scythia

Byzantium

Rome

Sasanian

Berbers

Libyan

Himyar

Bantu

A T L A N T I C

O C E A N

Eastern Hemisphere
around 250 CE

Eastern Han 220 CE

Xianbei

Xiongnu

Cao Wei

Luoyang •

Beekje

Tibetans

han

Shu

Eastern Wu

PACIFIC

a

OCEAN

akataka

Pallava

Funan

DIAN

CEAN

500   1000   1500 km

500   1000 miles

Around 400 CE, the Chinese poet Tao Yuanming penned his vision of the ideal world:

> The gentle south wind comes with the season,
> its whirling gusts blow open my robe.
> Breaking with social contacts, I enjoy leisure activities;
> lying around, or sitting up, I play with zither and books.
> Of garden vegetables, there is a surplus,
> last year's grain is still in storage.[1]

At the other end of Eurasia, Palladius Rutilius Taurus Aemilianus, a landowner in the Roman province of Gaul in the fourth or fifth centuries, embarked on a guidebook for novice farmers. His advice would help them tend a paradise as halcyon as that portrayed by Tao, one with inexhaustible wells, verdant fields, a clement atmosphere, orchards laden with fruit, and well-built roads.[2] After more than a thousand years, the dream of men living in harmony with nature had hardly changed.

But the Arcadian idylls of Tao and Palladius were written amid societies mired in political decay. Across Eurasia, the period between 250 and 500 was one of imperial regression. The Western Roman Empire was overrun by barbarians.

Remnants of the old imperial grandeur lived on in Constantinople, but the Eastern Roman Empire would never attain the same power as that of the first two centuries of imperial Rome. In China, barbarians swarmed over the kingdoms into which the Han Empire had splintered. In South Asia, the zenith of the Gupta Empire was comparatively short-lived. For a while, the newly established Sasanian Empire stood out as an exception, but by the end of the fifth century it too had degenerated. The rest of Eurasia comprised a cockpit of fighting and fluctuating alliances as relatively small polities – such as Funan, the Pandyan kingdom, Goguryeo, and the Yamato kingdom – along with nomadic societies and migrating peoples struggled for survival and supremacy.

The *Völkerwanderung*

The period from the third to the fifth century saw the two great centres of power, Rome and China, succumb to a combination of internal weakness and unrelenting migratory pressures. The fatal thrust came from the heart of Eurasia, where the plains and valleys of Mongolia and Central Asia were inhabited by the Xiongnu and the related people known collectively as the Huns, who comprised various tribal groupings – White Huns, Red Huns, Hephthalite Huns, to name but a few. The core of these genetically and culturally related societies consisted of confederated bands of nomads who followed their cattle from pasture to pasture on horseback. On the fringes of the Mongolian and Central Asian grasslands, semi-nomads and traders maintained relations with sedentary, agricultural societies, which looked down on the wandering peoples. They perceived them as wild, bow-legged beasts, hardened by the harsh climate. 'They can withstand wind and rain, fatigue, hunger, and thirst,' nervous Chinese officials reported.[3] Perhaps unsurprisingly, the Huns saw themselves rather differently. An inscription from northern India, for example, is fulsome in its praise of one Hun leader: 'His heroism . . . was specially characterised by truthfulness, the earth was governed with justice.'[4]

In the third century, relations between wandering tribes and agricultural centres were profoundly disturbed. This was partially caused by environmental changes. The climate became so severe in Mongolia and Central Asia that the Xiongnu and the Huns were forced to move. Dendrology shows that the steppes became drier between 242 and 293.[5] It was around this period that clashes between the Xiongnu, the Xianbei, and the Chinese along the Yellow River became more frequent. In 311, Xiongnu warriors sacked the Chinese capital, Luoyang. At about the same time, the Huns left their homeland on the banks of the Volga. Although we generally think of the Huns as exceptionally savage warriors, their 4,000-kilometre journey was appallingly tough and troubled by deprivation. In 370, they crossed the Don and reached the Danube a few years later, where they clashed with the Goths, who dwelt in that area. The exodus of the Goths panicked their fellow Germanic peoples who lived along the borders of the Roman Empire. They fled, overrunning the Roman *limes*. Bishop Ambrose of Milan explained the cataclysm. 'The Huns threw themselves upon the Alans, the Alans upon the Goths, and the Goths upon the Taifali and Sarmatians.'[6]

The same climatic change that drove the Huns out of their

plains, combined with overpopulation, accelerated the migration of the Germanic tribes from the Baltic region south towards the plains between the Rivers Elbe and Rhine, and onwards to the Black Sea. For centuries, the Baltic had been a transit zone for both trade and migration. But this exodus was far larger and more destabilizing. Consider the Goths. They originated in the Danish Peninsula; settled along the Elbe around the first century, where they clashed with the incumbent tribes; then moved on to the Danube around 350, where they clashed again, this time with the Roman legions. Gradually they became involved in Roman infighting over the imperial succession, resulting in the deaths of thousands. Conflicts between the Gothic tribes, over land and leadership, were also rife. And then they were plagued by famine and by the vanguard of the Hun incursion. In what was more an act of desperation than of aggression, the Goths finally crossed the Danube into the Roman Empire. Now they were at the mercy of local leaders, who allegedly enslaved Gothic children in exchange for food. In 405, the Goths could endure no more and marched on Rome to demand land and rights.

Another major Germanic people, the Vandals, did not fare any better. They had traversed the Baltic Sea in the second century, instantly coming into conflict with the tribes already there. Around 270, they moved on to the Danube, where they made a pact with Rome to stay on the northern bank. When the Goths arrived, they begged the Romans in vain for permission to relocate. But defeats by both the Goths and the Huns forced them west, following the Danube into present-day Slovakia, Austria, and Switzerland. Still dogged by the Huns, they reached the Rhine in 406, where they ran into the Franks and lost tens of thousands of lives in the ensu-ing battles. In 409, the Vandals crossed the Pyrenees into Spain, where their settlements were soon threatened by the migrating Visigoths. In 429, they finally traversed the Strait of Gibraltar to Africa, where they fought off Roman troops and Berbers to found the Vandal kingdom.

For the Vandals, Goths, Burgundians, Saxons, and the many other migrating peoples, their odysseys towards the temperate farmlands of Western and Southern Europe were long, arduous, and violent. These were not short, sharp, mili-tary invasions but a *Völkerwanderung*: sustained migration crises caused by a combination of climatic change, hardship, insecurity, and the lure of wealth. They rapidly spiralled out of control, first into wars with the peoples already inhabiting the lands they entered, and then, fatally, with the Roman Empire itself. The armies of the migrating peoples contained tens of thousands: the Hun army that reached the Roman heartland, for example, fielded around 60,000 warriors. But even hordes as large as this would probably not have prevailed if the im-perial structures had not already corroded from inside.

The Fall of Rome

In April 248, hundreds of thousands of Roman citizens flocked to the Colosseum and the Circus Maximus. Banquets were laid on, extra bread handed out to the poor. Special coins were stamped with slogans like *Romae Aeternae* and *Saecu-lum Novum* to commemorate a new age for the eternal city. According to the Roman calendar, the city had been founded exactly 1,000 years earlier, a millennium adorned by a long chain of triumphal arches. The Romans undoubtedly enjoyed their celebrations, even though many must have wondered whether the empire's future would continue to be triumphant. Rome had just recovered from a turbulent period during which five emperors ruled in less than a year. The city had been engulfed in religious strife between pagans and the growing community of Christians who no longer wished to stay hidden away in its underground catacombs. In 250, the new emperor, Decius, ordered that all citizens must pray to the gods of Rome. Ominously, the decree was followed by an outbreak of plague that, at its peak, killed 5,000 victims a day in the capital city.

The Christian writer and recently appointed Bishop of Carthage, Cyprian, wrote of a world order that was passing away.[7] Only heaven could bring salvation from plague and oppression. Meanwhile, messages reached the capital with news of emergencies on the empire's borders. The emperor at the time of Rome's millenary, Philip the Arab, had been forced to sign an embarrassing peace treaty with the Sasanians in the east, surrendering all claims on Armenia and paying a large indemnity, in order to have his hands free to defend the northern frontier. The late fifth-century Byzantine historian Zosimus wrote of universal confusion and feebleness at the time. 'Observing that the emperors were unable to defend the state, but neglected all without the walls of Rome, the Goths, the Scythians, the Burgundians, and the Carpi once more plundered the cities of Europe of all that had been left in them, while in another quarter, the Sasanians invaded Asia.'[8]

But if the humiliating treaty with the Sasanians showed

the limitations of Rome's power when faced by another empire, its military capabilities were still superior to those of the Goths and other Germanic tribes. The empire's northern frontiers were protected by major rivers serving as formidable natural barriers, by networks of fortresses, roads, and supply chains that had been built up over centuries, by warships that patrolled the rivers and seas, and, of course, by a formidable army. Numbering over 300,000 soldiers in total, the Roman army was equipped with better weapons and possessed heavy artillery, and engineering capabilities, that none of the barbarians had at their disposal.

Rome's problem for now, therefore, was not military but political weakness. Even if some emperors temporarily halted the forces of fragmentation within the empire, the average reign was only three years during the century that followed the millenary. In 293, Diocletian (284–305) attempted to stem the crisis in imperial authority by appointing three co-rulers, each responsible for governing part of the empire. Diocletian's reign was emblematic of the paradoxes that haunted the Roman Empire. On the one hand, there were no limits to its military ambition. Fortresses were refurbished, the army expanded, and campaigns launched against enemies outside the imperial borders. Foreign delegates were forced to abase themselves in the traditional Persian style, lying flat on the ground in the presence of the emperor. 'We – protectors of the human race – are agreed that justice must intervene,' Diocletian proclaimed, 'so that the long-hoped solution which men could not supply for themselves may, by our foresight, be applied to the general betterment of all.'[9] This was still the imperialist ethos at its purest.

On the other hand, Diocletian struggled to cope with social unrest within the empire caused by massive price inflation. The emperor tried his hand at populism, singling out wealthy speculators for blame: 'Although they each wallow in the greatest riches, with which nations could have been satisfied, they chase after personal allowances and hunt down their chiseling percentages. On their greed the logic of our shared humanity urges us to set a limit.'[10] More significant were his catastrophic policies of debasing the coinage, attempting to impose maximum prices, and increasing taxes to pay for the greater military expenditure. Tax revolts broke out all over the empire.

It required a renewed bout of civil war before the strong government and reforms of the Emperor Constantine (306–37) brought a period of relief. To help control the rampant inflation, he introduced a new gold coin, the *solidus*. He sought to end the blight of religious violence between pagans and Christians by issuing the Edict of Milan in 313, which recognized the right to religious freedom. Although Constantine did not convert to Christianity until he was on his deathbed, his edict is traditionally regarded as the point at which the Roman Empire formally ceased from persecuting Christians and began to adopt the faith. Of similar long-term significance for the empire was Constantine's decision to move the capital to the strategically situated old Greek city of Byzantium – refounded, in 330, as Constantinople – in order to increase his grip over the restive but wealthy eastern provinces and facilitate the renewed centralization of imperial authority.[11]

In reality, however, the fourth century saw the Roman Empire increasingly split into western and eastern halves, with rival emperors ruling from Rome and Constantinople. Nevertheless, the empire remained resolved to defend its northern borders, understanding very well that if the barbarians crossed the Rhine and seized the Alpine passes or traversed the Danube and conquered the Hungarian Plain, it would take them a matter of days to march into Central Italy. Although emperors like Constantine and, later, Valentinian I (364–75) could still inflict pulverizing defeats on their barbarian foes, the empire continued to fray. Rome increasingly came to rely on poorly trained barbarian manpower for its defence, both within its legions and as *foederati*, and on gold to buy peace. The turbulence harmed trade and agriculture in the provinces, while the rich living in the major cities spent like there was no tomorrow. Heavy taxation and tax revolts were the result. When several years of bad weather led to famine, the situation got completely out of hand.

In 356, open war erupted with a confederation of Germanic tribes known as the Alamanni. The neighbouring Salian Franks ultimately had to be granted the land they had settled on around the River Scheldt and accepted as *foederati*. In 363, Rome agreed on new annual payments of gold to pacify the Sasanians. This time, the senate decided to consult the oracular Sibylline Books. 'For all the wealth that Rome took from tributary Asia, three times as much shall Asia take from Rome, requiting upon her her cursed arrogance,' they prophesied. 'And for all the men who were taken from Asia to go and dwell in Italy, twenty times so many men of Italy shall serve in Asia as penniless slaves.'[12] A few years later, civil war broke out at the worst imaginable moment.

The arrival of the Huns on the Pontic-Caspian Steppe had driven the Goths from their homelands and forced them desperately to appeal for permission to cross the Danube into the empire and settle on the southern bank. Rome failed to take the situation seriously. 'When foreign envoys begged with prayers and protestations that an exiled race [the Goths] might be received on our side of the river,' wrote the soldier-historian Ammianus, 'the affair caused more joy than fear.'[13] The ensuing refusal triggered a major new border war that only ended in 382, when the Goths accepted the status of *foederati* in return for the right to remain south of the Danube. But still the situation continued to deteriorate. As the chronicler Prosper recorded: 'A savage storm of barbaric disturbance lay over Italy.'[14]

Following the death of the Emperor Theodosius in 395, the empire was formally divided. From now on, there would be two Roman Empires: the Western, with Rome as its capital; and the Eastern, ruled from Constantinople. But even with the empire split in two, at least the appearance of its traditional imperial prestige was maintained. Coins still depicted emperors slaying foreign foes, but were now minted from worthless copper. Triumphal arches were still erected, but the sculptures were often recycled from earlier monuments. On the pedestal of an obelisk in Istanbul, one can still see the Emperor Theodosius proudly looking down on kneeling barbarians. In the tradition of the Pax Romana, Constantine and Theodosius issued laws and protocols governing foreign relations. Writers like the late fourth-century statesman Quintus Aurelius Symmachus recounted how, during peace talks, the emperor was escorted by a host of splendidly equipped cavalry bearing magnificent standards in an attempt to intimidate barbarian opponents.

For most of their diplomacy, though, late Roman emperors relied on embassies – sometimes granted full authority to negotiate on behalf of their imperial masters – and envoys recruited for their familiarity with the language and culture of particular peoples. The senate still formally received foreign delegates and conferred over the taxes required to finance wars. But from the time of Diocletian onwards, most emperors were advised by a *sacrum consistorium* of senior officials in the imperial administration. After Theodosius, though, Roman diplomacy grew increasingly dysfunctional, with treaties no longer drafted as carefully as they once had been.[15]

At the end of 406, the northern border of the Western Roman Empire collapsed as the Alamanni, Vandals, and Suevi flooded over the Rhine into northern Gaul. Roman troops were rushed from Britain to meet the threat, leaving its shores undefended against major Saxon raids. 'The four plagues of sword, famine, pestilence and wild beasts rage[d] everywhere throughout the world,' recorded the chronicler Hydatius.[16] But worse was still to come. In 408, the Visigoths – those tribes that had been settled on the Danube in 382 – invaded Italy to avenge the massacre there of the families of Gothic *foederati* fighting in Gaul, whose loyalty had been doubted. As the Visigothic army descended on Rome, attempts to buy it off with vast amounts of tribute and the offer of extravagant honours failed. A long siege followed. 'Receiving no relief, and all their provisions being consumed, the famine, as might be expected, was succeeded by a pestilence, and all places were filled with dead bodies.'[17] It was left to slaves finally to open the gates.

It was the year 410. Rome had fallen to a foreign enemy for the first time in eight centuries. By the time the siege was over the city's population had halved to 500,000 inhabitants. 'The brightest light of the whole world is extinguished; indeed the head has been cut from the Roman empire,' lamented the historian and theologian Jerome.[18] The Visigoths soon abandoned the city laden with booty, but the death struggle of the Western Roman Empire continued for decades as the Huns, the Germanic peoples, and Roman warlords turned its provinces into a battlefield. Finally, in 476, Flavius Odoacer, a Roman general of barbarian stock, deposed the Emperor Romulus Augustulus. Although Odoacer purported to be acting under the auspices of the Eastern emperor, his troops soon proclaimed him king of Italy in his own right. The Western Roman Empire had finally fallen.

Across the Adriatic, however, the Eastern Roman Empire remained a formidable realm that reached from the Danube to the Red Sea. Its capital, Constantinople, contained around 500,000 inhabitants, and was augmented by shiploads of refugees from the Italian Peninsula. Its architecture already rivalled that of Rome. It had palaces, churches, a hippodrome, cisterns, aqueducts, bath houses, and a central square, the Augustaion, in the style of the Roman forum – all protected by mighty walls.

In the watershed year of 476, the Eastern Roman Empire

was ruled by Zeno (474–91), and he did everything in his power to uphold ancient glories. He received embassies seated on a high throne and robed in purple. Coins were issued with the diademed ruler spearing a fallen enemy. But he approached the turmoil in the west with a mixture of pomp and pragmatism. Unable to intervene militarily, he attempted to exert authority over Odoacer by granting him the highest honour, the title of patrician. When Odoacer shrugged off Zeno's imperial overlordship to become king of Italy, the emperor pursued a similar policy with the Gothic king Theoderic, who eventually defeated and murdered Odoacer in 493.

Meanwhile, in 482, Zeno had to address growing fissures between the Christian sects in the Eastern Empire. The *Henoticon*, his failed attempt to reconcile the opposing Church leaders, opens with an impressive fanfare of titles and epithets – 'the emperor Caesar Zeno, pious, victorious, triumphant, supreme, ever worshipful Augustus' – but ends up almost begging for peace and unity. 'The origin and constitution, the might and invincible defence, of our sovereignty is the only right and true faith.'[19] The seeds of a century-long schism between emperor and Church were sown. In 494, Pope Gelasius took the initiative to make the case for the supremacy of papal authority to Zeno's successor, Anastasius (491–518). 'There are two things, august emperor, by which this world is chiefly ruled, the consecrated authority of bishops and the royal power,' he expounded in a letter to Zeno. 'Of these, the bishops bear a burden which is so much the weightier as they must render an accounting in the divine judgment even for the kings of mankind.'[20] The emperor chose quietly to ignore the pope. He pragmatically continued to deploy bishops as diplomats and concentrated on the security of the empire instead.

Anastasius embarked on the refortification of the empire's eastern frontier, as well as the construction of a wall running from the Sea of Marmara to the Black Sea to protect Constantinople from landward attack. He continued the diplomatic fiction of bestowing imperial honours on various Germanic kings in the West: some were made patricians, others honorary consuls, some even 'ministers of public amusement' (*tribuni voluptatum*). The bishop-historian Gregory of Tours recorded the ceremony when the Frankish king Clovis was made consul after defeating the Goths in 507:

> Letters reached Clovis from the Emperor Anastasius to confer the consulate on him. In Saint Martin's church he stood clad in a purple tunic and the military mantle, and he crowned himself with a diadem. He then rode out on his horse and with his own hand showered gold and silver coins among the people present . . . From that day on he was called Consul or Augustus.[21]

Events such as Clovis's honorary consulship mark the start of an important new chapter in the history of Western Europe: the ambition of Christian kings to resurrect some of the greatness of the Roman Empire and adopt the mantle of its most illustrious rulers – Julius Caesar, Augustus, and the like. Europe's political order continued to evolve, but the imperial culture of Rome – its legends, its heroes, and its symbols – was preserved.

The Uprising of the Barbarians

In China, the collapse of the Han Dynasty in 220 was followed by an era of confusion, war, and genocide, in which tens of millions died. All traditional values were questioned: most notably, the Seven Sages of the Bamboo Grove suggested alcohol, individualism, free sex, and homosexuality as means of escaping the sorrows of the age.

Three kingdoms dominated the political map of China: the Wei, the Wu, and the Shu. The Wei ruled over most of the North China Plain. Power here had passed from the heirs of the Han Dynasty to warlords of the Cao family, who famously refused the heavenly mandate because becoming emperor, they feared, 'felt like being cooked on a stove'. To the south, on both sides of the Yangtze, the kings of Wu ruled over a fragmented, shifting realm that stretched all the way to the Red River. The kingdom of Shu ruled over the middle and upper reaches of the Yangtze; its centre of power was the Sichuan Plain, around the modern city of Chengdu. The three kingdoms maintained close trade relations, their different geographies and climates making their markets complementary. The Shu invested heavily in irrigation projects, became successful cotton growers, and traded luxury goods with Central Asia. The Wu had a flourishing agricultural economy, specialized in crafts like green glazed pottery, and built a merchant fleet that sailed to the Korean Peninsula and India. The situation of the Wei was more problematic. They were badly hit by climate change, drought, and depopulation. Wheat, consequently, had to be imported from the south. Under the threat of famine, the Wei were sharp-set and ambitious.

Trade relations between the three kingdoms notwith-standing, the overlapping spheres of interest turned the plains between the Yangtze and the Yellow River into a battleground. An early alliance between the Shu and the Wu did not survive tensions over the city of Jingzhou, a trade hub on the Yangtze. Aware of the turmoil in the Wei kingdom, the Shu launched five major expeditions in six years to con-quer it. On each of these occasions, hundreds of thousands of warriors were called to arms. The Shu bribed the Xianbei and Qiang to open a second front, but the Wei held firm, launched a counter-offensive, and conquered the rival capital in 263.

That same year, the Wei Dynasty was overthrown by a warlord called Sima Yan. Sima Yan had no problems with the imperial title: when he seized power from the Wei, he pro-claimed that he would avenge the Han Dynasty, a clear aim at the mandate of heaven. In 266, he assumed the title Emperor Wu, formally inaugurating the Western Jin Dynasty. Sima's eyes now turned to the kingdom of Wu. As the fourteenth-century *Romance of the Three Kingdoms* – one of the great prose classics of Chinese literature – put it: 'The towns and walls of Han were in new hands, the hills and streams of Wu would soon follow.'[22] He went all out to delegitimize his Wu rival. His advisors told him to move fast: 'Sun Hua's tyranny has reached the extreme of violence and cruelty. He can be conquered without a battle. But if Sun Hua should pass from the scene and a capable sovereign come to the throne, your majesty might find it very difficult to conquer the southern land.'[23] To reach the Wu capital across the Yangtze, Sima

Yan's troops reportedly worked for seven years on a fleet of warships. In 280, the Wu surrendered.

Most of the territory of the three kingdoms was reunified, but only in name. Sima Yan was never able fully to assert his power and had to rely on local princes to govern his realm. His successor lost control entirely. The annals describe how the Western Jin state was afflicted by infighting, hailstorms, earthquakes, fires, and the worship of mammon. Plagues of locusts devoured the rice crop; when one official informed the emperor that his people were eating grass because of this, he cynically retorted: 'Why don't they eat meat porridge?'[24] Writers from that time lambasted the Western Jin emperors for their decadence and immorality. 'To oppose the rites and injure the teachings [of Confucius] – there is no greater crime than this,' railed the Jin statesman Bian Kun.[25]

The mayhem that caused the demise of the Western Jin, as various members of the imperial family competed for the throne, was called the War of the Eight Princes (291–306). Meanwhile, dark clouds had also gathered over the outer borders of the disintegrating dominion of the Western Jin. Just west of the North China Plain, on the plateau of today's Shanxi Province, a charismatic leader had united many of the tribes of the Xianbei. Continuing merely to raid the plains, he argued, was not an option; they should conquer them once and for all. 'I have witnessed the past generations to raid and plunder the frontier peoples, and though there was some gain, the loot seized was not worth the cost in casualties, so they again had to call together raids and hostilities,' he said. 'The hundred surnames suffer in misery; it is not a long-term tactic.'[26]

The Xianbei leaned against an open door. Chinese princes, their own resources exhausted, turned once again to the barbarians to aid their internecine struggles. The Shu called on the Qiang and soon had to witness how their new allies captured their capital, Chengdu, in 304. A renegade general of the Western Jin now approached the Xiongnu, who had formerly been tied to the imperial court through marriage alliances and the taking of princely hostages. One of those erstwhile hostages, Liu Yuan, saw the invitation as an opportunity to declare himself emperor of the new state of Han Zhao, march on the great cities of Luoyang and Chang'an, capture the Jin emperor – and make him his butler.

The Xiongnu invasion was cataclysmic. The North China Plain was overrun by tens of thousands of barbarian warriors. 'Arrows flew like raindrops, and the light of the fires filled the sky.'[27] The Western Jin may have mobilized as many as 700,000 soldiers against them; records speak of 100,000 dead soldiers piled on top of one another in a single heap. Famine, disease, and depopulation afflicted the North China Plain. In an act of despair, the Jin wheedled the Xianbei with the titles of duke and prince of Dai. But it was too late, and the Xianbei took advantage of the turmoil to found their own kingdom in 310.

This period, known as the Uprising of the Five Barbarians (304–16), changed the political landscape entirely. The Jin realm had been reduced to the areas south of the Yellow River; henceforth, the dynasty was referred to as the Eastern Jin. The barbarians who took over great swathes of the North China Plain continued to war with local princes and each other with barely a break. In 340, a Xianbei warlord massacred 200,000 people. In 354, an Eastern Jin expedition against the Xianbei cost 40,000 lives. In 383, a war between the Eastern Jin and the Qiang state of Qin left 700,000 casualties. These were just the most noteworthy tragedies.

Exploiting the attritional conflict of the Eastern Jin and the Qin, the Xianbei made another bid for supremacy. This time, they expanded their realm from the middle reaches of the Yellow River down to the Yellow Sea. In 399, a convocation of Xianbei tribes declared their leader Emperor Daowu of the Northern Wei. This new barbarian dynasty aspired to be the equal of the great Chinese dynasties of the past. 'The mandate was sent down by high heaven,' Daowu proclaimed. 'My thoughts are to bring peace to the commoners. I have reverently carried out punishment in accordance with heaven. I have killed Liu Xian, slaughtered [Liu] Wei Chen, pacified the Murong, and settled the central Xia lands . . . May the deities of heaven and earth bestow their great blessing upon the court of Wei, and forever pacify the four directions.'[28] Daowu adopted the traditions of formal consultations with court advisors and of receiving the tribute of lesser rulers and keeping their family members as hostages. Ambassadors were dispatched to the Qin, the Eastern Jin, and the nomadic Rouran tribes.

For more than a century, the Northern Wei ruled over the northern banks of the Yellow River. Their first emperors kept at a distance from the ongoing struggles on the other side of the river to their south and between the nomadic tribes in the north. Most of them embraced Buddhism and pursued a policy of Sinicization. As the Northern Wei court grew ever more luxuriant, they constructed monumental shrines, like the temple caves at Yungang, where finely carved steles and statues of bodhisattvas blend nomadic and Chinese styles. Like previous imperial dynasties, they delegated the defence of the border to tribes on the periphery. Once again, the policy paved the way for ambitious generalissimos. By the turn of the sixth century, the Northern Wei Empire had started to crumble.

Meanwhile, the Eastern Jin had recovered and consolidated their power on the southern banks of the Yellow River. Most emperors were the puppets of military leaders who used the barbarian threat as a pretext to bolster their own status through countless campaigns. The threat of war hung permanently over the southern regions. Yet economically, at least, the Eastern Jin flourished. The leadership was strong enough to keep the realm nominally united, but was too weak to enforce strict control. This environment stimulated private initiative, trade, and agricultural innovation. The Eastern Jin capital, Jiankang, became an artistic and commercial centre with connections as far away as the Indian Ocean. This was the age of inventions like the mobile mill for grinding grains, and the mechanical puppet-theatre; the age when the use of paper for writing became widespread and calligraphy developed into an art form; and the age of great poets like Xie Daoyun:

> Looking toward Jiankang city,
> the little river flows against the current.
> in front, one sees sons killing fathers,
> and behind, one sees younger brothers killing older brothers.

These lines were written in around 420. The Eastern Jin Dynasty had just surrendered to the ambitions of their most prominent general, Liu Song. The Jin's reign was over; its realm ruptured, first into two and then four parts. The Chinese heartland would not be unified again before 581. It was in this context that the teachings of Pure Land Buddhism became very popular. Through enlightenment, adherents could leave behind the world of sorrows for a bird-filled paradise of peace and plenty. The escapism of the Pure Land's teachings coincided with a particular low in China's history. The period from the third to the sixth century was characterized by savage political anarchy far more than by imperial order. Even the dynasties of the Western and Eastern Jin were riven with weakness and struggled to control the heartland between the Yangtze and Yellow Rivers.

The Sasanians

Tremors from the twin downfalls of China and Rome were felt across much of the rest of Eurasia. 'From inside China I have heard worse, not better, news day by day,' wrote one Silk Road trader. 'I stay here in Guzang and I do not go hither and thither, and there is no caravan departing from here.'[29] Another merchant was astonished by what he had heard. 'The last emperor, so they say, fled from Luoyang because of the famine, and fire was set to his palace and to the city, and the palace was burnt and the city [destroyed],' he reported in a letter. 'Luoyang is no more . . . and the Indians and the Sogdians there had all died of starvation.'[30] At the other end of the Silk Road, in Palestine, Jerome described the sack of Rome in similar terms:

Who would believe that Rome, built up by the conquest
of the whole world, had collapsed, that the mother of
nations had become also their tomb; that the shores of the
whole East, of Egypt, of Africa, which once belonged to the
imperial city, were filled with the hosts of her men-servants
and maidservants; that we should every day be receiving in
this holy Bethlehem men and women who once were noble
and abounding in every kind of wealth, but are now
reduced to poverty?[31]

To the Sasanian Empire – the main power lying between
China and Rome – the fall of the two other empires was a
mixed blessing. The objective of the Sasanians was to build a
realm that was stronger and richer than that of their predecessors, the Parthians. Sasanian propagandists damned the
Parthians for corruption, tyranny, and incompetence, and
applauded the new dynasty for its kindliness, its encouragement of agriculture, and its protection of trade routes
against robbers.[32]

In the tradition of the Achaemenid Dynasty, the Sasanian
rulers claimed the Zoroastrian god Ahuramazda sanctioned
their status as 'kings of kings' (shahanshah). In the cliff face
at Naqsh-e Rustam – the burial place of the Achaemenids – a
rock carving of the first Sasanian king, Ardashir I, portrays
him on a horse trampling the last Parthian ruler. 'This is the
figure of the Mazda-worshipping Lord Ardashir, shahanshah
of Persia, who is descended from the gods.' The message
was spelled out in Persian, Parthian, and Greek, highlighting the heterogeneity of the Sasanian Empire. The Parthians
had sought to handle the challenges such diversity posed to

their rule with a policy of tolerance. Initially, the Sasanians followed suit; but as they became more successful, their attitudes hardened.

Benefiting from the weakness of Rome, Ardashir's son, Shapur I (240–70), overran Syria in 250, avenging an earlier defeat. According to Shapur:

> When at first we had become established in the empire, Gordian Caesar raised in all of the Roman Empire a force from the Goth and German realms and marched on Babylonia . . . Gordian Caesar was killed and the Roman force was destroyed. And the Romans made Philip Caesar. Then Philip Caesar came to us for terms, and to ransom their lives, gave us 500,000 *denars*, and became tributary to us . . . And Caesar lied again and did wrong to Armenia. Then we attacked the Roman Empire and annihilated at Barbalissos a Roman force of 60,000, and Syria and the environs of Syria we burned, ruined and pillaged all.[33]

The victories of Shapur I demonstrated the Sasanian Empire's ascendancy over Rome. Although a new treaty ceded the Sasanians control over a large part of Armenia in 271, it was not enough. In 315, Shapur II (309–79) invaded Armenia to 'reconquer what had belonged to his ancestors'. He declared Zoroastrianism the official religion of the Sasanian Empire. Its forced imposition led to the persecution of Jews, Christians, and Buddhists. Religious repression was partly a way to strengthen royal prestige, and partly a ploy against Rome and Constantinople, which by now had embraced Christianity. Rome retaliated: 'Our task is to wipe out a most pernicious people, on whose swords the blood of our kin is not yet dry.'[34] But the Sasanians prevailed. With the Roman threat waning, Sasanian attention moved to the east. Shapur II mounted several campaigns in Central Asia, which brought the Sasanians into competition with the Huns. To help counter the Hun threat, the Sasanians attempted to cultivate the friendship of the Xianbei, sending them envoys and a gift of tame elephants.

From the fifth century onwards, wars with the Huns along both the northern and eastern borders of the Sasanian Empire became more frequent. The Sasanian kings prevailed and used the opportunity provided by this victory to try to force concessions from the Eastern Roman Empire, which had been more seriously afflicted by Hunnic invasions. Constantinople proved a tougher military rival than the Huns, though. So the most King Bahram V could extract was a treaty that recognized the rights of Zoroastrians in the Eastern Roman Empire and Christians under the Sasanians. In 445, Ctesiphon and Constantinople signed a new deal: the Sasanians would be paid for defending Anatolia from incursions by the Huns through the eastern mountain passes.

At its peak, the Sasanian Empire stretched from the Euphrates to the Hindu Kush and from the Aral Sea to the Indian Ocean. Its riches impressed even Chinese envoys. The capital, Ctesiphon, had over 100,000 households, they reported. As for the rest of the empire: 'The land is fairly level and produces gold, silver, coral, amber, very fine pearls, vitreous ware and glass; crystals, diamonds, iron, copper, cinnabar, mercury; damask, embroidery, cotton, carpeting and tapestry. The climate is very hot and families keep ice in their houses.'[35] The reception of foreign dignitaries at the court was overwhelming. The Sasanians built immense vaulted brick halls. Their weight required the palace walls beneath them to look like fortresses. The impression of sturdiness was something the kings cultivated for themselves through heroic triumphal reliefs and martial statues, both in the tradition of the Achaemenids. But it was counterbalanced by the dazzling refinement of Sasanian tapestry, jewellery, glazed tiles, frescoes, poetry, and music.

The Sasanians pursued an aggressive policy to control trade along both the overland Silk Road and its maritime equivalent in the Indian Ocean. Ports and settlements were built near strategic chokepoints, like the Bab-el-Mandeb and the Strait of Hormuz, which connect the Red Sea and the Persian Gulf to the Indian Ocean. Even if trade was damaged by the turmoil in Rome and China, the Silk Road continued to serve markets like Egypt, the Levant, India, and Southeast Asia.

Merchants and envoys entering the Sasanian Empire had to announce themselves to the *marzbans*, noblemen who administered and guarded the border provinces. They were also part of the much larger martial aristocracy that furnished the empire's chief military asset: heavily armoured cavalry. As this suggests, Sasanian society was rigidly stratified. The *Denkard*, a compendium of Zoroastrian beliefs, warned: 'Know that the decadence of states begins when one permits the subjects to practice other than their traditional occupations.'[36] In fact, the empire does seem to have been plagued by social unrest at the end of the fifth century. A radical preacher named Mazdak attracted widespread support for a social revolution – involving land reform, subsidies

for the poor, and the abolition of the privileges of conservative clerics – in order to reverse growing inequality. At the
same time, tensions between the court and nobility, not least
among the *marzbans*, escalated into open conflict. The nadir
was reached after 458, when pretenders to the imperial throne
first brought the Hephthalite Huns into the empire from
which they had so long been kept at bay. In 475, the Hun presence was powerful enough to force the king to pay tribute.
Now 'chaos and famine ruled and women were shared by all'.[37]

The Guptas

About forty days' travel east from the Indus River border
of the Sasanian Empire lay a small kingdom in the Ganges
Valley. This was the homeland of the Guptas. Their early history is not well documented, but evidence of a marriage between the dynasty's founder, Chandragupta (320–35), and a
princess of the powerful Magadha kingdom attests to their
growing prominence. Through conquest and alliances, Chandragupta incorporated dozens of other small kingdoms along
the Ganges. Like the Sasanian rulers, he titled himself 'king
of kings' (*maharajadhiraja*). Sixty years later, the Gupta
realm stretched from the Indus to the Bay of Bengal. It was
the first time in centuries, after the Maurya dynasty, that
a native Indian dynasty had been so powerful. The Guptas
profited from the downfall of the Kushan Empire and the
fragmentation that followed, but their rise was also facilitated by the smooth succession of Chandragupta's son, the
potent king Samudragupta (335–80).

Samudragupta, like his father, was a capable strategist

and commander. Many neighbouring rulers were coaxed into matrimonial alliances. Others were bound by a ritual called the *Ashwamedha yajna*, whereby a ruler acknowledged his submission by accepting the gift of a horse. Those who refused the horse faced a formidable war machine, consisting of elephants, armoured cavalry, archers who used humidity-resistant steel bows, and a well-equipped riverine navy that allowed the Guptas to project their power along the banks of the Ganges and inland from coastal waters.[38] Because northern India was a patchwork of statelets and tribes, the Guptas' expansion was hard to stop. It was aided by the alliance they maintained throughout this period with the Vakataka kingdom, the dominant state on the northern Deccan Plateau.

The Gupta heartland was governed directly by the king, who was supported by a cabinet and an assembly, the *sabha*.[39] Vassal kings paid tribute and sent their sons to the Gupta court. Relations with tribes in the forests and kingdoms in the northern mountains were much less formalized. The ancient *Arthashastra* of Kautilya resurfaced as a practical guide to diplomacy. It inspired much of the work of the influential Gupta writer Kamandaka, who asserted that the anarchic nature of politics meant the ideal form of rule was paternal despotism (*nitisara*). A good king should always prioritize national interests, maintain a modern army – yet prevent it from depleting the treasury or causing the neglect of agriculture – and never expect foreign alliances to last. Kamandaka also made the case for just wars, arguing that force should be used only after the failure of strategies such as conciliation (*sama*), bribery (*dana*), or sowing dissension (*bheda*).

Gupta kingship had much in common with that of the

Maurya, as expressed not only in the *Arthashastra* but also in the edicts of Ashoka. The king was expected to uphold the rule of law (*dandaniti*) and refrain from harshness (*krodha*), unjust punishment, and the unwarranted seizure of property. As for more personal qualities, he should be well versed in the arts, music, science, and archery (*dhanurveda*), and not inclined to indulge in women, liquor, or gambling. Inscriptions paired the king's merits as a warrior with qualities like wisdom, calmness, compassion, refinement, and sensitivity. Despite the fact that, in the imperial hierarchy of the Gupta, the gods came first, then the law, and only then the monarch, the Gupta kings made sure their majesty was apparent to all. Their coins were emblazoned with images of them slaying tigers or human foes. Rock carvings proclaimed the Gupta monarch to be the *digvijaya* – the conqueror of the four quarters of the world.

The age of the Guptas witnessed a cultural and intellectual florescence. Sculptors melded Greek and Asian influences into works of exceptional sensuality. Vatsyayana compiled his great erotic treatise, the *Kama Sutra*. Scientists posited that the earth had to be round. Mathematicians developed the numerical system that we still use today. One of the 'nine gems' (*navarathnas*) of the Gupta court was the Sanskrit poet and dramatist Kalidasa, whose writings open a window directly on to its splendour and sensuality. Travellers who came from far afield – such as the Buddhist monk Fa-Hien at the beginning of the fifth century – marvelled at the wealth, luxury, and bounty of the Gupta kingdom.[40]

But the wisdom and majesty of the Gupta kings was soon challenged by the Hephthalite Huns. The Hephthalites had seized the rich trading cities and agricultural zones of the Amu Darya (Oxus) and Ferghana valleys, the heart of the former Bactrian kingdom. Under their aegis, the region flourished as a centre of commercial and cultural exchange, and as an important destination for Buddhist pilgrims, who flocked to its monasteries and religious schools.[41] Now the prospect of monopolizing the caravan routes through the Hindu Kush brought them into conflict with the Guptas, who had similar ambitions of their own. It led to a series of major wars, and caused havoc across the northwestern regions of the Gupta Empire.

At first, the Guptas prevailed. The king had 'accomplished his programme of conquests', it was stated. 'He can now devote himself to the tasks of peace and leave the sword for the flute as worshipper of Vishnu and his consort, Lakshmi.'[42] But the victory came at a price. Through force of circumstance, kings no longer adhered to the precepts of Kamandaka's statecraft, draining the treasury to finance the army, and levying new taxes that brought a halt to economic growth. By the end of the fifth century, a combination of economic weakness, unrest in the border kingdoms, and fresh attacks by the Hephthalite Huns brought the empire to its knees – and the Hephthalites to dominate, albeit briefly, much of Central Asia and northern India.

Killing Beasts for the Buddha

Until its collapse, the Gupta Empire served as the main hub of the trade system that had emerged during the previous centuries. Via the passes of the Hindu Kush, it traded with the Sasanians and Central Asia; via the Indian Ocean with China, Southeast Asia, Sri Lanka, the Arabian Peninsula, East Africa, and the Eastern Roman Empire. The expansion of trade coincided with the expansion of cities and kingdoms outside the traditional centres of power.[43] One of them was the kingdom of Funan. An inscription called it a 'realm of mud', because it had emerged from the marshy Mekong Delta.[44] The Chinese records described it as the place where East and West met, because its ports connected the South China Sea with the Indian Ocean. They were served by sailors from Malaysia, who perfected their skills in navigating between the hundreds of islands of the Southeast Asian Archipelago.[45] They transported gems, pearls, sandalwood, gum, and spices. In the third century, Funan seems to have paid tribute to the Eastern Jin, exchanged frequent diplomatic missions with them, and supplied them with significant numbers of trained elephants. The Chinese sources also indicated that five lesser kings in present-day Myanmar and Laos acknowledged Funan as overlord.

Chinese travellers marvelled at the abundance of luxurious goods in Southeast Asia, not only in Funan, but also in kingdoms like Taruma, in modern Indonesia, and Langkasuka, in modern Malaysia. Even though territories in the region specialized in the production of different wares, competition for trade and the control of sea lanes was merciless. The same held true in Southern Asia. The Guptas relentlessly tried to control trade; and after their downfall, competition continued between other kingdoms. The Pandyan Kingdom on the southeastern coast of India vied with Sri Lankan kings for domination over commerce in the Palk Strait. The rich natural resources of Sri Lanka made it an immense and tempting prize. In the fifth century, the Pandyans invaded the island in 429 and ruled it for several decades. In 455, they were pushed out, but this episode of oppression stirred Sri Lankan nationalism. The *Mahavamsa*, a historical and religious epic from the period, equated the killing of invaders with the killing of wild beasts: it was the will of the Buddha that the island's inhabitants should defend its independent sovereignty. 'Unbelievers and men of evil life' were 'not more to be esteemed than beasts,' it read. 'But as for thee, you will bring glory to the doctrine of the Buddha in manifold ways; therefore cast away care from your heart, O ruler of men!'[46]

Northeast Asia too saw the spread of Buddhism, trade, and migration. With China losing its imperial lustre, Manchuria, the Korean Peninsula, the East China Sea, and the Japanese Archipelago were transformed into a playground for several ambitious lesser powers: for example, the Yan – of Xianbei origin, but claiming the heavenly mandate – or the kingdoms of Baekje and Silla in the south of the Korean Peninsula. In Japan, the Yamato controlled most of Honshu, the largest of the archipelago's islands. Their king governed from a peripatetic court, and functioned more as the leader of a clan federation than a formal monarch.

The most powerful polity, however, was the Goguryeo kingdom in the Korean Peninsula. By 300, it had defeated its rivals in the Manchurian Plains. It embraced Buddhism and its arts reveal both Chinese and nomadic influences.[47] But it was also a martial society. For centuries, Goguryeo had competed with the Xianbei, Silla, and Baekje by means of both diplomacy and open war. Evidence for the scale of the turmoil is provided by the Stele of King Gwanggaeto (391–413), which credited the famed Goguryeo monarch with the unification of the Three Kingdoms of Korea, the defeat of the nomads, the construction of a chain of fortresses in Manchuria, and the imposition of tribute on smaller neighbours. In just one decade, he fought no fewer than ten major battles.[48]

Much further to the west, a similar regional conflict loomed over the Red Sea. With the downfall of the Western Roman Empire in the late fifth century and inability of the Eastern Roman Empire to project the same degree of influence as the earlier Roman Empire, two trading states rushed to fill the void: the Jewish kingdom of Himyar, in present-day Yemen, and the Christian kingdom of Aksum, in present-day Ethiopia. Himyar had already conquered neighbouring states like Hadhramaut and the ancient kingdom of Saba (Sheba), both famed for their production of frankincense. Aksum had grown rich from the export of ivory, elephants, and cotton. The influential third-century Sasanian prophet Mani regarded Aksum as one of the four great powers of the age, along with Rome, the Sasanian Empire, and China. Aksum maintained relations with Constantinople and copied its pomp. A Byzantine visitor reported how the Aksumite monarch received his guests on a golden chariot drawn by four elephants. The mid-fourth century Ezana Stone recorded how one ruler defeated neighbouring states to become the 'king of kings': 'After having subjected their kings, I ordered them to pay a tribute for their territory and to leave in peace navigation and land traffic.'[49] His attack on Himyar was described as a holy war in revenge for killing Christian envoys and as the reclamation of ancestral territory. Campaigns were also staged against the

Nubians, after they had robbed Aksum's envoys and refused demands for submission.

The Blending of Nations

The period between 250 and 500 unfolded like one long crisis of empire, at least for the Mediterranean, Western Europe, and China. Although the collapses of the Roman and Han Empires occurred at different times, they were remarkably similar. Both, at first, became hollowed-out states: they possessed garrisons and fortresses around their perimeters, but increasingly polarized societies within. Their seemingly hard outer shells weakened, however, as garrisons could no longer be paid and barbarians had to be incorporated within the empire. Even so, the pressure from the outside continued to mount, caused by the lure of the wealth that lay tantalizingly within reach and by the impact of environmental change and mass migration. When the borders finally gave way, the result was cataclysmic.

The decline of Han China and imperial Rome, therefore, was not a case of comparative shifts in power – of strong, prosperous states simply being overtaken by more dynamic ones. In both China and Rome, the imperial crisis sparked anarchy, hardship, famine, and population decline. The effect would be much the same if a foreign power invaded Washington today and forced its citizens to relocate to Mexico, or if contemporary Beijing was sacked and millions forced to flee to Korea. The fate of the Han and Roman Empires should also remind us that the barbarian invaders of today are often the citizens of tomorrow.

This blending of nations was not a smooth process. The relocations of people were often brutally violent events. At the same time, though, the assimilating pull of the old civilizations often proved very powerful. The barbarians that invaded China embraced the heavenly mandate with the same eagerness as the Frankish king Clovis cloaked himself in Roman consular purple. This was also true in the more newly established regimes in the Middle East and Southern Asia. The Sasanians adopted the imperial traditions of the great Achaemenid kings – and carved their portraits in the rocks beside those of their Persian forebears – with the same keenness as the Gupta rulers embraced the teachings of Kautilya and Ashoka.

This era witnessed another major geopolitical change: the growing importance of the Indian Ocean and the northern steppes as conduits between peoples. Trade in the Indian Ocean had certainly existed before, but from this period there is strong evidence of growing and more sustained connectivity. The Gupta Empire acted as an interface between the Middle East and Southeast Asia, where new trading kingdoms became prominent. The same was true for the northern steppes beyond the Caspian and Black Seas. The Scythians and other nomadic peoples had travelled over this highway of grass long before, but the speed with which the Huns moved along this corridor, and the magnitude of their migrations, were probably unprecedented. The continental Silk Road, revived after the Sasanians reunified much of the Middle East and Persia, thus now formed the central strand of a tripartite system of east–west trade routes: to the south was a maritime network spanning the Indian Ocean from the

Strait of Malacca to the Strait of Hormuz and the Bab-el-Mandeb; to the north, an overland transit zone across the steppes. Greater knowledge of the magnitude of the Eastern Hemisphere was gained both from expeditions of trade and from expeditions of conquest; and both stimulated the desire to push the boundaries of understanding ever onwards.

CHAPTER 8

In the Name of the Prophet

500–750 CE

North Sea

Baltic Sea

FRANKISH
EMPIRE

Magyar

Danube

Bulgars

• Rome

Constantinople

BYZANTINE
EMPIRE

A
T
L
A
N
T
I
C

O
C
E
A
N

Umayyads

• Córdoba

• Fez

Rustamids

Idrīsids

Aghlabids

Mediterranean Sea

• Tripoli

Fu

Egy

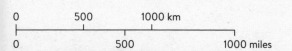

0   500   1000 km

0   500   1000 miles

The Caliphate in the Umayyad
and Early Abbasid Period c. 750

Aral
Sea

Caspian Sea

k Sea

Bukhārā •
• Samarqand

• Antioch

• Nīshāpūr

• Damascus
• Baghdad

Euphrates

• Isfahān

Jerusalem

Persian Gulf

• Medina

Red Sea

• Mecca

Arabian Sea

Gulf of Aden

The fall of the Western Roman Empire, the eclipse of the Han and Jin Dynasties, the failure of the Guptas to preserve power, and the struggles for survival of the Eastern Roman and Sasanian Empires – their cumulative effect was to produce an age of continued imperial crisis and political fracturing, as most of the Eastern Hemisphere was beset by fighting between lesser powers. At the same time, however, the *Völkerwanderung* and the mobility of the nomadic peoples across the steppes demonstrated that the fates of Europe and Asia had become more interconnected. The continuation of this trend over the following centuries was mostly the consequence of the rise of a new major power: the Islamic Caliphate.

Once again, a minor player on the periphery of great powers suddenly exploded to pre-eminence. The first Islamic armies contained a few hundred warriors, or *mujahedin*. But within barely a century the caliphate had conquered an immense realm. Not only had they done so faster than any major imperial power before them, but their realm was also larger than any previous empire, extending from the Pyrenees in the west all the way to the Gobi Desert in the east. Islamic warriors were soon followed by envoys and traders. The diplomatic network of the caliphate spanned almost the entire Eastern Hemisphere. So did its network of commerce, which encompassed most of the Silk Road, the Mediterranean, and the Indian Ocean.

The spectacular rise of the caliphate formed a backdrop to other great events: the struggles for survival of the Sasanian and the Eastern Roman (or Byzantine) Empires; and the rise of two new powers, the Franks in Western Europe and the Tang Dynasty in China. One of the most striking features is the lack of cooperation displayed by the established major powers – the Sasanian and Byzantine Empires – in trying to halt the threat posed by the Arabs. Another is the way that the era's three new powers – the Arabs, the Franks, and the Tang – quickly renounced their barbarian heritage and adopted the traditions and trappings of earlier cultures. The Tang claimed the heavenly mandate, the Franks claimed to inherit the legacy of Rome, and the caliphs abandoned the harsh Arabian desert for the luxurious ancient cities of the Levant. Old imperial practices persisted, but with new patrons.

The Birth of the Caliphate

In 497, in the Arabian city of Mecca, a man of great fame died. His name was Hashim ibn Abd Manaf. He had been an accomplished trader, selling his wares as far afield as Constantinople, Syria, and Ethiopia. But he was also a local benefactor, feeding travellers and arbitrating between the city's feuding clans. It was this combination of commercial cunning and selfless compassion that allowed his tribe, the Quraysh, to dominate Mecca, and Mecca – favourably located as it was not far from the Red Sea, water wells, and caravan routes – to dominate much of the trade across the Arabian Peninsula.

After Hashim's death, the Quraysh preserved their position by promoting harmony between the many tribes, who were torn apart by commercial rivalry and religious conflict. They proposed an annual truce and the establishment of a community of common rituals (*hums*). They sponsored a system of agreements (*ilafs*) guaranteeing access to wells in return for a fee. The Kaaba, a shrine where the Quraysh revered their gods, was declared a sanctuary (*haram*) where travellers could stay in peace, and its holy men arbitrated in conflicts. This all remained power politics on a small scale: Mecca, like other cities on the Arabian Peninsula, was home to only a few thousand people.

Nevertheless, the emergence of Mecca as a minor regional hegemon did attract some suspicion. In 570, the Christian king of Yemen, backed by Constantinople, attacked the city. He failed, but pestilence, internal rivalries, and conflict with other tribes in the so-called Fijar War (580–90) put the leadership of the Quraysh to the test. In an attempt to uphold justice and cooperation, they established a 'league of the virtuous'. It was in the context of such turmoil that the great-grandson of Hashim ibn Abd Manaf, a merchant named Muhammad (570–632), started to preach in favour of one god, Allah, and one community, the *umma*.

Muhammad's religious teachings sought to unite a deeply divided society. Yet the Meccan elite saw Muhammad as a threat, and attempted to counter him with violence. His followers first fled to Ethiopia, where they were offered sanctuary by a Christian king. In 622, after a murder attempt, Muhammad himself sought refuge in Medina, accompanied by his supporters. It was from this desert town that Muhammad's new religion spread. The teachings of Islam were adopted by the quarrelling clans of Medina and translated into a constitution which prescribed peace between all Muslims and kindness towards non-believers. By 631, the numbers of Muslim adherents had swollen to such an extent that Muhammad was able to march on Mecca with an army of 10,000 men. The capture of Mecca was the Prophet's last victory. He died in 632.

Muhammad's successor (*khalifah*, or 'caliph') was his father-in-law, Abu Bakr, who had been the earliest convert to Islam not related by blood to the Prophet. The first caliph subjugated most of the Arab tribes during the Ridda Wars (632–3) and initiated campaigns against the Byzantine and Sasanian Empires in Egypt, Syria, and Mesopotamia to seize the lucrative trade routes already familiar to Muslim merchants. The second caliph, Umar (634–44), completed the task, conquering the great cities of Ctesiphon, Basra, Damascus, Aleppo, Jerusalem, and Alexandria, and shattering the Sasanian Empire.

The imperial ideology of the early caliphs – much like that of many other nascent empires – was founded on the principles of compassion for believers, protection for subservient non-believers, and retribution for those who resisted. The Caliph Umar advised his successors to live soberly, respect the law, and support the poor. He employed heralds to read out proclamations informing citizens of their rights, and established administrative courts to investigate complaints against corrupt officials. He imposed a pact on non-Muslims, granting them security in exchange for submission. 'The dwellings of the non-Muslims must be low,' read one of its articles, 'so that exiting their houses would make them bend and would remind them of their low status.'[1] Even so, Muslims complained that Christians and Jews benefited from government spending while not being obliged to pay *zakat*, the main Islamic tax.

Around that time, clerics wrote down the texts of Muhammad's revelations and teachings – which had been preserved orally by his followers – to form the Quran. The holy book made clear the universal aspirations of Islam: 'Everything in the heavens and earth belongs to God; it is to Him that all things return.'[2] The good life was one of devotion: 'The love of desirable things is made alluring for men – women, children, gold and silver treasures piled up high, horses with fine markings, livestock, and farmland – these may be the joys of this life, but God has the best place to return to.'[3] Inside the *umma*, justice should prevail: 'Do not wrongfully consume each other's wealth . . . Do not kill each other . . . If any of you does these things, out of hostility and injustice, We shall make him suffer Fire.'[4] Outside the *umma*, hostile unbelievers should be subjugated: 'So if they neither withdraw, nor offer you peace, nor restrain themselves from fighting you, seize and kill them wherever you encounter them.'[5]

Although it is unlikely that Muhammad ever envisaged it, within a decade of his death Muslim armies had penetrated as far as the Hindu Kush, the Caucasus, and the Atlas Mountains. But the strains – and spoils – of such conquests ripped the *umma* apart, igniting a civil war. Fault lines existed between the Muslims east of the River Euphrates, who called

themselves Shia, and the Muslims of the western communities, who were known as Sunni. The Sunni Umayyad clan
prevailed, and proclaimed a new caliphate in 661. The centre
of Islamic power shifted from Mecca to the Levant, where
they ruled from Damascus. To aid them in their task, they
appointed *amirs* (governors), established *divans* (ministries), introduced a single currency, and promoted Arabic as
common language. Slavery was outlawed and land redistributed. As testament to the splendour – and devoutness – of
their regime, they constructed the architectural masterpieces
of the Great Mosque in Damascus and the Dome of the Rock
in Jerusalem, two of the holiest sites in Islam.

The Umayyad Dynasty continued relentlessly to expand
its empire, partly to bolster its prestige, partly to channel the
energy of the Arab tribes away from fighting each other, and
partly to take over the Byzantine trade in the Mediterranean.
This was one of the reasons why the first Umayyad caliph,
Muawiya, decided to build a navy, even though it had to be
manned mainly by Christians. He encountered widespread
resentment: those who sail in a ship 'are like worms in a log,'
one critic sneered, 'and if it rolls over they are drowned'.[6] But
the policy paid off. At its height, in the mid-eighth century,
the Umayyad Caliphate ruled a third of the world's population, and reached from the Atlantic to the River Indus and
from the Caucasus Mountains to the Bab-el-Mandeb.

The Impossible Peace

The chronicle of the eighth-century Syrian monk Theophilus
of Edessa, who also served as court astrologer to the caliph,

provides a unique perspective on the sufferings endured by the peoples of the Mediterranean during the Muslim conquests. Describing the campaigns of the Caliph Muawiya, for example, Theophilus recounted how 'The barbarian force had scattered throughout the land . . . to collect gold, slaves and expensive clothing . . . when they felt they had stayed long enough, they embarked their human loot on the ships. What misery and lamentation were seen then! Fathers were separated from their children, daughters from their mothers, brother from brother, some destined for Alexandria, others for Syria.'[7]

But what makes Theophilus' account especially valuable is that he was equally critical of Umayyad aggression and Byzantine ineptitude.[8] He discerned that the successes of the caliphate were to a great extent due to the failings of its enemies, in particular the inability of the Byzantines to cooperate with the other regional power – the Sasanian Empire – to see off the Islamic threat in the seventh century. To understand fully the triumph of the caliphate, therefore, it is vital to appreciate how fundamentally the centuries-old antagonism between the Byzantines and the Sasanians shaped the political situation in the Eastern Mediterranean and Middle East.

One of the chief reasons the Byzantine and Sasanian Empires became so consumed with mutual hostility and distrust was the way their spheres of influence overlapped in Armenia and the Caucasus. Both vied to control a region that acted as a buffer not only between them but also against the peoples of the Central Asian steppe. The wary stand-off was periodically inflamed by one side upgrading its border fortifications.

Despite protestations that this was merely a precautionary measure against the nomadic barbarian threat, each suspected the other of a ploy to tweak the status quo in their own favour. In the first year of his reign, for example, the Byzantine emperor Justinian the Great (527–65) ordered one of his generals to construct a fortress on the border in northern Mesopotamia. 'He accordingly with great haste began to carry out the decision of the emperor, and the fort was already rising to a considerable height by reason of the great number of artisans,' it was reported. 'But the Persians [Sasanians] forbade them to build any further, threatening that, not with words alone but also with deeds, they would at no distant time obstruct the work.'[9] Letters were sent, envoys dispatched, but the bickering sparked a full-scale war.

Friction was not confined to the Armenian–Mesopotamian border in the north. At the mouth of the Red Sea, in 522, the Jewish kingdom of Himyar called on the Sasanians for support against an invasion by the Christian kingdom of Aksum which was backed by Constantinople. In the north of the Arabian Peninsula, the Ghassanid and Lakhmid kingdoms fought proxy wars on behalf of the Byzantines and Sasanians respectively. The two empires also locked horns over the silk trade. In 531, the Emperor Justinian sought to bypass Sasanian control of the overland Silk Road by approaching the Arab kingdoms about trading directly with the East via the Red Sea. He also attempted to establish a Byzantine silk industry with silkworm eggs and knowledge smuggled back from China by Christian monks.

In 532, an eternal peace treaty was signed between Justinian and the Sasanian emperor Khosrow I (531–79). Under pressure from barbarians in the north, Constantinople paid 440,000 gold pieces for the privilege. The peace did not last even a decade. In 562, a fifty-year peace placed a moratorium on fortress building in Armenia; instituted a demilitarized zone between the empires; agreed that future disputes would be settled on the basis that the empires shared equal status; established immunities for diplomats; and designated frontier posts where cross-border trade would be allowed. A decade later, the two empires were at war again. Another eternal accord was signed in 591 – and another war erupted eleven years after. This time, the Sasanian armies reached the walls of Constantinople before the Emperor Heraclius was able to push them back. His counter-offensive took the Byzantine army to the banks of the River Tigris before the Sasanians sued for peace in 628.

Their endless wars left the two empires enfeebled and dependent on frontier kingdoms for their defence. This was the caliphate's chance. Even after Muhammad and his successors had embarked on their conquests, Ctesiphon and Constantinople continued to fight each other. In 637, a Muslim army marched on Ctesiphon. Fourteen years later, the caliphate brought the Sasanian Empire crashing down. In 674, the banners of Islam fluttered before the gates of Constantinople itself.

The Two Lights of the World

Before the Byzantine and Sasanian Empires were overwhelmed by the caliphate, each considered itself the centre of the world and the defender of the true faith. From a geopolitical viewpoint, the Byzantine Empire was both continental and maritime in its orientation, like the Roman Empire before it. It not only ruled an immense area of land, but also controlled much of the Mediterranean and Black Seas. Its population must have been around 40 million people. Constantinople alone had about 500,000 inhabitants. Its most famous landmark, Hagia Sophia – the Church of Holy Wisdom – was completed in 537, one of the prestige projects of Justinian the Great. But shortly before Hagia Sophia was opened, the Neoplatonic Academy of Athens was closed in an effort to stamp out the last vestiges of pagan thought.

Justinian the Great – renowned as the emperor who never slept – was tireless in his efforts to impose Orthodox Christianity as the empire's sole faith. The Musée du Louvre possesses an extraordinary ivory plaque of the triumphant emperor astride a rearing stallion and forcing back a defeated barbarian.[10] Beneath the charger's hooves cringe Asian tribute bearers, who offer him elephant tusks and a tiger. Before the emperor crouches a woman, one breast naked, who personifies the earth. With one hand, she clasps the emperor's foot in supplication; with the other she holds fruit. All this takes place beneath the gaze of Jesus Christ and two winged angels. The message is clear: subjugating the world for Christ was the emperor's mission.

To help further this end, Justinian issued the *Corpus Juris Civilis*, a compilation of Civil law, in 534. The emperor, it stated, was given God's blessing to conquer enemies of the faith. Once the code came into force, for example, any new Jewish synagogues were banned. Byzantine intellectuals debated the qualities of the ideal emperor, drawing on the examples of classical statesmen, generals, king, and emperors, as well as the monarchs of the Old Testament. The *Peri Politikes Epistemes* (*On Political Science*) represented him as a wise philosopher-king: 'The wealth and dearth of the times, which are bound to the rotations of the universe, are not in our power . . . Within our power, however, are justice and injustice, good government and bad government.'[11]

The Byzantines believed not only that they were the heirs of Rome, but that, as Christians, their glory would surpass the pagan Roman emperors. The late sixth-century emperor Maurice made the Byzantine worldview clear in his *Strategikon*. It reveals the Byzantine preoccupation with protecting its chief cities and emporiums: not just Constantinople, but also its commercial centres in the Levant and Egypt. This led them to create buffer zones and to seek to dominate the gateways to the Eastern Mediterranean. The *Strategikon* called for a vigilant policy of defensiveness, restraint, and concealment, 'unless a truly exceptional opportunity or advantage presents itself'.[12] A critical element in its strategic thinking was the navy, which guarded the capital and important trade routes.

The *Strategikon* also mocked the light-haired, faithless barbarians; although it sounded a note of caution about the military prowess of the 'wicked' Sasanians. Like Rome and China, the empire had a department to deal with such foreigners: the 'bureau of barbarians'. From the sixth century, envoys to Constantinople were received in the Chrysotriklinos Hall, a golden octagonal reception room at the heart of the Great Palace on the banks of the Sea of Marmara. 'When the curtain was drawn aside and the inner part was revealed, and when the hall of the gilded building glittered and Tergazis the Avar looked up at the head of the emperor shining with the holy diadem, he lay down three times in adoration and remained fixed to the ground,' we read in the *Strategikon*. 'The other Avars followed him in similar fear and fell on their faces.'[13]

The Sasanians regarded themselves as the equals of the Byzantines. King Khosrow I superscribed the peace treaty of 532 as follows: 'The divine, good, father of peace, ancient Khosro, king of kings, fortunate, pious and beneficent, to whom the gods have given great fortune and a great kingdom, giant of giants, formed in the image of the gods.'[14] He called Justinian his brother and described the empires as two lights, the moon of the west and the sun of the east.

Khosrow is indeed remembered as one of the Sasanian Empire's strongest rulers. While Zoroastrianism remained the empire's official religion, Khosrow pursued a policy of toleration and welcomed pagan Byzantines who fled Justinian's religious zeal. He organized a conference of scholars to discuss the respective merits of different religions and political systems. The brightest immigrants joined the Academy of Gondishapur, where learning flourished under the patronage of the Sasanian king so that it became the world's most important intellectual centre. The king improved irrigation infrastructure in Mesopotamia, built fortresses along the border, and embellished the capital, Ctesiphon, erecting a new palace, the Taq Kasra, where he received foreign guests in a vast vaulted hall. More significant in the long-term were his efforts to recruit cavalry from the lower nobility in exchange for land. While Khosrow had expected this reform to undermine the position of the upper nobility, it also created a new powerful interest group that would defy his weaker successors.

In the decades after Khosrow, the Sasanians continued to expand their borders, but the larger the empire became, the more it suffered from dynastic conflict, over-taxation, religious violence – one king even converted to Christianity – and plague. But the downfall of the Sasanians was also expedited by the alliance formed between the Byzantines and the emerging Göktürk Khaganate. The Göktürks were a nomadic confederacy, originating in Northern China, that had swept aside several other steppe peoples to seize control of much of Central Asia and the Silk Road. In 569, the Byzantines sent a delegation to establish direct trade with the Göktürks and so bypass the Sasanian intermediaries. The Byzantine envoy, Zemarchus, was deeply impressed by his audience with the khan, who was enrobed in silk embroidery, enthroned on gold, and surrounded by golden peacocks and silver animals. Out of these first diplomatic exchanges grew a coalition against the Sasanians. But as much as the Göktürks were valuable to Constantinople for the way their raids chipped away at the borders of the Sasanian Empire, their presence also forced nomadic societies such as the Avars further west, thereby destabilizing the borders of the Byzantine Empire too.

However, nobody at the beginning of the seventh century would have anticipated that these two mighty empires could be defeated by tribes from the Arabian desert. Even exhausted from fighting each other, their armies were immense, their cultural influence was huge, and their wealth unequalled. The armies of the caliphs may have been fresh and motivated, yet they were also divided. The caliphs may have possessed formidable cavalry, but so did the Sasanians and Byzantines. It was the failure of the great powers to make serious efforts to contain the caliphate when it was still small that proved critical. Another demonstration of the domino effect followed: once the Arab tribes had annexed towns on the peripheries of the empires, the caliphs could then draw on their resources to help take the major cities of the interiors. But even as the Muslim armies advanced ever closer, the Byzantines and Sasanians failed to work together. At the same time, the two empires were weakened by internal divisions. In Byzantine Egypt, for instance, Coptic Christians actively supported Muslim troops as a result of Constantinople's rigid Orthodoxy. For the Sasanian Empire, the cumulative effect of all these factors proved fatal. The Byzantine Empire was much reduced, but survived thanks to its powerful navy and the support of allies from elsewhere in Europe.

Western and Eastern Europe

Beyond the borders of the Byzantine Empire, Europe remained divided into small kingdoms. Many of the peoples from the *Völkerwanderung*, which had contributed to the collapse of the Western Roman Empire, had settled in its former provinces, but new fortune seekers and invaders continued to cause instability. For the time being, no one power in this region was able to emulate the conquests of the Islamic Caliphate. By the beginning of the eighth century – after Umayyad warlords had seized most of North Africa from the Byzantines and swept onwards as far as the Strait of Gibraltar – it stood poised on the threshold of Europe.

In 711, an Islamic army of probably no more than a couple of thousand soldiers crossed into Spain. They found the Visigothic kingdom in disarray. The *Mozarabic Chronicle* – compiled in the mid-eighth century by a Christian under Islamic rule – described how the region was afflicted by religious fighting, plague, Basque uprisings, and dynastic conflicts. In 717, the first Islamic troops traversed the Pyrenees and descended on the Western European Coastal Plain. They found it sparsely inhabited, with a scattering of small wood-built settlements, and with forest re-encroaching on the farmlands that had been needed to support the far greater population under the Roman Empire.

Most of the former Roman province of Gaul was controlled by the Franks, who had been united into a single state under the auspices of their king, Clovis (481–511). After his death, the kingdom was divided among his three quarrelsome sons and fell apart. Gregory of Tours wrote of a time of evil, bloodshed, and pillaging. 'What can we do when the entire population is steeped in vice and all delight in doing evil? No man fears the King, no man has any respect for his duke or his count.'[15]

By the early eighth century, this so-called Merovingian Dynasty was exhausted; the resultant anarchy provided the ideal pretext for a palace official called Charles Martel to seize power. The arrival of the Umayyads furnished another important opportunity to legitimize the new Frankish leadership, this time as figureheads in the Christian world's struggle against Islam. Charles Martel won immense prestige when he defeated the Muslim army at the Battle of Tours in 732. His son, Pepin the Short, continued to repel the Umayyads and expanded the Frankish realm as far as the Danube. In exchange for his continued protection of the Church, he received the blessing of the pope for his plan to take the place of the Merovingian king. 'It would be better for one who had power to be called a king than for one who remained without royal power,' the pope pronounced.[16] In 751, a new dynasty was born: the Carolingians.

Even if the Franks were seldom truly united, their kings tried hard to build a nation. They sought to establish some sort of common Frankish identity by the promotion of shared customs and the introduction of more standardized systems of government. More important, however, was the attempt to reconnect with the imperial legacy of the Romans. From the sixth century, kings took the old imperial title *Imperator Augustus* and emblazoned coins with the imperial laurels. Diplomatic exchanges with Constantinople were critical for upholding the king's standing as a faithful son of the emperor. When Clovis codified the Frankish civil law, he employed Gallo-Roman jurists who drew heavily on imperial Roman decrees.

Christianity provided one of the most important means of fostering Frankish unity and reinforcing the legitimacy of kings. Prelates like Gregory of Tours were expected to promote a common Frankish identity in their preaching. Kings explicitly portrayed themselves as the helpmeets of God. 'Let your servants, our kings, adorn the triumph of your virtue skilfully,' we read in a Merovingian Mass, 'so that they who are *principes* [rulers] by your command, may always be powerful in their duty and may rise above all the kingdoms.'[17] Clovis – the first Frankish king to convert – treated the subjection of Aquitaine and Burgundy as a holy war. His son Childebert backed bishops in their forced conversion of Jews. By the eighth century, Frankish kings called themselves *Rex Dei Gratia*: 'king by the grace of God'. They employed missionaries to expand Frankish influence beyond the northern and eastern borders. Churches were built in Frisia and prelates dispatched to the pagan Saxons. Whatever their personal aspirations, apostles like St Willibrord and St Boniface were pawns in what increasingly came to look like conquest under the banner of the cross. Christianity was increasingly used as a motive for war. Regions that refused to adopt Christianity were punished ruthlessly.

This was markedly different from earlier Christianity, which had averred that injustice should be countered peacefully and that suffering the scourge of suppression was the will of God.[18] In the third century, the theologian Clement of Alexandria had likened Christians to an army without weapons, a peaceful race; and Cyprian of Carthage had propounded that enemies are to be loved.[19] These were the views of Christians who lacked worldly power. As soon as the faith was adopted by political leaders, its attitudes to force changed. When Constantine marched against a rival emperor near Rome in 312, he inspired his troops by promising that their victory would be the will of God. In the early fifth century, the widely read Church father St Augustine of Hippo asserted that God had given the sword to kings and that it was just to defend the Christian peace.[20] In the Byzantine Empire, religion was commonly used to justify military campaigns. The *Strategikon*, for example, posited that Byzantine emperors commanded their armies under the aegis of God. Such religious zeal would only become more pronounced. By the late ninth century, the Emperor Leo VI even judged that in order to defend the Christian realm it was warranted to make use of 'contrivances of the devil'.[21]

The ardour of the Christian states was further tested by the Avars, who threatened their eastern borders as the caliphate encroached from the south. Like the Huns, the Avars originated from the steppes east of the Caspian Sea and settled in the plains north of the Black Sea. From there, they penetrated Anatolia, the Balkans, and Western Europe. Also like the Huns, they were feared for their sudden hit-and-run strikes. They perfected this form of warfare by introducing the stirrup, which kept riders more stable in the saddle, and a powerful, short, composite bow. These technological innovations, however, were offset by the fact that the Avar hordes were far smaller than those of the Huns and the peoples they encountered more organized.

At first, in the late sixth century, the Byzantines financed the Avars to fight the Gepids, the Bulgars, and other federations of nomadic tribes on the Danube. But it did not stop them from raiding the empire's northern frontiers. Moreover, the arrival of the Avars also upset the situation in the Italian Peninsula, where the Byzantines had been labouring to re-establish their rule. Having aided the Avars to defeat the Gepids, the Lombards increasingly feared their ally's military might. In a bid to evade it, they migrated into Northern Italy, where they took possession of much of the Byzantine territory. In 583, the Avar khagan exacted 120,000 gold pieces from Constantinople – along with a golden bed and an elephant. But Avar ambitions remained unsated. In 626, the Avars joined the Sasanians in besieging Constantinople. The defeat of the siege by the Emperor Heraclius the following year heralded the end of the Avar expansion.

In the Avars' stead, the Bulgars gained ground with the reluctant support of the Byzantines. The Avars initially responded by allying with the Slavs, but it was to no avail. By 680, the Bulgars had assimilated the Slav tribes in the former Avar territories of the northeast Balkans and proclaimed a new khanate. They forced the Byzantines to recognize their right to settle on the southern banks of the Danube, and exacted an annual payment of gold. In return for helping restore the Emperor Justinian II to his throne in 705, the Bulgar khan, Tervel, was granted the title of Caesar (*tsar*) and the emperor's daughter in marriage. Relations with Constantinople, however, remained tense. But when Islamic troops besieged the metropolis in 717–18, it was crucial Bulgar support that saved the city from falling. A barbarian – Khan Tervel – was now hailed as the saviour of Christian Europe.

Over 150 years after the fall of the Western Roman Empire, Europe remained a fragmented place. Spain was held by the Umayyads and would remain under the control of Islamic rulers for centuries. Protected by the Pyrenees, which acted as an important barrier between Islam and Christianity, the Western European Coastal Plain became dominated by the Franks. The Byzantines considered them barbarians; but their leaders increasingly came to see themselves as successors to the old Roman emperors. The Danube formed the other main fault line in Europe at this time. The region east of it was the domain of ambitious powers like the Avars and the Bulgars. Yet they remained small in population terms, hampered by environmental conditions that were less benign for agriculture; and they were far more affected than Western Europe by the incessant migrations and aggression that continued to sweep in from the steppes north of the Black Sea.

Armour in Chinese Fields

At the beginning of the sixth century, the fundamental political and social changes set in motion in China by the fall of the Western Jin state in 316 were still underway. The most important was the relocation of China's economic centre to the region south of the River Yangtze, which slowly transformed into a second food basket. The former centre of Chinese civilization, the North China Plain, was entirely ceded to barbarians like the Xiongnu and the Xianbei.

Chinese culture was no less alien to such peoples than Roman culture was to the Franks with their Germanic origins. But in much the same way that the Franks sought to align themselves with the former greatness of the Roman Empire and converted to Christianity, the barbarian peoples in China consciously embraced its imperial tradition and culture. They competed with each other to construct the most sumptuous temples and to perform the most extravagant ceremonial rituals at their royal courts – to the point that they came to look down on the native Chinese on the far side of the Yangtze. 'Your land is wet, cursed with malaria and crawling with insects,' reported one traveller. 'Frogs and toads share the same lairs, men and birds cohabit.'[22] Chinese making the journey in the opposite direction, however, were reluctantly impressed by the state of the cities in the north. As one visitor put it:

> Ever since Jin and Song times . . . Luoyang has been called a desolate region, and here we say that everyone north of the Yangtze is a barbarian; but on my recent visit to Luoyang, I found out that families of capped and gowned scholars live on the northern plains, where proper ceremonial and protocol flourish. I cannot find words to describe the magnificent personages I saw.[23]

Gradually, the ethnic composition of China changed entirely. The barbarians of the north blended with the native Chinese, and Chinese migrants in turn blended with the barbarians of the south. In the process, the old Confucian order was increasingly challenged by – and cross-fertilized with – the belief systems of Buddhism and Taoism, which first became widespread in this era.

Culturally, China flourished. Politically, however, it was a period of disunion and discord. 'The people had to wear armor to till the fields,' the records observed.[24] By the end of the sixth century, political power had crystallized into three kingdoms: the Southern Chen, the Northern Qi, and the Northern Zhou. The most powerful and extensive of the three was the Northern Zhou kingdom, which had been established by the Xianbei, and stretched from the Mongolian Steppes to the upper reaches of the Mekong River. This bestowed immense strategic advantages. It allowed the Northern Zhou to control all the valleys that gave access to the east of China. It meant they were the first to profit from important military innovations brought by nomads from the west, like the stirrup.[25] And it also let them benefit from the expertise of the highlanders of Sichuan in building and navigating ships that could be employed for warfare on often turbulent rivers.

Another major war for supremacy now loomed. In 577, the Northern Zhou overwhelmed the Northern Qi with a force said to number more than half a million men. In 588, they mounted an equally vast amphibious assault on the Southern Chen across the River Yangtze. The invasion had been preceded by the widespread distribution of pamphlets warning that the decadence and criminality of the Southern Chen rulers had caused them to lose the mandate of heaven. Their thesis was proved when their armies soon triumphed. For the first time in more than 350 years – since the collapse of the Han Dynasty in 220 – the majority of the Chinese heartland was firmly under the control of a single ruler. The Northern Zhou now established a new imperial dynasty, the Sui. Although it was to be short-lived, it was pivotal in the reunification of China. The Sui may have been descended from barbarian nomads, but their ambition was to restore the greatness of the Han Empire. Now, heaven ordained them to inaugurate a lasting era of harmony.

The Tang Dynasty

Heaven, however, was made to wait for another thirty years, until a new dynasty – also of Xianbei origin – arose to assume the imperial mandate. Worn out by border wars and domestic rebellions, the Sui were toppled by the Tang, with the aid of the powerful Göktürks, in 618. For a brief moment, China again stared into the abyss of civil war. But fortunately for the newborn dynasty, the first emperor was succeeded by a highly capable and experienced warrior, who ruthlessly murdered his two brothers to gain the throne. The new emperor, Taizong (626–49), mustered an army of hundreds of thousands to confront the troubled situation. 'The present disaster originated in the borderlands enjoying some small measure of peace, which allowed the ruler of men to roam at his ease and forget about warfare,' he asserted. 'We do not have you dig pools and construct parks, but instead allow you to focus on practicing the bow and arrow.'[26] Within five years, he had put down rebellion within the realm and restored stability along the border.

Once the survival of the young dynasty was guaranteed, Taizong shifted his focus to peaceful statecraft. Shoring up his legitimacy was imperative. In accordance with the ancient Confucian tradition, he formally adopted the heavenly mandate. The imperial dynasty was symbolized as a tree: the wisdom of the emperor flowed from the roots to his descendants, the branches, which had to grow strong, but not become too heavy. The emperor was also expected to manifest such qualities as compassion, benevolence, courtesy, respect for tradition, and thoughtfulness. To that end, Taizong worked hard to foster good governance, writing two essays on the subject, *The Model of an Emperor* and *The Emperor's Government Strategy*. Above all, he recommended avoiding military overstretch. 'A warlike country,' he warned, 'however huge and safe it may be, will end up declining and endangering its populace.'[27] To temper such martial ardour, he encouraged the growth of citizenship and civility through culture and education.

Between 618 and 683, the Tang Empire enjoyed stability, if not absolute harmony. Its population grew to between 50 and 60 million, reaching levels last seen during the Han Dynasty. Beliefs other than Confucianism were widely tolerated, including Taoism, Zoroastrianism, Christianity, and Islam; indeed, Taizong himself attended Buddhist services to commemorate the victims of war, and ordered the construction of Buddhist monasteries. Agricultural production was boosted by the use of prisoners to reclaim land on the empire's periphery and by technological innovations such as new water-lifting systems and a more advanced form of plough. This consequently allowed for growth in the output of silk factories, iron foundries, and ceramic workshops. One historian-official even hinted at surpluses: 'The prices of rice, corn and cloth kept on falling due to an abundance in supply.'[28] People flocked to the cities, like the capital, Chang'an, which now had around 300,000 inhabitants. 'Chang'an is a merchant's paradise,' a Silk Road trader testified. 'The market place has 3,000 stalls representing 200 merchant guilds. The city is beautiful with fruit trees and a lake.'[29] Like the Romans, the Tang laid out their cities according to grid systems and took great care in planning the water supply and other public amenities. These cities stimulated the spread of inventions, like woodblock printing, new medicines, and, above all, trade.

The early Tang emperors sought to encourage commerce along the Silk Road; although their attempts to develop a 'harmonious market' with the Göktürks, who controlled the route for much of its length through Central Asia, amounted to little more than demands to set trading terms unilaterally.

They also encouraged trade with Southeast Asia and onwards by sea with the countries around the Indian Ocean. 'A higher office will be rewarded to any official who can generate one million *min* annually in tariff revenue from maritime trade,' the court declared.[30] Tax rates for seaborne trade were lowered and official missions dispatched to establish relations with overseas countries. Several of China's trading partners were invited to establish permanent missions in the capital and they even received subsidies. Such efforts seem to have paid off: 'Rows of ships arrive from ten thousand countries,' a poet hymned, 'all trying to be the first to offer tributes and silk.'[31] Nevertheless, Tang China remained first and foremost a continental power. When Emperor Taizong first saw the great sea, he was profoundly scared of its thunderous waves; then he dismissed it as little more than a moat for the capital. The famous cartographer Jia Dan described shipping routes all the way to the Persian Gulf, but most of what survives of his work is devoted to China's continental neighbours, polities along the Silk Road, and the overland trade with the Middle East.

Although most East Asian powers were bound by common ties based on trade and Buddhism – which had become by far the most widespread belief system in the region – they still competed tirelessly over the control of that trade, and over the possession of strategic cities and natural resources. China's foreign policy, therefore, was characterized by a combination of hard and soft power. When the support of the Göktürks was no longer needed, the Tang expelled them from China by force; yet their elite became so assimilated with the Tang that they formally invited Emperor Taizong to become the Göktürk khagan. 'The sons of the nobles became the bondsmen of the Chinese people, their unsullied daughters became its slaves,' the Göktürk Orkhon Inscriptions recorded. 'While ensnaring them with their ingratiating talk and enervating riches, they have drawn the far-dwelling peoples nearer to themselves.'[32] Another threat in the west was posed by the Tuyuhun kingdom. Yet another branch of the Xianbei, the Tuyuhun were initially offered a marriage alliance in return for ceasing their border raids. When they baulked, the Tang emperor turned to the Tibetan kingdom. In exchange for a Tang princess, Tibet became an energetic ally, providing tens of thousand of troops for the campaign that put an end to Tuyuhun pretensions.

In the east, the Tang found itself in competition with the Korean kingdom of Goguryeo, which fought to maintain its primacy. After a large-scale invasion of the peninsula was routed, Taizong tried to wear down Goguryeo through border raids, disturbing its trade, and supporting its main Korean rival, the kingdom of Silla. In 668, Goguryeo was finally overwhelmed by a formidable Silla–Tang coalition. Much of the Korean Peninsula became a Tang protectorate – the so-called 'protectorate-general to pacify the East' – with the Silla king regarded merely as an adjunct to Chinese foreign policy.

Japan, meanwhile, remained torn between savage clan rivalries and efforts towards imperial reunification under its Yamato rulers. From China, they adopted Buddhism, urban planning, and the Confucian concept of imperial benevolence, which underpinned the famous Seventeen Article Constitution of Prince Shotoku in 604. Yet despite the beneficence of Shotoku's rule, he also managed to damage diplomatic relations with China. His attempt, in an official letter, to celebrate the close relationship between the two countries – describing Japan as the land of the rising sun, and China the land of the setting sun –was regarded by the Chinese emperor as an unconscionable insult for presuming that in some way the two states were equals.

Tang China also maintained contacts with the kingdoms in India. Even though Buddhism originated in India, the Tang considered themselves its chief upholders. Their policy of employing distinguished Buddhist monks to help spread Chinese influence, however, did not always go well. In 648, for example, Hindu priests in northern India threw the Chinese ambassador Wang Xuance into prison, fearing that the Tang presence in the region would bolster Buddhism and so undermine their own privileged status. Wang escaped to Tibet, where he mustered Tibetan troops and led them in a punitive expedition to avenge this insult to Tang honour. The Tibetan king was subsequently rewarded with honours, rolls of richly dyed silk, silkworm eggs, and craftsmen to make paper. Despite such temporary setbacks, the Tang continued to send missions to India.

When Taizong died in 649, the star of the Tang started to wane. Dynastic struggles broke out, and the next emperors could not emulate the success of the dynasty's founders. The storm clouds were further darkened by the appearance of the Islamic Caliphate on the western horizon. In 651, a first Arab envoy arrived in China, reportedly even trying to convert the emperor to Islam. A similar diplomatic mission seems to have been dispatched every four years subsequently. A worse humiliation was still to follow.

The expansion of the caliphate had caused many Central Asian kingdoms to seek aid from the Tang, but they were already too feeble to furnish military support. As resistance along the Silk Road crumbled before them, the troops of the caliphate marched relentlessly east. In 751, the forces of the Tang were crushed by the caliphate's armies at the Battle of the Talas River, in the Ferghana Valley. The era of Tang cosmopolitanism had come to an end.

The presence of the Islamic Caliphate in Central Asia established a powerful geopolitical bond between the extremities of the Eastern Hemisphere. Stimulated by the relentless competition of the major powers, transcontinental mobility steadily developed, not least with the growing commercial and diplomatic exchanges taking place between Europe, Africa, and Asia. But as much as the Eastern Hemisphere was beset by endemic violence, the same was also true of lands still far beyond the reach, knowledge, or imagination of either Asian or European lords. Centuries after the disappearance of the Olmec Civilization, it is time to return to the Western Hemisphere.

Spear-Thrower Owl

In Ross County, Ohio, in the Midwestern United States, there is a park with dome-shaped graves that were long a mystery. In those graves, archaeologists discovered copper that originated from the present-day border with Canada, sharks' teeth and mica from the east coast, obsidian and bears' teeth from the Appalachian Mountains, and seashells from the Gulf of Mexico. Eventually, the burials were attributed to a people known to historians as the Woodland Culture. They lived in the fifth century, in towns protected by wooden palisades, and used bows and arrows to make war on each other. They were among the first in North America to develop a hierarchical society, large settlements, and a trade network that spanned most of the continent.

While North America remained thinly populated – its development hampered by climate change in the late fifth century – matters were very different south of the Gulf of Mexico. Here the land was studded with settlements, some of which contained tens of thousands of inhabitants. At their heart, forming their political and religious centre, towered vast stone pyramids. The greatest – soaring more than seventy metres above its plaza – was the ancient Pyramid of the Sun in Teotihuacán, near present-day Mexico City. As early as the fourth century, the population of Teotihuacán was probably more than 120,000. It contained numerous temples, a royal citadel, wide streets, workshops, apartment blocks, and large reservoirs. Its extraordinary architectural and artistic treasures testify to its prosperity and power, which it owed to a combination of agriculture, trade, and conquest.

Teotihuacán lay at the centre of a web of smaller cities and towns, which it expected to contribute both troops and goods. Its ambitions were not confined to settlements in its immediate neighbourhood, though. Traders from Teotihuacán had long found the way south and east to the rich cities of the Yucatán Peninsula, in the most important of which they set up a kind of chamber of commerce.[33] These cities were all part of the Maya culture. They shared a common hieroglyphic script, calendar, architectural style, pantheon – and a passion for a highly competitive ritual ball game.

There were dozens of Maya city states in Yucatán. Their existence depended on the control of water resources: the peninsula is seasonally arid, so agriculture could only flourish when rulers built and maintained large reservoirs. The chief cities presided over a periphery of smaller satellite towns, which were required to participate in religious festivals and offer tribute (*patan*) of such highly valued commodities as cacao, obsidian, and brightly coloured feathers.[34] They erected steles to demarcate their territory and hosted the shrines of smaller towns. The Maya were warriors. Their arts, culture, and religion celebrated masculine strength. Temples were adorned with images of terrifying gods and warrior-kings. One plaque from the city of Tikal, for example, represents the king trampling the body of a fallen foe.[35]

In the late fourth century, Teotihuacáni traders in the Maya region were replaced by soldiers. The storm god of Teotihuacán had ordered King Spear-Thrower Owl – as archaeologists refer to him – to extend the city's power and prestige all the way to Yucatán. In city after city, Spear-Thrower Owl violently deposed the ruler in favour of one of his own relatives; in the major city of Tikal, Spear-Thrower Owl's son himself took the place of the executed king. Teotihuacán's conquests were aided by the state of discord that existed between Maya polities, as well as by superior weapons, such as spear-throwers (*atlatls*).[36] For over 150 years, Teotihuacán's hegemony cast a dark shadow over Yucatán. But then, in around 550, its star faded, probably as a result of famine and internal unrest.

The resulting power vacuum sparked a new contest for supremacy among the Maya cities. In the absence of metal weapons, the Maya fought with stone-tipped arrows, spears, and clubs, and wore primitive armour of padded cotton re-inforced with flakes of rock salt. Defeated soldiers were mas-sacred and leaders sacrificed to the gods. Around this time, cities began to invest in fortifications.[37] But victors often poisoned the reservoirs of captive cities, so that they had to be abandoned. By the early seventh century, two cities had emerged to dominate Yucatán: Calakmul and Tikal. The two had a long history of trade, diplomacy, royal visits, and joint rituals; but competition over trade along the Pasión River, and rivalry over the smaller cities in their overlapping spheres of influence, led to war. At least three major wars were fought before Calakmul was finally defeated in the mid-eighth century.

Despite such wars, the Maya civilization persisted into the ninth century, when it mysteriously collapsed. Popula-tion pressure may well have led to over-intensive farming that exhausted the soil, while a period of climate change would have exacerbated the situation. Whatever the cause, over a relatively short stretch of time, the Maya abandoned their cities – and the complex societies they supported – and returned to living in small villages. By the tenth century, many of the great Maya pyramid complexes had already been reconquered by the forest.

CHAPTER 9

The Earth between Hope and Calamity

750–1000 CE

Danes

Bulgars

Saxons

Slavs

• Aachen

Bavaria

Avars

Franks

Khazars

Aquitaine

Gokt

Bulgaria

Cordoba

Byzantium

• Constantinople

Umayyad

Mediterranean Sea

• Damascus

Umayyad

Libyan

• Medina

• Mecca

Red Sea

Ghana

Aksum

Bantu

A T L A N T I C

O C E A N

Eastern Hemisphere
around 750

Khagan of the Turks

Khitans

Balhae

Chang'an •

Tang

Silla

Yamoto

Tibet

Palas

ar

atihara

Chalukya

Rashtrakuta

Pallava

Lavo

Champa

Chenla

Anuradhapura

Malacca Strait

Srivijaya

Sunda Strait

PACIFIC

OCEAN

INDIAN

OCEAN

500 1000 1500 km

500   1000 miles

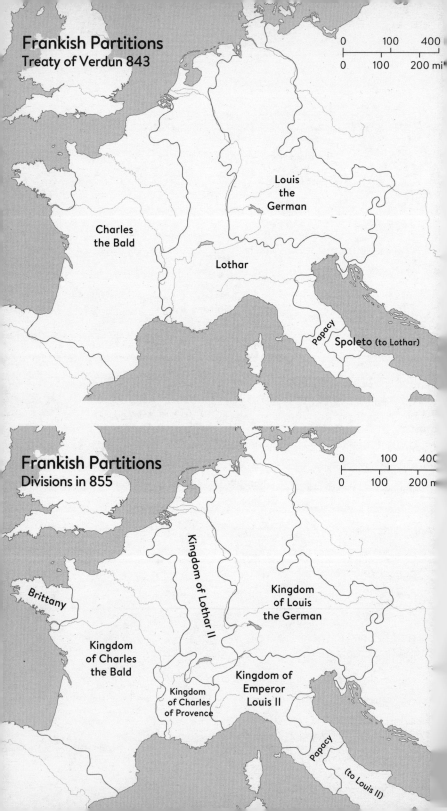

Frankish Partitions
Treaty of Verdun 843

0	100	400
0	100	200 mi

Louis
the
German

Charles
the Bald

Lothar

Papacy

Spoleto (to Lothar)

Frankish Partitions
Divisions in 855

0	100	400
0	100	200 m

Brittany

Kingdom of Lothar II

Kingdom of Louis
the German

Kingdom
of Charles
the Bald

Kingdom
of Charles
of Provence

Kingdom of
Emperor
Louis II

Papacy

(to Louis II)

The museum in the Chinese city of Luoyang possesses one of the world's finest collections of Tang Dynasty tomb sculptures. These small, playful terracotta figures portray elegant dancers, fierce warriors, and also prosperous merchants perched on top of the sort of heavily laden camels that regularly made the arduous trek along the Silk Road. The period in which they were made – the second half of the eighth century CE – is still considered a golden age not just of art but also of trade. Travellers described the crowded centres of commerce, filled with merchants from distant regions, thriving like true metropolises, and gleaming with 'pearls and jade like a fairyland' as 'thousands of lanterns shone over the clear, dark blue sky'.[1]

The Tang emperors were not the only rulers to encourage trade; so did their chief peers, the Frankish and Byzantine emperors, and the caliphs of the Abbasid Dynasty, who had succeeded the Umayyads. Numerous accounts – especially from the Abbasid Caliphate – attest to the increasing scope of the trans-Eurasian trade. 'There is the Tigris, to put us into trade contact with lands as far as China, and to bring us all that the seas yield as well as the foodstuffs of Mesopotamia,' recorded the ninth-century Persian polymath al-Tabari. 'And there is the Euphrates to transport to us all that Syria, al-Raqqah, and their regions have to offer.'[2] The tenth-century Arab geographer al-Muqadassi added: 'Caravans from Egypt and China will come by way of the desert, and all types of products will reach you from China via the sea, and from the realm of the Greeks and from al-Mawsil [Mosul] via the Tigris.'[3]

Men like al-Tabari and al-Muqadassi were cosmopolitans who highlighted the benefits of trade and the wonders of distant countries. To itinerant scholars like these, as well as to explorers and traders, the world literally became more open. 'Among the discoveries of this age of ours,' reported the tenth-century Persian scholar Abu Zayd al-Sirafi, 'is the previously unsuspected fact that the ocean on to which the Sea of China and India opens is connected to the Mediterranean Sea.'[4] As a result, in the eighth and ninth centuries new atlases and encyclopaedias began to be made of the Indian Ocean and the land routes to China, like Ibn Khordadbeh's *Book of Roads and Provinces*, or Jia Dan's famously detailed and vast map of China's western hinterland.

The first adherents of Islam were merchants: although the faith prohibited usury, it did not forbid profits earned through trade. To facilitate their increasingly long-distance ventures, Islamic merchants began to evolve a sophisticated commercial infrastructure. Contemporary sources record the widespread use of debt arrangements or payment instructions (*suftajahs*), so that traders did not need to carry cash. There was the *qirad*, a kind of joint-stock agreement in which multiple investors entrusted capital to a trader in the expectation of making profit from his activities.[5] The caliphate established trade zones (*funduqs*), rest houses, and relay stations for courier services, and financed the construction of bridges to improve routes like the ancient King's Highway and Royal Road. Trading with infidels was not an issue either: the Abbasids dealt profitably with the Franks, the Byzantine Empire, Tang China, and countless lesser powers. In turn, Constantinople reduced trade taxes and subsidized the building of merchant ships.[6] Far to the northwest, the Frankish court of Charlemagne at Aachen marvelled at the exotic goods and the copies of ancient Greek and Roman writings supplied to the palace school from all around the Middle East, to the point that his reign has traditionally been described as the Carolingian Renaissance.

But political obstacles to this nascent globalism remained. The whole Silk Road, we learn from Abu Zayd al-Sirafi, was lined with fortresses, dominating valleys, commanding passages over rivers, or looming over ports. They secured trade against robbery, but they also taxed and controlled it. On the Tang-administered section of the Silk Road, east of the Tian Shan, al-Sirafi recounted how guard posts blocked the road and traders needed to obtain permits to proceed with their goods.[7] At one stage, the Tang imposed a ban on dealing with 'the darker races', a measure primarily aimed at the Central Asian kingdoms.[8] Trade suffered from wars between the major powers, but also from political turmoil within states. 'The trading voyages to China were abandoned and the country itself was ruined,' wrote al-Sirafi about the downfall of the Tang. 'The Chinese placed undue impositions on merchants [and] seized their property by force.'[9]

Most importantly, the trade in luxuries and its accompanying cosmopolitanism were enjoyed by only a fraction of the people. There were, however, some improvements to their lot. In Europe, the climate became warmer. Iron horseshoes, the heavy plough, and the horse collar all made farmers' lives a little easier. But existence remained a daily fight against the wilderness. 'Wherever he spent the night he cut down trees . . . and made a circular fence for the protection of his ass, so that it would not be devoured by the wild beasts that were numerous there,' we read in the life of a wandering hermit in what is now Germany.[10] An abbot in northern France warned of the state of constant lawlessness: 'Brigandage is committed in the realm of our King Charles with impunity and there is nothing surer or more constant than violence and rapine.'[11] Similarly gloomy portraits were painted in the monastic annals of that time. Wherever the population grew, it sheltered as much as possible in the lee of fortress or city walls. This was the case not just in Europe but throughout most of the Eastern Hemisphere.

Abundant Goods and Honest People

In 734, the Tang emperor Xuanzong (712–56) wrote to the Yamato ruler in Japan informing him of the fate of three of the latter's ambassadors, who had failed to return home. A storm had blown their ship off course and wrecked it on the coast of Linyi, in present-day Vietnam, where they were robbed and sold into slavery. The emperor offered words of consolation: 'Linyi and other countries in the area pay tribute to China. I have already instructed the protector-general at Annan [Hanoi] to issue an edict to their rulers, ordering them to escort the Japanese diplomats to the protectorate, should any of them be spotted. I have also instructed the protector-general to comfort and send the Japanese home.'[12]

Diplomacy clearly remained a risky business; but Xuanzong's missive also reveals the sense of superiority that underlay his display of magnanimity. Such condescension was not reserved only for Japanese rulers. Xuanzong also referred to the khagan of the Turks as his son, for example, and refused a peace proposal from the Tibetan king because the latter addressed him as an equal. Precedence mattered, and the emperor – backed by an army of more than 600,000 men – was able to insist on it.

Xuanzong's reign was called 'the splendid age of original opening', an era of confidence, peace, and prosperity.[13] Amid the bustle of the capital, Chang'an, lay peaceful imperial gardens where exotic birds and animals gathered from across the realm reflected the natural harmony bestowed by the empire. This was the classical period of the Chinese arts. It was Xuanzong who founded the first Chinese opera school, known as the Pear Garden. He supported poets like Li Bo, and painters like Zhou Fang and Zhang Xuan, who created masterpieces celebrating the splendour and elegance of court life in return. Artisans blended techniques and styles from across Asia into sophisticated and sumptuous works of terracotta, gold, jade, and silk.

Xuanzong himself sought to excel in the arts of governance. Although he approved of the Confucian respect for tradition, he was a Taoist. He departed from legalist and Confucian principles to make the Tang legal code fairer. He also encouraged farming in order to replenish the state's granaries; built new locks on the Grand Canal, which ran between the River Yangtze and the Yellow River; and took various other steps to promote trade both inside and across the border. 'The Yellow River is clear and calm,' the Tang's historian recorded. 'The country enjoys peace and harmony. Goods are abundant and people are honest. Kingdoms like Anxi have submitted to, and were ruled by, the Tang . . . Everywhere enjoyed bumper harvests and the people were prosperous. Young men in the prime of life carried no weapons. No one would pick up and keep other people's property on the road.'[14]

To all appearances, this was still the heyday of the Tang Dynasty. But it was soon shown to be little more than a splendid façade. Natural disasters emptied the granaries. Famine and violence forced the emperor to evacuate the overpopulated capital. 'Inside rich men's doors, wine and meat went to waste,' wrote one of the era's greatest poets, Du Fu; 'while frozen corpses littered the roadside.'[15] Revolts broke out in northeast China, forcing the emperor to withdraw troops from the western border. The region's powers were quick to exploit the situation: the Tibetans broke their peace agreement; the nomadic Uighurs strengthened their hold on the region of modern Mongolia; and bands of the nomadic Khitan people raided across the border. The remaining Chinese forces were too feeble to defeat the armies of the Islamic Caliphate at the Battle of the Talas River in 751.

Worse was still to come. In 755, the warlord An Lushan took advantage of the hardship in the north to rebel. The uprising became one of the bloodiest episodes in Chinese history, costing tens of millions of lives. 'Each man of you has a bow and a quiver at his belt,' Du Fu wrote; 'And the sound of their sorrow goes up to the clouds.'[16] In 756, Emperor Xuan-zong was forced into retirement. Subsequent emperors restored a degree of stability, but could only do so by calling on the Uighurs and mercenaries from the caliphate to check Tibetan aggression. In 758, Arab and Persian pirates burned the city of Guangzhou; its port was not rebuilt for five decades. In 762, when the future emperor Dezong was dispatched to the Uighurs to affirm an alliance, they had the effrontery to try and make him dance.

This experience led Emperor Dezong (779–805) to reconsider relations with the Uighurs as soon as he ascended the throne. Advisors were invited to craft a strategy. But while some favoured an alliance with Tibet to resist the Uighurs, others considered Tibet to be the main rival and proposed attacking it. 'When the Tibetans are weak, they ask for an alliance, when they are strong, they invade,' one general counselled; 'now they have penetrated deep into our territory and they ask for a treaty, they certainly want to cheat us.'[17] The emperor nevertheless decided to forge ahead with negotiations. The Tibetans, however, declined to proceed as long as they were referred to as 'subjects'. They got their way, and an alliance was concluded in 783. When rebellion broke out in China a year later, Tibetan troops helped patrol the streets of Chang'an. But as soon as the capital had been secured, tensions between the Tang and Tibet rekindled. This time, China resolved to check the Tibetans by forging a grand alliance with the Uighurs and the caliphate. 'I think it would be best that Your Majesty build rapport with Uyghur in the north, Yunnan in the south, and [the] Arab Empire and Tianzhu in the west,' an imperial official advised. 'By doing this, we could isolate the

Tibetans.'[18] An alliance was established in 789, but did not last long, so that insecurity in the west continued to grow.

Meanwhile, the empire also fragmented domestically. When Emperor Dezong attempted a series of fiscal reforms to relieve the poor, he only exacerbated the problem. The existing taxation system, whereby a household's liabilities were based on the number of its members, had caused a rural exodus. But the new system, in which taxation was calculated on a family's wealth and assets rather than headcount, created an even more polarized society. Dezong's death was followed by a period of economic mismanagement, corruption, and instability. A number of taxes, including those on salt, were abolished, but this expedited the decline of the power of the imperial court. The difficulties were aggravated by climate change. 'A vast expanse of desert is covered with ice of a thousand feet,' wrote the poet Cen Shen, as a prolonged period of exceptionally cold weather caused bad harvests and renewed conflicts with the nomadic peoples in the north.[19] Emperor Xuanzong (846–59) temporarily restored order, but under his heirs the Tang Empire continued to decay economically and to disintegrate politically. When the wealthiest landlords resisted paying their dues, Emperor Xizong (873–88) reinstated the salt taxes. This, however, led to smuggling, crime, and further unrest. By the time the last Tang emperor was poisoned by a usurper in 907, the dynasty had ruled in little more than name for years.

The Tang collapse was followed by more than half a century of anarchy, an era known as 'the Five Dynasties and Ten Kingdoms' period (907–60). In reality, there were many more contenders, few of whom survived for more than a couple of decades. Fighting was incessant and accelerated the development of weapons like flamethrowers and the long *zhanmadao* sword. The north in particular suffered from depopulation. Cities became impoverished and the canal system that supported the food supply broke down. The country was rendered defenceless against foreign intrusion. The Tibetans, the Uighurs, and the Khitan now all commanded large territories inside what had been the Tang realm. Even Chinese kingdoms during this period, such as the Later Han, the Later Tang, and the Later Jin, were ruled by strongmen of Central Asian stock. The writer Wang Renyu decried how the quarrelling Chinese kingdoms of his day fell prey to barbarian rulers. The Later Jin, he recounted, 'lost control, while traitorous ministers sold out their country. Fierce armies and valiant warriors were helplessly surrendered, the common people were slaughtered one by one . . . Since the beginning of the world there had never been disorder like this.'[20]

By far the most formidable power during this period was the Khitan federation of tribes from the Mongolian and Manchurian steppes. In 907, its ruler crowned himself Emperor Taizu of the Liao Dynasty. He disparaged the Chinese for their decadence, laughed at their numerous uprisings, and expected Chinese kings – whom he addressed as his sons – to meet him in person and accede to his territorial demands. 'That my son in China had come to such troubles, I already knew,' he told one unfortunate envoy. 'But I had heard reports that this son kept two thousand women in his palace, and a thousand musicians, that he spent his days hawking and running his hunting hounds, that he was wallowing in drink and sex; he had no concern for his people.'[21] When

Taizu died in 926, the Liao Empire extended as far south as the Yellow River.

For a brief moment, the balance of power in East Asia had shifted to the north, where the plains and hills of Manchuria became an arena of power politics. On the coastal plains that bend around the Yellow and Bohai Seas, the Liao locked horns with the smaller kingdoms that controlled the southern banks of the Yellow River, such as the Later Zhou. In 954, the Later Zhou met a Liao-backed coalition in the Battle of Gaoping. The records explain that the northern coalition underestimated its rival and attempted to fight in the teeth of an intense southerly gale. It was decisively defeated, and its southward expansion stalled. Soon after the battle, in 960, a Zhou general founded one of China's most commercially minded dynasties: the Song. Although the Liao continued to control the area north of the Yellow River, the first Song emperors, Taizu and Taizong, increased their own domains at the expense of the other kingdoms to the river's south. But when, in 979, the Song attacked the Northern Han state, which had succeeded the Later Han and straddled the Yellow River, the Liao attempted to come to its defence. The rivalry between the Liao and the Song would continue for another 150 years.

Meanwhile, in the Korean Peninsula, the Silla kingdom – which had been the leading state since it had cast off the Tang dependency in the early eighth century – was overthrown in 936 by the recently founded kingdom of Goryeo, which considered itself the heir of Goguryeo. We do not know how exactly Goryeo prevailed, although Silla had long been in political decline. But with the advent of Goryeo, state building in Korea reached a new level: its achievement in unifying the peninsula still serves as an ideal of Korean unity today. The first king of Goryeo, Taejo, came from a wealthy mercantile family, and he had clear ideas about the preservation of his dominion. His principles of statecraft included devotion to the Buddha, the maintenance of probity at court, light taxation, openness to criticism, and guarding the country's independence.

Taejo remained constantly alert to potential threats, both internal and external. 'I only fear that my successors will give way to their passions and greed and destroy the principle of government,' he admitted shortly before his death, and then warned: 'Since our country shares borders with savage nations, always beware of the danger of their invasions.'[22] That danger would eventually become pressing. Initially, the Goryeo kingdom was separated from the Liao by the nomadic Jurchen, and the two agreed to join forces to prevent the Jurchen from raiding their towns. But after the Liao dealt a major defeat to the Jurchen in 991, they were left facing Goryeo across the Yalu River – and both felt entitled to establish a foothold on the other's side. 'Since your country does not take care of the people's needs,' pronounced a Liao general trying to justify aggressive action, 'we solemnly execute Heaven's punishment on its behalf.'[23]

Warriors of the Buddha

In Southeast Asia, the ninth century saw new dynasties establish the outlines of nations and cultures that are still visible today in Cambodia, Vietnam, Indonesia, and Myanmar.

The region's inhospitable geography of numerous rivers and forested mountains formed intractable barriers to overland communication – but this merely encouraged the forging of seaborne connections that tied its peoples together through the exchange of trade, the sharing of Hindu and Buddhist beliefs, and the creation of a common artistic language still visible in the remains of temples, palaces, and objects from the age. This same geography gave the region its immense strategic significance as the chief conduit for maritime commerce between China and India. The straits of Malacca and Sunda became crucial transit points, promoting the establishment of significant trading ports that, in turn, helped fuel the development of kingdoms, especially in Malaysia, Sumatra, and Java.

But trade, faith, and progress also bred war. The kingdom of Srivijaya, which emerged in the late seventh century on the island of Sumatra – strategically positioned between the straits of Malacca and Sunda – was the first to try and control the flow of trade by dominating these chokepoints.[24] It curried favour with China by dispatching tributary missions and offering pepper, turtles, pearls, and ivory in exchange for iron, ceramics, and silk. It proposed to the northern Indian Pala Dynasty that it build a Buddhist temple on its territory and it offered to donate gold to temples in southern Indian cities. Its king approached the caliphate, announcing that he was eager to trade and asking the caliph to 'send to me someone who might teach me Islam and instruct me in its Laws'.[25] Srivijaya tried to prevent others from siphoning off traffic by itself conquering the Malayan Peninsula and attacking trade cities in the kingdoms of Khmer and Champa in modern

Cambodia and Vietnam. Chinese sources report that ships were forced by Srivijaya to moor in the Strait of Malacca, so that they could be monitored and taxed.

Competition over commerce came with a religious dimension. In accordance with Buddhist doctrines, Srivijayan kings in the late seventh century embarked on a *siddhayatra*. What was meant to be a quest for spiritual enlightenment in reality involved the conquest of trade cities. Srivijayan troops destroyed Hindu temples on the Malayan Peninsula and erected Buddhist monasteries in their stead. Initially, Srivijaya extended its influence on the neighbouring island of Java through dynastic alliances. But by the ninth century, the two island states were locked in an increasingly bitter struggle for regional supremacy that simmered on into the next millennium.

On the continent, meanwhile, the threat of Srivijaya encouraged the unification of the Khmer under King Jayavarman II at the beginning of the ninth century. He relocated the Khmer political centre to the north, where it was safer for Srivijayan warships. In the process, the Khmer moved against the small kingdom of Lavo and turned it into a puppet state protecting their western border. Over the course of the next two centuries, the successors of Jayavarman steadily extended the bounds of the Khmer Empire and increased its wealth. At the end of the tenth century, civil war between rival claimants to the Khmer throne sucked in regional powers from as far afield as India.

As well as conflict, there was also intense diplomatic interaction between the states of Southeast Asia. Kings employed religion to propagate their influence, erecting temples

and monuments, and using priests and monks as envoys.
Nevertheless, warfare at some level was almost incessant,
although armies numbered only a few thousand soldiers –
closer in scale to contemporary European warfare than to
the huge battles fought in China or India. This situation was
to some degree both the cause and the effect of the emergence of the first significant monarchical states in the region
during this period. To these nascent dynasties, status was
almost everything. The king of Java was the 'saviour of the
universe' and the 'protector of Buddhism', for example,
while the Srivijayan monarch styled himself 'king of the
ocean lands'. 'Victory be to this king of Srivijaya,' one inscription proclaims, 'the glory of whose rule is worshipped
by the neighbouring rulers, and who has been created by the
creator of the universe as if intent on making firm the best
of religions.'[26] The reality of Southeast Asian politics, however, was a state of anarchy existing beneath the overlapping
shadows of Indian and Chinese spheres of influence.

India's Four Kingdom Period

'This prince's heart is sanctified with courtship, since he rec-
ognizes the merits of others. His pride is concealed under
genuine modesty.'[27] Thus the eighth-century poet-dramatist
Bhavabhuti described the qualities of a ruler in his *Exploits of
a Great Hero*. In the tradition of the ancient epics, this play
about the early life of the Hindu deity Rama is a struggle between the ideal form of justice championed by the priestly
upper caste of Brahmins and the evil caused by corrupt kings
and the devilish priests who supported them. Bhavabhuti's

plays are steeped in cruelty from which nobody could escape, not even women and small children.

India's population during the time of Bhavabhuti was probably around 60 million. Most of it was distributed across the Indo-Gangetic Plain where, much like the rest of the world, the vast majority lived in rural settlements. We can gain an impression of the daily struggles they faced from the large number of carved 'hero stones' that still survive from the period. These commemorate men and women who were important to their communities: a warrior who gave his life to defend his village; a husband who protected his family from robbers; a farmer who killed a leopard trying to eat his cattle. Increasingly large numbers of people, though, were also to be found clustered along the coasts of India, where trading cities thrived and connected the rich hinterland with export markets as far away as Europe and China.

The lives of city dwellers and peasants alike in this era were overshadowed by one major event: the struggle between the Palas, the Rashtrakutas, the Pratiharas, and the Islamic Caliphate over the fertile plains of the north. The conflict was one of competing religions as much as states: the caliphate of course was Muslim, but the Palas were Buddhists, the Pratiharas were Hindus, and the Rashtrakutas were Jainists. It seems that their respective areas of strength prevented the advantage from swinging decisively and permanently in favour of one of them; the Palas possessed the largest number of both war elephants and warships, the Rashtrakutas had the most infantry, the Pratiharas fielded the best cavalry.

The Pala Dynasty had its origins in around 750 on the

banks of the Padma River, the most important branch of the lower Ganges, in present-day Bangladesh. A group of tribal leaders granted the title of 'protector' (*pala*) to King Gopala, hoping that this would terminate a period of internecine conflict in the region. In the words of the inscription recording the event: 'To put an end to the state of affairs similar to what happens among fishes, people made the glorious Gopala, the crest jewel of the heads of kings, take the hand of Lakshmi, the goddess of fortune.'[28] Another inscription praised Gopala for 'releasing the war elephants' against the neighbouring tribes and states.[29] Clearly the Palas valued foreign conquest as much as domestic stability.

At about the same time as the emergence of the Palas, much of the Deccan Plateau and southern coasts of India fell under the control of the Rashtrakuta king Dantidurga. He was also the first of his dynasty to hold the *mahadana* (great gift) ceremony: to celebrate the king's birth from the golden womb of the divine universe, his weight in bullion was distributed to the needy. Similarly, the northwest of the Indo-Gangetic Plain was united by the first Pratihara king, Nagabhata, a descendant of the Huns, after he defeated an invasion by the forces of the caliphate and 'retrieved the earth from calamity'.[30] Despite this setback, the caliphate continued to try and force its way into northern India, as it had done ever since it reached the banks of the Indus in the late seventh century. This was the logical next step, given its control of the northern coastal plains of the Arabian Sea and the routes through the mountain ranges that gave on to the Indus Valley. The prize was not just to bring the word of God to the infidel, but also to seize the agricultural and mercantile riches of a land famed both for its bounty and as the recipient of the goods that flowed down from the Silk Road through the passes of the Karakoram to the Indian Ocean.

The struggle between these four powers ensued for almost two centuries. The Palas struck first, when King Dharmapala launched a sacred war over the Buddhist shrines in the north. His main target, however, was Kannauj, a prosperous trading city right in the centre of the Indo-Gangetic Plain. He defeated both the Pratiharas and the Rashtrakutas and, in around the year 800, his supremacy was recognized at an imperial *durbar* (assembly), where he appointed a puppet king to reign over the middle reaches of the Ganges. 'With a sign of his gracefully moved eye-brows he installed the illustrious king of Kanyakubja, who readily was accepted by the Bhôja, Matsya, Madra, Kuru, Yadu, Yavana, Avanti, Gandhâra and Kira kings, bowing down respectfully with their diadems trembling, and for whom his own golden coronation jar was lifted up by the delighted elders of Panchâla.'[31]

But Dharmapala failed to secure the region. These outwardly subservient kings soon rebelled, called in the Pratiharas, and collectively defeated the Palas. This was followed by a new attack by the Rashtrakutas, who prevailed over both the Palas and Pratiharas. In around 850, the Pratihara king Mihira Bhoja reignited hostilities with a series of offensives. The Pratiharas retained their influence in the northwest of the Indian subcontinent for about sixty years and were then defeated by the Rashtrakutas, who were now receiving assistance from the Arabs. By the turn of the ninth century, however, all three kingdoms began to suffer from internal unrest. Its causes are unclear, but the situation was instantly exploited by the Ghaznavids, a breakaway kingdom from the caliphate. In 1018, the city of Kannauj was captured not by an Indian dynasty, but by the Muslim ruler Mahmud of Ghazni.

This long-running contest for control of northern India was accompanied by great efforts by the participants to spread their cultural and religious influence. The Palas built Buddhist monasteries that became centres of learning. The Rashtrakuta capital, Manyakheta, was the residence of important Jain intellectuals, such as the mathematician Mahaviracharya and the poets Sri Ponna and Adikavi Pampa. The Hindu Pratiharas left awe-inspiring temple complexes, such as those at Osian, in modern Rajasthan, which are embellished with carvings that remain among the finest in the history of Indian art. Despite the fighting, the main powers also still traded with one another: their economies were largely complementary in terms of luxury goods. Everything – the art, the wars, the magnificent royal courts – was financed by heavy taxes on trade, land, salt, and minerals. Even if there is no definitive evidence for it, the burden must have fallen mainly on the shoulders of ordinary people, the local craftsmen and small farmers.

The Abbasid Takeover

In around 714, the Umayyad caliph Walid I ordered the construction of a new palace-city. Unusually, the site chosen was an arid and remote spot, two days away from his capital, Damascus. Anjar, as the place was called, came to boast spectacular colonnades, grand squares, and exquisitely carved marble. Here, in seclusion, the caliph intended to live in peace and devote himself to poetry, wine, and women. Walid, like the caliphs that came after him, brooked no disobedience of his wishes. These Umayyads upset traditional Islamic political thinking by asserting that they were the equals of the Prophet Muhammad.[32] Toleration of different Islamic opinions, let alone of completely different religions, gave way to a form of totalitarianism.

The schism between reality and the new doctrine of obedience, however, could not have been larger. The Umayyad Dynasty was crumbling. In the east, Persian subjects had become tired of the crackdown on Zoroastrianism, the influx of Arab migrants, heavy taxes exacted to support garrison towns, and the growing sense of Arab racial superiority that locked others out from government. In 719, a predominantly Shia resistance movement, the Hashimiyya, sprang up in the remote valleys of Central Asia. Its leaders claimed to be the heirs of the Banu Hashim clan to which Muhammad had belonged. They condemned the Umayyad caliphs as illegitimate and promised liberation from their tyranny. While preaching Shia Islam, they also incorporated Zoroastrian elements and struck a conciliatory tone towards Jews, Sunni, and Christians. Fuelled by the wider resentment in Persia and Mesopotamia, the Hashimiyya Movement spread like wildfire.

In 743, civil war erupted in Syria. When the Umayyad caliph was killed near Damascus, the victor ordered his head 'to be put on a lance, to have wine sprinkled on it and to be paraded around the city, announcing that "this is the head of the wine-lover."'[33] Thousands of camels carried the royal treasury out of the city.[34] There were 'beatings, pillaging, and violation of women in front of their husbands', the astrologer monk Theophilus of Edessa recorded.[35] Meanwhile, the ranks of the Hashimiyya Movement continued to swell and they descended on to the Mesopotamian plain. By now, the 'wearers-in-black' had formed an alliance with an influential Shia clan which claimed descent from the Prophet Muhammad's youngest uncle, Abbas, and which came to be known as the Abbasids.

In 749, the Middle East was struck by an earthquake that destroyed several cities. To the chroniclers, the ominous message was clear: a new era of anarchy had begun. 'Eyewitnesses affirmed that in Mesopotamia the ground was split along two miles and that out of the chasm there came up an animal like a mule, quite spotless, that spoke in a human voice and announced the incursion of a certain nation from the deserts against the Arabs.'[36] Disorder gripped the world not only in the sphere of civil affairs, Theophilus of Edessa wrote. There was fighting and bloodshed everywhere. In 750, an army of over 100,000 Umayyad troops was defeated by predominantly Shia warriors lead by the Abbasid chieftain Abu al-Abbas al-Saffah in the Battle of the Zab, in the north of what is now Iraq. After this victory, al-Saffah proclaimed himself the first caliph of the Abbasid Dynasty.

The downfall of the Umayyad Caliphate triggered a heated debate between scholars, jurists, and clerics on how the civil order of Islamic society should be maintained. All sides agreed that the Quran and the sayings of the Prophet remained the principle source of law, that the *umma* should be preserved, and that Islam should continue to be spread. But thereafter there was little consensus as to precisely how those fundamental principles should be translated into practice.

One of the ideas originating at this time which had the greatest long-term impact was the notion that all non-Muslim societies should be thought of as belonging collectively to a 'house of war', or Dar al-Harb. First proposed by the famous jurist Abu Hanifa, the concept and its ramifications were fleshed out in more detail by his disciple al-Shaybani in his *Introduction to the Law of Nations*. Al-Shaybani's treatise did not question *whether* jihad should be waged against infidels – they resided in the 'house of war', after all – but it did propose a framework for *how* jihad should be waged. Those refusing to accept the teachings of Islam should be fought by any means, and killed, pillaged, or enslaved, although a degree of mercy, on some occasions, could be shown to women, children, and the elderly.[37] But al-Shaybani also showed a degree of pragmatism, accepting that in certain circumstances peace treaties could be negotiated with the peoples of the Dar al-Harb, their merchants and envoys granted safe conduct, and trade conducted with them.

These views were later confirmed by the prominent eleventh-century jurist al-Mawardi, whose *Ordinances of Government* is one of Islam's most comprehensive works on justice, politics, and war. Al-Mawardi's priority is defence: the caliph's primary duty is to protect the lands of the believers – the Dar al-Islam, or 'house of peace' – and the holy sanctuaries. 'There is no benefit to a leaderless people when disorder reigns, and they will never have a leader if the ignorant amongst them leads.'[38] Only once such order has been achieved should the caliph turn to fulfilling the obligations of jihad. Like al-Shaybani, al-Mawardi declared that the inhabitants of the Dar al-Harb should be given the opportunity to sue for peace in return for paying tribute. Their lands would then become part of the 'house of conciliation', or Dar al-Sulh. 'It is not permitted to resume the jihad against them as long as they make the payments.'[39] If the infidels resisted, any means could be used 'to harry them from their houses and to inflict damage on them day and night, by fighting and burning'.[40] Women and children, however, should still not be killed, but merely enslaved.

To symbolize the zealousness of their allegiance to the Prophet, the Abbasid Dynasty took black as its official colour: black for its banners, black even for the tunic of its messengers. Black had been the colour of the flags borne by Muhammad's army in the decisive victory that led to the capture of Mecca over a century earlier. Coins hailed the caliph as the 'prince of believers' and 'servant of god'. New caliphs swore oaths at their accession. 'It is necessary to have a leader to keep religion and justice on the right road, protect the rights of all Muslims, and lead campaigns against pagan enemies,' one of them proclaimed. 'God, in His compassion and wisdom . . . has spared human beings the trouble of having to go in search of their leaders. He has designated them Himself and honored them by making them descendants of the Prophet.'[41] 'May Allah be a witness if he let me be Amir al-Mu'minin, and made me a caliph,' another vowed; 'and if he did make me a caliph then I would follow his word and Way of living, and that of the Prophet's, and would transmit that to my citizens, and I would not kill people or destroy places randomly, and I would not take someone's home or pillage their country, and be careful in making my decisions.'[42]

The first Abbasid caliphs recentralized power at the

same time as they expanded the Islamic empire. Although they were severely critical of the Umayyads for the laxness of their rule, they did adopt several of the most important administrative tools of their predecessors, such as *divans* (ministries) and *qadis* (judges in sharia courts), as well as introducing significant innovations, such as the role of *wazir* (vizier, or chief advisor). The caliphate now consisted of core provinces under direct rule, like Mesopotamia, Syria, Egypt, and Western Iran, and peripheral ones, like Armenia, North Africa, and Central Asia. Governors in the former provinces were often members of the royal family, rotated frequently, and monitored by the *barid* – a form of intelligence agency that reported directly to the caliph. In the latter provinces, military governors were deployed.

In 762, the second Abbasid caliph, al-Mansur (754–75), relocated the capital to the newly constructed city of Baghdad, officially known as Madinat al-Salam, or the 'city of peace'. Under al-Mansur, Baghdad became a centre of the arts, sciences, and philosophy. He dispatched envoys to Constantinople to request copies of the Greek philosophers for his library, the 'house of wisdom'. With the reign of Harun al-Rashid (786–809), the dynasty reached its peak. Harun is most widely remembered now for his presence in the entirely fictional *Book of One Thousand and One Nights*, which nostalgically portrayed his caliphate as a golden age of Islamic civilization. Court poets at the time, however, were also effusive in their praises:

'Through Harun, the light has shone forth in every region,
and the straight path has become established by the
justness of his conduct.

a leader who has ordered his affairs through the
attention to God's requirements . . .
People's eyes are unable to endure the brilliance of
his face.[43]

Perhaps such panegyrics were not entirely heartfelt. As al-Tabari slyly observed: 'The poets sang his praises, for which he rewarded them profusely.'[44]

Harun had gained precious experience as a prince in campaigns against the Byzantine Empire. One of his first deeds as caliph, therefore, was to fortify the Byzantine border and to behead dissident governors in the frontier provinces.[45] But despite such vigilance, it was under his rule that the still youthful Abbasid Caliphate started to weaken. Unrest in Syria, Egypt, and Persia never stopped. In Spain, the emirate of Córdoba recognized the new dynasty, but remained the last defiant outpost of Umayyad rule. In 788, the Idrisid Dynasty established itself in Morocco. In 793, the governor of Iran broke away. It required an expedition of 50,000 troops to restore order. Harun's death was followed by yet more disorder. By around 813, Baghdad was utterly lawless. Mutinous soldiers 'used to band together, go up to a man, seize his son and carry him off, and nothing could be done to stop them', wrote al-Tabari. 'There was no government authority which could restrain them . . . because the government authority itself depended on them.'[46] By 820, the caliphate had lost control over Syria and large swathes of its Central Asian territories.

An examination of the caliphate's treasury reveals a drop of 50 per cent in the ninth century.[47] Wars with the Byzantine

Empire helped drain the coffers. But it was also partly due to the neglect of agricultural production in Mesopotamia and the failure to collect taxes from Egypt and the eastern provinces. The more caliphs' incomes dropped, the greater the effort to levy new taxes – and the greater the unrest that followed. The caliphs became increasingly dependent on military men to maintain their rule, but they had to be rewarded with land. In 869, a massive slave uprising broke out near Basra, on the Persian Gulf. The caliphate had been importing large numbers of slaves for infrastructure works, farming, and the infantry. The Zanj Rebellion cost hundreds of thousands of lives. Young men became the slaves of slaves, women their concubines. 'I could hear their uproar, crying out "There is no God but Allah" as they were put to the sword,' recalled one eyewitness. The Zanj leader in Basra 'burned down the congregational mosque; he also burned the harbor from the cable to the bridge, the fire destroying all before it, including people, animals, goods, and merchandise . . . Anyone with some money was tortured to extract it and then killed, but anyone who was poor was killed straightaway.'[48] The rebellion lived on for another fourteen years before it was finally extinguished.

Meanwhile, the Abbasid Caliphate continued to fragment. Between 868 and 905, the Tulunids took control of Egypt and most of the Levant. Around 909, the Fatimid Dynasty started their expansion from Algeria. In the 930s, the Buyid Dynasty began to seize Persia and parts of Mesopotamia – including, in 945, Baghdad. But as the Islamic world tore itself apart, another small fringe power from the steppes of Central Asia was readying to strike.

The European Hellhole

The Abbasid Empire contained over 50 million inhabitants at its peak. With over a million citizens, Baghdad was the world's largest city.[49] By comparison, the Frankish Empire under Charlemagne numbered around 20 million people, the Byzantine Empire around 10 million, the Bulgarian Empire 2 million, and Umayyad Spain even fewer.[50] In Europe, the period saw the slow emergence of rich commercial cities: Córdoba, Seville, Palermo, the city states of the Italian Peninsula, Cologne, Mainz, Regensburg, Paris, London. Apart from a dozen or so, none had more than 20,000 inhabitants. The Arabic cities of Palermo and Córdoba and the Byzantine capital of Constantinople were the only cities with more than a quarter of a million residents.

Between the late eighth century and the early ninth century, Northern and Western Europe briefly became the focus of great power politics. The event with the most lasting significance was the founding of the first true empire in Western Europe since the fall of Rome. It was created by the Frankish king Charlemagne (768–814) out of his victories over the Frisians, the Saxons, the Bavarians, the Avars, and the Lombards; and it received formal acknowledgement of its status in Rome on Christmas Day, 800, when the pope crowned him 'emperor of the Romans'. Charlemagne's 'Holy Roman Empire' – as it is known to posterity – was built on the successes of his Carolingian predecessors. He inherited a realm much larger than those of potential rivals, so that he could muster more financial resources and troops against his enemies to the south and east. His cavalry, in particular, was a further strength. Shock attacks by heavily armoured horsemen – the distant forebears of the medieval knight – proved decisive in overcoming infantry; but mounted troops were equally valuable for clearing the territory around hostile cities, so that they could be starved into submission.[51]

Strong cavalry was also the most obvious military advantage held by one of the period's other important emergent powers, the pagan Bulgarian Empire of Khan Krum (795–814). Even though far less is known about Krum than Charlemagne, it is clear that he conquered a realm that encompassed large parts of Eastern Europe, benefiting from the weakness of the Avars due to the Frankish campaigns against them, and from the exhaustion of the Byzantine Empire as a result of its wars with the Abbasids. The other major new European state was the Umayyad emirate of Córdoba, in Spain, which came into being in 756 when the former province of the caliphate refused to acknowledge the Abbasid Dynasty.

The competition between Franks, Bulgars, Arabs, and Byzantines – between pagans, Christians, and Muslims – led to some remarkable alliances that overrode the claims of faith. Although the Franks took pride in their reputation as the defenders of Christendom, they were still prepared to form an alliance with the Abbasids to fight the Umayyads of Córdoba. Charlemagne addressed Harun al-Rashid in letters as his 'brother'. The caliph reciprocated with the gift of an elephant named Abul-Abbas, hunting dogs, horses, and swords of the finest steel. The Franks and the Abbasids shared another rival in the Byzantine Empire. The conquest of the Lombard kingdom in Italy in 774 brought the Franks into direct competition with Constantinople, which still retained some territorial interests in the Italian Peninsula. The Byzantines felt threatened by the presence of Frankish ships in the Adriatic Sea, and were especially displeased that Charlemagne's protection of Rome had earned him the pope's favour and honours.

Competition over the Adriatic – and particularly the increasingly autonomous but still formally Byzantine city of Venice, whose strategic situation was already obvious – caused relations between the Carolingians and Byzantines to deteriorate fast. Charlemagne's daughter, who had been betrothed to the Byzantine imperial heir, was kept at her father's court in Aachen.[52] Charlemagne also dispatched envoys to Khan Krum to propose a joint offensive against the Avars, and he imposed an embargo on selling arms to the latter. 'Let them not bring arms or breastplates to sell.'[53] After the Avars had been brought to their knees, Krum turned his cavalry south, against the Byzantine Empire. He defeated its army, killed its emperor, and turned his skull into a drinking cup. It was only when Krum stood poised to take Constantinople that the desperate Byzantines sued for peace. For years, diplomats travelled between the two courts, before a peace treaty was finally sealed in 815. Subsequently, the two states even organized a joint mission to demarcate the border.

European diplomacy at that time was mainly conducted by prelates. Their main task was to read the letters of their monarchs, not to negotiate. It took an envoy about fifty days to travel the dangerous road between Aachen and Constantinople. When the tired travellers finally arrived at their destination, they were sometimes treated poorly. One envoy lamented about his frugal reception by a Byzantine bishop. 'It is written, "God is love," and in that grace he is entirely lacking.'[54] On other occasions, the envoys appear to have been overwhelmed by what they encountered. Charlemagne's biographer Einhard, who was an official at his court, recounted how envoys prostrated themselves humbly before the emperor's cook, having mistaken him for the emperor himself.[55] Einhard also described the official reception that followed:

> The emperor was clad in gems and gold and glittered like the sun at its rising: and round about him stood, as it were the chivalry of heaven, three young men, his sons, who have since been made partners in the kingdom; his daughters and their mother decorated with wisdom and beauty as well as with pearls; leaders of the Church, unsurpassed in dignity and virtue; abbots distinguished for their high birth and their sanctity; nobles, like Joshua when he appeared in the camp of Gilgal; and an army like that which drove back the Syrians and Assyrians out of Samaria.[56]

The deaths of Charlemagne and Khan Krum in 814, together with the infighting that continued to ravage the Abbasid Caliphate after the death of Harun al-Rashid in 809, raised the prospect of a period of respite for Constantinople. Before long, however, the Byzantine Empire found itself hard pressed to contend with sustained attacks by Islamic troops from North Africa on its possessions in Sicily.[57] In 840, a Byzantine delegation was sent to Córdoba to propose an alliance against those interlopers, as well as against the Abbasids, and to suggest the emirate reclaim its ancestral lands in the

Levant. The Bulgars, meanwhile, were preoccupied with fighting Charlemagne's successor, Louis the Pious, and it was not until the 830s that they began to exert pressure again on the Byzantine border in the Balkans. The ability of the Carolingian Empire to encroach on the Byzantine sphere of influence was further diminished by the civil war which erupted after the death of Louis the Pious in 840, and by the Treaty of Verdun which brought it to an end in 843. The price of peace was the dismemberment of the Frankish Empire into three separate states – West, Middle, and East Francia.

Once again, Europe slumped into a morass of anarchy, as rulers struggled and failed to maintain their authority. It was a dreadful situation. Foreign travellers like the early tenth-century Abbasid envoy Ibn Fadlan described Europe as rich in trees, fruit, and honey, but nevertheless a cold, violent, and filthy hellhole.[58] From the early ninth century, Western Europe began to fall victim to the scourge of the Vikings. The annals of the West Frankish abbey of St Bertin, for example, recorded how in 841: 'Danish pirates sailed down the Channel and attacked Rouen, plundered the town with pillage, fire and sword, slaughtered or took captive the monks and the rest of the population.'[59] Worse was to follow: in 845, St Bertin fell victim to the vast Viking fleet that rowed up the Seine to attack Paris. 'The heathen broke in upon the Christians at many points,' the annals of the West Frankish abbey of Xanten noted in its entry for that year. 'Yet owing to his indolence Charles [the Frankish king] agreed to give them many thousand pounds of gold and silver if they would leave Gaul and this they did. Nevertheless the cloisters of most of the saints were destroyed and many of the Christians were led away captive.'[60] At the same time, local warlords also fought each other without restraint, afflicting their subjects with 'acts of devastation, burning, rape, sacrilege, and blasphemy'.[61]

Such havoc confirmed many Christians' view that the year 1000 heralded Doomsday, the Day of Judgment. 'Then will end the tyranny of kings and the injustice and rapine of reeves and their cunning and unjust judgments and wiles,' wrote one English monk. 'Then shall those who rejoiced and were glad in this life groan and lament. Then shall their mead, wine, and beer be turned into thirst for them.'[62] Instead of eternal salvation or damnation, however, the dawn of the eleventh century merely rose on a Europe that was still recovering from the downfall of the Roman Empire, and remained politically fragmented, economically backward, and thinly populated. Yet it also revealed the skeleton of a geopolitical order that, at first glance, is suddenly more recognizable to modern eyes: the Germanic states of the Holy Roman Empire, kingdoms of England, France, Poland, and Hungary – and the seemingly eternal twin poles of the papacy in Rome and the Byzantine Empire.

The Mirror of History

Let us try to draw some conclusions about the history of the first thousand years of the common era – the subject of the last four chapters – focusing, once again, primarily on the Eastern Hemisphere, and on five main aspects: the distribution of power; political organization; the nature of interactions between polities, including the causes of war and peace; the interaction of people and their environment; and the nature of thinking about world politics.

Throughout the first millennium, power still depended heavily on the size of populations. People meant hands; hands meant farmers, artisans, and fighters. Numbers mattered. But there were other factors that made societies more efficient in accumulating power. Mobility, for instance, allowed for large-scale trade, exploitation of resources, and conquest. The Romans led the way here. Their connective power was enhanced by an unequalled combination of transport capabilities on land: for example, standardized roads, courier services, and highly mobile legions. They also possessed a powerful navy and a large merchant fleet.

The most successful polities had it all: a large taxable population, economic cohesion, military strength, good administration, and capable leaders. The presence of the holy trinity of natural resources – water, fertile soil, and a temperate climate – was no longer sufficient by itself. Egypt and Mesopotamia, for instance, not only ceased to exist as independent polities, their populations barely grew. The North China Plain remained vital for China's agricultural production, but the northern plateaus and the southern hills became equally important. In South Asia, the centre of power extended out from the Indo-Gangetic Plain to encompass the trade routes in the north and the coastal cities in the south.

The political order in the first millennium was dominated by a series of empires, each of which controlled tens of millions of subjects at its height. One of the largest and most successful was Rome, which combined dominance over the Mediterranean with dominance over a significant portion of

Europe north of the Alps. Just as its rise had reshaped the political map of the Eastern Hemisphere, so its collapse in the fifth century defined the outlook of subsequent geopolitics. The downfall of the Han Empire in China in the third century, followed as it was by almost four centuries of political fragmentation, was of similar consequence. In both cases, the power vacuum that ensued was filled by peoples that were previously considered barbarians: the Qiang, the Xianbei, and the Xiongnu in China, the Germanic peoples in Europe.

The vast space between Rome and China was filled by other important polities. In the Middle East, the Parthian Empire gave way to the Sasanian, which was succeeded in turn by the Islamic Caliphate of the Umayyads, with its power base in the Levant, and then the Islamic Caliphate of the Abbasids, with its centre in Baghdad. South Asia, meanwhile, was dominated by a series of empires centred variously in the northwest around the Indus, such as the Kushans; in the south on the Deccan Plateau, such as the Rashtrakutas; and in the northeast along the middle and lower Ganges, such as the Guptas, who were unique in the extent of their command over the subcontinent.

By the turn of the tenth century, however, most of the Eastern Hemisphere's imperial order – the Tang, the Abbasids, the Carolingians, the Byzantines – appeared to be disintegrating. For a moment, it seemed as if there was no longer a place for great empires. Centrifugal forces prevailed; power fragmented. Across the entire globe, from Yucatán – the cradle of the Maya culture – through Europe and the Middle East, to the Japanese Archipelago, periods of violent upheaval were as common as periods of imperial stability.

Wars were fought for a handful of reasons that recurred time and again. Most obviously, they were fought because states had the power and the ambition to do so. In seventh-century China, for example, the Tang emperor Taizong was so convinced of his strength that he launched wars of conquest in all directions. In Central America, Teotihuacan pushed further and further into the Maya heartland because it realized the balance of power had tilted decisively in its favour. The motivations for such wars were often dressed up in ideas of justice or righteousness. The Sasanian kings of the third century, for instance, presented their wars with Rome as attempts to avenge earlier wrongs and reclaim what had been seized from their ancestors. Many imperial powers possessed a version of the doctrine that underlay the Pax Romana: that is, their conquests brought peace and prosperity to benighted realms. Indeed, in China, barbarian peoples like the Xianbei became as avid in using the heavenly mandate to justify their own wars of conquest as the states of the North China Plain had originally been in using it to legitimize attempts to conquer them.

Conversely, many wars occurred because states' weaknesses invited foreign intervention. In some cases, rebellion and unrest led rulers or pretenders to invite foreign powers to help restore order – only to find that their erstwhile allies created even greater instability. This happened, for example, with the Sasanian Empire and the Hephthalite Huns in the fifth century, and the enfeebled Tang Dynasty and Tibet in the late eighth. Elsewhere, imperial overstretch so weakened the sinews of the state that empires crumbled from within: in the late ninth century, for instance, the breakdown of the overburdened and exhausted Abbasid Caliphate saw the emergence of new states in North Africa, Persia, and the Levant. And sometimes it was the effect of environmental factors that forced desperate peoples into conflict. Perhaps the most obvious example of this was the climate change that drove the Xiongnu and Huns from their native lands, setting in motion the chain reaction of wars and migrations that culminated with the downfall of the Western Roman Empire at the hands of the Germanic peoples in 476.

Another major cause of war was a version of what theorists of international relations refer to as the 'security dilemma': namely, that the efforts made by a state to strengthen its security causes its neighbour to reciprocate, thereby creating tensions that ultimately lead to war. In an era when frontiers and spheres of influence were often only loosely defined, keeping potential enemies as far away as possible from one's heartlands was the best form of security. This factor led to recurrent tensions between the states of the North China Plain and their neighbours in the Korean Peninsula, the northern and western plateaus, and the southern hills. It also led to numerous clashes between the Roman and Byzantine Empires on the one hand and the Parthians and Sasanians on the other over the Armenian Highlands and the northern Mesopotamian plain.

A further catalyst for rivalry and confrontation was the desire to control the proceeds of trade. Many contested areas were important conduits for commerce: the eternal tussle for supremacy in Central Asia, for example, was in essence a struggle to monopolize the streams of wealth channelled by the Silk Road across most of the landmass of Eurasia. And when, partly in an attempt to bypass the obstructions on the overland route, long-distance maritime trade developed across the Indian Ocean, another theatre of conflict was born. Witness, for example, the efforts of the Sasanian Empire and the kingdom of Srivijaya to control the strategic chokepoints that lay at their respective ends of the Indian Ocean.

Finally, there was religion. Although religious differences did not necessarily prevent polities from forging ties of friendship and cooperation, at some time or another holy wars were fought by every faith and conviction – Hindus, Buddhists, Confucians, Taoists, Christians, Muslims, and pagans. The Buddhist kings of Srivijaya portrayed their late seventh-century wars of conquest as *siddhayatras*, or quests for spiritual enlightenment. The Christian kingdom of Aksum, in East Africa, attacked the Jewish kingdom Himyar, in the Arabian Peninsula, in revenge for the latter killing its envoys. The eighth-century Carolingian state mobilized troops under the holy cross in order to justify its wars against the Muslims to the south and the pagan peoples to its east. Religious differences could even cause adherents of the same faith to fight each other. In the eighth century, the Abbasids argued they were seizing the caliphate from the Umayyad Dynasty at least in part because of the latter's lack of true Islamic fervour. Only a couple of decades later, the papacy called on the Carolingians to protect its leadership of Christianity from the interference of the Lombard kingdom and, less obviously, the Byzantine Empire.

Undoubtedly, the ideal of peace remained a constant and fervent aspiration throughout the first millennium. But, more often than not, thinking about the nature of world politics was remarkably unfettered by sentiment or illusion. The interaction of states, cultures, and religions was characterized by struggle. Islamic scholars drew a very clear distinction between the community of believers (the *umma*) and the world of non-believers which formed the 'house of war' (Dar al-Harb). The teachings of the New Testament were far less belligerent; but, from the fourth century, most Byzantine theologians argued that Christian rulers were duty-bound to defend their subjects with force against pagan attacks. The influential Gupta theorist Kamandaka cautioned rulers always to be prepared because their alliances would never last. The Tang emperor Taizong warned that the state was dangerously weakened when men were allowed to roam at their ease and forget about war. One of the most accomplished rulers in Chinese history, Taizong, had another piece of wise advice for future leaders: study history thoroughly. 'Use history as a mirror so as to know the rise and fall of the dynasties.'[63]

CHAPTER 10

The Mongol
Shockwave

1000–1250 CE

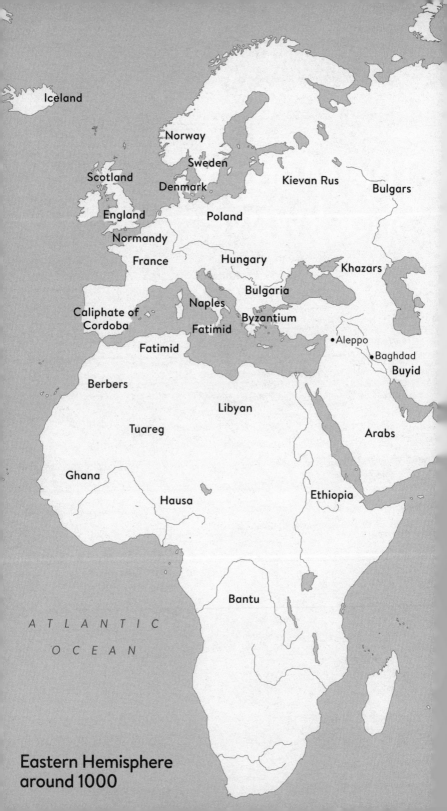

Iceland

Norway

Sweden

Scotland

Denmark

England

Poland

Normandy

Kievan Rus

Bulgars

France

Hungary

Khazars

Bulgaria

Naples

Caliphate of
Cordoba

Byzantium

Fatimid

Aleppo

Fatimid

Baghdad

Buyid

Berbers

Libyan

Tuareg

Arabs

Ghana

Hausa

Ethiopia

Bantu

ATLANTIC

OCEAN

Eastern Hemisphere
around 1000

Khitan

Goryeo   Japan

Kaifeng •

Northern Song

Pala

Pagan

Chalukya

Haripunjaya

PACIFIC

OCEAN

Champa

Chola

Khmer

Malays

Anuradhapura

Malacca •

Malays

D I A N

Srivijaya

C E A N

Sunda

500   1000   1500 km

500   1000 miles

In 974 CE, the Chinese emperor Taizu of Song held a naval review in which hundreds of warships fought a mock battle. His fleet consisted of galleys called 'sea hawks', which were armed with catapults and reinforced with iron, and junks equipped with landing gear.[1] In the following century, the Song emperors built the most powerful navy in the world. It contained 13,500 ships, engaged rivals with explosives, launched major expeditions to Vietnam and around the Korean Peninsula, maintained a base in the Philippines, and had the knowledge to navigate all the way to the Strait of Hormuz.[2] This naval prowess was backed by an immense domestic economy and industrial capability, and by a clear imperial vision of using that might against barbarians or pirates or whenever Chinese interests beyond its borders were threatened.[3]

If there seemed one power ready to spread its influence globally at the dawn of the second millennium, therefore, it was China. But it was not to be. Song China was far from united and so its naval power ended up being deployed mainly on rivers to quell domestic unrest. What held China back the most were invasions of barbarians in the north: first the Jurchen in the twelfth century and then the Mongols in the thirteenth.

The Mongol attacks halted China's economic growth and it would not recover until the Ming Dynasty over 150 years later.[4] This was a turning point which decisively altered the balance of power in the Eastern Hemisphere. Although the Mongols also struck at the Islamic powers and the kingdoms of Eastern Europe, they did not advance further west than Vienna, unlike the Huns before them. If they had, then the development of Western Europe at this time – the agricultural innovations, the expanding trade, the rise of cities as commercial centres, the construction of kingdoms – might have been completely annulled.

It is not known exactly why the Mongols aborted their campaigns in the West, but it seems to have been more a question of geography – and a stroke of luck – than a European military triumph. No longer at risk of imminent annihilation by external aggressors, Europe's polities devoted themselves to an ever more relentless contest for military, economic, and financial primacy. It involved not just kingdoms, principalities, and duchies, but also increasingly powerful and self-confident city states, of which Venice was the prime exemplar. Ambition and aggression, however, also spilled over into other arenas. But even the sacred war against the occupation of the Holy Land – the most notable of the various Crusades against unbelievers – involved only a few thousand knights at any one time. Such armies were accompanied by large throngs of both fortune seekers and the faithful, and were notorious for their equally deficient logistics and leadership. This was not yet the era of Europe's spectacular global conquests.

The Song

Following the Battle of Gaoping in 954 – which halted the nomadic forces in the north of China and allowed the south to be unified – the Song Dynasty announced in 960 that it had received the mandate of heaven. In accordance with the Confucian teachings, the first Song emperor, Taizu (960–76), promised to restore harmony, reassuring his subjects that: 'We model ourselves on the unselfishness of Heaven and earth.'[5] In reality, the first century of the Song Dynasty was characterized by a long struggle to overcome those states, and individuals, that still refused to accept their supremacy.

Taizu began the task of consolidating his power by building an army of hundreds of thousands of soldiers. Enemy warlords were given a stark choice: face overwhelming force, or accept a lifetime of retirement on some secluded country estate far from the centres of power. Loyal generals, however, were rewarded with provincial governorships. Civilian government was placed on a firmer footing, in the course of which it was reorganized into three distinct departments: a central secretariat; an advisory chancellery; and a department of state affairs, which itself consisted of ministries of personnel, finance, war, justice, public works, and rites. The last of these ministries oversaw foreign relations, court ceremonial, the civil service exams, and Buddhist and Taoist priests. All government functionaries had to swear subservience to the emperor, not to loot the countryside, and not to abuse civilians.

As domestic unification advanced, the main security

question became how to defend the border against the major states to the north: the Liao, and the kingdom of Xia, a Tibetan people. In 1005, the Treaty of Shanyuan was sealed with the Liao. It stipulated that the two powers mutually recognize each other as equals; but the Liao regarded the Song's annual 'gift' of silk and silver as tribute. Some time later, the Song court debated how best to deal with border raids by the Xia. Some favoured maintaining the existing policy of conciliation, albeit on pragmatic grounds.[6] 'Our generals are mediocre; our soldiers are not sharp,' one advisor said. 'We should wait until they are internally divided, and then launch a major attack.'[7]

Others argued against appeasement. A belligerent faction of officials cited the example of the Treaty of Shanyuan, referring to it as a humiliation. By effectively yielding the north to the Liao, they averred, the Song would never become as mighty as the Han or the Tang. 'Our soldiers are growing older, while the enemies are getting stronger day by day,' added another.[8] 'We have been in peace for too long. People do not know how to fight and are easily frightened,' asserted the statesman Fan Zhongyan. 'The Xia people dare to be our enemy because they have already secured help from our great enemy, the Liao', posited another official.[9] But, in the end, the emperor decided to negotiate a deal and once again buy peace with 'gifts' of tea, silver, and silk. 'We shall secure a century of peaceful relations,' he promised.[10]

What followed was indeed a period of prosperity. The Song emperors strengthened their control over both the North China Plain and the rich agricultural region south of the River Yangtze. Under Emperor Shenzong (1067–85), the so-called New Policies introduced a primitive form of welfare state. They included the redistribution of food, price controls, pensions, care for orphans, and the end of forced labour. Living conditions improved. Economic production per capita might even have doubled during this period, due to the re-establishment of peace, the introduction of more productive rice variants from Southeast Asia, and the rapid development of industries including iron and silk. Both internal and external trade flourished. In 1087, a new trade office was established in the southeastern city of Quanzhou, which became the chief entrepôt for China's foreign maritime commerce.

Song China became the world's largest economy, exercising a huge power of attraction over even hostile states. The neighbouring Liao rulers, for example, did everything in their might to emulate the opulence and refinement of the Song. The military balance shifted as well. Between 979 and 1041, the Song army trebled in size to 1.25 million men. The Song mastered the manufacture of gunpowder and introduced catapults with explosive bombs. They imposed an export ban on sulphur and saltpetre which, along with charcoal, formed the key ingredients of gunpowder. The emperor also ordered a breeding programme to reduce the Song army's dependence on horses imported from Central Asia. Alongside their military power, the Song resorted to economic coercion and cut off trade with neighbours if they refused to submit.

The era of tranquillity did not last. China's army may have been large and well-equipped, but it was never able to subdue the Song's foreign enemies. The peace treaty with the Xia failed to demarcate the border and so clashes continued.[11] In the south, the Song allied with the Champa to try to subdue the Ly Dynasty in Vietnam. The war sapped the imperial army's strength until, in 1077, it was forced to withdraw. Such campaigns, and the annual 'gifts' to the Xia and the Liao, drained the treasury. 'Eighty or ninety percent of our treasury income went to the military. Our troops can be said to be many. Our treasury can be said to be exhausted,' worried a senior imperial official.[12] The situation was worsened by the famine that ravaged northern China in 1074–6.

Setbacks now followed each other rapidly. Emperor Zhezong, who took the throne in 1085 when he was only eight, opted for a confrontational policy towards the Xia. His successor in 1100, Emperor Huizong, allegedly neglected his responsibilities in order to pursue his love of the arts. In 1125, as the emperor blissfully dabbled in poetry and painting, the Jurchen rebelled against their Liao overlords. Although Huizong chose to support the Jurchen in overthrowing the Liao, after their victory the Jurchen turned against the Song and launched a surprise attack on their capital. Faced with this invasion, Huizong abdicated in favour of his son. In 1127, both the new emperor and his father were captured and taken back to the Jurchen capital in Manchuria.

The speed and scale of the Jurchen triumph can be attributed to a combination of Song complacency and incompetence, and the fact that the Song's advantages in infantry, artillery, and warships were outweighed by the Jurchen's superior cavalry. The Jurchen 'were victorious only because they used iron-shielded cavalry, while we opposed them with foot soldiers', a Song general later explained.[13] The Jurchen Dynasty, called Jin, consolidated its rule over the northern plain, while the remnants of the Song retreated to the Yangtze where they continued to rule in the guise of the Southern Song Dynasty. In 1141, the two negotiated an agreement that fixed the border between them, in return for which the Southern Song agreed to pay a large annual tribute in silver and silk. For a while, both empires flourished. Thwarted in the north, the Song were ready to channel their energy overseas. The navy was again expanded, new ports opened, and maritime exploration was encouraged.

It was almost precisely at this point that the Mongol threat emerged. The Mongols dwelt around the Orkhon Valley in Mongolia, the same area where the Xiongnu had lived centuries before. In 1130, the Khamag Mongol confederation first clashed with the Jin. When a treaty was signed in 1147, the Mongols compelled the Jin to pay tribute. The peace was short-lived; and in the new skirmishes that followed, the Mongols were pushed back. But a series of exceptionally cold summers decimated the Mongol herds, causing them to re-intensify their efforts to advance south. In 1206, the Mongol tribes coalesced around one of the most legendary leaders in history, Genghis Khan, his name meaning 'universal ruler'. The khan propagated the idea of a holy war, ordered by the sky god Tengri, to unify the world under Mongol rule and avenge maltreatment from the past.

The Mongol force that attacked China in 1207 was probably no more than 150,000 strong, and entirely mounted on small but sturdy horses. It nevertheless made in-roads, thanks primarily to the Mongols' tactic of lightning charges, their lethal composite bows, their readiness to sacrifice thousands of men in order to seize strategic passes, and the defection of Jin generals. By 1234, the Jin Dynasty had been terminated, its death blow delivered by a combined Mongol–Southern Song army. 'Corpses sprawled, curled up beside the road – hordes of half-dead prisoners,' lamented the Jin poet Yuan Haowen. 'Our spirit's broken.'[14] The Jin's territory almost immediately became a launch pad for Mongol attacks against the Song.

The Southern Song offered intense resistance. Over the course of a war that lasted decades, the Mongols slowly won control of the devastated border provinces; as they became familiar with the Song's gunpowder weapons and siege engines, they increasingly used them against their inventors. In 1276, the Mongols finally took the Song capital, Lin'an (Hangzhou). 'The ruling senior ministers forgot their enmity and submitted to humiliation,' the invaders' chronicles boasted.[15] The carnage caused by the Mongol invasions was immense: tens of millions of people were killed. It would take almost three centuries for the population and agricultural output of China to recover.[16] Of equal geopolitical significance in the long term was the fact that the great upsurge of Chinese cosmopolitanism under the Song – one of the most outward-looking of Chinese dynasties – had been cut off at the roots.

Subduing Pagans into the Service of Christ

In some ways, the Mongols were merely the latest nomadic barbarian society from the fringes to take over the Chinese heartland. What made them different, however, was that they simultaneously entertained hopes of conquest as far as the Persian Gulf and the Mediterranean. The first Mongol campaigns back in the twelfth century may have been triggered by climate change and opportunism over the weakness of the Jin, but once the hordes started counting the spoils of their victories, they fell under the spell of Genghis Khan's promise that he would lead them to even greater wealth and to the empire ordained for them by the sky god Tengri. The descendants of Genghis Khan left little to the imagination. His grandson, Güyük Khan, referred to himself as the 'emperor of all men' when he wrote to Pope Innocent IV in 1246.

> From the rising of the sun to its setting, all the lands have been made subject to me. Who could do this contrary to the command of God? Now you should say with a sincere heart: 'I will submit and serve you.' Thou thyself, at the head of all the Princes, come at once to serve and wait upon us![17]

The Mongol khans between them plotted to conquer Eurasia as far as the 'great sea', or Atlantic Ocean. Between 1237 and 1241, they devastated Eastern Europe, killing half of its population. The reports that reached other European cities were shocking. 'They dragged men and women alike into the churches and shamefully mistreated and then killed them there,' wrote the prelate Roger of Apulia from the kingdom of Hungary. 'Their recreation was to rape the girls or wives before the fathers' or husbands' eyes.'[18] But the Mongols disappeared from Europe as quickly as they came. Climatic change was probably at work again: increased rainfall made the steppes of Eastern Europe swampy, slowing down the Mongol cavalry and depriving them of fodder. The Mongol hordes in Europe were smaller than in China too – and lacked their siege engines – so that heavily fortified European cities could hold out for longer. Many commanders were called back to elect a new leader after the death of Genghis Khan's successor, Ogodei. Western Europe had been spared from Mongol invasion. It remains an intriguing question as to what would have happened if the Mongols had not turned back.

In any case, the European political scene in the mid-thirteenth century remained fundamentally as disunited and multipolar as it had been when the sons of Charlemagne divided his empire between them 400 years earlier. By the early eleventh century, the six largest polities were the Holy Roman Empire – which dominated Europe from its geographic heart in Germany – the Byzantine Empire, and the kingdoms of France, England, Poland, and Hungary, although these bore only a limited resemblance to their later incarnations. None of them as yet possessed a strong centralized regime, or even well defined borders, but remained looser agglomerations of duchies, earldoms, autonomous cities, and even bishoprics. And there was also the papacy, whose position of spiritual authority imbued it with potentially tremendous political influence.

After the last Carolingian emperor of East Francia died without issue in 911, the leaders of the territories comprising what would become known as the Holy Roman Empire chose his successor in an election. For centuries thereafter, the emperor continued to be elected from candidates, all of whom belonged to the same successive, Germanic dynasties: the Ottonians, the Salians, the Hohenstaufen, and so on. It was the Ottonian emperors of the tenth century who first based their imperial authority on the principle of *translatio imperii* – namely, that there was a single imperial mandate, which had passed from the Romans to the Byzantines, from them to the Franks, and from them, in turn, to the Germans. Hence their assumption of the titles 'king of the Germans', 'emperor of the Romans', and the ancient honorific *Imperator Augustus*.[19] Their Christian aura was burnished by propagandists like the historian and canoness Hrotsvit of Gandersheim, who portrayed Otto I as a new biblical King David, 'subduing pagans into the service of Christ so that a stable peace for the holy church might be established'.[20]

Christian peace, however, was the thinnest of disguises for the Ottonians' profoundly worldly and expansionistic strategy. Their empire lacked restrictive natural borders. In the west, where it straddled the Rhine, possessions like Lorraine and the Low Countries brought it into conflict with France. In the south, the duchy of Bavaria bestrode the Alps so that the Brenner Pass giving access to Italy lay within it. In the open plains of the north and east, Ottonian troops fought ceaselessly with Denmark, Poland, and Hungary. The Ottonians were also not above exploiting the weakness of lesser monarchs to absorb their lands into their own realm. When Otto I intervened to free Queen Adelaide from imprisonment by the Lombards in 951, for example, he took the opportunity to have himself crowned king of Italy. Ten years later, when usurpers had seized the Italian throne in Otto's absence, he answered the pope's desperate plea that, for 'the love of God . . . the king would free the pope himself and his ward, the Roman church, from the tyrants' fangs, and return them to their original health and liberty'.[21] 'Considering not his own interests [and] having gathered his forces, Otto came quickly to Italy,' piously intoned the Italian churchman Liudprand, who was rewarded for his Ottonian loyalty with a bishopric.[22] Otto ensured that *his* reward was the pope's formal acknowledgement of his imperial supremacy.

In the seven decades that followed, emperors promoted and deposed pontiffs at their pleasure. But gradually the papacy underwent a process of renewal that enabled it to claw back many of its former prerogatives and much of its standing – to the point where it was even able to excommunicate Emperor Henry IV in 1076, thereby provoking a rebellion within the empire. One of the fiercest areas of conflict between pope and emperor, however, remained the right to appoint bishops. Finally, a compromise was reached in 1122 at the Concordat of Worms, which recognized the emperor's right to bestow bishops with secular authority and the pope's to grant them their spiritual authority. But tensions between the papacy and the emperor, as well as with other secular rulers, continued to seethe throughout the Middle Ages, exacerbating the discord and instability that blighted so much of the politics of the era.

The German expansion was possible because the French kings struggled to ward off the Norse raiders. By the tenth century, some of these Norsemen had been allowed to settle in the northwest of France, where they gave their name to the region: Normandy. Others continued to pillage the coasts of Western Europe. From the Baltic, they sailed their longships up the European rivers to loot towns, farms, and monasteries. Later on, the French kings also became ensnared in conflicts with the powerful Angevin kings of England, who also controlled much of the western coast of France, and the many barons who hedged opportunistically between them. In 1190, King Philip II sealed an alliance with the English king, Richard the Lionheart, but the agreement broke down, and in 1214 the armies of the two countries met on a battlefield near Bouvines, in what is now northern France. The French were victorious and could finally enforce sovereignty over Normandy and Brittany. King Louis IX of France (1226–70) made important steps in centralizing power and gradually the balance of power started to shift. By 1250, Louis was in command of the most populous country of Europe, the largest economy and the largest army. He called himself *le lieutenant de dieu sur terre*, 'the deputy of god on earth'.

This ushered in a period of relative stability for Europe, which would allow it to thrive again and, for the first time since the fall of the Roman Empire, wield influence far beyond its borders. There were growing hopes for a true Christian peace. From the monasteries, the churches, and the cities an embryonic pacifist movement emerged that advocated a 'peace of God' – or at least, a 'truce of God'. Particularly prominent were monks from the influential French monastery of Cluny, who organized a series of peace gatherings. 'No Christian should kill another Christian, for whoever kills a Christian undoubtedly sheds the blood of Christ.'[23] Although, in time, even kings and emperors propagated the idea, wars among European Christians continued to be fought.

But a more important evolution during the period was the weakening of external threats to Europe as the Muslim world fragmented. This permitted a Christian pushback. In 1095, Pope Urban II launched a holy war to recapture Jerusalem: the First Crusade. Between 1095 and 1271, at least nine military expeditions left Europe with the purpose of campaigning in the Holy Land. The fact that the disorganization and confusion among the crusaders did not elicit an immediate counterattack, shows the political vulnerability of the Islamic world. After immense hardships, the warriors of the First Crusade captured Jerusalem in 1099 and ruled it for nearly a century. The God-given victory was accompanied by apocalyptic violence, as the crusader chaplain Raymond of Aguilers recorded: 'Some of the pagans were mercifully beheaded, others pierced by arrows plunged from towers, and yet others, tortured for a long time, were burned to death in searing flames.'[24] By the time the fighting ended, many thousands of Jerusalem's Muslim and Jewish inhabitants had been massacred.

A warmer climate, the increased prevalence of iron tools, and the introduction of crop rotation allowed for the improved agricultural yields that fostered steady economic growth in this period. These so-called High Middle Ages were the first time since the heyday of the Roman Empire that agricultural surpluses were able to sustain the development of crafts and increasingly long-distance trade as well as the development of large cities. In recognition of their vital commercial role, cities began to receive, or to take for themselves, new liberties, which only incited further the competition for glory and prosperity. The era's economic growth also led to population growth: by the thirteenth century, Europe's population had reached 60 million, almost on a level with China, India, and the Middle East.[25] And population growth led in turn to migration. The overcrowding of cities and competition for land caused many young men from Western and

Northern Europe to seek their fortunes on the Crusades – where religious and economic motives went hand in hand – and in the far wilder reaches of the continent's east.

Beyond the Danube

If Hungary, Bulgaria, and Kievan Rus' cushioned Western Europe from the Mongol invasions between 1237 and 1241, the resulting destruction and depopulation created a void from which German princes, the Teutonic Knights in the Baltic area, and many others benefited. But the region recovered, thanks partly to migration from Central Europe and growing trade along rivers like the Danube, Vistula, and Dnieper. Poland under the Piast Dynasty revived and became one of two main Catholic realms, along with the kingdom of Hungary. Hungary grew rich from its gold and salt reserves and from controlling much of the trade between the Holy Roman Empire, the Adriatic, and the Black Sea region. From the trading city of Novgorod had sprung the federation of Kievan Rus', which after the Mongol attacks continued to prosper on the traffic between the Baltic and the Black Sea that was carried along the River Dnieper. This brought it into sustained contact with Constantinople, which led to its adoption of Orthodox Christianity in much the same way as had happened earlier with the Bulgarian Empire, near the Black Sea. These states were in permanent competition with each other, with neighbouring semi-nomadic peoples like the Cumans and the Pechenegs, and with the main power to their south: the Byzantine Empire.

At the beginning of the eleventh century, Constantinople

was still the largest city of Europe, squatting like an enormous spider at the heart of a giant web of commerce that spanned much of Eurasia. Its vast walls had been besieged nine times, but it had never fallen. Its empire had experienced a revival in the tenth century. Churches and monasteries, austere on the outside, richly decorated with mosaics and wall paintings on the inside, were built wherever the Byzantines controlled the trade: in Calabria, Chios, the Peloponnese, Athens, Cyprus, and so on. A network of fortified ports near strategic gateways like the Bosporus, the Strait of Messina, the Strait of Otranto, and the delta of the Danube collected immense amounts of revenue. Trade treaties were signed with monarchs who supplied furs and metal from the north. Domination of the Black Sea grain trade was vital.[26] To protect this commercial empire, the Byzantines deployed a large fleet of galleys, maintained a barrier of fortresses in Anatolia to guard its southern border, and sowed division among the states and peoples adjoining its northern frontier.

In his *De Administrando Imperio*, a work on imperial governance, the tenth-century Byzantine emperor Constantine VII had advised his son to show wisdom, to avoid relying on armed force, to foster the alliance with the Pechenegs against the Bulgars, the Kievan Rus', and the Turks – and never to sell them the incendiary weapon known as 'Greek fire', on which Byzantine naval supremacy in particular depended.[27] But the empire's security was challenged nevertheless: by an alliance between the Pechenegs and Bulgars; by the Normans, who took control of the Ionian Sea; by a civil war in 1047, which elicited an attack from the Pechenegs; by growing assertiveness from the Seljuk Turks in Anatolia, marked by their decisive defeat of the Byzantines at the Battle of Manzikert in 1071. 'It was my misfortune to find the Empire surrounded on all sides by barbarians, with no defence worthy of consideration,' said the Byzantine emperor Alexius I, according to his daughter, Anna Comnena.[28]

The new dynasty established by Alexius I Comnenus (1081–1118) eventually restored order, but at a very high price. Domestic unrest made the emperor neglect the navy, so that the Byzantines had to rely on the support of their former dependent and now up-and-coming economic rival, Venice. The Byzantine chronicler Niketas Choniates described how the lack of funds for the imperial navy strengthened the position of Venice, damaged trade, and diverted even more income from the treasury.[29] Protected by its shallow lagoon, the Venetian republic tried to isolate itself from the turmoil on the Italian Peninsula and turned to the sea. In 1082, in exchange for assisting the Byzantines in their attempts to resist the Norman encroachment into the Ionian Sea, the Venetians were granted the right to trade throughout the empire free from any taxes.

Under the Comnenian Dynasty, Constantinople flourished again for much of the twelfth century. It continued to look down on the Western Europeans, regarded the Orthodox Church as superior, and contented itself with the fact that the loss of its direct control of trade was compensated somewhat by the commercial activity that the merchants of Venice generated in Constantinople.[30] Yet continued military weakness forced the emperors to pursue alliances with the West. It was a Byzantine embassy at the Council of Piacenza in 1095 – informing Pope Urban II about the plight of Christians in the

East and begging for aid – that led to the preaching of the
First Crusade a few months later. Distrust between Constan-
tinople and Western Europe, however, remained deep-seated.
The Byzantines still thought of the Western Europeans as
barbarians. Westerners returned the favour by regarding the
Byzantines as lazy, overbearing, and deceitful.[31]

By the late twelfth century, the balance of maritime
power in the Mediterranean had shifted decisively to the
west. In 1180, Constantinople could only muster thirty vessels, Venice over a hundred. Meanwhile, distrust between the
Byzantines and the West, coupled with Venetian mercantile
and political ambitions, resulted in the sack of Constantinople in 1204 by a combined force of Venetians and troops
from France and the Low Countries, who had come east to
crusade in the Holy Land. To the horror of the Byzantines, a
count from tiny Flanders was crowned emperor. The empire
fragmented as territories refused to recognize the new ruler;
what was left of the trade fell almost exclusively to Venice.

Destroyer of the Infidels

East of Constantinople, no major power was able to match
the long-lasting success of the early Islamic caliphates or
previous empires like the Sasanians'. In the eleventh century,
the vast area between China and Europe remained fractured
as four main powers competed for supremacy: the Ghaznavids, with their power base in what is now Afghanistan,
the Buyids in Iran, the Seljuks in Anatolia, and the Fatimids
in Egypt. Although the Abbasid Dynasty also survived – and
their prestigious capital, Baghdad, remained an important

centre of culture and learning – they fell under the effective control first of the Buyids and then the Seljuks, who turned them into puppet kings and burnished their own credentials by association with the lustre of the caliphate.

The Seljuks had originated as part of a band of Turkish tribes living on the plains between the Caspian and Aral Seas, where they had converted to Islam in around 950. In 1034, at which point they numbered no more than about 10,000 people, they were forced to leave their homes on an arduous migration: 'From sheer necessity,' recorded the thirteenth-century Syriac chronicler Bar Hebraeus, 'they are compelled to depart to another quarter in order to find food for themselves and their beasts.'[32] Initially, they hoped to obtain a new home peacefully in the region of Khorasan – now Iran and Afghanistan – writing humbly to the Ghaznavid sultan: 'If the sultan sees fit, he will accept us as his servants . . . we have nowhere else to go.' But the sultan's vizier recommended caution: 'Up to this point, this has been an affair of dealing with shepherds, now they have become armies who seize provinces.'[33] When the Ghaznavids sought to drive the Seljuks away, they were defeated. Forced to grant the Seljuks' original demands, the Ghaznavids were powerless to stop them seizing the great caravan city of Merv as well in 1036.

But soon the Seljuks were no longer satisfied with what they held. In 1040, they defeated the Ghaznavid Empire, which by then was severely weakened by over-taxation and religious oppression. Its slow-moving troops were no match for the mobile Seljuk cavalry. In 1055, the struggling Abbasids called on the Seljuks' assistance against the Buyids. The Seljuks promptly drove the Buyids out of Baghdad, and kept the city for themselves, albeit nominally under Abbasid suzerainty. In 1071, they decisively defeated the Byzantine army at the Battle of Manzikert, which gave them control over most of Anatolia. By this time, the Seljuks were claiming to be the descendants of the ancient Achaemenid kings of Persia and to have inherited the divine right of the Sasanian rulers. They also aspired to universal rule, as the roll-call of titles belonging to Kilij Arslan II, a descendant of the victor of Manzikert, illustrates:

> The great sultan, the august *shahanshah*, chief of the
> sultans of the Arabs and the Persians, master of the
> nations, glory of the world and religion, pillar of Islam and
> the Muslims, glory of kings and sultans, defender of the
> law, destroyer of the infidels and the polytheists, helper
> of the fighters for faith, guardian of the countries of Allah,
> protector of the servants of Allah, sultan of the lands of
> Rum, Armenia, the Franks, and Syria.[34]

The conquest of Anatolia brought the Seljuks into direct confrontation with the Fatimid Dynasty in the Levant. The Fatimids were Shia and predominantly of Berber stock, having originated in what is now Tunisia. They had shifted their centre of power to Egypt in the late tenth century in furtherance of their primary objective, which was to oppose Sunni Arab expansion.[35] Their rulers were as much religious leaders as political ones: they claimed not only the title of caliph, but also that of imam, or leader of the Shia, and Mahdi – the saviour whom the Shia expected to restore justice just before the end of the world. 'The world is yours and your dynasty's,' sang a Fatimid poet. 'Young is your empire, O Mahdi, and the time is its slave.'[36] From Egypt, the soldiers of the Fatimids marched in the footsteps of the ancient pharaohs' armies across the Sinai Desert, into the Levant, and even on towards Mesopotamia. But after failing to overcome Abbasid resistance, the Fatimids then found themselves being driven back by the Seljuk advance out of Anatolia.

By 1076, the Seljuks had captured Damascus and were forcing their way deep into Egypt. A Jewish trader in Cairo was left dumbfounded: 'They entered Fustat [Cairo], robbed, murdered and ravished and pillaged the storehouses.'[37] The early thirteenth-century Arab historian Ibn al-Athir recounted: 'Wars between the rival sultans went on and on, corruption spread, possessions were plundered, blood was shed, the land was ruined, the villages were burned.'[38] Faced with the Seljuk threat, the Fatimids took advantage of the presence of the First Crusade, which had advanced through Anatolia and was inching towards Jerusalem. In 1098, the Fatimids proposed partitioning the Levant: Syria would go to the Franks and Palestine to them. The proposal fell on deaf ears, but by this time the danger posed by the Seljuks seemed less imminent. A succession conflict had split the Seljuk realm in two, with the sultanate of Rum in Anatolia and the Khwarazmian kingdom in Central Asia.

The Fatimids too fell prey to internal struggles, their authority having been weakened by their conflicts with Seljuks, crusaders, and North African tribes, and by the growing power of wealthy landowners. Finally, in 1171, an ambitious vizier named Saladin toppled the Fatimids and founded his own Ayyubid Dynasty in Egypt. Saladin pushed the Seljuk sultanate of Rum back to Anatolia and reconquered Jerusalem from the crusaders. Although a new crusader army led by Richard the Lionheart subsequently delivered a decisive defeat to Saladin at the Battle of Arsuf, it failed in its objective of taking back Jerusalem. By the time Saladin died eighteen months later, in 1193, Richard had abandoned the Holy Land, fearing attempts on his throne in England. It was left to the Mongols to deliver the fatal blow to the Islamic polities. In 1258, they sacked Baghdad, casting the Muslim world into disarray.

'The sultans were at loggerheads with each other,' wrote Ibn al-Athir about the Islamic Middle East in the late eleventh century. 'This enabled the Franks to occupy the country.'[39] After the fracturing of the Abbasid Caliphate in the ninth century, no single Islamic power was able to control Egypt, the Levant, Mesopotamia, and Persia at the same time. The irrigation systems in Egypt and Mesopotamia were neglected as elites focused on trade instead. But, protected by its Adriatic lagoon, Venice slowly undermined Islamic commercial dominance in the Eastern Mediterranean. Only under powerful Ottoman sultans like Selim I and Suleiman the Magnificent in the sixteenth century would the Islamic world regain a degree of unity.

The Gates of Hind

At first glance, the period from the eleventh to the mid-thirteenth century in the Indian subcontinent was an age of spectacular art and architecture, science and literature – at least for the large elite whose enviable lifestyle was supported by an immense economy. Ships traded with far-flung places, returning with rich and exotic goods. There were powerful merchants' guilds, thriving and tax-free trade villages, and royal agents to safeguard commerce across the border.[40] 'Gardens, filled for the enjoyment of all mankind with grapes, lecture-halls, wells with pellucid water and drinking fountains' – these were what distinguished India from the arid, dusty towns of Central Asia.[41]

Yet this was also an era in which over a dozen kingdoms struggled for supremacy. Many literary works describe a world rent by divisions and discord, a realm of spies, shifting alliances, overambitious kings, and fratricide. 'Royalty is a thorny creeper; it destroys family affection,' stated the king of a small realm in Kashmir.[42] Class struggle between the rich and poor castes of Hindu society was rife, and resentment against the ruling class widespread. 'Crabs kill their fathers, small bees their mothers, but the ungrateful Kayasthas, when they become rich, kill all,' observed the same Kashmiri king. The trader, he continued, 'differs from the tiger only in having a face smoothed with oil, in his power of speech, and his humble mien . . . Prostitutes, Kayasthas and big merchants are naturally deceitful. Men's energy, like that of sleeping serpents, is not known till they are angry.'[43]

During this period, the Hindu Chola kingdom in southeastern India emerged as one of Asia's most powerful trading nations. The Cholas invested heavily in irrigation systems to increase agricultural production, but also maintained a fleet of hundreds of vessels, which they deployed for trade as well as military expeditions. In the final years of the tenth century, they invaded Sri Lanka, having learned of internal strife on the island from a merchant. The Cholas turned Sri Lanka into a quasi-colony, destroying Buddhist monasteries, incorporating local chiefs, clearing forests, and establishing new settlements.[44] Afterwards, in around 1025, the Cholas ravaged its main commercial rival in the Indian Ocean, the Southeast Asian kingdom of Srivijaya. One of their goals was to take over the trade across the Kra Isthmus – the narrowest point of the Malayan Peninsula – which formed 'the general rendezvous of the ships of Siraf and Oman, where they meet the ships of China'.[45]

In India itself, the Cholas were at loggerheads with an alliance of Pandyan princes, who wanted to rid themselves of the Chola yoke. When they refused to pay their tribute, the Cholas razed the ancient Pandyan coronation hall, which merely intensified resistance. The Pandyans turned for support to rebellious princes in Sri Lanka and to the Chalukya kingdom – 'the terror of the Cholas'.[46] For decades, the Chalukyas and the Cholas, both Hindu kingdoms, had been locked in conflict over the fertile valleys and trade routes of the Deccan Plateau. The *Vikramankadevacarita* – a famous hagiography of the Chalukya king Vikramaditya VI (1076–1126) – described how 'The Chola again became proud and insolent', eliciting fear in their neighbours.[47] When attempts to conciliate them failed, war followed. But it was the Cholas who were defeated and forced to sue for peace by sending an ambassador to offer a princess in marriage to the triumphant Chalukya king.

It was divisions like these that encouraged foreign invaders from the north and benefited them when they attacked. Chinese and Muslim visitors were impressed by the size of Indian armies and by the 'necklace' of fortresses built by the northern kingdoms to defend the main routes from Central Asia, the so-called 'Gates of Hind'.[48] But, in the late eleventh century, neither succeeded in stemming a new wave of assaults. These were mounted by warlords originating from Khorasan, known as the Ghurids. 'The lords of the horse', the terrified Indians called them – as well as 'beef-eating barbarians', in recognition of their Islamic faith.[49] The kingdoms and tribes in the north offered fierce resistance, and depicted the Ghurids as the common enemy of all Hindus. But the main Hindu powers, such as the Chalukyas, were located far away from the fighting and initially showed little solidarity. This left the smaller realms exposed to relentless attacks from the Ghurids' mobile squadrons of horse archers, against which their infantry struggled to cope. After the Ghurid cavalry had inflicted serious losses on the northern Indian states between 1175 and 1186, resistance weakened. The Gates of Hind were now wide open; and yet more Ghurids poured in. In 1198, a great mosque was opened in Delhi to mark the establishment of Muslim rule in India.

Alliances Conducted at Sea

Despite the ways that the nomadic and tribal cultures of Eurasia had grown in strength and sophistication over the centuries, both the Byzantine and Song Empires still held to many of their ancient imperial traditions when it came to diplomatic dealings with them. Both still maintained dedicated offices to handle 'barbarian' affairs, although their main purpose was really no more than to manage protocol when envoys appeared at court. Those envoys' primary task continued to be to convey written or oral messages between monarchs. At the same time, diplomacy became to some degree global, or at least transcontinental, particularly along the Silk Road. Perhaps most remarkably, the Byzantine emperor Michael VII dispatched an envoy to the Song court in 1078 to negotiate a coalition against the Seljuks. The Song, however, considered the Byzantines' representative as an ordinary tribute payer. 'They have during former dynasties not sent tribute to our court. During the tenth month of the 4th year of the period Yüan-feng, their king, Mieh-li-i-ling-kai-sa, first sent the ta-shouling [high official] Ni-ssu-tu-ling-ssu-meng-p'an to offer as tribute saddled horses, sword-blades, and real pearls.'[50] This did not prevent the dispatch of another Byzantine mission, which was received in 1091.

In medieval Europe, churchmen and scholars – the two were indistinguishable – remained the main actors of diplomacy between states. They were also prominent in the pursuit of reconciling differences peacefully. St Francis of Assisi, for example, was one of the main advocates of tolerance and peace within the Christian community of the early thirteenth century; he even journeyed to Cairo in 1219 to try to end the Crusades by converting the Ayyubid sultan.

Increasingly, however, the period saw the papacy attempt to advance its spiritual and political authority through diplomatic endeavours. As well as sponsoring peace conferences, one of the chief papal strategies involved identifying common adversaries and seeking to build coalitions against them. Two of the chief targets were the Normans, whose ventures in Italy from the mid-eleventh century onwards were regarded by the popes as posing a threat to their security, and the Holy Roman Emperor. Pope Leo IX (1049–54), for example, referred to 'the most evil nation of the Normans' and called for the liberation of Christianity from the clutches of the Holy Roman Empire.[51] Gregory VII (1073–85), meanwhile, spoke of the Church as 'the legion of Christ' and promoted the idea of a 'militia of St Peter' recruited from knights across Europe to defend papal interests. In 1177, Venice hosted a large peace conference to try and resolve the longstanding differences between the Holy Roman Emperor, the papacy and its allies among the city states of Northern Italy, and the Norman kingdom of Sicily. A follow-up conference, held in Constance in 1183, confirmed the autonomy of the northern city states from imperial control.

The greatest common enemy of the Middle Ages, however, was Islam. In 1095, Pope Urban II summoned a conference to Clermont to call for unity and what would be the start of a holy war against the Muslims in the Levant that lasted for almost 200 years. 'You have seen for a long time the great disorder in the world,' he lamented. 'Although, O sons of God, you have promised more firmly than ever to keep the peace among yourselves and to preserve the rights of the church, there remains still an important work for you to do,' the pope continued. 'For your brethren who live in the east are in urgent need of your help . . . For, as the most of you have heard, the Turks and Arabs have attacked them.'[52]

The Crusades, as a multinational endeavour, were responsible for stimulating much medieval diplomacy. The crusader Geoffrey of Villehardouin, for example, observed how the barons that led the Fourth Crusade (1202–4) first held a summit at Soissons, then appointed envoys with full authority to negotiate, and subsequently sent them to Venice to ask for assistance. In Venice, the crusaders' delegates first had to make their case to the doge, then to the Great Council, and finally to a plenary session of the popular assembly in St Mark's Square – in a manner that recalls Thucydides' account of the Corcyran envoys addressing the Spartans and the Athenians. According to Geoffrey of Villehardouin, who acted as the crusaders' spokesman, they had been told 'to prostrate ourselves at your feet and not to get up until you have agreed to take pity on the Holy Land overseas'.[53] Venice consented to help, but continued to trade with the crusaders' enemies at the same time.

As this episode reveals, expediency was just as important as principles in determining medieval diplomatic strategy. Political alliances and trade agreements were forged and broken with equal impunity, while the force of circumstance overrode all. In 1096, for example, Urban II was prepared to help negotiate a peace on behalf of the duke of Normandy so that the latter could lead his army on the First Crusade. Around 1150, the abbot of the influential monastery of Cluny encouraged the Holy Roman Emperor and the Normans to make peace so that they could join in taking revenge on 'the worthless ruler' of the Byzantines for his role in the failure of the Second Crusade (1147–9). The Italians may generally have despised the Byzantines, too, but when Frederick Barbarossa descended on the northern cities in the 1170s, they scurried to secure Byzantine aid. After the sack of Constantinople in 1204, the Byzantines themselves were prepared to seek an alliance with their arch-enemies, the Seljuks, in their desperation to eject the crusaders from their capital. In 1220, Venice also signed trade agreements with the Seljuk sultans which provided for the mutual protection of ships and traders as well as the recognition of property rights.[54]

The Mongols, the other great common enemy of Christianity, did not elicit a united stance either. Some crusaders saw the Mongols as allies against the Muslims. Despite the stories of horrific Mongol atrocities emanating from the East, Pope Honorius III (1218–27) regarded the Mongols as potential associates in the fight against Islam, while Venice signed a trade treaty with the Mongols and rumours circulated that the French had tried to goad the Mongols into attacking the Holy Roman Empire.[55] But after the Mongols devastated Hungary in 1241, Pope Innocent IV called for a common front, a 'remedy against the Mongols'. In preparation for a council of European leaders in 1245, Innocent sent the Franciscan monk John of Plano Carpini, laden with gifts, to the court of the Mongol khan. His main task was to gain information about the plans of the Mongols concerning Europe and to deliver two letters from the pope explaining the Christian faith and calling for peace. Was not the whole world united by bonds of natural affinity, suggested the pope, and should not all men follow the teachings of Christ and 'live united in concord in the fear of God'?[56] Güyük Khan countered by proposing that if the pope and his fellow European rulers really wanted peace they should offer him fealty. In 1248, the first two Mongol envoys to Western Europe arrived in Rome where they delivered a blunt message: their khan was ordained by the gods to rule the whole world. Nevertheless, diplomatic endeavours continued. Over the next few years, Louis IX of France dispatched further envoys to the Mongols to try to convince them to aid a crusade to the Holy Land, while the Genoese hoped to be granted access to trade in the Black Sea region, which the Mongols controlled.

At the opposite end of Eurasia, in China, diplomatic practice was also characterized by opportunism. The Song brokered temporary alliances with the Tibetans, the Xia, the Jin, and many others – including even the Mongols. Sometimes these treaties were meant to sow discord so that other powers did not unite against them; at others their purpose was to obtain a truce that would allow the overstretched imperial troops time to regroup. The eminent Song official Tong Guan was a particular advocate of secretly negotiated deals, which came to be known as 'alliances conducted at sea'.

Like their European counterparts, the Song court recruited many of their envoys from the ranks of the intelligentsia, although the strategy did not always pay dividends. On one occasion, in 1075, the great polymath Shen Kuo was called in to try and break an impasse in long-running discussions with the Liao. For years, the Song and the Liao had been trying to fix their common border: cartographers had surveyed the region to create meticulous new maps, while other experts had researched historical precedents and legal arguments – but to no avail.[57] Shen Kuo and his staff spent further months trawling the imperial archives in search of fresh evidence to back the Song claim and learning their case by heart. But when they were finally admitted to the presence of the Liao king, all their assiduous efforts were angrily dismissed out of hand.[58]

The fiasco surrounding the negotiations between the Southern Song and the Jin in the early 1140s was arguably even worse. Although both states agreed on the Yellow River as their border, the treaty lasted barely a year before hard-liners on both sides, who considered its terms humiliating, sparked a new war. Concerned that the conflict was making his generals too powerful, the Song emperor appointed the senior official Qin Hui to negotiate peace. Qin was a prominent member of the peace party at court; he had also been a hostage of the Jin, developing close relations with them. Qin began by having the Song generals responsible for the war arrested and executed – a misstep that left the army leaderless and gave the Jin the upper hand in the rest of the negotiations. When the Treaty of Shaoxing was signed in 1141, the border had been shifted south almost to the River Yangtze – many miles in the Jin's favour – an immense indemnity had been forced on the Song, and their state was referred to as 'insignificant'.[59] The public outcry at what was widely perceived to be Qin Hui's treachery was immense, and has been used to fuel Chinese patriotism ever since.[60] Even today, in the former Song capital of Hangzhou, citizens passing by the tomb of Qin's victims still spit on his kneeling statue.

Why Europe?

The Mongol expansion was the most important political event between 1000 and 1250. Like the Scythians and the Huns before them, the Mongols enjoyed unequalled mobility across the Eurasian landmass via the long grass highway of the steppes that extend from Mongolia to Eastern Europe. In common with previous nomadic invasions, climate change also formed an important destabilizing factor: it was a period of exceptionally cold summers that forced the Mongols from their homeland. Their invasions were decisive in determining the distribution of power: they caused long-term instability and economic decline in Asia, but they left Western Europe unscathed to continue its heretofore unremarkable development.

This outcome was largely the consequence of geography. Both Western Europe and China were politically fractured: China between the Southern Song, the Jin, and the Xia; Western Europe between France, the Holy Roman Empire, and several other smaller powers. In both regions, the failure of polities to unite against the common Mongol threat produced a domino effect as the Mongols were able to deploy the resources of states they had conquered in the periphery against the centres of power. The only significant difference between the two scenarios is one of distance. The Mongol heartland of the Orkhon Valley is about 1,500 kilometres from the North China Plain and 6,500 kilometres from the nearest fringes of Western Europe. As a result, the Mongols could never muster the same forces in the west as in the east; and it was quite understandable that the Mongol troops did not attempt to return to Western Europe after they had trekked back east to bury their khan. At the same time, the ongoing fragmentation of the Muslim world meant that Western Europe had far less to fear from its southern borders than in previous centuries and could devote itself to propagating the seeds of development that had started to sprout since the year 1000. This 'lucky break' would prove crucial in Europe's history.

CHAPTER 11

Huddling in the Darkness

1250–1500 CE

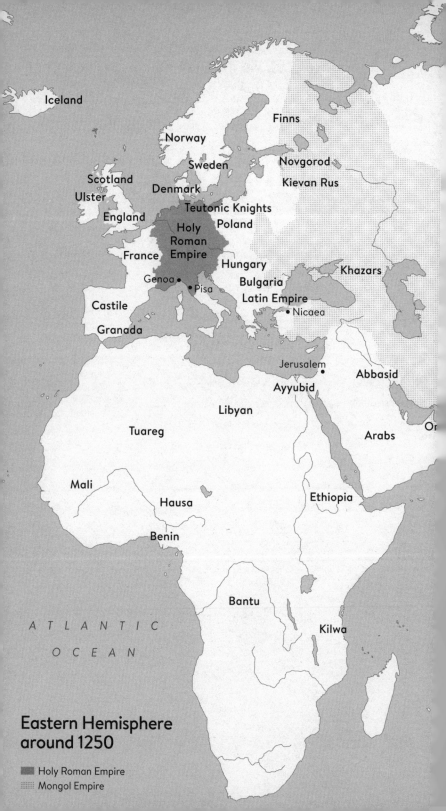

Iceland

Norway

Finns

Sweden

Novgorod

Denmark

Kievan Rus

Scotland

Ulster

Teutonic Knights

England

Poland

Holy
Roman
Empire

France

Hungary

Genoa •

Khazars

• Pisa

Bulgaria

Latin Empire

Castile

• Nicaea

Granada

Jerusalem

Abbasid

•

Ayyubid

Libyan

Arabs

Or

Tuareg

Mali

Hausa

Ethiopia

Benin

Bantu

ATLANTIC

Kilwa

OCEAN

Eastern Hemisphere
around 1250

Holy Roman Empire

Mongol Empire

Mongol

Ainu

Japan

• Delhi

hi Sultenate

Southern Song

wa

Vietnam

PACIFIC

Chola

Khmer

OCEAN

Malays

Srivijaya

DIAN

CEAN

500   1000   1500 km

500   1000 miles

'This slumber of forgetfulness will not last forever,' promised Petrarch in 1330 CE. 'After darkness has been dispelled, our grandsons will be able to walk back into the pure radiance of the past.'[1] The Italian poet and thinker was writing as Europe tentatively entered a new age of intellectual endeavour. Ancient works of literature and philosophy, industriously copied by scribes in monasteries, began to be more widely circulated. Classical treatises on science and mathematics, preserved by Islamic thinkers, were transmitted back to the West along with new ideas. Creative prodigies like Dante and Giotto produced extraordinary, innovative masterpieces. But Europe in the time of Petrarch also saw important economic breakthroughs: in the manufacturing of textiles, the production of steel, and the milling of grain. It was an era of revolutions in trade too, with developments in shipping, for example, and increasingly sophisticated financial instruments and networks.

Yet 'darkness', as Petrarch was all too well aware, still lingered. Rome, the city where he would soon live, remained little more than a scrapheap of imperial marble. Sacked by invading armies, looted by brigands, and abandoned by the popes, its population had shrunk to only 35,000. It would not begin to be rebuilt until the fifteenth century; this was not yet the age of imposing domes and elegant piazzas. Across Europe, from the late thirteenth century, the climate became colder and harsher as the world entered the Little Ice Age. Food production dropped, famine followed, making the population more vulnerable to disease. The plague epidemic known as the Black Death, which ravaged Europe between 1347 and 1351, killed at least 40 per cent of the population.

At the opposite end of Eurasia, life for many was similarly bleak in the fourteenth century. China too experienced the chilling effects of the Little Ice Age and suffered a plague pandemic, while the economic consequences of the Mongol invasion a century earlier were still being felt.[2] The whole region was scarred by immense hardship, violent social unrest, and cataclysmic wars whose destructiveness was magnified by the ever more widespread use of gunpowder artillery. Invented in China, this revolutionary weapon soon reached the Indian subcontinent, the Middle East, and Europe, heralding the dawn of a new age in warfare.

The period between 1250 and 1500 saw both renewed hopes of order and the reality of war shape diplomacy, politics, and government. It witnessed the advent of new imperial dynasties in Europe and China; new empires in the Middle East, Central Asia, and India; and the emergence of major powers in Central and South America for the first time since the collapse of the Maya civilization centuries before. This was an age of rebirth, of sorts.

Universal Peace

In the early 1250s, the citizens of Paris worshipped in the light of God that poured through the spectacular rose windows of the Gothic cathedral of Notre-Dame. Beyond the walls of the city's stone tribute to the deity, the worshippers were all too aware that the divine light also shone down on a world of war, destitution, and demons. Paris may have been the vibrant capital of a wealthy country, but the king and many of his nobles were fighting a crusade in Egypt, and brigands plagued the surroundings of the city. 'See the people of the nations, huddling in the darkness,' wrote the composer Pérotin in a mass for Notre-Dame. In more profane songs, the troubadour Guiraut Riquier lamented the carnal lust that drove lords to violent madness. Only devotional love could create a world of bliss and peace without end.[3] In the shadow of Paris's Gothic cathedral, the 'universal doctor' Albertus Magnus conjectured that, in anticipation of peace on earth, sacrifice in the cause of the Church was the highest good, and that the Christian realm needed to be protected.

Many other churchmen in the mid-thirteenth century thought along similar lines. Henry of Ghent, for example, argued that Christian lords should not fight wars against each other, but could band together to combat infidels.[4] Vincent of Beauvais, meanwhile, championed the idea that Christian unity and peace should be achieved by following the example of Christ, 'who won by sweetness and not by swords'.[5] The Italian theologian Thomas Aquinas (1225–74), meanwhile, adopted the middle ground. Kings could fight to defend their realms, as long as they were motivated by zeal for justice. And of all forms of governance, monarchy held the best chance of advancing the common good, which Aquinas defined as a combination of peace and virtuous living. But the authority of kings was to be checked by natural law, which was born out of God's eternal law. He drew confidence from his belief that men were innately social creatures, willing to transcend the monotony of their village life by aspiring to the common good and fighting tyranny.

But who should be king? The Florentine poet and statesman Dante Alighieri (1265–1321) advanced the theory of universal monarchy. In his political treatise *De Monarchia*, he proposed that the way to end the fighting between kings, and between the Holy Roman Emperor and the pope, was to vest supreme temporal authority in the emperor, with spiritual leadership reserved to the papacy. Dante's contemporary, the French political theorist Pierre Dubois, agreed with the concept of universal monarchy, but believed that the king of France was a better candidate for the role. The Holy See had the backing of thinkers like the archbishop Giles of Rome for its long-held belief that the supreme political power rightfully belonged to the pope. The Italian thinker Marsilius of Padua, meanwhile, weighed in on the side of the Holy Roman Emperor, but insisted that he had to be democratically elected in the first place. The English philosopher William of Ockham went a step further by arguing that both the pope and the emperor could be deposed if they conducted themselves unjustly, and that if Christians were not to be slaves, they had to be free to criticize the Church. The desperation of Europe's quest for a just ruler is perhaps best exemplified by the behaviour of Petrarch, who first begged the populist leader Cola di Rienzo to bring peace in Italy, then the pope, and finally the emperor. In sum: everyone agreed on the need for unity, justice, and peace, but they profoundly disagreed over who should be their ultimate guarantor.

A few thinkers, however, argued that diplomacy was the best way to bring about and maintain peace. 'The business of an ambassador is peace,' asserted the fifteenth-century French legal expert Bernard du Rosier. 'An ambassador labors for the public good . . . An ambassador is sacred because he acts for the general welfare.'[6] His contemporary, the envoy and memoirist Philippe de Commynes, was less idealistic, warning against diplomatic summits because they encouraged grandstanding and underhand methods of persuasion. 'There was scarce a day passed,' he wrote of one conference, 'but some artifice or other was made use of to debauch and bring over people from one side to the other . . . that place was afterwards called the Market, because the bargain was driven there.'[7] The Venetian diplomat Ermolao Barbaro was even more blunt. The role of ambassadors was not to advance the cause of universal peace, but 'to do, say, advise, and think whatever may best serve the preservation and aggrandizement of his own state'.[8] As the French king Louis XI instructed his envoys: 'If they lie to you, see to it that you lie more to them.'[9]

Nevertheless, the intensifying political and economic connections between states resulted in the emergence of a growing community of specialist diplomats. Although most were envoys employed on specific missions, permanent ambassadors also began to be appointed. They were dispatched to gather information, win allies and keep a wary eye on rival emissaries, and defend the political and economic interests of their own state. This expansion in diplomatic activity also led to the establishment of new bureaucracies to manage and archive official correspondence and to the evolution of conventions dictating the practice of diplomacy and the treatment of its exponents. As early as 1339, Venice had realized that any impediments or irritants it inflicted on other states' emissaries would be reciprocated on its own ambassadors 'who go continually throughout the world' – Venetian interests, therefore, would best be served by promoting the doctrine of diplomatic immunity.

Nowhere were the benefits of peace and stability – whether achieved through diplomatic cooperation or enforced by a universal monarch – so visible in the fourteenth and fifteenth centuries as in Italy. Trade boomed and the patchwork of cities and states negotiated hundreds of *pacta speciala* to facilitate commerce. The early fifteenth-century Venetian doge Tommaso Mocenigo even proposed making Italy a paradise of peace. 'You supply the whole world,' he asserted to his fellow citizens. 'Let us live in peace, so that our city will be made wealthy in gold and silver, in crafts, navigation, trade, nobility, in houses, wealthy citizens, in population growth.'[10] But trade was also a reason for conflict. Milan competed with Florence over silk production. Florence had tried to monopolize the production of alum, used for dyeing cloth, and had pressured the pope to prohibit imports from Muslim suppliers; while Milan had tried to control textile imports from Flanders via the Gotthard Pass. Venice, meanwhile, became embroiled in its own conflict with Milan over the River Po and so allied with Florence. When Milan relapsed into civil war and Venice became too powerful, Florence switched sides. Venice then formed an alliance with Naples. Further wars followed, increasingly involving the papacy, which was seeking to re-establish its political power in the Italian Peninsula after the end of a schism during which a second pope had resided in Avignon.

In 1454, Milan and Florence agreed the Peace of Lodi, vowing to preserve the status quo and to refrain from intervention in each other's domestic affairs. A few months later, they and the other Italian belligerents accepted the pope's proposal of a general peace and the formation of an Italic League of states. But tensions continued to simmer, fuelled by ancient rivalries between polities and the fierce personal ambitions of rulers. Increasingly it was pragmatic understanding of the balance of power that maintained stability rather than the high principles of treaty-based international order. As the leading Florentine statesman Lorenzo de' Medici put it: 'I care little about the universal league . . . I put more trust in desires and minds than in written provisions, which, as you know, are made and broken whenever necessary.'[11] His trust was not entirely misplaced: relative peace reigned in the Italian Peninsula until the end of the fifteenth century.

Italy could afford its anarchy as long as the Turks remained east of the Adriatic Sea and the powers of Northern Europe – in particular France and the Holy Roman Empire – were too busy sorting out their own problems to intervene south of the Alps. In the case of France, for much of the fourteenth and fifteenth centuries it was embroiled in a series of conflicts with England known collectively as the Hundred Years War (1337–1453). Originating in issues of succession and sovereignty relating to the

English and French crowns, the struggle spread to Spain, Portugal, Scotland, Flanders, and Germany, as the two main combatants battled each other through allies and proxies. Following the victory of Agincourt (1415) – where English longbows neutralized the might of the French cavalry – and an alliance with the wealthy and quasi-autonomous duchy of Burgundy, England briefly came to control much of northern France. But the death of the capable English king Henry V, who left an infant successor, and growing French resentment against the depredations of English rule led to a turning point.

Beginning with the siege of Orléans in 1429, where Joan of Arc inspired the French to victory, the English were slowly driven back. In 1435, France scored a major diplomatic coup at the Congress of Arras, where it persuaded the war-weary Burgundians to end their alliance with England. Although the final battle of the Hundred Years War was fought in 1453, the conflict was not formally ended until 1475, when the kings of the two belligerent nations met in person at Picquigny in northern France. Their encounter took place on a specially constructed wooden bridge over the River Somme; fearing assassination, the two monarchs and their parties were separated by 'a strong wooden grate or lattice, such as the lions' cages are made of', in the middle.[12]

The Hundred Years War cost the English crown every last vestige of the continental possessions that it had inherited from its Norman and Angevin predecessors – except for Calais, which was finally surrendered in 1558. The financial burden of the conflict, and the humiliation of defeat, sparked a civil war in England – the so-called Wars of the Roses (1455–85) – as rival magnates competed to control the throne. Victory for France was accompanied by a massive extension of royal authority, further transforming the kingdom from a collection of territories held together primarily by feudal ties of vassalage to a more recognizably modern centralized state. With the return of the duchy of Burgundy to direct rule by the crown in 1477, after French troops killed the last duke in battle – and despite continued attempts by the French nobility to regain their autonomy, most notably in the so-called Mad War (1485–8) – France was firmly established as one of the great powers of Europe. French self-confidence was now such that it interfered in Germany, Spain, and Scotland. In 1494, it invaded Italy, igniting a series of conflicts that lasted for over sixty years.

The other main combatant in these Italian wars was the Holy Roman Empire of the Habsburg Dynasty. One of the leading families in the empire, the Habsburgs had controlled the duchy of Austria since the late thirteenth century. A strategic marriage to the daughter – and only child – of the Emperor Sigismund in 1437 paved the way for a Habsburg candidate to be elected de facto emperor three years later. But it was not until 1452 that the Emperor Frederick III finally persuaded the pope formally to acknowledge his title with an imperial coronation in Rome.

Marriages, not war, continued to make the Habsburgs powerful. 'Let others wage wars, but you, happy Austria, shall marry,' became an informal motto of the family. Frederick III's own marriage to the *infanta* of Portugal in 1452 brought him a vast dowry that helped secure his position. His most important achievement was to marry his son, Maximilian, to the daughter and heir of the last duke of Burgundy. Although laws of inheritance allowed France to claim the duchy itself, the rich Burgundian possessions in the Low Countries came to Maximilian with his wife in 1477. France attempted to repel this takeover, but was finally forced to recognize the Habsburg claim in 1493. Resentments lingered, however, and the rivalry between France and the Habsburg Empire underlay much of the conflict in Europe for the next 300 years.

When Maximilian I succeeded his father as emperor in 1486, the star of the Habsburgs was rising. He portrayed himself as a new Clovis, Charlemagne, and Augustus, all rolled into one. His control over major trade routes attracted the interest of the immensely rich banker Jakob Fugger who, in exchange for economic privileges, financed the political projects of Maximilian, not least the machinations required to ensure the succession of his grandson and heir as emperor. When Maximilian died in 1519, he left staggering debts to his bankers, but also a realm that controlled some of the richest areas of Europe.

By the end of the fifteenth century, therefore, Europe's order was dominated by France and the Habsburg Empire. On their fringes lay several lesser powers. In the Iberian Peninsula, the centuries-old struggle to expel the Islamic invaders, the *Reconquista*, reached its triumphant end with the conquest of the emirate of Granada in 1492. The victors were the kingdoms of Castile and Aragon; united by marriage in 1469, they now ruled almost the entire peninsula except for Portugal. Since the early fifteenth century, Portuguese energies had increasingly become focused on the Atlantic and West Africa. Aided by innovations in cartography, navigation, and ship design, intrepid Portuguese explorers claimed the archipelagos of Madeira and the Azores and had voyaged down the entire length of Africa, reaching the Cape of Good Hope in 1488. Envy of Portuguese discoveries, and the prospect of establishing a direct sea route to the riches of the East, led the Spanish monarchs to sponsor a voyage by the Genoese navigator Christopher Columbus in 1492. A new arena for imperial ambition – and the promise of untold wealth – beckoned.

In the east of Europe, a series of states formed a buffer against invasion from the steppes. These kingdoms possessed vast territories but none of them had a population larger than 5 million.[13] Although trade between them was extensive, fierce competition for control of that trade – which stemmed from the vast natural resources of the continental hinterland – meant that they were too divided to constitute a danger to the more developed and populous states on their western borders.

One of the most significant polities was the kingdom of Poland, which was reunited under the Piast Dynasty in 1320 after an extended period of fragmentation. The Piast kings fostered a common, Catholic Polish identity, and achieved a measure of coexistence with the nobility which was formalized in the powerful assembly known as the *sejm*. Their achievements were later hailed in terms that consciously recalled the age of imperial Rome: they had found a primitive country built of wood, and left a modern state constructed in stone.

After the Piast line failed in 1370, the succession eventually passed to the Jagiellonians, who had previously ruled the last pagan state in Europe, the grand duchy of Lithuania. This combined, and now fully Christian, realm occupied the dominant position between the Baltic and the Black Sea for much of the fifteenth century. Jagiellonian monarchs also succeeded to the thrones of Bohemia and Hungary; but despite encroaching deep into the Habsburg sphere of influence, they did not pose a significant threat to the latter's empire. Instead it was Poland–Lithuania that found itself increasingly challenged – by the emergence to its east of the aggressive and ambitious grand duchy of Moscow.

Founded from a shard of Kievan Rus' in the aftermath of the thirteenth-century Mongol invasion, Moscow remained a tributary vassal of the Mongols until it succeeded in finally casting off the 'Tatar yoke' in 1480. Under Ivan III (1462–1505), the grand duchy tripled in size, laying the foundations of the Russian Empire. Through his marriage to the niece of the last Byzantine emperor, Ivan was able to claim that Moscow had inherited the imperial mantle of Byzantium as the 'Third Rome'. His decision to adopt the title of *tsar*, or Caesar, sent a clear message: here was the equal of any so-called Roman emperor in the West.

The Rise of the Ottomans

In 1258, a few hundred Turkish horsemen from Central Asia came to Anatolia to offer their services to the Seljuk sultanate of Rum, which had fallen into disrepair after repeated Mongol attacks. The new arrivals settled on a stretch of land in the northwest. As the sultanate unravelled into a dozen smaller kingdoms, they claimed independence. The leader of the band, Osman (1299–1323), had founded what would become one of the great imperial dynasties, the Ottomans.

From their landlocked home, the Ottomans initially set their eyes on the neighbouring rich coastal cities, such as Bursa. They benefited in their early campaigns from the weakness around them, and their conquests soon brought them into conflict with the Byzantine Empire. Constantinople and the Byzantine state had never recovered from the sack of the city during the Fourth Crusade in 1204, and the period of Western rule that ensued. The Palaiologos Dynasty, which had occupied the imperial throne since the mid-thirteenth century, was beset by exhausting wars with the Serbians and the Bulgars, internal conflicts, plague epidemics, and inflation.

In the face of Ottoman pressure, the Byzantines were forced to give up fortress after fortress. In 1345, the Ottomans crossed the Dardanelles into Europe. In 1355, Emperor John V desperately appealed to the pope in Rome for a campaign against the Turkish infidels. In 1387, Thessaloniki fell. By 1389, the Ottoman cavalry – supported by cannon and an elite force of slave infantry known as the Janissaries – had advanced as far as Kosovo. Even as the Ottomans established a hold on the Adriatic Sea, Venice and Genoa dispatched ambassadors to negotiate the right to import grain from the Black Sea at the lowest possible price. When the Ottomans slid into a short civil war, the Europeans did not use this crucial opportunity to repel them. And so the conquests were resumed. By 1450, all the lands around Constantinople were taken, and it was only a matter of time before 'the red apple', as it was called, would be attacked. In June 1453, after a long siege, the Ottoman sultan Mehmed II (1444–81) attended the first Friday prayers in Hagia Sophia, the great domed Byzantine church, which was then converted into a mosque.

The pope warned: 'You Germans who do not help the Hungarians, do not hope for the help of the French! And you Frenchmen, do not hope for the assistance of the Spaniards unless you help the Germans . . . Now that Mehmed has conquered the Orient, he wishes to conquer the West.'[14] Venice engaged the Ottomans at sea, destroying a small fleet near Gallipoli. But all the subsequent battles on land for Albania and Bosnia were lost.

Mehmed started to refer to himself as the Roman emperor. He compared himself to Alexander the Great and Julius Caesar, had the *Iliad* translated, and visited Troy to see the tomb of Achilles. He invited European scholars and artists to stay at his court, including the Venetian painter Gentile Bellini who painted his portrait. He incorporated elements of Roman and Byzantine law into his legal codification; established *millets*, or nations, where non-Muslims could preserve a degree of autonomy in exchange for paying taxes to the Ottoman state; appointed a new Orthodox patriarch of Constantinople; and allowed European traders to continue their activities in the Black Sea and the Eastern Mediterranean. Mehmed did not destroy the legacy of the Byzantine Empire; he wanted to do better. His propagandists announced that the Ottomans regarded Rome itself as the next great prize; its conquest would be followed by the invasion of all the lands of the 'blond people'.[15]

In 1470, a Venetian galley commander in Greece reported a most frightening evolution. 'The whole sea looked like a forest,' he wrote. 'It seems incredible to hear tell of it, but to see it is something stupendous!'[16] The 'forest' was a fleet which included over a hundred galleys that Mehmed II had secretly built at a new shipyard in the Golden Horn and fitted with cannon cast by Italian and Hungarian experts. The Ottomans had become a sea power, ready to challenge the Venetian republic and the other Christian powers. The Greek historian Michael Critobulus left no doubt about Mehmed's intentions: 'He did this because he saw that sea-power was a great thing, that the navy of the Italians was large and that they dominated the sea and ruled all the islands in the Aegean, and that to no small extent they injured his own coastlands, both Asiatic and European.'[17] In 1499, the Venetian navy was defeated at Zonchio, the first European sea battle where shipboard cannon were used.[18] Venice now depended on the Hungarians to defend the eastern seaboard of the Adriatic. In 1502, the republic signed an armistice that recognized all the Ottoman gains. Italy seemed to be ripe for the taking.

Earlier, Venice had hoped to open a second front against the Ottomans. In 1463 and 1471, the Venetian senate sent envoys to the Ottomans' nearest rival in the east, the White Sheep Turkomans. But both times, the Turkomans baulked. The White Sheep Turkomans were one of the many tribal federations that roamed Central Asia during the fourteenth and fifteenth centuries, as the pastoralist forces gradually fragmented and weakened. In the decades after the death of Genghis Khan in 1227, the Mongol realm had split into four parts: the Yuan Dynasty, which ruled China until 1386; the Golden Horde, which dominated Siberia and the Pontic-Caspian Steppe until it began to fall apart in the mid-fifteenth century; and the Chagatai Khanate and the Ilkhanate in Central Asia and Persia respectively, which survived until they were defeated by the Mongol-Turkish troops of

Timur, or Tamerlane (1370–1405). For about thirty years, Timur controlled a vast realm between the Levant and the Hindu Kush. He was a feared fighter, but his empire never achieved the sophistication of, say, the Achaemenids' or Sasanians' – nor their permanency. From the fifteenth century, the dramatic nomadic conquest characterized by swift mounted attacks began to encounter too much resistance from the gunpowder-armed forces of more sedentary societies. In this way, the White Sheep Turkomans were defeated in 1473, when thousands of their horsemen were cut down by Ottoman firearms and artillery.

The Sultan among Hindu Kings

The growth of powers like the Ottoman Empire and the grand duchy of Moscow ensured Western Europe was spared much of the volatility that spilled out from the centre of Eurasia. Matters were different in the Indian subcontinent, however, which would be dominated by Muslim rulers for over five centuries. In the late twelfth century, the Islamic warlords known as the Ghurids had swept in from Khorasan and conquered much of northern India. When the Ghurid ruler returned to his Central Asian domains in 1193, he left his new Indian possessions in charge of his most trusted commander and slave, Qutb al-Din Aibak. Following the death of his master in 1206, Aibak cast off Ghurid overlordship and established the independent Delhi Sultanate, consolidating his rule with the construction of fortresses and mosques.

Most of the Hindu kingdoms had large armies of infantry and war elephants, but lacked horses and failed to work together, so that they were too sluggish and divided to be able to cope with the lightning campaigns and raids of the Islamic cavalry-based armies. By the early fourteenth century, the sultanate was firmly in control of the Indo-Gangetic Plain and had either annexed or established indirect rule over the major kingdoms of the Deccan Plateau. Each victory strengthened the sultanate with immense tributes of gold, gems, pearls, and manpower. The sultans also launched charm offensives. They hired poets to rewrite traditional stories so that the Prophet Muhammad and his family appeared alongside much-loved Indian characters.[19]

But the Muslim aspect of the sultanate's rule undoubtedly also generated tensions, especially because some of the early sultans dramatically increased taxes, reserved trade monopolies for Muslims, and destroyed Hindu temples. Muhammad bin Tughluq (1325–51) was one of the sultans who pushed it too far. He commanded that the capital be transferred from Delhi to a city on the Deccan Plateau, ordered an impossible invasion of China across the Himalaya, and overburdened the realm with taxes so that numerous rebellions broke out.

It was in this context that a new political force emerged on the Deccan Plateau in the mid-fourteenth century: the kingdom of Vijayanagara. Often called an empire, Vijayanagara ruled much of the southern half of the Indian subcontinent as a rather loose federation. It was founded, however, on military might: there was frequent fighting between Vijayanagara and lesser Hindu kingdoms. Once defeated, each ruler continued to hold his own fortress and land in exchange for contributing infantry to the fight against the Muslims to the north.[20] There were multiple wars between Vijayanagara and the sultanate, sometimes involving hundreds of thousands of troops; but neither side was able to deliver the decisive blow.

Travellers from China, Europe, and the Islamic world were overawed by the capital of Vijayanagara, whose ruins are still visible at Hampi in Karnataka. 'The city is such that the pupil of the eye has never seen a place like it, and ear of intelligence has never been informed that anything existed to equal it in the world,' reported a Persian visitor in the 1440s.[21] He was particularly impressed by the wealth of the king, his 12,000 wives, and the zeal with which some of the city's 300,000 residents threw themselves under the wheels of royal processions.[22] The architecture of the city's main buildings drew on influences from other Hindu kingdoms and also the sultanate. Palaces were built on imposing platforms whose sides were sculpted with reliefs showing the king's armies and their prisoners of war, as well as hunting parties, dancers, and exotic foreigners. They were surrounded by markets, elephant stables, fortifications, water tanks, and temples. Yet more temples and fortresses in the same eclectic style were erected throughout the empire.

Although Vijayanagara's emblem was a wild boar facing a sword and crescent moon – an unmistakeable reference to its opposition to the Delhi Sultanate – its rulers were also influenced more constructively by the Islamic power to the north. They adopted elements of its fashions, artistic style, and military tactics – and, most curiously, came to use the title 'sultan among Hindu Kings'.[23] But Vijayanagara's laws and society remained essentially Hindu; the latter were rigidly stratified according to caste, with the priestly

Brahmins firmly at the top. The ideals of Vijayanagaran kingship, however, were similar to those of many other cultures: 'A crowned King should always rule with an eye towards *dharma*,' and he should 'counteract the acts of his enemies by crushing them with force, should be friendly, should protect one and all'.[24]

The strategic importance of trade was never far from the minds of Vijayanagara's monarchs. But in contrast to the Delhi Sultanate, which was primarily a continental power, they also sought outlets for their kingdom's energies through the Indian Ocean. They tried to gain access to strategic ports like Goa and attempted to invade Sri Lanka. More peaceably, they fostered maritime trade relations with China and even with Muslim emporiums like Alexandria and the cities of Yemen. A Portuguese visitor to Vijayanagara, for example, described how the king depended on horses imported from Islamic states near the Strait of Hormuz in order to be able to fight the Delhi Sultanate.[25] A carving on the central platform of the Hazara Rama Temple in the capital shows one of these Muslim traders selling horses to the king.[26] 'A king should improve the harbours of his country and so encourage its commerce that horses, elephants, precious gems, sandalwood, pearls, and other articles are freely imported,' advised one of Vijayanagara's later rulers. 'Make the merchants of distant foreign countries who import elephants and good horses attach to yourself by providing them with presents and allowing decent profits. Then those articles will never go to your enemies.'[27]

Asia in the Shadow of the Ming

In 1272, Kublai Khan, the great leader of the Mongols, had a message for the conquered people of China: '[We] have nobly accepted the splendid mandate covering the entire world,' he stated. 'We alone have brought peace to the myriad lands . . . In our endeavors there are continuities and discontinuities, but our Way connects Heaven and humanity.'[28] Although the name bestowed on the new dynasty – 'the great Yuan' – expressed ideas of primacy, its rulers were bent on emulating the prestige of previous Chinese imperial regimes.

The marriage remained an artificial one nevertheless. Confucian guidelines were used not only to reconstruct the imperial administration but also to build Kublai's new capital near the location of present-day Beijing – yet the khan had his private rooms lined with Siberian fur and his sons continued to live in tents next to the palace.[29] However much the Yuan Dynasty tried to Sinicize, they remained oppressors. Society was divided into three classes, with the Mongols at the top, followed by Muslim migrants from the West, and the Han Chinese at the bottom. Peasants may have benefited from new irrigation works, but they were also taxed heavily in order to finance wars of conquest.

Many of these campaigns failed. Mongol cavalry was not suited to the mountainous jungle of Southeast Asia. Nor were the former steppe warriors more fortunate at sea: two major naval expeditions against Japan never returned; and even the fleet of a thousand ships dispatched to punish Java for not paying tribute had only a brief impact. In 1279, the Yuan

Dynasty faced a serious financial crisis. Frustration grew as peasant uprisings were brutally repressed and Muslim minorities were prohibited from slaughtering their sheep ritually. In protest at the Yuan rule, the famous artist Zheng Sixiao painted his orchids without any soil to symbolize how the Mongol emperors had uprooted traditional Chinese society.[30]

The Yuan response to such widespread opposition had mixed success. They issued yet more Confucian propaganda, reinstalled traditional imperial exams, and built granaries. Culturally, China flourished, thanks in part to more intensive exchanges with the West. But the common people continued to endure taxation, inflation, discrimination, and famine. And by the late fourteenth century, China too was afflicted by sustained periods of exceptionally cold weather.[31] Succession problems and rivalry with the Mongol khanates to the northwest made it increasingly difficult to retain power. Eighty years after its formal foundation by Kublai, the Yuan Dynasty was faced with a nationwide uprising. As the warlords of the Red Turban Rebellion gained ground, the Yuan's heavenly mandate slipped away.

With the decline of the Yuan, support polarized around two powerful warlords. One of them was Zhu Yuanzhang, an orphaned peasant who had speedily climbed the ranks of the Red Turbans. In 1363, Zhu was able to defeat his rival in a decisive battle by using fire ships. Five years later, he adopted the title of 'the Hongwu Emperor' (1368–98) and claimed the heavenly mandate. His new dynasty was named 'Ming', meaning 'brilliance', and would rule China for more than 250 years. Having experienced hardship himself, the Hongwu Emperor transferred land to the peasants, cut taxes by slimming down the bureaucracy, instructed the army to feed itself, repaired irrigation networks, compiled a legal code that offered more protection to citizens, and colonized fertile areas in the south.

For the remainder of the fifteenth century, however, China remained restless. The Hongwu Emperor was pitiless in centralizing power. Tens of thousands of potential opponents were executed. This stoked resentment inside the elite, led to a brief civil war after his death, and prompted the Yongle Emperor (1402–24) to entrust his secret police and the military with excessive power. The whole economy was tightly centralized, but emperors struggled in particular to manage the food supply, sometimes shipping surpluses directly to provinces with agricultural deficits, at other times allowing such excess produce to be sold on the open market. As a result, there were famines, wild fluctuations in taxation levels, and violent uprisings in protest. But in the absence of any major invasions or civil wars, the population grew from 65 million in 1393 to 125 million in 1500.

Initially, Ming foreign policy was favourable to trade. 'Let there be mutual trade at the frontier barriers in order to supply the country's needs and to encourage distant people to come,' announced the Yongle Emperor, who opened three maritime trade offices.[32] As China was self-sufficient, it dominated its trade partners. Barbarian neighbours were expected to supply whatever the Ming court desired. They did so at officially designated maritime and overland trade emporiums overseen by Chinese officials. Many of them were also expected to proffer their goods as tribute. Such envoys were kept apart from Chinese citizens in special accommodation.

Sometimes there were hundreds of delegates from different countries, so that the resources of host cities were strained trying to feed them, not to mention their camels, horses, and elephants.[33] The climax of these missions was performing the kowtow before the emperor. Envoys could be kept waiting for weeks for the ritual and, even worse, be beaten for failing to execute it properly.

Trade policy became even more capricious later on. The Ming often closed the border with Tibet and the pastoralists in the northwest. In 1424, the Hongxi Emperor not only ended the frontier trade of tea for horses with Tibet, but also forbade the trade of gold for pearls with Vietnam, and ordered the imperial fleet to be burned. 'The security of the empire lay within the Great Wall,' he said, 'not on the sea.'[34]

Policies briefly changed again with the Xuande Emperor (1425–35), who followed in the wake of the Yongle Emperor when, in 1430, he ordered the launching of a vast armada to reaffirm Chinese might along its maritime trade routes: 'I send eunuchs Zheng He and Wang Jinghong with this imperial order to instruct these countries to follow the way of Heaven with reverence and to watch over their people so that all might enjoy the good fortune of lasting peace.'[35] Whether it was made for strategic reasons or purely ideological reasons, one decision of the emperor could reverse the trade relations of a society of almost 100 million people.

The wealth and power of the Ming Empire were the result not only of trade but also of military conquest. The Ming had the largest standing army of the world, close to 1 million soldiers. With it, they conquered territory beyond the borders of previous Chinese dynasties, annexing large parts of

Manchuria and Inner Mongolia, in order to expel remnants of the Mongols, as well as independent kingdoms in the south, in what is now Yunnan. From this new power base, Ming troops made incursions into other southern states, such as Vietnam, which was turned into a province in 1406. Whereas Ming expansionism in the north was partly driven by fears for security, the interventions in Southeast Asia were motivated solely by aggrandizement.

The latter coincided with a brief but unprecedented period of Chinese naval power projection. Between 1405 and 1433, Admiral Zheng He sailed seven times into the Indian Ocean, voyaging as far as the Horn of Africa and the Red Sea.[36] Although most of the expeditions' charts and logbooks have disappeared, there is evidence that Zheng's fleet intervened militarily in Java and Sumatra, where it defended Chinese colonists. Zheng was also probably responsible for the destruction of the Sri Lankan kingdom of Kotte. The Grand Secretary Yang Rong referred to its inhabitants as a noxious plague and as insignificant worms to be exterminated – women and children included. But Ming naval activities were not confined to the exploits of Zheng He. In 1400, for example, the emperor threatened to invade Japan and naval vessels engaged pirates near the Korean coast in 1406.

Throughout the fifteenth century, Ming China towered above its neighbours, such as the Korean kingdom of Goryeo with its 7 million inhabitants. In the thirteenth century, Goryeo failed to resist the Mongol invasions, becoming a tributary of the Yuan. It briefly regained its autonomy when the dynasty crumbled, even sending military forces to the border after an envoy of the Ming emperor came to claim

Korean territory, but finally accepted it would have to pay tribute. Coinciding with these frictions with the Yuan, internal unrest had weakened the Goryeo, so that a new dynasty saw the chance to seize power. The Joseon, who took their name from the ancient Gojoseon, adopted Confucianism in order to justify the fact that almost half of the Korean population were slaves.[37] The great Joseon king Sejong (1418–50) did much to consolidate his kingdom's security, adopting a pro-China diplomatic policy on one hand and, on the other, invading the Japanese island of Tsushima in order to eradicate the hordes of pirates that threatened strategic trade routes.

At the time of Sejong's intervention, the Japanese Archipelago was being devastated by the violent rivalry of its feudal lords. The prize for which they competed was the right to be recognized as shogun by the emperor, who was little more than a figurehead. As the imperial commander-in-chief – the title originally meant something like 'barbarian-quelling generalissimo' – whoever was shogun was de facto ruler of Japan. 'The four seas are disturbed and the fires of war darken the skies,' one emperor stated in the historical epic, the *Taiheiki*, or the *Chronicle of the Great Peace*. 'When shall peace return if the warmongers be not destroyed by the virtue of law?'[38] From the beginning of the thirteenth century, shoguns ruled over most of Japan, issuing the first Japanese law codes in an effort to promote civil harmony – although that remained little more than a dream.

After the attempted Mongol invasions of 1274 and 1281 were both miraculously destroyed by typhoons, Japan came to consider itself the chosen land of gods and of the divine wind known as *kamikaze*, a land ruled by an emperor blessed with the mandate of the sun goddess.[39] Mongols and Koreans were referred to as dogs, while the fourteenth-century political theorist Kitabatake Chikafusa argued that Japan's Buddhism endowed it with spiritual leadership over other Buddhist countries, such as China and India. In fact, the spread of Buddhism in Japan at this time was facilitated by exhaustion from the almost never-ending state of conflict. Civil wars, the threat of Mongol and Chinese invasions, and the cost of defensive fortifications caused peasant revolts and further internecine struggles. Yet, at the same time, economic competition between cities and regions resulted in important innovations in the arts, industry, and military technology, and Japan's population reached 10 million by 1500.

For much of the period between the thirteenth and fifteenth centuries, Southeast Asia was dominated by a handful of states: the kingdoms of Annam and Champa in Vietnam; the Khmer Empire in Cambodia; the Sukhothai kingdom in Thailand, followed by the Ayutthaya; and, in the Southeast Asian archipelago, the kingdom of Singhasari, which had taken Srivijaya's position as the leading trading power, and was replaced in turn by the Majapahit Empire. Despite their close interdependence, and the common threat they faced in the form of China's vast might, these states seldom cooperated politically. The history of the region in this period is an often bewildering catalogue of diplomatic machinations and wars. Other than repeated Chinese interference in Vietnam, perhaps the most significant event was the decline of the Khmer Empire in the face of internal conflicts and the rise of the formerly tributary kingdom of Sukhothai.

Nevertheless, much of Southeast Asia continued to thrive, due in no small part to the surpluses generated from bountiful rice yields. Regional trade flourished, especially in luxury products – and, along with it, so did diplomatic activity. One Majapahit poet celebrated his kingdom's ties with Angkor, Ayutthaya, Annam, Champa, and six other lesser kingdoms. The burgeoning wealth gave rise to growing cities, while kings sought to manifest the greatness of their majesty through the construction of vast temple complexes, such as Angkor Wat.

Come and Pay Tribute

As late as the fourteenth century, Africa was still inhabited by fewer than 50 million people. Most of them lived along the continent's coasts, especially those of the Mediterranean, the Indian Ocean, and the Gulf of Guinea. However, Africa was now in the middle of an important political transformation. The spread of iron tools, irrigation technology, and new crops had slowly increased agricultural production. New cities emerged that combined agriculture with pastoralism. Surpluses were limited, so they were traded mostly in local markets; but trade over longer distances was encouraged by a growing demand for gold, ivory, and slaves. One important network connected sub-Saharan Africa to the coast of the Red Sea and the Indian Ocean; another connected it across the Sahara to the Mediterranean.

The whole coast of East Africa was lined with trading cities that were supplied by kingdoms in the interior. In the Horn of Africa, the ports were controlled by small sultanates like Ifat, Adal, and Warsangali. Trade competition between them was fierce, but in the thirteenth and fourteenth centuries they were obliged to federate against the ambitions of the Christian kingdom of Ethiopia. Proclaiming themselves kings of kings and the heirs of King Solomon and the queen of Sheba in the Bible, the Solomonic Dynasty of Ethiopia had embarked on a campaign to gain control over the trade between the African hinterland and overseas markets and to turn the sultanates into tributaries. They sent envoys as far afield as Constantinople and Rome.[40]

Further south were the dozen or so trading cities of the Swahili people, including Mogadishu, Mombasa, Zanzibar, Kilwa, and Sofala. By the fourteenth century, Kilwa had annexed most of the others and dominated the channel between Africa and Madagascar.[41] The widely travelled Islamic scholar Ibn Battuta described mid-fourteenth-century Kilwa as one of the most beautiful towns in the world. He also recorded that it was engaged in a thriving slave trade and that it perpetually deployed its soldiers inland.[42]

These campaigns were waged against an important continental power, the kingdom of Great Zimbabwe. Like the Solomonic kingdom of Ethiopia, this polity had absorbed the numerous cattle-based chiefdoms of its surrounding highlands. At its height, around 1400, Zimbabwe's capital, with its great stone-walled structures, was home to about 18,000 people, before the inability of the grasslands to support this growing population led to the kingdom's decline. Its trade was taken over by its main rival, the kingdom of Mutapa, which monopolized the trade in gold, copper, and ivory in southern Africa. *Mutapa* means 'plunder', and its king called himself 'lord of the plundered lands'. The kingdom conquered lesser polities along the River Zambezi and on the east coast.[43]

It is more than likely that the states of southern and eastern Africa traded slaves and gold with Central Africa long before the arrival of the Portuguese in around 1485. Central Africa, with its rich lands, was a magnet for migration and settlement over many centuries. The ruins of an earthwork fortress near Bigo bya Mugenyi, in Uganda, might have been the centre of a loose empire known as Kitara, which dominated the Great Lakes region in the fourteenth and fifteenth centuries.[44] Kitaran trade routes might even have stretched as far as the River Congo. Mbanza-Kongo, located on a plateau not far from the Atlantic coast, was a regional node for trade in copper, iron, slaves, and agricultural produce in the fifteenth century. It was the capital of the kingdom of Kongo, which incorporated lesser states like Loango and Dongo through marriage and conquest.[45]

In the north, the trans-Saharan trade network consisted of the Mediterranean consumer markets, the Arab and Tuareg caravan traders, various polities that operated as gatekeepers in the Sahel – the belt of savannah to the south of the Sahara – and the main suppliers, which were various cities along the Gulf of Guinea. The most important of these was Edo, which functioned as the imperial capital of the Bini, meaning 'fighter', or kingdom of Benin. Until the fifteenth century, the region was controlled by chieftains who elected an *oba*, or king. After a period of internal strife, power was centralized in the mid-fifteenth century under a ruler who took the name Ewuare, which means 'the trouble has ended'. As well as his reform of the Bini state, Ewuare expanded their empire, conquering several other trading polities on the Gulf of Guinea. As the Bini flourished, they became known for their metallurgy, especially bronze work.

In the Sahel, three powers competed for control over towns like Gao and Timbuktu, which were trade hubs as well as vital sources of water for pastoralists. The Mossi kingdoms seized Timbuktu in 1400. Their capital was Ouagadougou, meaning 'come and pay tribute', and their ruler called himself 'king of the world'. They were challenged by the Songhai Empire, which emerged from the town of Gao, a major crossroads for the trade in gold, salt, ivory, and slaves between the Gulf of Guinea and the Niger River and North Africa. In 1468, Timbuktu succumbed to Songhai's camel fighters who, in the words of one Islamic historian, 'committed gross iniquity, burned and destroyed the town, and brutally tortured many people there'.[46] The Songhai also profited from the demise of the Mali Empire to their west. Mali too had thrived on the trade in gold and salt. At its peak in the fourteenth century, it had been able to mobilize 10,000 cavalry, as well as tens of thousands of infantry, drawn from its tributaries and equipped with arms imported from the Arabs. But infighting, raids by the nomadic Tuareg, and repeated attacks by the Mossi kingdoms and Songhai Empire caused its decline in the fifteenth century.

The Edge of the Flood

Before 1500, the Western Hemisphere remained a world of its own, with a population that probably did not exceed 40 million.[47] When the Spanish forced their way into Central

America, twenty-five years after Columbus discovered the island of Hispaniola in 1492, they found the coastal plains of the Gulf of Mexico were governed by the Aztec Empire.

The empire's origins can be traced back some 250 years earlier to one of the multitude of city states that thronged the region. It was inhabited by the Mexica, who were notorious for their skill as archers. At first, they were hired as mercenaries in the frequent wars that occurred between other cities, and they paid tribute to more prestigious states. Eventually, they forged a triple alliance with two other states, Texcoco and Tlacopan, and it was the military strength of this confederation that led to the founding of the Aztec Empire in around 1430. Its initial objectives were to dominate the coastal plains, followed by the trade routes of the Mexican Plateau. The latter led to a collision with the prominent kingdom of Tarascan. Both states built fortresses along the frontier, recruited other peoples to serve as proxies, and fought battles with tens of thousands of soldiers; but neither side was able to gain any lasting advantage.

The Aztecs were a warlike society. Monstrous figures on temples bore testament to bloody rituals and human sacrifice. One Aztec poem reminded citizens: 'You were sent to the edge of the flood, to the edge of the blaze. Flood and blaze is your duty, your fate.'[48] It was said that the empire's wars had been ordered by the sun god and that the realm was ruled by the son of the sun. In addition to the ties of shared religion and culture, the emperor further consolidated power through the appointment of governors in the provinces and the construction of public works. At the empire's heart was the capital of Tenochtitlan, now the historical centre of Mexico City.

Built on an island in a shallow lake, the city was adorned with causeways, canals, pyramids, plazas, and countless gardens, and was home to over 100,000 inhabitants.

In South America, the leading state by the end of the fifteenth century was the Inca Empire. Until the thirteenth century, the Pacific coast was spotted with small cities belonging to cultures like the Ichma, Chimu, and Picunche. Because these cities were isolated, they had few defences, and so easily fell prey to the emerging power of Cusco. Tucked away high in the Andes, the city had started raiding other towns in the fourteenth century in search of gold and slaves.[49] Before long, these raids became a holy war on behalf of the Inca sun god. As Cusco became more powerful, it invited neighbours to pay tribute voluntarily in exchange for protection, and invaded those that refused.[50]

By the late fifteenth century, Cusco had completed its transformation from city into kingdom and then into an empire that stretched for over 5,000 kilometres between the Andes and the Pacific. Like the Aztec ruler, the Inca emperor was venerated as the son of the sun. As such, he was entrusted with defending the realm and was expected to be the 'lover and benefactor of the poor'.[51] The Inca considered Cusco the navel of the world. The empire that surrounded it was divided into four large regions, each subdivided into provinces. The Inca pursued a policy of assimilation, imposing their language, arts, architecture, and tributary trade on subjugated states. As a chosen people, the Inca themselves were exempt from taxes; these were levied on defeated societies instead in the form of labour, which was used to construct the empire's vast network of roads, bridges, and military fortresses.[52]

Both the Aztec and Inca Empires were overthrown in the early sixteenth century by tiny armies of Spanish *conquistadores*. They achieved their stunning victories against seemingly overwhelming odds by adopting 'decapitation' strategies. The last Aztec emperor, Moctezuma, had over 200,000 soldiers under his command, whereas the Spanish *conquistador* Hernán Cortés led little more than 600. After Cortés landed in Yucatán in 1519, Moctezuma did not instantly respond, probably because he did not appreciate the relatively distant threat, and perhaps because the Aztec conventions for declaring war were not observed. After he established a foothold in Yucatán, Cortés first defeated some smaller states and made them join his forces. He then pressed on to Tenochtitlan, tricked his way into the Moctezuma's palace, and captured the emperor; without a ruler, the whole structure of the Aztec Empire foundered. Similarly, the Inca emperor, Atahualpa, who had an army of more than 80,000 soldiers, was slow to realize the threat from Francisco Pizarro and his 168 men in 1532. When the Spanish were invited to the city of Cajamarca to meet the Inca emperor, they mounted a surprise attack. Atahualpa was initially held hostage, then executed, and a puppet briefly installed in his place. Although the last pockets of resistance held out for another forty years, the former Inca Empire was to be ruled by the Spanish for the next three centuries.

In many ways, the Western Hemisphere and sub-Saharan Africa between 1250 and 1500 were not that different from

Asia, Europe, and North Africa. Here, too, polities wrangled over territory, trade, slaves, and religion, albeit on a much smaller scale. The key difference was that they lacked the technological capabilities that had given rise to force multipliers such as gunpowder weapons and true ocean-going ships – or even, in the case of the Americas, horses. Historians still debate the causes of this development gap, but the consequences were evident. The relative weakness of these regions' hard military power rendered them vulnerable to invaders from Europe and Asia, and to the large-scale colonization that followed in their wake.

The Scavengers of the Sea

When the Mongols arrived in Eastern Europe in the mid-thirteenth century, they appeared to their victims as brutal, merciless, and able to strike hammer blows as if out of nowhere. Like earlier invaders from the steppes, they benefited from a connective advantage: their mastery of the highway of grass through their nomadic lifestyle and skill with horses. The way that Spain and Portugal some 250 years later became masters first of the ocean and then of the Americas has certain similarities. Both Spain and Portugal were fringe powers, on the periphery of Western Europe and the Mediterranean. But their position on the Atlantic enabled them to exploit the highway of the oceans, which they achieved by developing fast, seaworthy caravels and advanced navigational skills. The ocean thus became to Spain and Portugal what the steppes were to the Mongol cavalry. From the viewpoint of native American and African peoples, the arrival of the Spanish and Portuguese out of the blue proved to be just as cataclysmic as the Mongol invasions had been to those who experienced them.

The global ventures of Spain and Portugal around 1500 opened an entirely new dimension for inter-state rivalry and strife. In this regard, China seems once again to have missed an opportunity. The fleet of the Ming Empire was absolutely enormous, and it reached the Indian Ocean and the shores of Africa decades before the Portuguese. It is not entirely clear what motivated the maritime voyages of the Ming; but what is clear is that once they had been halted by the conservative imperial court in 1433, they were never repeated later. By themselves, the obvious political differences between the giant, hierarchic, unipolar, centralized Ming Empire, and the fiercely competitive, relatively small, multipolar states of Western Europe, fail to explain this pivotal decision adequately. Although geographical factors undoubtedly played a role: the Chinese do not appear quite so inward-looking when one recalls the numerous rivals jostling against their continental borders and the enormous domestic economy that could be served primarily by shipping along rivers and canals and through coastal waters. What would have happened if China had continued its maritime ventures in the Indian Ocean and established a commercial – perhaps even colonial – presence in Africa? We can only guess. But the ramifications for global politics of not doing so were immense.

CHAPTER 12

A New Age of Islamic Conquest

1500–1750 CE

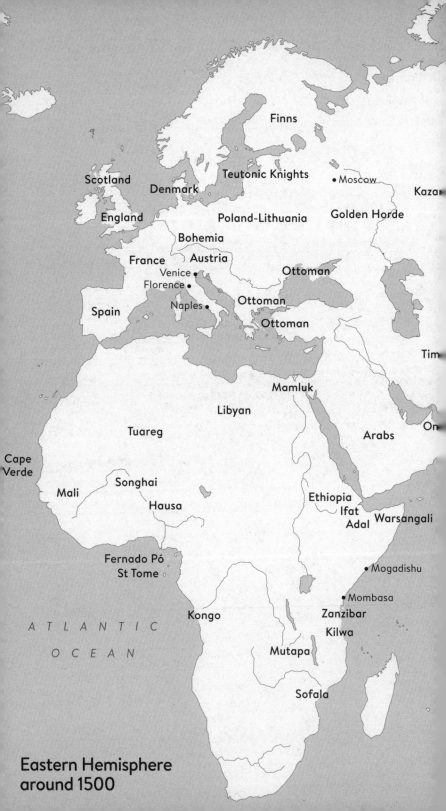

Finns

Teutonic Knights

• Moscow

Kaza

Scotland

Denmark

Golden Horde

England

Poland-Lithuania

Bohemia

France

Austria

Venice •

Ottoman

Florence •

Spain

Naples •

Ottoman

Ottoman

Tim

Mamluk

Libyan

Arabs

Tuareg

On

Cape
Verde

Songhai

Mali

Hausa

Ethiopia
Ifat
Adal

Warsangali

Fernado Pó
St Tome

• Mogadishu

Kongo

• Mombasa

Zanzibar

ATLANTIC

Kilwa

OCEAN

Mutapa

Sofala

Eastern Hemisphere
around 1500

kh

Mongol

Moghulistan

Tibet

• Delhi

lhi Sultenate

Ming

Joseon

Japan

P A C I F I C

O C E A N

Chola

Cambodia

Malacca

N D I A N

C E A N

| 500 | 1000 | 1500 km |

| 500 | 1000 miles |

The moment when Christopher Columbus discovered America in 1492 CE is widely considered to mark the advent of Europe's world domination. But, as this chapter shows, the main event shaping the world in the sixteenth and seventeenth centuries was not yet European expansionism. To be sure, the arrival of the *conquistadores* in the Americas spelled destruction for the indigenous peoples; and the Portuguese and Spanish crowns even divided the globe between them in the Treaty of Tordesillas (1494). Yet colonial possessions in America, Africa, and Asia by the mid-eighteenth century remained limited compared to what came later. Directly controlled overseas possessions were mostly confined to coastal fortresses, manned by a few dozen soldiers, which were gradually surrounded by the wooden huts of merchants and adventure seekers. Despite developments in agriculture, trade, banking, technology, and manufacturing, Europe's economy grew slowly. Wages and urbanization even stagnated throughout Europe, except in the Netherlands and Britain.[1] The spectacular effects of the industrial revolution did not occur until after 1760.

Between 1500 and 1750, the world population grew from around 400 million to over 700 million. Less than one fifth lived in Europe, while over half lived in Asia. Much more significant to those people was the rise of Muslim empires in the densely populated Middle East and South Asia. The Ottomans, the Safavids, and the Mughals subjugated about a quarter of the world's population. China, which accounted for another quarter of the world population, was thrown into confusion by the invasions of the Manchu, which culminated in the establishment of the Qing Dynasty. Europe, the other important demographic centre, remained beset by violence within and between states: the Eighty Years War (1568–1648), the Thirty Years War (1618–48), and the Wars of the Spanish and Austrian Successions (1701–13, 1740–48) – to name only the most familiar conflicts – were all fought over various combinations of territorial, religious, and commercial interests.

This world, where small kingdoms lived uneasily in the shadow of vast land empires, undoubtedly became more connected than ever before. The most compelling evidence remains the increasingly accurate globes and maps which were produced at the time in Europe, the Middle East, and in China, as well as the proliferation of travel journals and narratives whose exotic accounts of far-flung places were devoured by readers back home. Communication – both physical travel and the sharing of information – were advanced by the development of printing, the patronage of geographical exploration, and, most of all, by economic greed. Not since the junks of the Chinese admiral Zheng He plied the Indian Ocean in the early 1400s were ships with such firepower dispatched in the pursuit of gold, spices, and slaves. Now, however, there was no inward-looking Chinese emperor to stop this turn to the seas. European states competed with each other to monopolize overseas trade, while the ventures of increasingly enterprising merchants both stimulated and were emboldened by the emergence of modern capitalism, with its joint-stock companies, stock markets, and proliferation of financial products. The foundations of Europe's global supremacy were unquestionably laid during this period, but the road to primacy was still occupied by far more powerful actors.

The Ottoman Empire

Until the fifteenth century, the Ottomans considered themselves the underdogs in any wars they fought. After the conquest of Constantinople in 1453, however, the sultans regarded themselves as at least the equal of the Holy Roman Emperor and aspired to conquer the whole world.[2] This Ottoman bid for mastery was relaunched in the early sixteenth century by Sultan Selim I (1512–20).

Viewed from Constantinople, the three most important arenas were the Middle East, the Black Sea, and the Mediterranean. In the Middle East, the Ottomans were interested in the trade of the Levant and the Red Sea, the holy cities of Jerusalem, Medina, and Mecca, and in countering the Shia Safavid Empire which was centred in Persia. In a letter to the Safavid monarch, Selim I presented himself as the defender of Sunni Islam and accused his correspondent of tyranny, oppression, and, worst of all, alcoholism. He ordered 60,000 Ottoman troops to invade Mesopotamia. In the Battle of Chaldiran (1514), the Ottomans prevailed over the Safavids thanks to mobile artillery and flintlock rifles. Selim was unable to subdue the Safavids completely, but he gained control over the Levant and northern Mesopotamia. The success fuelled Ottoman ambitions for further conquests on the eastern border, running from Armenia in the north to Egypt and the Red Sea in the south.

Selim was succeeded by an even more accomplished conqueror, Suleiman the Magnificent (1520–66). Most of the Balkans and the western Black Sea region were already ruled by the Ottomans. Suleiman, however, took advantage of a civil war in Hungary, which controlled the trade along the Danube and some of the overland commerce with the Baltic, and launched an offensive. In the Battle of Mohacs in 1526, Ottoman gunpowder weapons proved superior against the old-fashioned Hungarian knights. The scale of the victory – the Hungarian king and at least 15,000 of his men were killed and the capital subsequently burned to the ground – sent a wave of panic flooding through the rest of Europe. In 1529, Suleiman stood before the gates of the imperial city of Vienna. His failure to take it was largely due to bad weather, which had prevented him bringing most of his heavy siege artillery, and other supply shortages. Only after the siege of Vienna had been lifted did the Holy Roman Emperor start improving his defences in the east.

Suleiman, meanwhile, turned his attention to the Mediterranean. 'If these scorpions [the Christians] are occupying the seas with their ships, if the flags of the Doge of Venice, the Pope and the kings of France and Spain are waved in the coasts of Thrace, this is because of our tolerance. I want a very strong navy large in number as well.'[3] These words were already spoken by Selim but mostly put into action by Suleiman. His vast naval build-up ensured the Ottoman fighting machine became as feared at sea as it was on land, defeating the fleets of major Christian alliances at the Battles of Preveza (1538) and Djerba (1560). In little more than two decades, the Ottomans had emerged as the leading naval power in the Mediterranean.

Under Suleiman's long rule, the empire reached its zenith. European diplomats were stunned by the beauty of Istanbul.[4] A poet himself, Suleiman patronized forty cultural societies; he ordered the building of the famous Süleymaniye Mosque in Istanbul and financed libraries, hospitals, schools, and public baths. The treasury was filled with booty, tribute, revenues from trade taxes, and the income from textile and armament industries. The construction and manning of galleys, the ranks of the Janissaries, labour on plantations and in palaces, not to mention the harems of wealthy Ottomans, required hundreds of thousands of slaves to be brought in from abroad.[5] They were collected through the so-called 'blood tax' from Christians in the Balkans; by warlords who 'harvested the steppes' of the Black Sea region; by slave caravans from sub-Saharan Africa; and by corsairs who supplied the slave markets of North Africa with Christian men, women, and children seized from ships in the Mediterranean and Atlantic or captured on raids as far afield as Ireland and Iceland. The corsairs were so active that a saying spread: it was 'raining Christians in Algiers'.[6]

The Ottoman Empire appeared eternal. Court advisors theorized that the sultan's power was based on a virtuous circle: as long as the sultan maintained justice, his subjects would flourish and support him. In reality, in the decades after the death of Suleiman the limits of Ottoman power became visible.

Throughout the seventeenth century, the empire struggled with inflation and the effects of currency debasements, even though the production of textiles and other goods grew.[7] By the end of the century, the custom whereby the new sultan secured his succession to the throne by killing all his brothers was also regularly causing civil wars, coups, and widespread instability. Increasingly, the Janissaries exploited the situation to control the succession, appoint viziers, and undermine the power of the sultans. The glory days of the empire were drawing to an end.

The failure to conquer the Safavid Empire forced them to keep many troops in the east. At the same time, the expansion of Russia made it difficult for the Ottomans to defend their territory around the Black Sea. The Ottomans also began to lag behind the maritime innovations of the European 'age of sail'. The turning point here had been marked by the Battle of Lepanto in 1571, where the victorious European fleet had matched the Ottoman one in size but had carried twice as many cannon. Although the Ottomans' galleys remained superior in the confined bays and straits of the Mediterranean, their sailing vessels never matched the quantity or quality of European ships. Despite a handful of naval expeditions in the Indian Ocean during the sixteenth century – one even ventured as far as the sultanate of Aceh on Sumatra in 1565 – the Ottomans were unable to contest the growing European mercantile and naval presence in the east.

In 1683, the Ottoman army returned to besiege Vienna once again. This time, the massed cavalry and artillery of the Holy Roman Empire and the Polish–Lithuanian Commonwealth shattered the Ottoman forces and lifted the siege. By the end of the seventeenth century, an alliance of Christian powers had driven the borders of the Ottoman Empire back into the Balkans in what were the first significant losses of territory in its history. Matters came to a head in 1703, when the Janissaries ousted the sultan in favour of his brother. Over the course of his reign, Ahmed III (1703–30) managed to establish a new status quo. Although the Ottomans were no longer able to threaten Western Europe, they continued to be the single largest power in the Mediterranean and the Middle East, for example seizing most of Venice's Greek possessions in 1717, and briefly annexing territory in Armenia and the southern Caucasus in 1724 from the weakening Safavid Empire.

The Safavid Empire

At the peak of its power, the empire of the Safavid Dynasty stretched from the Black Sea to the Hindu Kush and contained around 50 million people. It originated, however, as yet another minor power on the fringes of Mesopotamia and Persia when a religious leader called Ismail became king of the Qizilbash, or 'Redheads' – a coalition of Shia warrior tribes in the Caucasus – in 1501. Once he was firmly in power, Ismail imposed Twelver Shiism as the official form of Islam in his domains: 'With God's help, if the people utter one word of protest, I will draw the sword and leave not one of them alive.'[8] Nonetheless, he also continued to model himself on great ancient rulers of Persia, such as Cyrus, Darius, Khosrow, and Alexander the Great. He not only took the title of *shahanshah*, or 'king of kings', but also the Mongol title of 'khan', and the Indian title *bahadur*, meaning 'valiant war-rior'. This reflected the way that his subjects had grown to include Persians, Mongols, Turks, and Uzbeks.[9] But, above all, the Safavid shah was the semi-divine 'shadow of God upon earth', the spiritual leader of the mystical Sufi order of the Safaviyya – from which the dynasty takes its name – and the earthly representative of the Mahdi, or redeemer, whose coming would herald the end of the world.[10]

Benefiting from the decline of the Mongol-Turkish empire ruled by the heirs of Timur, or Tamerlane, Shah Ismail conquered Armenia in 1501, most of Persia by 1504, and parts of Uzbekistan in 1511. In 1514, he fought his first major war against the Ottomans. It was not only a holy war – of Shia Safavid against Sunni Ottoman – but one with the same huge territorial stakes as the conflicts between the Byzantines and the Sasanians a millennium earlier: control over the Caucasus and Mesopotamia. But when tens of thousands of Ottoman and Safavid soldiers faced each other at the Battle of Chaldiran, it was the Ottomans who prevailed. In the aftermath, they seized most of Mesopotamia and pillaged the Safavid capital, Tabriz. In 1555, the Ottoman ascendancy was such that they were able to impose the humiliating terms of the Peace of Amasya, which gave them access to the Persian Gulf, established large buffer zones between the two powers, and forced the Safavids to abandon some of their holiest cities, such as Najaf and Karbala.

Although the first Safavids lost their battles against the Ottomans, Shah Abbas I (1588–1629) became their nemesis. He profited from the civil war that followed the death of the Ottoman sultan Murad III in 1595 to thrust them out of Mesopotamia, recapturing Baghdad in 1623. This success was also the outcome of reforms at home. Abbas had transferred power from the Qizilbash warlords to a new political admin- istration and a new, more professional army equipped with modern European weapons, both of which were manned with slaves from the Caucasus. When the Georgians rebelled in 1614, Abbas crushed them ruthlessly, massacring tens of thou- sands, and forcing many more into captivity in Persia. He cas- trated the sons of the Georgian king, and tortured his mother to death for refusing to renounce Christianity. The Georgian monarch was left to weep 'an endless Nile of tears'.[11]

In the east, the Safavids developed close diplomatic rela- tions with the other rising Islamic power, the Mughal Empire. In 1544, the Safavid shah had provided sanctuary for the tem- porarily deposed Mughal emperor Humayun, welcoming him with a concert where 'Fair women, amiable and meek, expert in rendering service, stood in every corner like virgins in para- dise'; although he later wanted to execute Humayun for re- fusing to convert to Twelver Shiism.[12] Relations soured even further under Shah Abbas, who desired the recovery of trade routes that had been lost to the Mughals. Tensions were stoked by Uzbek princes to the north, who even invited the Mughals to join a grand alliance: 'If Prince Shah Jahan were to march north from the Deccan, we will also hurry there . . . After the victory, let us take Khurasan and whatever you wish of that country may be included in the imperial domains and the remainder granted to us', suggested one Uzbek to the Mughal emperor without success.[13] In 1622, Shah Abbas seized the chief prize at the heart of the conflict, the strategic fortress and trading city of Kandahar, in present-day Afghanistan.

The spoils of war, the control of trade, and the imperial silk factories allowed Abbas to spend lavishly on his new capital, Isfahan. The construction of buildings like the Ali Qapu palace marked the golden age of Safavid art and architecture. To the Safavids, Isfahan was the centre both of Islam and of global trade, as well as the seat of 'the great king, whose empire extends to the four cardinal points of the world, whose word can be broken by no force nor power'.[14] Soon after the death of Abbas, the glory of the Safavids began to wane. One of the reasons was that the start of almost every shah's reign was accompanied by a succession struggle, despite the custom whereby Safavid monarchs blinded family members who might become rivals. Another was the neglect of agriculture, so that the empire's cities relied excessively on international trade. Abbas's secretary and the historian of his reign, Iskandar Beg, described how the Safavid rulers prioritized the security of trade roads and the promotion of silk exports over agriculture, but also how they banned the export of bullion.[15] The lucrative Safavid silk trade was damaged by the Ottoman control of the Levant and the growing European presence in the Indian Ocean and Persian Gulf: in the seventeenth century, English traders began to bypass the Safavids' monopoly by shipping silk directly to Europe from the Bay of Bengal. The Safavids, who lacked even a coastal navy similar to that of the Ottomans, were unable to protect their interests.

Worst of all was the threat from the north posed by the rapidly expanding tsardom of Russia. Since the establishment of direct relations in the first half of the sixteenth century, the two powers had alternated between alliances against their common Ottoman enemy and confrontations over territory and trade in the Caucasus region. In 1722–3, the Safavids, internally weakened and externally challenged on all sides, were comprehensively defeated by both the Ottomans and Russia. In the Treaty of Constantinople the following year, the victors dismembered the Safavid Empire between themselves. A Turkic warlord, Nader Khan, deposed the last Safavid kings, ruling first as regent, then as shah in his own right from 1736. He briefly restored the realm's territorial integrity, and even lead Persian forces into Mughal India, where they sacked Delhi. But after his murder in 1747, Persia fragmented once again into anarchy.

The Mughal Empire

Like the Safavids, the Mughals originated in early sixteenth-century Central Asia. Around the year 1505, they crossed the Khyber Pass into the Indo-Gangetic Plain. The Delhi Sultanate initially resisted these incursions, but it was faced by threats on its other borders and could not sustain its defence. In 1526, the Mughal leader, Babur, formally founded his new dynasty, but it was his grandson Akbar (1556–1605) who turned the kingdom into a true empire. Akbar was a brilliant commander. Even if his troops were technologically no more advanced than those of other kings and sultans in South Asia, his tactical genius earned him victories like the decisive Battle of Panipat in 1556, which was fought against the sultan of Bengal.

Akbar prided himself on being a descendant of Genghis Khan. He took the title of *shahanshah*, like the Ottomans and Safavids; and, like the latter, he too claimed to be the shadow of God upon earth. Yet, at the same time, he also described royalty as a light emanating from god, a notion familiar to his tens of millions of Hindu and Buddhist subjects. Self-consciously presenting himself as the ruler of all religions, the Muslim Akbar embraced the Hindu and Buddhist concept of *dharma*, or righteousness, as a key principle of governance, sponsored the translation of classic Hindu texts like the *Mahabharata* and the *Arthashastra*, elevated lesser Hindu rulers to the Mughal nobility, and organized meetings for Muslim, Hindu, Buddhist, Zoroastrian, and Christian philosophers to expound their beliefs. Out of these discussions he distilled a syncretic creed called the *Din-i Ilahi*, or the 're-ligion of God', and promulgated the principle of *Suhl-i kul*, or universal harmony through religious tolerance.

In 1595, Akbar's vizier, Abu'l-Fazl, completed his official history of the Mughal emperor's reign. In the course of paying tribute to Akbar, the *Akbarnama*'s pages contain references to Plato, Aristotle, and Alexander the Great, as well as quotations from the *Mahabharata* and invocations of Hindu principles. The book concluded with some important advice for future princes. The prosperity of India's diverse society – which Abu'l-Fazl described as a vast market place – depended entirely on the king's being wise enough to preserve stability. Without a king, Abu'l-Fazl argued, the storm of strife would never subside as men were selfish, short-sighted, and intent solely on their own advantage. 'The superiority of man rests on the jewel of reason,'[16] he continued, explaining that this meant the king needed to resist self-aggrandizement, uphold justice, respect the religion of his subjects, be wary of unscrupulous advisors, reward merit, keep the army in good shape and neighbouring kingdoms from resorting to arms – and, in his personal life, abstain from womanizing and gambling.[17] 'All strife is caused by this,' Abu'l-Fazl summarized: 'that men neglecting the necessities of their state, occupy themselves with extraneous concerns.'[18]

One of the most important of Akbar's reforms was his formalization of the system known as *mansabdari*, in which the loyalty and service of military officers and civilian administrators was secured in exchange for the revenues from lands owned by the emperor. Another was the hiring of European and Ottoman soldiers and military engineers to modernize his army with matchlocks and artillery. This military revolution was so overwhelming that many of the lesser kings of the Indian subcontinent could no longer resist Mughal power. Uzbek and Dutch diplomats, for example, described how Mughal troops continued to campaign along the Indus, beheading captured local leaders and forcing villagers to sell their women and children into slavery.[19] To maintain the flow of trade, Akbar also built fortresses along the passes of the Hindu Kush and the Himalaya, and ensured that he controlled the ports of Gujarat and Bengal, which were the commercial gateways to the Middle East, Africa, and East Asia. By his death in 1605, the Mughal Empire encompassed present-day Pakistan, all of India except the southern most tip, and Bangladesh.

The Mughals established state monopolies in the production of salt, the saltpetre which was essential for making gunpowder, and textiles. Akbar commanded citizens buy locally in order to help shawl manufacturers in Lahore and carpet-weavers in Agra compete with wares imported from Persia.[20] Exports of textiles, tobacco, tea, and other commodities were immense, so that the empire profited from a large inflow of bullion. The drawback, however, was that those exports were to a large extent controlled by foreigners: English and Portuguese who settled in trading cities on the coast and lent money to local governors in exchange for licences to trade and protection of their activities.

This dependence on Europeans led to friction. In 1686, the East India Company – the state-backed English corporation that traded with South and East Asia – attempted to force the Mughal Empire into granting it commercial privileges. When English ships blockaded the coast, thereby preventing Indian pilgrims from voyaging to Mecca, the Mughal Emperor Aurangzeb dispatched a fleet of his own against the East India Company's base at Bombay (Mumbai). Eventually, in 1689, the English were forced to surrender and pay a substantial indemnity. European traders now started to develop the east coast of India as an alternative source of cotton and incited the Arakan kingdom in Myanmar to contest control of the Ganges Delta and the Bay of Bengal with the Mughals. To counter the threat, Aurangzeb ordered 300 ships to be built in the European fashion; but eventually, in order to protect his ports, he had to demand help from the Dutch and English, who saw this as an opportunity to strengthen their position in relation to the Portuguese. 'One ship manned with Europeans would rout 20 ships manned by the Mughals,' a vizier confided.[21] The Mughals may have continued to win wars on land throughout the seventeenth century, but at sea they remained at the mercy of more advanced and heavily armed European ships.

The death of Aurangzeb in 1707 sparked succession conflicts and civil war. These were exacerbated by the hardening of religious policies since the time of Akbar, so that relations with the Hindu majority had deteriorated. Meanwhile, the East India Company had assumed such a position of influence within the empire that it enjoyed tax-free trading rights for little more than a few thousand rupees a year, growing ever richer and more powerful at the expense of the Mughal administration. The concommitant neglect of the army and the defences in the north allowed the Persian ruler Nader Shah to invade in 1739. Mughal cavalry was overwhelmed by infantry with flintlock muskets and field artillery with horse-mounted swivel guns. The capital, Delhi, was sacked. 'Now commenced the work of spoliation, watered by the tears of the people,' wrote one Mughal courtier. 'Whole families were ruined. Many swallowed poison, and others ended their days with the stab of a knife . . . In short the accumulated wealth of centuries changed masters in a moment.'[22] Seven hundred elephants, 4,000 camels, and 12,000 horses were needed to carry the Mughal emperors' treasury away.[23]

A Universe United

Throughout much of the sixteenth century, China under the Ming Dynasty flourished as its economy boomed and population multiplied. The Forbidden City, the central palace complex in Beijing, whose construction had already begun in 1406, was now entirely completed. Foreign envoys were required to rehearse the ceremonial protocols for three days under the supervision of the ministry of rites before they were escorted to the main entrance to the palace at the Meridian Gate. After crossing a sequence of vast squares and passing through the immense Gate of Supreme Harmony, they were greeted by silk-robed eunuchs of the directorate of ceremonial, who ushered them up the flight of forty steps to the Hall of Supreme Harmony. Here, in the largest pavilion of all, they had to kowtow four times in front of the emperor, who was seated on the dragon throne and surrounded by gold, jade, and silks.

When the first Europeans arrived, the emperor prohibited trade, but took great interest in their powerful artillery. Eventually, thousands of 'red barbarian cannon' – copied from Western prototypes – were produced.[24] The Zhengde Emperor was criticized for being decadent, but he sealed an alliance with the Malacca Sultanate against Portugal, and in 1521 his junks defeated a small Portuguese fleet near Tunmen, near modern Hong Kong. Unable to break into the Chinese market, the Portuguese started to arm Japanese raiders with cannon and breech-loading swivel guns. These Japanese pirates soon revealed the weakness of China's coastal defences. They looted ports, marauded up the Grand Canal, laid siege to major garrison cities, and in the end forced the Ming to cooperate with the Portuguese. In 1554, Macao became Portugal's first trading settlement in China.

In the north, Mongol and Jurchen tribes now saw the chance to strengthen their position with regard to the Ming, and formed an alliance to invade China. In 1550, Mongol horsemen reached the suburbs of Beijing to demand trading rights. They were repelled, but wrested an agreement to trade horses for silk. The court ordered the Great Wall to be re-inforced, magnifying it to the monumental proportions that are still visible today. Fortifications were also erected on the coast to deter pirates. Other challenges emerged. In 1592, more than 150,000 Japanese troops invaded the Korean Peninsula. The Imjin War (1592–8) forced the Ming to intervene and caused a new drain on the treasure. Rebellions broke out in both the south and north of China. Although they were repressed, the Wanli Emperor decided to retreat from public life. The emperor's neglect of his responsibilities created a power vacuum that was filled by quarrelling factions at court, while the armed forces were no longer under unified command.

But now a much larger rebellion started to ferment in China's northern periphery. Here, peasants were troubled by Jurchen incursions, deserting imperial troops, and large gangs of bandits.[25] Meanwhile, a prolonged period of cold encouraged the Jurchen, like the Mongols four centuries before them, to leave their homeland and push south. Right from the outset, the Jurchen leader Nurhaci claimed to be fighting a holy war against the Ming.[26] In 1618, he formalized his complaints against Ming repression and violations of Jur-chen territory into a document known as the *Seven Griev-ances*, which to all intents and purposes was a declaration of war. 'The Wanli Emperor of the Ming Dynasty was unwise in politics. He did not attend to internal affairs,' Nurhaci later stated in justification of his actions. 'So Heaven con-demned him, and bestowed the Ming Emperor's land on the eastern side of the Yellow River upon me. Since Heaven fa-vored me and endowed land to me, I was afraid that if I did not govern the nation according to Heaven's will, I would be punished.'[27] In 1635, Nurhaci's successor formalized his people's growing ascendancy by ordering them to cast off their old Jurchen name, with its derogatory associations in China, and now be known as the Manchu.

In China itself, the climatic changes that had affected the Manchu were causing famine. The Grand Canal dried out so that cities fell short of food.[28] Particularly devastating typhoons wrought havoc again and again. Rebellion became nationwide as its leaders sought to establish a government more favourable to the peasants who formed the majority of the population. To subdue the rebels, panicking Ming officials courted the Manchu. They were now invited to cross the Great Wall, where they were joined by disgruntled Ming generals.[29] In the series of engagements known as the Battle of Song-Jin (1641–2), Ming loyalist forces were decisively defeated, dealing a deathblow to the dynasty. In 1644, the last Ming emperor hanged himself from a fruit tree beneath the red walls of the Forbidden City. The heavenly mandate had passed on to yet another barbarian dynasty: the Qing.

The Manchu rulers of the Qing Dynasty were quick to adopt the armature of Chinese imperial tradition. Ming officialdom was incorporated into the new government, critical infrastructure preserved, and the teachings of the ancient classics promoted. Buddhism was supported and Confucian values once again defined imperial doctrine. 'Evildoers are disliked by Heaven and their nations are subject to decline,' stated the Manchu leader. 'Those who do good deeds are blessed by heaven and their nations will be prosperous.'[30] At the same time, however, the first Qing rulers wanted to avoid complete assimilation. Manchu warriors were forbidden to marry Chinese women or to become farmers; hunting was practised as an expression of Manchu identity; and the rituals of the Manchu's traditional shamanism continued to be performed.

As regards foreign policy, the first Qing ruler of China, the Shunzhi Emperor (1644–61), restored the tributary tradition and received envoys from as far afield as the Vietnamese kingdom of Annam, the Ryukyu Islands south of Japan, and Tibet. 'Now, the universe is united under one rule, the four seas have become a family, the people of all the countries have all become my children,' he announced.[31] In reality, nothing was further from the truth. The southern provinces of Yunnan, Guangdong, and Fujian were held by warlords. In the north, Qing troops encountered armies from Russia, whose eastward expansion reached Manchuria, and competed with the Mongols of the Dzungar Khanate for control of Central Asian trade routes and for influence over the centre of Buddhism, Tibet.

It was the Kangxi Emperor (1661–1722) who did most to secure the Qing Empire from external threats. He believed that China could not rely on the protection afforded by the mountains and rivers that guarded its traditional borders. Defence through expansion was to be the strategy: 'use the Liuchiu [Ryukyu] to defend the southeast, Korea the northeast, Mongolia the northwest, and Vietnam the south.'[32] The Kangxi Emperor's first step was to negotiate a border treaty with Russia. Then he took advantage of the conflict between the Khalkha and Dzungar Mongols to attack the latter. The Dzungar menace would be exterminated, the Kangxi Emperor swore; heaven wanted it to happen.[33] During his reign, campaigns were also fought in Taiwan, Vietnam, Myanmar, and Tibet.

The Kangxi Emperor was succeeded by the Yongzheng Emperor (1722–35), who decided to engage the stubborn rebels of Yunnan. The Chinese spoke of its inhabitants as aboriginal thugs and frontier barbarians that killed for a living, while coveting its copper, salt, and tea and the direct route it provided to Tibet.[34] The campaign was a bloodbath: tens of thousands of civilians were killed, including women and children. Limbs were cut off those who protested against the Qing presence. 'If we do not kill a few at present, we will have to put to death many later on,' one Qing governor explained, but the region remained restless.[35] In Taiwan too policy hardened, with the Qing court classifying it as a strategically important place. Private settlers were followed by fully fledged colonization as more soldiers were deployed to the island.[36]

In the shadow of China, numerous lesser states continued to compete with each other. In the northeast, the Japanese regent Toyotomi Hideyoshi made use of matchlock muskets to unify the country and subsequently to invade Korea. Hideyoshi was praised for ruling the world 'wherever the sun shines'.[37] He was succeeded by almost three centuries of rule by shoguns from the rival Tokugawa clan. They kept the emperor as little more than a figurehead, repeatedly forced the Koreans to pay tribute, and mounted military expeditions as far away as Taiwan. However, concern began to mount about the growing influence of European traders: commercial and other interactions with non-Japanese should be restricted, it was argued. In 1633, the Tokugawa ruler ordered a policy of isolationism initially known as *kaikin*, or 'maritime restrictions', but later and more commonly referred to as *sakoku*, or 'closed country'.[38]

In Southeast Asia, European firearms also allowed the Buddhist Le emperors to strengthen their grip on most of present-day Vietnam. The Toungoo kingdom in Myanmar vied with the Ayutthaya kingdom of Thailand, in particular for control of the trade ports on the Andaman Sea. Ayutthaya in turn was later pushed back by the Malay Sultanate, which itself also faced competition from the sultanates of Johor, Aceh, and Banten for the Malayan Peninsula and strategic sea lanes like the Strait of Malacca. These sultanates were played off against one another as the first Dutch and Portuguese colonists sought to establish rival trading posts, heralding the start of centuries of European imperialism in the region.

Europe's Age of Iron

By the beginning of the eighteenth century, the world's four major powers – the Qing, the Safavids, the Mughals, and the Ottomans – all reluctantly engaged in trade with European colonists, copied European weapons, enquired into Western sciences, and welcomed Western artists. But none of them anticipated that this distant arena of squabbling pygmies was set to rule the globe. Christopher Columbus' discoveries might have finally tied the two hemispheres together, and the voyage of the Portuguese explorer Vasco da Gama round the Cape of Good Hope in 1497–9 might have opened up a new way to reach Asia, but Spanish and Portuguese colonization remained very modest.

In the Western Hemisphere, the armies of the *conquistadores* were tiny, as we have seen; most of the devastation wrought on the indigenous populations of the Americas was the result of European diseases, not force of arms. Even as late as 1700, there were still no more than 200 voyages across the Atlantic a year. Asian resistance to European encroachment via the Indian Ocean was far sterner, with the continent's vast land empires able to confine the initial colonial ventures to compact trading settlements along the coast and on islands.[39] By the late seventeenth century, the Qing and the Mughals each ruled more than 150 million people and the Ottomans more than 30 million; the Spanish Empire, meanwhile, contained fewer than 20 million souls.[40] Compared to the conquests of the Asian empires, European maritime colonialism was not necessarily more belligerent or aggressive.

In terms of political power, and the capacity to control large populations, therefore, Europe at this point might have only started its rise, but it already eclipsed the four major continental powers in significant ways. The most obvious was the continuing development of fast sailing ships, capable of voyaging vast distances and heavily armed with relatively long-range cannon. With their more lightly armed coastal fleets, it became increasingly difficult for the Asian empires to defend themselves against this naval might, which was soon converted into European maritime supremacy. As Asian trade, ports, and major cities came under threat, Europe began to take the economic lead. In China and India, economic production per capita did not increase between the sixteenth and early seventeenth centuries; in Western Europe, it improved by 30 per cent.

Growth in Europe was driven by increasingly fierce competition for markets and for technological advantage. In the fifteenth century, Northern Italy had been Europe's richest region, but gradually the centre of power began to shift to the north: first to the Flemish city of Bruges and then, after its main access to the sea had silted up and its competitiveness in the lucrative trade in woollen cloth had dwindled, to Antwerp in the sixteenth century. 'No other town in the world could offer me more facilities for carrying on the trade,' one of the Dutch city's leading businessmen explained. 'Antwerp can be easily reached; various nations meet in its marketplace; there too can be found the raw materials indispensable for the practice of one's trade; craftsmen for all trades can be easily found and instructed in a short time.'[41] In 1585, however, Antwerp too lost its access to the sea – due to a blockade by the Spanish – causing the centre of commercial activity to shift to Amsterdam.

By this time, the Low Countries had become the richest region on earth. The combination of the regional European trade in cloth and metals with the maritime trade in spices from South and East Asia transformed cities like Antwerp and Amsterdam into truly global commercial hubs. But over the course of the seventeenth century, military conflicts, trade wars, and diminishing competitiveness saw the lead in finance, manufacturing, and technology gradually shift once more – this time, to London. In the eighteenth century, breakthroughs in the automation of textile manufacturing, innovations in steel production, and the modernization of financial organization paved the way for the industrial revolution and Britain's ascendancy.

Several factors accounted for Europe's comparative success during this era: the absence of pandemics on the scale of the medieval plague; the climate slowly becoming warmer; widespread agricultural and industrial innovation; the growth of skilled craftsmanship and the birth of a recognizably modern consumer society in cities; the inflow of wealth from colonies; and the proliferation of new financial instruments and institutions.[42] Some of the latter had been employed by early medieval Islamic traders, others originated in late medieval Italy. But they were now avidly adopted in the Netherlands and England, where they were perfected and began to be employed globally. Joint-stock companies spread financial risk, thereby encouraging investment – both directly and through newly emergent stock markets – which in turn further promoted trade. The first central banks were founded, such as the Amsterdam Exchange Bank in 1609 and the Bank of England in 1694. The cumulative effect of these developments was to facilitate international credit and to pressurize rising trading nations into observing the rule of law and maintaining low commercial taxes if they wished to encourage foreign trade. More than ever, the competition for wealth between European states – and the cities within them – knitted the continent together through networks of commerce, capital, and information.

Throughout the period between 1500 and 1750, the signs of Europe's growing prosperity encouraged its thinkers to dream once again of the prospect of universal peace. 'A unified empire would be best if we could have a sovereign made in the image of God,' wrote the Dutch humanist Erasmus in 1530; 'but, men being what they are, there is more safety in kingdoms of moderate power united in a Christian league.'[43] His friend, the English statesman Thomas More, described his ideal world of Utopia as an island protected by the sea, where people lived in harmony. 'Most princes apply them-selves to the arts of war instead of to the good arts of peace,' he complained in 1516. 'They are generally more set on ac-quiring new kingdoms by hook or crook than on govern-ing well those they already have.'[44] He reckoned that peace would be better served by persuading princes of the benefits of supporting the trade of their country. Over a century later, the Flemish painter and diplomat Peter Paul Rubens was still of the same opinion. 'The interests of the whole world are in-timately connected at this moment,' he asserted.[45]

The sixteenth-century French political philosopher Jean Bodin was of the opinion that trade and communication would be the main facilitators of a *respublica mundana*, or 'global commonwealth'. Others believed the law of nations – founded on the common law of precedent and the natural law inherent to all human societies – would be more in-strumental. The Spanish philosopher and jurist Francisco de Vitoria stated: 'The sovereignty of the individual state is limited because it is part of a community of nations linked by solidarity and obligations.'[46] His fellow countryman and fellow philosopher Francisco Suárez also insisted on inter-national rules based on the shared needs of peoples, while still emphasizing the importance of separate sovereignties. The seventeenth-century Dutch jurist Hugo Grotius advo-cated a voluntary international common law. The French political theorist Émeric Crucé, in 1623, even argued for an association of states with a permanent assembly of ambas-sadors located in Venice. Decisions would be reached by ma-jority vote, and armed forces pooled.

Not all believed that the role of diplomacy was to further

some *respublica mundana*. The English envoy Henry Wotton famously claimed in 1604 that 'An ambassador is an honest man, sent to lie abroad for the good of his country'.[47] A year earlier, the French diplomat Jean Hotman had stated that the ambassador's primary duty was to conceal the follies of his country, like a child protecting a senile parent. The Dutch diplomat Abraham de Wicquefort explained in 1682 that the role of an ambassador merely 'consisted in maintaining effective communication between two Princes, in delivering letters in soliciting answers to them in protecting his Master's subjects and conserving his interests'.[48] Any ambassador, he concluded, also needed 'a Tincture of the Comedian' in his character.[49]

Peace summits like the Field of Cloth of Gold in 1520 and the Conference of Westphalia in 1648 raised hopes for a better future. When King Francis I of France and King Henry VIII of England met near Calais in June 1520, accounts of the splendour of the temporary accommodation and the monarchs' retinues – not to mention descriptions of the two kings wrestling together – dazzled the rest of Europe, concealing the fact that politically the gathering accomplished little of any value. 'Now all the Christian princes were conducting themselves as though they had, as one, accepted the humanist critique of war as correct,' wrote Henry's secretary of state.[50] Over the course of the sixteenth century, such meetings between kings gradually gave way to conferences of so-called plenipotentiaries, or ambassadors with a full mandate to negotiate on behalf of their rulers. In 1648, more than a hundred delegations gathered in northern Germany, in the imperial cities of Osnabrück and Münster. The

French diplomats alone brought twelve cooks, five bakers, and 300 barrels of wine. The delegates had come to negotiate an end to the Thirty Years War, the most recent and most destructive of the 'wars of religion' that had blighted Europe since the Protestant Reformation in 1517. The resulting Peace of Westphalia established one of the most fundamental principles of all subsequent Western diplomacy: that no state had any right to interfere with another's sovereignty or meddle in its domestic affairs.

Historians have referred to the Peace of Westphalia and other conferences and treaties from around that time as marking the beginning of modern diplomacy, in that they demonstrate the interests of a state's body politic being prioritized over a monarch's personal interests or those of more nebulous supranational bonds, such as the ties of Christendom, or Catholicism or Protestantism. Cardinal Richelieu, the chief minister of King Louis XIII of France from 1624 to 1642, for example, remarked that the state was no longer derived from divine provision, and advised governing rationally and strictly in accordance with the national interest, or *raison d'état*. However, it is difficult to judge whether the seventeenth century really did mark a diplomatic watershed. The concept of *ragion di stato* had first been defined in 1547 by the papal diplomat Giovanni della Casa; while around the beginning of the sixteenth century the Florentine politician Niccolò Machiavelli had summarized the primary pursuit of politics as 'the self-preservation of the state with all means at any price'.[51]

It also has to be asked how far conflicts like the Thirty Years War had ever been purely and genuinely about religion. King Henry IV of France famously switched his allegiance from Protestantism to Catholicism in 1593 in order to secure his hold on the throne during a civil war ostensibly fought along religious lines. In the period prior to the Thirty Years War, Henry's chief minister, the Duke of Sully, had envisaged fomenting discord in order to 'divide Europe equally among a certain Number of Powers, in such a Manner, that none of them might have Cause, either of Envy or Fear, from the Possessions or Power of others'.[52] In other words, religion and politics had always been – and remained – mixed. Colonization was still justified on religious grounds; kings continued to assert that they ruled with the blessing of God; and states continued to fight wars of religion.

The road towards the mid-seventeenth-century debate about sovereignty had also been paved decades earlier by the writings of thinkers like Jean Bodin, Giovanni Botero, and Thomas Mun on the role of the state in economic affairs. But whereas optimists still assumed that a common interest in prosperity would lead to cooperation, economic progress often resulted in yet more violence. The scientific and technological breakthroughs that boosted economic productivity also made guns more powerful and fortifications far more complex and sophisticated. States could now afford to maintain ever larger standing armies and subsidize allies to fight proxy wars. The consequence, as often as not, was military stalemate – but one produced at immense cost in men and materiel. 'Whenever this war ceases,' observed the English economic thinker Charles Davenant about the Nine Years War (1688–97), 'it will not be for want of mutual hatred in the opposite parties, nor for want of men to fight the quarrel . . . but that side must first give out where money is first failing.'[53] Economic competition also caused states to lock horns over strategic sea lanes, such as the English Channel, the Kattegat in the Baltic, and the Strait of Gibraltar in the Mediterranean, as well as over regions rich in commerce, manufacturing, or natural resources, both within Europe and increasingly across the globe.

The development of new financial and credit instruments caused instability too, especially when rulers, as they often did, borrowed beyond their means. Debt defaults, currency debasements, and extortionate taxation frequently led to social unrest. In 1568, for example, the cash-strapped Holy Roman Emperor tried to raise taxes in the Low Countries, causing riots that escalated into the Eighty Years War. In 1618, a currency debasement and tax increases prompted furious Bohemian politicians to throw Habsburg officials out of the meeting hall window, signalling the beginning of the Thirty Years War. Even those actively involved in the new financial markets, such as Joseph de la Vega, a Spanish Jewish merchant in late seventeenth-century Amsterdam, could regard speculation as 'the falsest and most infamous business in the world'.[54]

Economic competition gave birth to mercantilism: a system of protectionist government policies intended to build a strong national economy and to preserve a positive trade balance. All major powers, beginning with Spain and Portugal, established trading companies which were granted monopolies on the trade from particular colonies. English mercantilists claimed that their own national trading companies were the only way to change an unfair economic order and rectify the Spanish 'injustice toward the English, whom, *contra ius gentium* [against the law of nations], have excluded from commerce with the West Indies.'[55] At the same time, thinkers like the jurist John Selden were promulgating the notion of a *mare clausum* – a 'closed sea' – in order to try and lock out England's closest trading rival in the seventeenth century, the Dutch. Others – like Thomas Mun, one of the foremost mercantilist thinkers of the early seventeenth century and himself a director of the East India Company – argued that the import of all goods which were also domestically produced should be prohibited.

The outcome of these debates was a slew of protectionist legislation: in England, for example, the Navigation Acts of 1651 and 1673 required all trade to and from overseas colonies to be carried by English shipping; while the Calico Acts of 1700 and 1721 banned all cotton imports into England. Such measures, however, merely fanned the flames of European war. As the French finance minister Jean Colbert warned in 1669: Europe's commerce 'is carried on by 20,000 vessels and that number cannot be increased. Each nation strives to have its faire share and to get ahead of the others.'[56] Mercantilism, it appeared, was a zero-sum game.

The Rise and Fall of the Habsburgs

The sixteenth and seventeenth centuries set the stage for modern European power politics. At the beginning of the era, the continent was dominated by the Habsburg Empire. The dynasty's policy of imperial expansion by marriage culminated with Charles V (1519–56), whose dominions included Austria, Hungary, the Holy Roman Empire, Spain, Portugal, and the Low Countries – not to mention immense colonial possessions overseas. Spanning both hemispheres and the Atlantic, Pacific, and Indian Oceans, the Habsburg Empire was – as its propagandists proudly boasted – the first 'upon which the sun never set'.[57]

France, however, considered the Habsburg expansion along its borders a major threat. King Francis I went so far as to describe it as an evil empire, and was even prepared to forge alliances with Protestant England and the Islamic Ottoman Empire to fight it.[58] After Charles V divided his empire into a Spanish part, ruled by his zealously Catholic son Philip II, and an Austrian part, governed by his brother and successor as Holy Roman Emperor, Ferdinand I, the kings of France seized on the opportunities that arose to try to weaken the Habsburg hegemony.

The first chance was provided in 1568 by the start of the long-running popular uprising against Spanish rule in the Netherlands known as the Eighty Years War. But Philip II retaliated by inciting civil war between France's Catholics and Protestants. Another chance came with the Thirty Years War, which originated as a rebellion against Habsburg rule in Central and Northern Europe and spread to encompass most of the continent's powers at one time or another. Cardinal Richelieu outlined the French strategy in 1629.

We need to be constantly worried about stopping the rise of Spain and, unlike that nation, whose goal it is to enhance its domination and expand its borders, France must only think about fortifying itself and build and open gateways to enter the states of its neighbours in order to be able to save them from the oppression of Spain when the moment arises.[59]

To that end, France subsidized the large anti-Habsburg alliance of Protestant states spearheaded by the Swedish warrior-king Gustavus Adolphus, and eventually took up arms itself, before exhaustion brought all the parties to the negotiating table in Westphalia in 1648. Although the war often took the guise of a religious conflict between Catholics and Protestants, in reality it was a struggle for the political mastery of Europe. To the extent that the Habsburgs were undoubtedly left weaker than they had been in 1618, France benefited from the war. But fears of France's rising power had already emerged during the conference at Westphalia, where Sweden, the Netherlands, Austria, and Spain all sealed bilateral agreements with each other.

The formal conclusion to the Thirty Years War did not bring peace to Europe. Within a few years of Westphalia, the continent's leading trading nations – England and the Netherlands – were at war, Portugal was struggling to establish its independence from Spain, and Sweden was fighting the other northern powers for supremacy over the Baltic. Under the pretext of liberating Europe from the Habsburg yoke, France meanwhile continued its war with Spain and made repeated efforts to detach the German polities along the Rhine, the states of Northern Italy, and the provinces of Flanders from the Holy Roman Empire. The would-be beneficiaries of such French altruism, however, were far from welcoming. 'The nature of France is restless and can scarcely be suffered except at a distance,' wrote one Dutch pamphleteer. 'In the cold light of day, France aims at the expansion of its kingdom and of Catholicism, and finally even to obtain imperial dignity,' warned a Swiss diplomat.

In 1659, France and Spain finally agreed peace. In return for marriage to Philip IV of Spain's daughter, and a large dowry, Louis XIV of France would abandon his claims on Flanders. But the failure to pay the princess's dowry served France as a pretext to try and seize the Spanish Netherlands in lieu. This ignited a half century of conflicts – the War of Devolution (1667–8), the Dutch War (1672–8), the Nine Years War (1688–97), and the War of the Spanish Succession (1701–14) – in which shifting alliances of European powers fought to rein in French ambitions. Louis XIV may have been known as 'the Sun King' in recognition of the dazzling splendour of his court, but beneath the glittering surface the treasury coffers were increasingly bare. By the time of Louis's death in 1715, financially overburdened France had been checked and an uneasy balance of power established. A complete and lasting cessation of conflict, however, was another matter altogether.

Since the mid-sixteenth century, the various states surrounding the Baltic had engaged in a series of 'northern wars' for control of the region's lands and its lucrative trade in natural resources. With other contenders weakened by the Thirty Years War, the opportunity arose for Russia to flex its muscles. Under the Romanov Dynasty, which first came to the throne in 1613, the anarchy that blighted the realm was slowly expunged and a degree of order imposed. The first real sign of strength came during the Russo-Polish War of 1654–67, when Russia made significant territorial gains in Ukraine. In 1686, when Russia and Poland–Lithuania signed the alliance known as the Treaty of Perpetual Peace, the terms clearly demonstrated that it was the tsardom which was the senior partner. In 1700, Tsar Peter the Great (1682–1725) felt powerful enough to challenge Sweden for supremacy of the Baltic. Following the decisive victory at Poltava in 1709, Russia was able to take possession of Swedish territories in Estonia, Latvia, and Finland. By the time the war ended in 1721, Sweden's ascendancy in the Baltic had been shattered.

Peter the Great made the Russian Empire the leading power in Northern and Eastern Europe. He also took advantage of the weakening of the Safavids, as we have seen, to annex much of their former empire in the Caucasus and Caspian region. In addition, he built himself an entirely new capital – the city of St Petersburg, strategically located on the Baltic – brought in shipbuilders from the Netherlands in order to construct a powerful modern navy, founded his own trading company, and adopted mercantilist policies to try and strengthen the Russian economy. Peter was brutal in imposing his Westernizing reforms, but he also aspired to be an enlightened European monarch the equal of any king of France or Habsburg emperor. Just as 'Romans praise their first two tsars, Romulus and Numa, that one by war and the other by peace strengthened the fatherland, or as in sacred history David by arms and Solomon by politics created a blessed well-being for Israel,' wrote the great Orthodox preacher Theophan Prokopovich, so 'in our case both were achieved by Peter alone. For us he is Romulus, and Numa, and David, and Solomon – Peter alone.'[60]

But Russia was not alone, for the period saw a second rising power in the region: Prussia. The state originated in 1618 when the elector of Brandenburg inherited the duchy of Prussia. With its territories divided between the region around Berlin and the area surrounding Königsberg (modern

Kaliningrad), the priority of its first rulers was geographical consolidation. The Elector Frederick William seized the opportunities provided by the Thirty Years War, using French subsidies to build a standing army and assimilating some of his smaller war-exhausted neighbours. 'Alliances are certainly good, but a force of one's own, that one can confidently rely on, is better,' he wrote in 1667. 'A ruler is not treated with respect unless he has his own troops and resources.'[61]

To bolster Prussia's standing and security further, Frederick William's successor obtained international approval in 1701 for his state's elevation from an electorate of the Holy Roman Empire into a kingdom – the reward for Prussia's long-term contribution to various anti-French coalitions. Even though Prussia was now the largest German state after Habsburg Austria, diplomacy by itself was not felt to be sufficient. True to his electoral namesake's teachings, King Frederick William I (1713–40) expanded the army to such an extent that Voltaire, or so the story goes, quipped: 'Where some states possess an army, the Prussian army possesses a state.' In order to survive, let alone flourish, Prussia had to become a kingdom of iron. 'It is the duty of a God-fearing ruler,' Frederick William declared, 'to repress and not to tolerate the temple of Satan, that is, mistresses, operas, comedies, redoutes, ballets, and masques.'[62]

Europe's epoch of Renaissance, of global and scientific discovery, was no golden age; it remained, as Rubens put it, inherently an 'age of iron'.[63] 'Not even a Turk could be so cruel as to wish the Christians greater misfortune than the suffering they inflict upon each other,' lamented Erasmus in the early 1500s. The Flemish artist Pieter Bruegel the Elder painted his apocalyptic vision of *The Triumph of Death* in 1562. As armies fought across its war-torn landscape of ruined buildings and piles of bodies lit by flames on the horizon, the painting's message seemed to be that conflict spared no one, rich or poor. Three-quarters of a century later, Rubens expressed the tragedy of the Thirty Years War in his nightmarish masterpiece, the *Horrors of War* (1638). In England, the philosopher Thomas Hobbes wrote his influential political thesis *Leviathan* (1651) against the backdrop of a civil war that had resulted in the execution of the country's king. In order to escape from lives that were naturally 'nasty, brutish, and short', Hobbes urged, mankind had to submit to the rule of law in the form of an absolute monarch.

But subsequent events in Britain suggested that Hobbes's theory might not be entirely right. The so-called Glorious Revolution of 1688 introduced a framework of constitutional monarchy that, in its core principles, would prove lasting and would effect the gradual transformation of the government of England, Scotland, and Ireland from three personal monarchies loosely connected by a shared sovereign into a single, centrally administered state. Although sporadic incidences of rebellion would flare up in Scotland and Ireland during the eighteenth century, these changes ushered in an era of enduring domestic peace. They also established the context that would allow Britain – for so long a peripheral power – finally to forge ahead of its European rivals and occupy the centre of the global stage.

Outburst

Between 1500 and 1750, Europe was still far from being the world's centre of power. The initial colonization of the Americas, Africa, and parts of Asia may have appeared an extraordinary outburst of energy, ambition, and violence to Europeans at the time, but in reality such power was modest compared to that of the three Islamic empires – the Ottomans, the Safavids, and the Mughals – and the Chinese Qing Dynasty. Although the European conflicts of the period were undeniably savage, the main arena of great power competition was in Asia. Here, the causes of strife differed little from previous centuries: the desire to enhance security by controlling the gateways to imperial heartlands, and the quest for trade and profit.

Mercantilism – the policy of state intervention to protect and augment commerce – was in full swing all over the world. The Ottomans sought to control trade in the Mediterranean, the Safavids endeavoured to boost their silk exports, the Mughals protected their textile industries, and European rulers licensed lucrative monopolies to national trading companies. Most major powers had the ambition to go to sea. Yet it was here, in matters concerning maritime mobility, that European connective power started to make a major difference.

As in past eras, wars continued to be fought in order to prevent other states becoming too powerful. In Europe, for example, first the Habsburgs and then the French faced coalitions cobbled together to rein in their expansionist ambitions. Conversely, weakness too still elicited aggression.

The Ming tried to hide behind their newly reinforced Great Wall; but as the emperor became unable to rule, the court fell into disarray, and as hardship ignited social unrest, the Manchu seized their chance to take over their empire. It was the weakness of the Safavids that allowed numerically inferior Russian forces to destroy their dynasty, and weakness that permitted European colonists to shatter kingdoms in the Americas, Africa, and the Indian Ocean.

All these campaigns were justified by religious fervour, a burning sense of moral and cultural superiority, and a belief that the blessings of civilization and harmony were being bestowed on a world of benighted barbarians – even as rulers began to be governed by notions of national interest and diplomats elaborated the principles of national sovereignty. True sovereignty, it was understood, remained the preserve of the strong.

CHAPTER 13

The Primacy of the West

1750–2000 CE

A R C T I

ATLANTIC

OCEAN

PACIFIC

OCEAN

SOUTHER

Sw

Den

Nether

France   F
          R

          Ven

Spain   No

          Otto

Morocco

          Tuareg

Cape Verde

Fernando Pó
St Tome

A

World around 1750

British possessions
French possessions
Portuguese possessions
Dutch possessions
Spanish possessions

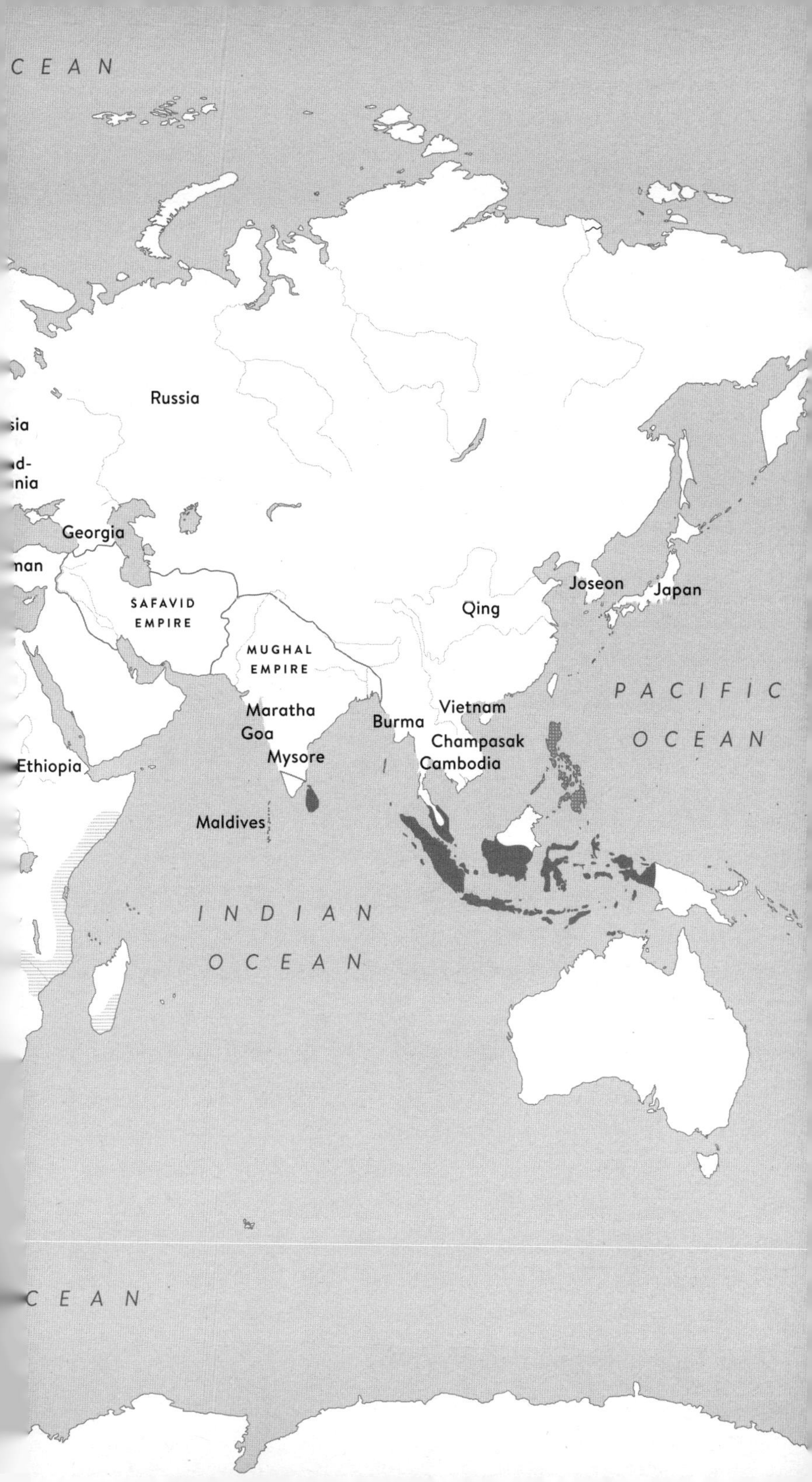

CEAN

Russia

sia

ad-
nia

Georgia

nan

SAFAVID
EMPIRE

MUGHAL
EMPIRE

Maratha
Goa
Mysore

Ethiopia

Maldives

Qing

Joseon   Japan

Vietnam
Burma
Champasak
Cambodia

PACIFIC

OCEAN

INDIAN

OCEAN

CEAN

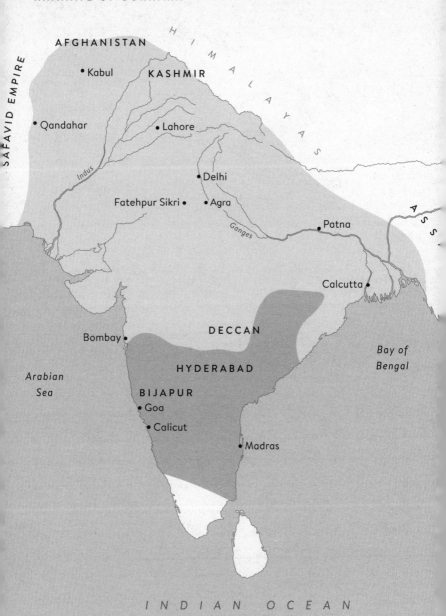

KHANATE OF BUKHARA

AFGHANISTAN

• Kabul

KASHMIR

HIMALAYAS

SAFAVID EMPIRE

• Qandahar

• Lahore

Indus

• Delhi

Fatehpur Sikri •

• Agra

Ganges

• Patna

ASSAM

Calcutta •

DECCAN

Bombay •

Bay of Bengal

HYDERABAD

Arabian Sea

BIJAPUR

• Goa

• Calicut

• Madras

INDIAN OCEAN

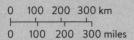

0   100   200   300 km

0   100   200   300 miles

The Mughal Empire 1605–1707

Mughal Empire to 1605

Mughal Empire to 1707

Black Sea

OTTOMAN
EMPIRE

• Chaldiran

Mosul •

Euphrates

Tigris

Karbala •
Najal •

• Baghdad

Basra •

Caspian Sea

Aral Sea

KHANATE
OF
KHIVA

KHANATE
OF
BUKHARA

Oxus

• Balkh

• Kabul

• Tehran
• Qum

SAFAVID
EMPIRE

• Herat

MUGHAL EMPIRE

• Isfahan

Indus

• Shiraz

Persian Gulf

• Hurmuz

Arabian
Sea

Red Sea

I N D I A N

O C E A N

0   200   400   600 km

0   200   400   600 miles

Safavid Iran in the 17th Century

Safavid Iran at its greatest
extent (17th century)

The eighteenth century CE witnessed an eruption of European progress on a scale never seen before. Propelled by steam engines, backed by unmatched firepower, incited by the competition for status and foreign markets, and facilitated by the domination of seas and oceans, the Europeans became unstoppable. By the end of the nineteenth century, a large part of the world had been colonized; and even the greatest powers that remained free from rule by those of white European stock – the Ottoman and Qing Empires – were tottering. In 1900, around 1.6 billion people lived on the planet. About 280 million of them inhabited Western and Central Europe, but those European societies governed at least 425 million people in their colonies.[1] Those ratios are perhaps not so exceptional, nor the violence with which this expansion happened. Many small polities had conquered vast empires and shown no mercy. Yet never before had it happened so rapidly and so widely. The eternal pursuit of imperialism had become industrialized and globalized.

Out of those 280 million Europeans, only a small elite held the reins of power. Until the twentieth century, most Europeans lived in poverty, worked in dangerous conditions, had almost no political rights, and risked being imprisoned or killed if they agitated for a better life. As Charles Dickens wrote ironically in 1859: 'It was the best of times, it was the worst of times.'[2] The real breakthrough in European democracy and welfare came when the continent's imperial dominance was in steep decline, after the two World Wars (1914–18 and 1939–45). Its global supremacy passed to the Soviet Union and the United States of America, with the latter becoming the ultimate victor of their rivalry in the Cold War (1947–91). The United States took centre stage as yet another exceptionalist power pledging to be a force for good. Its geographical position, separated by two oceans from the Eastern Hemisphere, meant that its leadership was expressed more indirectly, for example by developing unequalled potential in terms of air and sea power, by dominating digital and communications technology, and by spearheading the global economy. But the more power the United States gained, the more it too gave in to the temptation to use it.

What made this age truly different from previous ones was its immense economic progress. The gradual spreading of industrialization caused incomes to rise faster than ever before, the population to boom, international trade to expand, and mobility to increase. If production per capita, in constant dollar values, had increased by around $100 between 1500 and 1800, it grew by more than $5,000 between 1800 and 2000.[3]

This was the ideal of the European Enlightenment in practice: man using his intelligence to shape the world around him. But that other great ideal of the Enlightenment was realized much less, namely that rational man would come to see others' success as an opportunity instead of a threat, and compete by peaceful means instead of relapsing into war. As a result, progress in this period was what happened in between the hugely destructive wars, wars fought with the same ingenuity that had revolutionized the fields of industry, science, and medicine.

Prolific Abundance

In the Eastern Hemisphere, the rise of Europe first eclipsed and then contributed to the decline of some of its largest powers. The Mughal Empire was one of the first to collapse. By the mid-eighteenth century, European countries had been allowed to operate trading posts, or factories, on the coasts of South Asia for decades. But they wanted more. The British East India Company, for example, declared war on local Mughal rulers whenever they refused to allow them greater access to the interior. In 1757, its vastly outnumbered and outgunned forces won a decisive victory at the Battle of Plassey, which led to it gaining control over the Mughals' wealthiest province, Bengal. Over the next century, Indian rulers continued to resist the gradual British advance across the subcontinent. In 1858, after more than 100,000 people had been killed in the great rebellion traditionally known as the Indian Mutiny (1857–8), the British government took over the administration of the Raj from the East India Company. With the inauguration of crown rule, the Mughal Dynasty – for so long a shadow of its earlier mightiness – was formally ended.

The other powers to be weakened were the Safavid Dynasty's successors in Persia and the Ottoman Empire. Persia's new rulers were heavily pressurized by the growing strength of the Russian Empire. A famous dictum attributed to Tsarina Catherine the Great (1762–96) bluntly summed up Russia's policy of expansionism: 'I have no way to defend my borders but to extend them.'[4] In 1783, the Treaty of Georgievsk forced Georgia to accept Russian protection in place of its original dependence on Persia. In 1828, the Persian shah had to consent to the even more humiliating Treaty of Turkmenchay. Russia gained the last regions of the Caucasus not yet within its control, received a large indemnity, and was granted free access for its traders to all of Persia.

Meanwhile, Russia's desire to control the Black Sea region and gain access to the Mediterranean led it to support rebellions in the Ottoman Empire wherever they might further its goals. But when France incited an uprising in Ottoman Egypt, the Russians opportunistically agreed the Treaty of Hunkar Iskelesi with the Turks in 1833. In return for Russian military aid, the Ottomans promised to close the Dardanelles to foreign warships at Russia's behest. But as Russia resumed its strategy of chipping away at the Ottoman Balkans, the sultan became increasingly dependent on military and financial support from Western European powers seeking to maintain their own balance of power with the Russian Empire.

Europe also triggered decades of turmoil in what was still the world's wealthiest and most populous empire, China. Under the Qing, the Chinese Empire reached its greatest extent and ruled over a third of the global population.[5] 'Heaven has left us this vast wilderness,' explained the early nineteenth-century political theorist Wei Yuan.[6] Although some strategists proposed establishing clearly defined defensive borders, others, like the Qianlong Emperor (1735–96) – who ruled the Qing Empire at its apogee – considered expansion to be the best defence. 'What's this about "inner and outer" being divisible?' he asked rhetorically.[7]

> Since ancient times, the way of governing the country has been to manage civil affairs, while simultaneously exerting oneself in military affairs. Indeed, soldiers may not be mobilized for one hundred years, but they may not be left unprepared for one day. Although the state has been at peace for a long time, military preparedness should remain a top priority.[8]

The Chinese desire to dominate and to civilize other peoples was thus not very different from the views of European imperialists.

Although China's production per capita at the end of the eighteenth century was only half that of Western Europe, its economy remained the largest in the world. That led Great Britain to approach the Chinese emperor with proposals for closer trading relations in 1793. The British ambassador, Lord Macartney, brought the Qianlong Emperor a model steam engine, while the Chinese expected Macartney to fall on his knees and offer tribute.[9] The British delegation was dismissed with a letter from the emperor to the British king. 'Our Celestial Empire possesses all things in prolific abundance and lacks no product within its own borders,' it read. 'Should your vessels touch the shore, your merchants will assuredly never be permitted to land or to reside there, but will be subject to instant expulsion. In that event your barbarian merchants will have had a long journey for nothing.'[10]

Soon after, the British tried another tactic: addicting the Chinese to opium imported from India. Seeking to reduce the trade deficit with China, they discovered that opium produced in India was about the only commodity they had to offer for which there was much Chinese demand. The emperor's attempts to halt the destructive trade were violently resisted by the British in the two Opium Wars (1839–42 and 1856–60), which ended with both territorial and commercial concessions being forced from the defeated Chinese. 'The Qing government was already becoming weak and decadent,' assessed the historian Liang Qichao. 'The whole nation was drugged by the enjoyment of peace.'[11] The deliberate destruction of the Chinese emperors' Summer Palace outside Beijing by the British and their French allies in 1860, in retaliation for the murder of European prisoners, symbolized a watershed in the long era of Chinese instability between 1839 and 1949 – an unhappy period that China still refers to today as the century of humiliation. As the Qing Empire crumbled, Europe came to dominate perhaps not the whole world, but at least the whole Eastern Hemisphere.

France versus Britain

In 1761 the French philosopher Jean-Jacques Rousseau wrote down his proposals to end Europe's wars for ever. All the powers should combine in a system bound together by a shared religion, law, customs, commerce, and a sort of equilibrium that would prevent one state from upsetting others too easily.[12] Many British thinkers – from the economist Charles Davenant and the polemicist Daniel Defoe to the

THE PRIMACY OF THE WEST

philosopher David Hume – similarly vested their hopes for European harmony in a combination of commerce and the balance of power. The great liberal economist Adam Smith went further, arguing in *The Wealth of Nations* (1776) that the rising affluence of a neighbouring nation was less a political threat than an opportunity for trade. 'As a rich man is likely to be a better customer to the industrious people in his neighbourhood, than a poor, so is likewise a rich nation.'[13]

For a brief moment, when the Treaty of Paris brought an end to the Seven Years War (1756–63), it looked as if these intellectuals would be confirmed in their optimism. The war had been the first true world war: two coalitions, led by Great Britain on one side and France on the other, had fought in Europe, the Americas, and Asia, leaving more than a million people dead. In the treaty's first article, the signatories agreed that 'There shall be a Christian, universal, and perpetual peace, as well by sea as by land'.[14] But the assumptions on which the optimism of Rousseau and others rested were shaky from the outset. Previous treaties, such as the one that ended the War of the Spanish Succession in 1713, had also been founded on exactly the same principles of universal peace, mutual friendship, and the balance of power.[15]

The ink on the Treaty of Paris was barely dry before the states of Central Europe embarked on a new war with Russia, while France and the Netherlands continued their efforts to undermine British rule in North America. Much as the ancient Caledonian chieftain Calgacus had denounced Roman imperialism, or the states of Germany and the Dutch provinces rejected the fiscal, political, and religious oppression of the Habsburg Empire, the radical thinker Thomas Paine justified the revolt of the American colonies against the British Empire in 1776: 'Britain, with an army to enforce her tyranny, has declared that she has a right (*not only to* TAX) but "to BIND *us in* ALL CASES WHATSOEVER," and if being *bound in that manner*, is not slavery, then there is not such a thing as slavery upon earth.'[16]

Although American victory in the War of Independence (1775–83) was a severe setback, Great Britain remained Europe's greatest maritime power, its economic strength and still vast overseas possessions counterbalancing the might of the continent's leading land power, France. Indeed, it was France that suffered the most from the eighteenth century's many wars. The French population may have been far larger, but its production per capita declined to about half that of Britain's as the latter's steam engines, spinning machines, coke-fired blast furnaces, and countless other inventions spearheaded the industrial revolution. Despite the efforts of the finance minister Jacques Turgot to liberalize the French economy and control government spending, public debt was staggering, and so was the burden of taxation, especially on peasant farmers. 'Let them eat cake!' was Queen Marie Antoinette's alleged solution to bread shortages. These, in combination with King Louis XVI's feeble government and his reluctance to make the rich pay more taxes, led the citizens of Paris to start the French Revolution in July 1789. In comparison, Britain proved far more resilient, thanks mostly to more efficient taxation and the fact that, unlike France following the surrender of most of its North American colonies, British merchants managed to resume trade with the United States soon after the 1776 revolution.

When Louis XVI was dragged to the guillotine in January 1793, centuries of absolute rule were brought to an end in France. Even so, the First Republic wanted revenge for past French defeats, despite its continuing economic woes. Rumours spread in Paris that blue-blooded refugees in London were conspiring with foreign powers to restore the Bourbon monarchy. But while the more restless members of the republican leadership called for the revolution to be exported, others put the case for a new balance of power with Britain based on French annexation of the Low Countries. 'Your Indian Empire has enabled you to subsidize all the powers of Europe against us and your monopoly of trade has put you in possession of a fund of inexhaustible wealth,' one French official informed a British diplomat. 'Belgium, by belonging to France would remove what had been the source of all wars for two centuries past; and the Rhine being the natural boundary of France, would ensure the tranquillity of Europe for two centuries to come.'[17] To defend the republic, a new army was raised through mass conscription and sent into battle against Austria, the Netherlands, and Switzerland. A first British intervention to preserve the autonomy of Flanders failed in 1795, and so did a second expedition together with Russia to liberate Holland four years later. The coalitions sponsored by Britain against France failed miserably: Russia was distracted by rivalry with Austria, Prussia with Denmark, and Spain with Portugal. As the French attacked Europe from its heart, London's allies quarrelled with each other on the fringes. War and politics had stopped everything, wrote the German scientist and explorer Alexander von Humboldt in 1798: 'the world is closed'.[18]

By 1800, France had fallen under the spell of its leading general, the military genius Napoleon Bonaparte. The British government, led by William Pitt, tried to counter Napoleon's aggressive expansionism by establishing naval supremacy, blockading seaborne trade with France, and financially supporting new coalitions to wage war against the French. The cost of these strategies was immense, but Pitt had always been unapologetic about such expenditure. 'The relieving by every such means as my duty will suffer me to adopt, the burdens of the people and removing that load of debt by which it is oppressed, is the grand and ultimate end of my desire,' Pitt had explained in 1786. 'But let it be well understood. What a certain security there is in a defencible and powerful situation and how likely weakness and improvidence are to be the forerunners of war.'[19]

Napoleon, meanwhile, was frustrated by his inability to prevent Britain conquering French overseas colonies. The 'tyranny of the seas,' he later called it, while recognizing that war with Britain would always be inevitable because 'it is impossible for that country to remain long at peace. The territory of England is become too small for its population. She requires a monopoly of the four quarters of the globe to enable her to exist. War procures this monopoly, because it gives England the right of destruction at sea. It is her safeguard.'[20] In 1803, he proposed a deal with Britain: 'If you are masters of the seas, I am master of the land. Let us then think of uniting rather than going to war, and we shall rule at pleasure the destinies of the world.'[21] The idea was to buy time in which to defeat the threat posed by France's continental foes. Six weeks after Admiral Nelson annihilated the French and Spanish fleets at Trafalgar in October 1805, Napoleon won his great victory at Austerlitz, driving the Austrian Empire out of the war.

Austerlitz also led to the formal dissolution of the Holy Roman Empire in 1806 – but Napoleon had already granted himself imperial honours two years earlier. 'I am a true Roman Emperor,' he later declared; 'I am of the race of the Caesars, and of the best of their kind, the founders.'[22] The French artist Ingres painted Napoleon in 1806, seated in majesty on his throne, like a Roman god, a golden laurel wreath on his head, Charlemagne's sceptre in his hand, and an imperial eagle at his feet. Many Germans had considered Napoleon a counterweight to the rule of the Habsburgs – Goethe had hailed him as a demigod; Beethoven had dedicated a symphony to him – now they were horrified that he appeared to be the Habsburgs' successor.

Britain's main ally on the continent became the Russian Empire. Tsar Alexander I declared the fight against France a holy war, calling Napoleon the oppressor of Europe and the enemy of the Orthodox faith. But when Napoleon repeated the tactic he had tried with Britain and offered to divide the world between France and Russia, the tsar surrendered to temptation and, in 1807, made peace. Neither side kept their promises; relations worsened until 1812, when Napoleon invaded Russia. It was a disastrous miscalculation. As one soldier in the French army noted: 'There was no hospital for the wounded; they died of hunger, thirst, cold, and despair . . . our sick . . . were left to themselves; and only deathly white faces and stiffened hands stretched toward us.'[23] Of the more than 680,000 men in Napoleon's *Grand Armée* who invaded

Russia, barely a twentieth were still effective combatants by the end of the campaign. The Russian tragedy sealed Napoleon's fate, as the other continental powers now rebelled against French rule. He was decisively defeated in 1813 in the Battle of Leipzig, which led to his abdication, and finally in 1815 at Waterloo, when he attempted to return from exile.

The French Revolutionary and Napoleonic Wars (1792–1802, 1803–15) left millions dead and changed the political map of Europe. Against this bloody backdrop, however, the thinkers of the Enlightenment had never stopped issuing new proposals for European peace. In 1795, the German philosopher Immanuel Kant published his influential essay on 'Perpetual Peace'. He called for a political order without secret treaties and standing armies, but founded instead on three 'definitive articles' or principles: republicanism in place of belligerent monarchs, a league of nations, and the recognition of world citizenship. After the defeat of Napoleon, European countries competed for the moral high ground. The treaty between Russia and Prussia in 1813 had set the tone. 'The time will come,' it said, 'when treaties will no longer be mere truces, when they will once more be observed with that religious faith, that sacred inviolability which underlies the esteem, the power and the preservation of empires.'[24]

The Congress of Vienna

In 1814–15, Vienna hosted the biggest peace conference ever held in Europe. Over nine months, more than 16,000 delegates, correspondents, and what we would now call lobbyists participated in its deliberations. Plenipotentiaries – ministers with full responsibility to negotiate – combined formal talks with informal conversations and endless parties. The Austrian hosts laid on banquets, balls, hunts, and sleigh rides where Dutch milkmaids performed ballets on the ice. Delegates were often spotted drunk in the streets; when one of them was asked how much progress had been made in the talks, he quipped: 'Le Congrès ne marche pas: il danse.'[25] The conference's mastermind, the Austrian foreign minister Klemens von Metternich, believed this approach would facilitate diplomatic breakthroughs: 'The tongue is untied, the heart opens and the need to make oneself understood often takes over from the rules of cold and severe calculation.'[26] His British counterpart, Viscount Castlereagh, concurred: 'The advantage of this mode of proceeding is that you treat the Plenipotentiaries as a Body, with early and becoming respect.'[27]

The leaders of the war against Napoleon – Russia, Prussia, Austria, Britain, and Spain – formed a steering committee to ensure that their underlying aims would be achieved. These were threefold: to re-establish a multipolar European order in which no one power could predominate; to ensure that future disputes between states were resolved peacefully through regularly held diplomatic conferences; and to prevent the sort of revolution that had destabilized first France in 1789 and then the old European order from ever occurring again.

The outcome of the Congress of Vienna did not resemble in the least Kant's republican perpetual peace. Instead it upheld the power of the crowned heads of Europe. The main victors in Vienna were the absolute monarchies of Russia, Prussia, and Austria. Tsar Alexander received most of Poland and Finland. Prussian sovereignty was confirmed around the

Danzig Corridor, as well as in portions of Saxony and the Rhineland. Austria was cushioned from Prussia by a newly formed German Confederation and granted control of Tyrol, Lombardy, and Tuscany, as well as strategic Adriatic ports like Trieste. In France itself, the Bourbon dynasty was restored to power, while at the same time being kept in check by buffer states such as the Netherlands, Switzerland, and Piedmont. Great Britain, meanwhile, secured permanent ownership of many of the colonies it had acquired during the course of the Napoleonic War, including the Cape Colony (South Africa) and Ceylon (Sri Lanka). Guaranteeing these decisions was a series of further arrangements between the leading powers which became known as the Congress System, or Concert of Europe. These were formalized initially by Russia, Austria, and Prussia, in the socially conservative, politically reactionary Holy Alliance. This became the Quadruple Alliance when Britain joined them in November 1815, and the Quintuple Alliance with the addition of France three years later.

The Concert of Europe was soon being put to the test. When Prussia, Russia, and Austria agreed on repressing a liberal revolution in Naples in 1820, and then backed a French intervention to subdue a popular uprising in Spain in 1822, Britain opposed these interventions on the grounds that they were flagrant attempts to gain influence within other states and so alter the balance of power. Meanwhile, the French Revolution continued to inspire liberals and nationalists across Europe. In 1830, Greek independence from the Ottoman Empire was recognized by Britain, France, and Russia. In that same year, the French king himself was overthrown, Belgium seceded from the Netherlands, civil war continued to rage in Portugal, and there were uprisings in Italy and Poland to which Austria and Russia responded brutally.

It was the revolutions of 1848 that dealt the Concert of Europe its fatal blow. This Spring of Nations, as it was called, rippled through about a dozen European countries. Protesters demanded greater civil liberties and the end of imperial overlordship. These popular uprisings were exploited politically by the great powers. France backed an Italian rebellion against Austria. Prussia supported German rebels in Schleswig-Holstein against Danish rule. The revolutions were opposed by the Russian and Austrian Empires, but the tsar and the emperor themselves differed on how to handle turmoil in Poland and Hungary. In addition, unrest in the decaying Ottoman Empire elicited conflicting responses from Russia, France, and Britain. Britain wanted to avoid at any cost Russia establishing a naval presence in the Eastern Mediterranean.

The new French emperor, Napoleon III, was intent on increasing his prestige by becoming the protector of Christians in the Holy Land and by deploying a warship to the Black Sea. It incensed the Tsar, who responded by dispatching a small contingent to Moldavia in 1853. Even though France and Britain preferred a diplomatic settlement to the crisis in the Balkans, the Ottomans assumed their support for stronger measures and declared war on Russia. With anti-Russian passions inflamed, there was no way back. By 1854, a coalition of nearly a million mainly Ottoman, French, and British troops was fighting the Russian army in the Black Sea region. The Crimean War (1853–6) was the first industrial war in Europe. Long-range artillery was deployed and supplies were brought up to the lines by a purpose-built military railway. By the end of the war, which Russia lost, close to half a million soldiers had died, mostly from disease.

Prussia lay low throughout the Crimean War and focused on its economic development instead. Partly due to British investment, Prussia became the fastest industrializing country on the continent. Siemens led the development of the telegraph, Bayer in producing aspirin, and Krupp in armaments. The smaller German states were absorbed into a new Prussian-led customs union and slowly knit together with a network of Prussian railways. But it was not enough. In 1862, the newly appointed Prussian prime minister, Otto von Bismarck, proclaimed that the position of Prussia in Germany would not be determined by its promulgation of liberal values but by its military power: 'The great questions of the day will not be settled by speeches and majority decisions but by blood and iron.'[28] Prussia wanted German unity – but under its own leadership.

With Britain, France, and Russia still licking their wounds from the Crimean War and the Austrian Empire embroiled in another rebellion in its Italian domains, Bismarck got his way. In 1864, he provoked a new crisis in Schleswig-Holstein. Austria again sought to stop Prussian interference in Schleswig-Holstein, but this time it was utterly defeated thanks to the much more mobile and better commanded Prussian armed forces. Prussia's victory led to the establishment of the North German Confederation in 1867. Nominally it was a federal state, consisting of over twenty kingdoms, duchies, principalities, and free cities; in reality, it was a tool

THE PRIMACY OF THE WEST

of Prussian hegemony. Alarmed by the threat to the European balance of power posed by Prussia's ambitions for German unification, France mobilized against it in 1870. It was swiftly overwhelmed by the rapid Prussian advance, Napoleon III captured, and Paris occupied. In 1871, as France plunged once again into revolution and republicanism, the birth of the German Empire was proclaimed by Bismarck in Versailles's Hall of Mirrors.

Victory in 1871 left Germany as Europe's leading continental power. But Bismarck was afraid that it could lead to overconfidence and overreaching. To try and avert the dangers of German triumphalism, he refused to recognize the day of France's surrender as a national holiday, he invited Austria and Russia to re-establish the Holy Alliance, and he facilitated new diplomatic conferences and initiatives to resolve further European conflicts peacefully. Despite his reassurances that Germany was now a sated power, the next generation of political leaders were far from satisfied. In 1897, the new Kaiser, Wilhelm II, engineered Bismarck's downfall. Two years earlier, Bismarck had warned: 'The crash will come if things go on like this.'[29] Now he proffered a final piece of advice:

> We ought to do all we can to weaken the bad feeling which
> has been called out through our growth to the position
> of a real Great Power, by honourable and peaceful use of
> our influence, and so convince the world that a German
> hegemony in Europe is more useful and less partisan and
> also less harmful for the freedom of others than that of
> France, Russia, or England.[30]

The Rise of Germany

Despite Bismarck's counsel, frictions only increased between all the European powers in the decades following the unification of Germany. Revanchism simmered in France as a consequence of its defeat in 1871 and the reparations that had to be paid. Russia continued to distrust all the other European powers, who repaid the compliment. Austria, which considered the Balkans part of its sphere of influence, was angered by Russia's growing presence in the region after the latter defeated the Ottoman Empire there in 1878. And Britain distrusted any activities by Russia that brought it closer to the Mediterranean. France, meanwhile, collided with the recently unified kingdom of Italy over North Africa. The main source of tension, however, seemed to be envy at Britain's vast empire. Although, by the 1890s, Britain was mostly pursuing its imperialism indirectly, via protectorates instead of formal colonies, and was continuing to advocate free trade with other powers, the imperial ambitions of France, Germany, and Russia led to ever more frequent clashes with the United Kingdom.

This competition was partly about status and partly about economic interests. The industrial revolution led to growing demand for raw materials. As Europe's economic production often expanded faster than domestic demand, profits came under pressure. This led to protectionism, and it sparked an urgent search for export markets and opportunities to invest capital more profitably.[31] Writing in 1902, the English economist J. A. Hobson referred to over-production as the 'taproot of imperialism'.[32] Much as the British had developed imperial trading arteries in Africa and Asia, the French started building railways in Senegal and the Germans in the Ottoman Empire, while the United States joined the scramble for markets too. This economically motivated imperialism led to numerous minor wars and the deaths of countless young men in distant lands.

In 1880, the twenty-six-year-old Irish poet Oscar Wilde lamented the cost of empire:

> Wave and wild wind and foreign shore
>> Possess the flower of English land –
> Lips that thy lips shall kiss no more,
>> Hands that shall never clasp thy hand.
>
> What profit now that we have bound
>> The whole round world with nets of gold,
> If hidden in our heart is found
>> The care that groweth never old?[33]

The German foreign secretary, Bernhard von Bülow, summarized the situation more dramatically in a speech to the Reichstag in 1899:

> The rapid growth of our population, the unprecedented blossoming of our industries, the hard work of our merchants, in short the mighty vitality of the German people have woven us into the world economy and pulled us into international politics. If the English speak of a 'Greater Britain'; if the French speak of a 'Nouvelle France'; if the Russians open up Asia; then we, too, have the right to a greater Germany, not in the sense of conquest, but

indeed in the sense of peaceful extension of our trade and its infrastructures.[34]

The more the powers' foreign trade grew, the greater the steps they were prepared to take in order to defend their interests. The German Grand Admiral, Alfred von Tirpitz, was ordered to build a fleet strong enough to secure access to German colonies and deter Britain from challenging Germany at sea. The American naval captain and strategist Alfred Mahan also called for a larger fleet: 'Within, the home market is secured; but outside, beyond the broad seas, there are the markets of the world, that can be entered and controlled only by a vigorous contest, to which the habit of trusting to protection by statute does not conduce.'[35] At that time, Britain was officially referred to as a threat. It was often impossible, however, to discern the desire to defend trading interests from more aggressive objectives. Tirpitz's fleet, for instance, was ostensibly built to protect German trade, but it could also be used to deter Russia and Britain in the Baltic.

As Germany flexed its muscles, the French started building new fortifications along its Rhine frontier. In 1882, Germany formed a defensive triple alliance with Austria and Italy. France formed its own alliances, first with Russia in 1892 and then with Britain in 1904. With the establishment of an Anglo-Russian alliance in 1907, and finally the Triple Entente between France, Britain, and Russia in 1912, the battle lines were drawn across Europe.[36]

Tensions between the great powers increasingly focused on the Balkans, where the ever more fragile and fractious Russian, Austrian, and Ottoman Empires alternated between repressing nationalist insurrections within their own realms and fostering them in their neighbours. Matters came to a head in June 1914, when a Serbian nationalist assassinated the heir to the Austrian throne in Sarajevo. Austria responded by declaring war on Serbia, causing the Russians to intervene on the side of their fellow Slavs. Germany mobilized in support of Austria, then launched a pre-emptive strike on France to try and prevent it aiding Russia. The violation of Belgian neutrality by this German offensive ended any hopes that Britain might have stayed on the sidelines. Within five weeks from the firing of the fateful shot in Sarajevo, the five great powers of Europe were at war.

Most parties assumed the fighting would soon be over. Instead, it lasted more than four years and was fought over the entire Eastern Hemisphere. The mobilization of Europe's full industrial, technological, and imperial might resulted in battles of unprecedented scale and intensity, and the deaths of more than 15 million people. Writing in the first months of the conflict, H. G. Wells observed: 'Probably there have never been before in the whole past of mankind so many people convinced of the dreadfulness of war.'[37] Recollecting the fighting he took part in around the same time, one German infantryman wondered: 'What was it for that we soldiers stabbed each other, strangled each other and went for each other like mad dogs?'[38] His question remained unanswered.

The great war of 1914–18 was the tragic culmination of a century of great power politics; but, paradoxically enough, those hundred years had also been an age of political optimism. The French diplomat Dominique de Pradt, who attended the Congress of Vienna, vested new hopes in what he was the first to call 'public opinion'. 'The people have acquired a knowledge of their rights and dignity,' he announced.[39] The American diplomat Elihu Burritt encouraged working men to band together internationally in what he described as 'people-diplomacy'.[40] In Britain, even conservative statesmen acknowledged the influence of popular feeling: Lord Aberdeen, for example, joked that any prime minister had to please the newspapers, while Lord Salisbury praised the electric telegraph for 'assembling all mankind upon one great plane, whence they can see everything that is done and hear everything that is said and judge of every policy that is pursued at the very moment those events take place'.[41]

Peace conferences were held, assembling prominent intellectuals like the French diplomat Alexis de Tocqueville, the novelist Victor Hugo, and the English politician and free-trade campaigner Richard Cobden, who famously criticized the imperialism of his own country because it 'usurped the dominion of the ocean, and attempted to extend the sphere of human despotism over another element, by insolently putting barriers upon that highway of nations'.[42] There were international conventions on women's rights, humanitarian law, the abolition of slavery, constraints on maritime warfare, and free trade.

'Commerce,' wrote the British former prime minister Robert Peel in 1846, is 'the happy instrument of promoting civilization, of abating national jealousies and prejudices, and of encouraging the maintenance of general peace.'[43] By 1860, sixty commercial treaties were signed; by 1900 over 200. By the beginning of the twentieth century, the major powers had also agreed on an International Telegraph Union, an international bureau for trademarks and patents, the

Universal Postal Union, the Permanent International Peace Bureau, and the Permanent Court of Arbitration in The Hague. The series of world fairs that began in 1851 with the Great Exhibition in London became celebrations of cosmopolitanism and progress, leaving lasting monuments like the Crystal Palace in London and the Eiffel Tower in Paris. This was the *Belle Époque*, the time of playful art nouveau, Claude Monet's dreamy water lilies, and Auguste Renoir's bourgeois picnics at Le Moulin de la Galette. Less than a year before the First World War broke out, the Peace Palace was opened in The Hague.

But nineteenth-century bourgeois cosmopolitanism was also challenged by liberal and romantic nationalism. One of its early critics was the Italian revolutionary Giuseppe Mazzini. 'Is it enough,' he asked in 1847, 'to preach peace and non-intervention, and leave force, unchallenged ruler over three-fourths of Europe, to intervene, for its own unhallowed ends, when, where, and how, it thinks fit?'[44] He begged people to resist and to take their fate in their own hands. 'From the absence of this spiritual religion, of which but empty forms and lifeless formularies remain, and from a total lack of a sense of duty and a capacity for self-sacrifice, man, like a savage, has fallen prostrate in the dust, and has set up on an empty altar the idol "utility,"' Mazzini argued. 'Despots and the Princes of this world have become his High Priests; and from them has come the revolting formulary: "Each for his own alone; each for himself alone."'[45]

The Russian writer Leo Tolstoy, who quoted the preceding passage from Mazzini in his own work, argued that his compatriots should fight Western liberalism and re-establish their own, more spiritual traditions. 'Forgetting their relation to the Infinite,' he wrote following the Russian Revolution of 1905, 'the majority of men have descended, in spite of all the subtlety of their mental achievements, to the lowest grade of consciousness, where they are guided only by animal passions and by the hypnotism of the herd. That is the cause of all their calamities.'[46]

'Until we have created a romance of peace that would equal that of war, violence will not disappear from people's lives,' wrote the urbane and aristocratic German diplomat Harry Kessler.[47] His diaries, which he kept from 1880 to 1937, convey a gradual personal metamorphosis which mirrored that of the entire continent. Kessler's early years were a kaleidoscope of internationalism and high culture as he rediscovered the ancient world of the Mediterranean, dined with luminaries such as Nietzsche, and organized art exhibitions. When the drums of war started to roar, patriotism quickly took over. 'The whole population is as transformed and cast into a new form,' he wrote in 1914. 'This already is the priceless gain of this war; and to have witnessed it will certainly be the greatest experience of our lives.'[48]

The failure of the Concert of Europe in the nineteenth century and the consequent outbreak of the First World War had several causes. The Congress System had been devised by Metternich in 1815 to protect the power of Europe's main dynasties; but the most urgent threat they increasingly faced was not foreign armies but domestic unrest inspired by the examples of the American and French Revolutions, which had demonstrated the power of popular uprising, had enflamed nationalism, and propagated liberalism. Rapid urbanization and industrialization also created a new, far larger, and more self-confident bourgeoisie.

Another explanation for the system's breakdown was that the balance of power proved to be an illusion. The major powers harboured deep and enduring feelings of resentment and suspicion towards each other. They never found lasting solutions to the most serious territorial bones of contention: the repercussions of Italian and German unification; and the weakening of the Austrian and Ottoman Empires, so that nationalist unrest in their Balkan peripheries became an opportunity for others to interfere. The numerous lesser states of Europe, meanwhile, sought to enhance their own position by pitting the major powers against one another. Significantly, too, Great Britain failed to fulfil its self-appointed role as arbiter and enforcer of the balance. Although it held absolute authority at sea and had the strongest economy in the world, it generally lacked the interest or the military resources to check continental power politics. By the end of the nineteenth century, relations between European states were complicated even further by trade wars and imperial ambitions as the industrial revolution drove the quest for more export markets and for raw materials.

Japan and the United States of America

By the late nineteenth century, while the Mughal and Safavid Empires had long vanished, and the Ottomans and the Qing were severely weakened, two powers had managed to turn Europe's relentless rivalry and quest for foreign markets into an opportunity for their own advancement: Japan and the United States of America.

At first, the outlook for Japan had appeared far from promising. Much like China, it was forced to open itself up to trade with Western powers. In 1844, the Dutch king Willem II wrote to the Japanese emperor to warn him of the consequences if the country did not allow his merchants access. Then came the 'black ships' of Commodore Matthew Perry, which forced representatives of the shogun, the de facto ruler of Japan, to sign the Convention of Kanagawa in 1854, granting the United States trading rights. The British, Russians, and French promptly demanded – and received – similar benefits. High unemployment followed, along with epidemics of new diseases like cholera, rising tensions between the shogunate and the emperor, and widespread popular resentment against the ruling elite who were held responsible for agreeing such unequal treaties with foreigners.

In 1863, the emperor overrode the authority of the shogunate and ordered the expulsion of the foreign barbarians – but the barbarians fought back. Their punitive measures sparked a civil war which overthrew the shogun and, in an episode known as the Meiji Restoration (1868), returned the levers of day-to-day rule to the emperor, on condition that he modernized the country and 'sought knowledge throughout the world'. In 1871, the so-called Iwakura Mission was dispatched to the United States and Europe to try and renegotiate the treaties on more equal terms and to gather information on Western science and society. It returned to Japan in 1873 with blueprints for modernization and industrialization, and new ambitions which were soon realized. Supported by Germany, France, and Britain, the Japanese built their manufacturing base at a tremendous speed. Now it too needed foreign raw materials and export markets. In a few years, it had converted its newly gained industrial prowess into military might and built a formidable navy. In 1874, it attacked the island of Taiwan, still part of the Qing Empire. In 1876, it used gunboats to gain commercial access to the Korean kingdom of Joseon and to impose its first unequal treaty. In 1894, it attacked China, overwhelmed its army and navy, and forced the Chinese to cede Taiwan, pay a large indemnity, and grant it the same trading privileges as the Western powers. All this was stipulated in another unequal treaty, the Treaty of Shimonoseki of 1895.

Following this victory, the up-and-coming Japanese diplomat Hayashi Gonsuke cautioned against excessive belligerence, echoing Bismarck's warning to his fellow German politicians from around the same time. 'At present Japan must keep calm and sit tight, so as to lull suspicions nurtured against her; during this time the foundations of national power must be consolidated; and we must watch and wait for the opportunity that will surely come one day.'[49] That chance came in 1904–5, when Russia and Japan went to war over their rival claims to Manchuria. The Japanese victory, destroying most of Russia's navy, sent shockwaves round the world: it was the first time a European state had been defeated by a modern Asian power. In 1907, Japan issued its 'First Imperial National Defence Policy'. Russia was no longer regarded as a significant threat to Japanese interests. Instead, it stated, the most important and immediate hypothetical adversary facing Japan was the United States of America.[50]

The rise of the United States was spectacular by any standard. A tiny nation of rags and ramshackle towns at its creation in 1776, by the dawn of the twentieth century it was the world's largest economy, and its third most populous state. Its astonishing growth was not free from power politics and war. Already, in 1801–5, the young republic had deployed a small fleet in the Mediterranean to punish North African pirates for seizing American merchant ships. In 1812–15, it had fought a war with Britain that resulted in the burning down of the White House. In 1846–48, it had clashed violently with Spain over Texas and Mexico. Close to 1 million Americans died in the Civil War (1861–5) between the slave-holding agricultural states of the Confederacy in the south and the more industrialized Union in the north. Only in 1890 had the frontier in the American West been closed, following the decades-long subjugation of Native American tribes from the Appalachian Mountains, across the Great Plains, to the Pacific coast.

The United States' rise, therefore, was by no means peaceful. Yet, throughout their nation's history, American leaders have always sought to keep the United States apart from the political turmoil of the Eastern Hemisphere. In 1801, President Thomas Jefferson summarized America's foreign policy as 'peace, commerce, and honest friendship with all nations, entangling alliances with none'.[51] This was reaffirmed in the famous Monroe Doctrine of 1823. 'It is only when our rights are invaded or seriously menaced,' President James Monroe explained, 'that we resent injuries or make preparation for our defense.'[52] The United States would refrain from allying with any European power and at the same time it would shield both North and South America from European interference. Fortifications were built along the coast to keep its enemies – with Great Britain to the fore – at a distance.

Mirroring this early strategic restraint and defensive posture, the United States also adopted a policy of economic protectionism. Inspired by Prussia, the first secretary of the treasury, Alexander Hamilton, advocated the support of the nation's infant industries by means of import tariffs. Some two decades later, Jefferson realized that 'Experience has taught me that manufactures are now as necessary to our independence as to our comfort', and urged that nothing should be purchased from abroad.[53] In 1832, the trade secretary, Henry Clay, defended the 'American system'. Free trade, he argued, 'never has existed, it never will exist . . . if we throw our ports wide open to the admission of foreign productions, free of all duty, what ports of any other foreign nation shall we find open to the free admission of our surplus produce?'[54]

But while it maintained its own protectionist trade restrictions, the United States increasingly demanded that others open up their markets. In 1844, Washington wrested trading concessions for American exporters of cotton from the Qing emperor. In 1854, as we have seen, Commodore Perry forced Japan to grant access to American merchants and goods. In the 1870s, President Ulysses S. Grant used the principle of reciprocal trade tariffs to boost American exports to Cuba, Puerto Rico, and Hawaii. This meant that those countries could only export their goods freely to the United States if they allowed American imports similar access to their domestic markets. The more advanced and far larger US economy won the greater benefits. America's open-door trade policy was now fully under way.

With growing economic interests came greater political aspirations. Gunboats were dispatched to look after American interests in Fiji, Panama, Paraguay, Egypt, Haiti, Samoa, and Hawaii. Washington arbitrated in a conflict between Argentina and Paraguay, supported rebels against Spanish rule in Cuba, and aspired to naval supremacy in the Caribbean. In his seminal essay of 1890, Alfred Mahan advised how sea power could support American imperialism, recommending the construction of naval bases across the Pacific and the conquest of Hawaii. Theodore Roosevelt was a fervent believer in Mahan, and during his presidency (1901–9) he ordered military outposts to be built in Cuba, Panama, Hawaii, Guam, and the Philippines. While continuing to pay lip service to the Monroe Doctrine, Roosevelt now added a proviso: it might be necessary to intervene in a foreign power if domestic turmoil within it posed a significant enough threat to the interests and security of the United States.

Despite such expressions of *realpolitik*, and despite the vast social inequalities caused by the nation's economic boom – a handful of families, such as the Carnegies and Rockefellers, revelled in the so-called Gilded Age as tens of millions of their fellow citizens struggled in the direst poverty – the United States continued to preach its message of liberty, democracy, and American exceptionalism to the world. Washington, after all, had been reconstructed on a grandiose scale and in a neoclassical style that simultaneously recalled the austere morality of the Roman Republic and the might and majesty of imperial Rome. By the eve of the First World War, one thing was very clear: the old empires of the Eastern Hemisphere were now challenged by the new power in the West.

From War to War

In 1916, as the young men of Europe fought and died in the morass of trenches that have come to epitomize the suffering of the First World War, the American president Woodrow Wilson was re-elected to the White House under the slogans 'He Has Kept Us Out of War' and 'America First'. The United States had remained neutral when the conflict erupted in August 1914. It was only in April 1917, after Germany's adoption of unrestricted submarine warfare led to the sinking of American shipping, and the disclosure of the so-called Zimmermann Telegram – a secret German offer to support Mexico in regaining territory it had lost to the US in the nineteenth century – that America finally entered the war on the side of Britain, France, and, until the revolution in November, Russia. The prospect of America's reserves of manpower and full economic might being brought to bear against Germany forced it to overreach itself and led to the end of hostilities in November 1918.

With the European powers exhausted, and either dependent on American loans or, in the case of Russia and Germany, riven by revolution, the end of the war provided another opportunity for the United States to augment its standing and realign the shifting global dynamics more firmly in its favour. In January 1919, slightly more than a hundred years after the Congress of Vienna, the powers gathered in Paris for yet another major peace conference. When Woodrow Wilson arrived in France, well aware of his clout, he brought with him a programme of fourteen points ostensibly designed to remodel the world order on principles of national self-determination, free trade, non-aggression, and liberalism. Although, in 1917, the president had publicly assured the world that the United States 'had no selfish ends to serve', privately he had confessed to his advisor: 'When the war is over we can force them to our way of thinking, because by that time they will, among other things, be financially in our hands.'[55] It was clear that his manifesto would pose a fundamental challenge to the traditional great powers.

The Paris Peace Conference attracted over a thousand delegates. It was organized into sixty specialized committees, a plenary conference, and five commissions. In practice, however, everything was decided by the chief victorious Allies: the United States, France, Britain, and Italy. The journalist Ray Stannard Baker, who served as Wilson's press secretary, enthusiastically hailed the conference as a new way of conducting diplomacy:

> The old way was for a group of diplomats, each
> representing a set of selfish national interests, to hold
> secret meetings, and by jockeying, trading, forming private
> rings and combinations with one another, come at last to a
> settlement . . .
>   The new way so boldly launched at Paris was, first,
> to start with certain general principles of justice, such

as those laid down by President Wilson and accepted by all the world; and, second, to have those principles applied, not by diplomats and politicians each eager to serve his own interests, but by dispassionate scientists – geographers, ethnologists, economists – who had made studies of the problems involved.[56]

The British prime minister, David Lloyd George, was rather more cynical. 'I was seated between Jesus Christ and Napoleon,' he later said, referring to the American president and the French prime minister, Georges Clemenceau. The latter in turn joked that 'Wilson had 14 points, while Moses had only 10.'[57] Another attendee, the cabinet minister Winston Churchill, was similarly sceptical: he thought the conference little different from pre-war diplomatic endeavours and just as ineffective. In many ways Churchill was right. Even though, at Wilson's behest, the conference led to the establishment of a League of Nations to provide collective security for members and arbitrate between them in case of conflict, the US Senate never ratified America's accession to this forerunner of the United Nations lest it constrain the country's autonomy.

There were no European victors in Paris. The resulting Treaty of Versailles (1919) dismantled the German Empire, with Japan promptly snapping up many of its Asian possessions. Germany was also forced to surrender most of the Rhineland to France, burdened with massive war reparations, and had its military capability severely constrained. The parallel Treaty of Saint-Germain (1919) carved the Austrian Empire up into several new states – the republic of Austria;

Czechoslovakia; Poland; the kingdom of Slovenes, Croats, and Serbs, soon renamed Yugoslavia – and prohibited from forming new alliances with Germany. The Treaty of Sèvres (1920) dismembered the Ottoman Empire, which had sided with Germany and Austria during the war. The remnants of its historical possessions in Mesopotamia and the Levant were divided between Britain and France – ostensibly as mandates under the aegis of the League of Nations – and its last sultan was deposed in a civil war that ended with the founding of the Turkish Republic under Kemal Ataturk.

Despite their territorial gains, the victors of the war did not have everything their own way. France remained dissatisfied about the amount of economic compensation it received for the destruction wrought by German occupation of its land. Britain, meanwhile, had to accept that the United States was now a leading oceanic power. At the Washington Naval Conference of 1921–2, the two countries formally agreed on naval parity. Japan had to be satisfied with a fleet two thirds the size. Although this meant Japan was the third greatest naval power, it inflamed Japanese nationalism. 'War is not out of the question,' warned one not-untypical Japanese naval officer, 'especially as a large part of the American Fleet has come through the Panama Canal into the Pacific.'[58] If there was a winner of the Paris and Washington conferences, however, then it was the United States.

Even in 1919, the English economist John Maynard Keynes was warning of the devastating consequences of the treaties that ended the First World War. 'Paris was a nightmare,' he wrote. 'A sense of impending catastrophe overhung the frivolous scene.'[59] Keynes resigned his position as the British treasury's official representative to the Paris Peace Conference in protest at the proposed treaty terms, arguing that Europe would slip back into turmoil without a far-reaching economic recovery plan and that the size of Germany's reparations and its war debt would lead to revanchism. What disturbed him the most, however, was the way that the cosmopolitan elite of Europe and the United States, just as they had before the outbreak of the First World War, remained blind to the malign forces that still lurked beneath the spirit of internationalism:

> The inhabitant of London could order by telephone, sipping his morning tea in bed, the various products of the whole earth . . . he could at the same moment and by the same means adventure his wealth in the natural resources and new enterprises of any quarter of the world, and share, without exertion or even trouble, in their prospective fruits . . . The projects and politics of militarism and imperialism, of racial and cultural rivalries, of monopolies, restrictions, and exclusion, which were to play the serpent to this paradise, were little more than the amusements of his daily newspaper.[60]

It did not take long for Keynes's fears to be confirmed. The destruction of Europe's factories during the First World War had led the United States to expand its industrial capacity even faster than before. As the European nations recovered in the twenties, overcapacity caused prices to collapse and protectionism to spread. 'Our investments and trade relations are such,' warned President Calvin Coolidge in 1928, 'that it is almost impossible to conceive of any conflict anywhere on earth which would not affect us injuriously.'[61] Influential American financiers like John Pierpont Morgan Jr proposed that German reparations should be reduced, and that the US should lend money to Berlin so that it could pay its debts to other European nations, and in this way prop up demand for American exports. In 1924, the American banker and politician Charles Dawes oversaw the negotiation of an agreement in which the French and Belgian occupation of the German industrial heartland in the Ruhr Valley was ended, in the hopes this would make it more likely that Germany would be able to pay its war reparations.

Both the Dawes Plan and its successor, the American-sponsored Young Plan of 1929, failed to ease the strain on the European economy caused by the scale of Germany's reparations. As a result of the difficulties in Europe, American exports to the region dropped by around a fifth between 1921 and 1928.[62] The Wall Street Crash of 1929 was followed by a great economic depression. The hardship was felt by ordinary people on both sides of the Atlantic. 'It was a time of terrible suffering,' one American citizen recalled. 'Have you ever seen a child with rickets? Shaking as with palsy. No proteins, no milk . . . People who were independent, who thought they were masters and mistresses of their lives, were all of a sudden dependent on others.'[63] American financiers withdrew their loans from Europe as Austria, Germany, and other countries defaulted on their national debts. The world economy fractured as protectionist barriers were raised ever higher: the Smoot–Hawley Tariff Act increased import duties in the United States to 59 per cent; in Europe, they climbed to 43 per cent.

In 1928, the United States, Britain, Germany, France, and most of the other countries of Europe signed the Kellogg–Briand Pact, committing them not to use violence to resolve international disputes. But the Great Depression merely intensified tensions between states, the suffering it inflicted on their populations fuelling a sudden upsurge in violent nationalism – nowhere more so than in Germany. In 1933, the new German chancellor, Adolf Hitler, withdrew his country from the League of Nations, claiming that it was no more than a tool to keep Germany down and that international organizations were unfit to preserve order. 'If it is the task of the League of Nations only to guarantee the existing state of the world and to safeguard it for all time, then we might just as well entrust it with the task of regulating the ebb and flow of the tides,' he fulminated.[64]

Hitler came to power promising to undo the humiliation of the Treaty of Versailles, to defend Germany against the alleged bullying of France and Britain, and to provide the economic resources and 'living space' (*Lebensraum*) for the nation to fulfil its destiny and flourish. Peace conferences continued to be staged, but Hitler was unstoppable in his remilitarization. First, in 1936, he sent German troops into the demilitarized Rhineland, openly violating the Treaty of Versailles; then, in 1938, he began to push into resource-rich eastern neighbours, occupying the Sudetenland in Czechoslovakia. Once again, the rectification of perceived wrongs and the desire for security had become ruthless aggression and imperialist expansionism.

The Nations United

In August 1939, the foreign ministers of Nazi Germany and the Soviet Union met in Moscow to agree a treaty of mutual non-aggression and to establish spheres of influence that implied the two states would divide Europe between them. Nine days after the signing of the Molotov–Ribbentrop Pact, German tanks advanced into Poland. The Second World War (1939–45) had begun. The brutality of its horrific battles and ruthless campaigns of extermination were magnified by the industrial might and technological innovation brought to bear on the conflict. In just six years, 60 million people lost their lives. The Holocaust alone was responsible for the deaths of 6 million Jews: a massacre of civilians planned and implemented with the callous efficiency of a factory production line.

The reasons for Germany's eventual defeat were partly strategic and partly economic. Hitler's prime advantage was the speed with which his troops were able to conquer large parts of Europe. But holding on to this territory proved much more difficult. The tide turned in 1942, following the entry of the Soviet Union and the United States into the war following surprise attacks by Germany on the former and Germany's ally Japan on the latter. The combination of the Soviet Union's far greater reserves of manpower and the United States' overwhelming economic superiority – by 1945, its economy was five times larger than Germany's – proved decisive.

The picture was similar in the war against Japan in Asia and the Pacific, which accounted for at least a third of all casualties during the Second World War. Like Germany, Japan's aggression was motivated by a toxic mixture of revenge for perceived slights at the hands of other powers, a belief in racial and cultural superiority, and the need for raw materials – oil, rubber, and metals – to feed its industries. Like Germany, Japan found it far harder to hold on to the vast swathes of territory it had captured than to conquer it in the first place. And, like Germany, Japan was unable to contend with the financial firepower of the United States: its economy was ten times larger than Japan's by 1945, its ammunition production thirty times greater. Even Japan's advantage in military manpower – despite the United States deploying more troops in the Pacific than in Europe – was outweighed by America's technological superiority. Within days of the destruction of Hiroshima and Nagasaki by atomic bombs in August 1945, Japan surrendered.

Three and a half months earlier, as the war in Europe entered its final days, more than 800 official delegates and 2,000 other attendees gathered in San Francisco to embark on the negotiations that would culminate, in October 1945, with the establishment of the most ambitious project of multilateralism the world had ever seen: the United Nations. The opening words of its charter proclaimed: 'We the peoples of the United Nations determined to save succeeding generations from the scourge of war, which twice in our lifetime has brought untold sorrow to mankind.'[65] The UN system was to be built on the principles of national sovereignty and self-determination, military restraint and peaceful arbitration, and collective security should any member be at risk. Its General Assembly would include all signatories. 'A perfect plan for perpetual peace and one world,' an American congressman hailed it.[66] Yet effective power continued to be held by a small group: the five main victors of the war against Germany and Japan, who formed the permanent members of the Security Council – the United States, the Soviet Union, the United Kingdom, France, and China.

The new spirit of idealism and internationalism that gave rise to the United Nations proved unable to suppress the old ethos of suspicion, national competition, and great power rivalry. Even as the first tentative steps were being taken in the formulation of the United Nations, the major powers had been discussing once again how to divide up Europe between them. In October 1944, Churchill and Stalin scribbled on a small piece of paper – which the former later dubbed the 'naughty document' – how influence in the Balkans would be split. But the prime minister was already well aware that Britain itself now had to tread carefully around its much more powerful allies. 'What a small nation we are,' he recalled, describing the Tehran Conference in October 1943. 'There I sat with the great Russian bear on one side of me with paws outstretched, and on the other side the great American buffalo, and between the two the poor little English donkey who was the only one who knew the right way home.'[67] During the Yalta Conference in February 1945, Stalin reiterated his demand for a Soviet sphere of influence encompassing Central and Eastern Europe. The United States countered by insisting on the need for democratic elections in the newly liberated countries of Europe, hoping these would check the Soviets. By the time the last of the major conferences between the Allies took place at Potsdam in July–August 1945,

Soviet control over Eastern Europe was a fait accompli. Germany itself was divided into four occupation zones. Although Britain and France shared in this partition – and despite their status at the United Nations – the Europeans were finished as great powers. In their place, not only in Europe but across the globe, stood the United States and the Soviet Union.

The conclusion of the Second World War heralded the end of the old European empires in Asia and Africa. In Southeast Asia, the retreat of Japanese forces left a power vacuum in former colonies such as Dutch Indonesia and French Indochina which new independence movements sprang up to try and fill. In South Asia, Britain realized it no longer had the resources to maintain its empire in the Indian subcontinent against growing opposition. In August 1947, the British Raj was replaced by the independent republics of India and Pakistan. By 1950, eleven countries had gained independence from their former colonial masters; a decade later, there were twenty-eight more. In China, meanwhile, the appalling state of anarchy and civil war that had endured since the fall of the Qing Dynasty was finally ended in 1949 by the victory of the communists under Mao Zedong and the proclamation of the People's Republic of China.

However, independence did not automatically bring peace: in the absence of the old imperial powers, ancient enmities resurfaced in contemporary rivalries that broke out in a rash of conflicts. In 1947, Pakistan and India clashed over Kashmir. In 1948, Egypt, Jordan, and Syria declared war on the newly established state of Israel. In 1950, the People's Republic of China invaded the Korean Peninsula. In an attempt to end such conflicts, and also to resist being absorbed

CHAPTER 13

into the rival global hegemonies of the United States and the Soviet Union, many of the newly independent states of Asia and Africa joined with countries in South America and Europe in 1961 to form a Non-Aligned Movement. But despite committing their nations to peaceful coexistence based on the core values already promulgated by the United Nations, the premiers of the non-aligned countries soon quarrelled over which of them should be the group's leader.

In the years immediately following the Second World War, it was the United States that ultimately held the best cards. Its economy was now bigger than that of all the Western European nations combined. To serve its economic interests, security objectives, and desire for status, the United States sought to reshape the international order around it in a manner that resembled so many empires in the past.

Foremost were the measures it took to open up the global economy to American businesses and investment. The conference held at Bretton Woods in 1944 led to the establishment of the World Bank and the International Monetary Fund, along with other measures that cemented the position of the US dollar as the global reserve currency. In 1947, the Global Agreement on Tariffs and Trade (GATT) was negotiated in order to liberate American firms from the import taxes that reduced their competitiveness abroad. The Marshall Plan, which offered US aid to rebuild Western Europe so that it could form a bulwark against communism, was rolled out in 1948 on condition that the recipients adopted open markets.

A new world order was being created. In April 1950, the US president Harry Truman was briefed by his staff: 'In a

THE PRIMACY OF THE WEST

shrinking world, which now faces the threat of atomic warfare, it is not an adequate objective merely to seek to check the Kremlin design, for the absence of order among nations is becoming less and less tolerable. This fact imposes on us, in our own interests, the responsibility of world leadership.'[68]

The Cold War

One power, however, was determined to prevent an American takeover. The Union of Soviet Socialist Republics had been established in 1922 and formed the successor state to the old tsarist Russian Empire, which had been toppled five years earlier in the two revolutions of 1917. Ever since the Western powers had supported the tsarists in the Russian Civil War (1917–22), the Soviet state had felt itself under existential threat from abroad. Its first leader, Vladimir Lenin, spoke repeatedly of 'capitalist encirclement'; his successor, Joseph Stalin, of a 'socialist island' surrounded by enemies.[69] Soviet fears were worsened by the German invasion in 1941, and the apparent unwillingness of the United States to open a second front in Western Europe to relieve the pressure in the east. By the end of the Second World War, although Soviet troops occupied Berlin, at least 20 million of their fellow citizens had died and a quarter of their country's economic capacity had been destroyed.

Suspicions on the Western side grew as well, fuelled not least by Soviet attitudes at the Potsdam Conference and the USSR's behaviour subsequently. In February 1946, the American diplomat George Kennan described in his famous 'long telegram' the Soviet regime as neurotic, driven by an instinctive sense of insecurity, and incompatible with an open, capitalist world.[70] Less than a fortnight later, Winston Churchill – who had been an outspoken supporter of the Western intervention in the Russian Civil War – warned that Soviet actions to strengthen their influence in Eastern and Central Europe by establishing communist regimes there meant that 'an iron curtain has descended across the Continent'.[71] Churchill's speech outlining the nature of this new world order presaged the onset of the Cold War.

The Cold War was unique, not so much for the fact that the main adversaries never fought each other directly in open conflict, but for the fact that their main centres of power were concentrated in different hemispheres and separated by wide oceans. As such, the rivalry focused on the states on the peripheries of the two superpowers. Just as the Soviet Union feared encirclement of its heartland by US-aligned states in what the influential political theorist Nicholas Spykman dubbed the 'rimland' of Eurasia, so the United States feared the presence of communist regimes on its geopolitical doorstep in Central and South America.[72]

As the Soviet Union tried to spread communism from the heart of Eurasia, the United States advanced its own values and interests through the North Atlantic Treaty Organization in Europe (NATO), the Central Treaty Organization in the Middle East (CENTO), the Southeast Asian Treaty Organization (SEATO), and a pact with Australia and New Zealand (ANZUS). The two superpowers engaged in numerous proxy wars, like the Yom Kippur War (1973), the Korean War (1950–53), the Vietnam War (1955–75), and the Angolan Civil War (1975–91). Meanwhile troops massed on both sides of the Iron Curtain in Europe, and a furious arms race was conducted in an effort to establish air, sea, and most lethally nuclear supremacy. Only once did the United States and the Soviet Union reach the brink of full-scale nuclear war: the Cuban Missile Crisis of 1962, when the Kremlin attempted to deploy ballistic missiles in Cuba, some 300 kilometres away from the continental United States.

The main struggle, however, was economic. Throughout the Cold War, the American economy remained twice as large as the Soviet Union's. The Soviets spent 17 per cent of their wealth on defence; the United States only 7 per cent. The average Soviet citizen never earned more than one third the salary of an American. In most areas of advanced technology – computers, communications, life sciences, materials science, robotics, propulsion – the United States held the leading edge.

America was ruthless in defence of its economic advantage, even turning on their closest allies to maintain it. In 1967, for example, West Germany – by now the economic powerhouse of Western Europe – was faced with the stark choice of propping up the dollar or facing a reduction in the American forces protecting it from the Soviets. In 1985, the Plaza Agreement saw Britain, France, West Germany, and Japan the leading Asian economy, forced to implement a major devaluation of the dollar in order to render American exports more competitive.

Cracks in the Soviet regime started to appear in the 1970s, when the USSR was forced to buy grain from the United States and faced technological shortcomings that prevented it from developing new oil wells. As Soviet production per capita stagnated, poverty and food rationing became prevalent. It was in this context that the American president Ronald Reagan decided to boost defence spending in the early 1980s and unleash a financial battle of attrition. The Soviet economy could not cope. 'There was a visible decline in the rate of growth, then its complete stagnation,' a senior intelligence officer recalled. Opposition to the communist regime grew within the Soviet Union. 'Our society, our people, the most educated, the most intellectual, had become tired of the model that oppressed them spiritually and politically,' wrote the Russian essayist Mikhail Antonov in 1987.

Although a new premier, Mikhail Gorbachev, attempted to liberalize the political and economic systems with his far-ranging policies of *perestroika* (restructuring) and *glasnost* (openness), his reforms proved too little, too late. His refusal to crack down on increasingly widespread protests against Soviet rule in the Baltic states during the late 1980s emboldened dissidents elsewhere in the Soviet Union. The genie was out of the bottle, and the reformist leadership was unwilling and unable to put it back. In elections held in 1990, the communist party was defeated in six of the USSR's fifteen constituent republics by nationalist movements determined on independence. The short-lived coup the following year, mounted by communist hardliners trying to prevent Gorbachev from turning the centralized Soviet Union into a looser federation of states, merely hastened the denouement. By the end of 1991, Gorbachev had left power and the Soviet Union had been dissolved. The Cold War was over: the United States was now the world's sole superpower.

America's Unipolar Moment

Writing in 1989, the American political scientist Francis Fuku-yama famously argued that the collapse of the communist re-gimes of Eastern Europe marked 'the triumph of the West', the unabashed victory of liberalism, and the end of history as we had known it.[73] The unipolar moment of the United States, however, was as much the result of the weakness of the rest of the world as of America's own military strength. Neverthe-less, with the downfall of the Soviet Union, the stage was left clear for two decades of unrestrained American foreign policy.

In 1991, President George Bush put it thus: 'American leadership is indispensable. We must not only protect our citi-zens and our interests, but help create a new world in which our fundamental values not only survive but flourish. We must work with others, but we must also be a leader.'[74] Being 'a leader' meant that America was ready to use military force to uphold its liberal order. To that end, the United States now accounted for 40 per cent of the world's total defence spend-ing. At the same time as maintaining its immense strategic nuclear capability, its sustained investment in overseas mili-tary bases, eleven aircraft carrier battle groups – more than the rest of the world combined – a vast arsenal of cruise mis-siles, and advanced stealth bombers gave it an unrivalled cap-acity to project power around the globe.

Under America's military umbrella, NATO expanded right up to Russia's doorstep by granting membership to the Baltic states and many of the Soviet Union's former satel-lites in Eastern Europe. In Asia, the United States bolstered its alliances with South Korea, Japan, and Australia, and deployed its navy in the Strait of Taiwan, in order to deter Chinese expansionism. In the Middle East, it built up its presence in the Persian Gulf in order to check the regional ambitions of Iran's Islamic fundamentalist government. Regimes that refused to comply with the American vision for world order had to risk the consequences. The US-led retaliation against Iraq's invasion of Kuwait in 1991 left the world awestruck as it watched waves of smart bombs and cruise missiles rain down on Baghdad. US air power was demonstrated again during the Yugoslav Wars (1991–9), when NATO intervened militarily to end Serbian attacks on Kosovo in 1999. Less high-profile operations were mounted all over the world, some to defend clearly defined American interests, others to uphold national prestige – most lay somewhere between the two. The US secretary of state Madeleine Albright justified such actions in 1998: 'If we have to use force, it is because we are America; we are the indispensable nation. We stand tall and we see further than other countries into the future.'[75]

The United States also continued to dominate the key international organizations that regulated the economic order, such as the International Monetary Fund, the World Bank, and the World Trade Organization, established in 1995 to replace GATT. As the world's most innovative economy, it took measures to reinforce protections for intellectual property rights, for example the Agreement on Trade-Related Aspects of Intellectual Property Rights (TRIPS) in 1994, as well as for the independence of the Internet with the establishment of the Internet Corporation for Assigned Names and Numbers (ICANN) in 1998. The American political scientist

Richard Rosecrance described such developments in terms of the rise of the US as a 'virtual state', one reliant less on trade in tangible goods and more on transnational companies that take the lead with technology and absorb the industries of other countries in vertically integrated production chains.[76] His influential fellow scholar Joseph Nye stressed the importance of America's soft power: the ability to lead through the example of its efficient and liberal governance.[77]

Increasingly, critics of US-led globalization saw it as simply the latest incarnation of American imperial hegemony. As other Western states – perhaps most obviously France and Germany – became more wary of American unilateralism, resistance to the United States coalesced in the sphere of economics. In Western Europe, the first steps in economic and political integration may have originated in the conditions set by the United States for rolling out the Marshall Plan in 1948, but gradually one of the drivers for closer cooperation became frustration with American influence. One French finance minister, for instance, referred to the dominant position of the US dollar as the global reserve currency as an 'exorbitant privilege', because it allowed Washington to borrow cheaply abroad.

In 1973, the nine member states – including France, West Germany, and Britain – of the European Economic Community agreed to coordinate their foreign policies more closely, declaring: 'The growing concentration of power and responsibility in the hands of a very small number of great powers mean that Europe must unite and speak increasingly with one voice if it wants to make itself heard and play its proper role in the world.'[78] Yet although the Treaty of Maastricht in

1992 transformed the community, now comprising twelve states, into the European Union, the full political integration foreseen by the founding fathers of the European project remained incomplete. And the European monetary union, which instituted a single European currency the euro as an alternative to the US dollar, was shaky from its outset in 1990.

Meanwhile, the world's second largest economy after the collapse of the Soviet Union was Japan. It tried to compete with America's economic power by means of a robust, export-led industrial policy, but faced demographic stagnation. In China, however, the communist party retained its hold on power by embarking on a programme of industrialization and economic liberalization that saw the living standards of its population rise significantly – although its economy remained several times smaller than the United States, and depended heavily on American investors. These reforms, which were started in the late seventies by China's de facto leader Deng Xiaoping, were accompanied by a newfound spirit of nationalism that saw the People's Republic deliberately position itself as an alternative to the American-led global order.

At the same time as these developments in Eurasia, the domestic engine of American progress started to splutter. The United States had a balanced current account in 1990, but by 2000 it had incurred a vast deficit, to the tune of 4 per cent of its domestic production. The Americans were spending beyond their means and this was only possible because other countries financed the difference by buying US government bonds. By 1998, over 50 per cent of American treasury bonds were in foreign hands.[79] This reflected the position of the dollar as the primary global reserve currency, raising concerns about the durability of that position. In terms of innovation, the American economy continued to be world leading, but it relied increasingly heavily on imported oil, Asian consumer goods, and European high-end products. Furthermore, investment was excessively concentrated in high-tech sectors, causing stock market bubbles and crashes. When the American sociologist Robert Putnam published his book *Bowling Alone* in 2000, he found that his compatriots were increasingly isolated and less empathetic towards one another. For many, as the gap between rich and poor widened, the American dream became unreachable.

In 1999, the American politician and publicist Pat Buchanan sounded a note of warning: 'America's leaders are reenacting every folly that brought these great powers to ruin – from arrogance and hubris, to assertions of global hegemony, to imperial overstretch, to trumpeting new "crusades," to handing out war guarantees to regions and countries where Americans have never fought before.'[80] Two years later, Islamic terrorists struck at New York and the Pentagon – the symbolic hearts of American capitalism and militarism – killing almost 3,000 people. The most conspicuous attack on the American global order since the end of the Cold War had been mounted not by a powerful rival nation, but by a small group of religious fundamentalists.

An Age of Extremes

In the period between 1750 and 2000, a true global arena was shaped. Never before had the world's continents been so connected – not just by ships, railways, and aeroplanes, but by trade, capital exchanges, personal travel, cultural interaction, and diplomacy. The fundamental cause of this transformation was the industrial revolution. The production of men and women was no longer dependent on their own hands or on animals. Horsepower per capita surged from below 0.4 in 1750, to 3 in 1900, and 120 in 2000.[81] As a result, world economic production grew, in constant dollars, from about $130 billion in 1750 to $1,100 billion in 1900, and $41,000 billion in 2000.[82] Average life expectancy increased from below thirty years in 1750, and thirty-three years in 1900, to sixty-nine years in 2000.[83] The world's population expanded from around 600 million in 1750 to 1.5 billion in 1900, and then to 6 billion in 2000.[84] Transportation and communication became much faster. If it took over forty days on average to cross the Atlantic in 1750, this decreased to twenty days by 1800, five days in 1900, and less than five hours by 2000.[85] The industrial revolution was followed in the late twentieth century by the start of a digital revolution. In the context of such extraordinary developments, the assumption more than ever was that progress was based on rational behaviour – and therefore progress would prevail over darkness and bring peace.

These changes were accompanied by more intense diplomatic interaction. The number of international governmental organizations, for instance, grew from only a handful in the nineteenth century to around thirty-seven in 1900, and then to 6,556 in 2000.[86] Major peace conferences were held, as we have seen – in Vienna, in Paris, in San Francisco – which had lasting consequences. The principles of national sovereignty and self-determination were globally enshrined in law. The United Nations Charter of 1945 remains the most ambitious attempt to preserve peace by means of universal principles. But the world did not become more peaceful. The twentieth century was extremely bloody, not just in absolute terms but also if one measures the number of deaths as a proportion of the total world population. On the one hand, there was this steep acceleration in economic production, communication, and international organization. On the other hand, there was little if any change in the frequency of wars. Throughout the era, periods of about twenty years of relative stability continued to be followed by periods of about twenty years of significant conflict.

One of the reasons why the unprecedented progress did not seem to lead to durable peace was that it was not spread evenly over the globe. Growth in one place was often at the expense of another, or it elicited intense envy and distrust that found expression in conflict. Moreover, periods of economic growth and political confidence were inseparable from periods of recession, inflation, growing inequality, social unrest – which, in turn, impelled self-defeating policies of economic protectionism and ugly nationalism. 'La terre est un vaste théâtre où la même tragédie se joue sous des noms différents,' wrote Voltaire in 1756.[87] The centuries following the industrial revolution witnessed no change in the nature of power politics or lessening of their effects; they merely became more extreme.

Horror as a Friend

The dream of peace is eternal and universal. Throughout history and across the globe, farmers have wished to take in their harvest unharmed, traders to arrive safely at the next city, and kings to go down in the annals as just and peaceful rulers. Peace means tranquillity, the absence of the trauma of war, its killing, mutilation, torture, rape, and destruction. To be sure, war has also been celebrated; some people still do so today. The dark side of man, Abraham Lincoln called it. Yet once war becomes reality, jingoism always makes way for despair, even among the young men ready to pick up arms. Witnessing comrades being maimed, not seeing the end of the bloodshed, and not being able to protect the family at home, are some of the greatest agonies men and women can suffer. As Colonel Kurtz put it in Francis Ford Coppola's Vietnam War movie *Apocalypse Now* (1979): 'You must make a friend of horror.'

I found this sentiment of disillusion, of fortitude turned into bitterness, expressed most clearly in the diaries of the Flemish writer Stijn Streuvels (1871–1969). Once an enthusiastic supporter of the First World War, he became sceptical:

I have had enough of it. I am not interested in how it ends, but it must end. I am starting to doubt what England and France so confidently promised; I do not expect anything from Russia; and I no longer trust the moralizing, which today just seems silly and false. The newspapers have lied to us, written things that appear scandalous with hindsight. What we get to read today is so censored, nonsensical, inarticulate, insipid, vague, and idiotic that one is inclined to throw it all away in disgust. There should have been a law limiting the duration of this war, so that we soldiers, after every day of suffering, could at least see the end coming nearer. Just think – they told us this war would be over in a few weeks . . . [1]

The feelings that Streuvels committed to paper are not very different from those in some of the ancient Chinese poems quoted in this book.

When wars have ended, exhausted societies have usually rallied behind rulers that promised an era of tranquillity and cheered the delegates who negotiated peace treaties. Peace has been celebrated most by men and women who have experienced its loss. Yet wars have continued to break out again and again. 'The world is like a chariot run wild,' the Roman poet Virgil concluded. But perhaps such views give a false impression, by highlighting periods of war instead of periods of peace. Still, out of 3,000 years of Chinese history, at least 1,100 of them have featured wars. The Roman Empire was at war during at least 50 per cent of its existence. Since 1776, the United States of America has spent over a hundred years at war.

Even those eras of peace that have been celebrated as golden ages were not so harmonious after all. They have often coincided with vicious social conflicts arising from slavery and other extreme inequalities between the destitute masses and decadent elites. The peace enjoyed by empires – such as the Pax Romana – was primarily experienced by a small circle of privileged people, a gilded and gated community of magnates and political leaders; then, to a lesser degree, by the wealthy middle classes of the capital and its rural environs; then by the mass of poorer citizens and, in some situations, by more fortunate slaves; and finally all the subjugated peoples eking out an insecure existence on the empire's fringes. This meant that force had to be deployed on the periphery to guarantee the supply of slaves, gold, food, horse, or other resources. In other words, imperial peace, for most, meant exploitation. Exploitation inevitably created hatred, resistance, and conflict. The peace enjoyed by inhabitants at the heart of empires, therefore, was often only possible because of the wars waged on the frontiers, to conquer new lands, repel invaders, or control migration. Families still had to sacrifice their sons and pay high taxes. War always loomed as an ominous cloud on the horizon.

The Moral High Ground

One of the conclusions of this book is that war is universal. Time and again, great powers have promised that their rise would be benevolent, that they would refrain from aggression, and that they stood for a just new order. Time and again, however, this promise has ended in disappointment – irrespective of when or where it was made. The West has been no more aggressive than China, India, or Africa. It is true that, in more recent centuries, the West has been more successful in waging war, colonizing others, and exploiting the world's richness. And it is true that the West was also the first to do so over a sustained period on a genuinely global scale. But there is ample evidence that all great powers throughout history have been similarly brutish. China's history does not bear testament to a comparatively benign strategic culture based on Confucian principles of harmony, as the country's current leadership would have the rest of the world believe. Most of the territory that forms the People's Republic of China was colonized by the Han Chinese in one way or another in the past. China's colonization was predominately continental, therefore, not necessarily less savage or smaller scale. The same was true for other civilizations. Before the arrival of the European empires, the populations of Asia, Africa, and the Americas fought their neighbours frequently, enslaved each other, and created empires of their own. There is no absolute moral high ground in history.

That said, history does show that claims to occupy the moral high ground have been an important excuse for waging war. Many times, powers have fought to overturn what they believed to be injustices or an unfair world order. At the end of the third century BCE, Hannibal led the Carthaginian army in a war to avenge the humiliating losses of an earlier war with Rome. The Sasanian Empire repeatedly fought the Romans in the third and fourth centuries CE over perceived injustices relating to the buffer state of Armenia. In the eighth century, the Abbasids attacked the Umayyad

Caliphate because of its un-Islamic behaviour. In the thirteenth century, the Mongols broke their peace with the Chinese Empire on the grounds that it was based on an unequal treaty. In the twentieth century, Hitler came to power in Germany by promising to reverse the losses of the Treaty of Versailles, while imperial Japan claimed to be building a new East Asian order liberated from European interference. Even today, China's occasional bouts of sabre rattling are justified as part of the process of reversing the damage caused by the century of humiliation. Throughout history, therefore, the need to avenge past humiliations and mistreatment and the promise to restore justice has provided popular justifications for war and for rising polities to attack the incumbent great power. The more one state criticizes the belligerence of another, the more there are reasons for concern.

Another recurrent pretext for going to war has been the claim by aggressors that they brought the benefits of superior civilization to backward peoples. All great empires have considered themselves to be the centre of the world, and those living beyond their borders to be barbarians that required subduing or unfree peoples needing to be liberated. Similarly, fighting unbelievers also served as an excuse for war. The Greeks led by Alexander the Great claimed to be fighting a holy war against the Persians in the fourth century BCE. In ancient Rome, priests were responsible for proclaiming war after having sought the approval of the gods. Chinese emperors fought to fulfil the 'mandate of heaven'. In Southeast Asia in the seventh century CE, the kings of Srivijaya represented their wars of conquest as Buddhist quests for enlightenment. Islamic caliphs campaigned to spread the true faith across the Dar al-Harb as much as medieval European lords crusaded in the service of Christ. Even the Mongol conquests of Genghis Khan and his descendants were promoted as a holy war to unite the world at the behest of the sky god. But the battle to establish the true faith was also fought between the adherents of different strands of the same religion: Orthodox Christians against Catholics, Catholics against Protestants, Shia Muslims against Sunnis – not to speak of the numerous conflicts between different branches of Hinduism and Buddhism. If most religions and their holy books called for peace, they equally provided the arguments for war.

The same was true of the principles of law and justice. How many times have powers shattered the peace they claimed to be protecting, or violated treaties as they purported to defend them? Throughout history, polities signed up to international agreements to limit the use of force. After the downfall of the Zhou Dynasty in China at the end of the 3rd century BCE, the rival states convened numerous diplomatic conferences; but they did not resolve the conflicts precisely because they were regarded either as serving the interests of the strongest state or as the means by which lesser polities could check the dominant kingdom. In Europe, King Louis XIV of France campaigned against Habsburg Spain in the seventeenth century CE on the grounds that the latter had allegedly violated the terms of the Peace of Westphalia; while Russia justified its interventions in the Balkans and Eastern Europe throughout the nineteenth century as upholding the balance of power established by the Congress of Vienna. Even as late as 2003, the United States and its allies desperately tried to rationalize their invasion of Iraq as a measure to counter the proliferation of weapons of mass destruction. Truces, treaties, and pacts promising eternal peace were sealed with the most solemn oaths and dire curses, and with the exchange of sons and daughters as marriage partners or hostages. And yet none of them lasted. There were always ambiguities that one side could exploit if they sought a reason for attacking the other – the minor infraction of an imprecise border, the unintentional breaching of a vaguely defined sphere of influence, the refurbishment of fortifications in response to another's construction programme, and so on.

Competition for the moral high ground frequently resulted in states accusing each other of being the aggressor. Although the blame in some cases is blatantly obvious, in many more the primary responsibility is far from clear. For example, take the First Punic War in the third century BCE: both Rome and Carthage had good reason to feel threatened by the other's activities in the Western Mediterranean before they fell to blows over the control of Sicily. Similarly, throughout its history France time and again argued that it needed natural borders – the Rhine, the Alps, the Pyrenees – to be secure. Was that so strange with powerful rivals like the Habsburgs lurking on its fringes? In Asia, the lack of clarity about borders led Chinese rulers to clash numerous times over the plains in the northeast, with the nomads as well as with the Korean kingdom of Goguryeo. Historians – not to mention politicians and diplomats at the time – have endlessly debated whether the Monroe Doctrine of 1823 was an act of aggressive imperialism by the United States, an attempt to seize a vast and exclusive sphere of influence covering most of the Western Hemisphere, or a proportionate act of self-defence against the encroachment of the European empires. The answer here, as in so many cases, lies somewhere between the two – just as one side should not bear the full burden of responsibility, neither should the other be entirely absolved from it.

Then there were wars waged by major powers because they were called on by lesser ones. Russia's direct military intervention in the Syrian civil war since 2015 is a good recent example, since it was formally invited by the Syrian government to help fight rebels and jihadists on its territory. In the same vein, the king of Egypt marched into the Levant in the early ninth century BCE in support of his erstwhile ally, the king of Israel. The ancient historians recorded how the Peloponnesian War in the fifth century was ignited when small states turned to the great powers for aid. At the end of the fifteenth century CE, the conflicts between the states of Italy were inextricably interwoven with the competition between the papacy, the Habsburgs, and France. Again and again, small states have thought to mastermind a game of divide-and-rule between the great powers. But very often the major powers have played such overtures to their own advantage in order to legitimize the annexation of lesser states – including those that invited their involvement in the first place.

Treaties, justice, peace, and religion: all have been used to justify wars. Even the lengthiest investigations can leave us uncertain about the exact causes of specific wars, about who was in the right and who was in the wrong. The tragedy is that the search for the moral high ground, claims of benign exceptionalism, and promises of changing the course of power politics for the better have rarely advanced the cause of peace, but merely been employed to vindicate the decision to go to war. This is true of all history, across all regions of the globe, all religions, and all political systems. As soon as great powers start preaching about a moral cause, then conflict is usually never far away.

The Limits of Diplomacy

In much the same way that this book has exposed the failure of morality to maintain peace, it has also demonstrated the limitations of diplomacy. The body of diplomats has expanded enormously over the centuries, but it has never prevented war. In the ancient Mediterranean world, city states maintained close diplomatic relations but were at war almost permanently. In ancient China, the sources record how envoys hurried back and forth between rival kingdoms, but to little avail. Monks, scholars, and even artists were employed as emissaries to smooth relations, only to be confronted with the limitations of their influence. When permanent ambassadors became relatively widespread in Renaissance Europe, idealistic political theorists argued that they would become workers for the common good and the general welfare more than mouthpieces for their rulers' personal ambitions. In reality, however, their primary roles were still to gather information on the assumption that the state where they had been posted was a potential enemy, to negotiate alliances against rival powers, to defend their rulers' often unprincipled actions, and to show off the strength of their country with extravagant entertainments and endless bickering over ceremonial precedence.

The history of diplomatic conferences has followed a similar pattern. Time and again, onlookers yearned for such events to mark a watershed in international politics, a change for the good in the way power politics was pursued. In the Spring and Autumn period of Chinese history (771–476 BCE), hopes were vested in summits convened to discuss arms limitations and restrictions on fortress building, and even to chart the way towards collective security and the reduction of barriers on trade. Their outcomes were affirmed by the most solemn and binding pledges, which were never kept for long. The city states of classical Greece repeatedly held conferences under the aegis of their shared gods to establish leagues of cooperation and collective security against shared enemies – who were far more likely to be fellow Greeks than external threats like the Persian Empire. In Renaissance Italy following the Peace of Lodi in 1454 CE, a similar venture – consciously modelled on classical precedents – brought only partial peace. The spectacular meeting of the kings of France and England at the Field of Cloth of Gold in 1520 failed to end the rivalry between the two nations. Within a few years of the Peace of Westphalia, which brought an end to the Thirty Years War in 1648, and has often been celebrated for introducing the principle of national sovereignty, most of Europe was once again embroiled in conflict. To a greater or lesser degree, much the same can be said about the long-term impact of the Congress of Vienna in 1815, the peace negotiations of Paris in 1919, and the United Nations Conference on International Organization at San Francisco in 1945.

Diplomatic summits may have grown ever greater in scale and ambition, but, as Philippe de Commynes so shrewdly observed in the late fifteenth century, this did not necessarily mean they were any more successful in achieving lasting peace. His more idealistic contemporary, the legal expert Bernard du Rosier, stated that establishing harmony between nations was the most important task of diplomacy. Yet history reveals that, in reality, it has primarily been about advancing the selfish interests of polities. Sometimes these interests converged, so that peace agreements, truces, and cooperation became possible. Far more often, they did not.

The Liberal Case

The liberal idea that peace brings prosperity, and vice versa, has been advanced for centuries. But, as this book has explored, the reality is far from straightforward. The historian Thucydides, for example, summarized the causes of the Peloponnesian War when he wrote: 'What made war inevitable was the growth of Athenian power and the fear which this caused in Sparta.' It was Athens's economic success – which it converted in part into a larger and more capable navy – that frightened Sparta into fighting a war before it was too late. Even if the economic growth of one country benefited others in the long run – as Adam Smith so famously argued in *The Wealth of Nations* – politics always focused on inequalities in the short term and the fear that the shifting economic balance might render a state vulnerable to aggression. Thus, in the nineteenth century CE, France was so alarmed when the industrial might of its neighbours, first Britain and then Prussia, overtook its traditional economic supremacy. Today, the United States is concerned that

China's economic rise and increasing military expenditure will lead to a challenge to its own global position. Prosperity means power and power leads others to be fearful.

Economic success exacerbates rivalry, but so does economic failure. Fiscal overburdening, for instance, triggered – or at least aggravated – numerous internal conflicts. There were violent tax revolts against the Zhou in China in the ninth century BCE, the Assyrian Empire in the Levant in the seventh century, the Persian Empire in Asia Minor in the fifth century, the Roman Empire in Macedonia and Syria in the first century CE, the Habsburg Empire in the Netherlands in the sixteenth century and Central Europe in the seventeenth – to mention just a few. Inflation was also an important destabilizing factor: in Rome in the third century, Yuan China in the fourteenth century, the Ottoman Empire in the seventeenth century, and so on. Then there was the problem of overpopulation which, as we have seen, was a prominent factor driving ancient Greek colonization, the wars of the Roman Republic and early Empire, and the medieval Crusades. Much later, from the nineteenth century onwards, industrial overcapacity in Europe fuelled both revolutionary social unrest and ferocious competition between states for export markets. Economic crises sparked protectionism, causing trade wars and inflaming political rivalries.

As we have seen, economic weakness leads to political weakness – which is an open invitation for others to interfere. Whether caused by natural disasters, trade routes being cut off, misguided economic policies, or government overspend, economic weakness forces empires to retreat and retrench, so that challengers step in to fill the void, gaining in power as they expand while their rival's contraction only weakens them further. We have observed this phenomenon in the downfall of numerous great empires: the Roman, the Byzantine, and many of the major dynastic realms of China and the Middle East. However strong the armies, walls, and fortifications built and maintained by the Roman and Han Empires to keep barbarians at a distance, they could not protect societies that increasingly were administratively feeble, immobilized by decadence, and fragmented by social conflicts.

Trade has rarely fostered peace either, though the expectation that it would is very old. As early as the fourth century BCE, for example, Xenophon argued the case for free trade. In the eighteenth and nineteenth centuries CE, economists like Adam Smith and David Ricardo developed the argument further. Greater trade allowed greater economic specialization. The resulting efficiencies allowed more growth, which benefited all parties. In reality, though, what generally happened was that, once trade increased, rulers and states sought to monopolize it. And, in any case, free trade and economic openness tended disproportionately to reflect the interests of the strong. This was true both of the British Empire in the nineteenth century and the United States in the second half of the twentieth: both pressurized weaker foreign states into opening their markets to competition and investment, which overwhelmingly benefited their own more developed and powerful economies.

Indeed, when it comes to trade, many great powers follow a similar cycle. During their rise, they are protectionist in order to defend their own infant industries. Once these have grown sufficiently, the government takes an interest in helping to develop their position abroad, by such means as economic coercion, military pressure, and colonization. If this succeeds and the companies establish a position of dominance, then the government starts to promote a narrative of free trade, peace, and harmony of interests. This is when trading powers are at their zenith. By then, however, new challengers have arisen, who benefited from the incumbent's pioneering work in developing markets, production methods, and technology, as well as from the fact that rich societies often lose some of their earlier dynamism. If the competition becomes too fierce, the leading power is liable to defend its position by resorting to protectionist measures once again.

Economic openness, and trade more generally, often co-incide with military aspirations. Their most straightforward manifestation is the control and conquest of trade routes. Merchants and commercial interest groups have been important lobbyists for imperialism. As far back as the third-century BCE, the so-called 'Campanian connection' of Roman businessmen advocated the conquest of Sicily and war with the mercantile state of Carthage. In the nineteenth century CE, German, American, and Japanese industrialists all demanded their governments secure them access to markets and raw materials overseas. As long-distance trade became increasingly maritime, the concomitant build up of naval power elicited jealousy and distrust among land powers, who feared that this was less a means of protecting commerce and the freedom of navigation and more an instrument of imperialist power projection. Consider, for instance, the relations between Britain and France at the beginning of the nineteenth century, Britain and the German Empire at the beginning of the twentieth, or China and the United States at the beginning of the twenty-first. Seemingly liberal economic orders, therefore, have often been the epitome of power politics, not an antidote to them – which is why they have so frequently elicited such violent resistance. As the great maritime and commercial power of Venice so bluntly expressed it: wealth to obtain power, power to obtain wealth.

Cosmopolitan Peace

In the history of power politics, cosmopolitanism often marked the crowning point of imperialism. The greatest cosmopolitan cities were invariably imperial capitals, and the greatest patrons of foreign sciences, of tolerance between religions, of cultural cross-pollination, and of exploration, were almost always imperial courts. Consider the palace library of the Assyrian king Ashurbanipal, the Academy of Gondishapur under the Sasanian emperors, the so-called Carolingian Renaissance under Charlemagne, or the Mughal emperor Akbar's synthesis of the different religious creeds of his subjects, the *Din-i Ilahi*. Imperial courts and capitals became display cases of all the exotic riches brought back as tribute, booty, or through trade from their subject lands. With them came reports of extraordinary new cultures, and tales of unbelievable wealth that only intensified the appetite for yet more gold, slaves, trade, and conquest.

In fact, as we have seen, cosmopolitanism is more innate to imperialism than we have often realized. In many cases,

what we have traditionally regarded as single civilizations –
China, say, or India – are actually the outcome of a long process of amalgamation out of numerous distinctive cultures.
Often, imperial civilizations have evolved into their most
characteristic and recognizable forms from the assimilation of conquered peoples. But just as often, they have been
shaped by the influx of conquering dynasties or peoples who
brought with them their own traditions. Some of these were
then imposed on or voluntarily adopted by their new subjects; at the same time, they themselves adopted many of
the old customs, fashions, and beliefs of the previous rulers.
Ancient Egypt, for instance, was at various times ruled by
Libyan and Nubian dynasties. The Achaemenid kings of
Persia self-consciously modelled their rule on the ancient
imperial traditions of the Mesopotamian peoples they conquered. The heartland of China was repeatedly ruled by alien
dynasties from 'barbarian' peoples like the Xiongnu, the
Xianbei, the Mongols, and the Manchu. Throughout recorded history, the great Indo-Gangetic Plain was governed by a
succession of invaders from Central Asia, such as the 'Indo-
Ayrans', the Yuezhi, and the Mughals. The result was often
cultural crosspollination, the blending of artistic styles, languages, and religions – but, equally often, the process of cultural intermingling was accompanied by appalling suffering
and violence.

But might not a more peaceful form of cosmopolitanism –
a genuine world community of common interests – evolve
if more ordinary citizens had a say in their countries' foreign policy? Unfortunately, the assumption that democratic or popular participation in politics would act as a brake

on imperialism or aggression does not stand up to closer inspection. Was Rome less bent on conquest when it was a republic than when it was ruled by emperors – or republican France less belligerent than the Bourbon monarchy? Popular politics can easily be enflamed, not least by the malign forces of nationalism, as the history of the twentieth century only too painfully showed.

Humility

Just as sobering are the limitations of trying to maintain peace by preserving the balance of power. So-called 'realist' theorists of international power politics are sceptical of the roles of treaties, conferences, trade, and other forms of connectivity in fostering peace, believing that the only way to avoid war is by keeping the ambitions of states mutually in check. In theory, if no one state is significantly more powerful than any other, then the risks of aggression are too great, irrespective of any jealousies or other tensions that might exist. In reality, though, the practice of fetishizing the balance of power ensures its transformation into the archetypal 'security dilemma' – as occurred in Europe between 1815 and 1914.

Even if we did accept the fundamental assumption of these 'realists' – that all polities are primarily motivated by security not aggrandizement – it is frequently impossible to tell from a state's actions how far they are prompted by defensive fears and how far by offensive ambitions. As we have seen, building a powerful navy or trying to exert an exclusive sphere of influence can appear equally to be both. In practice, there is often only the finest of lines between maximizing security and maximizing power. So much so, that countless leaders through history have surmised that the best guarantee of security is to maximize power, and have acted accordingly – with devastating consequences.

As this book has shown, there is no one-size-fits-all theory to explain why the ideal of peace has been overruled so frequently by the reality of war. History reveals a plenitude of possible causes of conflict. It can be said, however, that peace generally depends on the behaviour of many actors. Those actors, whether they are cities, states, or empires, are primarily concerned with their own prosperity and security.

Even today, the majority of people remain neither particularly cosmopolitan nor internationalist in outlook; they hardly travel, and align their interests with a specific territory, ethnicity, culture, religion, nation, or leader. The world is fragmented by default. In addition, prosperity is always unequal. Together, these factors trigger envy and fear among those societies that lag behind; and when they attempt to rectify the situation, it is not always through peaceful channels. Similarly, those societies occupying the top of the table invariably use their power to warp international relations to their advantage: sometimes pacifically, sometimes aggressively.

This should not make onlookers or participants in international relations either desperate or disillusioned, though. Diplomats, politicians, experts, and opinion makers all have a responsibility to manage the destabilizing effects caused by shifts in power. I believe diplomacy starts with humility – in the first place, towards the wrecking forces of fear and envy.

It is not because trade grows or that there is more diplomatic interaction that the world becomes more stable. Tranquillity should never be taken for granted, the ideal of peace never be confused with reality. It is beyond the scope of this conclusion to formulate any strategies or framework of policies for bringing about or maintaining peace, but one other quality in particular should be highlighted: sensitivity. Diplomats and other foreign-policy practitioners should remain alert to whatever is happening at home – not least because any negotiator that makes too many compromises is doomed to face a backlash when they step off the return flight. At the same time, however, they need to have empathy for their counterparts: they should try to understand how historical experiences have shaped their expectations, what lies at the root of the behaviour of states and their representatives, why what might seem fair to one party might be rank injustice to another, and so on. Humility and sensitivity cannot guarantee that peace will be achieved. Yet they are critical in order to avoid miscalculations, ameliorate suspicions, and so optimize the chances of diplomatic success.

Humanity's natural state – if it is possible to deduce such a thing from the 3,000 years of history outlined in this book – is not unbridled peace. It appears to me that, for individuals to survive, their most fundamental need is the maximization of power, preferably at the lowest possible cost. On the one hand, power is the best form of security. The weak will always be dominated by the strong – meaning, at the worst, exploitation, penury, abuse, and even death. On the other hand, power stems from want and greed. People's needs are never satisfied: progress creates new desires, while the successes of others cause envy. Security and greed, therefore, are two sides of the same coin. When it comes to states, these will always be under pressure to pursue power, irrespective of whether they are motivated by greed or security. It is precisely because of this that history is filled with so much misunderstanding and strife.

Notes and References

INTRODUCTION: WHY HISTORY MATTERS

1. Estimated annual average global military expenditure in 2016 US dollars: 1980s: $1,350 billion; 1990s: $1,050 billion; 2000s: $1,300 billion; 2010s: $1,650 billion. Source: SIPRI, 2018. SIPRI Military Expenditure Database. Stockholm International Peace Research Institute. Retrieved from: https://www.sipri.org/databases/milex.
2. Cicero, Marcus Tullius, G. L. Hendrickson and H. M. Hubell, trans., 1939. *Brutus. Orator*. Cambridge, MA: Harvard University Press, p. 395.
3. See, for example, the brilliant reconstruction of the Congress System (or the 'Concert of Europe') in Kissinger, Henry, 1994. *Diplomacy*. New York: Simon & Schuster.
4. For example, Bueno de Mesquita, Bruce, 1981. *The War Trap*. New Haven, CT: Yale University Press.
5. Notable examples include: Kennedy, Paul, 1987. *The Rise and Fall of the Great Powers: Economic Change and Military Conflict from 1500 to 2000*. New York: Random House; Organski, A. F. K., 1968. *World Politics*. New York: Knopf; Landes, David S., 1999. *The Wealth and Poverty of Nations: Why Some Are So Rich and Some So Poor*. New York: W. W. Norton.
6. Dahl, Robert, 1957. The Concept of Power. *Systems Research and Behavioral Science*, vol. 2, no. 3, pp. 201–15.
7. Morgenthau, Hans, 1948. *Politics among Nations: The Struggle for Peace and Power*. New York: McGraw-Hill.

CHAPTER 1: HEAVENS OBSCURED

1. Smith, John D., trans., 2009. *The Mahabharata*. London: Penguin, p. 590.
2. Lal, B. B. 1992. The Painted Grey Ware Culture of the Iron Age. In A. H. Dani and V. M. Masson, eds. *History of Civilizations of Central Asia*, vol. 1, *The Dawn of Civilization: Earliest Time to 700 B.C.* Paris: UNESCO, pp. 421–41.
3. Rousseau, Jean-Jacques, John T. Scott, trans., 2012. *The Major Political Writings of Jean-Jacques Rousseau: The Two Discourses and the Social Contract.* Chicago, IL: University of Chicago Press, p. 93.
4. Drennan, Robert D., and Christian E. Peterson, 2008. Centralized Communities, Population, and Social Complexity after Sedentarization. In Jean-Pierre Bocquet-Appel and Ofer Bar-Yosef, eds. *The Neolithic Demographic Transition and Its Consequences.* Dordrecht: Springer, p. 383.
5. Similar carvings and paintings are found all over the globe: in Valcamonica in Italy, the Akakus Mountains in Libya, Fulton's Cave in Lesotho, Tassili n'Ajjer in Algeria, and Bhimbetka in India.
6. Meyer, Christian, et al. 2015. The Massacre Mass Grave of Schöneck-Kilianstädten Reveals New Insights into Collective Violence in Early Neolithic Central Europe. PNAS, vol. 112, no. 36, pp. 11217–22.
7. Image retrieved from: https://www.pinterest.com/pin/436919601323913392/visual-search/?x=1&y=72&w=99&h=28. Similar finds are discussed in: The Metropolitan Museum of Art, 1996. *Ancient Art from the Shumei Family Collection.* New York: The Metropolitan Museum of Art, pp. 23–5.
8. Image retrieved from: https://s-media-cache-ako.pinimg.com/originals/25/4b/16/254b16811f97f13735f4cf56b63ca37f.jpg.
9. For the Dashly Complexes, see: Kohl, Phil, 1987. The Ancient Economy, Transferable Technologies and the Bronze Age World-System: A View from the Northeastern Frontier of the Ancient Near East. In Michael Rowlands et al., eds. *Centre and Periphery in the Ancient World.* Cambridge: Cambridge University Press, pp. 19–22.
10. Evelyn-White, Hugh G., trans., 1914. The Homeric Hymns. In *Hesiod, the Homeric Hymns and Homerica.* London: William Heinemann, pp. 433–5. Note: the hymns were once attributed to Homer, but this is now disputed.
11. Van De Mieroop, Mark, 2016. *A History of the Ancient Near East, ca. 3000–323 BC.* Chichester: Wiley Blackwell, p. 151.
12. Bryce, Trevor, 2003. *Letters of the Great Kings of the Ancient Near East: The Royal Correspondence of the Late Bronze Age.* London: Routledge, p. 102.
13. Anderson, Kenneth, 1985. *Pharaoh Triumphant: The Life and Times of Ramesses* II, *King of Egypt.* Warminster: Aris & Phillips, p. 75.

14. Barras, Colin, 2016. World War Zero Brought down Mystery Civilisation of 'Sea People'. *New Scientist*, no. 3074 (21 May).

15. Morkot, Robert G., 2005. *The Egyptians: An Introduction*. London: Routledge, p. 185. Haring, B. J. J., 1997, *Divine Households: Administrative and Economic Aspects of the New Kingdom Royal Memorial Temples in Western Thebes*. Leiden: Nederlands Instituut voor het Nabije Oosten, p. 375.

16. Walker, Cameron, 2004. Ancient Egyptian Love Poems Reveal a Lust for Life. *National Geographic* (20 April).

17. Musée du Louvre, inv. no. E27069.

18. Moran, William L., 1987. *Les lettres d'El Amarna: correspondence diplomatique du pharaon*. Paris: Éditions du Cerf, p. 8.

19. Weinstein, James M., 1998. The World Abroad. Egypt and the Levant in the Reign of Amenhotep III. In David O'Connor and Eric H. Cline, eds. *Amenhotep III: Perspectives on His Reign*. Ann Arbor, MI: University of Michigan Press, p. 227.

20. Niebuhr, Carl, J. Hutchinson, trans., 1901. *The Tell El Amarna Period: The Relations of Egypt and Western Asia in the Fifteenth Century B.C. According to the Tell El Amarna Tablets*. London: David Nutt, p. 39.

21. Lichtheim, Miriam, 1976. *Ancient Egyptian Literature: A Book of Readings*, vol. 2, *The New Kingdom*. Berkeley, CA: University of California Press, p. 71.

22. Bauer, Susan Wise, 2007. *The History of the Ancient World: From the Earliest Accounts to the Fall of Rome*. New York: W. W. Norton, p. 238.

23. Lichtheim, Miriam, 1973. *Ancient Egyptian Literature: A Book of Readings*, vol. 1, *The Old and Middle Kingdom*. Berkeley, CA: University of California Press, pp. 141–2. Note: this poem was first written in the twentieth century BCE.

24. Abulhab, Saad D., 2016. *The Epic of Gilgamesh: Selected Readings from Its Original Early Arabic Language*. New York: Blautopf, p. 172.

25. Dalley, Stephanie, 2013. *The Mystery of the Hanging Garden of Babylon: An Elusive World Wonder Traced*. Oxford: Oxford University Press, p. 48.

26. Drake, Brandon, 2012. The Influence of Climatic Change on the Late Bronze Age Collapse and the Greek Dark Ages. *Journal of Archaeological Science*, vol. 39, no. 6, pp. 1862–70. Kaniewski, David, et al. 2015. The Late Bronze Age Collapse and the Early Iron Age in the Levant: The Role of Climate in Cultural Disruption. In Susanne Kerner et al., eds. *Climate and Ancient Societies*. Copenhagen: Museum Tusculanum Press, pp. 157–76.

27. Younger, K. Lawson, Jr, 2007. The Late Bronze Age / Iron Age Transition and the Origins of the Arameans. In K. Lawson Younger Jr, ed. *Ugarit at Seventy-Five*. Winona Lake, IN: Eisenbrauns. pp. 159, 161.

28. Li, Feng, 2006. *Landscape and Power in Early China: The Crisis and Fall of the Western Zhou, 1045–771 BC*. Cambridge: Cambridge University Press.

29. Keightley, David N., 1985. *Sources of Shang History: The Oracle-bone Inscriptions of Bronze Age China*. Berkeley, CA: University of California Press, pp. 33–4. Peterson, Barbara Bennett, et al., eds., 2015. *Notable Women of China: Shang Dynasty to the Early Twentieth Century*. Abingdon: Routledge, p. 14.

30. Modern estimates vary between 50,000 and 70,000 combatants for each army.

31. The oldest text containing the characters meaning 'the centre under heaven', or 'Middle Kingdom' is inscribed on the He *zun* (wine vessel), which dates from 1039.

32. Shaughnessy, Edward L., 1991. *Sources of Western Zhou History: Inscribed Bronze Vessels*. Berkeley, CA: University of California Press, pp. 188–9.

33. Wyatt, Don J., 2010. Shao Yong's Numerological-Cosmological System. In John Makeham, ed. *Dao Companion to Neo-Confucian Philosophy*. Dordrecht: Springer, p. 24.

34. Cartier, Michel, 2002. La Population de la Chine au fil des siècles. In Isabelle Attané, ed. *La Chine au seuil de XXIe siècle: questions de population, questions de société*. Paris: INED, p. 22.

35. The 'Indo-Aryan Migration' remains the focus of debate between those scientists who believe that the Aryan tribes originated in South Asia and those who argue that they originated elsewhere.

36. Smith, John D., trans., 2009. Op. cit., p. 322.

---

2. SOLOMON'S PEACOCK

1. Younger, K. Lawson, Jr, 2016. *A Political History of the Arameans: From Their Origins to the End of Their Polities*. Atlanta, GA: SBL Press, p. 224.

2. The city of Nimrud already existed, but it had not served as the Assyrian capital.

3. Pritchard, James B., ed., 1969. *Ancient Near Eastern Texts Relating to the Old Testament*. Princeton, NJ: Princeton University Press, p. 560.

4. Bonatz, Dominik, ed., 2014. *The Archaeology of Political Spaces: The Upper Mesopotamian Piedmont in the Second Millennium BCE*. Berlin: De Gruyter.

5. Cohen, Ada, and Steven E. Kangas, eds., 2010. *Assyrian Reliefs from the Palace of Ashurnasirpal II: A Cultural Biography*. Hanover, NH: University Press of New England.

6. Clare, Israel Smith, 1897. *Library of Universal History*, vol. 1, *Ancient Oriental Nations*. New York: R. S. Peale and J. A. Hill, p. 151.

7. Rittner, Robert K., trans., 2009. *The Libyan Anarchy: Inscriptions from Egypt's Third Intermediate Period*. Atlanta: Society of Biblical Literature, pp. 219–20.

8. Edwards, I. E. S., 1982. Egypt: From the Twenty-Second to the Twenty-Fourth Dynasty. In John Boardman et al., eds. The Cambridge Ancient History, vol. III, part 1, *The Prehistory of the Balkans; and the Middle East and the Aegean World, Tenth to Eighth Centuries B.C.* Cambridge: Cambridge University Press, p. 554.

9. Myśliwiec, Karol, 2000. *The Twilight of Ancient Egypt: First Millennium B.C.E.* Ithaca, NY: Cornell University Press, pp. 49–51.

10. 2 Chronicles 9:21.

11. Hagelia, Hallvard, 2005. Philological Issues in the Tel Dan Inscription. In Lutz Edzard and Jan Retsö, eds. *Current Issues in the Analysis of Semitic Grammar and Lexicon I*. Wiesbaden: Harrassowitz Verlag, p. 235.

12. Brinkman, J. A., 1968. *A Political History of Post-Kassite Babylonia, 1158–722 B.C.* Rome: Pontificium Institutum Biblicum, p. 280.

13. Waltke, Bruce K. and Charles Yu, 2011. *An Old Testament Theology: An Exegetical, Canonical, and Thematic Approach*. Grand Rapids, MI: Zondervan, p. 319.

14. Van De Mieroop, Marc, 2016. *A History of the Ancient Near East, ca. 3000–323 BC*. Chichester: Wiley Blackwell, p. 278.

15. Taylor, Jonathan, 2015. The Black Obelisk of Shalmaneser III. In *Nimrud: Materialities of Assyrian Knowledge Production*. The Nimrud Project. Retrieved from: http://oracc.museum.upenn.edu/nimrud/livesofobjects/blackobelisk/.

16. Musée du Louvre, inv. no. AO 19913. Note that this relief is from the palace of Ashurbanipal at Nineveh, so from a slightly later period (around 640 BCE).

17. Arnold, Bill T., and Bryan E. Beyer, eds., 2002. *Readings from the Ancient Near East: Primary Sources for Old Testament Study*. Grand Rapids, MI: Baker Academic, p. 101.

18. Faraone, Christopher A., 1993. Molten Wax, Spilt Wine and Mutilated Animals: Sympathetic Magic in Near Eastern and Early Greek Oath Ceremonies. *The Journal of Hellenic Studies*, vol. 113, p. 62.

19. Deuteronomy 1:28.

20. Judges 21:25.

21. Deuteronomy 17:15–20.

22. Deuteronomy 20:10–14.

23. Deuteronomy 7:23–4.

24. Carter, Martha L., and Keith N. Scoville, eds., 1984. *Sign, Symbol, Script: An Exhibition on the Origins of Writing and the Alphabet*. Madison, WI: University of Wisconsin-Madison, p. 44.

25. De Jong, Matthijs J., 2007. *Isaiah among the Ancient Near Eastern Prophets: A Comparative Study of the Earliest Stages of the Isaiah Tradition and the Neo-Assyrian Prophecies*. Leiden: Brill, p. 204.

26. Makhortykh, S., 2008. About the Question of Cimmerian Imports and Imitations in Central Europe. In P. F. Biehl and Y. Ya. Rassamakin, eds. *Import and Imitation in Archaeology*. Langenweißbach: Beier & Beran, pp. 167–86.

27. Panyushkina, Irina P., 2012. Climate-Induced Changes in Population Dynamics of Siberian Scythians (700–250 B.C.). In L. Giosan et al., eds. *Climates, Landscapes, and Civilizations*. Washington, DC: American Geophysical Union, pp. 145–54.

28. Barnett, R. D., 1967. *Phrygia and the Peoples of Anatolia in the Iron Age*. Cambridge: Cambridge University Press, pp. 9–10.

29. Morris, Ian, 2005. The Eighth-Century Revolution. Princeton/Stanford University Working Papers in Classics no. 120507, p. 9. Hall, Jonathan M., 2013. *A History of the Archaic Greek World, ca. 1200–479 BCE*. Chichester: John Wiley, p. 111.

30. Chew, Sing C., 2007. *The Recurring Dark Ages: Ecological Stress, Climate Changes, and System Transformation*. Lanham, MD: Altamira Press, pp. 65–80.

31. Shaughnessy, Edward L., 1999. Western Zhou History. In Michael Loewe and Edward L. Shaughnessy, eds. *The Cambridge History of Ancient China: From the Origins of Civilization to 221 B.C.* Cambridge: Cambridge University Press, p. 310.

32. Legge, James, trans., 1879. *The Sacred Books of China: The Texts of Confucianism*, vol. 1. Oxford: Clarendon Press, p. 201.

33. Legge, James, trans., 1861. *The Chinese Classics*, vol. 1. London: Trübner &. Co., p. 275.

34. Legge, James, 1885. *The Sacred Books of China: The Texts of Confucianism*, vol. 3. Oxford: Clarendon Press, p. 289.

35. Shaughnessy, Edward, L., 1999. Op. cit., p. 318.

36. Legge, James, trans., 1865. *The Chinese Classics*, vol. 3, part 2. London: Trübner & Co., p. 624.

37. Shaughnessy, Edward L., 1988. Historical Perspectives on the Introduction of the Chariot into China. *Harvard Journal of Asiatic Studies*, vol. 48, part 1, pp. 189–237.

38. The Xianyun were also known as the Quanrong.

39. Legge, James, trans., 1885. *The Sacred Books of China: The Texts of Confucianism*, vol. 3. Oxford: Clarendon Press, p. 229.

40. Minford, John, 2009. The Triumph: A Heritage of Sorts. *China Heritage Quarterly*, vol. 9, no. 19. Retrieved from: http://www.chinaheritagequarterly. org/articles.php?searchterm=019_triumph.inc&issue=019.

41. Shaughnessy, Edward L., 1999. Western Zhou History. In Michael Loewe and Edward L. Shaughnessy, eds. *The Cambridge History of Ancient China: From the Origins of Civilization to 221 B.C.* Cambridge: Cambridge University Press, p. 322.

42. Legge, James, trans., 1871. *The Chinese Classics*, vol. 4, part 2. London: Trübner & Co., p. 258.

43. Shaughnessy, Edward L., 1999. Op. cit., p. 324.

44. Shaughnessy, Edward L., 1991. *Sources of Western Zhou History: Inscribed Bronze Vessels*. Berkeley, CA: University of California Press, p. 265.

45. Ibid., p. 141.

46. Ibid., p. 171.

47. Habu, Junko, 2004. *Ancient Jomon of Japan*. Cambridge: Cambridge University Press.

48. Pool, Christopher A., 2007. *Olmec Archaeology and Early Mesoamerica*. Cambridge: Cambridge University Press, p. 136.

49. Coe, Michael D., et al., eds., 1981. *The Olmec and Their Neighbors: Essays in Memory of Matthew W. Stirling*. Washington, DC: Dumbarton Oaks Research Library.

50. Rice, Prudence M., 2007. *Maya Calendar Origins: Monuments, Mythistory, and the Materialization of Time*. Austin, TX: University of Texas Press, pp. 96–7.

51. Hassig, Ross, 1992. *War and Society in Ancient Mesoamerica*. Berkeley, CA: University of California Press, pp. 23–30.

3. THE PERSIAN TAKEOVER

1. Kuhrt, Amélie, 2007. *The Persian Empire: A Corpus of Sources from the Achaemenid Period*, vol. 1. Abingdon: Routledge, pp. 53–4.

2. Isaiah 8:7–9.

3. Holloway, Steven W., 2002. *Aššur Is King! Aššur Is King! Religion in the Exercise of Power in the Neo-Assyrian Empire*. Leiden: Brill, p. 92.

4. Edelman, Diana, 2006. Tyrian Trade in Yehud under Artaxerxes I: Real or Fictional? Independent or Crown Endorsed? In Oded Lipschits and Manfred Oeming, eds. *Judah and the Judeans in the Persian Period*. Winona Lake, IN: Eisenbrauns, p. 223.

5. Parpola, Simo, 2007. *Letters from Assyrian Scholars to the Kings Esarhaddon and Ashurbanipal*, vol. 2. Winona Lake, IN: Eisenbrauns, p. 488.

6. Galil, Gershon, 2007. *The Lower Stratum Families in the Neo-Assyrian Period*. Leiden: Brill.

7. Nahum 2:9.

8. Luckenbill, Daniel David, 2005. *The Annals of Sennacherib*. Eugene, OR: Wipf and Stock, p. 18.

9. British Museum, inv. no. 1856,0909.16.

10. British Museum, inv. no. 1856,0909.53.

11. Smith, John M. P., trans., 1901. Annals of Ashurbanipal. In Robert Francis Harper, ed. *Assyrian and Babylonian Literature: Selected Translations*. New York: D. Appleton and Company, p. 107.

12. Carter, Elizabeth, 1996. *Excavations at Anshan (Tal-e Malyan): The Middle Elamite Period*. Philadelphia, PA: The University of Pennsylvania, pp. 1–6. Hansman, John, 1985. Anshan in the Median and Achaemenian Periods. In Ilya Gershevitch, ed. *The Cambridge History of Iran*, vol. 2, *The Median and Achaemenian Periods*. Cambridge: Cambridge University Press, pp. 25–35. Curtis, Vesta Sarkhosh, and Sarah Stewart, eds., 2005. *Birth of the Persian Empire*. London: I.B. Tauris.

13. Tuplin, Christopher, 2004. Medes in Media, Mesopotamia, and Anatolia: Empire, Hegemony, Domination or Illusion? In *Ancient West and East*, vol. 3, no. 2, pp. 223–51.

14. Grayson, A. Kirk, 2000. *Assyrian and Babylonian Chronicles*. Winona Lake, IN: Eisenbrauns, p. 108.

15. Ibid. p. 111.

16. Kuhrt, Amélie, 2007. Op. cit., pp. 47–8.

17. Xenophon, Walter Miller, trans., 1914. *Cyropaedia*, vol. 2. Cambridge, MA: Harvard University Press, p. 283.

18. Ibid., p. 343.

19. Finitsis, Antonios, 2011. *Visions and Eschatology: A Socio-Historical Analysis of Zechariah 1–6*. London: T & T Clark, pp. 64–86.

20. Trotter, James M., 2001. *Reading Hosea in Achaemenid Yehud*. London: Sheffield Academic Press.

21. Wiesehöfer, Josef, 2001. *Ancient Persia: From 550 BC to 650 AD*. London: I.B. Tauris, p. 77.

22. Kuhrt, Amélie, 2007. Op. cit., p. 486.

23. Esther 3:12.

24. See, for example, the series of relief panels from the palace of Sargon II at Khorsabad depicting the transportation of cedar from Lebanon: Musée du Louvre, inv. no. AO 19888–19891.

25. De Jong, Matthijs J., 2007. *Isaiah among the Ancient Near Eastern Prophets: A Comparative Study of the Earliest Stages of the Isaiah Tradition and the Neo-Assyrian Prophecies*. Leiden: Brill, p. 221.

26. Makhortykh, S. V., 2004. The Northern Black Sea Steppes in the Cimmerian Epoch. In E. Marian Scott et al., eds. *Impact of the Environment on Human Migration in Eurasia*. Dordrecht: Kluwer, p. 38.

27. Panyushkina, Irina P., 2012. Climate-Induced Changes in Population Dynamics of Siberian Scythians (700–250 B.C.). In L. Giosan et al., eds. *Climates, Landscapes, and Civilizations*. Washington, DC: American Geophysical Union, p. 145.

28. Grousset, René, 1970. *The Empire of the Steppes: A History of Central Asia*. New Brunswick, NJ: Rutgers University Press.

29. Rolle, Renate, 1989. *The World of the Scythians*. Berkeley, CA: University of California Press, p. 100.

30. Ibid., p. 54.

31. McGlew, James F., 1993. *Tyranny and Political Culture in Ancient Greece*. Ithaca, NY: Cornell University Press, p. 54.

32. Hesiod, Hugh Evelyn-White, trans., 1914. *Hesiod, the Homeric Hymns and Homerica*. London: William Heinemann, p. 21.

33. Ibid., p. 5.

34. McGlew, James F., 1993. Op. cit., pp. 52–86.

35. Gerber, Douglas E., trans., 1999. *Greek Elegiac Poetry: From the Seventh to the Fifth Centuries* BC. Cambridge MA: Harvard University Press, p. 57.

36. Sage, Michael M., 1996. *Warfare in Ancient Greece: A Sourcebook*. London: Routledge, p. 28.

37. Barnstone, Willis, trans., 2010. *Ancient Greek Lyrics*. Bloomington, IN: Indiana University Press, p. 16.

38. Ibid., p. 88.

39. Morris, Ian, 2006. The Growth of Greek Cities in the First Millennium BC. In Glenn R. Storey, ed. *Urbanism in the Preindustrial World: Cross-Cultural Approaches*. Tuscaloosa, AL: University of Alabama Press, pp. 37–8.

40. Thucydides, Rex Warner, trans., 1972. *The Peloponnesian War*. Harmondsworth: Penguin, pp. 148, 122.

41. Aubet, Maria Eugenia, 1993. *The Phoenicians and the West: Politics, Colonies and Trade*. Cambridge: Cambridge University Press.

42. We do not know a lot about Tarsus, not even where it was located, although it was most probably part of the Phoenician sphere of influence. Culican, W., 1991. Phoenicia and Phoenician Colonization. In John Boardman et al., eds. *The Cambridge Ancient History*, vol. III, part 2, *The Assyrian and Babylonian Empires and Other States of the Near East from the Eighth to the Sixth Centuries B.C.* Cambridge: Cambridge University Press, p. 519.

43. Zolfagharifard, Ellie, 2015. Huge Tomb of Celtic Prince Unearthed in France. *Daily Mail* (6 March).

44. Livy, B. O. Foster, trans., 1919. *History of Rome: Books I–II.* Cambridge, MA: Harvard University Press, p. 81.

45. Bodhi, Bhikkhu, trans., 2012. *The Numerical Discourses of the Buddha: A Translation of the Anguttara Nikaya.* Boston: Wisdom Publications, p. 300.

46. Ibid., p. 747.

47. Legge, James, trans., 1872. *The Chinese Classics*, vol. 5, part 1. London: Trübner & Co., p. 2.

48. Von Falkenhausen, Lothar, 1999. The Waning of the Bronze Age: Material Culture and Social Developments, 770–481 B.C. In Michael Loewe and Edward L. Shaughnessy, eds. *The Cambridge History of Ancient China: From the Origins of Civilization to 221 B.C.* Cambridge: Cambridge University Press, pp. 450–544. Hsu, Cho-yun, 1999. The Spring and Autumn Period. In ibid., pp. 545–86.

49. Milburn, Olivia, trans., 2015. *Urbanization in Early and Medieval China: Gazetteers for the City of Suzhou.* Seattle, WA: University of Washington Press, p. 222. Schinz, Alfred, 1996. *The Magic Square: Cities in Ancient China.* Stuttgart: Edition Axel Menges, p. 54.

50. Miller, Harry, 2015. *The Gongyang Commentary on* The Spring and Autumn Annals: *A Full Translation.* New York: Palgrave Macmillan, p. 14. This summit took place in 498.

51. Liu, Daqun, 2014. International Law and International Humanitarian Law in Ancient China. In Morten Bergsmo et al., eds. *Historical Origins of International Criminal Law*, vol. 1. Brussels: Torkel Opsahl, p. 91.

52. Ibid.

53. Ibid., p. 92.

54. Legge, James, trans., 1872. *The Chinese Classics*, vol. 5, part 2. London: Trübner & Co., p. 534.

55. Zhong, Guan, W. Allyn Rickett, trans., 2001. *Guanzi: Political, Economic, and Philosophical Essays from Early China: A Study and Translation*, vol. 1. Boston, MA: Cheng and Tsui Company, pp. 111, 206, 96, 210, 99.

56. Legge, James, trans., 1861. *The Chinese Classics*, vol. 1. London: Trübner &. Co., pp. 122, 139, 120.

57. Lao, Tzu, Arthur Waley, trans., 1997. *Tao Te Ching*. Ware: Wordsworth Editions, p. 31.

58. Ibid., p. 82.

59. Sun, Tzu, Lionel Giles, trans., 1910. *Sun Tzu on the Art of War: The Oldest Military Treatise in the World*. London: Luzac & Co., p. 2.

60. Ibid., p. 13.

4. GOLD AND IRON

1. National Archaeological Museum, Athens, inv. no. 1818. See: https://www.pinterest.com/pin/23643966768039280/.

2. Nawotka, Krzysztof, 2010. *Alexander the Great*. Newcastle: Cambridge Scholars Publishing, p. 58.

3. British Museum, inv. no 1848,1020.62. Llewellyn-Jones, Lloyd, 2012. The Great Kings of the Fourth Century and the Greek Memory of the Persian Past. In John Marincola et al., eds. *Greek Notions of the Past in the Archaic and Classical Eras: History without Historians*. Edinburgh: Edinburgh University Press, pp. 339–40.

4. Wiesehöfer, Josef, 2001. *Ancient Persia: From 550 BC to 650 AD*. London: I.B. Tauris, p. 33.

5. Briant, Pierre, 2002. *From Cyrus to Alexander: A History of the Persian Empire*. Winona Lake, IN: Eisenbrauns, p. 460.

6. Demosthenes, J. H. Vince, trans., 1939. *Orations*, vol. 2. Cambridge, MA: Harvard University Press, p. 425.

7. Thucydides, Rex Warner, trans., 1972. *The Peloponnesian War*. Harmondsworth: Penguin, p. 295.

8. Ibid., pp. 45–6.

9. Demosthenes, Henry Owgan, trans., 1866. *The Three Olynthiacs, Prolegomena, Orations on the Peace and the Chersonesus*. Dublin: William B. Kelly, p. 38.

10. Plato, Desmond Lee, trans., 2003. *The Republic*. London: Penguin: p. 233.

11. Aristotle, Jonathan Barnes, ed., 1984. *The Complete Works of Aristotle: The Revised Oxford Translation*, vol. 2. Princeton, NJ: Princeton University Press, p. 2162.

12. Herodotus, Aubrey de Sélincourt, trans., 1972. *The Histories*. Harmondsworth: Penguin, p. 57.

13. Thucydides, Rex Warner, trans., 1972. Op. cit., p. 49.

14. Ibid., p. 87.

15. Ibid., p. 104.

16. Hees, Brigitte, 1991. Honorary Decrees in Attic Inscriptions, 500–323 B.C. Unpublished PhD dissertation, University of Arizona, p. 49. Retrieved from: http://hdl.handle.net/10150/185480.

17. Acropolis Museum, Athens, inv. no. 2996, 2985.

18. Xenophon, Carleton L. Brownson, trans., 1921. *Hellenica*. vol. 2. Cambridge, MA: Harvard University Press, p. 155.

19. Xenophon, Ashley Cooper et al., trans., 1832. *The Whole Works of Xenophon*. London: Jones & Co., p. 683.

20. Adolf, Antony, 2009. *Peace: A World History*. Cambridge: Polity Press, p. 42.

21. Reardon, B. P., ed., 1989. *Collected Ancient Greek Novels*. Berkeley, CA: University of California Press, p. 702. Note: this quote is from the so-called *Alexander Romance*. The exact origin of this document is unknown.

22. Plutarch, Bernadotte Perrin, trans., 1920. *Lives*, vol. 9. Cambridge, MA: Harvard University Press, p. 417.

23. Polybius, Evelyn S. Shuckburgh, trans., 1889. *The Histories of Polybius*, vol. 1. London: Macmillan and Co., p. 10.

24. Xenophon, Edward Bysshe, trans., 1889. *The Memorable Thoughts of Socrates*. London: Cassell & Company, p. 81.

25. Mookerji, Radha Kumud, 1966. *Chandragupta Maurya and His Times*. Delhi: Motilal Banarsidass, p. 165.

26. Kautilya, R. Shamasastry, trans., 1915. *Kautilya's Arthasastra*. Bangalore: The Government Press, pp. 321, 324.

27. Dhammika, Ven. S., trans., 1993. The Fourteen Rock Edicts. In *The Edicts of King Ashoka*. Retrieved from: https://www.cs.colostate.edu/~malaiya/ashoka.html.

28. Xunzi, John Knoblock, trans., 1990. *Xunzi: A Translation and Study of the Complete Works*, vol. 2. Stanford, CA: Stanford University Press, p. 197.

29. Lewis, Mark Edward, 2007. *The Early Chinese Empires: Qin and Han*. Cambridge, MA: Belknap Press, p. 19.

30. Schinz, Alfred, 1996. *The Magic Square: Cities in Ancient China*. Stuttgart: Edition Axel Menges, p. 89.

31. Deng, Gang, 1999. *The Premodern Chinese Economy: Structural Equilibrium and Capitalist Sterility*. London: Routledge, p. 140.

32. Lewis, Mark Edward, 2007. Op. cit., p. 14.

33. Legge, James, trans., 1861. *The Chinese Classics*, vol. 2. London: Trübner & Co., p. 76. Legge, James, trans. 1885. *The Sacred Books of China: The Texts of Confucianism*, vol. 3, p. 289.

34. Yang, Shang, J. J. L. Duyvendak, trans., 1998. *The Book of Lord Shang*. Ware: Wordsworth Editions, p. 214.

35. Zhang, Ellen Y., 2015. 'Weapons Are Nothing But Ominous Instruments': The *Daodejing's* View on War and Peace. In Ping-cheung Lo and Sumner B. Twiss, eds. *Chinese Just War Ethics: Origin, Development, and Dissent*. London: Routledge, p. 260.

36. Xunzi, John Knoblock, trans., 1990. Op. cit., p. 191.

37. Bramwell Bonsall, 2011. *The Annals of the Warring States*, World Heritage Encyclopedia:

5. THE WORLD LIKE A CHARIOT RUN WILD

1. Most of our sources for the Qin, including Sima Qian's *Records of the Grand Historian*, date from the subsequent Han period and are thus often coloured by the way the Han tried to delegitimize their predecessors.

2. Sima, Qian, Burton Watson, trans., 1993. *Records of the Grand Historian: Qin Dynasty*. New York: Columbia University Press, p. 45.

3. Mott, William H., and Jae Chang Kim, 2006. *The Philosophy of Chinese Military Culture: Shih vs. Li*. New York: Palgrave Macmillan, p. 56.

4. Zhang, Longxi, 2009. Heaven and Man: From a Cross-Cultural Perspective. In Jin Y. Park, ed. *Comparative Political Theory and Cross-Cultural Philosophy: Essays in Honor of Hwa Yol Jung*. Lanham, MD: Lexington Books, p. 144.

5. Luo, Yuming, 2011. *A Concise History of Chinese Literature*, vol. 1. Leiden: Brill, pp. 125–46.

6. Nishijima, Sadao, 1986. The Economic and Social History of Former Han. In Denis Twitchett and Michael Loewe, eds. *The Cambridge History of China*, vol. 1, *The Ch'in and Han Empires, 221 B.C.–A.D. 220*. Cambridge: Cambridge University Press, p. 552.

7. Luo, Yuming, 2011. Op. cit., p. 140.

8. Kinney, Anne Behnke, trans., 2003. The Annals of [Emperor Hsiao]-Wen. In Anne Behnke Kinney, trans., *The History of the Former Han Dynasty*. Retrieved from: http://www2.iath.virginia.edu:8080/exist/cocoon/xwomen/texts/hanshu/d2.14/1/0/english.

9. Husmann, Lisa Eileen, 1993. Territory, Historiography, and the Minorities Question in China. Unpublished MA dissertation, University of California, Berkeley, p. 9.

10. Schuman, Michael, 2015. *Confucius and the World He Created*. New York: Basic Books, p. 174.

11. Golden, Peter, 2013. Courts and Court Culture in the Proto-Urban and Urban Developments among the Pre-Chinggisid Turkic Peoples. In David Durand-Guédy, ed. *Turko-Mongol Rulers, Cities and City Life*. Leiden: Brill, p. 32.

12. Lewis, Mark E., 2000. The Han Abolition of Universal Military Service. In Hans van de Ven, ed. *Warfare in Chinese History*. Leiden: Brill, pp. 46–7.

13. Sima, Qian, Burton Watson, trans., 1993. *Records of the Grand Historian: Han Dynasty*, vol. 2. New York: Columbia University Press, 251–3.

14. Rawlinson, H. G., 1912. *Bactria: The History of a Forgotten Empire*. London: Probsthain & Co.

15. Diodorus Siculus, G. Booth, trans., 1814. *The Historical Library of Diodorus the Sicilian*, vol. 1. London: W. McDowall, p. 104.

16. Thiruvalluvar, P. S. Sundaram, trans., 2005. *The Kural*. London: Penguin, p. 109.

17. Altekar, A. S., 2002. *State and Government in Ancient India*. Delhi: Motilal Banarsidass, p. 292.

18. Polybius, Evelyn S. Shuckburgh, trans., 1889. *The Histories of Polybius*, vol. 1. London: Macmillan and Co., p. 23.

19. Ibid., pp. 10–11.

20. Lazenby, J. F., 2016. *The First Punic War: A Military History*. London: Routledge, p. 40.

21. Plutarch, Bernadotte Perrin, trans., 1914. *Lives*, vol. 2. Cambridge, MA: Harvard University Press, p. 383.

22. Ibid., p. 329.

23. Von Ungern-Sternberg, Jürgen, 2004. The Crisis of the Republic. In Harriet I. Flower, ed. *The Cambridge Companion to the Roman Republic*. Cambridge: Cambridge University Press, p. 91.

24. Virgil, Smith Palmer Bovie, trans., 1956. *Virgil's Georgics: A Modern English Verse Translation*. Chicago, IL: University of Chicago Press, p. 102.

25. Tibullus, J. P. Postgate, trans., 1962. *Catullus, Tibullus, Pervigilium Veneris*. Cambridge, MA: Harvard University Press, p. 247.

26. Horace, C. E. Bennett, trans., 1912. *The Odes and Epodes*. Cambridge, MA: Harvard University Press, p. 345.

27. Tempest, Kathryn, 2011. *Cicero: Politics and Persuasion in Ancient Rome*. London: Continuum, p. 47.

28. Stelkens, Wilhelm, 1867. *Der römische Geschichtsschreiber Sempronius Asellio*. Hamburg: J. B. Klein, p. 81.

6. BARBARIANS AT THE GATES

1. Virgil, Robert Fitzgerald, trans., 1983. *Aeneid*. New York: Random House, p. 13.
2. Everitt, Anthony, 2009. *Hadrian and the Triumph of Rome*. New York: Random House, p. 173.
3. Augustus, Thomas Bushnell, trans., 1998. *The Deeds of the Divine Augustus*. The Internet Classics Archive. Retrieved from: http://classics.mit.edu/Augustus/deeds.html.
4. Ibid. Arabia Felix ('that part of Arabia which is called Happy') was the Roman name for the southern part of the Arabian Peninsula.
5. Ibid.
6. Tacitus, Alfred John Church and William Jackson Brodribb, trans., 1877. *The Agricola and Germany of Tacitus and the Dialogue on Oratory*. London: Macmillan and Co., 1877, p.29.
7. Tacitus, Michael Grant, trans., 1996. *The Annals of Imperial Rome*. London: Penguin, p. 44.
8. Ibid., p. 209.
9. Ibid., p. 242.
10. Ibid., pp. 322–3.
11. Musée du Louvre, inv. no. MA 1009.
12. Dio, Cassius, Earnest Cary, trans., 1927. *Roman History*, vol. 9. Cambridge, MA: Harvard University Press, p. 271.
13. Ibid., p. 239.
14. Ibid., p. 299.
15. Ibid., p. 471.
16. Ibid., p. 359.
17. Tacitus, Michael Grant, trans., 1996. Op. cit., p. 83.
18. Jongman, Willem, 2003. Slavery and the Growth of Rome: The Transformation of Italy in the Second and First Centuries BCE. In Catharine Edwards and Greg Woolf, eds. *Rome the Cosmopolis*. Cambridge: Cambridge University Press, p. 108.
19. Milanovic, Branko, et al., 2007. *Measuring Ancient Inequality*. Washington, DC: World Bank, Policy Research Working Paper, WPS 4412, p. 66–8. Retrieved from: http://documents.worldbank.org/curated/en/803681468135958164/Measuring-ancient-inequality.
20. Harvey, Brian K., 2016. *Daily Life in Ancient Rome: A Sourcebook*. Indianapolis, IN: Focus, p. 19.
21. Dio, Cassius, Earnest Cary, trans., 1927. Op. cit., p. 483.
22. Arafat, K. W., 1996. *Pausanias' Greece: Ancient Artists and Roman Rulers*. Cambridge: Cambridge University Press, p. 90.

23. Ibid.

24. Herodian, Edward C. Echols, trans., 1961. *History of the Roman Empire: From the Death of Marcus Aurelius to the Accession of Gordian* III. Berkeley, CA: University of California Press, p. 125.

25. Howard, Michael C., 2012. *Transnationalism in Ancient and Medieval Societies: The Role of Cross-Border Trade and Travel.* Jefferson, NC: McFarland & Co., p. 65.

26. Ibid.

27. Pliny the Elder, John Bostock and H. T. Riley, trans., 1893. *The Natural History of Pliny*, vol. 2. London: George Bell & Sons, p. 63.

28. McLaughlin, Raoul, 2010. *Rome and the Distant East: Trade Routes to the Ancient Lands of Arabia, India and China.* London: Continuum, p. 134.

29. Schoff, Wilfred H., trans., 1912. *The Periplus of the Erythraean Sea: Travel and Trade in the Indian Ocean by a Merchant of the First Century.* London: Longmans, Green, and Co.

30. Ibid., p. 35.

31. Ibid., p. 48.

32. Ibid., p. 39.

33. Ibid.

34. Young, Stuart H., 2002. *Biography of the Bodhisattva Aśvaghoṣa.* Retrieved from: http://buddhism.lib.ntu.edu.tw/FULLTEXT/JR-AN/103180.htm.

35. Ibid.

36. Sims-Williams, Nicholas, 2012. Bactrian Historical Inscriptions of the Kushan Period. *The Silk Road*, vol. 10, pp. 77.

37. Rosenfield, John, M., 1967. *The Dynastic Arts of the Kushans.* Berkeley, CA: University of California Press, p. 16.

38. Dio, Cassius, Earnest Cary, trans., 1917. *Roman History*, vol. 6. Cambridge, MA: Harvard University Press, p. 305.

39. Elvin, Mark, 1973. *The Pattern of the Chinese Past: A Social and Economic Interpretation.* Stanford, CA: Stanford University Press, p. 31.

40. Dash, Mike, 2011. Emperor Wang Mang: China's First Socialist? *Smithsonian* (9 December). Retrieved from: http://www.smithsonianmag.com/history/emperor-wang-mang-chinas-first-socialist-2402977/#S71e97Gbvdie37vF.99.

41. Clark, Anthony E., 2008. *Ban Gu's History of Early China.* Amherst, NY: Cambria Press, p. 155.

42. Lewis, Mark E., 2000. The Han Abolition of Universal Military Service. In Hans van de Ven, ed. *Warfare in Chinese History.* Leiden: Brill, pp. 33–76.

43. Chin, Tamara T., 2010. Defamiliarizing the Foreigner: Sima Qian's Ethnography and Han-Xiongnu Marriage Diplomacy. *Harvard Journal of Asiatic Studies*, vol. 70, no. 2, p. 317.

44. Lewis, Mark E., 2000. Op. cit., p. 45.

45. Ibid., p. 46.

46. Lewis, Mark Edward, 2007. *The Early Chinese Empires. Qin and Han.* Cambridge, MA: Belknap Press, pp. 145–6.

47. Yü, Ying-shih, 1986. Han Foreign Relations. In Denis Twitchett and Michael Loewe, eds. *The Cambridge History of China*, vol. 1, *The Ch'in and Han Empires, 221 B.C.–A.D. 220.* Cambridge: Cambridge University Press, p. 415.

48. Lewis, Mark E., 2000. Op. cit., p. 69.

49. Ebrey, Patricia, 2008. Estate and Family Management in the Later Han as Seen in the *Monthly Instructions for the Four Classes of People.* In Jos Gommans and Harriet Zurndorfer, eds. *Roots and Routes of Development in China and India: Highlights of Fifty Years of* The Journal of the Economic and Social History of the Orient (1957–2007). Leiden: Brill, pp. 124–68.

50. Cai, Zong-qi, 2008. Pentasyllabic *Shi* Poetry: The 'Nineteen Old Poems'. In Zong-qi Cai, ed. *How to Read Chinese Poetry: A Guided Anthology.* New York: Columbia University Press, p. 107.

51. De Crespigny, Rafe, 2007. *A Biographical Dictionary of Later Han to the Three Kingdoms* (23–220 AD). Leiden: Brill, p. 50.

52. Tse, Wai Kit Wicky, 2012. Dynamics of Disintegration: The Later Han Empire (25–220 CE) and Its Northwestern Frontier. Unpublished PhD dissertation, University of Pennsylvania. Retrieved from: https://repository.upenn.edu/edissertations/589/.

53. Ibid., p. 142.

54. Ibid., p. 22.

55. Cotterell, Arthur, 2014. *A History of Southeast Asia.* Singapore: Marshall Cavendish Editions, p. 73.

56. Maspéro, Georges, 2002. *The Champa Kingdom: The History of an Extinct Vietnamese Kingdom.* London: White Lotus Press, p. 24.

57. Westermann, William L., 1955. *The Slave Systems of Greek and Roman Antiquity.* Philadelphia, PA: The American Philosophical Society. Scheidel, Walter, 2007. The Roman Slave Supply. Princeton/Stanford Working Papers in Classics no. 050704, p. 2. Scheidel, Walter, 2013. Slavery and Forced Labor in Early China and the Roman World. Princeton/Stanford Working Papers in Classics, no. 041301, p. 6. Both Scheidel papers retrieved from: https://www.princeton.edu/~pswpc/papers/authorMZ/scheidel/scheidel.html.

58. The work of Walter Scheidel is particularly instructive. See, for instance: Scheidel, Walter, 2010. Physical Wellbeing in the Roman World. Princeton/Stanford Working Papers in Classics, no. 091001. Retrieved from: https://www.princeton.edu/~pswpc/papers/authorMZ/scheidel/scheidel.html.

59. Gallant, Thomas W., 1991. *Risk and Survival in Ancient Greece: Reconstructing the Rural Domestic Economy*. Stanford: Stanford University Press, pp. 20–21, 40–38.

---

7. THE GREAT IMPERIAL CRISIS

1. Tian, Xiaofei, 2005. *Tao Yuanming and Manuscript Culture: The Record of a Dusty Table*. Seattle, WA: University of Washington Press, p. 186.
2. Palladius, T. Owen, trans., 1807. *The Fourteen Books of Palladius Rutilius Taurus Æmilianus on Agriculture*. London: J. White.
3. Margy, Nagit, 2010. A Hun-Age Burial with Male Skeleton and Horse Bones Found in Budapest. In Florin Curta, ed. *Neglected Barbarians*. Turnhout: Brepols, pp. 137–75.
4. Biswas, Atreya, 1971. *The Political History of the Hunas in India*. New Delhi: Munshiram Manoharlal Publishers, p. 69.
5. McCormick, Michael, et al., 2012. Climate Change during and after the Roman Empire: Reconstructing the Past from Scientific and Historical Evidence. *Journal of Interdisciplinary History*, vol. 43, no. 2, pp. 169–220.
6. Maenchen-Helfen, J. Otto, 1973. *The World of the Huns: Studies in Their History and Culture*. Berkeley, CA: University of California Press, p. 33.
7. Cyprian, Rose Bernard Donna, trans., 1964. *Letters 1–81*. Washington, DC: Catholic University of America Press.
8. Zosimus, James J. Buchanan and Harold T. Davis, trans., 1967. *Historia Nova: The Decline of Rome*. San Antonio, TX: Trinity University Press, p. 201.
9. Williams, Stephen, 1997. *Diocletian and the Roman Recovery*. London: Routledge, p. 129.
10. Kropff, Antony, 2016. An English Translation of the Edict on Maximum Prices, also Known as the Price Edict of Diocletian (Edictum de pretiis rerum venalium). *Academia. edu*. Retrieved from: http://www.academia.edu/23644199/ New_English_translation_of_the_Price_Edict_of_Diocletianus.
11. Heather, Peter, 1998. Senators and Senates. In Averil Cameron and Peter Garnsey, eds. *The Cambridge Ancient History*, vol. 13, *The Late Empire, A.D. 337–425*. Cambridge: Cambridge University Press, pp. 185–6.
12. Bate, H. N., trans., 1918. *The Sibylline Oracles: Books III–V*. London: Society for Promoting Christian Knowledge, p. 62.

13. Themistius, Peter Heather and David Moncur, trans., 2001. *Politics, Philosophy, and Empire in the Fourth Century: Select Orations of Themistius.* Liverpool: Liverpool University Press, p. 201.

14. Lewis, Naphtali, and Meyer Reinhold, eds., 1955. *Roman Civilization: Selected Readings*, vol. 1, *The Republic.* New York: Columbia University Press, p. 377.

15. Blockley, R. C., 1984. The Romano-Persian Peace Treaties of A.D. 299 and 363. *Florilegium*, vol. 6, pp. 28–49.

16. Merrills, Andy, and Richard Miles, 2009. *The Vandals.* Chichester: Wiley-Blackwell, p. 42.

17. Zosimus, 1814. *The History of Count Zosimus, Sometime Advocate and Chancellor of the Roman Empire.* London: J. Davis, p. 164.

18. Malamud, Martha, trans., 2016. *Rutilius Namatianus' Going Home: De Reditu Suo.* Abingdon: Routledge, p. 6.

19. Maas, Michael, 2010. *Readings in Late Antiquity: A Sourcebook.* Abingdon: Routledge, p. 138.

20. Benson, Robert L., 1982. The Gelasian Doctrine: Uses and Transformations. In Dominique Sourdel, ed. *La Notion d'autorité au Moyen Age: Islam, Byzance, Occident.* Paris: Presses Universitaires de France, p. 14.

21. Gregory of Tours, Lewis Thorpe, trans., 1974. *The History of the Franks.* London: Penguin, p. 154.

22. Luo, Guanzhong, Moss Roberts, trans., 1991. *The Romance of the Three Kingdoms: A Historical Novel.* Berkeley, CA: University of California Press, p. 923.

23. Chen, Shou, 1977. *San guo zhi* [*Records of the Three Kingdoms*]. Taipei: Dingwen Printing, p. 210.

24. Cheng, Qinhua, 2000. *Sons of Heaven: Stories of Chinese Emperors through the Ages.* Beijing: Foreign Languages Press, p. 118.

25. Tanner, Harold M., 2009. *China: A History.* Indianapolis, IN: Hackett, p. 143.

26. Ibid.

27. Dreyer, Edward L., 2009. Military Aspects of the War of the Eight Princes, 300–307. In Nicola Di Cosmo, ed. *Military Culture in Imperial China.* Cambridge, MA: Harvard University Press, p. 124.

28. Duthie, Nina, 2015. Origins, Ancestors, and Imperial Authority in Early Northern Wei Historiography. Unpublished PhD dissertation, Columbia University, p. 112. Retrieved from: https://doi.org/10.7916/D8NC601F.

29. Sims-Williams, Nicholas, trans., 2004. *The Sogdian Ancient Letters.* Retrieved from: https://depts.washington.edu/silkroad/texts/sogdlet.html.

30. Ibid.

31. Wace, Henry, and Philip Schaff, eds., 1893. *A Select Library of Nicene and Post-Nicene Fathers of the Christian Church: Second Series*, vol. 6, *St. Jerome: Letters and Select Works.* Oxford: James Parker and Company, p. 500.

32. Boyce, M., trans., 1968. *The Letter of Tansar*. Rome: Istituto Italiano per il Medio ed Estremo Oriente, pp. 40–46.

33. Frye, Richard N.; 1984. *The History of Ancient Iran*. Munich: C. H. Beck'sche Verlagsbuchhandlung, p. 371.

34. Marcellinus, Ammianus, Walter Hamilton, trans., 1986. *The Later Roman Empire (A.D. 354–378)*. Harmondsworth: Penguin, p. 263.

35. Sykes, P. M., 1915. *A History of Persia*, vol. 1. London: Macmillan and Co., p. 484.

36. Darling, Linda T., 2013. *A History of Social Justice and Political Power in the Middle East: The Circle of Justice from Mesopotamia to Globalization*. Abingdon: Routledge, p. 42.

37. Sykes, Percy, 1915. Op. cit. p. 390.

38. Nieminen, Timo A., 2010. The Asian War Bow. In E. Barbiero et al., eds. *19th Australian Institute of Physics Congress*, ACOFTAOS, p. 4. Retrieved from: https://arxiv.org/abs/1101.1677.

39. Ramachandra Dikshitar, V. R., 1993. *The Gupta Polity*. Delhi: Motilal Banarsidass, pp. 151–2.

40. Singh Jina, Prem, 1995. *Famous Western Explorers to Ladakh*. New Delhi: Indus Publishing Company, pp. 139–40.

41. Litvinsky, B. A., 1996. The Hephthalite Empire. In B. A. Litvinsky et al., eds. *History of Civilizations of Central Asia*, vol. 3, *The Crossroads of Civilizations: A.D. 250 to 750*. Paris: UNESCO, pp. 135–62.

42. Quoted in Mookerji, Radhakumud, 1989. *The Gupta Empire*. Delhi: Motilal Banarsidass, p. 55.

43. Wicks, Robert S., 1992. *Money, Markets, and Trade in Early Southeast Asia: The Development of Indigenous Monetary Systems to AD 1400*. Ithaca, NY: Cornell Southeast Asia Program.

44. Cœdès, George, 1931. Deux Inscriptions Sanskrites Du Fou-Nan. *Bulletin de l'École française d'Extrême-Orient*, vol. 31, nos. 1–2, p. 2.

45. Shaffer, Lynda Norene, 1996. *Maritime Southeast Asia to 1500*. Armonk, NY: M. E. Sharpe.

46. Peebles, Patrick, ed., 2015. *Voices of South Asia: Essential Readings from Antiquity to the Present*. Abingdon: Routledge, p. 59.

47. Chŏn, Ho-t'ae, 2008. *Goguryeo: In Search of Its Culture and History*. Elizabeth, NJ: Hollym International.

48. Kim, J. Y., 1988. The Kwanggaet'o Stele Inscription. In Ian Nish, ed. *Contemporary European Writing on Japan: Scholarly Views from Eastern and Western Europe*. Woodchurch: Paul Norbury, pp. 79–81.

49. Robin, Christian Julien, 2012. Arabia and Ethiopia. In Scott Fitzgerald Johnson, ed. *The Oxford Handbook of Late Antiquity.* New York: Oxford University Press, p. 277.

8. IN THE NAME OF THE PROPHET

1. Meri, Josef W., 2006. *Medieval Islamic Civilization: An Encyclopedia*, vol. 1. London: Routledge, p. 203.
2. Abdel Haleem, M. A. S., 2008. *The Qur'an.* Oxford: Oxford University Press, 3.109.
3. Ibid., 3.14.
4. Ibid., 4.29–30.
5. Ibid., 4.91.
6. Rogerson, Barnaby, 2006. *The Heirs of the Prophet Muhammad and the Roots of the Sunni–Shia Schism.* London: Little Brown, p. 160.
7. Theophilus of Edessa, Robert G. Hoyland, trans., 2011. *Theophilus of Edessa's Chronicle and the Circulation of Historical Knowledge in Late Antiquity and Early Islam.* Liverpool: Liverpool University Press, p. 133.
8. Ibid., p. 159.
9. Procopius, H. B. Dewing, trans., 1914. *History of the Wars*, vol. 1. London: William Heinemann, p. 103.
10. Musée du Louvre, inv. no. AO 9063.
11. Bell, Peter N., 2009. *Three Political Voices from the Age of Justinian: Agapetus, 'Advice to the Emperor'; 'Dialogue on Political Science'; Paul the Silentiary, 'Description of Hagia Sophia'.* Liverpool: Liverpool University Press, p. 175.
12. Maas, Michael, 2010. *Readings in Late Antiquity: A Sourcebook.* Abingdon: Routledge, p. 90.
13. Ibid., p. 382.
14. Menander, R. C. Blockley, trans., 1985. *The History of Menander the Guardsman.* Liverpool: Cairns, p. 63.
15. Gregory of Tours, Lewis Thorpe, trans., 1974. *The History of the Franks.* London: Penguin, p. 461.
16. James of Viterbo, R. W. Dyson, ed., 2009. *De Regimine Christiano: A Critical Edition and Translation.* Leiden: Brill, p. xxxi.
17. Hen, Yizhak, 2010. Converting the Barbarian West. In Daniel E. Bornstein, ed. *A People's History of Christianity*, vol. 4, *Medieval Christianity.* Minneapolis, MN: Fortress Press, p. 42.

18. Cadoux, C. John, 1919. *The Early Christian Attitude to War: A Contribution to the History of Christian Ethics*. London: Headley Bros, pp. 86–201.

19. Ibid., p. 81.

20. Augustine, Saint, Henry Bettenson, trans., 2003. *Concerning the City of God against the Pagans*. London: Penguin, p. 267.

21. Leo VI, George T. Dennis, trans., 2010. *The Taktika of Leo VI*. Washington, DC: Dumbarton Oaks, p. 5.

22. Lovell, Julia, 2006. *The Great Wall: China against the World, 1000 BC–AD 2000*. New York: Grove Press, p. 109.

23. Wang, Mei-Hsiu, 2007. Cultural Identities as Reflected in the Literature of the Northern and Southern Dynasties Period (4th–6th Centuries A.D.). Unpublished PhD dissertation, University of Leeds, p. 160. Retrieved from: http://etheses.whiterose.ac.uk/364/.

24. Dien, Albert E., 2007. *Six Dynasties Civilization*. New Haven, CT: Yale University Press, p. 6.

25. Dien, Albert E., 1986. The Stirrup and Its Effect on Chinese Military History. *Ars Orientalis*, vol. 16, pp. 33–56.

26. Chen, Jack W., 2010. *The Poetics of Sovereignty: On Emperor Taizong of the Tang Dynasty*. Cambridge, MA: Harvard University Asia Center, p. 39.

27. Ebrey, Patricia Buckley, 1993. *Chinese Civilization: A Sourcebook*. New York: Free Press, p. 114.

28. Zhang, Qizhi, 2015. *An Introduction to Chinese History and Culture*. Heidelberg: Springer, p. 196.

29. Whitfield, Susan, 2015. *Life along the Silk Road*. Berkeley, CA: University of California Press, p. 14.

30. Li, Kangying, 2010. *The Ming Maritime Trade Policy in Transition, 1368 to 1567*. Wiesbaden: Harrassowitz Verlag, p. 8.

31. Li, Qingxin, 2006. *The Maritime Silk Road*. Beijing: China Intercontinental Press, p. 40.

32. Ross, E. Denison, 1930. The Orkhon Inscriptions: Being a Translation of Professor Vilhelm Thomsen's Final Danish Rendering. *Bulletin of the School of Oriental Studies*, University of London, vol. 5, no. 4, pp. 864–5, 862.

33. Drew, David, 1999. *The Lost Chronicles of the Maya Kings*. Berkeley, CA: University of California Press, p. 197.

34. Ibid., pp. 285–6.

35. The so-called Leiden Plaque: National Museum of Ethnology, Leiden, inv. no. RV-1403-1193.

36. Cowgill, George L., 1997. State and Society at Teotihuacan, Mexico. *Annual Review of Anthropology*, vol. 26, p. 145.

37. Van Tuerenhout, Dirk, 2002. Maya Warfare: Sources and Interpretations. *Civilisations: Revue internationale d'anthropologie et de sciences humaines*, vol. 50, p. 129–52.

9. THE EARTH BETWEEN HOPE AND CALAMITY

1. Schinz, Alfred, 1996. *The Magic Square: Cities in Ancient China*. Stuttgart: Axel Menges, p. 206.
2. Heck, Gene W., 2006. *Charlemagne, Muhammad, and the Arab Roots of Capitalism*. Berlin: Walter de Gruyter, p. 66.
3. Ibid., p. 67.
4. Al-Sirafi, Abu Zayd, Tim Mackintosh-Smith, trans., 2014. Accounts of China and India. In Tim Mackintosh-Smith and James E. Montgomery, eds. *Two Arabic Travel Books*. New York: New York University Press, p. 87.
5. Heck, Gene W., 2006. Op. cit., pp. 111, 98.
6. Treadgold, Warren, 1988. *The Byzantine Revival, 780–842*. Stanford, CA: Stanford University Press, p. 118.
7. Al-Sirafi, Abu Zayd, Tim Mackintosh-Smith, trans., 2014. Op. cit., p. 51.
8. Lewis, Mark Edward, 2009. *China's Cosmopolitan Empire: The Tang Dynasty*. Cambridge, MA: Belknap Press, p. 158.
9. Al-Sirafi, Abu Zayd, Tim Mackintosh-Smith, trans., 2014. Op. cit., pp. 67, 71.
10. Noble, Thomas F. X., and Thomas Head, eds., 2000. *Soldiers of Christ: Saints and Saints' Lives from Late Antiquity and the Early Middle Ages*. University Park, PA: Pennsylvania State University Press, p. 171.
11. Riché, Pierre, 1978. *Daily Life in the World of Charlemagne*. Philadelphia, PA: University of Pennsylvania Press, p. 17.
12. Wang, Zhenping, 2005. *Ambassadors from the Islands of Immortals: China–Japan Relations in the Han–Tang Period*. Honolulu, HI: University of Hawaii Press, p. 158.
13. Makeham, John, ed., 2008. *China: The World's Oldest Living Civilization Revealed*. London: Thames & Hudson, p. 218.
14. Zhang, Qizhi, 2015. *An Introduction to Chinese History and Culture*. Heidelberg: Springer, pp. 59–60. Anxi was the protectorate established by the Tang in 640 to control the Tarim Basin.
15. Ibid., p. 60.
16. Birch, Cyril, ed., 1965. *Anthology of Chinese Literature*, vol. 1, *From Early Times to the Fourteenth Century*. New York: Grove Press, pp. 240–41.

17. Slobodnik, Martin, 1997. The Early Policy of Emperor Tang Dezong (779–805) towards Inner Asia. *Asian and African Studies*, vol. 6, no. 2, p. 193.

18. Keng, Chen-hua, 2012. The Impact of Tang-Tubo War on the Transformation of Military System and Heqin Politics in Tang Dynasty. *Mongolian and Tibetan Quarterly*, vol. 21, no. 1, p. 20. Rong, Xinjiang, A Study of Yang Liangyao's Embassy to the Abbasid Caliphate. In Victor H. Mair and Liam C. Kelley, eds. *Imperial China and Its Southern Neighbours*. Singapore: ISEAS, p. 245.

19. Wu, Chong, 2007. Drought Blamed for Tang Collapse. *China Daily* (8 January). Fan, Ka-Wai, 2010. Climatic Change and Dynastic Cycles in Chinese History: A Review Essay. *Climatic Change*, vol. 101, no. 3–4, pp. 565–73.

20. Dudbridge, Glen, 2013. *A Portrait of Five Dynasties China: From the Memoirs of Wang Renyu (880–956)*. Oxford: Oxford University Press, p. 156.

21. Mote, F. W., 2003. *Imperial China, 900–1800*. Cambridge, MA: Harvard University Press, p. 46.

22. Lee, Peter H., et al., eds., 1997. *Sources of Korean Tradition*, vol. 1, *From Early Times through the Sixteenth Century*. New York: Columbia University Press, pp. 154, 156.

23. Ibid., p. 172.

24. Bronson, Bennet, and Jan Wisseman, 1976. Palembang as Srivijaya: The Lateness of Early Cities in Southern Southeast Asia. *Asian Perspectives*, vol. 19, no. 2, p. 222.

25. Fatimi, S. Q., 1963. Two Letters from the Maharaja to the Khalifah: A Study in the Early History of Islam in the East. *Islamic Studies*, vol. 2, no. 1, p. 127.

26. Chatterjee, Bijan Raj, and Niranjan Prasad Chakravarti, 1933. *India and Java: Inscriptions*. Calcutta: Greater India Society, p. 43.

27. Bhavabhuti, John Pickford, trans., 1871. *Maha-Vira-Charita: The Adventures of the Great Hero Rama*. London: Trübner & Co., p. 75.

28. Sengupta, Nitish, 2011. *Land of Two Rivers: A History of Bengal from the Mahabharata to Mujib*. New Delhi: Penguin India, p. 40.

29. Ibid.

30. Sharma, Shanta Rami, 2001. Evolution of Deities and Syncretism in Rajasthan, *c.* A.D. 600–1000: The Dynamics and Material Implications. *Indian Historical Review*, vol. 28, p. 20.

31. Kielhorn, F., 1896–7. Khalimpur Plate of Dharmapaladeva. In E. Hultzsch, ed. *Epigraphia Indica*, vol. 4. Calcutta: Office of the Superintendent of Government Printing, India, p. 248.

32. Judd, Steven, 2008. Reinterpreting al-Walid b. Yazid. *Journal of the American Oriental Society*, vol. 128, no. 3, pp. 439–58.

33. Theophilus of Edessa, Robert G. Hoyland, trans., 2011. *Theophilus of Edessa's Chronicle and the Circulation of Historical Knowledge in Late Antiquity and Early Islam.* Liverpool: Liverpool University Press, p. 246.

34. Ibid., p. 253.

35. Ibid., p. 256.

36. Ibid., p. 270.

37. Al-Shaybani, Majid Khadduri, trans., 2001. *The Islamic Law of Nations: Shaybani's Siyar.* Baltimore, MD: Johns Hopkins University Press.

38. Al-Mawardi, Asadullah Yate, trans., 1996. *Al-Akham as-Sultaniyyah: The Laws of Islamic Governance,* London: Ta-Ha, p. 28.

39. Bostom, Andrew G., ed., 2008. *The Legacy of Jihad: Islamic Holy War and the Fate of Non-Muslims.* Amherst, NY: Prometheus, p. 193.

40. Ibid., p. 190.

41. Cooperson, Michael, 2005. *Al-Ma'mun.* London: Oneworld, pp. 40–41.

42. Mahal, Talab Sabbar, 2015. *The Manners, Norms, and Customs (Rusoom) of the House of Governance in the First Age (Era) of the Abbasid Caliphate, 750–865 AD.* New York: Xlibris, p. 94. 'Amir al-Mu'minin', or 'commander of the faithful', was a traditional title adopted by many caliphs.

43. Al-Tabari, C. E. Bosworth, trans., 1989. *The History of al-Tabari*, vol. 30, *The Abbasid Caliphate in Equilibrium.* Albany, NY: State University of New York Press, p. 100.

44. Ibid., p. 116.

45. Ibid., p. 102.

46. Al-Tabari, C. E. Bosworth, trans., 1987. *The History of al-Tabari*, vol. 32, *The Reunification of the Abbasid Caliphate.* Albany, NY: State University of New York Press, pp. 55–6.

47. Waines, David, 1977. The Third Century Internal Crisis of the Abbasids. *Journal of the Economic and Social History of the Orient*, vol. 20, no. 3, p. 285.

48. Al-Tabari, David Waines, trans., 1992. *The History of al-Tabari*, vol. 36, *The Revolt of the Zanj.* Albany, NY: State University of New York Press, p. 132.

49. Shatzmiller, Maya, 1994. *Labour in the Medieval Islamic World.* Leiden: Brill, pp. 56–7. Stansfield, Gareth, 2007. *Iraq: People, History, Politics.* Cambridge: Polity Press, p. 96.

50. Russell, Josiah, 1972. Population in Europe, 500–1500. In Carlo M. Cipolla, ed. *The Fontana Economic History of Europe*, vol. 1, *The Middle Ages.* London: Fontana, pp. 25–70.

51. Rogers, Clifford J., 2014. Carolingian Cavalry in Battle: The Evidence Reconsidered. In Simon John and Nicholas Morton, eds. *Crusading and Warfare in the Middle Ages: Realities and Representations*, Farnham: Ashgate, pp. 1–12.

52. Scholz, Bernhard Walter, and Barbara Rogers, trans., 1970. *Carolingian Chronicles: Royal Frankish Annals and Nithard's Histories*. Ann Arbor, MI: University of Michigan Press.

53. Cave, Roy C., and Herbert H. Coulson, 1936. *A Source Book for Medieval Economic History*. Milwaukee, WI: Bruce Publishing, p. 151.

54. Grant, A. J., ed., 1907. *Early Lives of Charlemagne by Eginhard and the Monk of St. Gall*. London: Chatto and Windus, p. 111.

55. Ibid., p. 113.

56. Ibid., p. 114.

57. Treadgold, Warren, 1997. *A History of the Byzantine State and Society*. Stanford, CA: Stanford University Press, p. 436.

58. Ibn Fadlan, Paul Lunde and Caroline Stone, trans., 2012. *Ibn Fadlan and the Land of Darkness: Arab Travellers in the Far North*. London: Penguin.

59. Nelson, Janet L., trans., 1991. *The Annals of St-Bertin: Ninth-Century Histories*, vol. 1. Manchester: Manchester University Press, p. 50.

60. Robinson, James Harvey, ed., 1904. *Readings in European History*, vol. 1, *From the Breaking up of the Roman Empire to the Protestant Revolt*. Boston, MA: Ginn & Company, p. 159.

61. Nelson, Janet L., trans., 1991. Op. cit., p. 52.

62. Landes, Richard, 2000. The Fear of an Apocalyptic Year 1000: Augustinian Historiography, Medieval and Modern. *Speculum*, vol. 75, no. 1, p. 103.

63. Hung, Hing Ming, 2013. *Li Shi Min, Founding the Tang Dynasty: The Strategies That Made China the Greatest Empire in Asia*. New York: Algora, p. 176.

10. THE MONGOL SHOCKWAVE

1. Deng, Gang, 1997. *Chinese Maritime Activities and Socioeconomic Development, c. 2100 B.C.–1900 A.D*. Westport, CT: Greenwood Press, p. 70.

2. Lo, Jung-Pang, Bruce A. Elleman, ed., 2012. *China as a Sea Power, 1127–1368: A Preliminary Survey of the Maritime Expansion and Naval Exploits of the Chinese People during the Southern Song and Yuan Periods*. Singapore: NUS Press, p. 57. Lo, Jung-Pang, 1955. The Emergence of China as a Sea Power during the Late Sung and Early Yuan Periods. *The Far Eastern Quarterly*, vol. 14, no. 4, pp. 489–503. Hall, Kenneth R., 2011. *A History of Early Southeast Asia: Maritime Trade and Societal Development, 100–1500*. Lanham, MD: Rowman & Littlefield, pp. 331–2. Chenzhen, Shou, 2002. *Tushuo zhongguo haijun shi* [*An Illustrated History of the Chinese Navy*]. Fuzhou: Fujian Education Press, pp. 17–30.

3. Anderson, James, 2007. *The Rebel Den of Nùng Trí Cao: Loyalty and Identity along the Sino-Vietnamese Frontier*. Seattle, WA: University of Washington Press, pp. 88–118.

4. Broadberry, Stephen, et al., 2017. China, Europe and the Great Divergence: A Study in Historical National Accounting, 980–1850. University of Oxford Discussion Papers in Economic and Social History, no. 155. Retrieved from: https://www.economics.ox.ac.uk/materials/working_papers/ . . ./155aprilbroadberry.pdf.

5. Chen, Guanwei, and Chen Shuguo, 2015. State Rituals. In John Lagerwey and Pierre Marsone, eds. *Modern Chinese Religion I: Song-Liao-Jin-Yuan (960–1368 AD)*, vol. 1. Leiden: Brill, p. 152.

6. Wang, Yuan-kang, 2011. *Harmony and War: Confucian Culture and Chinese Power Politics*. New York: Columbia University Press, p. 34.

7. Ibid., pp. 60–61.

8. Ibid., p. 63.

9. Ibid., p. 61.

10. Mote, Frederick W., 2003. *Imperial China, 900–1800*. Cambridge, MA: Harvard University Press, p. 71.

11. Twitchett, Denis, and Klaus-Peter Tietze, 1994. The Liao. In Herbert Franke and Denis Twitchett, eds. *The Cambridge History of China*, vol. 6, *Alien Regimes and Border States, 907–1368*. Cambridge: Cambridge University Press, p. 122.

12. Wang, Yuan-kang, 2011. Op. cit., p. 63.

13. Smith, Paul J., 1991. *Taxing Heaven's Storehouse: Horses, Bureaucrats, and the Destruction of the Sichuan Tea Industry, 1074–1224*. Cambridge, MA: Council on East Asian Studies, Harvard University, p. 16.

14. Manyard, Kevin, 2013. Yuan Haowen's June 12th, 1233 – Crossing North: Three Verses. *Welling out of Silence*, vol. 2, no. 2. Retrieved from: http://poetrychina.net/wp/welling-magazine/yuan-haowen-three-verses.

15. McLaren, Anne, 2011. Challenging Official History in the Song and Yuan Dynasties: The Record of the Three Kingdoms. In Lucille Chia and Hilde de Weerdt, eds. *Knowledge and Text Production in an Age of Print: China, 900–1400*. Leiden: Brill, p. 333.

16. Broadberry, Stephen, et al., 2017. Op. cit., p. 26.

17. Dawson, Christopher, 1980. *Mission to Asia*. Toronto: University of Toronto Press, p. 86.

18. Roger of Apulia, János M. Bak and Martyn Rady, trans., 2010. *Master Roger's Epistle to the Sorrowful Lament upon the Destruction of the Kingdom of Hungary by the Tatars*. Budapest: Central European University Press, pp. 201, 209.

19. Müller-Mertens, Eckhard, 1999. The Ottonians as Kings and Emperors. In Timothy Reuter, ed. *The New Cambridge Medieval History: Volume III, c. 900–c. 1024*, Cambridge: Cambridge University Press, pp. 233–67.

20. Lees, Jay T., 2013. David *Rex Fidelis*? Otto the Great, the *Gesta Ottonis*, and the *Primordia Coenobii Gandeshemensis*. In Phyllis R. Brown and Stephen L. Wailes, eds. *A Companion to Hrotsvit of Gandersheim (fl. 960): Contextual and Interpretive Approaches*. Leiden: Brill, p. 215.

21. Liudprand of Cremona, Paolo Squatriti, trans., 2007. *The Complete Works of Liudprand of Cremona*. Washington, DC: The Catholic University of America Press, p. 219.

22. Ibid., pp. 220–21.

23. Mastnak, Tomaž, 2002. *Crusading Peace: Christendom, the Muslim World, and Western Political Order*. Berkeley, CA: University of California Press, p. 37.

24. Fletcher, Richard, 2003. *The Cross and the Crescent: Christianity and Islam from Muhammad to the Reformation*. London: Allen Lane, p. 123.

25. Coleman, David, 2006. Migration as a Primary Force in Human Population Processes. In Graziella Caselli et al., eds. *Demography: Analysis And Synthesis. A Treatise in Population Studies*. Amsterdam: Elsevier, pp. 34–5.

26. Gieysztor, Aleksander, 1987. Trade and Industry in Eastern Europe before 1200. In M. M. Postan and Edward Miller, eds. *The Cambridge Economic History of Europe*, vol. 2, *Trade and Industry in the Middle Ages*. Cambridge: Cambridge University Press, pp. 485–92.

27. Constantine VII Porphyrogenitus, R. J. H. Jenkins, trans., 1967. *De Administrando Imperio*. Washington, DC: Dumbarton Oaks Center for Byzantine Studies.

28. Comnena, Anna, E. R. A. Sewter, trans., 1969. *The Alexiad*. Harmondsworth: Penguin, p. 157.

29. Choniates, Niketas, Harry J. Magoulias, trans., 1984. O *City of Byzantium: Annals of Niketas Choniates*. Detroit, MI: Wayne State University Press.

30. Poly, Jean-Pierre, 1997. Europe in the Year 1000. In Robert Fossier, ed. *The Cambridge Illustrated History of the Middle Ages: Volume II, 950–1250*. Cambridge: Cambridge University Press, p. 23.

31. Neocleous, Savvas, 2009. Is the Contemporary Latin Historiography of the First Crusade and Its Aftermath 'Anti-Byzantine'? In Savvas Neocleous, ed. *Papers from the First and Second Postgraduate Forums in Byzantine Studies: Sailing to Byzantium*. Newcastle: Cambridge Scholars Publishing, pp. 32–50.

32. Peacock, A. C. S., 2015. *The Great Seljuk Empire*. Edinburgh: Edinburgh University Press, p. 46.

33. Ibid., p. 33.

34. Korobeinikov, Dimitri, 2013. 'The King of the East and the West': The Seljuk Dynastic Concept and Titles in the Muslim and Christian Sources. In A. C. S. Peacock and Sara Nur Yildiz, eds. *The Seljuks of Anatolia: Court and Society in the Medieval Middle East*. London: I.B. Tauris, p. 73.

35. Canard, Marius, 1947. L'impérialisme des Fatimides et leur propaganda. *Annales de l'institute d'études orientales*, vol. 6, pp. 180–86.

36. Black, Antony, 2011. *The History of Islamic Political Thought: From the Prophet to the Present*. Edinburgh: Edinburgh University Press, p. 46.

37. Peacock, A. C. S., 2015. Op. cit., p. 61.

38. Ibid., p. 72.

39. Karsh, Efraim, 2006. *Islamic Imperialism: A History*. New Haven, CT: Yale University Press, p. 73.

40. Meenakshisundararajan, A., 2009. Rajendra Chola's Naval Expedition and the Chola Trade with Southeast and East Asia. In Hermann Kulke et al., eds. *Nagapattinam to Suvarnadwipa: Reflections on the Chola Naval Expeditions to Southeast Asia*. Singapore: ISEAS, pp. 174–5.

41. Bilhana, Georg Bühler, ed., 1875. *The Vikramankadevacharita: A Life of King Vikramaditya-Tribhuvanamalla of Kalyana Composed by his Vidyapati Bilhana*. Bombay: Government Central Book Depôt, p. 12.

42. Kahlana, Jogesh Chunda Dutt, trans., 1887. *Kings of Kashmira: Being a Translation of the Sanskrita Work Rajatarangini of Kahlana Pandita*, vol. 2. Calcutta: J. C. Dutt, p. 17.

43. Ibid., pp. 9, 12, 15.

44. Spencer, George W., 1976. The Politics of Plunder: The Cholas in Eleventh-Century Ceylon. *Journal of Asian Studies*, vol. 35, no. 3, pp. 405–19.

45. Lo, Jung-Pang, Bruce A. Elleman, ed., 2012. Op. cit., p. 11.

46. Bilhana, Georg Bühler, trans., 1875. Op. cit., p. 15.

47. Ibid., p. 44.

48. Wink, André, 1997. *Al-Hind: The Making of the Indo-Islamic World*, vol. 2, *The Slave Kings and the Islamic Conquest, 11th–13th Centuries*. Leiden: Brill, p. 146.

49. Nizami, K. A., 1998. The Ghurids. In M. S. Asimov and C. E. Bosworth, eds. *History of Civilizations of Central Asia*, vol. 4, part 1, *The Age of Achievement, A.D. 750 to the End of the Fifteenth Century: The Historical, Social and Economic Setting*. Paris: UNESCO, p. 188.

50. Hirth, F., 1885. *China and the Roman Orient: Researches into Their Ancient and Mediaeval Relations as Represented in Old Chinese Records*. Leipzig: Georg Hirth, p. 62.

51. Robinson, I. S., ed., 2004. *The Papal Reform of the Eleventh Century: Lives of Pope Leo IX and Pope Gregory VII*. Manchester: Manchester University Press, pp. 8, 11.

52. Thatcher, Oliver J., and Edgar H. McNeal, eds., 1905. *A Source Book for Mediaeval History: Selected Documents Illustrating the History of Europe in the Middle Age.* New York: Charles Scribner's Sons, p. 516.

53. Joinville and Villehardouin, Caroline Smith, trans., 2008. *Chronicles of the Crusades.* London: Penguin, p. 10.

54. Martin, M. E., 1980. The Venetian-Seljuk Treaty of 1220. *English Historical Review.* vol. 95, no. 375, pp. 321–30.

55. Jackson, Peter, 2005. *The Mongols and the West, 1221–1410.* Harlow: Longman, p. 131.

56. Dawson, Christopher, 1980. Op. cit., p. 76.

57. Lamouroux, Christian, 1997. Geography and Politics: The Song-Liao Border Dispute of 1074/75. In Sabine Dabringhaus and Roderich Ptak, eds. *China and Her Neighbours.* Wiesbaden: Harrassowitz Verlag, pp. 1–28.

58. Chang, Yachin, 1975. Chenkuo yu Song Liao hua jie jiaoshi [Shen Kua and the Border Negotiations between Sung and Liao]. *Shihi*, vol. 12, pp. 10–25.

59. Fenby, Jonathan, 2015. *The Dragon Throne: China's Emperors from the Qin to the Manchu.* London: Quercus, p. 167.

60. Liu, Shi-Yee, 2010. Epitome of National Disgrace: A Painting Illuminating Song-Jin Diplomatic Relations. *Metropolitan Museum Journal*, vol. 45, pp. 55–82.

11. HUDDLING IN THE DARKNESS

1. Panofsky, Erwin, 1960. *Renaissance and Renascences in Western Art*, vol. 1. Stockholm: Almqvist & Wiksell, p. 10.

2. Qian, Weihong, and Yafen Zhu, 2002. Little Ice Age Climate near Beijing, China, Inferred from Historical and Stalagmite Records. *Quaternary Research*, vol. 57, no. 1, pp. 109–19. Sussman, George D., 2011. Was the Black Death in India and China? *Bulletin of the History of Medicine*, vol. 85, no. 3, pp. 319–55.

3. Topsfield, L. T., 1975. *Troubadours and Love.* Cambridge: Cambridge University Press, p. 251.

4. McGrade, Arthur Stephen, et al., eds., 2001. *The Cambridge Translations of Medieval Philosophical Texts*, vol. 2, *Ethics and Political Philosophy*. Cambridge: Cambridge University Press, p. 331.

5. Jarrett, Bede, 1968. *Social Theories in the Middle Ages, 1200–1500.* London: Frank Cass, p. 185.

6. Mattingly, Garrett, 1955. *Renaissance Diplomacy.* Boston, MA: Houghton Mifflin, p. 42.

7. Commynes, Philippe de, 1817. *The Historical Memoirs of Philip de Comines*. London: J. Davis, pp. 54–5.

8. Boone, Rebecca Ard, 2007. *War, Domination, and the 'Monarchy of France': Claude de Seyssel and the Language of Politics in the Renaissance*. Leiden: Brill, p. 53.

9. Der Derian, James, 1987. *On Diplomacy: A Genealogy of Western Estrangement*. Oxford: Blackwell, p. 2.

10. Modelski, George, and Sylvia Modelski, eds., 1998. *Documenting Global Leadership*. Basingstoke: Macmillan, pp. 27, 20–21.

11. Fubini, Riccardo, 1996. The Italian League and the Policy of the Balance of Power at the Accession of Lorenzo de' Medici. In Julius Kirshner, ed. *The Origins of the State in Italy, 1300–1600*. Chicago, IL: University of Chicago Press, p. 195.

12. Commynes, Philippe de, 1817. Op. cit., p. 222.

13. Gieyztor, Aleksander, 1998. The Kingdom of Poland and the Grand Duchy of Lithuania, 1370–1506. In Christopher Allmand, ed. *The New Cambridge Medieval History: Volume VII, c. 1415–c. 1500*. Cambridge: Cambridge University Press, p. 728.

14. Babinger, Franz, 1978. *Mehmed the Conqueror and His Time*. Princeton, NJ: Princeton University Press, p. 235.

15. Kiss, Tamás, 2016. Cyprus in Ottoman and Venetian Political Imagination, c. 1489–1582. Unpublished PhD dissertation, Central European University, p. 155. Retrieved from: www.etd.ceu.hu/2016/kiss_tamas.pdf.

16. Setton, Kenneth M., 1978. *The Papacy and the Levant (1204–1571)*, vol. 2. Philadelphia, PA: The American Philosophical Society, p. 301.

17. Kritovulus, Charles T. Riggs, trans., 1970. *History of Mehmed the Conqueror*. Westport, CT: Greenwood Press, p. 185.

18. Guilmartin, John Francis, 2003. *Gunpowder and Galleys: Changing Technology and Mediterranean Warfare at Sea in the Sixteenth Century*. London: Conway Maritime, pp. 102–4.

19. Gosh, Pika, 2005. *Temple to Love: Architecture and Devotion in Seventeenth-Century Bengal*. Bloomington, IN: India University Press, p. 86.

20. Roy, Kaushik, 2015. *Warfare in Pre-British India, 1500 BCE to 1740 CE*. Abingdon: Routledge.

21. Sewell, Robert, 1900. *A Forgotten Empire (Vijayanagar): A Contribution to the History of India*. London: Swan Sonnenschein & Co., p. 88.

22. Ibid., p. 82.

23. Wagoner, Phillip B., 1996. 'Sultan among Hindu Kings': Dress, Titles, and the Islamicization of Hindu Culture at Vijayanagara. *Journal of Asian Studies*, vol. 55, no. 4, pp. 851–80.

24. Verma, H. N., and Amrit Verma, 1992. *100 Great Indians through the Ages*. Campbell, CA: GIP Books, p. 163.

25. Stein, Burton, 1982. Vijayanagara, *c.* 1350–1564. In Tapan Raychaudhuri and Irfan Habib, eds. *The Cambridge Economic History of India: Volume 1, c. 1200–c. 1750*. Cambridge: Cambridge University Press, pp. 117–18.

26. Anon., 2009. *Great Monuments of India*. London: Dorling Kindersley, p. 133.

27. Stein, Burton, 1982. Op. cit., p. 117.

28. Langlois, John D., Jr, 1981. Introduction. In John Langlois ed. *China under Mongol Rule*. Princeton, NJ: Princeton University Press, pp. 3–4.

29. Rossabi, Morris, 1994. The Reign of Khublai Khan. In Herbert Franke and Denis Twichett, eds. *The Cambridge History of China*, vol. 6, *Alien Regimes and Border States, 907–1368*. Cambridge: Cambridge University Press, pp. 455, 457.

30. McCausland, Shane, 2011. *Zhao Mengfu: Calligraphy and Painting for Khubilai's China*. Hong Kong: Hong Kong University Press, pp. 287–8.

31. Schurmann, Herbert Franz, 1956. *Economic Structure of the Yüan Dynasty: Translation of Chapters 93 and 94 of the Yuan Shih*. Cambridge, MA: Harvard University Press, pp. 325–30.

32. Levathes, Louise, 1996. *When China Ruled the Seas: The Treasure Fleet of the Dragon Throne, 1405–1433*. New York: Oxford University Press, p. 88.

33. Tsai, Shih-shan Henry, 1996. *The Eunuchs in the Ming Dynasty*. New York: State University of New York Press, p. 142.

34. Hybel, Alex Roberto, 2010. *The Power of Ideology: From the Roman Empire to Al-Qaeda*. Abingdon: Routledge, p. 39.

35. Levathes, Louise, 1996. Op. cit., p. 169.

36. Li, Kangying, 2010. *The Ming Maritime Trade Policy in Transition, 1368 to 1567*. Wiesbaden: Harrassowitz Verlag. Levathes, Louise, 1996. Op. cit.

37. Ebrey, Patricia, and Anne Walthall, 2006. *Pre-Modern East Asia to 1800: A Cultural, Social, and Political History*. Boston, MA: Wadsworth, p. 257.

38. McCullough, Helen Craig, trans., 1959. *The Taiheiki: A Chronicle of Medieval Japan*. New York: Columbia University Press, p. 214.

39. Rawski, Evelyn S., 2015. *Early Modern China and Northeast Asia: Cross-Border Perspectives*. Cambridge: Cambridge University Press, p. 211–12.

40. Dombrowski, Franz Amadeus, 1985. *Ethiopia's Access to the Sea*. Leiden: E. J. Brill, p. 14.

41. Roland, Oliver, and Anthony Atmore, 2001. *Medieval Africa, 1250–1800*. Cambridge: Cambridge University Press, p. 199.

42. Dunn, Ross E., 2005. *The Adventures of Ibn Battuta: A Muslim Traveler of the 14th Century*. Berkeley, CA: University of California Press, p. 127.

43. Mlambo, Alois S., 2014. *A History of Zimbabwe*. Cambridge: Cambridge University, pp. 22–3. Marks, Shula, and Richard Gray, 1975. Southern Africa and Madagascar. In Richard Gray, ed. *The Cambridge History of Africa: Volume 4, from c. 1600 to c. 1790*. Cambridge: Cambridge University Press, pp. 385–93.

44. Roland, Oliver, and Anthony Atmore, 2001. Op. cit., p. 141.

45. Maret, Pierre de, 2013. Recent Farming Communities and States in the Congo Basin and its Environs. In Peter Mitchell and Paul Lane, eds. *The Oxford Handbook of African Archaeology*. Oxford: Oxford University Press, p. 876–8.

46. Levtzion, Nehemia, 1977. The Western Maghrib and Sudan. In Roland Oliver, ed., *The Cambridge History of Africa: Volume 3, from c. 1050 to c. 1600*. Cambridge: Cambridge University Press, p. 421.

47. McEwan, Gordon F., 2006. *The Incas: New Perspectives*. Santa Barbara, CA: ABC-Clio, pp. 95–6.

48. Bierhorst, John, 2011. Translating an Esoteric Idiom: The Case of Aztec Poetry. In Brian Swann, ed. *Born in the Blood: On Native American Translation*. Lincoln, NE: University of Nebraska Press, p. 383. 'Blaze' was an Aztec poetic idiom for 'battle'.

49. Covey, R. Alan, 2006. *How the Incas Built Their Heartland: State Formation and the Innovation of Imperial Strategies in the Sacred Valley, Peru*. Ann Arbor, MI: University of Michigan Press, p. 169.

50. Rostworowski de Diez Canseco, María, 1999. *History of the Inca Realm*. Cambridge: Cambridge University Press, p. 41.

51. Vega, Garcilasso de la, Clements R. Markham, trans., 1869. *First Part of the Royal Commentaries of the Yncas*, vol. 1. London: Hakluyt Society, p. 90.

52. Bauer, Brian S., 1992. *The Development of the Inca State*. Austin, TX: University of Texas Press.

12. A NEW AGE OF ISLAMIC CONQUEST

1. Broadberry, Stephen, 2016. The Great Divergence in the World Economy: Long-Run Trends of Real Income. In Joerg Baten, ed. *A History of the Global Economy: From 1500 to the Present*. Cambridge: Cambridge University Press, p. 37. Allen, Robert C., 2001. The Great Divergence in European Wages and Prices from the Middle Ages to the First World War. *Explorations in Economic History*, vol. 38, no. 4, pp. 411–47. De Vries, Jan, 1984. *European Urbanization, 1500–1800*. London: Methuen.

2. Palabiyik, Mustafa Serdar, 2012. The Changing Ottoman Perception of War: From the Foundation of the Empire to Its Disintegration. In Avery Plaw, ed. *The Metamorphosis of War*. Amsterdam: Rodopi, p. 130.

3. Bostan, Idris, 2007. *Ottoman Maritime Arsenals and Shipbuilding Technology in the 16th and 17th Centuries*. Manchester: Foundation for Science, Technology and Civilization, p. 3. Retrieved from: http://www.muslimheritage.com/article/ottoman-maritime-arsenals-and-shipbuilding-technology-16th-and-17th-centuries.

4. Forster, Edward Seymour, trans., 2005. *The Turkish Letters of Ogier Ghiselin de Busbecq, Imperial Ambassador at Constantinople, 1554–1562*. Baton Rouge, LA: Louisiana State University Press.

5. Faroqhi, Suraiya, 2014. *Travel and Artisans in the Ottoman Empire: Employment and Mobility in the Early Modern Period*. London: I.B. Tauris, pp. 129–42. Zilfi, Madeline C., 2010. *Women and Slavery in the Late Ottoman Empire: The Design of Difference*. New York: Cambridge University Press.

6. Braudel, Fernand, 1995. *The Mediterranean and the Mediterranean World in the Age of Philip II*, vol. 2. Berkeley, CA: University of California Press, p. 882.

7. Berument, Hakan, and Asli Günay, 2004. Inflation Dynamics and Its Sources in the Ottoman Empire, 1586–1913. Turkish Economic Association Discussion Paper 2004/3. Retrieved from: https://ideas.repec.org/p/tek/wpaper/2004-3.html.

8. Savory, Roger, 1980. *Iran under the Safavids*. Cambridge: Cambridge University Press, p. 29. Twelver Shiites believe that Allah concealed the twelfth and last of the imams – the spiritual and political leaders who were divinely ordained successors of the Prophet Muhammad – who would then emerge as the Mahdi to liberate the world on the Day of Judgment.

9. Dale, Stephen F., 2010. *The Muslim Empires of the Ottomans, Safavids, and Mughals*. New York: Cambridge University Press, p. 78.

10. Savory, Roger, 1980. Op. cit., pp. 2–3, 33.

11. Rayfield, Donald, 2016. The Greatest King among Poets, the Greatest Poet among Kings. In Hans-Christian Günther, ed. *Political Poetry across the Centuries*. Leiden: Brill, p. 55.

12. Mitchell, Colin P., 2009. *The Practice of Politics in Safavid Iran: Power, Religion and Rhetoric*. London: I.B. Tauris, pp. 94, 89.

13. Nicoll, Fergus, 2009. *Shah Jahan*. New Delhi: Penguin, p. 168.

14. Chick, H., trans., 2012. *A Chronicle of the Carmelites in Persia: The Safavids and the Papal Mission of the 17th and 18th Centuries*, vol. 1. London: I.B. Tauris, p. 74.

15. Eskander Beg Monshi, Roger M. Savory, trans., 1978. *History of Shah Abbas the Great*. Boulder, CO: Westview Press.

16. Abul Fazl-i-Allami, H. S. Jarrett, trans., 1894. *The Ain I Akbari*, vol. 3. Calcutta: Asiatic Society of Bengal, p. 382.

17. Ibid., pp. 235–43.

18. Ibid., p. 399.

19. Major, Andrea, 2012. *Slavery, Abolitionism and Empire in India, 1772–1843*. Liverpool: Liverpool University Press, pp. 26–7.

20. Edwardes, S. M., and H. L. O. Garrett, 1995. *Mughal Rule in India*. New Delhi: Atlantic Publishers, p. 265.

21. MacDougall, Philip, 2014. *Naval Resistance to Britain's Growing Power in India, 1660–1800: The Saffron Banner and the Tiger of Mysore*. Woodbridge: Boydell Press, p. 30.

22. Dalrymple, William, 2016. The Beautiful, Magical World of Rajput Art. *New York Review of Books* (24 November).

23. Ibid.

24. Swope, Kenneth M, 2015. Bringing in the Big Guns: On the Use of Artillery in the Ming–Manchu War. In Kaushik Roy and Peter Lorge, eds. *Chinese and Indian Warfare: From the Classical Age to 1870*. Abingdon: Routledge. p. 136.

25. Dardess, John W., 1972. The Late Ming Rebellions: Peasants and Problems of Interpretation. *Journal of Interdisciplinary History*, vol. 3, no. 1, pp. 103–17.

26. Meng, Huiying, 2011. Characteristics of Shamanism of the Tungusic Speaking People. In Xisha Ma and Huiying Meng, eds. *Popular Religion and Shamanism*. Leiden: Brill, p. 402.

27. Ibid., p. 405.

28. Swope, Kenneth M., 2014. *The Military Collapse of China's Ming Dynasty, 1618–44*. Abingdon: Routledge, pp. 214–15.

29. Wakeman, Frederic, Jr, 1986. *The Great Enterprise: The Manchu Reconstruction of Imperial Order in Seventeenth-Century China*. Berkeley, CA: University of California Press, pp. 175–225.

30. Meng, Huiying, 2011. Op. cit., p. 405.

31. Schottenhammer, Angela, 2010. Characteristics of Qing China's Maritime Trade Policies, *Shunzi* through *Qianlong* Reigns. In Angela Schottenhammer, ed. *Trading Networks in Early Modern East Asia*. Wiesbaden: Harrassowitz Verlag, p. 111.

32. Liu, Xiaoyuan, 2004. *Frontier Passages: Ethnopolitics and the Rise of Chinese Communism, 1921–1945*. Washington, DC: Woodrow Wilson Center Press, p. 16.

33. Johnston, Alastair Iain, 1995. *Cultural Realism: Strategic Culture and Grand Strategy in Chinese History*. Princeton, NJ: Princeton University Press, pp. 217–30.

34. Giersch, C. Patterson, 2006. *Asian Borderlands: The Transformation of Qing China's Yunnan Frontier*. Cambridge, MA: Harvard University Press, pp. 49–50.

35. Geary, D. Norman, et al., 2003. *The Kam People of China: Turning Nineteen*. London: RoutledgeCurzon, p. 13.

36. Li, Guo-rong, 2009. Archives of the Qing Dynasty: Emperor Yongzheng and Taiwan. Paper Presented at the First International Symposium Organized by the Palace Museums across the Strait: The Complexities and Challenges of Rulership – Emperor Yongzheng and His Accomplishments in Time (Taipei, 4–6 November).

37. Dening, Walter, 1904. *A New Life of Toyotomi Hideyoshi*. Tokyo: Kyōbun-Kwan, p. 320.

38. Toby, Ronald P., 1984. *State and Diplomacy in Early Modern Japan: Asia in the Development of the Tokugawa Bakufu*. Princeton, NJ: Princeton University Press, p. 11.

39. Engerman, Stanley L., and João César das Neves, 1997. The Bricks of an Empire, 1415–1999: 585 Years of Portuguese Emigration. *Journal of European Economic History*, vol. 26, no. 3, pp. 471–509.

40. Roy, Kaushik, 2011. *War, Culture and Society in Early Modern South Asia, 1740–1849*. Abingdon: Routledge, p. 29. Rowe, William, T., 2009. *China's Last Empire: The Great Qing*. Cambridge, MA: Belknap Press, p. 91.

41. Spufford, Margaret, 1995. Literacy, Trade and Religion in the Commercial Centres of Europe. In Karel Davids and Jan Lucassen, eds. *A Miracle Mirrored: The Dutch Republic in European Perspective*, p. 238.

42. On climate change, see: Zhang, David D., et al., 2011. The Causality Analysis of Climate Change and Large-Scale Human Crisis. PNAS, vol. 108, no. 42, pp. 17296–17301.

43. Vollerthun, Ursula, 2017. *The Idea of International Society: Erasmus, Vitoria, Gentili and Grotius*. Cambridge: Cambridge University Press, p. 44.

44. More, Thomas, Robert M. Adams, trans., 2016. *Utopia*. Cambridge: Cambridge University Press, p. 14.

45. Lamster, Mark, 2010. *Master of Shadows: The Secret Diplomatic Career of the Painter Peter Paul Rubens*. New York: Anchor, p. 169.

46. Moratiel Villa, Sergio, 1997. The Philosophy of International Law: Suárez, Grotius and Epigones. *International Review of the Red Cross*, vol. 37, no. 320, pp. 539–52.

47. Walton, Izaak, 1858. *Walton's Lives of Dr. John Donne, Sir Henry Wotton, Mr. Richard Hooker, Mr. George Herbert, and Dr. Robert Sanderson*. London: Henry Washbourne and Co., p. 134.

48. Craig, Gordon A., and Alexander L. George, 1990. *Force and Statecraft: Diplomatic Problems of Our Time*. Oxford: Oxford University Press, p. 13.

49. Wicquefort, Abraham de, trans. John Digby, 1716. *The Embassador and His Functions*. London: B. Lintott, p. 294.

50. Cailes, Michael John, 2012. Renaissance Ideas of Peace and War and the Humanist Challenge to the Scholastic Just War. Unpublished PhD dissertation, University of Exeter, p. 87. Retrieved from: https://ore.exeter.ac.uk/repository/handle/10036/3683.

51. Küng, Hans, 1998. *A Global Ethic for Global Politics and Economics*. New York: Oxford University Press, p. 17.

52. Schröder, Peter, 2017. *Trust in Early Modern International Political Thought, 1598–1713*. Cambridge: Cambridge University Press, p. 62.

53. Corzo, Teresa, et al., 2014. Behavioral Finance in Joseph de la Vega's Confusion de Confusiones. *Journal of Behavioral Finance*, vol. 15, no. 4, p. 342.

54. Pocock, J. G. A., 2016. *The Machiavellian Moment: Florentine Political Thought and the Atlantic Republican Tradition*. Princeton, NJ: Princeton University Press, p. 438.

55. Beer, George Louis, 1908. *The Origins of the British Colonial System, 1578–1660*. New York: Macmillan, p. 8.

56. Wilson, George W., ed., 1964. *Classics of Economic Theory*. Bloomington, IN: Indiana University Press, p. 19.

57. Coleman, David, 2000. Spain. In Andrew Pettegree, ed. *The Reformation World*. London: Routledge, p. 296.

58. Knecht, R. J., 1982. *Francis I*. Cambridge: Cambridge University Press.

59. Zwierlein, Cornel, 2014. The Thirty Years' War – A Religious War? Religion and Machiavellism at the Turning Point of 1635. In Olaf Asbach and Peter Schröder, eds. *The Ashgate Research Companion to the Thirty Years' War*. Farnham: Ashgate, p. 237.

60. Riasanovsky, Nicholas V., 2005. *Russian Identities: A Historical Survey*. New York: Oxford University Press, p. 82.

61. Clark, Christopher, 2006. *Iron Kingdom: The Rise and Downfall of Prussia, 1600–1947*. London: Allen Lane, p. 48.

62. Macartney, C. A., ed., 1970. *The Habsburg and Hohenzollern Dynasties in the Seventeenth and Eighteenth Centuries*. London: Macmillan, p. 311.

63. Lamster, Mark, 2010. Op. cit., p. 137.

---

13. THE PRIMACY OF THE WEST

1. European populations in millions: Germany: 55; British Isles: 50; Austrian Empire: 47; France: 41; Italy: 34; Spain: 22; Scandinavia: 12; Netherlands 7.5; Belgium: 7; Portugal: 5. Source: McEvedy, Colin, and Richard Jones,

1978. *Atlas of World Population History.* New York: Facts on File. Colonial populations in millions: Britain: 309; France: 56; Netherlands: 29; Spain: 8.4; Belgium: 8; Portugal: 6.3; Italy: 5.4; Germany: 3.3. Source: Engerman, Stanley L., and Kenneth L. Sokoloff, 2013. Five Hundred Years of European Colonization: Inequality and Paths of Development. In Christopher Lloyd et al., eds. *Settler Economies in World History.* Leiden: Brill, pp. 70–77.

2. Dickens, Charles, 1859. *A Tale of Two Cities.* London: Chapman and Hall, p. 1.

3. Agnus Maddison's estimates in 1990 International Geary-Khamis dollars: $566 in 1500, $666 in 1820, and $6,038 in 2000. Bradford De Long's estimates in 1990 international dollars: $138 in 1500, $195 in 1800, and $6,539 in 2000. Sources: Maddison, Angus, 2010. Historical Statistics of the World Economy, 1–2008 AD, table 1. Retrieved from: www.ggdc. net/maddison/historical_statistics/horizontal-file_02-2010.xls. De Long, J. Bradford., 1998. Estimating World GDP: One Million B.C.–Present. Retrieved from: https://delong.typepad.com/print/20061012_LRWGDP.pdf.

4. Cooper, Robert, 2004. *The Breaking of Nations: Order and Chaos in the Twenty-First Century.* London: Atlantic Books, p. 78.

5. In 1800, the world population stood at around 900 million, of which at least 300 million were inhabitants of Qing China. Rowe, William, T., 2009. *China's Last Empire: The Great Qing.* Cambridge, MA: Belknap Press, p. 91.

6. Perdue, Peter C., 2005. *China Marches West: The Qing Conquest of Central Eurasia.* Cambridge, MA: Belknap Press, p. 501.

7. Millward, James A., 1998. *Beyond the Pass: Economy, Ethnicity, and Empire in Qing Central Asia, 1759–1864.* Stanford, CA: Stanford University Press, p. 38.

8. Waley-Cohen, Joanna, 2006. *The Culture of War in China: Empire and Military under the Qing Dynasty.* London: I.B. Tauris, p. 19.

9. Peyrefitte, Alain, 1989. *L'empire immobile, ou le choc des mondes.* Paris: Fayard.

10. Backhouse, E., and J. O. P. Bland, 1914. *Annals and Memoirs of the Court of Peking: From the 16th to the 20th Century.* Boston, MA: Houghton Mifflin, pp. 326, 331.

11. Yü, Ying-shih, 2016. *Chinese History and Culture*, vol. 2, *Seventeenth Century through Twentieth Century.* New York: Columbia University Press, p. 157.

12. With this interpretation Rousseau built on Abbé de Saint-Pierre's 'Plan for Perpetual Peace'. See: Spector, Céline, 2008. Le Projet de paix perpétuelle: De Saint-Pierre à Rousseau. In Rousseau, Jean-Jacques, B. Bachofen and C. Spector, eds. *Principes du droit de la guerre: Écrits sur la paix perpétuelle.* Paris: J. Vrin, pp. 229–94.

13. Smith, Adam, 1776. *An Inquiry into the Nature and Causes of the Wealth of Nations*, vol. 2. London: W. Strahan and T. Cadell, p. 84.

14. Anon., 1785. *A Collection of All the Treaties of Peace, Alliance, and Commerce, between Great-Britain and Other Powers: From the Treaty Signed at Munster in 1648 to the Treaties Signed at Paris in 1783*, vol. 3. London: J. Debrett, p. 179.

15. Anon., 1785. Op. cit., vol. 2, p. 5.

16. Paine, Thomas, Moncure Daniel Conway, ed., 1894. The Writings of Thomas Paine, vol. 1. New York: G. P. Putnam's Sons, p. 170.

17. Harris, James Howard, third Earl of Malmesbury, ed., 1844. *Diaries and Correspondence of James Harris, 1st Earl of Malmesbury*, vol. 3. London: Richard Bentley, p. 353.

18. Wulf, Andrea, 2015. *The Invention of Nature. The Adventures of Alexander von Humboldt, the Lost Hero of Science*. London: Hodder & Stoughton, p. 44.

19. Pitt, William, R. Coupland, ed., 1915. *The War Speeches of William Pitt the Younger*. Oxford: Clarendon Press, pp. xi–xii.

20. O'Meara, Barry E., 1822. *Napoleon in Exile; or, A Voice from St. Helena: The Opinions and Reflections of Napoleon on the Most Important Events of His Own Life and Government, in His Own Words*, vol. 1. London: W. Simpkin and R. Marshall, p. 263. Anon., 1817. *Manuscript Transmitted from St. Helena, by an Unknown Channel*. London: John Murray, p. 45.

21. Thiers, M. A., D. Forbes Campbell, trans., 1845. *History of the Consulate and the Empire of France under Napoleon*, vol. 4. London: Henry Colburn, p. 157.

22. Nicassio, Susan Vandiver, 2009. *Imperial City: Rome under Napoleon*. Chicago, IL: University of Chicago Press, p. 31.

23. Walter, Jakob, Marc Raeff, ed., 1991. *The Diary of a Napoleonic Foot Soldier*. New York: Doubleday.

24. Zamoyski, Adam, 2007. *Rites of Peace: The Fall of Napoleon and the Congress of Vienna*. London: HarperPress, p. 221.

25. Nicolson, Harold, 1946. *The Congress of Vienna: A Study in Allied Unity, 1812–1822*. London: Constable, p. 292.

26. Zamoyski, Adam, 2007. Op. cit., p. 250.

27. Ibid., p. 265.

28. Steinberg, Jonathan, 2011. *Bismarck: A Life*. Oxford: Oxford University Press, pp. 180–81.

29. Taylor, A. J. P., 1967. *Bismarck*. New York: Vintage, p. 264.

30. Bismarck, Otto von, A. J. Butler, trans., 1898. *Bismarck, the Man and the Statesman: Being the Reflections and Reminiscences of Otto Prince von Bismarck*, vol. 2. London: Smith, Elder &. Co., p. 289.

31. Blattman, Christopher, et al., 2002. Who Protected and Why? Tariffs the World Around, 1870–1938. Paper presented to the Conference on the Political Economy of Globalization, Trinity College, Dublin. Retrieved from: https://pdfs.semanticscholar.org/50d9/32085c399cf4913423846d54b69 off01d186.pdf.

32. Hobson, J. A., 1902. *Imperialism: A Study.* London: James Nisbet & Co., p. 85.

33. Wilde, Oscar, 2000. *The Collected Poems of Oscar Wilde.* Ware: Wordsworth Editions, p. 5.

34. Bülow, Bernhard von, Richard Hacken, trans., 2010. Hammer and Anvil Speech before the Reichstag, December 11, 1899. In Richard Hacken, ed. *World War I Document Archive.* Retrieved from: http://net.lib.byu.edu/estu/ wwi/1914m/buloweng.html.bak.

35. Mahan, A. T., 1918. *The Interest of America in Sea Power, Present and Future.* Boston: Little, Brown and Company, p. 4.

36. In fact, Italy initially remained neutral when the First World War broke out, before joining on the side of Britain, France, and Russia in 1915. Germany, however, was able to use its immense loans and investments in infrastructure to entice the Ottoman Empire into an alliance, which was signed at the beginning of August 1914.

37. Wells, H. G., 1914. *The Peace of the World.* London: *The Daily Chronicle*, p. 9.

38. Rieth, John K., 2014. *Imperial Germany's 'Iron Regiment' of the First World War: War Memories of Service with Infantry Regiment 169, 1914–1918.* Canal Winchester, OH: Badgley Publishing, pp. 101, 100.

39. Pradt, M. de, 1816. *The Congress of Vienna.* London: Samuel Leigh, p. 21.

40. Burritt, Elihu, 1854. *Thoughts and Things at Home and Abroad.* Boston, MA: Phillips, Sampson, and Company, pp. 329–33.

41. Briggs, Asa, and Peter Burke, 2009. *A Social History of the Media: From Gutenberg to the Internet.* Cambridge: Polity Press, p. 133.

42. Cobden, Richard, 1867. *The Political Writings of Richard Cobden*, vol. 1. London: William Ridgway, p. 264.

43. Lechner, Frank J., and John Boli, eds., 2015. *The Globalization Reader.* Chichester: Wiley Blackwell, p. 18.

44. Mazzini, Giuseppe, 1847. *Address of the Council of the Peoples' International League.* London: Palmer and Clayton, p. 12.

45. Tolstoy, Leo, Louise and Aylmer Maude, trans., 1907. *The Russian Revolution.* Christchurch: The Free Age Press, p. 1.

46. Ibid., p. 31.

47. Kessler, Harry, Laird Easton trans., 2011. *Journey to the Abyss: The Diaries of Count Harry Kessler, 1880–1918.* New York: Alfred A. Knopf, p. 867.

48. Easton, Laird McLeod, 2002. *The Red Count: The Life and Times of Harry Kessler*. Berkeley, CA: University of California Press, p. 221.

49. Kennedy, Paul, 1987. *The Rise and Fall of the Great Powers: Economic Change and Military Conflict from 1500 to 2000*. New York: Random House, p. 208.

50. Asada, Sadao, 2007. *Culture Shock and Japanese–American Relations: Historical Essays*. Columbia, MO: University of Missouri Press, p. 107.

51. Powaski, Ronald E., 1991. *Toward an Entangling Alliance: American Isolationism, Internationalism, and Europe, 1901–1950*. Westport, CT: Greenwood Press, p. xvi.

52. Richardson, James D., ed., 1896. *A Compilation of the Messages and Papers of the Presidents, 1789–1897*, vol. 2. Washington, DC: Government Printing Office, p. 218.

53. Randolph, Thomas Jefferson, ed., 1829. *Memoir, Correspondence, and Miscellanies, from the Papers of Thomas Jefferson*, vol. 4. Charlottesville, VA: F. Carr and Co., p. 282.

54. Mallory, Daniel, ed., 1844. *the Life and Speeches of the Hon. Henry Clay*, vol. 1. New York: Robert P. Bixby & Co., p. 17.

55. Baker, Ray Stannard, 1923. *Woodrow Wilson and World Settlement: Written from His Unpublished and Personal Material*, vol. 1. London: William Heinemann, p. 19. Striner, Richard, 2014. *Woodrow Wilson and World War I: A Burden Too Great to Bear*. Lanham, MD: Rowman & Littlefield, p. 113.

56. Baker, Ray Stannard, 1923. Op. cit., p. 112.

57. Humes, James C., 2016. *Presidents and Their Pens: The Story of White House Speechwriters*. Lanham, MD: Hamilton Books, p. 48.

58. Ishimaru, Tota, 1936. *Japan Must Fight Britain*. London: Hurst & Blackett, p. 161.

59. Keynes, John Maynard, 1919. *The Economic Consequences of the Peace*. London: Macmillan, pp. 3–4.

60. Ibid., pp. 9–10.

61. Williams, William Appleman, 1954. The Legend of Isolationism in the 1920s. *Science & Society*, vol. 18, no. 1, p. 16.

62. US Department of Commerce, 1930. *Statistical Abstract of the United States*. Washington, DC: US Department of Commerce, p. 486.

63. Terkel, Studs, 2005. *Hard Times: An Oral History of the Great Depression*. New York: New Press, pp. 461–2.

64. Baynes, Norman H., ed., 1969. *The Speeches of Adolf Hitler: April 1922–August 1939*, vol. 2. London: Oxford University Press, p. 1343.

65. United Nations, 1945. Charter of the United Nations and Statute of the International Court of Justice, preamble. Retrieved from: https://treaties. un.org/doc/Publication/CTC/uncharter-all-lang.pdf.

66. US Congress, 1945. *Congressional Record. Proceedings and Debates of the 79th Congress*, Washington, DC: Government Printing Office, vol. 91, part 11, p. A3125.

67. Charmley, John, 2001. Churchill and the American Alliance. *Transactions of the Royal Historical Society*, vol. 11, p. 368.

68. US Departments of State and Defense, 1950. A Report to the National Security Council by the Executive Secretary on United States Objectives and Programs for National Security. NSC 68 (14 April), p. 9. Retrieved from: https://www.trumanlibrary.org/whistlestop/study_collections/ coldwar/ . . ./10-1.pdf.

69. Service, Robert, 1995. *Lenin: A Political Life*, vol. 3, *The Iron Ring*. Basingstoke; Macmillan, p. 201. Shachtman, Max, 1931. Stalin in 1921: More about the Theory of Socialism in One Country Before Lenin's Death. *The Militant*, vol. 4, no. 18, p. 4. Retrieved from: https://www.marxists.org/ archive/shachtma/1931/08/stalin1921.htm.

70. Kennan, George, 1946. Telegram, George Kennan to George Marshall, 22 February 1946. Harry S. Truman Administration File, Elsey Papers, Harry S. Truman Presidential Library. Retrieved from: https://www.trumanlibrary. org/whistlestop/study_collections/coldwar/documents/pdf/6-6.pdf.

71. Churchill, Winston, David Cannadine, ed., 2007. *Blood, Toil, Tears and Sweat: The Great Speeches*. London: Penguin, p. 301.

72. Spykman, Nicholas J., 2017. *America's Strategy in World Politics: The United States and the Balance of Power*. Abingdon: Routledge.

73. Fukuyama, Francis, 1989. The End of History? *The National Interest*, no. 16, p. 3.

74. White House, 1991. National Security Strategy of the United States, p. v. Retrieved from: http://nssarchive.us/national-security-strategy-1991/.

75. US Department of State, 1998. Transcript of Secretary of State Madeleine K. Albright Interview on NBC-TV 'The Today Show' with Matt Lauer (19 February). Retrieved from: https://1997-2001.state.gov/ statements/1998/980219a.html.

76. Rosecrance, Richard, 1999. *The Rise of the Virtual State: Wealth and Power in the Coming Century*. New York: Basic Books.

77. Nye, Joseph S., Jr, 1990. Soft Power. *Foreign Policy*, no. 80, pp. 153–71.

78. Secretariat of the Commission of the European Communities, 1973. Declaration on European Identity. *Bulletin of the European Communities*, no. 12, p. 120.

79. Sobol, Dorothy Meadow, 1998. Foreign Ownership of U.S. Treasury Securities: What the Data Show and Do Not Show. *Federal Reserve Bank of New York: Current Issues in Economics and Finance*, vol. 4, no. 5, p. 2.

80. Buchanan, Patrick J., 1999. *A Republic, Not an Empire: Reclaiming America's Destiny*. New York: Regnery, p. 4.

81. Figures are only for the USA: Carroll Roop Daugherty, 1928. The Development of Horsepower Equipment in the United States. In C. R. Daugherty, et al. *Power Capacity and Production in the United States*. Washington, DC: Department of the Interior, p. 45. Ristinen, Robert A., and Jack J. Kraushaar, 2006. *Energy and the Environment*. New York: John Wiley, p. 6.

82. De Long, J. Bradford, 1998. Op. cit.

83. Riley, James C., 2005. Estimates of Regional and Global Life Expectancy, 1800–2001. *Population and Development Review*, vol. 31, no. 3, pp. 537–42.

84. Maddison, Angus, 2010. Op. cit.

85. Hugill, Peter J., 1993. *World Trade since 1431: Geography, Technology, and Capitalism*. Baltimore, MD: Johns Hopkins University Press, p. 128.

86. Union of International Associations, 2013. Historical Overview of Number of International Organizations by Type, 1909–2013. Retrieved from: https://www.uia.org/sites/uia.org/files/misc_pdfs/stats/Historical_overview_of_number_of_international_organizations_by_type_1909-2013.pdf.

87. Voltaire, 1878. *Œuvres complètes de Voltaire*, vol. 12, *Essai sur les mœurs*. Paris: Garnier Frères, p. 430.

CONCLUSION: HORROR AS A FRIEND

1. Streuvels, Stijn, 1916. *In oorlogstijd: Het volledige dagboek van de Eerste Wereldoorlog*. Den Haag: DBNL, p. 540.

Further Reading

Readers wishing to find out more about any of the subjects covered in *A Political History of the World* may find the following selection of recommended works more useful than a conventional and lengthy list of the sources consulted in the course of writing this book. Works have been listed under the period for which they are most relevant.

BEFORE 750 BCE (CHAPTERS 1–2)

Avari, Burjor, 2016. *India: The Ancient Past. A History of the Indian Subcontinent from c. 7000 BCE to CE 1200*. Abingdon: Routledge.

Cline, Eric H., 2014. *1177 B.C.: The Year Civilization Collapsed*. Princeton, NJ: Princeton University Press.

Cohen, Raymond, and Raymond Westbrook, eds., 2000. *Amarna Diplomacy: The Beginnings of International Relations*. Baltimore, MD: The Johns Hopkins University Press.

Di Cosmo, Nicola, 2002. *Ancient China and Its Enemies: The Rise of Nomadic Power in East Asian History*. Cambridge: Cambridge University Press.

Diehl, Richard A. 2004. *The Olmecs: America's First Civilization*. London: Thames & Hudson.

George, Andrew, trans., 2003. *The Epic of Gilgamesh: The Babylonian Epic Poem and Other Texts in Akkadian and Sumerian*. London: Penguin.

Kriwaczek, Paul, 2014. *Babylon: Mesopotamia and the Birth of Civilization.* London: Atlantic Books.

Morkot, Robert G., 2005. *The Egyptians: An Introduction.* London: Routledge.

Romer, John, 2013–15. *A History of Ancient Egypt*, 2 vols. London: Penguin.

Singh, Sarva Daman, 1997. *Ancient Indian Warfare, with Special Reference to the Vedic Period.* Delhi: Motilal Banarsidass.

Singh, Upinder, 2008. *A History of Ancient and Early Medieval India: From the Stone Age to the 12th Century.* Delhi: Pearson Longman.

Smith, John D., trans., 2009. *The Mahabharata.* London: Penguin.

Thorp, Robert L., 2006. *China in the Early Bronze Age: Shang Civilization.* Philadelphia, PA: University of Pennsylvania Press.

750–500 BCE (CHAPTER 3)

Aubet, Maria Eugenia, 1993. *The Phoenicians and the West: Politics, Colonies and Trade.* Cambridge: Cambridge University Press.

Confucius, 1861. *The Analects.* In James Legge, trans., *The Chinese Classics*, vol. 1, *Confucian Analects, The Great Learning, and The Doctrine of the Mean.* London: Trübner & Co.

Coogan, Michael D., et al., eds., 2018. *The New Oxford Annotated Bible: New Revised Standard Version with the Apocrypha.* Oxford: Oxford University Press.

Frahm, Eckart, ed. 2017. *A Companion to Assyria.* Chichester: John Wiley.

Grousset, René, 1970. *The Empire of the Steppes: A History of Central Asia.* New Brunswick NJ: Rutgers University Press.

Kuhrt, Amélie, 2007. *The Persian Empire: A Corpus of Sources from the Achaemenid Period.* Abingdon: Routledge.

Lao, Tzu, Arthur Waley, trans., 1997. *Tao Te Ching.* Ware: Wordsworth Editions.

Loewe, Michael, and Edward L. Shaughnessy, eds., 1999. *The Cambridge History of Ancient China: From the Origins of Civilization to 221 B.C.* Cambridge: Cambridge University Press.

Rolle, Renate, 1989. *The World of the Scythians.* Berkeley, CA: University of California Press.

Simpson, St John, and Svetlana Pankova, eds., 2017. *Scythians: Warriors of Ancient Siberia.* London: Thames & Hudson.

Sun, Tzu, Lionel Giles, trans., 1910. *Sun Tzu on the Art of War: The Oldest Military Treatise in the World.* London: Luzac & Co.

500–250 BCE (CHAPTER 4)

Adcock, Frank, and D. J. Mosley, 1975. *Diplomacy in Ancient Greece.* London: Thames & Hudson.

Aristotle, Jonathan Barnes, ed., 1984. *The Complete Works of Aristotle: The Revised Oxford Translation.* Princeton, NJ: Princeton University Press.

Briant, Pierre, 2002. *From Cyrus to Alexander: A History of the Persian Empire.* Winona Lake, IN: Eisenbrauns.

Herodotus, Aubrey de Sélincourt, trans., 2003. *The Histories.* London: Penguin.

Kagan, Donald, 2005. *The Peloponnesian War: Athens and Sparta in Savage Conflict, 431–404 BC.* London: Harper Perennial.

Kautilya, R. Shamasastry, trans., 1915. *Kautilya's Arthasastra.* Bangalore: The Government Press.

Lewis, Mark Edward, 2007. *The Early Chinese Empires: Qin and Han.* Cambridge, MA: Belknap Press.

Plato, Desmond Lee, trans., 2003. *The Republic.* London: Penguin.

Thapar, Romila, 1997. *Asoka and the Decline of the Mauryas.* Delhi: Oxford University Press.

Thucydides, Steven Lattimore, trans., 1998. *The Peloponnesian War.* Indianapolis, IN: Hackett.

Wiesehöfer, Josef, 2001. *Ancient Persia: From 550 BC to 650 AD*. London: I.B. Tauris.

250–1 BCE (CHAPTER 5)

Allen, Charles, 2012. *Ashoka: The Search for India's Lost Emperor*. London: Little, Brown.

Eilers, Claude, ed., 2009. *Diplomats and Diplomacy in the Roman World*. Leiden: Brill.

Freeman, Philip, 2011. *Alexander the Great.* New York: Simon & Schuster.

Goldsworthy, Adrian, 2016. *Pax Romana: War, Peace and Conquest in the Roman World*. London: Weidenfeld & Nicolson.

Grainger, John D., 2017. *Great Power Diplomacy in the Hellenistic World*. Abingdon: Routledge.

Liu, Xinru, 2001. Migration and Settlement of the Yuezhi-Kushan: Interaction and Interdependence of Nomadic and Sedentary Societies. *Journal of World History*, vol. 11, no. 2, pp. 261–92.

Man, John, 2009. *The Terra Cotta Army: China's First Emperor and the Birth of a Nation*. Cambridge, MA: Da Capo Press.

Miles, Richard, 2010. *Carthage Must Be Destroyed: The Rise and Fall of an Ancient Civilization*. London: Allen Lane.

Polybius, Ian Scott-Kilvert, trans., 1979. *The Rise of the Roman Empire*. Harmondsworth: Penguin.

Powell, Anton, 2016. *Athens and Sparta: Constructing Greek Political and Social History from 478 BC*. Abingdon: Routledge.

Qian, Sima, Raymond Dawson, trans., 2007. *The First Emperor: Selections from the Historical Records*. Oxford: Oxford University Press.

Rawlinson, H. G., 1912. *Bactria: The History of a Forgotten Empire*. London: Probsthain & Co.

Verstandig, André, 2001. *Histoire de l'empire parthe (250–227): À la découverte d'une civilisation méconnue*. Brussels: Le Cri.

1–250 CE (CHAPTER 6)

Dio, Cassius, Earnest Cary, trans., 1917–27. *Roman History*, vols. 6–9. Cambridge, MA: Harvard University Press.

Goldsworthy, Adrian, 2014. *Augustus: From Revolutionary to Emperor.* London: Weidenfeld & Nicolson.

Harmatta, János, et al., eds., 1994. *History of Civilizations of Central Asia*, vol. 2, *The Development of Sedentary and Nomadic Civilizations: 700 B.C. to 250 A.D.* Paris: UNESCO.

Kim, Hyun Jin, 2016. *The Huns.* London: Routledge.

Souza, Philip de, and John France, eds., 2008. *War and Peace in Ancient and Medieval History.* Cambridge: Cambridge University Press.

Tacitus, Michael Grant, trans., 1996. *The Annals of Imperial Rome.* London: Penguin.

Veyne, Paul, ed., 1992. *A History of Private Life*, vol. 1, *From Pagan Rome to Byzantium.* Cambridge, MA: Belknap Press.

250–500 CE (CHAPTER 7)

Brent, Allen, 2010. *Cyprian and Roman Carthage.* Cambridge: Cambridge University Press.

Daryaee, Touraj, 2009. *Sasanian Persia: The Rise and Fall of an Empire.* London: I.B. Tauris.

Gibbon, Edward, David Womersley, ed., 2000. *The History of the Decline and Fall of the Roman Empire.* London: Penguin.

Gregory, Timothy E., 2010. A *History of Byzantium.* Chichester: Wiley-Blackwell.

Halsall, Guy, 2007. *Barbarian Migrations and the Roman West, 376–568.* Cambridge: Cambridge University Press.

Lewis, Mark Edward, 2009. *China between Empires: The Northern and Southern Dynasties.* Cambridge, MA: Belknap.

Marcellinus, Ammianus, Walter Hamilton, trans., 1986. *The Later Roman Empire (A.D. 354–378).* Harmondsworth: Penguin.

Merrills, Andy, and Richard Miles, 2009. *The Vandals*. Chichester: Wiley-Blackwell.

Mookerji, Radhakumud, 1989. *The Gupta Empire*. Delhi: Motilal Banarsidass.

Norwich, John Julius, 1988. *Byzantium: The Early Centuries*. London: Viking

Qian, Sima, Burton Watson, trans., 1993. *Records of the Grand Historian. Han Dynasty*, 2 vols. New York: Columbia University Press.

Swartz, Wendy, et al., eds., 2014. *Early Medieval China: A Sourcebook*. New York: Columbia University Press.

Wickham, Chris, 2009. *The Inheritance of Rome: A History of Europe from 400 to 1000*. London: Allen Lane.

Zosimus, James J. Buchanan and Harold T. Davis, trans., 1967. *Historia Nova: The Decline of Rome*. San Antonio, TX: Trinity University Press.

500–750 CE (CHAPTER 8)

Abdel Haleem, M. A. S., 2008. *The Qur'an*. Oxford: Oxford University Press.

Chen, Jack, W., 2010. *The Poetics of Sovereignty: On Emperor Taizong of the Tang Dynasty*. Cambridge, MA: Harvard University Asia Center.

Coe, Michael D., and Stephen D. Houston, 2015. *The Maya*. London: Thames & Hudson.

Graff, David A., 2002. *Medieval Chinese Warfare: 300–900*. London: Routledge.

Gregory of Tours, Lewis Thorpe, trans., 1974. *The History of the Franks*. London: Penguin.

Le Goff, Jacques, 1988. *Medieval Civilization, 400–1500*. Oxford: Basil Blackwell.

Maas, Michael, ed., 2005. *The Cambridge Companion to the Age of Justinian*. Cambridge: Cambridge University Press.

Maurice, George T. Dennis, trans., 1984. *Maurice's Strategikon: Handbook of Byzantine Military Strategy*. Philadelphia, PA: University of Pennsylvania Press.

Theophilus of Edessa, Robert G. Hoyland, trans., 2011. *Theophilus of Edessa's Chronicle and the Circulation of Historical Knowledge in Late Antiquity and Early Islam*. Liverpool: Liverpool University Press.

Wells, Colin, 2006. *Sailing from Byzantium: How a Lost Empire Shaped the World*. New York: Delacorte Press.

750–1000 CE (CHAPTER 9)

Barbero, Allesandro, 2004. *Charlemagne: Father of a Continent*. Berkeley, CA: University of California Press.

Bennison, Amira K., 2009. *The Great Caliphs: The Golden Age of the Abbasid Empire*. London: I.B. Tauris.

Clot, André, 2005. *Harun al-Rashid and the World of the Thousand and One Nights*. London: Saqi Books.

Hawting, G. R., 2000. *The First Dynasty of Islam: The Umayyad Caliphate, AD 661–750*. London: Routledge.

Hulbert, Homer B., Clarence Norwood Weems, 1999. *The History of Korea*, vol. 1. Richmond: Curzon.

Kaldellis, Anthony, 2017. *Streams of Gold, Rivers of Blood: The Rise and Fall of Byzantium, 955 A.D. to the First Crusade*. New York: Oxford University Press.

Lewis, Mark Edward, 2009. *China's Cosmopolitan Empire: The Tang Dynasty*. Cambridge, MA: Belknap Press.

Wilson, Peter H., 2016. *Heart of Europe: A History of the Holy Roman Empire*. Cambridge, MA: Belknap Press.

1000–1250 CE (CHAPTER 10)

Asbridge, Thomas, 2010. *The Crusades: The War for the Holy Land*. London: Simon & Schuster.

Crowley, Roger, 2011. *City of Fortune: How Venice Won and Lost a Naval Empire*. London: Faber and Faber.

Farooqui, Salma Ahmed, 2011. *A Comprehensive History of Medieval India: Twelfth to the Mid-Eighteenth Century*. Delhi: Longman.

Hall, Kenneth R., 2011. *A History of Early Southeast Asia: Maritime Trade and Societal Development, 100–1500*. Lanham, MD: Rowman and Littlefield.

Huffman, Joseph P., 2000. *The Social Politics of Medieval Diplomacy: Anglo-German Relations (1066–1307)*. Ann Arbor, MI: University of Michigan Press.

Jackson, Peter, 2005. *The Mongols and the West, 1221–1410*. Harlow: Longman.

Joinville and Villehardouin, Caroline Smith, trans., 2008. *Chronicles of the Crusades*. London: Penguin.

Kaldellis, Anthony, 2017. *Streams of Gold, Rivers of Blood: The Rise and Fall of Byzantium, 955 A.D. to the First Crusade*. New York: Oxford University Press.

Kuhn, Dieter, 2009. *The Age of Confucian Rule: The Song Transformation of China*. Cambridge, MA: Belknap Press.

Massie, Suzanne, 1981. *Land of the Firebird: The Beauty of Old Russia*. New York: Simon & Schuster.

Morgan, David, 2015. *Medieval Persia, 1040–1797*. Abingdon: Routledge.

Peacock, A. C. S., 2015. *The Great Seljuk Empire*. Edinburgh: Edinburgh University Press.

Runciman, Steven, 2016. *A History of the Crusades*, 3 vols. London: Penguin.

Shaffer, Lynda Norene, 1996. *Maritime Southeast Asia to 1500*. Armonk, NY: M. E. Sharpe.

Weatherford, Jack, 2005. *Genghis Khan and the Making of the Modern World*. New York: Broadway Books.

1250–1500 CE (CHAPTER 11)

Abu-Lughod, Janet, L., 1991. *Before European Hegemony: The World System, A.D. 1250–1350*. New York: Oxford University Press.

Crowley, Roger, 2005. *1453: The Holy War for Constantinople and the Clash of Islam and the West*. New York: Hyperion.

Dunn, Ross E., 2005. *The Adventures of Ibn Battuta: A Muslim Traveler of the 14th Century*. Berkeley, CA: University of California Press.

Erasmus, 2003. *The Complaint of Peace*. New York: Cosimo.

Frigo, Daniela, ed., 2000. *Politics and Diplomacy in Early Modern Italy: The Structure of Diplomatic Practice, 1450–1800*. Cambridge: Cambridge University Press.

Huizinga, Johan, 1999. *The Waning of the Middle Ages*. Mineola, NY: Dover Publications.

Ibn Battutah, Tim Mackintosh-Smith, ed., 2003. *The Travels of Ibn Battutah*. London: Picador.

McKissack, Patricia and Frederick, 1994. *The Royal Kingdoms of Ghana, Mali, and Songhay: Life in Medieval Africa*. New York: Henry Holt.

Oliver, Roland, and Anthony Atmore, 2001. *Medieval Africa, 1250–1800*. Cambridge: Cambridge University Press.

Polo, Marco, Ronald Latham, trans., 1958. *The Travels of Marco Polo*. Harmondsworth: Penguin.

Rivère de Carles, Nathalie, ed., 2016. *Early Modern Diplomacy, Theatre and Soft Power: The Making of Peace*. Basingstoke: Palgrave Macmillan.

Rostworowski de Diez Canseco, María, 1999. *History of the Inca Realm*. Cambridge: Cambridge University Press

Strathern, Paul, 2003. *The Medici: Godfathers of the Renaissance*. London: Jonathan Cape.

Townsend, Richard F., 2010. *The Aztecs*. London: Thames & Hudson.

Tuchman, Barbara, 2017. *A Distant Mirror: The Calamitous 14th Century*. London: Penguin.

1500–1750 CE (CHAPTER 12)

Braudel, Fernand, 1992. *Civilization and Capitalism, 15th–18th Century*, 3 vols. Berkeley, CA: University of California Press.

Braudel, Fernand, 1995. *The Mediterranean and the Mediterranean World in the Age of Philip II*, 2 vols. Berkeley, CA: University of California Press.

Brook, Timothy, 2010. *The Troubled Empire: China in the Yuan and Ming Dynasties*. Cambridge, MA: Belknap Press.

Dale, Stephen F., 2010. *The Muslim Empires of the Ottomans, Safavids, and Mughals*. New York: Cambridge University Press.

Eraly, Abraham, 2004. *The Mughal Throne: The Saga of India's Great Emperors*. London: Phoenix.

Ferguson, Niall, 2003. *Empire: How Britain Made the Modern World*. London: Allen Lane.

Finkel, Caroline, 2005. *Osman's Dream: The Story of the Ottoman Empire, 1300–1923*. London: John Murray.

Ginzburg, Carlo, 1980. *The Cheese and the Worms: The Cosmos of a Sixteenth-Century Miller*. Baltimore, MD: Johns Hopkins University Press.

Kant, Immanuel, Ted Humphrey, trans., 2003. *To Perpetual Peace: A Philosophical Sketch*. Indianapolis, IN: Hackett.

Lamster, Mark, 2010. *Master of Shadows: The Secret Diplomatic Career of the Painter Peter Paul Rubens*. New York: Anchor.

Machiavelli, Niccolò, Tim Parks, trans., 2011. *The Prince*. London: Penguin.

MacQuarrie, Kim, 2008. *The Last Days of the Incas*. New York: Simon & Schuster.

Madariaga, Isabel de, 2005. *Ivan the Terrible: First Tsar of Russia*. New Haven, CT: Yale University Press.

Mancall, Mark, 1984. *China at the Center: 300 Years of Foreign Policy*. New York: Free Press.

Mattingly, Garrett, *Renaissance Diplomacy*. Boston, MA: Houghton Mifflin.

Newman, Andrew J., 2006. *Safavid Iran: Rebirth of a Persian Empire*. London: I.B. Tauris.

Norwich, John Julius, 2016. *Four Princes: Henry VIII, Francis I, Charles V, Suleiman the Magnificent and the Obsessions That Forged Modern Europe*. London: John Murray.

Wilson, Peter H., 2009. *Europe's Tragedy: A History of the Thirty Years War*. London: Allen Lane.

1750–2000 CE (CHAPTER 13)

Clark, Christopher, 2006. *The Iron Kingdom: The Rise and Downfall of Prussia, 1600–1947*. London: Allen Lane.

Clark, Christopher, 2012. *The Sleepwalkers: How Europe Went to War in 1914*. London: Allen Lane.

Dalrymple, William, 2006. *The Last Mughal. The Fall of a Dynasty, Delhi, 1857*. London: Bloomsbury.

Dower, John W., 1999. *Embracing Defeat. Japan in the Aftermath of World War II*. London: Allen Lane.

Figes, Orlando, 1986. *A People's Tragedy: The Russian Revolution, 1891–1924*. London: Jonathan Cape.

Frank, Anne, Susan Massotty, trans., 2009. *The Diary of a Young Girl*. London: Puffin.

Fromkin, David, 2009. *A Peace to End All Peace: The Fall of the Ottoman Empire and the Creation of the Modern Middle East*. New York: Henry Holt.

Gaddis, John Lewis, 2006. *The Cold War*. London: Allen Lane.

Hopkirk, Peter, 2006. *The Great Game: On Secret Service in High Asia*. London: John Murray.

Jansen, Marius B., 2000. *The Making of Modern Japan*. Cambridge, MA: Belknap Press.

Judt, Tony, 2005. *Postwar: A History of Europe Since 1945*. London: Heinemann.

Keegan, John, 1998. *The First World War*. London: Hutchinson.

Kissinger, Henry, 1994. *Diplomacy*. New York: Simon & Schuster.

Knight, Roger, 2013. *Britain against Napoleon: The Organization of Victory, 1793–1815*. London: Penguin.

Macmillan, Margaret, 2001. *Peacemakers: The Paris Conference of 1919 and Its Attempt to End War*. London: John Murray.

Polanyi, Karl, 2000. *The Great Transformation: The Political and Economic Origins of Our Time*. Boston, MA: Beacon Press.

Rowe, William T., 2009. *China's Last Empire: The Great Qing*. Cambridge, MA: Belknap Press.

Steinberg, Jonathan, 2011. *Bismarck: A Life*. Oxford: Oxford University Press

Taylor, A. J. P., 1963. *The Origins of the Second World War*. London: Penguin.

Troyat, Henri, 2000. *Catherine the Great*. London: Phoenix.

Weinberg, Gerhard L., 2005. *A World at Arms: A Global History of World War II*. Cambridge: Cambridge University Press.

Zamoyski, Adam, 2007. *Rites of Peace: The Fall of Napoleon and the Congress of Vienna*. London: HarperPress.

Zimmermann, Warren, 2002. *First Great Triumph: How Five Americans Made Their Country a World Power*. New York: Farrar, Straus and Giroux.

GENERAL

Anderson, M. S., 1993. *The Rise of Modern Diplomacy, 1450–1919*. London: Longman.

Diamond, Jared, 2017. *Guns, Germs, and Steel: The Fates of Human Societies*. New York: W. W. Norton.

Frankopan, Peter, 2017. *The Silk Roads: A New History of the World*. London: Bloomsbury.

Kennedy, Paul, 1987. *The Rise and Fall of the Great Powers: Economic Change and Military Conflict from 1500 to 2000*. New York: Random House.

Landes, David S., 1999. *The Wealth and Poverty of Nations: Why Some Are So Rich and Some So Poor.* New York: W. W. Norton.

Parker, Geoffrey, ed., 2005. *The Cambridge History of Warfare.* Cambridge: Cambridge University Press.

Pomeranz, Kenneth, 2001. *The Great Divergence: China, Europe, and the Making of the Modern World Economy.* Princeton, NJ: Princeton University Press.

Ralph, Philip Lee, et al., 1997. *World Civilizations: Their History and Their Culture.* New York: W. W. Norton.

Satow, Ernest, Ivor Roberts, ed., 2017. *Satow's Diplomatic Practice.* Oxford: Oxford University Press.

Toynbee, Arnold J., D. C. Somervell, ed., 1987. *A Study of History*, 2 vols. Oxford: Oxford University Press.

Twitchett, Denis, and John K. Fairbank, eds., 1978–2016. *The Cambridge History of China*, 15 vols. Cambridge: Cambridge University Press.

ECONOMIC AND DEMOGRAPHIC STATISTICS

Throughout this book, I have tried to give readers a rough idea of the size of populations, the magnitude of economies, and so forth, in order to contextualize political events. Any such figures should be treated as estimations, as rough indicators, not as exact data. For anyone interested in historical demographic and economic data, I can recommend the following:

Broadberry, Stephen, et al., 2017. China, Europe, and the Great Divergence: A Study in Historical National Accounting, 980–1850. University of Oxford Discussion Papers in Economic and Social History, no. 155. Retrieved from: https://www.economics.ox.ac.uk/materials/working_papers/ . . ./155aprilbroadberry.pdf.

De Long, J. Bradford, 1998. Estimating World GDP: One Million B.C.–Present. Berkeley University. Retrieved from: https://delong.typepad.com/print/20061012_LRWGDP.pdf.

Maddison, Angus, 2010. Historical Statistics of the World Economy, 1–2008 AD, table 1. Retrieved from: www.ggdc.net/maddison/historical_statistics/horizontal-file_02-2010.xls.

McEvedy, Colin and Richard Jones, 1978. *Atlas of World Population History*. New York: Facts on File.

ACKNOWLEDGEMENTS

This book would not have been possible without the support of my university and, as is perhaps not so often acknowledged, my fellow citizens, who remain indispensable sponsors of our work as academics. They allow us the time and freedom to read, think, and write. I would particularly like to thank my students, for their input and patience, my exceptional copy editor, Kit Shepherd, for his meticulousness and encyclopaedic knowledge, my commissioning editor at Penguin, Laura Stickney, for giving me the opportunity to be published by my favourite publishing house, her editorial assistant, Shoaib Rokadiya, who helped me out on the maps, Lynn Tytgat, for accompanying and encouraging me throughout the last few years of exploring and writing, and my family, Ann, Aline, and Julia, for giving me the inspiration and encouragement – day after day.

Index

A

Aachen, 323, 348
Abbas I, Shah of the Safavids, 444–6
Abbasid Caliphate: rise and decline of,
  340–5, 378–80
– and trade, 321, 323
Abd Manaf, Hashim ibn, 286–7
Aberdeen, George Hamilton-Gordon, 4th
  Earl, 502
Abu Bakr (caliph), 288
Abu Hanifa (Islamic jurist), 341
Abu Simbel, Egypt, 37
Abu'l-Fazl (Mughal vizier), *Akbarnama*
  (Mughal history), 448–9
Aceh sultanate, 457
Achaean League, 147
Achaemenid dynasty, 93, 100, 104, 123, 130,
  152, 162–3, 552
Adad-nirari II, King of Assyria, 58–9, 68, 87
Adelaide, Queen, 371
Adikavi Pampa (poet), 338
Adriatic sea, 152, 189, 348, 409
Afghanistan, 28, 378, 379, 446
African continent: Angolan Civil War
  (1975–91), 524
– Chinese voyages to (15th century),
  420, 431
– colonization by Europe, 473–4
– population (14th century), 423
– Portuguese exploration of, 406–7
– trade networks in, 423–6
– tribal wars, 199–200 *see also* Egypt;
  North Africa

Agincourt, Battle of (1415), 404
Ahmed III, Sultan of the Ottomans, 443
Ahuramazda (Zoroastrian god), 264
Ai, Emperor of the Han, 181, 228
Aibak, Qutb al-Din, 412
Akbar, Mughal Emperor, 447–50, 551
Akkad, Mesopotamia, 33, 40
Aksum kingdom, 274, 292, 356
Alamanni (Germanic tribe), 251, 253
Alans (nomadic people), 245
Albania, 410
Albright, Madeleine, 528
Alcaeus, 108
Aleppo, Syria, 288
Alexander I, Tsar, 491, 493
Alexander the Great, 98, 130, 135–7, 148,
  152, 541
Alexandria, 98, 288
Alexius I, Byzantine Emperor, 377
Allah, 287
Alpide Belt, 23
Amarna, Egypt, 33
Amarna Tablets, 36
Amasya, Peace of (1555), 444
ambassadors, permanent, 401–2, 545
Ambrose of Milan, 245
American War of Independence
  (1775–83), 488
Americas: European discovery of, 407, 437,
  457–8 *see also* Central America; North
  America; South America; United States
  of America
Ammianus (Roman historian), 252
Ammon, kingdom of, 64

Amphictyonic League, 108, 109

Amsterdam, Netherlands, 459

Amsterdam Exchange Bank (founded 1609), 460

Amu Darya (Oxus River), 28, 182, 271

Anastasius, Eastern Roman Emperor, 255–6

Anatolia: and the Assyrian Empire, 59
– and the Byzantine Empire, 266, 302, 376
– and the Cimmerians, 71
– Hittite kingdom in, 31–2
– and the Ottoman Empire, 408
– under the Seljuk Turks, 376, 380–1
  see also Asia Minor

Anaximander, 112, 200

Andaman Sea, 457

Angevin kings of England, 372

Angkor Wat temple, 423

Anjar (Umayyad city), 338

Anna Comnena (Byzantine historian), 377

Annam kingdom, 422, 455

Antalcidas, Treaty of (387 BCE), 147–8

Antigonids, 149, 162

Antigonus I, 149

Antiochus I, 149, 156

Antonov, Mikhail, 526

Antwerp, Netherlands, 459

ANZUS (alliance between the US, Australia and New Zealand), 524

Apocalypse Now (film, 1979), 537

Apuleius, Lucius, The Golden Ass, 217

Aquinas, Thomas, 399–400

Arab-Israeli War (1948), 521 see also Yom Kippur War (1973)

Aragon, Spain, 406

Arakan kingdom, 450

Arameans, 42, 58, 62–3, 64, 65, 87, 98

Arcadian League, 146

Archaic period, of Greek art, 112

Archilochus, 108

Ardashir I of the Sasanians, 222, 264

Aristides, 219

Aristophanes, 142

Aristotle, 136, 143

Armenia, 24, 215, 222, 248, 265, 293, 443, 444, 540

Arpad, Syria, 65, 68

Arras, Congress of (1435), 404

Arsuf, Battle of (1191 CE), 382

Artaxerxes I, King of Persia, 141

Artaxerxes II, King of Persia, 134, 138, 141

Artaxerxes III, King of Persia, 134, 135

Arthashastra (Hindu epic), 448

Arukka (Persian prince), 93

Aryabhata (mathematician and astronomer), 156

Ashoka, King of the Mauryan Empire, 155, 163, 170, 183

Ashurbanipal, King of Assyria, 93, 95, 97, 98–9, 551

Ashur-dan II, King of Assyria, 58–9

Ashurnasirpal II, King of Assyria, 59, 60

Ashvaghosha (Buddhist monk), 225–6

Asia Minor, 73, 96, 102, 133–7, 149, 162 see also Anatolia

Assyrian Empire, 40, 86–7, 105, 123
– rise of, 58–62, 64–8, 75–6
– zenith of, 94–100

Assyrians, 31, 32, 41, 42

Atahualpa, Inca Emperor, 429

Ataturk, Kemal, 514

Athens: Neoplatonic Academy, 294
– in the Peloponnesian War, 134, 142–5, 147
– under Persian rule, 140–1
– in the Persian wars, 132
– rise of, 109–10

atlases and encyclopedias, 322

atomic bomb, 519

Atoyac river, 203

Attalids, 149, 162

Augustine of Hippo, 301

Augustus Caesar (Octavian), Roman Emperor, 196–7, 207, 209–12

Aurangzeb, Mughal Emperor, 450–1

Austerlitz, Battle of (1805), 491

Austria: Duchy of, 405, 466
– republic of, 513

Austrian Empire: 1848 revolutions, 495
– and the Congress of Vienna (1814–15), 492–4
– creation of, 467
– dissolution of, 513
– and the First World War, 500–1

– and the Napoleonic Wars, 491
– and the Schleswig-Holstein crisis, 496
Autocles, 147
Avars, 297, 302–3, 346, 348
Avignon, France, 403
Ayutthaya kingdom, Thailand, 422, 457
Ayyubid Dynasty, 381
Azores, 407
Aztec Empire, 427–8

B

Babur, Mughal Emperor, 447
Babylon, city of, 95, 96, 101, 149
Babylonians, 40, 42, 59, 64, 68, 96, 99, 131
Bactria, kingdom of, 100, 131, 170, 183
Baekje kingdom, 273
Baghdad (Madinat al-Salam): under the
    Abbasid Dynasty, 343, 344, 346, 378
– recaptured by the Safavids, 445
– sacked by the Mongols (1258), 382
– seized by the Seljuk Turks (1055), 379–80
Bahram V of the Sasanians, 266
Baker, Ray Stannard, 512
Balkans: Bulgarian khanate in, 303
– crisis in, 495, 498, 500
– and the Gauls, 150
– invaded by the Avars, 302
– Ottoman Empire in, 440, 441, 443, 484
– Roman campaigns in, 191
– and the Scythians, 105
Ban Chao (Han Chinese military
    general), 231
Ban Gu (Han historian), 229, 230
Bank of England, 460
banks, central, foundation of, 460
Banten sultanate, 457
Bantu people, 200
Bar Hebraeus (Syrian chronicler), 379
Barbaro, Ermolao, 401
Barbarossa, Frederick, 388
Barga'yah, Levantine king, 68
Basra, Syria, 288
Bavaria, duchy of, 371
Bavarians, 346
Bayer (company), 496
Beethoven, Ludwig van, 491

Behistun, Mount, 186
Beijing, China, 451
Belgium, 489, 494
Bellini, Gentile (painter), 410
Bengal, 483
Benin, kingdom of, 425
Bhavabhuti (Indian poet), *Mahaviracharita*
    (Exploits of a Great Hero), 334
Bian Kun (Jin statesman), 259
Bilsk, Ukraine, 106
Bimbisara, King of Magadha, 115, 153
Bindusara Maurya, 154, 156
Bini people, 425–6
Bismarck, Otto von, 496–7
Black Obelisk of Shalmaneser III, 67
Black Sea, 442
Black Sea region: 1st millenium BCE, 42,
    71–2, 96, 107
– and the Byzantine Empire, 294
– Crimean War (1853–56), 495
– Germanic tribes in, 246
– and the Ottoman Empire, 409, 410,
    439–42
– and the Roman Empire, 207, 216,
    219, 221
– and the Russian Empire, 484
– trade with Europe, 375–6, 390
Bodin, Jean, 461, 464
Bohemia, 408
Bombay (Mumbai), 450
Boniface, St, 301
Book of Documents (Chinese), 78
*Book of One Thousand and One
    Nights*, 343
Book of Rites (Zhou dynasty), 77–8, 159
Book of the Later Han, 225
Bosnia, 410
Botero, Giovanni, 464
Bouvines, Battle of (1214), 373
Brennus (Gallic leader), 150
Bretton Woods Conference (1944), 522
Britain: 18th century, 459
– East India Company, 450, 451, 466, 483
– Glorious Revolution (1688), 472
– Great Exhibition (1851), 503
– industrial revolution, 488, 498
– maritime supremacy of, 488, 490

– and the Opium Wars, 486
– under the Roman Empire, 219 *see also* England
British Empire, 483, 498–9, 505
British Museum, 98
Bronze Age Collapse, 31, 61, 75
Bruegel the Elder, Pieter, *The Triumph of Death* (1562), 471–2
Buchanan, Pat, 531
Buddhism: in China, 261–3, 305, 311, 454
– in the Goguryeo kingdom, 273
– in the Goryeo kingdom, 331
– and holy war, 331–4
– in India, 116, 155, 163, 227, 335, 338
– in Japan, 310, 422
– spreads in Asia, 273, 309
Bulgarian Empire, 346, 347, 350, 375, 376
Bulgars, 302, 303
Bülow, Bernhard von, 499
Burgundy, duchy of, 247, 404, 405
Burritt, Elihu, 502
Bush, George H. W. (US President), 527
Buyid Dynasty, 345, 378–9, 379
Byblos, Temple of, 61
Byzantine Empire (Eastern Roman Empire): created by division of the Roman Empire, 252–6
– fragmentation of, 375–8
– and Orthodox Christianity, 294
– Palaiologos Dynasty, 409
– population of, 346
– relations with the Song Dynasty, 385–6
– rivalry with the Sasanian Empire, 291–3
– *Strategikon*, 295–6, 301
– threatened by Bulgarian Empire, 348
– threatened by Frankish Empire, 347–8
– threatened by Islamic Caliphate, 286, 291
– and Western Europe, 370, 377–8
– worldview of, 293–6
Byzantium *see* Constantinople

C

Cadusians, 100
Caesar, Augustus *see* Augustus Caesar
Caesar, Julius, 196, 197
Cajamarca, Inca city of, 429

Calais, France, 404
Calakmul, Yucatán, 315
Caledonian tribes, 212, 217
Calgacus (Caledonian leader), 212
Caligula, Emperor, 213
Callias, Peace of, 133, 134, 141, 147, 148
Cambodia, 331, 332, 422
Cambyses I, King of Persia, 99
Cambyses II, King of Persia, 102, 131
Cannae, Battle of (215 BCE), 189, 191
Cape of Good Hope, 407, 457
capitalism, emergence of, 439
Caracalla, Emperor, 214, 215, 222
Carchemish, Battle of (605 BCE), 99
Carolingian Empire, 300, 323, 346, 348, 350, 356, 370 *see also* Frankish Empire
Carolingian Renaissance, 323, 551
Carthage/ Carthaginians, 111, 112, 150–1
– and the Punic Wars, 170, 188–91, 194, 540
cartography: Ancient Greek, 200
– Chinese, 322, 390
– increasing accuracy of, 438
– and Portuguese exploration, 406
– and trade routes, 322
Cassius Dio (Roman historian), 214–15, 217, 219
Castile, Spain, 406
Castlereagh, Robert Stewart, Viscount, 493
Catherine the Great, Tsarina, 484
Cato the Elder, 192, 194, 201
Cen Shen (Chinese poet), 328
Central Africa, trade networks in, 425–6
Central America: Aztec Empire, 427–8
– Olmec civilization, 83–6, 202
Central Treaty Organization in the Middle East (CENTO), 524
Chagatai Khanate, 411
Chaldeans, 96
Chaldiran, Battle of (1514), 439, 444
Chalukya kingdom, India, 384–5
Champa kingdom, Vietnam, 332, 366, 422
Chandragupta I of the Guptas, 268
Chandragupta Maurya, 153–4
Chang'an (city), 175, 177, 260, 308, 325, 327
Changping, Battle of (260 BCE), 171
Chao Cuo (Han imperial counsellor), 176, 182, 231

Charlemagne, 323, 346, 347–50, 551

Charles V, Holy Roman Emperor, 466, 467

Chavín people, South America, 83, 203

Cheng, Prince of Zhou, 77, 78

Chengdu (city), 260

Chengzhou, China, 77

Childebert, King of the Franks, 301

China: Communist revolution (1949), 521

– ethnic composition (6th century CE), 304–5

– 'Five Dynasties and Ten Kingdoms' period (907–60), 328–9

– Gaoping, Battle of (954), 330, 363

– Han dynasty, 169, 174–81, 257

– Hundred Schools of Thought, 160

– imperial tradition, 43–4

– Jin Dynasty, 366–7, 390, 392

– Later Han kingdom, 329

– Later Jin kingdom, 329

– Later Tang kingdom, 329

– Later Zhou kingdom, 330

– Liao Dynasty, 329–31, 390

– Ming Dynasty, 417–21, 451–4, 474

– Mongol rule in, 392, 416–17

– naval power of, 361, 420, 431

– Northern Qi, 305–6

– Northern Zhou, 305–6

– Pear Garden (first opera school), 325

– population, 158, 175

– Qin dynasty, 171–3

– Qing Dynasty, 438, 454–6, 484–6

– Red Turban Rebellion, 417

– Seven Sages of the Bamboo Grove, 257

– Shang dynasty, 43–4

– Song Dynasty, 330, 363–8, 385–6, 390

– Song-Jin, Battle of (1641–42), 454

– Southern Chen, 305–6

– Southern Song Dynasty, 367–8, 390–1, 392

– Spring and Autumn period (771–476 BCE), 81, 94, 116–22, 546

– Sui dynasty, 306

– Tang Dynasty, 286, 306–12, 324–8

– Three Kingdoms period, 257–9

– Treaty of Shanyuan (1005 CE), 364

– Treaty of Shaoxing (1141 CE), 391

– Uprising of the Five Barbarians (304–316 CE), 260

– War of the Eight Princes (291–306 CE), 259

– Warring States period (476–221 BCE), 81, 156–62

– Wars of Unification, 171

– Xia kingdom, 392

– Zhenge Emperor, 452

– Zhou dynasty, 44, 76–83, 87, 88, 116–17 *see also* People's Republic of China

Chola kingdom, India, 225, 383–4

Christianity: adopted by the Franks, 300–1

– adopted by the Roman Empire, 250

– in China, 308

– Coptic, 298

– as motive for war, 300–2

– Orthodox, 294, 298, 375

– and peace movements, 373, 399–400

Christians: in the Roman Empire, 248, 250

– in the Sasanian Empire, 266

Chu (Chinese state), 78–80, 117, 119, 157, 172, 173–4

Churchill, Winston, 513, 520, 524

Cicero, Marcus Tullius, 5, 197, 199, 201

Cimmerians, 42, 71–2, 95, 96, 97, 98

Cincinnatus, 192

Cirrha (Greek city), 109

Claudius, Emperor, 213

Clay, Henry, 509

Clemenceau, Georges, 513

Clement of Alexandria, 301

climate change: 1st millenium BCE, 51

– 3rd century CE, 245–6, 247

– 8th century CE, 324

– 9th century China, 328

– 16th century China, 453–4

– and European expansion, 459–60

– and migration and war, 355

– and the Mongol invasions, 369, 391

Clovis, king of the Franks, 256, 276, 299, 300–1

Cluny, monastery of, 373, 388

Cobden, Richard, 502

Code of Hammurabi, 40–1, 139, 185

coins, introduction of, 94, 104

Colbert, Jean, 466

Cold War (1947–91), 482, 523–6
Cologne, 346
Columbus, Christopher, 407, 427, 437, 457
commercial treaties (19th century), 502–3
Commodus, Emperor, 218
communism, 524, 530
Commynes, Philippe de, 401, 546–7
Concert of Europe, 494, 504
conferences and summits, diplomatic, 546–7
Confucianism: adopted by the Han Dynasty, 174–5, 178–80, 232
– adopted by the Qing Dynasty, 454
– adopted by the Yuan Dynasty, 416
– and foreign policy, 201
– in Korea, 421
– and realism, 161
– and trade, 159
Confucius, 116, 117, 121, 122, 124
Constance, Peace of (1183 CE), 387
Constantine, Roman Emperor, 250–1, 301
Constantine VII, Byzantine Emperor, *De Administrando Imperio*, 376
Constantinople: 11th and 12th centuries
– captured by Islamic Caliphate (674 CE), 293
– Comnenian Dynasty, 377
– created capital of Eastern Roman Empire, 250, 252, 254
– fall of (1453), 409, 439
– Hagia Sophia, 294, 409
– population of, 346
– sack of (1204), 378, 388
– and trade, 323 see also Istanbul
Constantinople, Treaty of (1724), 447
constitutional monarchy, 472
Coolidge, Calvin (US President), 515
Coppola, Francis Ford, *Apocalypse Now* (1979), 537
Coptic Christians, 298
Córdoba, Spain, 344, 346, 347, 349
Corinth, 107, 109–10, 194 see also League of Corinth
Corsica, 188–9
Cortés, Hernán, 429
cosmopolitanism, 551–3
Crimean War (1853–56), 495–6

Critobulus, Michael, 411
crop rotation, 374
Crucé, Émeric, 461
Crusades, 362, 373–4, 375, 378, 382, 386, 387–8
Ctesiphon (city), 222, 266, 288, 293, 296
Cuba, 510, 525
Cuban Missile Crisis (1962), 525
Cuman people, 375
Cusco, Inca city of, 428
Cyaxares, King of the Medes, 99
Cylon (Greek tyrant), 108
Cyprian, Bishop of Carthage, 248, 301
Cyprus, 95, 133
Cypselus (Greek tyrant), 107, 109
Cyrus II, King of Persia, 100–1, 102, 115
Czechoslovakia, 514, 517

D

Da Gama, Vasco, 457
Dacians, 218
Dahl, Robert, 8
Damascus, Syria, 288, 290, 381
Dante Alighieri, *De Monarchia*, 400
Dantidurga, king of the Rashtrakuta Dynasty, 336
Danube river, 303, 375
Daowu, Emperor of the Northern Wei, 261
Dargom dam, 226
Darius I, King of Persia, 102, 103–4, 131, 132, 136–7, 138, 140
Darius III, King of Persia, 135
Dark Ages, 31, 58
Davenant, Charles, 464, 486
David, King of Israel, 63, 69
Dawes, Charles, 516
Decius, Roman Emperor, 248
Defoe, Daniel, 486
Delhi, India, 385, 451
Delhi Sultanate, 412, 447
Delian League, 10, 133, 141, 146
Della Casa, Giovanni, 463
Delos island, 103
Delphi, oracle of, 74, 108
Demetrius I, 149
Demosthenes, 143

Deng Xiaoping, 530

Dezong, Emperor of the Tang dynasty, 327, 328

Dharmapala, king of the Pala Dynasty, 337

Dickens, Charles, 482

digital revolution, 532

Ding of Jin, Duke, 118–19

Diocletian, Roman Emperor, 249–50, 253

Diodorus Siculus, 183

Dionysius of Halicarnassus, 219

diplomacy: ancient Greek, 141, 145–6, 152
- Byzantine, 385–6
- in China, 78, 118–20, 179, 324–5, 385–6, 390–1
- European, 348–9, 386–90, 401–2, 461–3
- in India, 269
- in the Iron Age, 88
- limits of, 545–7
- Roman, 253
- in the Ugarit kingdom, 30–1

Djerba, Battle of (1560), 441

Dnieper river, 375

Dong Zhongshu, 175, 201, 229

Dongyi people, 78–9

Dorians, 42

Du Fu (Chinese poet), 326

Dubois, Pierre, 400

Dutch War (1672–78), 469

Dzungar Khanate, 455

E

East Africa, trading cities of, 423–4

East Francia, 350, 370

East India Company, 450, 451, 466, 483

Eastern Europe, 407–8

Eastern Jin Dynasty, 260–3

economic competition, 464–5

economic protectionism, 498, 509, 515, 533, 548–50

Edict of Milan (313 CE), 250

Egypt: Assyrian rule in, 98
- Ayyubid Dynasty, 381
- Fatimid Dynasty, 378, 380–1
- imperial tradition of, 25, 33–9, 66
- Libyan dynasty, 38, 61
- New Kingdom era (1550–1069 BCE), 37

- Persian rule in, 102, 104
- Ptolemiac kings, 170, 198

Eighty Years War (1568–1648), 438, 465, 467

Einhard (biographer of Charlemagne), 349

Elamites, 40, 42, 64, 93, 95, 96, 98

An, Emperor of the Han, 233

England: Angevin kings, 372
- Calico Acts (1700 and 1721), 466
- early 11th century, 370
- Hundred Years War (1337–1453), 403–4
- kingdom of, 1000 CE, 351
- Navigation Acts (1651 and 1673), 466
- Wars of the Roses (1455–85), 404 see also Britain

Enlightenment, European, 482–3, 492

Epaminondas, 147

Ephesus, Battle of (498), 132

Epic of Gilgamesh, 41, 98, 139

Epirote League, 147

Erasmus, 460, 471

Estonia, 470

Ethiopia, 424

Etruscans/ Etruria, 112–13, 114, 150

Euphrates river, 40, 101, 199, 222

Euripides, 142

Europe: 9th century, 350
- 14th and 15th centuries, 399–408
- 16th and 17th centuries, 457–66
- 18th century, 481–3
- 1848 revolutions, 495
- Belle Époque, 503
- Concert of Europe, 494, 504
- Congress of Vienna (1814–15), 494
- Crimean War (1853–56), 495–6
- Dutch War (1672–78), 469
- Eighty Years War (1568–1648), 438, 465, 467
- European Economic Community (EEC), 529
- European Union (EU), 530
- First World War (1914–1918), 501, 504, 511
- Habsburg Dynasty, 466–72
- High Middle Ages, 373–5, 386–8
- Holy Roman Empire, 370–2
- industrial revolution, 459, 482, 532
- League of Nations, 513, 514
- maritime supremacy of, 458

- monetary union, 530
- and Mongol invasion, 362, 369, 375, 389–90
- Nine Years War (1688–97), 464, 469
- Paris Peace Conference (1918), 512–15
- Renaissance, 471–2
- Schleswig-Holstein crisis (1864), 496
- Thirty Years War (1618–48), 438, 463, 465, 467
- Treaty of Saint-Germain (1919), 513
- Treaty of Sèvres (1920), 514
- Treaty of Versailles (1919), 513
- War of Devolution (1667–68), 469
- War of the Austrian Succession (1740–48), 438
- War of the Spanish Succession (1701–13), 438, 469
European Economic Community, 529
European Union, 530
Ewuare, king of the Bini, 425–6
Ezana Stone, 274

F

Fa-Hien (Buddhist monk), 270
Fan Li (Chinese economist), 118
Fan Zhongyan (Song dynasty statesman), 364
Fatimid Dynasty, 345, 378, 380–1
Fenghao, China, 45
Ferdinand I, Holy Roman Emperor, 467
Field of the Cloth of Gold (1520), 462, 546
Fijar War (580–90 CE), 287
financial instruments and institutions, 460, 465
Finland, 470, 493
First Crusade (1095–1099), 373–4, 378, 381, 388
First Sacred War (595–585 BCE), 109
First World War (1914–1918), 501, 504, 511
Forbidden City, Beijing, 451–2
Fourth Crusade (1202–04), 387, 409
France: Belle Époque, 503
- early 11th century, 370
- kingdom of, 351
- Mad War (1485–8), 405
- restoration of the Bourbon dynasty, 494

- Revolution (1789), 488–9
- rivalry with the Habsburg Empire, 406, 467–9
Francis I, King of France, 462, 467
Francis of Assisi, 386
Franco-Prussian War (1870), 497
Frankfurt, Germany, mass grave at, 27
Frankish Empire: divided into West, Middle and East Francia, 350
- population of, 346
- rise of, 286
- as successors to the Roman Empire, 303
- and trade, 321, 323
- united under Clovis, 299–301
- and the Vandals, 247
Frederick III, Holy Roman Emperor, 405
Frederick William I, King of Prussia, 471
free trade, 148, 498, 502, 509, 549–50
French Indochina, 521
French Revolution (1789), 488–9
French Revolutionary Wars (1792–1802), 489
Frisians (Frisii), 217–18, 218, 346
Fu Hao tomb, 43
Fugger, Jakob, 406
Fukuyama, Francis, 527
Funan kingdom, 244, 272

G

Gaius Marius (Roman consul), 194
Gallic migrations, 150
Gaoping, Battle of (954), 330, 363
Gaozu, Emperor of Han (Liu Bang), 173–4
Gaugamela, Battle of, 136
Gaul, 253, 299–300
Gauls, 189, 192, 198
Gelasius, Pope, 255
Genghis Khan, 367–70
Geoffrey of Villehardouin, 387–8
geographical exploration, 438
geopolitics, 23–5
Georgia, 445, 484
Georgievsk, Treaty of (1783), 484
Gepids (nomadic tribe), 302
Germanic tribes, 215–18, 245, 246, 251
Germany: divided after the Second World War, 521

– German Empire proclaimed by Bismarck, 497
– Molotov-Ribbentrop Pact (1939), 518
– reparations after the First World War, 513, 516
– rise of, 498–500
Ghassanid kingdom, 292
Ghaznavid Empire, 338, 378, 379
Ghurids, 385, 412
Giles of Rome, 400
Global Agreement on Tariffs and Trade (GATT), 522, 528
Goethe, Johann Wolfgang von, 491
Gogukcheon, King, 236
Goguryeo kingdom, 235–6, 244, 273–4, 310, 543
Gojoseon dynasty, in Korea, 157, 160, 162
Göktürks, 297, 306, 308, 309–10
Golden Horde, 411
Gondishapur, Academy of, 296, 551
Gopala, king of the Pala Dynasty, 336
Gorbachev, Mikhail, 526
Goryeo kingdom, 330–1, 420–1
Goths, 245, 246
Gracchus, Tiberius, 194
Granada, Spain, 406
Grant, Ulysses S. (US President), 509
Great Depression (1930s), 516
Great Exhibition (1851), 503
Great Wall of China, 172, 453
Greece: 10th–8th centuries BCE, 72–4
– city states, 106–12, 546
– independence from the Ottoman Empire (1830), 494
– Peloponnesian War (431–404 BCE), 129, 134, 142–8, 152
– under the Roman Empire, 219
Gregory of Tours, 256, 299, 300
Gregory VII, Pope, 387
Grotius, Hugo, 461
Guan Zhong, 120, 122, 124
Guangwu, Emperor of the Han (Liu Xiu), 208, 229–31
Guangzhou (city), 327
Guifang people, 78–81
Guiling, Battle of (354 BCE), 158
Gupta Empire, 244, 268–71, 276

Gustavus Adolphus, King of Sweden, 468
Güyük Khan, 369, 389
Gwanggaeto, king of the Goguryeo, 274

H

Habsburg Dynasty, 405–6, 466–72
Hadhramaut kingdom, 274
Hadrian, Emperor, 214, 222, 237
Hagia Sophia, Constantinople, 294, 409
Hague, The, Permanent Court of Arbitration, 503
Hainan, China, 180
Halule, Battle of (691 BCE), 96–7
Halys, Battle of (585 BCE), 99
Hamath, Syria, 70
Hamilton, Alexander, 509
Hammurabi see Code of Hammurabi
Hampi, Karnataka, 414
Han (Chinese state), 171, 172, 173
Han Anguo (Han general), 179–80
Han Empire, 130, 169, 174–81, 199, 201–2, 207–8, 228–38
– collapse of, 257, 275, 353
– 'Eastern Han,' 229
Han Fei, 160, 163
Han Wudi, 185
Hangzhou (city), 391
Hannibal, 189–90, 192, 198, 540
Harappa Civilization, 46
Harun al-Rashid (Abbasid caliph), 343, 344, 347, 349
Hashimiyya Movement, 339–40
Hathigumpha Inscription, 183
Hattusha (Hittite city), 31–2
Hattushili III, Hittite ruler, 32
Hayashi Gonsuke (Japanese diplomat), 507
Hazara Rama Temple, 415
Hecataeus, 200
Helen of Troy, 29
Helvetii, 198
Henri IV, King of France, 463–4
Henry IV, Holy Roman Emperor, 372
Henry of Ghent, 399
Henry V, King of England, 404
Henry VIII, King of England, 462
Hephthalite Huns, 244, 268, 270–1, 354

Heraclius (Byzantine Emperor), 293, 303
Herodian (Roman historian), 223
Herodotus, 99, 109, 139, 142, 143, 200–1
Hesiod, 106–7, 111, 123
Hexi Corridor, 180
Hideyoshi, Toyotomi, 456
Himyar kingdom, 274, 292, 356
Hinduism, 46–7, 335, 414–15
Hipparchus, 200
Hispaniola, Columbus' discovery of, 427
Hitler, Adolf, 517, 518, 541
Hittites, 31–2, 42, 59
Hobbes, Thomas, *Leviathan* (1651), 472
Hobson, J. A., 498–9
Hohenstaufen dynasty, 370
Holocaust, 518
Holy Roman Empire: conflict with papacy, 372, 386–7, 400
– creation of, 346–7
– dissolution of, 491
– and Germanic dynasties, 370–1
– and the Habsburg Dynasty, 405–6
holy wars, 356, 541–2
– Crusades, 387
– in Europe, 463–4
– Inca Empire, 428
– Islamic, 444
– the Mongol invasions, 367, 368
Homer, 29–30, 86, 106, 111
Hong Bang kingdom, Vietnam, 82
Hongwu Emperor of the Ming, 417
Hongxi Emperor of the Ming, 419
Honorius III, Pope, 389
Horace (poet), 197
Hormuz, Strait of, 361, 415
Hotman, Jean, 462
Hrotsvit of Gandersheim, 371
Hua Yi, 81
Huainanzi (Chinese scholarly texts), 178
Hugo, Victor, 502
Huizong, Emperor of the Song Dynasty, 366
Humayun, Mughal Emperor, 445
Humboldt, Alexander von, 489
Hume, David, 487
Hundred Schools of Thought (China), 160
Hundred Years War (1337–1453), 403–4
Hungary, 351, 370, 375, 408, 440

Hunkar Iskelesi, Treaty of (1833), 484
Huns: migration, 245, 247, 252
– origins of, 244–5
– wars with the Sasanian Empire, 266
Hydatius (Roman chronicler), 253
Hyrcanians, 100

I

Ibn al-Athir (historian), 381, 382
Ibn Battuta, 424
Ibn Fadlan, 350
Ibn Khordadbeh, *Book of Roads and Provinces*, 322
Idrisid Dynasty, 344
Ilkhanate, 411
Illyrians, 189
Imjin War (1592–8), 453
imperialism: American, 510
– Assyrian, 60
– and cosmopolitanism, 551–3
– Egyptian, 33–9
– European and American, 498–9
– Mesopotamian, 39–42
– Persian, 138–41
– Roman, 209–21, 256
– and trade, 550–1
Inca Empire, 428–9
India: British Raj, 483, 521
– Chalukya kingdom, 384–5
– Chola kingdom, 225, 383–4
– Deccan Plateau, 384, 413
– Delhi Sultanate, 412–15
– Four Kingdom period, 334–8
– 'Gates of Hind,' 384–5
– Ghurids, 412
– independence (1947), 521
– Indian Mutiny (1857–58), 483
– Kashmir, 183, 383, 521
– *Mahajanapads*, 82, 94, 115–16
– Muslim rule in, 385, 412–13
– Pandyan kingdom, 183, 225, 244, 272–3, 384
– relations with Tang dynasty China, 311
Indian Mutiny (1857–58), 483
Indian Ocean: Chinese reach, 420, 431

- European presence in, 446, 458
- maps of, 322
- and trade in 1st millenium, 63
- trade routes, 130, 170, 267, 272, 276–7, 356, 415
'Indo-Aryan Migration,' 46
Indo-Gangetic Plain: Delhi Sultanate in, 413
- in the Four Kingdom period, 335–7
- Harappa Civilization in, 45–8
- Mahajanapads in, 82, 115
- Mauryan Empire, 162, 170
- Mughal Empire in, 447
- political and demographic centre in, 22, 23, 45–6, 57
- warring states in, 183
Indonesia, 331, 521
Indus river, 45, 115, 131, 153
industrial revolution, 437, 459, 482, 505, 532–3
infant mortality, in the Roman and Han empires, 238
Ingres, Jean-Auguste-Dominique, 491
Innocent IV, Pope, 369, 389
innovations, technological: agricultural, 93, 159
- bronze casting, 81, 82
- crossbow, 118
- gunpowder, 365
- mechanical puppet-theatre, 262
- medicines, 308
- mobile mill, 262
- paper and calligraphy, 262
- printing, 438
- sewage system, 114
- use of iron, 93, 158
- waterwheel, 93
- wet-rice cultivation, 81
- woodblock printing, 308 see also industrial revolution
Insubres tribe, 113
intellectual property rights, 528
International Monetary Fund, 522, 528
Internet Corporation for Assigned Names and Numbers (ICANN), 528
Ionian Revolt (499), 132, 140, 146, 163
Ionian Sea, 376, 377
Ipsus, Battle of (301), 149, 154

Iran, 343, 344, 378, 379, 548 see also Persia
Iraq, 528, 542–3
'iron curtain,' 524
Isfahan (city), 446
Isfet (chaos), 36
Iskander Beg, 446
Islam: birth of, 287–90
- in China, 308
- and the Crusades, 387–8
- in India, 385, 412–13
- principles and teachings of, 340–2
- and trade, 322–3
- Twelver Shiism, 443, 445
Islamic Caliphate, 285–90, 311–12, 335–8
  see also Abbasid Caliphate; Umayyad Caliphate
Islamic terrorism, 531
Ismail, Shah of the Safavid Empire, 443–4
Israel: Biblical, 63–4, 69–70, 75, 96, 544
- modern state of, 521
Istanbul: under the Ottoman Empire, 441
  see also Constantinople
Isthmian Games, 109
Italy: 14th and 15th centuries, 402–3
- 15th century, 458 see also Lombards; Rome
Ivan III, Tsar of Russia, 408

J ——————————————

Jade Gate (Silk Road pass), 233, 237
Jagiellonians, 407–8
Jainism, 184, 335, 338
Janissaries, 409, 441, 442, 443
Japan: 13th to 15th centuries, 421–2
- 19th and 20th centuries, 505–8, 514
- Buddhism in, 422
- economic competition with US, 530
- failure of Mongol invasion, 416, 421
- invade Korean Peninsula (1592), 453
- Iwakura Mission (1871), 506
- Meiji Restoration (1868), 506
- pirate raids on China (16th century), 452
- relations with Tang dynasty China, 310
- and the Second World War, 518–19
- Seventeen Article Constitution (604 CE), 310

- *Taiheiki* (Chronicle of the Great Peace), 421
- Tokugawa rule, 456
- Treaty of Shimonoseki (1895), 507
- unification of (16th century), 456
- war with Russia (1904–05), 507
- Yamatai kingdom, 236
- Yamato kingdom, 244, 273, 310, 324
Java, 333–4, 416, 420
Jayavarman II, king of the Khmer, 333
Jefferson, Thomas (US President), 508, 509
Jerome (theologian and historian), 254, 263
Jerusalem, 103, 288, 290, 381–2
Jesus Christ, 220
Jews, 102–3, 301, 518
Jia Dan (cartographer), 309, 322
Jia Yi, 179
- *Faults of the Qin*, 172
Jiankang (city), 262
jihad, in Islamic teaching, 341
Jin (Chinese state), 117, 119, 157
Jin Dynasty, China, 390
Jing, Emperor of the Han, 175
Joan of Arc, 404
John (evangelist), 220
John of Plano Carpini, 389
John V, Byzantine Emperor, 409
Johor sultanate, 457
Jordan Rift Valley, 62
Joseon Dynasty, Korea, 421, 507
Josephus, Flavius, 220
Judah, kingdom of, 63–4, 96, 103
Jurchen people, 331, 361, 366, 452–4 *see also* Manchu (Qing dynasty)
Justinian II (Byzantine Emperor), 303
Justinian the Great (Byzantine Emperor), 292, 294

K ———————————————

Kadesh, Battle of (1274 BCE), 32
Kadesh, Treaty of (1259 BCE), 32
Kalidasa (poet), 270
Kalinga, kingdom of, 183
Kalisz, Treaty of (1813), 492
Kama Sutra, 270
Kamandaka (Gupta theorist), 357

Kanagawa, Convention of (1854), 506
Kandahar (city), 446
Kang, King of the Zhou, 79
Kangxi Emperor of the Qing, 455
Kanishka, Kushan Emperor, 226, 227
Kannauj (city), 337, 338
Kant, Immanuel, 492
Karmandaka (Gupta writer), 269
Kashmir, 183, 383, 521
Kassites, 42
Kautilya, *Arthashastra*, 11, 154–5, 163, 172, 269–70
Kennan, George, 523
Kessler, Harry, 504
Keynes, John Maynard, 514–15
Khalkha Mongols, 455
Khan Krum (Bulgarian Emperor), 347, 348, 349
Khitan people, 326, 329
Khmer Empire, 333, 422
Khorasan region, 379, 385, 445–6
Khosrow I (Sasanian Emperor), 292, 296
Khwarazmian kingdom, 381
Kievan Rus', 375, 376, 408
Kilij Arslan II, Seljuk Sultan, 380
Kilwa, city of, 424
Kissinger, Henry, 3
Kitabatake Chikafusa (Japanese theorist), 422
Königsberg (Kaliningrad), 470
Korea: annexed by the Han dynasty, 180
- Goguryeo kingdom, 235–6, 273–4, 310, 543
- Gojoseon dynasty in, 82, 157, 160, 162
- Goryeo kingdom, 330–1, 420–1
- Imjin War (1592–8), 453
- Joseon Dynasty, 421, 507
- Silla kingdom in, 330
Korean War (1950), 524
Kosovo, 528
Kotte kingdom, Sri Lanka, 420
Krupp (company), 496
Kshaharatas, kingdom of, 225
Kublai Khan, 416
Kushan Empire, 170, 183, 185, 199, 208, 224–8
Kuwait, 528

L

Lade, Battle of (494), 132
Lakhmid kingdom, 292
Lakshmi (Hindu goddess), 47
Langkasuka, 272
Lao Tzu, 121, 122, 124
Latvia, 470
Lavo, kingdom of, 333
law, codes of, 40–1, 69, 74, 103
League of Corinth, 135, 146
League of Nations, 513, 514, 517
leagues, Greek, 146–7
legalism (Chinese philosophy), 160–1, 172
Leipzig, Battle of (1813), 492
Lelantine War (c.710–650), 108
Lenin, Vladimir, 523
Lentulus Crus, Lucius Cornelius (Roman consul), 187
Leo IX, Pope, 386
Leo VI, (Byzantine Emperor), 302
Leonidas, King of Sparta, 133
Lepanto, Battle of (1571), 442
Levant: under the Assyrian Empire, 95–7
– conflict and trade in first millenium BC, 62–71, 87, 88
– conquered by Alexander the Great, 136
– divided between Britain and France, 514
– and the Fatimid Dynasty, 381
– under the Ottoman Empire, 439–40
– under the Persian Empire, 105, 111
Li Bo (Chinese poet), 325
Liang Qichao (historian), 486
Liao Dynasty, China, 329–31, 364, 390
liberalism, 547–51
libraries, at Ninevah, 98
Lin'an (Hangzhou), 368
Lincoln, Abraham, 537
Linqu canal, China, 172
Linzi, China, 159
Lithuania, 407–8
Liu Bang (Han ruler) see Gaozu, Emperor of Han (Liu Bang)
Liu Song (Chinese general), 263
Liu Yuan, Emperor of the Han Zhao, 260
Liudprand, Bishop of Cremona, 372
Livy (Roman historian), 113, 114, 209

Lloyd George, David, 513
Lodi, Peace of (1454), 403, 546
Lombards, 302, 346, 347, 371
London, England, 346, 459, 503
Louis IX, King of France, 373, 389
Louis the Pious, 350
Louis XI, King of France, 401
Louis XIII, King of France, 463
Louis XIV, King of France, 469, 542
Louis XVI, King of France, 488–9
Louvre, Musée de, 35, 40, 67, 214, 294
Low Countries see Netherlands
Lu (Chinese state), 116
Lu, Dowager Empress of the Han, 174
Lu Buwei, 159
Luoyang (city), 245, 263
An Lushan (Chinese warlord), 326
Ly Dynasty, Vietnam, 366
Lycurgus, 74, 86
Lydia, kingdom of, 99, 101

M

Maastricht, Treaty of (1992), 529–30
Maat (divine force), 36
Macao, China, 452
Macartney, George, 1st Earl, 485
Macedon, Greece, 135–6
Machiavelli, Niccolò, 463
Madagascar, 424
Madeira, 407
Magadha kingdom, 115–16, 153
Magnus, Albertus, 399
Mahabharata (Indian epic), 21–2, 36, 47, 70, 448
Mahan, Alfred, 500, 510
Mahapadma Nanda, 153
Mahavamsa (Sri Lankan epic), 273
Mahaviracharya (mathematician), 338
Mahmud of Ghazni, 338
Mainz, 346
Majapahit Empire, 422
Malacca, Straits of, 332, 333
Malacca Sultanate, 452
Malayan Peninsula, 457
Mali Empire, Africa, 426
Malthus, Robert, 107

Man Bac, Vietnam, Bronze Age cemetery, 27

Manchu (Qing dynasty), 454–5

Manchuria, 329–30, 366, 420, 507

Mani (Sasanian prophet), 274

Manneans, 72, 97

al-Mansur (Abbasid caliph), 343

Manusmriti (Hindu text), 184, 202

Manzikert, Battle of (1071), 377, 380

Mao Zedong, 521

maps *see* cartography

Marcus Aurelius, Emperor, 214

Mardonius (Persian satrap), 140, 146

Marie Antoinette, Queen, 488

Marshall Plan (1948), 522, 529

Marsilius of Padua, 400

Martel, Charles, 299–300

Mathura Inscription, 226

Mati'ilu, king of Arpad, 65, 68

Matti'el, Levantine king, 68

Mauretania, 199

Maurice (Byzantine Emperor), *Strategikon*, 295–6

Mauryan Empire, 47, 130, 153–6, 162, 163, 170, 183, 185

al-Mawardi, *Ordinances of Government*, 341

Maximilian I, Holy Roman Emperor, 405–6

Maya civilization, 203, 313–15, 354

Mazdak (Zoroastrian preacher), 267

Mazzini, Giuseppe, 503

Mecca, 286–8

Medes, 40, 95, 97, 98–9, 99–100

Median Empire, 99–100

Medici, Lorenzo de,' 403

Medinet Habu, Egypt, 37, 66

Megabazus, 141

Megalopolis, 146

Megara, Greece, 108

Megasthenes, 156

Mehmed II, Sultan of the Ottomans, 409–11

Mehmed Pasha, Piri, 440

Mekong Delta, 23, 272

Meliac War (c.690–670 BCE), 109

Memphis, Egypt, 33, 97, 103, 134

Mencius (philosopher), 116, 159

Menes of Egypt, 34

mercantilism, 465–6, 473

Merovinigian Dynasty, 299–300

Merv (city), 379

Meshwesh (Libyan tribe), 38

Mesopotamia: decline of, 352
- divided between Britain and France, 514
- earthquake (749 CE), 340
- imperial culture, 25, 39–42
- invaded by the Ottomans, 439
- recaptured by the Safavids, 445

Messenian Wars (743–724, 685–668 BCE), 108

Messina, Sicily, 150–1

Metternich, Klemens von, 493, 504

Mexica people, 427

Mihira Bhoja, king of the Pratihara Dynasty, 337

Ming, Emperor of the Eastern Han, 231

Ming Dynasty, China, 417–21, 431, 451–4, 474

Mitanni kingdom, 40

Mithridates I, King of the Parthians, 186

Mithridates II, King of the Parthians, 186

Moab, kingdom of, 64

Mocenigo, Tommaso, 402

Moche people, South America, 203

Moctezuma, Aztec Emperor, 429

Mogadishu, 424

Mohacs, Battle of (1526), 440

Mohenjodaro, India, 46

Moldavia, 495

Molotov-Ribbentrop Pact (1939), 518

Mombasa, 424

Monet, Claude, 503

Mongolia, 181–2, 367, 392, 420

Mongols: in China, 361–2, 367–8, 452
- division of, 411
- in Europe, 369–70, 375, 391–2
- failure to invade Japan, 416, 421
- Hungary (1241), 389
- and Moscow, 408
- sacking of Baghdad (1258), 382
- Yuan Dynasty, 411, 416–17, 420–1

Monroe, James (US President), 508–9

Monte Albán, Central America, 202

More, Thomas, *Utopia*, 460

Morgan, John Pierpoint Jr, 516

Morgenthau, Hans, 10

Morocco, 344

Moscow, Duchy of, 408, 412

Mossi kingdoms, Central Africa, 426
Mozarabic Chronicle, 299
Mu, King of the Zhou, 79
Muawiya (caliph), 290, 291
Mughal Empire, 438, 445, 447–51, 457, 483
Muhammad, Prophet, 287–9
Mun, Thomas, 464, 466
al-Muqadassi (geographer), 322
Murad III, Sultan of the Ottomans, 445
Mutapa kingdom, 424–5
Muye, Battle of (1046 BCE), 44, 76
Myanmar, 331, 450, 455, 457
Mycenae, 29

N

Nader Khan, 447
Nader Shah, 451
Nagabhata, king of the Pratihara
    Dynasty, 336
Nanda kingdom, 153
Nanyue, kingdom of, 180
Napoleon Bonaparte, 490–2
Napoleon III, Emperor of France, 495, 497
Napoleonic Wars (1803–15), 490–2
Naqsh-e Rustam, 264
Native Americans, 508
NATO *see* North Atlantic Treaty
    Organization in Europe (NATO)
'natural state' politics, 25–8, 49
navigation: British supremacy (18th and
    19th centuries), 488, 490
– Chinese naval power, 361, 420, 431
– European supremacy (16th and 17th
    centuries), 458
Nelson, Admiral Horatio, 490
Nero, Emperor, 213
Netherlands, 406, 459, 467
New Testament, 220
Nicias, Peace of (421 BCE), 147
Niketas Choniates (Byzantine
    chronicler), 377
Nile valley, 23, 33, 34, 39, 57
Nimrud, Assyrian city, 59, 60, 97
Nine Years War (1688–97), 464, 469
Ninevah, Assyrian city, 93, 97, 97–8, 99
Non-Aligned Movement, 522

Normandy, France, 372, 373, 376, 377, 386–7
North Africa: Carthage / Carthaginians,
    150–1, 190–1
– European colonization of, 498
– Islamic rule in, 298–9, 343, 355
– Romans in, 190–1, 199
– slave markets in, 441
– Vandal kingdom in, 247
North America: British rule in, 487
– geography, 24
– Woodland Culture, 312–13 *see also* United
    States of America
North Atlantic Treaty Organization in
    Europe (NATO), 524, 527, 528
North China Plain: human settlement in,
    23, 43–5, 48–9, 57–8 *see also* China
North German Confederation, 496
Northern Wei Empire, 261–2
Nubians, 35, 38
Numerical Discourses of the Buddha, 116
Numidia, 199
Nurhaci, leader of the Jurchen, *Seven
    Grievances*, 453–4
Nye, Joseph, 529

O

Odoacer, Flavius, 254, 255
Ogodei (Mongol leader), 370
Old Testament, 63, 68–70, 86, 96, 97, 104
Olmec civilization, 83–6, 202
Olympic Games, 74, 109
Opium Wars (1939–42 and 1856–60), 486
Orkhon Valley, Mongolia, 181, 367, 392
Orléans, siege of (1429), 404
Orthagoras (Greek general), 108
Orthodox Christianity, 294, 298, 375
Osman I, 408
Osorkon II of Egypt, 61, 62
Osorkon IV of Egypt, 96
Otto I, Holy Roman Emperor, 371–2
Ottoman Empire: dissolution of, 514
– dominance of, 439–43
– naval power of, 441
– rise of, 408–12, 438
– and the Russian Empire, 484
– trade with Europe, 457

Ottonian dynasty, 370–2
Ouagadougou, Central Africa, 426

P

Paine, Thomas, 487–8
Pakistan, 521
Pala Dynasty, India, 332, 335–8
Palaiologos Dynasty, 409
Palermo, Sicily, 346
Palladius Rutilius Taurus Aemilianus, *Opus agriculture*, 243
Pallas, Marcus Antonius, 216
Pandyan kingdom, 183, 225, 244, 272–3, 384
Panipat, Battle of (1556), 447
papacy: authority of, 370, 372
– conflict with Holy Roman Emperor, 372, 386–7, 400
– schism, 403
Papremis, Battle of (460), 133
Paris: attacked by Vikings, 350
– Eiffel Tower, 503
– emergence of, 346
– Notre-Dame Cathedral, 399
Paris, Treaty of (1763), 487
Paris Peace Conference (1918), 512–15, 546
Parthian Empire, 170, 185–8, 198, 199, 208
– collapse of, 353
– and Rome, 211, 215, 221–3
Parthians, 98
Pataliputra (capital city of the Mauryan Empire), 156
Pausanias (Greek geographer), 219
Pax Romana, 197, 538
Pecheneg people, 375, 376
Peel, Robert, 502
Peloponnesian League, 146
Peloponnesian War (431–404), 129, 134, 142–8, 152, 544, 547
Pengcheng, Battle of (205 BCE), 173
People's Republic of China, 521, 530 *see also* China
Pepin the Short, 300
Periander (Greek tyrant), 109
Pericles, 10, 110
Pérotin (composer), 399
Perry, Matthew, 506, 509

Persepolis, 103, 138
Persia, 447, 451, 483–4 *see also* Achaemenid dynasty; Iran; Parthian Empire; Safavid Empire
Persian Empire: establishment of, 100–5
– fall of, 131–7
– imperial tradition of, 138–41
– roads and communication, 103–4
– trade, 104–5
Persian Wars (499–449 BCE), 132–3, 141
Persians: under the Assyrian Empire, 95, 98
– rebel against the Median Empire, 99–100
Peter the Great, Tsar, 469–70
Petrarch, 401
Philip II, King of France, 373
Philip II, King of Macedon, 135–6
Philip II, King of Spain, 467
Philip IV, King of Spain, 469
Philip the Arab, Roman Emperor, 214, 248
Philistines, 64
Philo of Alexandria, 220
philosophers and thinkers, European, 460–2, 486–8, 492
Phoenicians, 62, 73, 76, 87, 102, 111
– and the Punic Wars, 151
Phrygia, 72, 95, 96
Piacenza, Council of (1095), 377
Piast Dynasty, Poland, 407
Picquigny, Treaty of (1475), 404
Pilate, Pontius, 220
Pitt, William, 490
Pizarro, Francisco, 429
Plassey, Battle of (1757), 483
Plato, 143
Plaza Agreement (1985), 525
Pliny the Elder, 223–4
Plutarch, 137
Poem of Pentaur, 37
Poland: early 11th century, 370
– Jagiellonians, 407–8
– kingdom of, 351
– Piast Dynasty, 375, 407
– under the Russian Empire, 493
Poltava, Battle of (1709), 470
Polybius, 151, 152, 188, 189, 191, 192
Pompeius Trogus, 221
Pompey (Roman Emperor), 196

Pontic-Caspian Steppe, 72, 105, 130, 131, 252
Pontus, kingdom of, 198
population: in ancient Greece, 107
 – of China (3rd century BCE), 158
 – European, in the Middle Ages, 374
 – and migration, 548
 – and power, 352
 – world (1000 BCE), 24
 – world (1500–1750 CE), 437
 – world (1900 CE), 481
 – world (2000), 532
Portugal: discoveries and exploration, 406–7, 430–1, 437, 457
 – trade with China, 452
Potsdam Conference (1945), 520, 523
Pradt, Dominique de, 501–2
Pradyota, Chanda, 115
Pratihara Dynasty, India, 335–8
Preveza, Battle of (1538), 441
printing, development of, 438
Prokopovich, Theophan, 470
Prussia: and the Congress of Vienna (1814–15), 493–4
 – economic development, 496
 – rise of, 470–1
 – treaty with Russia (1813), 492
Ptolemies, 130, 149, 162
Ptolemy II, 149, 151
'public opinion,' first reference to, 501–2
Punic Wars (264–146 BCE), 151, 188–91, 193, 543
Pure Land Buddhism, 263
Putnam, Robert, 531
Pyrenees, 303
Pyrrhus, King of Epirus, 150, 151
Pythagoras, 112

Qarqar, Battle of (853 BCE), 64, 76
Qi (Chinese state), 117, 119, 157, 159, 172
Qiang people, 157, 232, 234–5, 260
Qianlong Emperor of the Qing, 485
Qin (Chinese state), 117, 157, 261
Qin Empire, 158, 160, 162, 171–3
Qin Er Shi, Emperor of the Qin, 173
Qin Hui (Song dynasty official), 391

Qin Shi Huang (Ying Zheng), Emperor of the Qin, 171, 172
Qing Dynasty, China, 454–6, 457, 484–6
Qizilbash people, 443–4, 445
Quanzhou (city), 365
Quran, 289, 340
Quraysh (tribe), 286–7

R

Rabatak Inscription, 226
Rajasthan, India, 338
Ramayana (Indian epic), 47
Ramesses II of Egypt, 37
Ramesses III of Egypt, 37, 66
Rashtrakuta Dynasty, India, 335–8
Raymond of Aguilers, 374
Reagan, Ronald, 526
Reformation, Protestant, 463
Regensburg, 346
religions *see* Buddhism; Christianity; Confucianism; Hinduism; Islam; Jainism; shamanism; Zoroastrianism
Renoir, Auguste, 503
Ricardo, David, 159, 549
Richard I, King of England ('Lionheart'), 373, 382
Richelieu, Cardinal, 463, 467
Ridda Wars (632–33 CE), 288
Rienzo, Cola di, 401
Riquier, Guiraut, 399
Roger Apulia, 369
Roman Empire: fall of, 247–56, 275
 – Pax Romana, 207–17
 – rise of, 169, 188–99, 202
 – slavery in, 238
 – splits into Eastern and Western halves, 251, 252
 – transport networks, 352
 – Western, 243–4, 252, 254, 355
Romance of the Three Kingdoms, 258
Romanov Dynasty, Russia, 469
Rome: civil wars (49–31 BCE), 196
 – early history of, 113–14
 – emergence as major power, 149–51
 – falls to the Visigoths (410 CE), 253–4
 – flourishes under Augustus, 210

- foundation of, 74–5
- Pax Romana, 197, 538
- and the Punic Wars, 190–1
- Social War (91–88 BCE), 195
- warrior cult, 192–3
Romulus and Remus, 75
Romulus Augustulus, Roman Emperor, 254
Roosevelt, Theodore (US President), 510
Rosecrance, Richard, 529
Rosier, Bernard du, 401, 547
Rouen, 350
Rousseau, Jean-Jacques, 26, 486, 487
Rubens, Peter Paul, 461, 471, 472
Rubicon river, 196
Rum, Anatolia, 381, 408
Russian Civil War (1917–1922), 523, 524
Russian Empire: expansion of, 442, 446–7, 455, 484
- foundation of, 408
- Napoleon invades, 491–2
- under Peter the Great, 470
- Romanov Dynasty, 469
- toppled in the 1917 revolutions, 523
Russo-Japanese War (1904–05), 507
Russo-Polish War (1754–67), 469
Ryukyu Islands, 455

S

Saba (Sheba) kingdom, 274
Sabines, 75
Sacians, 100
Safavid Empire, 438, 439, 442, 443–7, 457, 470
Safaviyya (Sufi order), 444
al-Saffah, Abu al-Abbas, 340
Sahel, Africa, 425–6
Saladin, 381–2
Salamis (Greek island), 110
Salian dynasty, 370
Salian Franks, 251
Salisbury, Robert Gascoyne-Cecil, 3rd Marquess, 502
Sam'al, kingdom of, 70
Samarkand, 226
Samguk Sagi, 236
Samudragupta of the Guptas, 268

Sang Hongyang, Discourses on Salt and Iron, 180
Sarajevo, 501
Sardinia, 188–9
Sargon II, King of Assyria, 105
Sarmations, 245
Sasanian Empire, 223, 248, 251, 288, 291–8, 540
Satavahanas, kingdom of, 183, 225
satraps (Persian governors), 102, 104, 139, 140
Saul, King of Israel, 63, 69
Saxons, 247, 346
Schleswig-Holstein crisis (1864), 495, 496
Scotland, Caledonian tribes, 212, 215, 217
Scythians, 3, 72, 97, 98–9, 105–6, 131, 186, 276
Sea Peoples, 32, 37, 42, 58, 65
Second Crusade (1147–49), 388
Second World War (1939–1945), 518–19
Sefire Stele, 68
Sejong, Joseon king, 421
Selden, John, 466
Seleucid Empire, 170, 183, 186, 198
Seleucids, 130, 149, 162
Seleucus, King, 149, 153–4
Selim I, Sultan of the Ottomans, 382, 439–40
Seljuk Turks, 376, 378–81, 388
Sempronius Asellio, 199
Seneca, 187, 217
Senegal, 499
Sennacherib, King of Assyria, 95, 96–7
Servius Tullius, King of Rome, 113
Seven Years War (1756–63), 487
Severus, Septimius, Emperor, 214–15, 222
Seville, Spain, 346
Shalmaneser III of Egypt, 67
shamanism, 455
Shamash (Babylonian god of justice), 41
Shang dynasty, China, 43–4
Shang Yang, 159, 160
Shanyuan, Treaty of (1005 CE), 364
Shao Bowen, 45
Shaoxing, Treaty of (1141 CE), 391
Shapur I of the Sasanians, 265
Shapur II of the Sasanians, 265–6
al-Shaybani, Introduction to the Law of Nations, 341
Sheba, Queen of, 63

Shen Kuo (Song dynasty scholar), 390
Shenzong, Emperor of the Song
 Dynasty, 364
Shia Muslims, 290, 339–40, 380, 444
Shoshenq I of Egypt, 38, 61, 62, 63
Shotoku of Japan, Prince, 310–11
Shu (Chinese state), 160
Shu kingdom, 235, 257–8, 260
Shunga kingdom, 183, 184
Shunzi Emperor of the Qing, 455
Sibylline Books, 251
Sicily, 188–9, 190, 349
Siemens (company), 496
Sigismund, Emperor, 405
Silk Road trade: competition to control,
 170, 208, 221–4, 228
– controlled by the Göktürks, 297, 308
– Sasanian control of, 267, 276, 292
– taxes and controls, 323
Silla kingdom, 273, 310, 330
Sima Qian (Chinese historian), 171, 173
Singhasari kingdom, 422
al-Sirafi, Abu Zayd, 322, 323
Slavs, 303
Smith, Adam, 487, 547, 549
Sofala, city of, 424
Solomon, King of Israel, 63, 69, 87
Solon, 110
Song (Chinese state), 117, 119
Song Dynasty, China, 330, 363–8, 385–6, 390
Songhai Empire, Central Africa, 426
Song-Jin, Battle of (1641–42), 454
South America, 203, 428–9
Southeast Asia: 13th to 15th centuries, 422–3
– European traders in, 457
– post-Second World War, 521
Southeast Asian Treaty Organization
 (SEATO), 524
sovereignty: European debate on,
 460–3, 464
– Kautilya on (3rd century BCE), 154
– Tang Dynasty China, 307
Soviet Union: break up of, 525–6
– and the Cold War, 482, 523–6
– and Eastern Europe, 521
– Molotov-Ribbentrop Pact (1939), 518
– and the Second World War, 518, 520–1

Spain: under the Carthaginians, 189, 190
– discovery of America, 407
– overthrow Aztec and Inca Empires,
 426–31, 437, 457–8
– *Reconquista*, 406
– under the Umayyad Caliphate, 303, 344
Sparta: culture of, 73–4
– in the Messenian Wars, 108
– in the Peloponnesian War, 134,
 142–4, 147
– under Persian rule, 140–1
– in the Persian wars, 132
– rivalry with Corinth, 109
Spykman, Nicholas, 524
Sri Lanka, 273, 383, 415
Sri Pona (poet), 338
Srivijaya kingdom, 332–4, 384
St Bertin Abbey, 350
St Petersburg, Russia, 470
Stalin, Joseph, 520, 523
stenochoria, 107, 115
Strabo (Greek geographer), 219
Streuvels, Stijn, 537–8
Suárez, Francisco, 461
Suetonius (Roman historian), 213
Suevi (Germanic tribe), 253
Sufism, 444
Sukhothai kingdom, Thailand, 422
Suleiman the Magnificent, Sultan, 382,
 440–1
Süleymaniye Mosque, Istanbul, 441
Sulla, Lucius Cornelius, 187, 195–6
Sully, Maximilien de Béthune, Duke
 of, 464
Sumatra, 332, 420, 442
Sumerians, 40
Sun Tzu, 11, 117, 121, 122, 124
Sunda Strait, 332
Sunni Muslims, 290, 380, 439, 444
Swahili people, 424
Swat Valley, Pakistan, 46
Sweden, 468, 470
Symmachus, Quintus Aurelius, 253
Syracuse, 150
Syria: civil war (743 CE), 339
– civil war (2015 –), 544
– invaded by the Sasanians (250 CE), 265

T

al-Tabari (Persian scholar), 321–2, 344

Tabriz (city), 444

Tacitus (Roman historian), 212, 213, 216, 219, 222, 224

Taejo, king of Goryeo, 331

Taharqa of Egypt, 97

Taifali (Germanic people), 245

Taiwan, 180, 455, 507

Taizong, Emperor of the Song Dynasty, 330

Taizong, Emperor of the Tang Dynasty, 307, 309, 311, 354, 357

Taizu, Emperor of the Liao Dynasty, 329–30

Taizu, Emperor of the Song Dynasty, 330, 361, 363

Talas River, Battle of (751 CE), 312, 326

Tang Dynasty, China, 286, 306–12, 321, 323, 354

Tanumshede, Sweden, 27

Tao Yuanming (poet), 243

Taoism, 121, 305, 308, 325

Tarascan kingdom, Central America, 427

Tarentum, 150

Tarquinius Priscus, Lucius, 114

Tarquinius Superbus, King of Rome, 113, 114

Tarsus, 111

Taruma kingdom, 272

Tehran Conference (1943), 520

Tel Dan Stele, 64

Temple of Apollo, Corinth, 112

Tenochtitlan, Aztec city, 427–8, 429

Teotihuacan, Central America, 203, 313–14, 354

Terracotta Army, 173

Tervel (Bulgar khan), 303

Texcoco state, Central America, 427

Thailand, 422, 457

Thebes, Egypt, 33, 38

Themistocles, 110

Theoderic, king of the Goths, 255

Theodosius (Roman Emperor), 252

Theophilus of Edessa, 290–1, 340

Thessaloniki, 409

Thirty Years War (1618–48), 463, 467, 468

Thiruvalluvar (poet), 184, 202

Thuc Phan, Prince, 160

Thucydides, 139, 142, 143–6, 152, 163, 192, 547

Thymbra, Battle of (546 BCE), 101

Tiberius, Emperor, 212

Tibet, 310, 311, 390, 455

– and Tang dynasty China, 326, 327, 329, 354

Tibullus (poet), 196

Tiglath-Pileser III, King of Assyria, 94–5

Tigris river, 39

Tikal, Yucatán, 315

Timbuktu, Africa, 426

Timur (Tamerlane), 411–12, 444

Tirpitz, Alfred von, 500

Tlacopan state, Central America, 427

Tocqueville, Alexis de, 502

Tolstoy, Leo, 503–4

Tong Guan (Song dynasty official), 390

Torah, 69, 103

Tordesillas, Treaty of (1494), 437

tortilla, 85, 87

Toungoo kingdom, Myanmar, 457

Tours, Battle of (732 CE), 300

Trade-Related Aspects of Intellectual Property Rights (TRIPS), 528

Trafalgar, Battle of (1805), 490–1

Trajan, Emperor, 214, 220, 222

Treaty of Perpetual Peace (1686), 469

triremes (Greek warships), 109

Trojan War, 29–30

Truman, Harry (US President), 10, 522

Trung Sisters (Vietnam), 236

Ts'ui Shih, *Monthly Instructions for the Four Classes of People*, 233

Tsushima, Japan, 421

Tuareg people, 426

Tughluq, Muhammad bin, Sultan, 413

Tulunid Dynasty, 345

Tunisia, 380

Tunmen, China, 452

Turgot, Jacques, 488

Turkish Republic, 514

Turkmenchay, Treaty of (1828), 484

Tuthmosis III of Egypt, 37

Tuyuhun kingdom, 310

Twelver Shiism, 443, 445

Tyre (city), 62, 63, 73, 76, 97, 105

Tyrtaeus, 'Spartan Creed' of, 108

U

Ugarit, Syria, 30–1
Uighurs, 326, 327, 329
Umar (caliph), 288
Umayyad Caliphate: downfall of, 338–40
– expansion of, 290, 291
– in Gaul, 300
– in Spain, 298–9, 303, 347
United Nations, 519–22, 532, 546
United States of America: Civil War (1861–65), 508
– and the Cold War, 524–6
– Dawes Plan (1924), 516
– dominance after WW2, 482, 520–1, 521
– economic deficit (2000), 530
– economic protectionism, 515–17
– in the First World War, 511
– Great Depression (1930s), 516–17
– imperialism of, 510
– industrial expansion, 515
– Monroe Doctrine (1823), 508–9, 510, 543
– post-Cold War foreign policy, 527–9
– rise of, 508–11
– and the Second World War, 518
– terrorist attacks, 9/11, 531
– war with Britain (1812–15), 508
– Young Plan (1929), 516
Ur, Mesopotamia, 40
Urartu, kingdom of, 40, 72, 95, 96
Urban II, Pope, 373, 377, 387, 388
Uzbekistan, 444

V

Vakataka kingdom, 269
Valentinian, Roman Emperor, 251
Vandals, 246–7, 253
Vasudeva I, Kushan Emperor, 227–8
Vatsyayana, *Kama Sutra*, 270
Vedic Civilization, 46–7
Vega, Joseph de la, 465
Velleius Paterculus, 194
Venice: commercial dominance of, 348, 377, 382, 551
– in the Crusades, 387–8
– and diplomatic immunity, 402
– and the Ottoman Empire, 410–11
– sack of Constantinople (1204), 378
– trade with the Mongols, 389
Venice, Peace of (1177 CE), 387
Verdun, Treaty of (843 CE), 350
Versailles, Treaty of (1919), 513, 541
Vienna, threatened by the Ottoman Empire, 440, 442–3
Vienna, Congress of (1814–15), 492–3, 542, 546
Vietnam: Annam kingdom, 422, 455
– Au Lac state, 160
– Bronze Age cemetery, Man Bac, 28
– Champa kingdom, 332, 422
– Hong Bang kingdom, 82
– Le Emperors, 457
– Ly Dynasty, 366
– province of the Ming Empire, 420
– Trung Sisters' rebellion, 236
Vietnam War (1955–1975), 524
Vijayanagara, kingdom of, 413–15
Viking invasions, 350, 372
Vikramaditya VI, Chalukya king, 384
Vikramankadevacarita, 384
Vincent of Beauvais, 399
Virgil (poet), 195, 217, 538
– *Aeneid*, 209
Vishnu (Hindu god), 47
Visigoths, 247, 253–4, 299
Vistula river, 375
Vitoria, Franciso de, 461
Völkerwanderung, 244–7, 285, 298
Volsci, 150
Voltaire, 471, 533

W

Walid I, Umayyad Caliph, 338–9
Wang Hui, 179
Wang Jinghong, 419
Wang Mang (military commander of the Han), 229, 230
Wang Renyu (Chinese writer), 329
Wang Xuance, 311
Wanli Emperor of the Ming, 455
war, justifications for, 539–45
War of Devolution (1667–68), 469

War of the Spanish Succession
(1701–13), 469
Washington Naval Conference
(1921–22), 514
Waterloo, Battle of (1815), 492
Wei kingdom, 235–6, 257–8
Wei peoples, 157–8, 172
Wei Yuan (political theorist), 484
Wells, H. G., 501
Wen, Emperor of the Han, 174, 178
Wen of Wei, 157
Western Jin Dynasty, 258–9, 260
Westphalia, Conference of (1648), 462–3,
468, 542, 546
White Sheep Turkomans, 411–12
Wicquefort, Abraham de, 462
Wilde, Oscar, 499
Wilhelm II, Kaiser, 497
Willem II, King of the Netherlands, 506
William of Ockham, 400
Willibrord, St, 301
Wilson, Woodrow (US President), 511,
512–13
Woodland Culture, North America,
312–13
World Bank, 522, 528
world fairs, 503
World Trade Organization, 528
Worms, Concordat of (1122), 372
Wotton, Henry, 462
writing systems, early, 94
Wu (Chinese state), 117
Wu, Emperor of the Han, 170, 175, 180, 185
Wu, Emperor of the Western Jin dynasty
(Sima Yan), 258–9
Wu kingdom, 235, 236, 257–9
Wuhuan people, 231, 232

X

Xanten Abbey, 350
Xanthos, 139
Xenophon, 100, 139, 140, 152, 163, 549
Xerxes, King of Persia (486–465), 132
Xi Jia, 80–1
Xi Jinping, 10
Xia kingdom, 364, 365–6, 390

Xianbei people, 231, 232, 245, 259–61,
304, 310
Xianyun people, 78, 87
Xiao of Qin, 158
Xie Daoyun (poet), 262
Xiongnu people, 157–8, 170, 172, 178–83,
230–2, 244, 245, 260
Xizong, Emperor of the Tang dynasty, 328
Xuande Emperor of the Ming, 419
Xuang, King of the Zhou, 80–1
Xuanzong (712–56), Emperor of the Tang
dynasty, 324–5, 327
Xuanzong (846–59), Emperor of the Tang
dynasty, 328
Xun Kuang (Chinese philosopher), 163
Xunzi (Confucian philosopher), 161

Y

Yalta Conference (1945), 520
Yamato kingdom, 244, 273
Yan (Chinese state), 157, 160, 273
Yang Rong (Ming official), 420
Yellow River, China, 43
Ying Zheng see Qin Shi Huang
Yom Kippur War (1973), 524
Yongle Emperor of the Ming, 418
Yongzheng Emperor of the Qing, 456
You, King of the Zhou, 81
Yuan, Emperor of the Han, 181
Yuan Dynasty (Mongols), 411, 416–17, 420–1
Yuan Haowen (poet), 368
Yucatán, Central America, 203, 313–15, 429
Yue (Chinese state), 117
Yuezhi people, 170, 182–3, 185, 225–6
Yugoslav Wars (1991–99), 528
Yugoslavia, 514
Yunnan, China, 420, 455, 456

Z

Zab, Battle of the (750 CE), 340
Zagros Mountains, 23, 40, 93, 96, 99, 103
Zakkur, king of Hamath, 70
Zama, Battle of (202 BCE), 190
Zanj Rebellion (869–883 CE), 345
Zanzibar, 424

Zapotec culture, 202
Zeno, Eastern Roman Emperor, 255
Zhang, Emperor of the Eastern Han, 231
Zhang Qian (Chinese explorer), 178, 183, 200–1
Zhang Xuan (painter), 325
Zhao, King of the Zhou, 79
Zhaoxiang, King of the Qin, 171
Zheng He (Chinese Admiral), 420
Zheng Sixiao (painter), 417
Zhenge Emperor of the Ming, 455

Zhezong, Emperor of the Song Dynasty, 366
Zhou, Duke of, 77
Zhou dynasty, China, 44, 76–83, 87, 88, 157, 158, 171
Zhou Fang (painter), 325
Zhu Yuanzhang, 417
Zimbabwe, 14th century, 424
Zonchio, Battle of (1499), 411
Zoroastrianism, 264, 265, 266, 267, 296, 308, 339
Zosimus (Byzantine historian), 248